Kate Stechschulte

202-244-0548

SECOND EDITION

GOVERNMENTAL AND NONPROFIT ACCOUNTING

THEORY AND PRACTICE

SECOND EDITION

GOVERNMENTAL AND NONPROFIT ACCOUNTING

THEORY AND PRACTICE

PATRICIA P. DOUGLAS
University of Montana

THE DRYDEN PRESS
Harcourt Brace College Publishers

Fort Worth   Philadelphia   San Diego   New York   Orlando   Austin   San Antonio
Toronto   Montreal   London   Sydney   Tokyo

Acquisitions Editors: **Tim Vertovec and Bill Teague**
Developmental Editor: **Glenn Martin**
Project Editor: **Jim Patterson**
Art Director: **Brian Salisbury**
Production Manager: **Ann Marie Coburn**
Marketing Manager: **Diana Farrell**
Director of Editing, Design, and Production: **Diane Southworth**
Publisher: **Elizabeth Widdicombe**

Copy Editor: **Carolyn Crabtree**
Compositor: **Beacon Graphics**
Text Type: **10/12 ITC Garamond Book**

Address for orders:
The Dryden Press
6277 Sea Harbor Drive
Orlando, FL 32887-6777
1-800-782-4479, or 1-800-433-0001 (in Florida)

Address for editorial correspondence:
The Dryden Press
301 Commerce Street, Suite 3700
Fort Worth, TX 76102

ISBN: 0-03-006639-5

Library of Congress Catalog Card Number: 94-70133

Printed in the United States of America

4 5 6 7 8 9 0 1 2 3   0 9 0   10 9 8 7 6 5 4 3 2 1

The Dryden Press
Harcourt Brace College Publishers

The Dryden Press Series in Accounting

Introductory

Bischoff *Introduction to College Accounting* Third Edition

Principles

Hanson, Hamre, and Walgenbach *Principles of Accounting* Sixth Edition

Computerized

Bischoff and Wanlass *The Computer Connection: General Ledger and Practice Sets to accompany Introductory Accounting* Second Edition

Wanlass *Computer Resource Guide: Principles of Accounting* Fourth Edition

Financial

Backer, Elgers, and Asebrook *Financial Accounting: Concepts and Practices*

Beirne and Dauderis *Financial Accounting: An Introduction to Decision Making*

Porter and Norton *Financial Accounting: The Impact on Decision Makers*

Stickney and Weil *Financial Accounting: An Introduction to Concepts, Methods, and Uses* Seventh Edition

Managerial

Ketz, Campbell, and Baxendale *Management Accounting*

Maher, Stickney, and Weil *Managerial Accounting: An Introduction to Concepts, Methods, and Uses* Fifth Edition

Intermediate

Williams, Stanga, and Holder *Intermediate Accounting* Fifth Edition

Advanced

Huefner and Largay *Advanced Financial Accounting* Third Edition

Pahler and Mori *Advanced Accounting* Fifth Edition

Financial Statement Analysis

Stickney *Financial Statement Analysis: A Strategic Perspective* Second Edition

Auditing

Guy, Alderman, and Winters *Auditing* Third Edition

Rittenberg and Schwieger *Auditing; Concepts for a Changing Environment*

Theory

Belkaoui *Accounting Theory* Third Edition

Bloom and Elgers *Foundations of Accounting Theory and Policy*

Bloom and Elgers *Issues In Accounting Theory and Policy*

Taxation

Everett, Raabe, and Fortin *1995 Income Tax Fundamentals*

Madeo, Anderson, and Jackson *Sommerfeld's Concepts of Taxation* 1996 Edition

Reference

Miller and Bailey *Miller Comprehensive GAAS Guide* College Edition

Williams and Miller *Miller Comprehensive GAAP Guide* College Edition

Governmental and Not-For-Profit

Douglas *Governmental and Nonprofit Accounting: Theory and Practice* Second Edition

Ziebell and DeCoster *Management Control Systems in Nonprofit Organizations*

The Harcourt Brace College Outline Series

Campbell, Grierson, and Taylor *Principles of Accounting I* Revised Edition

Emery *Principles of Accounting II*

Emery *Intermediate Accounting I* Second Edition

Emery *Intermediate Accounting II*

Frigo *Cost Accounting*

Poteau *Advanced Accounting*

PREFACE

TEXT PURPOSE AND ORGANIZATION

Governmental and Nonprofit Accounting: Theory and Practice, Second Edition, provides the fundamental knowledge necessary for understanding the operation of governmental and nonprofit entities, their accounting, auditing, and financial reporting practices, and the standards that shape their accounting and financial reporting systems.

Accounting Practices

Because an appropriate blanace between theory and practice is always an important goal, all governmental and nonprofit textbooks attempt to integrate theory and practice. This textbook uses an early emphasis on a conceptual framework for governmental accounting and financial reporting to introduce readers to that desirable blend of theory and practice. Chapters 1 and 2 expose them to the Governmental Accounting Standards Boards (GASB) concept statement and trace the evolution of that work in relation to earlier conceptual work done by the National Council on Governmental Accounting. These first two chapters also describe the efforts being made to develop generally accepted accoutning principles from a conceptual framework.

Organization

Governmental accounting, financial reporting, and auditing are described in the first 13 chapters of this book. After assigning Chapters 1 to 3, which provide the fundamental concepts, professors may order the material to suit their particular needs. (This book is intended to be as current as possible. However, because governmental accounting is developing so rapidly, the instructor may want to update some topics as needed.)

Colleges and universities, hospitals, volunteer health and welfare organizations, and other nonprofit organizations are covered in Chapters 14–16. Similarities and differences among these organizations, and between them and governmental entities, are highlighted. Here too, chapters can be interchanged without any loss of efficacy.

Relation to Business Accounting

Most students who take a course in nonprofit accounting are already familiar with business accounting. And to avoid the burden of learning a "new accounting language," this book frequently brings in the relationship between governmental or nonprofit accounting and business accounting. Chapter 3, for example, provides an overview of the significant similarities and differences between governmental and business accounting.

"Future and Current" GAAP

Governmental accounting will change markedly in the future. The GASB has issued a pronouncement changing the measurement focus and basis of accounting for governmental funds. Currently, those funds use current financial resources and the modified accrual basis of accounting. Future GAAP will be total financial resources and the accrual basis of accounting. The effective date of the pronouncement has been deferred to allow the GASB more time to develop implementation aids and to complete related projects such as the one on financial reporting. Until the effective date and during the transition period, practitioners need to understand and apply current GAAP. Thereafter, future GAAP will be important. Therefore, each chapter covers both the current and future GAAP. Current GAAP is covered in the body of each chapter. Future GAAP is covered in an appendix to the appropriate chapters.

Capturing the Essence of Change

Because the rapidly evolving nature of governmental and nonprofit accounting is important to overall understanding, change constitutes a major focal point of the textbook. The Governmental Accounting Standards Board has passed the five-year structure review with its purview unchanged and its credibility substantiated. In addition to the measurement focus/basis of accounting project, the Board is addressing and expected to finalize soon standards relating to the financial reporting, capital assets, and a host of other accounting and financial reporting issues. Some of those may be finalized by the time this book is published.

The Financial Accounting Standards Board (FASB) is taking an increasingly active role in establishing accounting standards for the nonprofit organizations within its jurisdiction. Recently issued standards related to financial reporting, contributions, and pledges all reflect the Board's concern for the inconsistent accounting and reporting practices of nonprofit organizations. Other nonprofit topics, such as investments, are on the Board's agenda.

Within the last few years, the American Institute of Certified Public Accountants has issued several auditing standards that relate directly or indirectly to governmental and nonprofit organizations. More are expected in the years ahead. The Institute is also in the process of revising several auditing guides related to these entities.

These rapid and fundamental changes in the accounting and financial reporting for governmental and nonprofit entities lend excitement to teaching and learning. Providing professors and students a guide to current accounting and reporting practices and, at the same time, giving a flavor of possible future practices was also challenging.

Pedagogy

Governmental and Nonprofit Accounting provides an extensive array of pedagogic elements. Each chapter ends with both review questions and exercises. Additionally, the book offers cases that allow discussion of practical and theoretical issues to create an awareness of the accounting and standard-setting environment impossible to achieve with problems and exercises alone.

The review questions tend to focus on specific issues and can be used to reinforce major points made in the text. Most exercises integrate several concepts and are especially useful for providing a broader review of the chapter material. Most chapters in Part 1 also contain an exercise related to the financial statements of Raleigh, North Carolina, which appear in the Appendix to the book. This continuing example helps integrate the separate topics.

Observation Blocks

Fact and editorial license are often confused in textbooks. To avoid that confusion and to add an occasional theoretical or practical implication, the text is sprinkled with personal observations. They are clearly marked as such. Students who have used this book have commented that these made the "text come alive" or "the theory clearer." They also represent yet another attempt to blend theory and practice.

ANCILLARY MATERIALS

A solutions Manual and Test Bank accompany the textbook. The Test Bank includes true-false, multiple-choice, and essay questions, as well as miscellaneous problems and exercises. Solutions to all Test Bank questions are provided, with detailed calculations where appropriate.

ACKNOWLEDGMENTS

This textbook has only one author who assumes responsibility for the accuracy and quality of material. Many people, however, helped make it better than it would otherwise have been. First among them is Professor Robert Anthony whose critical questions helped shape the way in which the FASB standards on contributions and financial reporting were incorporated into the nonprofit chapters.

Many students assisted by reading selected chapters and evaluating the ease with which material can be understood and the relationship between the text and the end-of-chapter materials.

Two graduate students, Darlene Bay and Dong Feng Lin, merit special attention. Darlene Bay has patiently read the chapters for typographical errors, conceptual flaws, and author inconsistencies as well as helped check the Solutions Manual and Test Bank. Dong Feng Lin prepared an outstanding Index and offered insightful observations which make the text easier for students to understand.

Sherry Rosette handled all of the tough typing assignments with only general guidance and lots of author frustration. To say that she served as typist greatly understates her editorial talents.

Harcourt Brace also has a fine staff of editors, and I most grateful for the patient assistance of Jim Patterson who kept everyone on schedule and always explained perfectly the limitations and potential of modern typesetting.

I am grateful, too, for the encouragement from Kenneth Rethmeier, Tim Vertovec, and Bill Teague, without whose support the textbook would not have been published. Thanks also to Brian Salisbury, art director; Ann Marie Coburn, production manager; Diana Farrell, marketing manager; and Glenn Martin, developmental editor.

Professors Michael Emerson, Harding University; Marc Rubin, Miami University; John L. Farbo, University of Idaho; Alexander E. C. Yuen, San Francisco State University; and Henry H. Davis, Eastern Illinois University; all provided an excellent critique of the first edition. Those critiques provided an excellent basis for sometimes subtle but always significant changes in the second edition. Bobbe M. Barnes, Economics Institute — affiliated with the University of Colorado at Denver — checked accuracy in the textbook and the solutions manual for this edition.

I extend my thanks once more to Joyce Watson of the City of Raleigh for making sure that the Appendix was available in the form desired and was received in a timely fashion.

Most of those acknowledged here are different from those acknowledged for their work on the first edition. Positions and lives change. One person, however, has remained in the same position, provided the same encouragement, and withstood the additional demands related to a textbook. He is Chuck Douglas, my husband, and I am deeply appreciative of his willingness to put life on the back burner while I finished this second edition.

BRIEF TABLE OF CONTENTS

CONTENTS

PART I

INTRODUCTION TO GOVERNMENTAL
ACCOUNTING SECTION

Chapters 1–12 describe accounting and financial reporting for governmental entities. The environment in which governmental units operate and the general concepts and accounting principles are discussed in the first two chapters. Chapter 3 gives a broad overview of the differences between accounting for governments and businesses.

Beginning with Chapter 4 and ending with Chapter 9, each individual fund and account group used in governmental accounting is described in detail, along with the general reporting practices of each one. Because the basis of accounting for many of these funds will change sometime in the future, the text provides guidance to the reader for both current and future standards. The current standards are described in the body of the chapter, and the future standards are described in the appendix to each chapter.

Chapter 10 covers the annual and interim financial reporting requirements for governmental entities. It includes illustrations of the various financial statements and describes the format and inclusions for the comprehensive annual financial report.

Auditing considerations relating to governmental units are discussed in Chapter 11 and Chapter 12, including the requirements of the Single Audit Act. Generally accepted auditing standards for governmental entities are described, and illustrative note disclosures are provided.

The final chapter in this section, Chapter 13, covers several important current topics in the governmental area. The continued concern over the jurisdiction of the Governmental Accounting Standards Board and the Financial Accounting Standards Board is one such topic. Others include pension accounting and the accounting and reporting for general fixed assets.

Governmental accounting is changing rapidly and will continue to do so. The first section of the textbook provides direction to those who will be examining these changes. It also will help those making the transition from current, generally accepted accounting principles to the principles applicable in the future.

CHAPTER 1

Governmental and Nonprofit Entities: An Overview of Accounting, Reporting, and Auditing

In its broadest sense, the term *nonprofit* refers to all entities that are not in business to make a profit. Thus, the term encompasses both governmental and all other not-for-profit entities. Frequently, the term is used in a narrower sense to refer to all nongovernmental not-for-profits, such as colleges and universities, hospitals, voluntary health and welfare organizations, and health care organizations. As sometimes happens when different meanings are attributed to a single term, the reader may have to determine the context in which the term is being used before the meaning is clear. Although this textbook uses the term in the narrower sense, quotes from other authors or from standard-setting bodies may not always be entirely consistent with this usage.

Governmental and nonprofit entities are a critically important force in our society. The federal government alone employs 3 million people, and its annual budget exceeds $1 trillion. In addition, local governments (states, counties, cities, towns, and school districts) spend billions of dollars and employ over 14 million workers. Nonprofit organizations, such as hospitals, colleges and universities, foundations, churches, and health care organizations, also spend considerable sums and employ a substantial work force.

Everyone regardless of occupation, locale, or status, comes into daily contact with governmental and nonprofit entities. When paying taxes, attending school, using public services, or working for local charities, people contribute to or benefit from these organizations.

The pervasive influence and economic significance of governmental and nonprofit organizations require the public to understand how they are organized and managed, and how they can be held accountable for the resources they spend. Accountants, in particular, need that understanding because they audit these organizations or prepare the information that others will audit. In addition, accountants frequently are called upon to assist laypersons in interpreting financial statements and to develop ways in which performance can be improved.

Chapters 1 and 2 of this text define the environment and character of governmental and nonprofit entities. In this first chapter, the external environment is discussed. The importance of these entities and their impact on society are briefly described. This chapter also covers the standard-setting process for governmental and nonprofit organizations: its historical development, significance, and current status. Another major topic covered is the nature and scope of auditing in the governmental and nonprofit area, including a description of the forces that are expanding the audit function.

THE DISTINCTION BETWEEN FOR-PROFIT AND NONPROFIT ORGANIZATIONS

Accounting and reporting for governmental and nonprofit organizations differ markedly from that of for-profit organizations. In a profit-making organization, management decisions are made, theoretically at least, to increase owners' welfare, which is usually measured in terms of profitablility.

Acctg & reporting differences

Because both investors and managers are interested in maximizing profits, there is a single purpose, and everyone associated with the business acts to contribute to the attainment of an agreed-upon objective. The same criterion can be used to evaluate decisions. This notion of a single goal is so deeply ingrained in our society that many people equate profit maximization with capitalism and democracy.

Judging the performance of entities whose goal is not profit maximization is more difficult and subjective. For most governmental and nonprofit organizations, the goal is to provide the best and highest level of service possible with the available resources. In government, an organization's objectives and its management actions may not coincide with the will of its elected officials. Evaluating performance to determine whether any service was "best" or at the "highest" level possible is not simply an economic judgment but a social and political one as well.

goals

This basic distinction between for-profit and nonprofit entities results in a number of reporting and managerial differences. In for-profit organizations, the unit as a whole is evaluated. For example, consolidated financial statements are prepared for companies with subsidiaries. In governmental and nonprofit entities, certain activities or functions tend to be examined separately, combining those activities in only the most superficial way. The premise is to provide accountability at the lowest level feasible. Because no one element of information is a good substitute for "the bottom line," lots of detail is typically shown.

reporting

In the governmental and nonprofit arena, operating activities tend to be segregated from long-term financing and activities related to the purchase of long-lived assets. This separation helps decision makers focus on which services or facilities are funded from current revenue sources and which ones are financed through longer-term debt commitments.

debt/ assets

Without a single criterion to measure performance of these units, it is difficult to compare the operating results of one entity to those of another. Is sheer size important? How can one set of services be compared to another? What makes one better or worse than the other? This lack of a single criterion also makes goal formation more complicated in the governmental and nonprofit sector. Each contributing and benefiting party has a notion of what the goals ought to be but those notions differ and, without a single evaluation criterion, it is difficult to build a consensus about good or bad performance.[1]

ACCOUNTING AND REPORTING SUPPORT FOR PUBLIC POLICY

Goals for governmental and nonprofit units cannot be established by asking which are best solely from an economic perspective: they are established for governmental and nonprofit units in political and social realms. For example, the city of Dallas does not decide that the marginal revenue of another social worker will enhance the city's profitability. Instead, the city council, with input from the citizens, decides that another social worker is or is not "needed" and ultimately whether that need is greater or less than the need for other services. Sometimes the decision may be based on the relative voter appeal of several services. Social needs and political votes often determine which programs are funded and at what levels.

Social political goals

Once programmatic decisions have been made, accounting and financial reporting enable the citizenry to determine whether the programs responded to the public mandate. In the 1988 revision of the audit standards of governmental organizations, the Comptroller General states:

> Our system of government today rests on an elaborate structure of interlocking relationships among all levels of government for managing public programs. Officials and employees who manage these programs must render a full account of their activities to the public.... Public officials, legislators, and private citizens want and need to know not only whether government funds are handled properly and in compliance with laws and regulations, but also whether government organizations and programs are achieving the purposes for which they were authorized and funded and are doing so economically and efficiently.[2]

Those few words describe explicitly the context in which accounting information is used to evaluate the extent to which public policy is being implemented. Accounting information and financial reports are used to determine if program managers have complied with the purpose and level of funding. Was less spent than authorized? More? If so, how much more? Were the program objectives achieved?

Comparisons of budgeted versus actual figures are particularly important for determining how much was spent, and in what areas expenditure patterns differed from what was anticipated. In fact, because budgets are considered an expression of public policy, such presentations are frequently a part of public financial reporting. Overspending may result in a fine or a more serious consequence. Compliance is not just an indication of good man-

---

[1] Specific accounting differences between business and governmental entities are the subject of Chapter 3.

[2] Comptroller General of the United States, *Government Auditing Standards* (Washington: GAO, July 1988), 1–3.

agement but a legal requirement. Accountants prepare information that enables public bodies or private boards to judge financial compliance.

Accountants also prepare nonfinancial reports that enable governmental entities to judge the programs' efficiency and effectiveness. **Efficiency** involves determining whether an entity is using its resources economically. Should the entity have been able to provide more service with a given level of resources? Evaluating an entity's **effectiveness** involves determining if the program is achieving its intended consequences. Is crime or hunger being reduced? By how much have juvenile delinquency rates declined since the program's initiation?

Accountants and public officials have begun to recognize that governmental financial reports do not contain sufficient information to judge the effectiveness and efficiency of an entity's activities. Other avenues are being explored to better measure these nonfinancial qualities. One such approach is referred to as *service efforts and accomplishments (SEA) reporting,* and its goal is to provide performance measures or indicators that will enable financial statement users to assess the accountability of the entity. Accounting practitioners, standard setters, and governing boards are all struggling with such issues as the extent to which such indicators ought to be mandated for all governmental entities, whether they should be included within the audit scope, and which ones best fit specific types of activities.

SEA

accountability

STANDARD SETTING IN THE GOVERNMENTAL AND NONPROFIT SECTOR

Standards

FASB

associations

state laws.

NCGA

Until 1984, the standard-setting process represented a combined effort of the Financial Accounting Standards Board (FASB), its predecessors, and associations of practicing professionals. Also, state laws addressed the accounting practices of many state and local governmental units. Little consistency existed among these laws and, as a result, they provided little benefit to the overall standard-setting process. With the exception of the FASB and the National Council on Governmental Accounting (NCGA), none of the professional associations' committees or commissions had official status, so a governmental unit or nonprofit entity could decide whether to follow their pronouncements. For many nonprofits, peer pressure was the only incentive to follow these early versions of generally accepted accounting principles.

Governmental Accounting and Reporting Standards

The development of accounting and financial reporting standards for governmental entities is easily traced. In 1948, a committee was formed by the Municipal Finance Officers Association (MFOA) to follow up on earlier recommendations the MFOA had made regarding accounting matters. The committee reviewed the recommendations, suggested some changes in accounting practices, and then dissolved.

1968 GAAFR

1979 NCGA

Statement I

Eleven years later, the MFOA formed another committee that wrote a document called *Governmental Accounting, Auditing, and Financial Reporting.*[3] Published in 1968, it was known as the 1968 GAAFR and served as the primary guide for accounting and financial reporting of governmental entities for about ten years. The 1968 GAAFR described some underlying accounting principles for governmental units, but most of the publication described how the principles were to be applied to particular transactions and events.

In 1979, the MFOA established another group called the National Council on Governmental Accounting that assumed responsibility for updating the 1968 GAAFR. Task forces were assigned to update parts of the document, but it soon became clear that the update would take some time and NCGA believed some accounting issues needed immediate attention. In March 1979, it addressed those immediate accounting concerns by issuing *Statement 1,* which iterated 12 basic accounting principles and discussed annual financial reporting requirements for governmental units. The statement included recommendations for annual audits.

About a year later, the American Institute of CPAs (AICPA) issued *Statement of Procedure 80-1* to incorporate into the Audit Guide for State and Local Governments changes necessitated by *Statement 1.* This action indicated that as far as the AICPA was concerned NCGA was promulgating preferred accounting practices for governmental entities.

Although *Statement 1* superseded the 1968 GAAFR, any of the 1968 illustrations that were consistent with the new guidelines could still be used. By 1980, the update of the 1968 GAAFR was completed. The foreword stated that, unlike the 1968 issue,

> this text neither establishes nor authoritatively interprets GAAP for governments. This edition ... is intended to provide government finance officers, elected officials, independent auditors, and others with detailed guidance to the effective application of ... *Statement 1.*[4]

For roughly five years, the NCGA provided the official accounting pronouncements. But by 1981, the forces were growing to establish a body that would carry the same status as the FASB, including a substantial research budget and full-time board members. (NCGA had 21 members, all of whom were volunteers from various segments of the governmental accounting profession, an annual budget of $50,000, and little support for research.) Culminating a long struggle and overcoming the self-interests of various facets of the governmental accounting profession, not to mention a territorial squabble with the FASB, the Governmental Accounting Standards Board (GASB) was formed in mid-1984.

1984 GASB formed

In May 1986, the Council of the American Institute of CPAs voted in favor of a resolution giving the GASB further status in the standard-setting process.

[3]Municipal Finance Officers Association of the United States and Canada, *Governmental Accounting, Auditing, and Financial Reporting* (Chicago: MFOA, 1968).

[4]Municipal Finance Officers Association of the United States and Canada, *Governmental Accounting, Auditing, and Financial Reporting* (Chicago: MFOA, 1980), 1.

[handwritten margin notes: Council AICPA / Rule 203 ↓ GASB to est GAAP for gov't entities]

The Council gave the GASB what is referred to as "Ethics Rule 203 support" for its standards. Rule 203 states:

> A member shall not (1) express an opinion or state affirmatively that the financial statements or other financial data of any entity are presented in conformity with generally accepted accounting principles or (2) state that he or she is not aware of any material modifications that should be made to such statements or data in order for them to be in conformity with generally accepted accounting principles, if such statements or data contain any departure from an accounting principle promulgated by bodies designated by Council to establish such principles that has a material effect on the statements or data taken as a whole.[5]

By adopting this resolution, the AICPA Council designated the GASB as the body to establish generally accepted accounting principles for governmental entities. Essentially, this placed the GASB on equal footing with the FASB insofar as its standard-setting process and application were concerned. Auditors who review the financial statements of a state or local governmental unit must assess the unit's financial statements in relation to the GASB standards, or they violate professional standards of conduct.

Like the FASB, the GASB is an independent board governed by articles of incorporation and is under the broad tutelage of the Financial Accounting Foundation (FAF). The articles of incorporation make it clear that the GASB will have purview over all governmental entities, but standards for all other organizations remain under the FASB's authority (the pertinent ones for this book are, of course, the nonprofit organizations).

The GASB has a full-time chairman and vice chairman, a full-time director of research, and three other part-time board members. It uses the same due process as the FASB to establish accounting and reporting standards. Typically, exposure drafts or discussion memoranda are issued, followed by public hearings and periods of comment. A pronouncement is issued after the deliberative process is completed. A pronouncement may be followed by an interpretation or a technical bulletin.

OBSERVATION ▲

To date, the GASB has issued 23 statements, one concepts statement, and several technical bulletins and interpretations. Some statements have been easy to develop while others have been very difficult. Difficulties sometimes arise because of changes in the composition of the Board. New board members do not always agree with the positions taken by their predecessors. This causes delay in the issuance of the statements. In other cases, the issues faced by the GASB are exceedingly complex and therefore difficult to resolve. Also, the GASB would find some statements easier to develop had they worked harder to complete the conceptual framework before undertaking so many topical issues.

---

[5]American Institute of Certified Public Accountants, *AICPA Professional Standards: Code of Conduct/Bylaws, as of January 14, 1992* (New York: AICPA, 1992), 14.

Standard Setting for Nonprofits

The standard-setting path for nonprofits is not nearly as straightforward or focused as that for governmental units. The original mandate of the FASB and its predecessors could easily be interpreted to encompass nonprofits, but it was not until 1980 that the FASB issued anything of consequence pertaining to these entities. As part of its conceptual framework project, the Board issued *Concepts Statement No. 4* on the objectives of financial reporting by nonbusiness organizations.

With the exception of the AICPA audit guides[6] and with limited guidance from the FASB, nonprofits turned to their own professional organizations for assistance in developing accounting and reporting practices. For example, the National Association of College and University Business Officers has developed detailed preferred accounting practices for colleges and universities. Similarly, the American Hospital Association developed descriptions of the chart of accounts and other materials relating to hospital accounting. The United Way, the National Health Council, the Health Care Financial Management Association, and others have developed standards of accounting and financial reporting for health care and voluntary health and welfare organizations. Professional organizations for church administrators or foundation officers have addressed particular accounting and reporting issues of their member organizations sporadically over the years. Without the several audit guides for nonprofit organizations, very little can be said about preferred accounting practices of these organizations.

The GASB operated for more than a year before the FASB revised its concepts statement pertaining to the elements of financial statements to incorporate nonprofit organizations.[7] Replacing *Concepts Statement No. 3* and designed to mark the FASB's active involvement with the nonprofit area, it contributed little to the literature. The term *nonprofit* was simply added to much of the existing language in the document.

Two items of particular importance to nonprofit organizations were discussed: the nature of its net assets (assets minus liabilities) and the effect of donor restrictions on those net assets. The document makes it clear that while net assets for both for-profit and nonprofit organizations represent the difference between the entity's assets and its liabilities, those for nonprofit entities do not represent an ownership interest. The limited discussion of nonprofits asserts that there are three classes of net assets. Some are permanently restricted by donor-imposed stipulations, others are temporarily restricted for purposes imposed by donors, and still others are unrestricted.

Before the issuance of this concepts statement, considerable debate surrounded these restricted assets. The central question was whether donor-imposed restrictions created liabilities, and whether those restrictions should be identified with specific assets or with net assets. The statement makes

---

[6]The AICPA has published four audit guides relevant to these organizations: volunteer health and welfare organizations, colleges and universities, health care entities, and other nonprofits.

[7]Financial Accounting Standards Board, *Statement of Financial Accounting Concepts No. 6* (Stamford, Conn.: FASB, 1985).

clear that in the FASB's opinion, donor restrictions do not constitute liabilities and restrictions pertain to total net assets, not particular ones.

    Other developments include issuance of a statement requiring depreciation of fixed assets. The FASB *Statement No. 93* is controversial because most nonprofits had depreciated only operating assets, and the development of asset records necessary to depreciate most other assets was costly and considered by many practitioners to add little to the financial reporting of these organizations. The FASB also has tackled recognition issues related to contributions and the appropriate financial statements for nonprofits.[8]

FASB No. 93 Depreciation

THE GASB/FASB DISPUTE

Dividing the authority of the two boards between governmental and nonprofit entities was meant to define clearly the jurisdiction of the FASB and the GASB. However, it has not turned out that way. Because some organizations that are similar in function and economic substance can be either governmentally or privately owned, similar units can have different accounting and reporting standards. For example, colleges and universities, utilities, and hospitals can be either governmentally or privately owned. Governmentally owned units derive their standards from the GASB; those operated in the private sector receive guidance from the FASB. If the two boards issue different accounting practices applicable to colleges, for example, it would be difficult to compare the results of operations or the financial position of one type of college or university to those of another type.

    When the possibility of conflicting standards for similar organizations first became evident, a flurry of activity began. Meetings were held with representatives of the two boards and the Financial Accounting Foundation (FAF) to see if the problem could be resolved before dissimilar standards were issued for similar organizations. The Financial Accounting Foundation established a structure committee to address the matter and, in December 1986, the committee issued its report. As the committee described the problem, "the two Boards, acting entirely within their defined jurisdiction, can establish different standards for the same types of transactions (e.g., pension costs and depreciation) and entities (e.g., utilities and hospitals) not justified by the fact that there are differences in circumstances."[9]

Conflicts

    The committee took as a given the FAF's reluctance to revise the structure agreement that was signed at the time the GASB was formed and, within that context, provided recommendations that were later adopted by the FAF. Excerpts from those recommendations follow:

---

[8]Financial Accounting Standards Board, *Statement of Financial Accounting Standards No. 116, Accounting for Contributions Received and Contributions Made* (Norwalk, Conn.: FASB, 1993), and *Statement of Financial Accounting Standards No. 117, Financial Statements of Not-For-Profit Organizations* (Norwalk, Conn.: FASB, 1993).

[9]Financial Accounting Foundation, "Structure Committee Report to Trustees Regarding Consistent Standards by FASB and GASB" (Committee Report, Stamford, Conn.: 1986), 6.

1. Each Board and its technical staff should give more emphasis to communicating with the other about projects that are in process and planned.
2. While each Board must exercise due process in coming to its conclusions, each should, where possible, avoid duplication of efforts and unnecessary use of FAF resources on research and other activities regarding issues that already have been researched and studied by the other Board.
3. To implement 1 and 2 above, the Chairmen and Directors of Research of the two Boards should develop, for review and approval by the Trustees, specific mechanisms for communication between the Boards and their respective staffs about present and planned projects and about sharing or performing joint research on technical subjects of mutual interest.
4. When adding an agenda item that could result in one Board reaching a conclusion different from one already published by the other Board (or its predecessor) on a particular technical issue, or which could result in a standard applicable to the types of entities or activities also within the jurisdiction of the other Board, each Board should report to the Trustees for information purposes the background and basis for adding the subject to its agenda.
5. In each case of proposing or issuing different standards on a particular technical issue, each Board should state explicitly its justification for coming to a conclusion different from that already published by the other Board (or its predecessor).[10]

In adopting these recommendations, the FAF also decided to review the structure and operations of the two boards and their advisory councils in 1989. Although the structure review resulted in considerable turmoil, the standard-setting process remained unchanged. The GASB has governmental entities and the FASB has all other nonprofits and business entities. Chapter 13 describes this structure review in more detail.

OVERSIGHT RESPONSIBILITY AND THE AUDIT FUNCTION

Most governmental and nonprofit organizations are governed by a board, commission, or council. As with for-profit boards of directors, these governing boards establish overall policy and set the level of the annual operating budget. Usually they are self-perpetuating. They act as the conduit through which the unit's functions and programs are explained and interpreted for the public, the constituency, and other interested parties.

Whether revenues are derived from taxes or from contributions, governmental and nonprofit organizations operate on funds furnished by others. Managers have a fiduciary responsibility for converting those resources into viable services, and they should be held accountable for the way in which they make the conversion. Without a generalized way to characterize operating re-

---

[10]Ibid., 8–9.

sults, such as "profitability," the board measures accountability by evaluating the manager's compliance with public or board policy and the effectiveness and efficiency with which the resources were converted to planned services.

The evaluation is conducted in a number of ways: regular meetings to assess policy directions, often in a public forum with an opportunity for citizens to challenge the decisions being made by the oversight board; internal audits designed to provide information on selected financial or managerial activities; and external independent audits. Both internal and external audits are important; one is not a substitute for the other.

Internal audits are not necessarily financial in nature. They can be designed to examine any aspect of the operations, from internal control procedures to pricing and space allocation issues. The existence of a professional internal audit staff reduces the amount of effort required by external auditors. However, external audits are still necessary because they bring independent judgment that is so critically important in maintaining credibility with the public.

External Audits

Nothing comparable to the Securities and Exchange Commission (SEC) exists in the nonprofit arena. No national body forces governments and nonprofits to provide audited financial statements. Nonetheless, there is considerable pressure (and it is escalating) on these organizations to follow generally accepted accounting principles (GAAP) in accounting and reporting. Some state laws or local regulations make GAAP accounting and reporting a requirement for governmental entities. Others require periodic audited financial statements that serve the same purpose. Since the AICPA Rule 203 makes the GASB standards GAAP, auditors would have to give, at best, a qualified opinion if the unit did not use GAAP as defined by the GASB.

Governmental units and nonprofits may obtain state or federal funding. Reporting requirements associated with the funding encourage units to adopt GAAP accounting and reporting. Also, some credit-rating firms emphasize the importance of improved governmental financial reporting by issuing policy statements urging issuers of governmental debt to prepare financial statements according to GAAP.

OBSERVATION ▲

Use of the phrase *generally accepted accounting principles* does not imply that they are the same as those for profit-making entities. Rather, the principles are those generally accepted within the context of governmental and nonprofit accounting, as Rule 203 and subsequent chapters make clear.

A program begun by the Government Finance Officers Association (GFOA) in 1945 took hold in the mid-1970s and brought accounting practices within many governmental units into conformity with GAAP. GFOA's Certificate of Achievement Program recognizes excellence in financial reporting. Any governmental unit that receives this certificate may publish it in the comprehensive annual financial report (CAFR), enhancing its public image. One requirement for earning distinction under the program is to "enhance understanding of current GAAP theory." A report cannot enhance understanding of GAAP if GAAP is not used in preparing the report. Governmental units are encouraged through the certificate program and other forms of peer pressure to adopt GAAP accounting and reporting standards.

Not least of the forces increasing governments' and nonprofits' interest in and use of GAAP is the public's demand for greater accountability. Although it may not be totally justified, the public senses that reports prepared according to GAAP will be easier to understand. The public also feels that the data will be more consistent and credible.

Types of External Audits

In contrast with the private sector, in which almost all audits are financial in nature, those in the public sector are financial and compliance, or performance audits. In a financial and compliance audit, the auditor expresses an opinion on the audited unit's financial statements—the fairness of presentation in conformity with GAAP—and its compliance with the various legal and contractual provisions used to ensure acceptable governmental organizational performance and effective public-sector management.

Performance audits are designed to assess the economy and efficiency of an entity's operations, or the effectiveness of the programs offered. In an economy and efficiency audit, the auditor determines: "(a) whether the audited entity is managing and utilizing its resources ... economically and efficiently; (b) the causes of inefficiencies or uneconomical practices; and (c) whether the entity has complied with laws and regulations concerning matters of economy and efficiency."[11]

The effectiveness audit (or "program audit" as it is often called) was established during the late 1960s and early 1970s when local and state governments relied heavily on federal funding. Geared specifically to determine if the unit complied with the conditions and other requirements under which it accepted the grant or revenue-sharing funds, program audits focus on performance and management actions.

Single Audit

With several federally financed programs from different agencies, a local unit could potentially be under constant audit. A new audit concept, the single audit, addresses the possible duplication of audit effort and the inefficiencies at the local level caused by almost continual requests for information or analyses from federal program auditors. A federal law, the Single Audit Act,[12] sets the parameters for the single audit, and the Office of Management and Budget (OMB) provides the interpretations and detailed guidelines for implementing

[11]Comptroller General, *Government Auditing Standards,* 1, Sec. 5.
[12]*Single Audit Act of 1984,* Public Law 98–502.

the act. A single audit is required if a governmental entity receives $100,000 or more in federal funding.

Under the OMB's implementation regulations, state and local governments have one audit performed to satisfy all federal agencies. One federal agency, called the cognizant agency, is responsible for seeing that the audit is actually performed and that the audit report is distributed to the appropriate funding agencies. Under a single audit, the auditor tests for compliance with applicable laws and regulations as well as adequacy of matching requirements, efficiency of administration, and proper allocation of indirect charges.

OBSERVATION ▲

Ironically, the Single Audit Act, applicable to audit years after December 31, 1984, is being implemented at a time when federal funding of state and local programs is declining. Therefore, it is more difficult to judge the effectiveness of the act. During the heyday of federal assistance, the legislation was bogged down in the political process. Now that federal funding has declined, the audit requirements are in place!

The OMB has extended the single audit concept to nonprofits as well. Circular A-133, *Audits of Institutions of Higher Education and Other Nonprofit Institutions,* requires an organization-wide audit for nonprofits receiving a certain amount of federal financial assistance. The organization-wide audit is conceptually very similar to the single audit required for qualifying governmental entities.

Audit Standards

Developing and applying audit standards for business entities is straightforward. The FASB develops generally accepted accounting principles; the AICPA establishes the audit standards. If a firm falls within the purview of the SEC, its accounting must follow GAAP. Other firms are urged to follow GAAP; many lenders require audited financial statements, and the audit reveals the extent to which GAAP is being followed. In complying with professional standards, an auditor must adhere to the AICPA's audit standards and judge the extent to which a unit's accounting is in accordance with GAAP.

This relationship between the SEC, the FASB, and the AICPA encourages firms to use GAAP and requires attestation to that use. To obtain public financing from investors and creditors, financial institutions, and others, a business certainly attempts to follow accounting practices that will lead to a "clean opinion," an attestation that generally accepted accounting principles are being applied to business transactions. Auditors want to audit according to accepted auditing standards; to do otherwise leads to a violation of their professional standards of conduct and could lead to loss of the CPA designation, without which they could not practice. All parties concerned benefit by supporting the use of GAAP and the development of clear, concise general, field, and reporting audit standards.

[handwritten marginalia: Operate according to state laws / local ①]

The audit environment pertaining to governmental entities is quite different. The first requirement is to operate within the constraints of state law and local regulations. Some state laws and local regulations require accounting practices not defined as GAAP by the GASB and its predecessors. If state law requires non-GAAP accounting, the financial audit must address the extent to which the unit complied with the state's required accounting practices.

A governmental unit could be operating within the state's requirements and still receive an "unclean" opinion because GAAP was not followed. If the same unit received federal funds, the cognizant agency would require a single audit. The basis for the single audit opinion would be the GASB's GAAP. Conceivably, the federal audit standards could differ markedly from those required under state law, resulting in a confusing audit opinion.

Although the potential for confusion exists, diverse practices are gradually being eliminated. In recent years, many states have revised statutes to reference generally accepted accounting principles instead of specifying their own accounting practices. Also, the U.S. General Accounting Office (GAO) incorporates, by reference, the AICPA audit standards for all federal financial audits unless they are specifically excluded by formal announcement. To date, no exclusion has been issued. However, because the interests and needs of many users in government are broader than those that can be satisfied by financial audits, the GAO has included additional standards for expanded scope auditing (the performance audits referred to earlier).

Nonprofits, relying largely on public solicitations for operating resources, have an incentive to follow GAAP and obtain periodic financial audits. Bond-rating agencies encourage the use of the GAAP by those nonprofit entities issuing bonds. Also, those receiving federal assistance are audited and therefore pressured to use GAAP. The remainder may have no such incentive. They tend to use accounting practices that are perceived as being understood by their governing boards. Management reports, or perhaps a compilation or review, are considered adequate for reporting purposes.

The Adequacy of Governmental Audits

Audit standards and the competency of those performing the audits have recently received considerable national attention. In 1986, the General Accounting Office reviewed the quality of audits performed by CPAs of recipients of federal money. In its review, the GAO defined audit quality as "compliance with professional standards and contractual terms set out for the particular type of audit being conducted." The GAO concluded that 34 percent of the audits sampled did not comply with professional standards, and 20 percent of the standards violations were severe.

The two most serious deficiencies were insufficient testing of compliance with governmental laws and regulations, and insufficient evaluation of internal accounting controls, including controls over federal expenditures. The GAO developed a number of recommended actions for strengthening the audit capabilities of practicing professionals. Those actions include required peer reviews, better college preparation in governmental accounting, and continuing professional education requirements for CPAs performing governmental audits. Numerous new audit standards have been developed that address specific audit concerns related to governmental entities.

Since 1986, reviews by the GAO and inspectors general for federal agencies have indicated that auditors are doing a better job. However, failures to comply with generally accepted auditing standards persist, and the profession is devoting considerable time and resources to addressing this problem.

TEXTBOOK ORGANIZATION

The first 12 chapters of this book discuss the accounting, financial reporting, and auditing of governmental organizations. The discussion begins with the conceptual framework within which accounting, reporting, and auditing take place. Much of the text is devoted to making sure the reader understands the workings of the accounting and reporting system as well as the standards governing the accounting and reporting system. The rate of change in accounting standards makes a basic understanding critical for financial statement preparers, auditors, and laypersons who sit on oversight boards. The earlier standards as well as the current ones are covered.

Chapter 13 summarizes current issues in the governmental sector. It is followed by three chapters on accounting and reporting for other nonprofit organizations. While many accounting and reporting issues are similar for the two types of organizations, this division is necessary because the standard-setting process and, accordingly, the resolution of these issues are frequently different for governmental and other nonprofit entities. Clearer exposition and hopefully better understanding result from separating the discussions.

QUESTIONS

1-1 "The accounting and reporting standards for governmental and nonprofit entities are not nearly as well developed as those for businesses." Do you agree with that statement? Explain why or why not.

1-2 Accountants are unaccustomed to providing information on a governmental or nonprofit entity's efficiency and effectiveness. Explain why.

1-3 From what you have learned previously about the standard-setting process for businesses, contrast for-profit development with that of nonprofit entities.

1-4 Speculate why the preface to the 1980 GAAFR made it clear that its purpose was not to establish or interpret GAAP for governments.

1-5 Discuss the similarities and differences between the organization of the GASB and that of the FASB.

1-6 In the context of current accounting standards, who owns (a) a city? (b) a nonprofit foundation?

1-7 What is the principal characteristic that distinguishes governmental and nonprofit from for-profit entities? Explain why that creates accounting and reporting differences between the two types of organizations.

1-8 Of the pronouncements issued by the FASB pertaining to nonprofit entities, which do you think will have the most long-run significance? Why?

1-9 The 1986 FAF Structure Committee's recommendations have been described by some as weak and ineffectual. Explain why you believe they have been described that way. Do you agree? Why?

1-10 "Without a body similar to the SEC, there is no pressure on governmental and nonprofit entities to utilize GAAP." Explain why you believe that statement to be true or false.

1-11 Why are some goods and services provided by governmental and nonprofit entities?

1-12 Discuss the role of the FASB and the AICPA in establishing GAAP for nonprofit entities.

1-13 *Compliance* is a term frequently used to describe the accounting and reporting for governmental entities. Explain the context in which the term is used.

1-14 Explain why an external auditor is not required to issue an opinion on the efficiency and effectiveness of a governmental organization.

1-15 What is the purpose of performance audits? Speculate why they were developed.

1-16 How would a single audit assist a governmental entity in using its resources more effectively?

1-17 In a single audit, what is the responsibility of the cognizant agency?

1-18 Why was inclusion in Ethics Rule 203 an important developmental step for the GASB?

1-19 What developments have been responsible for narrowing the accounting principles used by governmental entities?

1-20 If you were a member of your state's legislative body, how would you have reacted to the GAO's report on the quality of federal audits and the competency of those conducting the audits?

CASES

1-1 The Milltown City Council has recently hired a new city manager. Because the city has previously had some financial difficulties, the manager wants assurance that the unaudited financial statements presented during the interview are accurate.

The city has a total population of 200,000, and its main source of revenue is property taxes. However, the city has been very active in soliciting federal grants for a sewer treatment plant and exploratory research for several potential solid waste dump sites. Its federal grant money totaled $132,000 during the last fiscal period.

Many Milltown hourly and salaried employees have worked for the city for a number of years. Turnover is low, and a recent federal review of personnel hirings suggested that recruitment procedures are somewhat lax. The city offers the typical array of social services, from administrative and planning assistance to public assistance for the aged and the needy. The newly hired manager made some comparisons with cities of comparable size and determined that either on an absolute or on a per-capita basis, the cost of services is relatively expensive. The city council assured the manager that the differences in costs stem from different accounting practices among cities. The differences also trace, according to the city council, to higher salary scales. Finally, the longevity of the employees means that many are being paid at the higher end of the salary scale.

REQUIRED

1. What advice would you give the new city manager for ensuring the accuracy of Milltown's financial statements?
2. Without prejudicing your answer to the first question, assume that the city council decided to utilize an audit to respond to the manager's questions. Describe what type(s) of audit(s) you would recommend, and explain why.
3. When the audit(s) is (are) completed, what assurances does the manager have that the financial statements are accurate and the city's operations are being managed efficiently and effectively? Relate your answer to specific types of audits.

1-2 It has been suggested that you, a newly elected member of the Socorro City Council, review the revenue and expenditures, budget and actual, for the operating activities during the previous year. Other council members think this is a good way to get a feel for the city's operations. You profess ignorance about governmental accounting procedures, but finally agree to review the data. The following summary is handed to you, and you are told that it represents the budget and actual data for the city's general fund, its operating entity.

Socorro City
General Fund
Revenue and Expenditures, Budget and Actual
Fiscal Year 19X9

	Budget	**Actual**	**Difference**
Revenue:			
Property Taxes	$214,000	$276,000	$ 62,000
Fees and Fines	29,000	19,000	(10,000)
Revenue Sharing	104,000	104,000	-0-
Sales Taxes	150,000	123,000	(27,000)
Licenses and Permits	20,000	21,000	1,000
Miscellaneous	37,000	25,000	(12,000)
Total	$554,000	$568,000	$ 14,000

(continued)

(continued)	Budget	Actual	Difference
Expenditures:			
Personal Services	$310,000	$311,000	$ 1,000
Contracted Services	-0-	11,000	11,000
Supplies and Materials	133,000	129,000	(4,000)
Equipment	28,500	25,000	(3,500)
Current Debt Obligations	82,500	82,500	-0-
Total	$554,000	$558,500	$ 4,500

REQUIRED

1. What conclusions would you draw from the budgetary information?
2. Is it significant that the revenues and expenditures are both over budget?
3. What importance would you place on the fact that numerous line items are considerably over budget or under budget?
4. Presuming the operating segment is reflective of the total operations of the city, what can you gauge about its financial position from the operating results?

1-3 You have been contacted by a member of the FAF, who would like you to consult on an important issue. Congress has proposed legislation that would force consolidation of the GASB and the FASB. The sponsoring congressperson believes the proposal would assure cooperation between the two boards, avoid future territorial disputes, and assure the consistency of accounting and reporting standards for governmental entities and nonprofit organizations. In addition to consolidating the two boards, the legislation would provide an appropriation of $500,000 per year to assist financially in operating the combined board.

The FAF wants your recommendation about supporting or opposing the bill. Some members of the Foundation are impressed with the legislation. Others are adamantly opposed to the proposition. The Foundation's board members are confident that if they receive an analysis from you concerning the reasons for supporting or opposing the legislation, FAF will be able to develop a consensus.

REQUIRED

1. What arguments can you identify to support passage of the bill? Those opposed?
2. What position would you recommend the FAF take? Why? (Be specific, and draw on opinions formed from other classes in addition to the materials presented in this chapter.)
3. What public reaction would likely develop over this bill? Why?

1-4 The Seattle Opera Association faces a dilemma. Because of the economic climate, fund-raising has not been as easy as in the past. The Association has rarely had to ask for money in recent years. Being the only professional opera company in the area, it has been placed high on the donation list of leading businesses and philanthropists. Proof that their contributions were well spent was seen in the excellent productions offered by the Association. Now businesses are being asked to justify donations to their own boards of directors, and with the formation of a new ballet company in the greater Seattle area, wealthy residents have competing uses for their contributions to the performing arts.

The board is asking for assistance in developing a strategy for increasing its fund-raising capabilities. One particular proposal is to issue audited financial statements to potential donors.

REQUIRED

1. Evaluate the merits of providing audited financial statements. Indicate how the board should weigh the advantages against the costs of an audit. If an audit is desirable, what type should it be?
2. What explanation could you give board members to counteract the opponents who argue that, if the activities of the Opera Association are so beneficial, it should be a for-profit organization?
3. What accounting and reporting difficulties would be encountered if the Opera Association and the ballet company were merged? Would the standards and the nature of the reports be comparable?

1-5 As the accountant for a local church, you are asked to explain the item called "depreciation" on the operating statement. One member of the church's finance committee does not understand what depreciation signifies. Furthermore, the committee member cannot understand why it should affect the financial status of the church. She reasons that the capital program is separate from the operating activities. When additional capital needs are identified, the church develops a funding campaign and solicits funds for the capital program; therefore, depreciation has no relevance to the annual operating activities.

REQUIRED

1. What is the meaning of depreciation? Is it necessary to take depreciation in nonprofit organizations? In governmental units?
2. Is the board member correct that depreciation should not be taken on a nonprofit organization's assets? Explain.
3. How might the financial statement presentation be changed to make the concept of depreciation clearer and more understandable to the lay reader?

CHAPTER 2

Objectives and Principles of Accounting for Governmental Entities

Governmental units, including incorporated cities, towns, counties, school districts, states, and the federal government, are established to provide service to citizens who live within their geographical boundaries. They are funded, in large part, from taxes assessed against real and personal property and certain transactions. Some governmental units also charge for facility use and some services.

Governmental units have substantial influence over their constituencies. Their boards, commissions, legislative houses, or councils have broad taxation authority. These oversight bodies also have authority to define acceptable behavior on the part of citizens and businesses. In order for the governmental unit to be accountable to the electorate, there must be some way to hold the oversight body responsible for its actions. Periodic elections are one common way of making sure the ultimate power is in the hands of the governed.

Another important way of demonstrating accountability is by issuing periodic financial reports to the governed. For those reports to be understandable and to serve their intended purpose, some broad accounting objectives and principles are necessary. This chapter describes the broad objectives and accounting principles underlying the accounting and reporting practices of state and local governments. It also describes a fund and the accounting used as a basis for their reports. The chapter ends with a brief overview of governmental budgeting and accounting.

THE REPORTING UNIT

Cities, towns, states, and school districts are all governmental organizations (the federal government is one, too, but it is excluded here because its accounting practices are quite different from those of other governmental units). Each organization is described as a **reporting unit** and prepares financial statements used by citizens, creditors, bond rating agencies, and others to evaluate the financial position and operating results for purposes of making public policy and financing decisions. Other governmental organizations, such as sewer and water districts, airports, seaport authorities, special development projects, and multicounty or city recreational entities, usually are not reporting units. Their financial reports are included with a major reporting unit—a city, county, or state. The discussion that follows concentrates on the primary reporting units, such as counties, incorporated cities, towns, and states.

Historically, the primary public policy issue was whether those operating governmental units had adequately protected the resources entrusted to them. The financial statements were developed to assist in evaluating stewardship for the year; the accounting system was designed to enable users to view each activity separately. How could one tell if construction activities, for example, were handled effectively—the bonds sold at the right time, the contractor paid the correct amount, or the interest and principal payments made properly—if these activities were mixed in with the general operating activities of a unit?

When businesses want to evaluate an activity separately, they create a division, segment, or department. These subunits enable management to evaluate managers of particular production facilities, product or service lines, or manufacturing processes. Depending upon the precision necessary, general overhead, financing, and other administrative costs may be allocated to each division, segment, or department. An operating statement, perhaps even a cash flow statement, is sometimes prepared for each unit. These financial statements are used primarily for internal evaluation purposes. The financial statements contained in the annual report to stockholders depict the overall profitability of the firm; all divisions and departments are consolidated to determine the net income and financial position of the business as a whole.

Governmental units also segregate particular activities, but much differently than in industry. General operating activities are identified separately from construction activities, as are activities operated to recover costs, charge-back divisions, and long-term assets. Unlike the division or segment in the private sector, the governmental activities that are accounted for separately remain so in the financial reporting system. In fact, the segregation is primarily for external reporting and not for internal management purposes. Operating statements show the operating results for each activity; the balance sheet shows its status. No attempt is made to consolidate all of the activities into one operating unit.

A FUND: THE BASIC ACCOUNTING UNIT

Segregating activities for external reporting results in separate accounting and reporting entities within a unit. Each unit—a city, county, state, school district, or town—has within it several activities that are separate and distinct from others for purposes of accounting and reporting. For example, a governmental entity establishes a separate entity for all construction activities. These separate accounting and reporting entities are referred to as **funds**. The accounting and reporting entities for fixed assets and long-term

*account
    groups*
fixed assets
long term debt

debt are referred to as **account groups,** rather than funds. Exhibit 2-1 depicts the differences between the subunits of government and those of private industry.

No common basis, such as the product line, factory location, and the like found in business, exists for the various separate funds or account groups. Some funds were established because of intense interest by governing bodies or debt holders. Others were established for activities that have unique accounting requirements, for example, to satisfy a requirement that revenues cover all costs. Still others were developed as a result of legal mandates relating to gifts or assets held in trust. The diversity of origin has led to a diversity of accounting practices for the funds, another reason why separate financial statements are prepared for each fund.

To complicate matters further, similar activities may be accounted for separately. For instance, a governmental unit may be operating several construction projects simultaneously, in which case each project may be accounted for in a separate fund. The same is true for debt servicing activities; better reporting may be achieved by reporting the debt service activities for each debt issue in a separate fund.

Types of Funds and Account Groups

*10 funds
2 acct groups*

State and local governmental units have ten funds and two account groups. As Exhibit 2-2 indicates, a general fund is used to account for the unit's general operating activities. All general operating activities are accounted for in a single fund, so there is only one general fund. A governmental

---

Exhibit 2-1

Comparison of Business and Governmental Accounting Structure

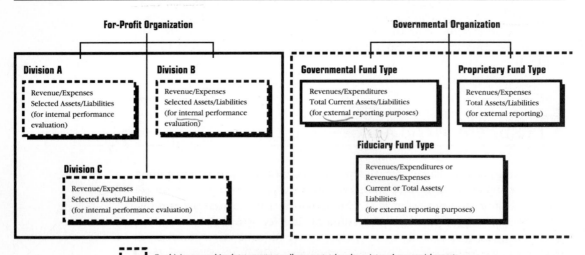

For-Profit Organization | Governmental Organization

Division A
Revenue/Expenses
Selected Assets/Liabilities
(for internal performance
evaluation)

Division B
Revenue/Expenses
Selected Assets/Liabilities
(for internal performance
evaluation)

Division C
Revenue/Expenses
Selected Assets/Liabilities
(for internal performance evaluation)

Governmental Fund Type
Revenues/Expenditures
Total Current Assets/Liabilities
(for external reporting purposes)

Proprietary Fund Type
Revenues/Expenses
Total Assets/Liabilities
(for external reporting)

Fiduciary Fund Type
Revenues/Expenditures or
Revenues/Expenses
Current or Total Assets/
Liabilities
(for external reporting purposes)

Combining or combined statements, usually memo totals only, or internal managerial reports

Entity-audited financial statements

Exhibit 2-2

Funds and Account Groups
Governmental Entities

Fund/Account Group	Purpose
General Fund	To account for all current financial resources except those to be accounted for in another fund.
Special Revenue Funds	To account for the proceeds of specific revenue sources (other than fiduciary sources or major capital projects) that are legally restricted to expenditure for specified purposes.
Capital Projects Funds	To account for current financial resources to be used for the acquisition or construction of major capital facilities (other than those financed by proprietary funds and trust funds).
Debt Service Funds	To account for the accumulation of resources for, and the payment of, general long-term debt principal and interest.
Enterprise Funds	To account for operations that are financed and operated in a manner similar to private enterprises—where the intent is to provide goods or services to the general public.
Internal Service Funds	To account for the financing of goods or services provided by one department or agency to other departments or agencies of the governmental unit.
Fiduciary Funds (4 funds)	To account for assets held by a governmental unit in a trustee capacity or as an agent for individuals, private organizations, other governmental units, and/or other funds.
General Fixed Asset Account Group	To account for all general fixed assets of a governmental unit.
General Long-Term Debt Account Group	To account for all unmatured general long-term liabilities of the governmental unit.

Source: Adapted from *Governmental Accounting, Auditing and Financial Reporting* (Chicago: GFOA, 1988), 11.

unit may have several capital projects funds, which account for expenditures pertaining to the construction or acquisition of fixed assets. Special revenues, those from an earmarked source and usually expended for specified projects, are accounted for in special revenue funds. Servicing of debt, an item of particular interest to bondholders, bond rating services, and others, is segregated in debt service funds.

Two funds, internal service and enterprise, account for activities that are operated on a break-even or for-profit basis within a governmental unit. These are commonly referred to as "business-type" or proprietary funds.

OBSERVATION ▲

Interestingly, although the idea of separate entities was a natural outgrowth of a desire to measure stewardship by government managers, accounting professionals did not support the logical extension of this idea, a fund for each program. It is not clear why a fund was established for "construction activities" rather than one for highway or street maintenance. Similarly, if stewardship was the primary focus, why is there no fund for public parks and recreation, commerce, social welfare, public health and safety, and so forth?

Funds also are maintained to segregate moneys held in a fiduciary capacity; agency, pension, expendable trust, and nonexpendable types of trust funds all fall in this category.

Measurement Focus of the Funds

The fund types suggest that stewardship focused on several functions: operating—general operations, special operations, and business activities; debt and its servicing; acquisition or construction of long-term assets; and fiduciary. For general and special operations, debt service, and asset acquisition functions, the primary interest of those monitoring stewardship is what money flowed in and out, and what financial resources remain to be spent in a subsequent period. For business operations, on the other hand, the idea of the "bottom line" and the maintenance of the capital entrusted to those managers is of predominant concern.

Governmental units use the term *measurement focus* to describe what is being measured. When the focus is on inflows and outflows and balances of financial assets and liabilities at year end, **financial resources** are being measured. Which financial resources are included also affects the measurement focus. The focus could be on **current** financial resources (current assets and liabilities) or **total** financial resources, which would include all financial resources but exclude fixed, intangible, and other nonfinancial resources. If, on the other hand, the focus is on how well the governmental unit maintained its assets, **capital maintenance** is being measured. Exhibit 2-3 indicates the measurement focus appropriate for each fund type.

The two account groups, general fixed asset and general long-term debt, are not listed in Exhibit 2-3. They are nothing more than single entries

Exhibit 2-3

A Summary of Fund Accounting

Fund Type	Fund Categories	Measurement Focus	Primary Means of Spending Controls	Basis of Accounting
General	Governmental	Financial Resources	Annual Operating Budget	Modified Accrual
Special Revenue	Governmental	Financial Resources	Annual Operating Budget	Modified Accrual
Debt Service	Governmental	Financial Resources	Bond Indentures	Modified Accrual
Capital Projects	Governmental	Financial Resources	Bond Indentures	Modified Accrual
Enterprise	Proprietary	Capital Maintenance	Marketplace	Accrual
Internal Service	Proprietary	Capital Maintenance	Budgetary—indirectly	Accrual
Trust and Agency	Fiduciary	—	—	
Expendable Trust	—	Financial Resources	State Laws	Modified Accrual
Nonexpendable Trust	—	Capital Maintenance	State Laws	Accrual
Pension Trust	—	Capital Maintenance	Pension Agreement	Accrual
Agency	—	—	—	

forced into self-balancing sets of accounts and therefore have no measurement focus. A general fixed asset account group is a listing of fixed assets (debits) offset on the credit side by a series of accounts defining the source of these assets. The general long-term debt account group itemizes the long-term debt (credits); the offsetting debit accounts indicate whether money has been set aside to pay these debts.

The following sections explain how the objectives and principles of accounting for governmental units embody these rudimentary ideas about measuring management's stewardship of public resources. These objectives and principles have been developed by the standard-setting bodies for governmental entities: the Governmental Accounting Standards Board and its predecessor, the National Council on Governmental Accounting. Because the GASB has been in existence for a relatively short time, its conceptual framework is incomplete. As a result, and as will be discussed, there are some internal inconsistencies in the framework for governmental accounting.

[handwritten margin note: GASB NCGA]

THE CONCEPTUAL FRAMEWORK FOR GOVERNMENTAL ACCOUNTING

Financial Reporting Objectives

The GASB's first concept statement on financial reporting objectives parallels the efforts of the Financial Accounting Standards Board. As with the FASB statement, it defines the objectives of financial reporting for governmental entities and establishes the framework for developing accounting principles and practices. The GASB's *Concepts Statement No. 1* supersedes an earlier NCGA pronouncement on the same subject.

[handwritten margin note: GASB St #1 objectives framework]

Underlying Concepts The GASB's objectives of financial reporting rest, to a considerable extent, on two basic concepts: accountability and interperiod equity. In introducing the concept of accountability, the GASB states that "governmental financial reporting should provide information to assist users in (a) assessing accountability and (b) making economic, social, and political decisions."[1]

Use of the term *accountability* represents a subtle attempt to broaden the focus of governmental entity reporting from the earlier emphasis on stewardship. Used extensively in public policy literature, but rarely in the context of state and local government accounting, **accountability** implies:

[handwritten margin note: objectives 1-accountability 2-interperiod equity]

- Providing information about decisions and actions taken during the course of operating an entity
- Having external parties review the information
- Taking corrective action where necessary

[handwritten margin note: P info provided R review C correct]

---

[1]Governmental Accounting Standards Board, *Concepts Statement No. 1, Objectives of Financial Reporting* (Stamford, Conn.: GASB, 1987), ¶76.

[handwritten margin notes: Compliance Conservation]

Stewardship, on the other hand, is interpreted more narrowly; compliance with law and conservation of the principal are adequate conditions for stewardship. If managers complied with local rules and documented the inflow, outflow, and balance of funds, they would have met their stewardship requirements. However, they may not have been accountable. To be accountable, they would also have had to make wise use of the resources during the period. In *Concepts Statement No. 1,* the GASB stated that accountability requires "governments to answer to the citizenry—to justify the raising of public resources and the purposes for which they are used."[2]

[handwritten margin notes: revenues to cover expenses]

Interperiod equity is the second concept used by the GASB as a foundation for the reporting objectives. It is the extent to which revenues generated during a given period are sufficient to cover expenditures made during the period. As stated by the GASB, interperiod equity is the "extent to which the services which the constituency existing during a particular reporting period has paid for the services which the constituency used during the period."[3] Many state laws address the issue of interperiod equity by: (1) requiring balanced budgets, (2) requiring that any deficit generated in one period be made up in the subsequent year, or (3) establishing limited time periods for debt issues, forcing a given generation to repay the debt incurred for the assets it uses.

[handwritten margin notes: ① A vs B ② Compliance ③ assess fin cond ④ eff + eff]

Uses of Financial Reports   Four uses of governmental financial reports are identified by the Board: (1) to compare actual financial results with the legally adopted budget; (2) to assist in determining compliance with finance-related laws, rules, and regulations; (3) to assess financial condition and results of operations; and (4) to assist in evaluating efficiency and effectiveness.[4] The first two uses emphasize accountability. How much was spent in relation to the approved amount? Were the operations in compliance with laws and regulations? The last two enable users to evaluate interperiod equity as well as an entity's current performance. Interpreted broadly, these uses certainly provide a basis for financial reporting objectives that would extend far beyond the traditional bounds of stewardship.[5]

The GASB Objectives   The GASB objectives were stated in very broad terms. The Board noted that the objectives apply to financial reporting by all governmental units (the federal government is, of course, outside the jurisdiction of the GASB). "Business-type" activities operated by governmental units also must apply these objectives.

---

[2] Ibid., 21.

[3] Emerson O. Henke, "Governmental Financial Statements—Generational Equity Reporting," *The Government Accountants Journal* XXXVI, No. 1 (Spring 1987): 20.

[4] GASB, *Concepts Statement No. 1,* 27.

[5] The preceding is a brief summary of *Concepts Statement No. 1.* The environment in which government operates is also discussed in some detail, as are the qualitative characteristics of information, such as understandability, reliability, relevance, timeliness, consistency, and comparability. Unlike the FASB's work, however, no hierarchy of these characteristics is provided.

As shown in Exhibit 2-4, *Concepts Statement No. 1* identifies three objectives of financial reporting for state and local units. Three subelements amplify and clarify each objective. The first objective addresses the necessity of accountability and interperiod equity. The first subelement indicates that the information should be prepared in enough detail to assess the adequacy of current-year revenues to cover current-year services. The other two subelements focus on compliance with the budget and on measurement of service efforts and accomplishments.

The second objective deals with the evaluation of operating results: the inflows, outflows, and financing of current-year operations. It seems to emphasize compliance with budgets and how the unit met its cash requirements. Some professionals hoped the second objective would have addressed the efficient and effective use of the resources, not merely their stewardship.

The third objective is all-encompassing: financial position should be assessable from a government's reports. Lest the objective be interpreted narrowly to include only financial resources, the second subelement expands the coverage to "physical and other nonfinancial resources having useful lives that extend beyond the current year."

Exhibit 2-4

Objectives of Financial Reporting
Governmental Entities

GASB
Concepts St #1

F

A. Financial reporting should assist in fulfilling government's duty to be publicly accountable and should enable users to assess that accountability.   *accountability / int. equity*

A

 1. Financial reporting should provide information to determine whether current-year revenues were sufficient to pay for current-year services.
 2. Financial reporting should demonstrate whether resources were obtained and used in accordance with the entity's legally adopted budget; it should also demonstrate compliance with other finance-related legal or contractual requirements.
 3. Financial reporting should provide information to assist users in assessing the service efforts, costs, and accomplishments of the governmental entity.

B. Financial reporting should assist users in evaluating the operating results of the governmental entity for the year.   *Operating results*

O

 1. Financial reporting should provide information about sources and uses of financial resources.
 2. Financial reporting should provide information about how the governmental entity financed its activities and met its cash requirements.
 3. Financial reporting should provide information necessary to determine whether the entity's financial position improved or deteriorated as a result of the year's operations.

C. Financial reporting should assist the users in assessing the level of services that can be provided by the governmental entity and its ability to meet its obligations as they become due.

L

level of services
obligations

 1. Financial reporting should provide information about the financial position and condition of a governmental entity.
 2. Financial reporting should provide information about a governmental entity's physical and other nonfinancial resources having useful lives that extend beyond the current year, including information that can be used to assess the service potential of those resources.
 3. Financial reporting should disclose legal or contractual restrictions on resources and risks of potential loss of resources.

Source: Governmental Accounting Standards Board, *Concepts Statement No. 1, Objectives of Financial Reporting* (Stamford, Conn.: GASB, 1987), 27–30.

▲   **OBSERVATION**

The third objective may turn out to be the most controversial. By mentioning service potential, the Board has opened the door for depreciation and other accounting practices that are outside the current realm of governmental GAAP.

A Context for the GASB Objectives

The objectives of financial reporting for governmental entities were developed within the context of the environment in which government operates. Significant characteristics of that environment include the following:

Citizens

- Citizens, through their representatives and their own participation in the governing process, and not market forces, ultimately determine which services are provided by governmental entities and the amount to be spent on those services.

taxes & benefits not related

- Governmental entities impose taxes to support the services that have been approved by the citizens. In some instances, they charge fees for services rendered. The benefits received by individual citizens are not directly related to the amount of taxes paid. Taxes are usually assessed according to the value of one's property or the amount of one's income, whereas the amount of the services may be based on need for the services or usage.

public policy

- A governmental entity's budget is a plan showing the relationship between taxes and charges on one hand and approved services on the other. It represents an expression of public policy. The public has an opportunity to be involved in its development, both through its elected officials and by commenting on proposed aspects of the budget.
- Government operates at several levels: local government (city, county, school district); state or regional governments; and the federal government. Services consumed may be provided by any one of these levels, and sometimes tax dollars collected by one level are passed through or granted to other levels to pay for particular services.

These characteristics—and others—make accounting and reporting for governmental entities conceptually difficult. For example, in order for citizen representation to work, tax and service levels must satisfy the public's notion of what is needed and how much it should cost. Since no direct relationship exists between the amount of taxes paid and the services used by individual citizens, government needs to demonstrate that it is achieving "the common good." As members of society become increasingly interested in their personal gain, achieving a consensus about the common good becomes more difficult. Also, as government representatives become entrenched in the processes rather than the ultimate goal and as the bureaucracy surrounding government services becomes more complex, citizens tend to feel disenfranchised and ineffectual in getting their voices heard. Special interest groups sometimes overshadow and out shout the voices for the common good. The way governmental entities account for their activities and report them to the public can make a difference.

The financial reporting objectives address these issues. Adhering to the words and the spirit in which they were defined means that the resulting financial statements can be understood and used in the decision-making process. These financial statements should demonstrate whether the adopted budget was followed and whether current resources were sufficient to provide current services (or if not, the amount being shifted to future generations). They should also provide information about what specific services were offered and how those services were funded.

Governmental Versus Industry Reporting Objectives

Both the FASB and the GASB chose to focus their statements on financial **reporting** instead of financial **statements** to reflect their concern for information presented both in the statements and in other reports. As the GASB put it, "not all financial reporting objectives of state and local governmental entities can be accomplished through general purpose financial statements."[6]

The two statements also are similar in the emphasis placed on sources and uses of funds, or funds flow. The FASB statement identifies the assessment of amounts, timing, and uncertainty of future cash flows; the GASB statement discusses sources and uses of financial resources as well as financing of activities and meeting cash requirements.

The FASB and the GASB statements have two other similarities. Some FASB objectives concern the solvency of the enterprise. Several subelements of the GASB statement reference solvency, but couch it in slightly different terms, such as "financing its activities," "meeting its cash requirements," or the "extent to which inflows meet outflows."

The GASB statement emphasizes the importance of maintaining interperiod equity. One such reference is "financial reporting should show whether current-year revenues are sufficient to pay for current-year services." If current-year revenues are sufficient to pay for current-year services and price-level adjustments are ignored, whatever net assets existed at the beginning of the year will remain at year end. The FASB's *Concepts Statement No. 5* contains a similar concept called *financial capital maintenance*. In FASB terms, financial capital is maintained whenever net assets at the end of a period equal the financial amount of net assets at the beginning of the year, after excluding the effects of transactions with owners. The FASB concept also ignores price-level changes. Financial statements prepared for businesses are based on this concept of financial capital maintenance. If the GASB uses interperiod equity as a cornerstone of its financial accounting principles, users could expect some similarity between the financial statements of businesses and governmental units.

The two statements differ in one important respect. Earning power—the ability to generate income—is conspicuously absent from the GASB document.

[6]GASB, *Concepts Statement No. 1*, 4.

Not even the "business-type" activities are expected to generate a profit (though some do), only to cover direct and any indirect costs appropriately allocated to such activities.

Having established three fundamental objectives for financial reporting, the GASB has embarked on the task of providing accounting and reporting standards that will satisfy these objectives. Some who commented on the objectives statement argued that the scope remained too broad and that the Board would be unable to achieve those objectives. An appendix to the statement describes the standard-setting process as ongoing and evolutionary. In other words, the objectives had to be broad enough to satisfy tomorrow's reporting requirements as well as those in existence today.

▲ **OBSERVATION**

Some respondents argued against the broad scope for another reason: the only type of financial reporting for which the Board can require adherence to its standards is audited financial statements. It cannot require a city, county, or state to issue other reports to interested persons acording to GAAP. Since no enforcement mechanism exists for other financial reports, why extend the scope of the concepts statement beyond the point of assured influence?

The development of accounting standards is a bit awkward; until the GASB has an opportunity to issue its own standards statements, the accounting profession has to use the accounting principles developed by the NCGA and last updated in their entirety in 1979. These principles do not entirely mesh with the recently developed reporting objectives.

BASIC PRINCIPLES OF GOVERNMENTAL ACCOUNTING AND FINANCIAL REPORTING[7]

12 Principles developed to carry out objectives

Generally accepted accounting principles represent a refinement of the goals and objectives; they constitute the mechanism through which goals and objectives are applied to the everyday practice of accounting. Ideally, the goals and objectives would be established first, and the principles would describe the way in which the goals and objectives should be met. Unfortunately, the accounting profession began only recently to define the concepts underlying financial accounting and reporting, so there is no such thing as a "clean slate." The principles were developed from practice and, gradually, they will be changed and refined to reflect the objectives.

[7]The statements of the 12 principles are reproduced with permission from the Governmental Accounting Standards Board. They are taken from National Council on Governmental Accounting, *Statement 1, Governmental Accounting and Financial Reporting Principles* (Chicago: Municipal Finance Officers Association of the United States and Canada, 1979). Copyright 1979 by the Municipal Finance Officers Association of the United States and Canada, as amended by subsequent statements. The 12 principles have been reordered for ease of exposition. They also have been modified to reflect recent GASB statements.

This is certainly the case for state and local government accounting. The GASB completed the objectives statement in 1987, and the principles document practitioners use to implement the objectives was last revised in 1979. Some principles are still applicable; they are broad enough to fit any objectives statement applicable to governmental units. Others are being revised or changed as the GASB develops alternative accounting practices that better enable the profession to meet the objectives.

The first ten chapters of this textbook explain the principles[8] as well as illustrate their application to accounting and financial reporting of governmental entities. Some additional value is derived by seeing those principles all together as a cohesive whole so they can be explained in the context of the reporting objectives, and in terms of their importance to accounting practice. Thus, they are covered here with brief explanations designed to enable readers to better understand the financial reports of governmental entities.

Accounting and Reporting Capabilities

The first accounting principle is very broad and uses words familiar to most accountants—"to present fairly with full disclosure;" regardless of the type of organization or location in the world, a common principle is fair presentation with full disclosure. The first principle for governmental units also emphasizes the importance of complying with legal and contractual provisions.

1. A governmental accounting system must make it possible both (a) to present fairly and with full disclosure the financial position and results of financial operations of the funds and account groups of the governmental entity in conformity with generally accepted accounting principles; and (b) to determine and demonstrate compliance with finance-related legal and contractual provisions.

(1) present fairly full disclosure compliance

Fund Accounting

Several principles relate to fund accounting. The second principle requires that the accounting system should be organized and operated on a fund basis. Each fund (general fund, special revenue fund, and so on) is identified as a separate accounting and reporting entity and separate financial statements are prepared for each one. Because financial reports for governmental units focus on "available spendable resources," the balance sheet differs from that found in industry. (The operating statement is different, too, but as we will see later, those differences are related to the method of accounting, not to the fund structure.) It includes only current financial resources and liabilities. Fixed assets and their related debt are accounted for in the general fixed asset and general long-term debt account groups respectively.

(2) fund basis

[8]Just as the principles may change over time, so may the language used to describe them. Many NCGA promulgations refer to the "basic principles of accounting," whereas the GASB *Concepts Statement No. 1* refers to the development of "standards" as being next in the hierarchy of the accounting framework. The terms are used interchangeably here.

2. Governmental accounting systems should be organized and operated on a fund basis. A fund is defined as a fiscal and accounting entity with a self-balanacing set of accounts which are segregated for the purpose of carrying on specific activities or attaining certain objectives in accordance with special regulations, restrictions, or limitations.

The types and number of funds are the subjects of the third and fourth principles. Exhibit 2-2 describes each fund.

③

Types of funds

3. The following types of funds should be used by state and local governments: the general fund, special revenue funds, capital projects funds, debt service funds, enterprise funds, internal service funds, and fiduciary funds (expendable trust, nonexpendable trust, pension trust, and agency funds).

Every governmental unit does not necessarily use all fund types while some units need two or more funds of a given type. With the exception of the general fund, the number of funds depends upon the nature of an organization's activities, ease of accounting, and local statutes or regulations. A general fund, the major operating fund, is required for all governmental units; only one general fund is permitted under GAAP. The other funds depend on whether an activity is undertaken by the unit; a capital projects fund, for example, would not be needed if the unit were not constructing or acquiring fixed assets. A limited capital construction or acquisition program could be accounted for in the general fund without losing the identity of the activity. Purchase of a single asset with a single payment represents a circumstance in which the unit could record the activity in the general fund without establishing a capital projects fund. On the other hand, if the governmental unit were purchasing or constructing numerous assets and each facility was being financed with a different bond issue, several capital projects funds should be opened. When in doubt, fewer funds, not more, are preferable.

④

Fewer funds as possible

4. Governmental units should establish and maintain those funds required by law and sound financial administration. Only the minimum number of funds consistent with legal and operating requirements should be established, however, since unnecessary funds result in inflexibility, undue complexity, and inefficient financial administration.

Basis of Accounting

The basis of accounting refers to **when** revenues and expenditures or expenses are recognized in the accounts. Under the modified accrual basis, revenues are recognized in the accounting period in which they become **available** and **measurable** — in other words, when they can be spent for ongoing operations. Under the accrual basis, which applies to all business accounting, revenues are recognized when earned, usually when the earnings process is complete. Clearly, under the accrual basis, revenue is implicitly required to be **measurable**, just as under the modified accrual basis. However, under the accrual basis, revenues normally do not have to be **available**.

On the expense side, the accrual and the modified accrual bases of accounting have the same recognition criteria: when the related liability is incurred. However, the modified accrual basis uses the term *expenditures* rather than *expenses,* as is done under the accrual basis. *Expenditures* is used because it relates to financial outflows, whereas *expenses* can be either outflows or using up of assets (cost expiration), such as applied to fixed assets by taking depreciation.

Historically, the emphasis in governmental accounting has been on stewardship. Reviewers of financial statements were provided information on what resources were spent and what "spendable" resources remained at year end. The basis of accounting used to provide this information was the modified accrual basis. The problem with this accounting basis is that it does not permit statement users to evaluate the total performance of the entity, which is achieved more easily with the accrual basis.

Consistent with its emphasis on accountability and interperiod equity, the GASB has changed the basis of accounting used for some funds. Effective sometime in the future, all governmental fund types will use the accrual basis of accounting. As is explained later in this chapter and more fully in Chapter 3, the fact that both governmental and business entities use accrual accounting does not necessarily make their accounting practices identical.

The ten funds used by governmental entities are grouped into three broad categories: governmental (general fund, special revenue funds, capital projects funds, and debt service funds); proprietary (enterprise and internal service funds); and fiduciary (expendable trust funds, nonexpendable trust funds, pension trust funds, and agency funds). The groupings, for the most part, were created to simplify a discussion of accounting and reporting practices for each type of fund. The principle that describes the basis of accounting uses this grouping.

5. The modified accrual basis of accounting should be utilized in measuring financial position and operating results for **governmental funds.** The accrual basis of accounting should be used for **proprietary funds. Fiduciary fund** revenues and expenses or expenditures (as appropriate) should be recognized on a basis consistent with the fund's accounting measurement objective....**Transfers** should be recognized in the accounting period in which the interfund receivable and payable arise.

Fixed Assets and Long-Term Liabilities

Accounting for a fund's fixed assets and long-term liabilities follows naturally from the fund's measurement focus. For those funds having a primary focus of financial resources, only financial assets/liabilities are reported in the balance sheet. Fixed assets (referred to as capital assets by the GASB) are not financial assets; the liabilities used to fund these capital assets are capital-related, not financial, liabilities. Neither are shown in the fund making the purchase or incurring the debt. On the other hand, funds having a focus of capital maintenance show all assets and liabilities in the fund.

(b)

Fixed assets
LT L/Debt

6. A clear distinction should be made between (a) fund fixed assets and general fixed assets and (b) fund long-term liabilities and general long-term debt.

   a. Fixed assets related to specific proprietary funds or trust funds should be accounted for through those funds. All other fixed assets...should be accounted for through the General Fixed Assets Account Group.

   b. Long-term liabilities of proprietary funds and trust funds should be accounted for through these funds.

   c. All unmatured general long-term liabilities of governmental funds should be accounted for in the General Long-Term Debt Account Group.

▲ **OBSERVATION**

When the accrual basis of accounting is adopted, only capital-related debt should be accounted for in the general long-term debt account group. All other long-term liabilities will be recorded in the fund incurring the debt. Thus, Item 6.c above will change to the following: All noncapital unmatured general long-term liabilities of governmental funds should be accounted for through these funds. All capital-related unmatured general long-term liabilities should be accounted for through the general long-term debt account group.

Business practices are followed by a governmental unit in recording asset acquisitions but thereafter the practices differ. An asset's basis is its cost, unless acquired by donation, in which case its basis is the fair market value. However, depreciation is not taken on a governmental unit's general fixed assets. Under GASB standards, the using up of the assets does not represent a use of financial resources, so depreciation is not recorded. Instead the expenditure for the asset is recognized when it is made, that is, when the outflow of financial resources occurs.

Depreciation is taken only in the proprietary and trust funds where capital maintenance—and not financial resources—is the focal point.

(7)
Fixed assets
at cost

(8)
Depreciation

7. Fixed assets should be accounted for at cost, or if the cost is not practicably determined, at estimated cost. Donated fixed assets should be recorded at their estimated fair value at the time received.

8. Depreciation of general fixed assets should not be recorded in the accounts of governmental funds.... Accumulated depreciation may be recorded in the General Fixed Assets Account Group. Depreciation of fixed assets accounted for in a proprietary fund should be recorded in the accounts of that fund. Depreciation is also recognized in those trust funds where expenses, net income, and/or capital maintenance are measured.

Budgetary Accounting

As the objectives of financial reporting make clear, compliance with laws, regulations, and governing body mandates is an important aspect of accountability. The public and governing bodies assess financial compliance, particularly for such funds as the general and special revenue funds, by comparing the budget with the actual revenues and expenditures. If the actual and budgeted amounts match, the money has theoretically been generated and spent as the governing board intended. Because managers know their performance will be judged in part by variances from the budget, the budget must be a good reflection of agreed-upon goals and objectives for a particular year. For this reason, budgeting is very important in governmental units.

Budgeting is also important because it represents one avenue for citizen involvement in government. Typically, hearings are scheduled on various budget categories. Citizens present oral arguments about why some parts of the budget should be increased or decreased; often, citizen input is very important in shaping the budget. After the budget has been developed, elected officials want to demonstrate that citizen input was heeded, which can be accomplished by presenting both the budget and the actual revenue and expenditures in the governmental unit's financial statements.

Whenever possible, the budget should be based on generally accepted accounting principles. Use of some other basis complicates both the budgeting process and the preparation of financial statements. For example, if state laws require a cash basis budget, governmental organizations must maintain the accounts and prepare interim and annual financial statements according to the cash basis. For an auditor to provide an unqualified opinion, the governmental unit also must maintain sufficient information to prepare financial statements according to GAAP.

9. An annual budget should be adopted by every governmental unit. The accounting system should provide the basis for appropriate budgetary control. Budgetary comparisons should be included in the appropriate financial statements and schedules for governmental funds for which an annual budget has been adopted.

Not only is the budgetary information included in the financial statements, but the budget is also integrated into the general ledgers of some governmental funds. This integration is especially important for the general and special revenue funds, and is accomplished by establishing accounts for estimated revenues and estimated expenditures. If the legally adopted budget is not amended, the budgetary accounts remain unchanged and are closed at year end. For interim statements, the revenue and expenditures can be summed and compared to the budgetary amounts.

Financial Reporting

The frequency and detail of governmental **interim** financial reports vary, and such reports are used largely for internal purposes. Because compliance with the legal budget is important, interim reports must be prepared frequently enough to detect any major deviation from the plan. With enough lead time, the governing body can adjust expenditure authorizations or raise additional revenues, such as user charges. The amounts presented must be detailed enough to pinpoint the deviations to determine, for instance, whether a revenue decline can be traced to property taxes, income taxes, or use rates for services or facilities. Typically, the same level of detail presented in the original budget is used for interim reporting.

CAFR

Comprehensive **annual** financial reports are used for a variety of purposes. Taxpayers, managers, bonding authorities, governing bodies, employees, and grantors or general creditors all are interested in the annual financial reports. Although each group's specific interests vary, clearly the financial information is used for purposes other than judging economic performance. As noted earlier, political and social decisions also are based, at least in part, on the financial information. A taxpayer, for example, might decide that too little was spent for a favorite governmental service, and consequently vote against a tax levy or for a political candidate who has similar views.

The comprehensive financial report covers all funds and account groups. An operating statement and a balance sheet are prepared for each fund; then combining statements are included for each fund type. Combining statements show each fund in a column with a total column for all funds of that type. The next level in the hierarchy combines the various types of funds and the account groups into a combined operating statement and balance sheet. Not all users understand these detailed statements, so highly summarized and largely narrative reports are sometimes prepared and offered as a substitute for, or as a supplement to, the comprehensive annual financial report.

Also included in the comprehensive annual financial report are the auditor's opinion, notes to the financial statements, and a detailed statistical section. Typically, the report is organized into three sections: the introductory section, including the unit's letter of transmittal and other information about the unit; the financial section, including the individual and combined financial statements, notes, supporting schedules, and the auditor's opinion; and a statistical section, including historical trend data and information about the organizations that comprise the reporting unit.

(10)

CAFR
fin st/reports

interim statement/ reports

10. Appropriate interim financial statements and reports of financial position, operating results, and other pertinent information should be prepared to facilitate management control of financial operations, legislative oversight, and, where necessary or desired, for external reporting purposes. A comprehensive annual financial report covering all funds and account groups . . . should be prepared and published. General purpose financial statements may be issued separately from the comprehensive annual financial reports. Such statements should include the basic financial statements and notes to the financial statements that are essential to fair presentation of financial position and operating results.

Classification and Terminology

The final two principles combined in *Statement 1* relate to the classification of governmental and proprietary funds' revenues and expenditures, to interfund transfers, and to terminology used in the accounting process. They are discussed more fully in succeeding chapters.

11. (a) Interfund transfers and proceeds of general long-term debt issues should be classified separately from fund revenues and expenditures or expenses.

(b) Governmental fund revenues should be classified by fund, function (or program), organization unit, activity, character, and principal classes of objects.

(c) Proprietary fund revenues and expenses should be classified in essentially the same manner as those of similar business organizations, functions, or activities.

12. A common terminology and classification should be used consistently throughout the budget, the accounts, and the financial reports of each fund.

[margin handwritten notes:]
⑪ Interfund Transfers
Gov't rev/exp
Propri rev/exp
⑫ common terminology

Relating Reporting Objectives and Accounting Principles to the Accounting Process

The concepts, uses of financial reports, objectives, and principles discussed in the preceding sections are all interrelated in a hierarchical scheme. As depicted in Exhibit 2-5, the reporting goal provides a basis for developing objectives and principles. The objectives represent an expanded version of the goal, that is, the translation of broad concepts into a usable form for practice. Finally, the principles explain how each objective should be achieved.

[margin handwritten notes:]
goal
obj.
principle

The transition from the theoretical to the practical can be facilitated by tracing the goal of assisting users in assessing accountability. Interpreted for financial statement purposes, assisting users in assessing accountability means enabling users to compare actual and budgeted amounts, and to assess compliance. The key term, accountability, is carried through to the first objective; the objective, however, represents a more definitive explanation of what accountability and its assessment really means. It means determining the adequacy of revenues to cover current-year costs, examining compliance with the budget and other finance-related rules, and assessing the accomplishments and service efforts.

At the detailed level of accounting principles, a number of principles give guidance for implementing this objective. First, the activities are divided into separate funds so each element of the total budget or effort can be measured (Principle 2). A basis of accounting is determined. This determination enables preparers to "present fairly" the results of operation and the financial position for each fund (Principle 5). A budget is adopted formally so comparisons can be made between the anticipated and actual revenues and expenditures (Principle 9). Finally, this information is displayed in a usable and understandable fashion; in order to be usable and understandable, the accounting principles and terminology must be applied consistently throughout the report and from one year to the next (Principle 12). Each principle makes the accounting process more definitive.

The hierarchical relationships of accounting goals, objectives, and principles for governmental units are not as explicit as they are in the for-profit

Exhibit 2-5

Government Accounting Framework

Reporting Goal

> Governmental financial reporting should provide infomation to assist users in (1) assessing accountability and (2) making economic, social, and political decisions

Uses of Financial Reports

- To compare actual financial results with the legally adopted budget
- To assess financial conditions and results of operations
- To assist in determining compliance with finance-related laws, rules, and regulations
- To assist in evaluating efficiency and effectiveness

Objectives of Financial Reporting

- Financial reporting should assist in fulfilling government's duty to be publicly accountable and should enable users to assess that accountability.

- Financial reporting should assist users in evaluating the operating results of the governmental entity for the year.

- Financial reporting should assist the users in assessing the level of services that can be provided by the governmental entity and its ability to meet its financial obligations as they become due.

Principles of Governmental Accounting and Reporting

Accounting and Reporting Capabilities
(1) Accounting system to assure fair presentation and full disclosure

Fund Accounting
(2) Organized and operated on a fund basis
(3) Types of funds
(4) Number of funds as necessary

Basis of Accounting
(5) Modified accrual basis for governmental and some fiduciary; accrual plus depreciation for proprietary and some fiduciary

Fixed Assets and Long-Term Liabilities
(6) Distinguish between fund and governmental fixed assets and liabilities
(7) Account for assets at cost
(8) Depreciation is not recorded

The Budget and Budgetary Accounting
(9) An annual budget is required and is included in financial statements and schedules

Financial Reporting
(10) Appropriate interim and comprehensive financial statements

Classification and Terminolgy
(11) Classification of interfund transfers, revenues, and expenditures
(12) Common terminology and consistent use

sector. In contrast to for-profit principles, accounting principles for governmental units stress structure and form over accounting process. For example, in the private sector the objective relating to information about enterprise resources is supported directly by the concept of assets, liabilities, and owners' equity; the principles of "monetary unit" and "consistency" are used in measuring the elements.

If the GASB had a complete conceptual framework, the relationship among various levels in the hierarchy would be clearer. The first concepts statement on reporting objectives was meant to provide room for changes in governmental accounting, rather than simply a foundation for existing principles. Thus, as the GASB details the principles, a clearer relationship will emerge between the principles and the objectives. At present, however, the accounting foundation must be supplemented with practices being used by governmental entities.

AN OVERVIEW OF GOVERNMENTAL BUDGETING AND ACCOUNTING

The Budget and Accounting Cycle

The budget is a plan for the year. The accounting system provides assistance in implementing the plan and preparing statements that permit comparisons between the plan and actual operations. The budget cycle normally begins at least three months before the close of the fiscal or calendar year. Operating complexities, local laws or regulations, and preferences of the governing body determine which funds require a formal budget. Under GAAP, a budget should be established for the general fund and usually for special revenue funds. Many units also prepare budgets for capital projects and debt service funds.

At the beginning of a budget cycle, managers of operating departments or divisions present their plans for the coming year to key administrators. Tentative spending plans are discussed and revenue estimates are made. The preliminary budgets for all departments comprising a given fund are combined for presentation to the governing body.

OBSERVATION ▲

Programs or departments are not organized according to the accounting funds, so a program run by a manager may cross fund lines or be only a small portion of the operations covered by a given fund. For example, the director of the social services department would have a budget for his or her department and that program, along with many others, would comprise the expenditure budget for the general fund. The department might also have a budget for special revenue funds. Therefore, considerable consolidation of departmental budgets occurs before the budget can be presented for a given fund.

After the preliminary budgets for programs and funds have been determined, key administrators present those budgets to the governing body. Although the governing body reviews the overall budget by fund, it may have the departmental detail as well. If spending or revenue decisions have to be altered, the governing body can examine the impact on individual programs. The governing body also requests input from the citizens affected by the budget. Sometimes there is active involvement and diverse opinion; other times, the galleries are empty, and the governing body has only a limited sense of public mandate, usually the ideas of a vocal minority.

Formal adoption of the budget means decisions regarding the best way for the unit to achieve its short-term objectives have been finalized. The unit's managers are then responsible for adhering to the plan, constantly monitoring operations, and making reports to the governing body about the extent to which the objectives are being achieved. Depending on the sophistication of the accounting and reporting system, reports to the governing body range from daily printouts for operating results and financial position to monthly or even quarterly, hand-prepared summaries comparing budget to actual.

The Accounting Process

As succeeding chapters will make clear, the accounting process varies by type of fund. Only the overall process is explained here. When the budgets have been established for the general fund, for example, the budgetary amounts are entered into the general ledger control accounts:

Estimated Revenues	1,000,000	
Appropriations		1,000,000

Appropriations refer to authorized spending levels; they can be described as estimated expenditures.

In the general ledger control accounts, total estimated revenues are compared to actual revenues and total appropriations are compared to actual expenditures. Unless the budget is changed during the year, these amounts do not change; they serve as a reminder of the plan, standards against which to compare the revenues and expenditures to date. If budget changes are approved, the budgetary accounts should be changed accordingly. If, for example, the revenue estimate and authorized expenditures are reduced by $100,000 during the year, the correct procedure is to reduce both appropriations and estimated revenues by the amount of the reduction.

Appropriations	100,000	
Estimated Revenues		100,000

The entry would be the reverse if the revenues and appropriations were increased during the year.

Subsidiary ledgers contain a detailed breakdown of the total revenues by source, such as property taxes, fines, fees, user charges, and the like, and the total expenditures by object code (salaries, supplies, equipment, and so on) and perhaps by program (social services, highway or street maintenance, planning, and so forth). Most subsidiary ledgers contain a column for the budgeted amount and a column for actual revenues or expenditures, making it possible to immediately assess the remaining balance by type of revenue or expenditure classification.

By including budgetary amounts in the control accounts and the subsidiary ledgers, managers can better determine the amount of uncommitted resources without having to prepare interim financial statements. Because delays occur between the order date for materials or the contract date for services and the time when the liability is incurred (when an expenditure is recognized), the format alone does not ensure accurate estimates of remaining balances. Managers must also know what commitments are outstanding.

Encumbrance Accounting

The accounting convention used to register commitments that are not yet liabilities is called *encumbrance accounting*. When a purchase order is sent, the amount is encumbered and a like amount of net assets (called the *fund balance*) is reserved for purposes of alerting managers and statement users to budgetary commitments:

Encumbrances	1,000	
Reserve for Encumbrances		1,000

When the order is received, this entry is reversed, and the appropriate expenditure account is debited and accounts payable or vouchers payable is credited for the actual cost.

Reserve for Encumbrances	1,000	
Expenditures	1,000	
Encumbrances		1,000
Accounts Payable		1,000

If the order is not received by year end, the encumbrance account is closed as though it were an expenditure. The closure is to fund balance; in business accounting, the comparable account is retained earnings. Because governmental units are not operated for profit, the net assets (assets minus liabilities) is referred to as the fund balance.

Fund Balance	1,000	
Encumbrances		1,000

The reserve account remains open and is placed in the Fund Balance section of the balance sheet; its presence alerts statement users to outstanding commitments. At the beginning of the subsequent period, the encumbrance account would be reopened by:

Encumbrances	1,000	
Fund Balance		1,000

As the T-Account shown illustrates, had this been the only transaction for the preceding year, this last entry leaves the fund balance unchanged from the beginning of the year. This is as it should be; no liability has been incurred, but a commitment has been authorized.

	Fund Balance	
Closing, 1st year	1,000	
Reversing, 2nd year		1,000

To make it clearer that the commitment is against the resources authorized for the prior year, a second entry probably would have been made on the first day of the second year:

Reserve for Encumbrances	1,000	
Reserve for Encumbrances—prior year		1,000

This entry avoids any confusion between commitments made against the current year's budget and those for the prior period.

In the typical situation, when numerous transactions occurred throughout the year, and after any necessary adjusting entries have been made, the closing entries eliminate all nominal accounts:

Revenues
Appropriations
      Estimated Revenues
      Expenditures
      Encumbrances
      Fund Balance

The credit to the Fund Balance assumes that the revenues and appropriations exceeded the estimated revenues, expenditures, and encumbrances. Otherwise, the fund balance would have been debited.

Once the closing entries have been made, financial statements are prepared. For fund types using budgetary accounts, the primary financial statements are a Balance Sheet; Statement of Revenues, Expenditures, and Changes in Fund Balance; and a Statement of Revenues, Expenditures, and Changes in Fund Balance, Budget and Actual. For governmental types of funds not using budgetary accounts, the last statement is excluded. A Balance Sheet; Statement of Revenues, Expenses, and Changes in Retained Earnings; and a Cash Flow Statement are required for proprietary funds and some fiduciary funds.

THE EVALUATION PROCESS

Presentation of budget and actual figures in the financial statements constitutes one aspect of performance evaluation. Although they may be necessary, variances indicate the extent to which managers did not adhere to the mandates of the governing board. In some states or locales, variances pertaining to specific line items are tolerated as long as the managers stayed within the totals, for example, total appropriations.

The GASB is encouraging governmental entities to use additional measures to evaluate performance, specifically measures that relate to achievement of programmatic or efficiency objectives. Further, the GASB is urging governmental entities to report these additional measures in the financial statements. Services efforts and accomplishments (SEA) reporting describes this development in performance evaluation. The GASB is publishing a second concepts statement describing the necessity for SEA reporting. The Board also has produced numerous research reports detailing specific measures that governmental entities might use for individual functions, such as police, fire, or secondary education. SEA reporting is discussed more fully in a later chapter.

SUMMARY

This chapter has provided an introduction to the governmental unit and the foundation for the accounting and reporting system, includng the objectives and principles of accounting. Governmental organizations use the **fund** as the basic accounting and reporting entity. Many governmental accounting principles are designed to achieve a fair presentation and full disclosure of financial information about individual funds.

Although the budgeting, accounting, and reporting processes bear some resemblance to those in the for-profit sector, some marked differences exist: budgetary accounts may be integrated into the ledgers, commitments are incorporated into the accounting system, the reporting of assets and liabilities varies by fund type, most funds do not utilize a cash flow statement, and one primary statement for some governmental funds compares budgeted and actual revenues and expenditures.

Other less obvious differences exist between the accounting and reporting for governmental and for business organizations. These differences will be explored further in Chapter 3.

QUESTIONS

2-1   What is the difference between the reporting unit and the accounting and reporting entity in governmental accounting?

2-2   In your opinion, what funds most closely parallel operating programs of a governmental entity? Why?

2-3   Describe briefly the framework for governmental accounting and reporting.

2-4   What is the meaning of the term *interperiod equity*? *Accountability*?

2-5 Explain why the concept of accountability is so important in governmental accounting.

2-6 From the descriptions provided in this chapter, what fund would you look at first to get an understanding of a governmental entity's operations? Why?

2-7 Describe the similarities and differences between governmental and for-profit reporting objectives.

2-8 Reexamine the 12 accounting principles discussed in the chapter and determine which one best fits with the GASB's overall reporting objectives. Explain your selection.

2-9 Explain the rationale for placing a governmental entity's general fixed assets in an account group rather than in the fund accounting for the activities in which those assets are used.

2-10 If the laws of a particular state require a non-GAAP basis for budgeting and reporting, on what basis should the comprehensive annual financial report be prepared? Does an entity have any options?

2-11 Do you think the GASB reporting objectives suggest a change in the accounting for general fixed assets? Explain why or why not.

2-12 What is the difference between the "accrual" and the "modified accrual" bases of accounting?

2-13 One accounting principle contains the following statement:

"Budgetary comparisons should be included in the appropriate financial statements and schedules for governmental funds for which an annual budget has been adopted."

What does it mean to integrate the budget into the accounting records? Why is this done?

2-14 What role do the four uses of financial reports enumerated in the GASB's *Concepts Statement No. 1* have in the accounting framework for governmental entities?

2-15 George Miller, a member of your constituency, calls and asks you to explain why he cannot find the budget for the public health department in the report you sent him when he inquired about the city's latest budget. What would your response be? Can you provide information that will enable him to analyze that department in more depth?

2-16 Why is it necessary to integrate the budgetary accounts into the general ledger? Why couldn't the general ledger have only operating accounts that could then be compared with the budget data to develop a budget versus actual report?

2-17 What is the difference between a fund and an account group?

2-18 The city manager wants to know why the city comptroller opened two separate capital projects funds. Without knowing the specifics of the situation, explain why that decision might have been made.

2-19 The terms *expenditures* and *expenses* are sometimes used interchangeably. Why is that practice incorrect?

2-20 Describe what you think will be the long-run benefits of the GASB's *Concepts Statement No. 1*.

CASES

2-1 The city of Treetony is newly incorporated; it developed initially as a suburb for a major eastern city. The city council has been elected and has hired a chief financial officer, Derrick Jones. Although he has considerable experience in corporate accounting, he has only recently completed his one and only course in nonprofit accounting. He is asking that you do some basic consulting work for Treetony. Mr. Jones explains that the following major activities are contemplated by the city council within the next year or two:

- To construct and equip a city hall. It is anticipated that the state might contribute some money toward this project, but most of the cost will be funded by 20-year general obligation bonds. Because market rates are increasing, it is anticipated that general tax revenues will be used to commence the project, and then, later in the year when bond rates fall, the bond issue will be sold.
- To construct and operate a major recreational facility that will serve the citizens of Treetony as well as those from the metropolitan area. Because it will be used by people outside the city, the city council decided to fund both the debt and operational costs by user charges.
- To attract additional tourists to the area. Treetony does not have the resources to conduct a major tourist campaign, so the city council decided to levy a bed tax (this tax has been approved by the state legislature), and earmark those revenues for maintenance of tourist facilities and promotion of the tourist industry.

REQUIRED

1. In your consulting role, describe what fund(s) and/or account group(s) will be required for Treetony. Explain why you have chosen to include each one.
2. Without prejudicing your answer to Item 1, presume that one of the funds you recommended was the debt service fund. Mr. Jones argues vehemently that a debt service fund is not required. If he argues against the establishment of such a fund, give his likely arguments. What are the counter arguments?
3. The data processing bureau that will be processing the accounting records for Treetony wants to make sure that there is some flexibility in the system it is designing. The bureau asks you what additional fund(s) or account group(s) might be established at a later date. Describe other aspects of the system that would require flexibility for future growth of Treetony.

2-2 Redrock County has just received notice that the GASB is considering issuing a pronouncement that will change the accounting for general fixed assets. The Board is proposing that depreciation be taken on all facilities, and that this cost allocation be charged against current operations. Further, the GASB has asked Redrock for comment: How will this pronouncement affect the county's operating statement? How would the county present its financial statements to indicate clearly the fact that depreciation is not a use of cash or working capital? What is the theoretical justification, if any, for the taking of depreciation? Is that posture reconcilable with the modified accrual basis of accounting?

Last year, Redrock had an excess of revenues over expenditures of $87,000. It has the following assets (roads, bridges, and streets have been excluded because the GASB asked for comment only on the facilities described below); the cost and the remaining useful lives are noted for each type of asset.

Description	Amount	Useful Life in Years
Swimming Pool Funded by User Fees	$ 210,000	25
Courthouse and Annex	5,800,000	40
Furniture and Fixtures for General Government Offices	180,000	10
Data Processing Facility Serving All Government Departments	900,000	20
Vehicles and Transportation Equipment	3,200,000	8

REQUIRED

1. Respond to the questions raised by the GASB.
2. Aside from the rationale for taking depreciation in governmental entities, analyze the accuracy of the depreciation you estimated for purposes of completing Part 1.

2-3 At a recent social gathering, a financial analyst for a regional brokerage firm indicated that he had read an auditor's opinion statement covering the city of Hinsdale. The statement said that Hinsdale's combined financial statements present fairly the financial position of the city, the financial position of the individual funds, and the results of operations of such funds. He is confused by the wording of the opinion statement because he had always thought that either a city had single entity or consolidated financial statements, and the term *combined* suggests something else. He is also uncertain about the implications of giving an opinion for the combined financial statements as well as the individual funds.

REQUIRED

1. Why is the reference to combined financial statements rather than to consolidated financial statements?
2. What does it mean when the auditor says that the financial statements "present fairly" the financial position? Does that term mean the same when used in nonprofit and for-profit opinion statements?
3. Why do you suppose the auditors would mention both the combined financial statements and those for the individual funds? (Hint: Consider the implications of different accounting practices for different funds, and the impact those differences have on the opinion statement.)

2-4 A friend majoring in medieval history noticed that your governmental textbook was open to a page describing accounting concepts. She wondered what concepts could be used in accounting. She thought that specific rules govern every action taken by accountants and a college education in that field involved memorizing the rules. Particularly in relation to governmental accounting, she felt that there was no need for concepts because laws and local regulations prescribe the accounting process.

REQUIRED
1. Discuss how accounting concepts are used to guide and structure the accounting and auditing process.
2. What is the relationship between accounting concepts and the objectives of governmental financial accounting and reporting?
3. Discuss the interaction of laws/regulations and accounting concepts in the development of governmental accounting and reporting standards.

2-5 Carbon County recently hired a new manager for its Social Services Department. The manager submitted the budget shown below for your review as the county's chief financial officer. With only a cursory review, you know that the manager has made some serious errors in presenting the budget; you decide that you should draft a written evaluation of the budget so that both you and the manager have something to refer to when you are discussing the problems.

Social Services Department
Preliminary Budget
Fiscal 19X9

Revenues:		
General Tax Allocation	$ 260,000	
Earmarked State Revenue Sharing	100,000	
Proceeds from Bonds for Construction	3,000,000	
Total Revenue		$3,360,000
Expenditures:		
Salaries and Wages	$ 260,000	
Supplies	50,000	
Equipment	60,000	
Construction of New Facility	3,000,000	
Total Expenditures		3,370,000
Excess of Revenues over Expenditures		$ (10,000)

REQUIRED
1. Identify the major weaknesses in the departmental budget, including the appropriate detail.
2. Has the manager commingled the general fund operations with those of other funds? If so, identify the different funds in which those items would be budgeted.

EXERCISES

2-1   Selected financial statements for the city of Raleigh, North Carolina, are presented as Appendix A of your textbook. The first exercise of each chapter in Part 1 concerns those financial statements. Review the statements and then answer the questions.

1. What types of funds and account groups are used by Raleigh? Are they consistent with those described in the text? If there are differences, please explain.
2. Are the financial statements prepared in accordance with GAAP? How do you know whether that is the case?
3. Are the financial statements audited? If so, what type(s) of audit(s) was (were) conducted? Did the city receive a "clean opinion"?
4. For what funds, if any, was the budgetary data shown in the financial statements?

2-2   The listing below describes the general nature of revenue and expenditures (expenses) earned or incurred by Salem Heights. Based on the description given, decide which fund (account group) is being used by the city for each activity. Justify your decision.

1. An intergovernmental grant was received from the state to be earmarked for specific programs.
2. Bonds in the amount of $1 million were issued to fund renovation and construction of the jail.
3. Property tax revenues were collected for general operating use.
4. Salem Heights has a retirement program for its employees; contributions were received from the city to fund this year's costs.
5. Depreciation expense was recorded on the city's swimming pool, which is funded through charges to the public.
6. The city purchased supplies for use.
7. A wealthy citizen gave Salem Heights 200 shares of corporate stock; the dividends from the stock are to be used to supplement the Public Library holdings.

2-3   A year-end operating statement prepared on the accrual basis for the city of Dentor appears below. Using the following information, recast the statement into a modified accrual statement.

1. The property tax revenues shown on the statement were levied in 19X9 and were available to meet current liabilities when they became due in 19X9.
2. Of the sales tax revenue shown, only one-half has been received to date; the remaining 50 percent is not expected to be received until four months into the next fiscal period.
3. Miscellaneous revenues were received in cash.

4. Miscellaneous equipment totaling $3,000 was purchased during the year. (Hint: Under the GASB's GAAP, the equipment would be recorded as an expenditure this period.)
5. Of the total salary expense, $1,500 was for accrued year-end wages. *exist*
6. The supplies were purchased and used within the current operating period.
7. The insurance was purchased in the preceding fiscal period.

Dentor
Operating Statement
For the Period Ending June 30, 19X9

Revenues:		
Property tax revenues	$160,000 *wouldn't change*	
Sales tax revenues	10,000 *5,000*	
Miscellaneous fees and fines	8,000 *No change*	
Total Revenues		$178,000
		173,000
Expenses:		
Salaries and wages	$ 85,000 *same*	*no inventory*
Supplies expense	9,000 *same*	
Depreciation expense	~~42,000~~ *source*	
Insurance expense	~~1,200~~ *0*	
Repair and maintenance	7,000 *same*	
Travel, lodging and per diem	5,800 *same*	
equip	*3,000*	*169,800*
Total Expenses		150,000
Net Income	*no depreciation on*	$ 28,000
	modified accrued	*~~28,000~~*

2-4 Select the best answer for each of the following questions. *16.*

1. A fund can be described as:
   a. an accounting entity
   b. a reporting unit
   c. a separate group of accounts
   d. an accounting and reporting entity
2. The GASB concepts statement on objectives provides:
   a. guidance on what accounting practices to use for various types of transactions
   b. a review of the environment in which governmental entities operate
   c. goals to be achieved in governmental financial reporting
   d. a summary of the differences between governmental and nonprofit reporting objectives
3. General fixed assets of a governmental unit would be recorded in:
   a. the general fixed asset account group and the general fund
   b. the fund that pertained to the purpose of those assets
   c. the general fixed asset account group
   d. the general fund
4. Stewardship refers, among other things, to:
   a. conservation of the principal of assets
   b. the same thing as accountability

    c. guarding the reputation of those managing an entity's assets

    d. all of the above

5. Which of the following statements does not relate to the GASB's reporting objectives?

    a. assessing the service costs of an entity

    b. determining compliance with legal requirements

    c. evaluating the potential debt capacity of an entity

    d. measuring the cash-flow requirements of an entity

6. Business-type funds in a governmental entity are used to segregate those activities that:

    a. are expected to generate revenues to cover costs

    b. relate to special revenue and/or expense classifications

    c. are designed to generate profits for the entity

    d. need special attention because of low profitability

7. A reporting unit:

    a. would be included in the financial statements of another governmental entity

    b. prepares consolidated financial statements

    c. prepares financial statements for those entities combined within it

    d. none of the above

8. General operations of a governmental entity would be recorded in:

    a. the general fund

    b. the general fixed asset account group

    c. the general long-term debt account group

    d. the general long-term debt and fixed asset account groups

9. When a purchase previously ordered is received, which of the following accounts would not be debited?

    a. encumbrances

    b. expenditures

    c. reserve for encumbrances

    d. none of the above

10. In addition to integrating the budget into the general ledger, what other accounting convention enables governmental entities to closely monitor their compliance with the budget?

    a. expenditure accounting

    b. estimating revenues

    c. posting to subsidiary ledgers

    d. encumbrance accounting

2-5 During fiscal 19X9, Dodge Park had the following transactions relating to its budget appropriations and expenditures. Make the journal entries to reflect these transactions.

1. On July 1, 19X8, the budget was approved; estimated revenues were $980,000 and estimated expenditures were $980,000.

2. On August 7, 19X8, an order was placed for supplies; the amount was $27,000.

3. On September 5, 19X8, the supply order was received and vouchered; it cost what had been anticipated.
4. On December 8, 19X8, an order for equipment amounting to $40,000 was placed. The equipment had to be manufactured and was not received during the fiscal period.
5. On January 15, 19X9, the revenue estimate was reduced by $18,000; appropriations were left unchanged.
6. On April 15, 19X9, appropriations were reduced by $6,000.

2-6   An inexperienced bookkeeper has been making the entries for the city of Crowsnest. He asked for your advice in determining where and how certain transactions should be reflected in the books. For each circumstance described below, indicate which accounting principle provides guidance in determining the appropriate accounting treatment. Also, indicate what the accounting treatment is and why you selected a particular principle. (Each circumstance is independent of the others.)

1. The general ledger shows an expenditure for equipment amounting to $100,000; the bookeeper explains that the equipment will be used by the manager in charge of a central facility for repairing the city's vehicles.
2. In preparing a schedule of long-term debt, the bookkeeper omitted all detail regarding the increases and decreases in particular debt categories; instead, he just showed the net change for that type of debt.
3. The bookkeeper has not made any entries for depreciation because he has forgotten for which activities it is appropriate.
4. At year end, accrued wages and salaries have not been booked because he cannot remember if that is appropriate for a government entity.
5. The bookkeeper has begun to prepare this year's financial statements, but he does not want to send all of the required statements to the city council. He argues that most of those required disclosures will not have much meaning to the council members.
6. Looking forward to next year, the bookkeeper does not know for which funds he should prepare a budget and he thinks the budget would be most meaningful if prepared on the cash basis.

CHAPTER 3

Differences Between Business and
Government Accounting

As explained in Chapter 2, a **fund** is a separate accounting and fiscal entity. The next six chapters discuss each fund and account group individually: its measurement focus, basis of accounting, and financial statements. This approach emphasizes the similarities among and differences between the funds and account groups. It also allows readers to compare entries and financial statements of governmental, proprietary, and fiduciary types of funds.

Most readers will approach the next six chapters with a background in business accounting. For this reason, accounting for proprietary and certain fiduciary funds, those which use the accounting practices of business entities, tends to be easier to understand. Conversely, accounting for governmental funds involves enough departures from the business approach that the description may seem confusing. The confusion is reduced considerably with a general overview of the major differences between business accounting and accounting for governmental funds. This chapter provides that overview. Exhibit 3-1 depicts the major differences highlighted in this chapter.

The chapter begins with a brief historical review of accounting practices for governmental **entities**. A general description of accounting practices for governmental **funds** is provided, followed by a discussion of accounting practices that contrast accounting for governmental funds with that of businesses. Each distinction is explained and journal entries are used to contrast the accounting for specific transactions in governmental funds with those made by business entities.

A word of caution is in order. This overview will not give comprehensive knowledge about the accounting practices for governmental entities. Only

---

Exhibit 3-1

Differences in Accounting Practices
Business Entities and Governmental Funds

	Business Entity	Governmental Funds
Accounting for Fixed Assets	One Entity/Capitalize	Several Entities/Expenditure
Accounting for Long-Term Debt	One Entity/Interest is Expensed	Several Entities/Principal and Interest Are Expenditures
Budgetary Accounting	Not Integrated	Integrated
Departure from Accrual Basis Accounting	Revenue Recognition	Revenue and Expenditure Recognition
Fund Accounting	Not Used	Used

---

selected transactions and events that illustrate the primary differences between business entities and certain funds of governmental entities are discussed. For this reason, many of these differences are discussed again in the chapters in which the accounting practices for specific funds are described.

GENERAL ACCOUNTING PRACTICES FOR ALL GOVERNMENTAL FUNDS

Recurring governmental activities are accounted for in one of four governmental funds. The capital projects funds account for capital construction, asset acquisitions, or capital leases. The debt service fund accounts for principal and interest payments on general governmental debt. Earmarked revenues are accounted for in special revenue funds. All general recurring governmental activities not accounted for in one of these three funds are accounted for in the general fund. These four funds constitute the "governmental funds" category.

Historical Review of Accounting for Governmental Funds

Governmental fund accounting practices have changed several times during the twentieth century. Initially, many state laws and local ordinances limited expenditure authority to the amount of taxes and other revenues collected during the period. Governmental units therefore operated on a cash basis. In the 1930s when the emphasis shifted to overall performance measurement, the modified accrual basis of accounting was adopted for governmental funds.

Under the modified accrual basis the focus is on current financial resources, the amount that can be spent. Revenues of governmental funds are recognized when available and measurable, which generally means recognizing those revenues received during the current year or soon enough thereafter to satisfy current-year claims. Revenues susceptible to accrual, such as property taxes, are recognized when earned. Expenditures are recognized when the related liability is incurred. The decrease in financial resources is an *expenditure* rather than an *expense*. Expenses are cost expirations, and therefore the term is inappropriate for an accounting basis that focuses on financial resources.

Recent Change in the Accounting Basis

One of the Governmental Accounting Standards Board's initial agenda items was the basis of accounting. The GASB "measurement focus/basis of accounting" project responded to the long-standing criticism that the modified accrual basis of accounting did not capture the essence of many transactions. As the GASB observed,

> some are concerned that the evolution of the governmental accounting model has not kept pace with financial and technological changes in the environment.[1]

[1]Governmental Accounting Standards Board, *Discussion Memorandum, Measurement Focus and Basis of Accounting — Governmental Funds* (Stamford, Conn.: GASB, 1985), ¶19.

Increased sophistication of statement users was also given as a reason for re-examining the basis of accounting. In addition, the project was undertaken because many considered it inconsistent that a unit's governmental funds used the modified accrual basis of accounting while enterprise funds and certain trust funds used the accrual basis of accounting.

The GASB discussion memorandum, issued in early 1985, outlined four options: (1) flow of economic resources (accrual basis), (2) flow of total financial resources (accrual basis with modifications for fixed assets and related debt), (3) flow of current financial resources (modified accrual), and (4) the cash basis. After public hearings and written comments, the Board issued an exposure draft proposing the flow of total financial resources for all governmental funds. In 1990, it issued an opinion statement that would require adoption of the flow of total financial resources basis of accounting for all governmental, expendable trust, and agency funds.[2] Although not the same definition as in the 1985 exposure draft, the statement basically requires accrual accounting without depreciation.

▲ **OBSERVATION**

Had the GASB adopted the model described as the flow of total economic resources, little more would need to be said about government accounting practices. This model is identical to the one used in business. Accountants would already know the principles implicit in accrual accounting — cost, matching, periodicity, and so on. These principles could be applied to all accounting transactions.

An effective date of 1994 was specified as part of the pronouncement. However, in 1993 when it became obvious that the companion pronouncements could not be completed by the proposed effective date, the GASB deferred the implementation date indefinitely. Because of the uncertainty of the effective date, both the *Statement No. 11* model (total financial resources and accrual basis) and the current GAAP model (current financial resources and modified accrual basis) must be understood in order to work for or audit governmental entities. Both models are presented in this chapter and contrasted to accounting in the for-profit sector. Thereafter, the *Statement No. 11* model is described in an appendix to each chapter.

The Flow of Total Financial Resources Model

The flow of total financial resources model requires governmental units to recognize the effect of transactions **when they occur,** regardless of when cash is received or paid. As such, many accrual accounting procedures are applied to the accounting for governmental funds. For example, revenues are

---

[2]Governmental Accounting Standards Board, *Statement No. 11, Measurement Focus and Basis of Accounting — Governmental Fund Operating Statements* (Norwalk, Conn.: GASB, 1990).

generally recognized when earned; expenditures are generally recognized when the related liability is incurred.[3]

Although the accrual basis of accounting is applied for recognition purposes, the term *expenditures* rather than *expenses* is used. Perhaps the GASB chose to refer to the outflows as expenditures rather than expenses because the modifications to the accrual basis system were so substantial. It also could have been a bow to tradition. Whatever the reason, the resulting inconsistencies are confusing. For example, although most expenditures occur when financial resources decline, inventories and prepaids are treated differently. They are initially recorded as assets in the governmental funds. They become expenditures only when consumed or used, despite the fact that there is no financial outflow at that point.

Adoption of the flow of total financial resources model has implications not only for specific accounting transactions but also for what is reported in each fund. "Financial resources" include cash, claims to cash, and claims to goods or services (the inventories and prepaids discussed above are encompassed by this definition) arising from past transactions or events. Since the purpose of the model is to measure only financial resources, nonfinancial resources, such as fixed assets, are excluded from individual governmental funds. In contrast, principal and interest payments on debt represent actual flows of financial resources; they are reported in the operating statement. Specific attributes of the GASB's basis of accounting are discussed further in the following sections.

Accounting for Fixed Assets Financed by Current Operations or Debt

Under accrual accounting any purchase of a fixed asset is reflected by a debit to the asset and a credit to cash or the liability incurred to finance the purchase. However, since fixed assets are nonfinancial resources, only their initial purchase or eventual sale —*not their use*— is reflected under the flow of financial resources model. Therefore, if cash is paid for the asset, an expenditure occurs. If the asset is sold for cash, a financial resource is generated and recognized.

Issuing long-term debt to acquire a fixed asset is treated as two separate transactions in the governmental funds. When the debt is issued, cash is debited and an account called "other financing sources" is credited. (Other financing sources is used to distinguish other financial inflows from revenues, an important distinction when trying to measure the performance of a governmental fund.)

Cash	xx	
Other Financing Sources		xx

---

[3]The term *when earned* is used in its broadest sense. Revenues from income taxes are recognized when the income is earned by the taxpayer, not the governmental unit. Property taxes are not "earned" as such; they are generally considered "earned" for purposes of accrual when levied.

Financial resources are increased, but because the debt is related to a long-term asset whose use *does not* affect financial resources, the debt is not reported as a liability in the general fund. The asset purchase is recorded as a debit to expenditures and a credit to cash.

Expenditures	xx	
Cash		xx

Combining the two transactions results in the entry:

Expenditures	xx	
Other Financing Sources		xx

Both expenditures and other financing sources appear in the operating statement. Expenditures reduce financial resources. The "other financing sources," even though in a different section from revenues and expenditures, increase financial resources. Therefore, the net effect on financial resources is zero.

Contributed Assets   Recording contributed assets follows a different pattern from that of assets purchased with debt. Donated assets are reported in the general fixed asset account group by a debit to assets and a credit to investment in general fixed assets, and as an addition to fixed assets in the notes to the financial statements. No entry would be made in the general fund when the asset is donated. If it is later sold, the following entry is made in the general fund:

Cash	xx	
Other Financing Sources—Gifts		xx

If the governmental entity intends to sell the donated asset and does so before the financial statements are issued, the donated asset would be reported as an asset held for resale in the general fund:

Asset Held for Resale	xx	
Revenues		xx

Depreciation of Fixed Assets   Under the GASB pronouncement, fixed assets are not depreciated in governmental funds. Governmental units may reflect the *effects* of depreciation in the general fixed asset account group, but no depreciation is actually shown in the operating statement. The entry in the general fixed asset account group to reflect accumulated depreciation is:

Investment in General Fixed Assets	xx	
Accumulated Depreciation		xx

Under the financial resources model, assets purchased from operating resources are shown as expenditures when purchased. To also reflect depreciation expense in the operating statement would result in double counting the asset's cost.

OBSERVATION ▲

As will be explained in a subsequent section, debt service payments are recorded as expenditures. If the payment for debt service principal is approximately the same amount as depreciation, this payment can be used as a surrogate for depreciation.

Governmental units are increasingly inclined to show the effects of depreciation in the general fixed asset account group. Some federal and state grants allow governmenal units to include depreciation—called a **use rate**—as one of the costs to be reimbursed by grant funds. Unless a governmental unit systematically computes the amount of depreciaton and reflects the accumulated depreciation in the general fixed asset account group, it may lose this opportunity.

Principal and Interest Payments on Debt   The GASB's *Statement No. 11* distinguishes between principal and interest payments on capital debt from those on operating debt. It provides recognition criteria for only the operating debt. For such debt, the expenditure is recognized as interest accrues, and is based on the debt's effective interest rate. This accounting practice is the same as that used by business entities.

No guidance for recognizing expenditures related to capital debt is provided pending completion of other projects on the GASB's agenda. Therefore, governmental entities will continue their past practice of recording the expenditure when the payments are due. Only if the budget for the current year includes amounts for the payment of principal and interest in the first part of the next year is the accrual allowed at year end. For example, if the fiscal year end is June 30 *and the budget for that period includes $100,000* for principal and interest payments due July 5, the $100,000 would be reported as an expenditure in the fiscal period ending June 30.

Used consistently, this convention will yield the same results as regular accrual accounting. The problem is that some governmental units are inconsistent. Taking the preceding example, if the second fiscal-year budget does not include debt payments for the third fiscal year, a full two year's interest would be recorded in one fiscal year and none in the next. In such circumstances, the Board advised governmental entities to adjust debt service expenditure recognition so that one year's payments are reported in each year.

The Inconsistencies in the GASB's Model for Fixed Assets   Accounting for general fixed assets represents an area in which the GASB's measurement focus of financial resources is inconsistent with its accrual basis of accounting. Measuring financial resources dictates that only flows of financial resources be recognized as expenditures. The accrual basis of accounting, on the other hand, focuses attention on expenses, or expired costs. Only the portion of the fixed asset "expired" during the year is an expense (through a charge called *depreciation*). A single operating statement cannot be structured to reflect both the flow of financial resources and expired costs for any item, such as a fixed asset that is not used up in a single period.

The financial resources measurement focus <u>may not enable governmental units to measure interperiod equity</u>. The GASB has not provided a very explicit definition of interperiod equity. Interperiod equity measurement is:

> the measure of whether current-year revenues are sufficient to pay for current-year services. A measure of interperiod equity would show whether current-year citizens received services but shifted part of the payment burden to future-year citizens or used up previously accumulated resources. Conversely, such a measure would show whether current-year revenues were not only sufficient to pay for current-year services, but also increased accumulated net resources.[4]

Whether citizens receive benefits unaccompanied by the burden when fixed assets are purchased depends upon the circumstances. If an asset is purchased with existing resources (no debt financing), citizens today are assuming the entire burden of an asset that will benefit future periods, so the equity of future generations has been increased at the expense of today's citizens.

Circumstances change if the asset is purchased with long-term debt. The purchase is shown as an expenditure but it is offset by a credit to "other financing sources," so the net effect on financial resources is zero in the year of acquisition. In future periods, the debt principal payments are shown as expenditures. If these payments match the "expiration" pattern of the asset, each year citizens benefiting from the asset's use are bearing their share of the burden. For example, level principal payments would be the same as straight-line depreciation. Declining principal payments could be a surrogate for one of the accelerated depreciation methods. <u>A lump sum payment</u> on the due date would not <u>maintain interperiod equity</u>. The citizens making that payment would bear the entire burden when the asset has benefited the citizens over several years.

Supplies Inventory and Prepaid Items   Under the flow of total financial resources model, operating expenditures are generally recognized when the transactions or events occur. In other words, supplies and other prepayments are recognized as expenditures when consumed, just as they are under the accrual basis of accounting.

When Received:	Supplies Inventory	40,000	
	Accounts Payable		40,000
When Used:	Expenditures	36,800	
	Supplies Inventory		36,800

The GASB made sure, however, that financial statement users could look at the net fund balance (net financial resources) to determine how much could

---

[4]GASB, *Statement No. 11,* ¶3.

be budgeted for expenditures in a subsequent period. Supplies inventories and prepayments do not represent expendable amounts. Therefore, at year end, the portion of the fund balance representing supplies inventory or other prepayments is reserved. Continuing with the preceding example, $40,000 of supplies were purchased and $36,800 consumed. A balance of $3,200 remains at year end.

Year End:	Unreserved Fund Balance	3,200	
	Reserve for Supplies		
	Inventory		3,200

Interfund Transactions   Because each fund is a separate accounting and reporting entity, transactions among the funds are inevitable. Interfund transactions can be of four types: (1) operating transfers, (2) residual equity transfers, (3) reimbursements, or (4) quasi-external transactions.

Recurring transactions among funds are called **operating transfers** and include such items as a general fund transfer of cash to the debt service fund for debt repayment. When one fund transfers cash to another, the following entry is made:

Operating Transfers Out	XX	
Cash		XX

The receiving fund has the opposite entry:

Cash	XX	
Operating Transfers In		XX

Operating transfers are not revenues or expenditures; they are shown in a separate section of the operating statement as "other financing sources and uses" along with the proceeds of debt used to finance capital assets. The transfers reduce or increase a fund's financial resources but do not affect the relationship between revenues and expenditures.

Nonrecurring transactions among funds are called **residual equity transfers.** A contribution by the general fund to the equity of an internal service or enterprise fund is one example of a residual equity transfer. Another is the transfer made to close out a fund, such as when a capital projects or debt service fund has a cash balance that is no longer needed. Residual equity transfers are *not* reported in the operating statement. Rather, they are shown as additions to or deletions from the beginning fund balance of governmental funds.

Another interfund transaction is a **reimbursement**. One fund may reimburse another for supplies or other items purchased on its behalf. For example, the general fund might pay the entire rental on a facility even though the facility is used by both the general and special revenue funds. When the expenditure is made by the general fund, the entry is:

Expenditures	XX	
Cash		XX

When the reimbursement is received from the special revenue fund for its share of the rent, the general fund includes the following entry:

Cash	xx	
Expenditures		xx

The special revenue fund debits expenditures and credits cash.

quasi-external
rev, exp,
expense

The last type of interfund transaction is called a **quasi-external transaction.** It represents a payment from one fund to another that is treated as a revenue, expenditure, or expense. As an example, a proprietary fund might make a payment to the general fund that is in lieu of taxes. Another example is a charge by the internal service fund and payment by the receiving fund for goods or services rendered. Although quasi-external transactions represent movement of resources from one fund to another, they are legitimate arm's-length transactions and are treated as revenues, expenses, or expenditures.

Interfund Loans   To use idle cash effectively or to avoid borrowing from external sources, one fund may loan money to another. Interest is charged on these loans only when the borrowing or lending fund is mandated to operate on a self-sufficient basis (usually the proprietary funds). If a short-term extension of credit is made, it is recorded as a **due to** or **due from** in the borrowing and lending funds, respectively. Whenever a loan is for an extended period, an **advance to** or **advance from** account is used by both funds. Using two different account titles helps financial statement users determine the nature of the loan.

▲   **OBSERVATION**

When accounting for a specific fund, the name of the fund that the money is due from or due to may be included in the account title, for example, "due to general fund." Since a number of different funds may be shown on a single financial statement, the more generic description, "due to other funds," is used.

In summary, the flow of total financial resources model portends the following accounting practices for governmental entities:

1. By and large, governmental fund revenues will be recognized when earned and expenditures recognized when an asset or resource is acquired, either by cash or by incurring a liability.
2. Governmental entities will continue to use fund accounting.
3. Each fund will account for its own long-term liabilities unless they are associated with the acquisition or construction of general fixed assets, in which case the debt is recorded in the general long-term debt account group.
4. Some funds will continue to use a different measurement focus and basis of accounting; business-type activities and nonexpendable trust funds will use the total economic resources model, including taking depreciation, whereas governmental funds will use the flow of total financial resources model.

Practical Problems of Implementation Rarely do standard-setting bodies issue a pronouncement with an indefinite delay between the issuance and effective dates. The GASB did this because so many other projects on its agenda impinge upon the basis of accounting. The implementation date also was delayed because the statement requirements represent a sharp departure from previous accounting methods. Governmental entities need lead time to develop data bases and procedures that allow a smooth transition to new accounting methods.

OBSERVATION ▲

Between the adoption of *Statement No. 11* and its scheduled implementation date, the composition of the GASB changed, making the deferral necessary. The newer members did not support the model adopted by the earlier Board. Consequently, any implementation guidance would have been adopted on a three-to-two vote, an unacceptable majority for such a vital undertaking.

Because of the interrelationships among GASB projects, accounting principles used for governmental funds are not yet defined completely. For example, all long-term debt except that related to the purchase of general fixed assets will appear in the fund incurring the debt, usually the general fund. This means literally moving the noncapital debt from one place to another as depicted in Exhibit 3-2. Given that most governmental units do not retain large fund balances in governmental funds, the shift of noncapital long-term debt from an account group (where it sits off to the side without affecting the fund balance of any governmental fund) to an operating fund is apt to make the fund balance negative, as shown in this example. The GASB and

Exhibit 3-2

**Impact of the Change in Accounting Basis on Governmental Funds
A Hypothetical Example**

Current Accounting Model (Modified Accrual)

	Governmental Fund		General Long-Term Debt Account Group	
	Dr.	Cr.	Dr.	Cr.
Current Assets	$1,000			
Balancing Account*			$5,000	
Current Liabilities		$ 500		
Long-Term Debt:				
General				$3,000
Related to Fixed Assets				2,000
Fund Balance		500		
Totals	$1,000	$1,000	$5,000	$5,000

(continued)

| Exhibit 3-2 | (continued) |

Future Accounting Model (Accrual)

	Governmental Fund		General Long-Term Debt Account Group	
	Dr.	Cr.	Dr.	Cr.
Current Assets	$1,000			
Balancing Account*			$2,000	
Current Liabilities		$ 500		
Long-Term Debt:				
General		$3,000		
Related to Fixed Assets				$2,000
Fund Balance		(2,500)		
Totals	$1,000	$1,000	$2,000	$2,000

*Because the general long-term debt account group is only a single-entry system, a balancing account is used to make the account group "a self-balancing set of accounts." It is called "amount to be provided" in the general long-term debt account group.

practitioners are concerned about the implications of the negative fund balance. Will some financial statement users immediately conclude that the governmental unit is in financial trouble?

The GASB also has not decided how to handle all the transactions related to the acquisition, disposal, and debt servicing of general fixed assets. These transactions are scattered among several funds and account groups. The GASB is considering whether the financial statement display would be as clear or clearer if some of the separate funds and/or account groups were merged into one.

GASB pronouncements related to these areas of the measurement focus/basis of accounting project could markedly alter specific differences between business and governmental-fund accounting. Whatever the GASB conclusions, some underlying differences will persist. They are discussed in the following sections, as are the differences between business accounting and the current model used by governmental entities.

MAJOR DIFFERENCES IN ACCOUNTING PRACTICES

Historically, governmental accounting methodologies were developed to enable managers to gauge the status of funding at any time. Governmental managers wanted to know how much of the budget had been spent and how each activity was progressing. In contrast, business managers focus on profitability for a given period. Most differences in accounting between the two types of entities trace to this difference in perspective.

Both entities use the double-entry system of accounting. Eventually both also will use accrual accounting. However, many accounting entries are different because governmental entities report various transactions in separate

[margin notes: - diff funds | - fin vs. econ resources | - budgetary accts | - encumb. acctg.]

funds. Even if funds were collapsed into one entity, differences would persist. Governmental-fund accounting focuses on **financial** resources whereas business accounting focuses on **economic** resources. Some accounting transactions also appear differently because budgetary accounts are integrated into the accounting system. Other accounts used for governmental funds, such as those related to encumbrances, have no or only limited application in business.

Fund Accounting

The concept of a fund was discussed in Chapter 2. Simply put, it is a means of segregating activities into identifiable and measurable segments. A manager can then tell which assets relate to a particular program, how much has been spent on the program, and whether unspent resources remain at year end.

The idea of segregating resources or activities is not unique to government. Businesses also use this concept. Businesses establish a *sinking fund* for the repayment of debt or some other long-term obligation. Cash is segregated into a restricted account, and retained earnings are appropriated for the total amount in the sinking fund to dissuade stockholders from the idea that sinking-fund assets are available for other purposes, such as dividends. Governmental entities could use the same approach to segregate assets and liabilities related to specific activities without using separate funds. Because governmental entities have several such activities for every one in business, early accountants probably chose to make a physical separation by using individual fiscal and accounting entities: funds.

Fund accounting complicates recording financial transactions. Before an event can be recorded, the accountant must not only determine the nature of the transaction but also the type of activity. For example, a voucher from a vendor could represent a payment on a construction activity, in which case it generally would be recorded in a capital projects fund. Alternatively, the payment might represent a charge for supplies used by the governmental unit. If so, unless the governmental unit used a central supply entity, the charge would be recorded in the general fund. If a central supply warehouse provided supplies for all governmental activities, the transaction would be recorded in an internal service fund.

[margin note: nature type]

In contrast, a business records an invoice in a single entity. Also, when the purchase involves assets (fixed assets or inventories), the amount is capitalized. The nature of the invoice does not determine the entity, and the entity does not determine whether the item is an expense or a capital asset. Further, a business has a single balance sheet, for example, and all sinking funds are shown on it. Governmental units prepare a balance sheet for each fund.

Fund accounting also tends to reduce comparability among governmental units. One governmental entity may account for supplies in the general fund. Another may use an internal service fund to centralize purchasing and control over supplies. Although accrual accounting is used for both funds, depreciation is taken in the internal service fund, but not in the general fund. All other operating characteristics being equal, the governmental unit providing supplies from a central facility would tend to have more stable earnings than

[margin note: reduces comparability]

the other one. Fixed assets would be depreciated over their useful lives rather than expensed when purchased.

Encumbrance Accounting

As explained in Chapter 2, encumbrance accounting is used to refine the process of keeping track of the budget. Commitments that are not yet liabilities are recorded by debiting an encumbrance account and crediting a reserve for encumbrances when an order is placed. The entry is reversed when the order is received.

Encumbrance accounting is helpful in tracking the budgetary commitments during the year. It also enhances an entity's ability to determine orders placed in one fiscal period that will be paid for during the next. Appropriations may lapse at the end of each fiscal period. Purchases made in good faith cannot be canceled just because they were not received before the appropriation expired. Therefore, the first commitments under the new appropriation are for orders placed in a prior year but received in the current one.

Governmental entities use encumbrance accounting for irregular purchases and for those involving a delay between the order and receipt dates. Supplies and capital purchases meet this description and usually are encumbered. Salaries and fringe benefits would normally not be encumbered because it is easy to determine the amount unspent by multiplying monthly salary and benefit costs times the number of payroll periods remaining. However, if the activity involves a great deal of part-time or seasonal employment, encumbrances should be used.

Businesses may use encumbrance accounting for internal control purposes. If encumbrance accounting is used, however, it is not integrated into the accounting system. Since businesses focus on profit, orders impact the accounting system only when expensed. In contrast, governmental units' budget authorizations are related to the flow of financial resources. If the outflow did not occur in the current year, it will in the next. The governmental unit needs to make some provision for the anticipated outflow. The fund balance is reserved for encumbrances outstanding at the end of the year, which alerts the managers to outstanding commitments against financial resources.

Integrating the Budgetary Accounts into the Accounting System

Governmental and business entities both prepare detailed budgets for planning purposes. The difference is that in governmental accounting, budgetary accounts are integrated into the accounting system. Suppose, for example, that a governmental unit expects to collect revenues of $1,000,000 and to expend the same amount during the next fiscal year. Rather than use the anticipated revenues and expenditures as a basis of some secondary control system, as a business would do, the estimated revenues and expenditures are entered into the general ledger accounts by the following entry:

Estimated Revenues	1,000,000	
Appropriations		1,000,000

The subsidiary accounts in the general ledger show the various types of revenues and expenditures; each subsidiary account carries the budgetary amounts. For example, if property tax revenues are anticipated to account for $800,000 of the total estimated revenues of $1,000,000, the subsidiary account for property taxes will show the following after the estimated revenue entry (shown above) was made:

PROPERTY TAX REVENUES

Date	Description	Dr.	Cr.	Balance
1/1	Budget Authorization	800,000		800,000

As revenue is accrued the governmental unit debits a receivable and credits revenue. The amount of the revenue is entered into the subsidiary ledger account as a credit. The amount in the balance column of the subsidiary ledger allows managers of governmental units to see at a glance the difference between the amount budgeted for the year and the amount earned to date.

Integrating the budgetary accounts into the general ledger does not alter the report of operating results for the year. Actual revenues and actual expenditures are reported on a governmental unit's operating statement. It does, however, allow governmental entities to easily compare actual and projected performance at any point during the year. Together with encumbrance accounting, it enables managers to determine exactly how much budgetary authority remains. The integration of budgetary accounts also facilitates the preparation of one required financial statement, the Statement of Revenues, Expenditures, and Changes in Fund Balance—Budget and Actual.

The differences just discussed—fund accounting, encumbrance accounting, and integrating the budgetary accounts—are the same regardless of whether the governmental entity uses the modified accrual or the accrual basis of accounting. For the following topics, the nature of the differences depends on whether governmental entities are using the accrual or the modified accrual basis of accounting.

Departures from Generally Accepted Accounting Principles

The accrual and modified accrual bases of accounting provide general recognition criteria for revenues and expenditures/expenses. Some generally accepted accounting practices for government and business depart from general recognition criteria. Usually these departures pertain to specific transactions or types of entities. Businesses, for example, recognize some installment sales revenues as cash is received instead of when the income is earned.

Governmental entity accounting practices also diverge from modified accrual accounting principles. For example, under the modified accrual basis of accounting, expenditures are recognized when the related liability is incurred, just as they are under the accrual basis of accounting. However, payments on *all* types of long-term debt are recognized when due. This is a

property taxes

significant departure. The modified accrual basis generally means that revenues are recognized when **measurable and available.** Recognition of property tax revenues represents a departure from this recognition criteria; property tax revenue is recognized when the tax is levied on the condition that such revenue is "susceptible to accrual."

The specific departures from the accrual basis are different for governmental accounting and business accounting. Accountants cannot assume that a departure from one basis of accounting applies to another, even under similar circumstances. This complicates matters for statement preparers and users alike.

Treatment of Fixed Assets and Related Debt

Differences due to
- measurement
  focus
- fund acctg

Whether governments are using the modified accrual or accrual basis, the most significant difference between governmental and business accounting practices is the treatment of fixed assets. This difference results both from the differences in the measurement focus and from the fact that governmental units use fund accounting while businesses do not.

Purchasing Fixed Assets for Cash   When a governmental entity purchases assets for general government purposes, the flow of financial resources— the cash outflow—is recorded in a governmental fund. This means that the asset's cost is recorded as an expenditure when it is purchased. For example, if a governmental unit spent $100,000 from a governmental fund to purchase an asset, the entry is:

Expenditures	100,000	
Cash		100,000

Under either governmental model, additional entries are necessary to maintain control over the asset. Unless some type of subsidiary record is maintained, the $100,000 appears only as an expenditure in the operating statement. To maintain a permanent record of the asset, the governmental entity keeps a list of the assets and the sources of funding for those assets. This listing is maintained in a self-balancing set of accounts called a general fixed asset account group. When the expenditure entry is made in the governmental fund, an entry is also made in the account group:

Asset	100,000	
Investment in General Fixed Assets—Source		100,000

Under either governmental model, assets are not depreciated. Therefore, the $100,000 remains in the general fixed asset account group until the asset is sold or scrapped, at which time the entry made above is reversed. Any proceeds from the sale are revenue in the governmental fund receiving the cash.

Business treatment of fixed assets is much simpler. The cost of the asset is capitalized and depreciated over the asset's estimated useful life. All accounting transactions pertaining to fixed assets—purchase, depreciation, disposal—appear in a single entity. Any difference between the book value and the sales price is shown as a gain or loss on the disposition of the asset.

Purchasing Assets with Long-Term Debt   As explained earlier, the issuance of long-term debt provides financial resources; this inflow must be reported in the operating statement to maintain the integrity of the model. A governmental entity avoids confusing inflows from revenues with those from other sources, such as the proceeds from the debt issuance, by recording these latter financial inflows as other financing sources:

Cash	100,000	
Other Financing Sources		100,000

A problem arises when long-term debt is issued to finance fixed assets. Because the long-term debt relates specifically to the acquisition or construction of fixed assets, a governmental entity must make sure it reports accurately the effect on interperiod equity. If a governmental entity records the long-term debt in the governmental funds, it implies that the debt must be repaid by the current generation of taxpayers. This implication is incorrect. Since the asset benefits future generations, the related debt should likewise be a burden of future generations. Thus, the debt has to be reported *outside* the governmental funds. Governmental entities use a second self-balancing account group for this purpose. When the proceeds are reflected in the governmental funds, the debt is recorded in the general long-term debt account group:

Amount to Be Provided for the Repayment of		
Long-Term Debt	100,000	
Long-Term Debt Payable		100,000

The account entitled "amount to be provided for the repayment of long-term debt" is not an asset or an expenditure account. Although it carries a debit balance and will be shown on the asset side of a balance sheet, it is simply a balancing account to achieve equality between the debits and the credits. The account group provides a listing of the long-term debt outstanding. The "amount to be provided..." account translates that listing into a self-balancing set of accounts.

Servicing Long-Term Debt   Interest and principal payments on debt used to finance asset acquisitions are usually accounted for in the debt service fund. From earmarked revenue sources or transfers from the general fund, cash is deposited in the debt service fund to make principal and interest payments. Because the payments involve an outflow of financial resources, they are reported as expenditures. If, for instance, the first year's interest payment on the $100,000 debt was $7,000, the entry in the debt service fund is:

Expenditures	7,000	
Cash		7,000

If a principal payment of $10,000 was due at the same time, the following entry is made in the debt service fund:

Expenditures (10,000 + 7,000)	17,000	
Cash		17,000

As this entry illustrates, no distinction is made between principal and interest. Both are outflows of resources and therefore both are shown as expenditures.

Once a principal payment is made, the amount carried in the long-term debt account group must be changed:

Long-Term Debt Payable	10,000	
Amount to Be Provided for the Repayment		
of Long-Term Debt		10,000

Because only the principal portion of the debt is shown in the general long-term debt account group, only the principal amount paid is used to reduce the long-term debt.

ILLUSTRATED EXAMPLE OF THE DIFFERENCES RELATED TO FIXED ASSETS

Differences between the treatment of assets under the future governmental (total financial resources) and the business (total economic resources) models can be best illustrated by showing the respective journal entries and resulting financial statements. The following illustration is for a construction project with a total cost of $28,000. The project is financed by $28,000 of 5-year, 7 percent serial bonds requiring level debt-service payments. Expenditures for the project will be $12,000 in Year 1 and $16,000 in Year 2. Other governmental activities include noncapital expenditures of $50,000 in Year 1 and Year 2, and expenditures for equipment of $2,000 in Year 1 and $1,000 in Year 2. Property tax revenues total $63,000 per year.

Transactions and Financial Statements, Year 1[5]

As Exhibit 3-3 indicates, when the governmental entity issues the bonds, both the capital projects fund and the general long-term debt account group are affected. The inflow of financial resources is reported in the capital projects fund, and the entity maintains a record of the debt in the account group. In contrast, the business entity simply debits cash and credits the long-term liability.

Except for transactions related to capital acquisitions, revenues and expenses are reported similarly for the two entities (entries 2, 3, and 4). Reve-

---

[5]This display concentrates on the differences between business GAAP and the model that will be adopted by governments in the future. Differences between current GAAP and this "future" model are illustrated in a subsequent section.

Exhibit 3-3

Journal Entries, Year 1

	Business Model		Governmental Model		
1. Issuance of Bonds					
Cash	28,000		CP	28,000	
Bonds Payable		28,000			
OFS—Bond Proceeds					28,000
Amount to Be Provided			GLTDAG	28,000	
Bonds Payable					28,000
2. Property Taxes Collected*					
Cash	63,000		G	55,400	
Revenues, Taxes		63,000			55,400
Cash			DS	7,600	
Revenues, Taxes					7,600
3. Payment of Operating Expenses and Equipment Purchases					
Operating Expenses	50,000				
Operating Expenditures			G	50,000	
Equipment	2,000				
Capital Expenditures				2,000	
Cash		52,000			52,000
Equipment			GFAAG	2,000	
Investment in Assets					2,000
4. Construction Expenditures Paid					
Construction in Progress	12,000				
Capital Expenditures			CP	12,000	
Cash		12,000			12,000
Construction in Progress			GFAAG	12,000	
Investment in Assets					12,000
5. Debt Service Paid					
Bonds Payable	5,500				
Expenditures			DS	7,500	
Interest Expense	2,000				
Cash		7,500			7,500
Bonds Payable			GLTDAG	5,600	
Amount to Be Provided					5,600

Key to Fund Designations:
G   = General Fund
CP   = Capital Projects Fund
GFAAG   = General Fixed Asset Account Group
GLTDAG = General Long-Term Debt Account Group
DS   = Debt Service Fund

*The amount deposited in the debt service fund is sufficient to cover assumed principal ($5,500) and interest ($2,000) payments, and a small ($100) cushion to keep the fund open. These amounts could have been recorded as revenue in the general fund and then transferred to the debt service fund.

nues are recognized when earned and expenses/expenditures are reported when the related liability is incurred. In entry 3, capital and operating expenditures are reported separately only to make the example clearer, not because two different control accounts are actually used in practice. Separate subsidiary accounts must be maintained, however, in order for the governmental entity to determine which amounts are capital expenditures that must be simultaneoulsy reported in the general fixed asset account group (the second entry under the governmental model).

In entry 5, bonds are reduced by $5,500 under either model. The difference is, once again, that the governmental unit must make entries in two entities—the debt service fund and the general long-term debt account group. Further, because the entire payment of $7,500 represents an outflow of financial resources, it is shown as an expenditure in the debt service fund. Under the business model, only the amount paid for interest reduces economic resources and therefore is reported as an expense.

As Exhibit 3-4 shows, the financial statements provide a very interesting contrast between the two models. Because the government uses fund ac-

---

Exhibit 3-4

Financial Statements, Year 1

Balance Sheet	Business Model	General Fund	Debt Service	Capital Projects	GFAAG	GLTDAG
		Governmental Model				
Cash	$ 19,500	$ 3,400	$ 100	$ 16,000	$ —	$ —
Construction in Progress	12,000	—	—	—	12,000	—
Equipment	2,000	—	—	—	2,000	—
Amount to Be Provided	—	—	—	—	—	22,500
Total Assets	$ 33,500	$ 3,400	$ 100	$ 16,000	$14,000	$22,500
Bonds Payable	$ 22,500	$ —	$ —	$ —	$ —	$22,500
Equity	11,000	—	—	—	—	—
Fund Balance	—	3,400	100	16,000	—	—
Investment in Fixed Assets	—	—	—	—	14,000	—
Total Liabilities and Equity or Fund Balance	$ 33,500	$ 3,400	$ 100	$ 16,000	$14,000	$22,500

Operating Statement	Business Model	General Fund	Debt Service	Capital Projects	GFAAG	GLTDAG
		Governmental Model				
Revenues	$ 63,000	$ 55,400	$ 7,600	$ —	NA	NA
Operating Expenses (Expenditures)	(50,000)	(50,000)	—	—	NA	NA
Capital Expenditures	—	(2,000)	—	(12,000)	NA	NA
Interest Expense/ Debt Service	(2,000)	—	(7,500)	—	NA	NA
Other Financing Sources—Bonds	—	—	—	28,000	NA	NA
Excess (before depreciation)	$ 11,000	$ 3,400	$ 100	$ 16,000	NA	NA

[handwritten annotation: Fund balance]

Cash Flow Statement	
Income (before depreciation)	$ 11,000
Cash Provided by Operations	$ 11,000
Cash Provided by Borrowing	28,000
Cash Used to Repay Debt	(5,500)
Cash Used for Capital Assets	(14,000)
NET INCREASE IN CASH	$ 19,500

(No cash flow statement is prepared under the governmental model)

counting, the entity's $19,500 cash balance is split up among three different entities. The government's balance sheet shows two account titles that are foreign to business accounting: amount to be provided and investment in fixed assets. These accounts are necessary to make the two account groups self-balancing.

The total assets are different as well. The business entity shows a total of $33,500; for the governmental entity, total assets are derived by adding the assets of the three funds together with the fixed assets in the general fixed asset account group and the two accounts in the general long-term debt account group. Although these are not true assets, they carry debit balances and therefore must be included in the total for the assets.

The operating statement shows the results of including the bond proceeds as financing sources and total debt payments as expenditures within governmental entities. The excess of revenues and other sources over expenses/expenditures and other sources totals $19,500 for the governmental entity compared to $11,000 for the business entity, a difference of $8,500. The following table reconciles the difference:

Additional Revenues/Sources:	
Bond Proceeds ~ other financing sources	$ 28,000 —op state
Additional Expenditures/Uses:	
Principal Debt Service Payment	$(5,500) -- not on business op st.
Capital Expenditures	(14,000)
Total	$(19,500)
Net Difference	$ 8,500

Transactions and Financial Statements, Year 2

Similar results are evident for the second year. As Exhibit 3-5 indicates, the journal entries for the governmental entity are made in several different funds/account groups. Any capital outlays are reported as expenditures in the incurring fund and as assets in the general fixed asset account group. Also, the total debt service payment is recorded as an expenditure; the principal portion of the payment is shown in the general long-term debt account group as a reduction of the long-term liability.

As the balance sheet (Exhibit 3-6) reveals, total assets and equities of the governmental entity exceed those of the business entity by $16,900. This is the exact amount of the debit balance in the long-term debt account group. This account is necessary to maintain the self-balancing phenomenon of the account group. If the two account groups were collapsed into one fund, the total assets (or liabilities and equity) of the business and governmental entities would be the same.

The operating statements for both years ignore depreciation. Depreciation would be taken by the business entity, but not by the governmental entity. This difference in accounting practice leads to different financial statements throughout the life of the asset. All other things being equal, the business

Exhibit 3-5

Journal Entries, Year 2

	Business Model		Governmental Model		
1. Collection of Property Taxes					
Cash	63,000		G	55,400	
Revenues, Taxes		63,000			55,400
Cash			DS	7,600	
Revenues, Taxes					7,600
2. Payment of Operating Expenses and Equipment Purchases					
Operating Expenditures			G	50,000	
Operating Expenses	50,000				
Equipment	1,000				
Capital Expenditures				1,000	
Cash		51,000			51,000
Equipment			GFAAG	1,000	
Investments in Assets					1,000
3. Construction Completed					
Construction in Progress	16,000				
Capital Expenditures			CP	16,000	
Cash		16,000			16,000
Building	28,000		GFAAG	28,000	
Construction in Progress		28,000			12,000
Investment in Assets					16,000
4. Debt Service Payments					
Interest Expense (Expenditures)	1,900		DS	7,500	
Bonds Payable	5,600				
Cash		7,500			7,500
Bonds Payable			GLTDAG	5,600	
Amount to Be Provided					5,600

Exhibit 3-6

Financial Statements, Year 2

Balance Sheet	Business Model	Governmental Model				
		General Fund	Debt Service	Capital Projects	GFAAG	GLTDAG
Cash	$ 8,000	$ 7,800	$ 200	$ —	$ —	$ —
Building	28,000	—	—	—	28,000	—
Equipment	3,000	—	—	—	3,000	—
Amount to Be Provided	—	—	—	—	—	16,900
Total Assets	$ 39,000	$ 7,800	$ 200	$ —	$31,000	$16,900
Bonds Payable	$ 16,900	$ —	$ —	$ —	$ —	$16,900
Equity	22,100	—	—	—	—	—
Fund Balance	—	7,800	200	—	—	—
Investment in Fixed Assets	—	—	—	—	31,000	—
Total Liabilities and Equity or Fund Balance	$ 39,000	$ 7,800	$ 200	$ —	$31,000	$16,900

(continued)

| Exhibit 3-6 | *(continued)* |

Operating Statement	Business Model	Governmental Model				
		General Fund	Debt Service	Capital Projects	GFAAG	GLTDAG
Revenues	$ 63,000	$ 55,400	$ 7,600	$ —	NA	NA
Operating Expenses (Expenditures)	(50,000)	(50,000)	—	—	NA	NA
Capital Expenditures	—	(1,000)		(16,000)	NA	NA
Interest Expense/ Debt Service	(1,900)	—	(7,500)	—	NA	NA
Other Financing Sources—Bonds	—	—	—	—	NA	NA
Excess (before depreciation)	$ 11,100	$ 4,400	$ 100	$(16,000)		

Cash Flow Statement						
Income (before depreciation)	$ 11,100					
Cash Provided by Operations	$ 11,100	(No cash flow statement is prepared				
Cash Used to Repay Debt	(5,600)	under the governmental model)				
Cash Used for Capital Assets	(17,000)					
NET DECREASE IN CASH	$(11,500)					

entity's excess of revenues over expenditures will be less than that for the governmental entity by the amount of the depreciation.

DIFFERENCES BETWEEN THE TWO GOVERNMENTAL MODELS

The preceding section described the differences between the business model and the governmental model (total financial resources) that will be used when the GASB sets an effective date. Understanding the differences between current GAAP (current financial resources) and the governmental model of the future also is important because the adoption date is uncertain.

Both the current and future governmental accounting practices involve the treatment described above for general fixed assets and any related debt financing. Also, fund accounting, encumbrance accounting, and integration of the budget into the accounting records are the same under both models. The GASB might reduce the number of funds by the adoption date, but that change will not affect any of these aspects of current GAAP.

Two primary differences exist between the total financial resources and current financial resources models. Under the current financial resources model now being used, all long-term debt is recorded in the general long-term debt account group. When the total financial resources model is adopted, debt as issued to cover operating deficits should be recorded in the fund incurring the debt. Interest and principal payments on capital-related debt will be recognized when due. Interest on operating debt will be recognized as an expenditure as it occurs, and when a principal payment is made on such debt, it will reduce the amount of debt outstanding.

The second difference relates to revenue recognition. Under current GAAP, revenues are recognized when **measurable and available.** The only exception is property tax revenue, which is recognized when it is levied because, according to the applicable accounting standards, it is **susceptible to accrual.** Under future GAAP, revenues generally will be recognized **when earned,** provided the due date is before the end of the period.

This general recognition principle almost becomes revenue specific. For example, property taxes should be recognized when the underlying event has taken place and the government has demanded the taxes by establishing a due date on or before the end of the period. Other revenues, such as interest income, are recognized as they accrue.

These differences are further delineated in the following chapters. In each case, current GAAP is included in the body of the text and the total financial resources/accrual model is discussed in an appendix.

SUMMARY

Accounting for governmental and business entities differs in a number of ways. Governmental entities use fund accounting and integrate budgetary accounts into the accounting records of some funds. Another difference relates to the departures from accrual-based accounting: both governmental and business entities are allowed certain departures, but the departures differ for each type of entity.

Although these differences are important, the most significant difference relates to the accounting treatment accorded the acquisition, use, and disposition of general fixed assets and related debt. Because the accounting for governmental entities focuses on the flow of **financial resources,** asset acquisitions are reported as expenditures and are charged against revenues in the year in which they are acquired. In contrast, under the **economic resources** model used by business entities, the asset is capitalized and its cost is charged against revenue over its useful life.

The issuance of debt to finance an asset acquisition is reported as an "other financing source" by governmental entities. Business entities report the issuance of debt as a liability, a transaction that does not affect their operating statement. When servicing the debt, governmental entities record the total payment as an operating transaction—an expenditure. Business entities report only the interest portion of the payment as an expense. The remainder reduces the balance of the outstanding liability.

Under the governmental model, neither the asset nor the related debt is shown in the fund making the expenditure. Two account groups, self-balancing sets of accounts, are used as a way of tracking the asset and the debt.

This overview of governmental and business accounting provides a general context in which to study the individual funds and account groups. The next six chapters discuss the specific types of funds used by governmental entities, beginning with the general and special revenue funds. Following that chapter, Chapters 5, 6, and 7 cover capital assets and related debt. The two proprietary funds are discussed in Chapter 8, followed by a chapter on fiduciary funds.

QUESTIONS

3-1 What activities are accounted for in governmental funds?

3-2 Contrast the current financial resources model with the total financial resources model. Which one focuses on the amount available for spending?

3-3 Which accounting model uses full accrual accounting—the current financial resources or the total financial resources model? Explain.

3-4 Both the total financial resources and total economic resources models use accrual accounting. How do they differ?

3-5 Contrast the journal entries to record the purchase of an asset under the total financial resources and total economic resources models. Explain the basis for each one.

3-6 Explain why depreciation expense is not recognized under a financial resources model.

3-7 A governmental entity purchased $11,000 in supplies and throughout the year, used $7,000 of those supplies. Show the entries that would be made under the total financial resources and total economic resources models.

3-8 Explain the distinction between operating and residual equity transfers under the governmental accounting model.

3-9 Describe the major characteristics of the total financial resources model to be used by governmental entities.

3-10 What are the major differences between generally accepted accounting principles for governmental and business entities?

3-11 What conclusions might a user reach about a governmental entity whose financial statements show a negative fund balance in its general fund? Explain how these conclusions relate to the change from the modified accrual to the accrual basis of accounting.

3-12 Why do governmental entities place so much importance on budgeting in their accounting practices?

3-13 Explain the rationale of fund accounting.

3-14 What differences between governmental and business accounting result from government's use of fund accounting?

3-15 Explain how budgets are integrated into a governmental entity's accounting records.

3-16 Record and explain the entries a governmental entity would make if it purchased a fixed asset costing $62,000 for cash. How do those entries differ from the ones made by a business entity?

3-17   Debt principal and interest payments made by governmental entities are made in the debt service fund. Explain the basis for debiting expenditures for the full amount of the payment.

3-18   What is the difference between a residual equity transfer and an operating transfer? Give examples of each type of transfer.

3-19   Why do governmental units segregate general fixed assets and the debt relating to those assets from the fund making the purchase and incurring the debt?

3-20   Describe the treatment of operating transfers and expenditures in the statement of revenues, expenditures, and changes in fund balance. What is the reason for treating the two differently?

CASES

3-1   The city of Radnor has been using the modified accrual basis of accounting. Assume it is time to adjust to the accrual basis of accounting as defined by the GASB. Explain how the following revenues/expenditures would be recognized under the accrual basis of accounting.

Revenues
     Property Tax Revenues
     Interest Revenues on Investments
Expenditures
     Principal and Interest Payments on Noncapital Debt
     Fixed Assets/Depreciation
     Supplies

3-2   The finance director for the city of Dextor recently hired an accounting graduate who has had little exposure to governmental accounting. After struggling with his assignments for about a month, the accountant asks the manager to assist him in the area of fixed asset accounting. The accountant indicates that he has been making the entries, but he cannot understand the reason for the practices. For example, he cannot understand why capital outlays are recorded both as an expenditure and as an asset. He also is confused by the practice of recording an expenditure for the interest and principal payments on debt.

REQUIRED
Prepare a report that addresses the accountant's concerns, bearing in mind that the purpose of the report is to teach the accountant why the governmental unit uses the accounting procedures just discussed.

3-3   The Institute of Management Accounting (IMA) has a standing committee called the Management Accounting Practices Committee (MAP). On behalf of IMA, MAP promulgates accounting practices for management accounting. It also responds to the standard-setting bodies when they ask for comments on proposed accounting practices for businesses and governmental entities. Most MAP members represent large manufacturing concerns and national public accounting firms and have limited interest in governmental accounting practices.

Assume that the GASB has just issued a proposed accounting standard that would require governmental units to depreciate all fixed assets. As the MAP committee member responsible for drafting responses to the GASB, you have to convince the rest of the committee that your response ought to be adopted by the full committee.

REQUIRED

Presume that you have drafted a letter to the GASB opposing the accounting statement that would require depreciation on all fixed assets. Keeping in mind the background of the MAP committee members, write a short statement justifying the position you took in the response to the GASB.

3-4 Adopting the flow of total financial resources model has implications for all long-term debt not associated with capital acquisition or construction. Prior to the effective date of the pronouncement requiring use of the new model, Shelby County has the following debt:

1. 7 percent bonds issued to finance the new addition on the courthouse, $1,000,000.
2. 10 percent serial bonds used to build county roads, $510,000.
3. 8 percent long-term note issued when the general fund ran an unexpected deficit two years ago, $500,000.
4. A 7 percent mortgage assumed when the county bought land and two houses for later expansion of the city offices, $110,000.

REQUIRED

Assuming the general fund has a fund balance of $50,000 (cr.), prepare a statement contrasting the city's general fund balance sheet before and after the adoption of the flow of total financial resources model. What entries would be made to make the adjustment to the new model?

3-5 A new member of the Ronan City Council who sits on its budget committee has been familiarizing herself with governmental budgetary and accounting procedures. She was appointed to the committee because she heads the budget committee for a large retailer in a metropolitan area. After several hours poring over the records, she has a number of questions to ask the city's finance director:

1. What entry or entries are made when the budget is approved?
2. Why are those entries incorporated in the accounting records?
3. What are the first debits made in the revenue subsidiary accounts? The initial credits to the expenditure subsidiary accounts?
4. How is the integration of the budgetary accounts used when financial statements are prepared?
5. Why are the budgetary practices so different from those used in industry?

REQUIRED

Prepare a statement responding to the questions of the budget committee member.

3-6   A recently elected county commissioner is confused by the operating and equity transfers found on the financial statements. An operating transfer out of $110,000 is found in the operating section of the statement of revenues, expenditures, and changes in fund balance, while an equity transfer of $66,000 is found in a subsequent section entitled "other sources and uses." She has been informed that both relate to debt service: The $110,000 reflects a transfer from the general fund to the debt service fund for interest and principal payments. The $66,000 is a transfer from the capital projects fund to the debt service fund, also for interest and principal payments.

REQUIRED

1. Explain why two payments for debt service could be classified differently, that is, one as an equity transfer and one as an operating transfer.
2. Explain why one of the payments may be in the operating section of the statement and one in the other financing sources and uses section. Is this treatment correct?
3. How could the GASB pronouncements be improved to reduce the kind of confusion experienced by the county commissioner?

EXERCISES

3-1   Select the best answer for each question.

1. In its *Statement No. 11* on measurement focus/basis of accounting, the GASB requires:
   a. governmental units to depreciate their fixed assets
   b. governmental units to use accrual accounting for their governmental funds
   c. governmental units to use the modified accrual basis of accounting for their governmental funds
   d. none of the above
2. Which of the following is *not* a difference between the accounting for governmental entities and businesses?
   a. the acquisition, and disposition of fixed assets are accounted for in several funds/account groups
   b. governmental and business entities have different departures from GAAP
   c. budgetary accounts are integrated into the accounting records
   d. governmental entities recognize expenditures when the related liability is incurred
3. Under governmental accounting, capital assets are:
   a. recorded as fixed assets when purchased and depreciated
   b. recorded as an expenditure in the debt service fund and capitalized in the general fixed asset account group
   c. recorded as an expenditure in the captial projects fund only
   d. recorded as an expenditure in the capital projects fund and listed in the general fixed asset account group

4. Principal and interest payments on long-term debt associated with captial assets are:
   a. recorded as an expenditure in the debt service fund when the payments are due
   b. recorded as expenses in the general long-term debt account group
   c. shown as a reduction in the amount of debt in the general long-term debt account group
   d. none of the above

5. The major difference between the accrual and the modified accrual bases of accounting is:
   a. the treatment of fixed assets
   b. the recognition of revenues
   c. the recognition of expenditures
   d. the treatment of long-term debt

6. Fund accounting means that:
   a. revenues are recognized when earned
   b. expenditures are recognized when the related liability is incurred
   c. both (a) and (b)
   d. activities are segregated into separate fiscal and reporting entities

7. Other financing sources are: *distinguish from revenues.*
   a. the same as revenues
   b. inflows of financial resources that are not revenues
   c. outflows of financial resources that are not expenditures
   d. transfers to other funds

8. Principal and interest payments on long-term debt would be accrued if: *perticula*
   a. they were not due until next period
   b. the payment was made one day after the fiscal year end
   c. the current year's budget included amounts to be paid early in the succeeding fiscal period
   d. none of the above

9. One departure from current GAAP allowed for governmental entities is:
   a. recognizing sales tax revenues
   b. recognizing repairs expenditures
   c. recognizing salaries and wages expenditures
   d. recognizing expenditures related to debt payments

10. The concept of fund accounting is:
    a. used for businesses to establish sinking funds for long-term debt payments
    b. never used by business entities
    c. used occasionally by governmental entities
    d. both (b) and (c)

3-2 Select the best answer for each question.

1. The GASB placed a deferred effective date on its statement related to measurement focus/basis of accounting because:
   a. it wanted to give governmental entities time to prepare for the change

   b. not all related issues had been decided
   c. it was not sure to which entities the statement would apply
   d. both (a) and (b)

2. Encumbrance accounting:
   a. allows governmental entities to refine the budget process by keeping track of future obligations
   b. is used to segregate certain types of expenditures
   c. provides a basis for estimating remaining budgetary authority for salary amounts pertaining to full-time employees
   d. is used exclusively to reflect upcoming payments on debt

3. Debt issued to finance the purchase of fixed assets would be recorded as:
   a. a debit to cash and a credit to long-term debt
   b. a debit to other financing sources and a credit to long-term debt
   c. a debit to cash and a credit to other financing sources
   d. a debit to fixed assets and a credit to other financing sources

4. An interfund transfer to service debt payments that will occur for the next ten years would be classified as:
   a. a reimbursement
   b. an operating transfer
   c. a residual equity transfer
   d. either (a) or (b) depending on the type of debt

5. A governmental entity that uses the "when consumed" method for supply purchases and expenditures for the year would make the following entry at year end reflecting the inventory on hand:
   a. debit reserve for inventory, credit inventory supplies
   b. debit inventory and credit reserve for inventory supplies
   c. debit unreserved fund balance and credit reserve for inventory supplies
   d. none of the above

6. Fund accounting complicates the financial statements of governmental entities. One such complication is:
   a. to derive total operating results, the user has to look at several different entities
   b. depreciation is not shown on the face of the statement
   c. fixed assets are not reported
   d. the long-term debt is reflected only in the footnotes

7. If total governmental revenues were $100,000 of which $10,000 was earmarked for debt payments, the general fund would show total revenues of:
   a. $110,000
   b. $100,000
   c. $90,000
   d. $0

8. The balancing account in the general long-term debt account group is entitled:
   a. amount to be provided for debt service
   b. investment in general fixed assets

    c. net amount due on long-term debt

    d. none of the above

9. If the general fund purchased equipment for $50,000, the entry to re-cord the transaction in the general fund would be:

    a. debit asset, credit other financing sources

    b. debit asset, credit cash or long-term debt

    c. debit expenditures, credit cash

    d. debit expenditures, credit debt or cash

10. When governmental entities adopt the new statement on measure-ment focus/basis of accounting, it will change:

    a. the basis reported for fixed assets

    b. the recognition basis for revenues

    c. the entity in which debt related to capital acquisition is recorded

    d. the focus from total financial resources to total current financial resources

11. The measurement focus/basis of accounting project of the GASB refers to:

    a. an examination of the appropriate accounting basis for special revenue funds

    b. a review of revenue and expense recognition practices for govern-mental funds

    c. a project to determine whether spending or capital maintenance ought to be the focus for governmental funds

    d. both (b) and (c)

12. When a governmental unit receives a donated asset an entry is made in:

    a. general fund

    b. general fixed asset account group

    c. general fixed asset account group and capital projects funds

    d. general fund and general fixed asset account group

13. When debt is issued to construct a general governmental facility, en-tries would be made in the following fund(s) and/or account group(s):

    a. general fund and general long-term debt account group

    b. capital projects fund and general long-term debt account group

    c. general fund and capital projects fund

    d. general fund, capital projects fund, and general long-term debt ac-count group

14. An oversight board approved the payment of debt service within the current-year budget of the general fund. The payment is for serial debt, and it is normal for the general fund to provide the resources with which to make debt service payments. When the payment is made to the debt service fund, it should be classified as:

    a. quasi-external transaction

    b. operating transfer

    c. residual equity transfer

    d. reimbursement

3-3 Selected transactions from Grenville County's records are described below:

1. The general operating budget was established.
2. An asset was purchased for cash from general operating funds.
3. The county issued an order for general office supplies.
4. Interest on long-term debt related to the acquisition of fixed assets was paid; the payment also included some reduction of principal.
5. A short-term note was issued to provide working capital before the county issued its annual property tax levy.

REQUIRED

Identify the funds/account groups in which each of these transactions would be recorded (remember some may be recorded in more than one place). Assume Grenville County is operating under the total financial resources model.

3-4   Taking the information from Exercise 3-3, briefly explain the differences in accounting practices, if any, between governmental entities and businesses.

3-5   Selected information from the City of Orondo's post-closing trial balance appears below:

City of Orondo
Selected Account Balances
Post-Closing Trial Balance
June 30, 19X1

	Dr.	Cr.
Cash	$ 15,000	
Taxes Receivable, Net	800,000	
Buildings	1,200,000	
Equipment	870,000	
Short-Term Notes Payable		$ 540,000
Long-Term Debt:		
Related to Operations		200,000
Related to Fixed Assets		1,100,000
Totals Related to Selected Accounts	$2,885,000	$1,840,000

Upon further investigation you learn that, of the total cash shown, $2,000 has been set aside in the fund through which debt service payments are made.

REQUIRED

Prepare a balance sheet for the appropriate funds/account groups of Orondo as of June 30, 19X1, under the total financial resources model.

3-6   Forest City is operating under the GASB's total financial resources model. Selected transactions from its records for fiscal 19X4 are described below:

1. The city council approved its annual budget, containing estimated revenues and expenditures of $200,000.
2. Taxes of $199,000 were levied and collected, of which $42,000 was earmarked for debt service payments.
3. The city manager ordered supplies of $11,000.
4. Equipment of $57,000 was purchased with operating funds.
5. Debt of $620,000 was issued to buy a bulding adjacent to city property.
6. The asset described in Item 5 was purchased.
7. A debt payment totaling $42,000 was made. Of the total, $7,000 was principal and the remainder interest. The debt related to general fixed assets and the necessary amount was on hand in the debt service fund.
8. Miscellaneous revenues of $43,000 were received in cash.
9. Depreciation of $11,400 and $62,000 was taken on the assets described in Items 4 and 5 respectively.
10. General operating money of $20,000 was transferred for debt payments coming due in the next fiscal year.
11. General operating expenses of $100,000 were incurred and paid.

REQUIRED

Prepare the journal entries recording these transactions. Indicate in which fund/account group each entry would be made.

3-7   Using the information in Exercise 3-6, prepare the same entries for a business organization.

3-8   The following statements describe certain accounting procedures. Read each statement carefully, and indicate whether or not it is correct for a governmental entity after adoption of the total financial resources model. If the statement is incorrect, explain what makes it so.

1. Using a perpetual inventory system, a governmental entity would debit inventories and credit cash/accounts payable when supplies it had purchased were received.
2. If a capital projects fund was opened by a transfer from the general fund, operating transfers would be debited and cash would be credited.
3. Long-term debt issued to cover an operating deficit would be recorded as a debit to cash and a credit to revenues in the capital projects fund.
4. Payment of interest and principal on general long-term debt would be recorded as a debit to other financing uses and a credit to cash in the debt service fund.
5. Purchase of an asset acquired by issuing long-term debt would be recorded as a debit to expenditures and a credit to cash in the capital projects fund. Another entry debiting the asset and crediting the net investment in assets would be made in the general fixed asset account group.
6. Fixed assets are depreciated by debiting depreciation expense and crediting accumulated depreciation in the general fixed asset account group.

7. Accrual of an obligation would be recorded as a debit to expense and a credit to cash or a payable.
8. Under a periodic inventory system and at the end of the period, a governmental entity would make a single entry debiting expenditures and crediting supplies inventory for the amount of supplies used during the period.
9. A contributed asset would be recorded as a debit to fixed assets and a credit to revenues in the general fund.
10. If the general fund purchased items for other funds, the repayment by those other funds would be classified as an operating transfer in the general fund.

3-9   Based on the entries made in Exercise 3-6 and Exercise 3-7, prepare an operating statement and a balance sheet for a business and a governmental entity.

CHAPTER 4

Accounting and Budgeting for the General Fund and Special Revenue Funds

The general fund and special revenue funds are discussed together in this chapter. Although their purposes are different, they are both in the governmental fund category, and their accounting and reporting practices are similar. The everyday affairs of government—receiving tax levies and other general revenues and paying the operating bills—are accounted for in the general fund.

A special revenue fund is used to account for revenues and expenditures associated with an earmarked tax or other source of revenue. Governmental entities often levy a particular type of tax (a tax on gasoline, lodging, cigarettes, or alcoholic beverages, to name a few) to finance specific activities. Oversight boards want detailed revenue and expenditure data related to the specific levy; thus a separate fund is opened for this purpose. A governmental entity may have several special revenue funds if it has more than one earmarked source of revenue.

This chapter explains the general budgeting and accounting procedures for governmental funds, including the integration of the budgetary accounts into the general ledger. The accounting treatment for capital assets and long-term liabilities, insofar as it relates to these funds, also is discussed. Specific accounting procedures applicable to the general and special revenue funds are explained. Finally, illustrative transactions for the general fund are presented, along with the related financial statements.

GENERAL BUDGETARY PROCEDURES

State and local governments obtain a large portion of their revenue from taxes. For local governments, the primary source is property taxes; for states, the income tax, sales tax, and specialty-item taxes all contribute significant amounts of revenue to the treasuries. The general fund accounts for all of the revenues except the earmarked tax revenues that are generally accounted for in special revenue funds.

Oversight boards—city councils, county commissioners, legislatures—try to assure that the tax and other revenue sources are sufficient to pay for the services provided during the year. This practice assures that future generations will not be paying for the current generation's services. Interperiod equity is maintained only so long as revenues equal the expenditures made during the year. The process of "balancing the budget" is complicated by the fact that the resources available to a governmental unit are mainly unrelated to the goods and services being financed by those resources.

Estimating Revenues

Budgetary estimates usually begin with estimating revenues. Unless new taxes or higher rates are imposed, revenues from ad valorem (based on value, such as property and sales) and income taxes, fees, fines, and certain other revenues usually do not change markedly in the aggregate. Therefore, oversight boards find it helpful to begin the budgetary process with revenues. They like to see what programs could be funded with existing sources of revenue.

Property Tax Revenue　　For most local governments, property taxes are a primary source of revenue. Unlike other revenue sources, property tax revenues can be controlled and estimated within a small margin of error. Estimating property tax revenues begins with determining the assessed or taxable value of the property. The estimated revenue is determined by applying a tax rate (typically referred to as a mill) to the assessed value.

Not all property is taxed. Property owned by governmental units and religious and certain other nonprofit organizations is excluded, and must be deducted from the total property values when estimating revenues. Also, certain groups, such as senior citizens and veterans, may be exempted from paying taxes. Although property taxes represent a lien on the property, not all taxes are collected, and the revenue estimate must be further reduced to allow for these delinquencies. The following example demonstrates the steps in the estimation process:

Gross Assessed Valuation	$ 7,800,000
Less: Exempted Individuals	(400,000)
Excludable Properties:	
Governmental Properties	(1,500,000)
Charitable Organizations	(900,000)
Net Assessed Valuation	$ 5,000,000
Mill Levy: 25 mills per $1,000 of	
assessed value	
(25 × $5,000)	$　125,000
Collection Estimate, 97 percent	.97
Estimated Property Tax Revenue	$　121,250

Because property taxes represent the most determinable source of revenue, they are sometimes used as the "balancing" item for the budget. In the preceding example, the $121,250 would be a preliminary estimate of property tax revenues. Once other revenue sources are examined, it may be necessary to adjust the mill levy to balance the budget.

Other Revenue Sources   Other revenue sources include licenses and permits, fines and forfeitures, intergovernmental revenues, and sales and income taxes. Unlike property tax revenues, the governmental unit cannot determine the exact amount of total revenue to be derived from each source. The governmental unit can determine the income tax rate, for example, but not the amount of revenue that will be collected.

The estimation process for these other revenues is based largely on historical data. The amount collected over the past several years and the trend in those collections are primary indicators of the amounts that can be expected currently. Of course, adjustments are made for changing economic conditions or other factors likely to distort historical trends.

Oversight boards may request alternative revenue estimates. Changing the property or income tax rate may substantially affect total revenues. Before looking at the executive expenditure budget, the board may find it helpful to have in mind the financial consequences of possible rate or assessment changes.

Estimating Expenditures

Oversight boards or their staffs may become intimately involved in the revenue estimates, but the initial expenditure budget is typically prepared by the chief executive and department heads. The chief executive sets the overall limits or incremental changes, and the department heads make estimates by object code, program, or function.

No satisfactory expenditure budgeting technique has yet been devised. Because governments lack a profit motive, no natural constraint exists. As a result, department heads are inclined to think that "more is better," particularly if constituents are clamoring for additional services. Department heads also have little incentive to reexamine or restructure existing services; without a profit motive that responds to market pressures, it is easier to simply continue to offer the same services in the same way as always. Typically programs are reassessed only when taxpayers eventually refuse to approve additional taxes.

Budgeting Techniques   Numerous budgeting techniques have been advanced over the years to force program managers or department heads to request only realistic budgets or to reassess programs. One technique, popular in the 1970s, was zero-based budgeting (ZBB). Under ZBB, a program's existence is not guaranteed; in each budget cycle the program manager starts over from "zero," and projects various levels of expenditures at which a given program or service could be offered. The oversight board ranks the various levels of service for all programs and funds the highest priority levels possible for each program.

Another budgeting technique, planning-programming-budgeting systems (PPBS), originated in the mid-1960s. They were first implemented in the federal government's Department of Defense. The emphasis under PPBS is the long-run consequences of alternative courses of action. First, a plan is

Budgeting Techniques

ZBB

PPBS

developed for accomplishing specific objectives; a resource budget is then developed that will enable managers to accomplish the objectives.

The problem with these and other budgeting techniques is that they change neither the basic character of the people doing the budgeting nor the oversight board's insistence on controlling expenditures by department. Budgeting techniques can easily be manipulated to produce preconceived notions of appropriate funding levels. Governmental units may use these techniques to help plan and structure governmental programs, but typically the budget presented to the oversight board is object-of-expenditure (or line-item) based with incremental increases from one year to the next.

▲   **OBSERVATION**

While zero-based and PPBS budget techniques have been implemented at various levels of government, none has been used with continuing success. They are difficult to understand and, with understanding, easy to manipulate. Most oversight boards tend to revert back to incremental budgeting.

Incremental Budgeting   Under incremental budgeting, certain percentage increases or other parameters are set for various segments of the budget. For example, expected inflation rates may be used to increase the supplies and rent budgets. Cost-of-living increases ratified by comparable labor organizations may be used to adjust budgeted salaries. The increments are applied to either budgeted or actual figures for the prior year, and the result becomes the budget request for the upcoming year.

The executive officer (governor, mayor, manager) provides considerable detail for the expenditure budget. Usually, the budget document shows both line-item and program totals. The line-item classification scheme is similar to the one used by business, including salaries and wages, fringe benefits, supplies, utilities, rent, and so forth.

The breakdown by program depends upon the specific programs being offered and the sophistication and complexity of the governmental unit. A small unit might group program expenditures by broad functional classifications, such as health and welfare, education, public safety, recreation and cultural activities, roads and streets, and general government. A large complex unit may use subprogram titles under each of the major functions. For example, health and welfare might include public awareness, infectious diseases, aid to dependent children, and other specific programs.

Presenting and Implementing the Budget

The budget document presented to the oversight board or budget subcommittee includes summary data as well as revenue and expenditure details and the basis upon which the estimates were made. A summary page will show revenues by major source and expenditures either by line item, by department, or both. The following example shows an object-of-expenditure format:

Proposed Budget
Governmental Unit
General or Special Revenue Fund
Fiscal Period 19X1

Estimated Revenues:		
Property Taxes	$440,000	
Income Taxes	364,000	
Licenses and Permits	73,000	
Fees and Fines	26,000	
Charges for Services	110,000	
Intergovernmental	50,000	
Investment Income	8,000	
Other	1,000	
Total Estimated Revenues		$1,072,000
Appropriations:		
Salaries and Wages	$588,000	
Fringe Benefits	118,000	
Supplies	100,000	
Utilities	80,000	
Maintenance	25,000	
Rent	16,000	
Other Operating Expenditures	87,000	
Total Appropriations		1,014,000
Excess of Estimated Revenues over Appropriations		$ 58,000
Estimated Beginning Fund Balance (deficit)		(10,000)
Estimated Ending Fund Balance		$ 48,000

Supplementary schedules will show the line-item expenditures by major function or department. Another schedule might show the cash flows by month so an oversight board can see the periods in which short-term borrowing or investing are necessary.

Obtaining Budget Authorization   Most state laws require public comment and formal authorization before budgetary amounts can be spent. Before approval, and depending upon public input, the budget may be altered numerous times. Department heads appear before the oversight board or budget subcommittee to explain their programs, justify proposed budget levels, or comment on estimating procedures. Estimated revenues typically are less than what is needed for desired levels of service. Thus, many oversight boards are faced with the dilemma of raising taxes or curtailing services.

When adopted, a budget may be binding on administrators either in total or by line item or function. Most state laws provide some formal process through which an administrator can amend the budget for unforeseen events. For example, actual revenues may exceed or fall short of the estimate. Without some mechanism to adjust expenditures — particularly when it is a shortfall — administrators would have little guidance in determining which functions or programs to curtail or expand. An amendment process usually provides an opportunity for public review and comment.

▲ **OBSERVATION**

Presenting the budget and obtaining approval has been described here in a matter-of-fact way. Sometimes the process is anything but routine: frequently public members who testify regarding the budget are personally affected by the decisions and therefore emotionally involved in representing specific points of view; politicians vote along party lines creating impasses in the decision-making process; and department heads may be more interested in job security than in serving the public.

Implementing Budget Decisions   As pointed out in Chapter 2, the general fund and typically the special revenue fund budgets are integrated into the accounting system at both the control and subsidiary account levels. This integration, along with encumbrance accounting practices, enables administrators to closely monitor compliance with budget authorizations.

A subsidiary account for one revenue and one expenditure item is presented in Exhibit 4-1. As shown there, when the budget is approved, the estimated revenues are debited. The tax levy is reported as a credit, and the balance shows the difference between the amount budgeted and actual amount levied. The expenditures subsidiary ledger shows the same general pattern, except when maintenance work is authorized, encumbrances are

Exhibit 4-1

Governmental Unit Sample Revenue and
Expenditure Subsidiary Ledgers

REVENUE SUBSIDIARY LEDGER

Revenue Type: Property Taxes

Date	Explanation	Estimated Revenues Dr.	Revenues Cr.	Balance Dr./(Cr.)
1/1	Budget Approved	650,000		650,000
2/1	Levied Tax		643,500	6,500

EXPENDITURE SUBSIDIARY LEDGER

Function: General Government
Object Code: Repairs and
Maintenance

Date	Encumbrances Dr.	Expenditures Dr.	Appropriations Cr.	Unencumbered Balance Dr./(Cr.)
1/1			197,000	(197,000)
1/15	27,000			(170,000)
2/2	(27,000)	31,000		(166,000)

debited. The encumbrance entry is reversed when the invoice for completed work is received.

ACCOUNTING FOR GENERAL AND SPECIAL REVENUE FUNDS

Until the GASB implements *Statement No. 11,* governmental units will use the modified accrual basis of accounting for all governmental fund types. *Statement No. 11* mandates the accrual basis for these same fund types. This means students of governmental accounting must understand both accounting methodologies. The modified accrual basis is explained in the body of each chapter, and the significant differences between the accrual and the modified accrual bases are explained in an appendix to the appropriate chapters.

The same accounting procedures are used for general and special revenue funds. The modified accrual basis of accounting is applied to both funds. The measurement focus for both funds is current financial resources, so their capital assets and all long-term debt are recorded in the general fixed asset and general long-term debt account groups, respectively.

Accounting for Revenues

Under the modified accrual basis of accounting, revenues are recognized when **measurable and available.** *Measurable* means that the entity must be able to put a value on the potential revenue transaction and *available* means that the resulting revenue must be available to finance expenditures of the current fiscal period. For many types of revenues, including fines and fees, licenses and permits, forfeits, and charges for services, the amount may not be measurable before actually received. Even if the amount is known, it may not be available to meet current liabilities until paid in cash. For example, if a dispute exists over the amount of fines and fees due, the availability is uncertain until the appeal process has been exhausted. Therefore, most of these revenues are not recognized until received in cash. In other words, the **cash basis** and the **modified accrual basis,** as defined for governmental accounting entities, yield the same results for some revenues. For other revenues, the modified accrual accounting basis yields different results.

Property-tax revenues are one important exception to the general recognition criteria. Such revenues are said to be "susceptible to accrual" and therefore recognized as revenue when the tax is levied. The amount is determined at the time of the levy, so it is measurable. Most property taxes also are "available" to pay liabilities incurred for expenditures made during the period. To assure that the availability criterion is met, the property taxes must be "collected within the current period or expected to be collected soon enough thereafter to pay liabilities of the current period. Such time thereafter shall

property taxes when levied

not exceed 60 days."[1] If a governmental entity had a July 1 through June 30 fiscal year, for example, taxes levied within that period and expected to be collected by August 31 of the following fiscal period would qualify for recognition in the period levied.

Other revenues that can and should be recorded on the accrual basis include charges for routine and regularly provided services, revenue entitlements from other governments, and certain other transactions where the receivable is established and collectibility is assured or losses can be reasonably estimated. The accountant must use judgment in applying the recognition criteria to such revenues. Materiality and practicality would also affect whether the revenues should be accrued. Thus, differences may exist among governmental entities.

The "when measurable" and "available" criteria are applied differently to governmental revenue than to restricted grants or contracts. Revenue from such sources is recognized **when earned.** In this case, *when earned* is defined as when qualifying expenditures are made on the grant. Also, if matching requirements pertain to such revenues, recognition of the revenue would not occur until any matching requirements had been met.

Accounting for Expenditures

Because governmental entities use a current financial resources focus, they do not distinguish among operating, capital, and debt service payments. All three are reported as expenditures. Expenditures incurred for operating expenses are reported only in the fund making the expenditure. Capital and debt service payments are reported as expenditures in the fund making the disbursement or commitment. Simultaneously they are reported as assets, in the case of capital expenditures, in the general fixed asset account group. In the case of a debt service payment, the total payment is reported as an expenditure in the fund making the payment. The principal portion of that payment is also recorded as a reduction to the principal amount of the debt in the general long-term debt account group.

Recognition Principles   Expenditures are generally recognized when transactions or events giving rise to claims against current financial resources take place. Operating expenditures are recognized when incurred. For example, salaries and wages should be reported as expenditures during the period in which the employees perform the work.

As noted in the *Codification,* one exception to this recognition principle concerns expenditures related to *all* long-term debt:

The major exception to the general rule of expenditure accrual relates to unmatured principal and interest payments on general long-term debt. Financial resources usually are appropriated in other funds to transfer to a debt service

[1]Governmental Accounting Standards Board, *Codification of Governmental Accounting and Financial Reporting Standards* (Norwalk, Conn.: GASB, 1993), sec. P70.103. Interestingly, the GASB is now considering a standard that would extend the "susceptible to accrual" criterion to all taxpayer assessed revenues.

fund in the period in which maturing debt principal and interest must be paid. Such amounts thus are not current liabilities of the debt service fund as their settlement will not require expenditure of existing fund assets.[2]

Recognition of expenditures related to inventory costs has a unique application under the modified accrual basis of accounting. Governmental units may use either the "when consumed" or the "when purchased" method. The "when consumed" method is what businesses use under accrual accounting. This method results in an expenditure for only the amount used during the period. Under the "when purchased" method, an expenditure is recognized for the entire amount of the inventory when it is received. The following illustrates the differences between the two methods:

Supplies of $1,000 were purchased on January 15. By year end $600 had been consumed.

When consumed:

1/15	Supplies Inventory	1,000	
	Accounts Payable		1,000
12/31	Expenditures	600	
	Supplies Inventory		600

When purchased:

1/15	Expenditures	1,000	
	Accounts Payable		1,000

Prepaid items, such as insurance, rent, and payments for similar services that apply to more than one period, may be shown as expenditures in the period of acquisition. Therefore, the accountant does not need to allocate these items among several periods.

Encumbrance Accounting   An important part of the expenditure recognition process is encumbrance accounting. Encumbrances are commitments pertaining to contracts for goods that have not yet been received or services that have not yet been performed. A supplies order represents such a commitment; the goods have not been received (the contract is unperformed), but the commitment exists to pay for the goods if and when they are received.

Encumbrance accounting is used for those items that are nonrecurring and vary in amount, such as supplies, contractual services, and repairs. Personal services ordinarily are not encumbered because the monthly amounts usually are constant, making it easy to estimate what portion of the appropriation remains at any time. If a unit has seasonal fluctuations in employees or if much of the staff consists of part-time help, encumbrance accounting also would be used for this budget category.

Encumbrance accounts are affected when an order is placed and when the goods or services are received. As discussed in Chapter 2, when the order is placed, the encumbrance account is debited:

---

[2]GASB, *Codification*, sec. 1600.121.

Encumbrances   XX
    Reserve for Encumbrances   XX

This entry is reversed when the order is received. If only a portion of the order is received, only the portion of the encumbered amount pertaining to the goods received is reversed.

▲ | **OBSERVATION**

The extent to which encumbrance accounting works well depends, in part, on how meticulous the receiving clerk is in determining exactly what portion of the goods was received.

The accounting treatment of any outstanding orders at year end depends upon state or local practices related to appropriations. If appropriations lapse at year end and no obligation exists to pay for services ordered before but received after that date, the reserve for encumbrances and the encumbrances for outstanding orders are both closed:

Reserve for Encumbrances   Balance in Account
    Encumbrances   Balance in Account

In the most common situation, the appropriation lapses but the governmental unit has an obligation to pay for orders placed in one fiscal period and received in another. Under these circumstances, the reserve for encumbrances remains open, and the encumbrance account is closed, along with expenditures, to unreserved fund balance. Providing the subsequent year's appropriation gives authority to complete these transactions, the encumbrances account is reopened at the beginning of the subsequent period:

Encumbrances   Amount Outstanding
                                                  at Prior Year End
    Unreserved Fund Balance   Amount Outstanding
                                                  at Prior Year End

After reversing the entry, the encumbrances and the reserve for encumbrances both carry the balance of the order outstanding at the end of the prior year. When the goods arrive, the encumbrances and reserve for encumbrances accounts are closed.

As the sequence of entries makes clear, encumbrances are not treated as expenditures. Any encumbrances outstanding at year end, although closed to the unreserved fund balance, are not reported with the expenditures in the operating statement. The debit to unreserved fund balance reduces the equity section of the balance sheet, but the credit amount remaining in the reserve account offsets the effect of closing the encumbrances account. The net effect is zero.

Expenditure Classification Schemes   Several different expenditure classification schemes are used by governmental units. Almost all units use an object classification, that is, salaries and wages, fringe benefits, supplies, rent, utilities, insurance, and so forth. Because governmental units sometimes report debt service payments and capital outlays as expenditures in the general or special revenue funds, these two items are also object classes.

Another classification scheme is by function. Typical functional classifications would include highways and streets, health and welfare, education, general administration, and public safety. Each classification represents a major service or area of responsibility. Comparative analyses among governmental units are often based on a functional classification scheme.

Governmental units frequently use two other classification schemes for assigning administrative responsibility. One is program classification. For example, several programs, such as police protection, sanitation, and pollution monitoring, might all be located within the public safety function. Each program would be administered by a different individual; by reporting expenditures for each program, oversight boards can monitor the financial performance of each director.

Classifying expenditures by organizational unit also helps oversight boards evaluate performance and fix responsibility. Expenditures are grouped according to the government's organizational structure. Depending upon how closely the unit is organized around functions, the organizational and functional classification schemes may be very similar.

Classification schemes are often combined for internal or external reporting. Exhibit 4-2 combines the object and functional classifications in one possible format. If more detail were needed, this same exhibit could be expanded to include the program classification as a subset of the functional areas.

Application of Accounting Principles to Selected Transactions

Some accounting conventions used for general and special revenue funds do not follow from the general recognition principles described above. In some cases, governmental entities are allowed to depart from GAAP. In others, generally accepted accounting principles have not been fully defined, so governmental units use optional treatments. Sometimes, the accounting treatment is not obvious from a description of the general recognition criteria; these transactions are discussed in this section.

Accounting for Assets and Liabilities   Governmental entities using the modified accrual basis of accounting record only current assets and liabilities in the general and special revenue funds. All general fixed assets are recorded in the general fixed asset account group. Usually other long-term assets are not recorded because the focus is on "available" resources and other long-term assets do not reflect available resources. For example, if a governmental entity had a long-term lease receivable, the portion representing measurable and available revenues/other financing sources should be recognized during the period. The remainder of the receivable should be deferred.

Exhibit 4-2

Governmental Expenditures, by Function and Object Code

	General Government	Health and Welfare	Public Safety	Streets and Highways	Total
Expenditures:					
Personal Services					
Salaries and Wages	$100,000	$ 82,000	$ 77,000	$216,000	$475,000
Fringe Benefits	20,000	16,500	15,400	43,200	95,100
Part-time Salaries	—	—	—	—	—
Overtime Pay	—	—	—	—	—
Total Personal Services	—	—	—	—	—
Other Operating Expenditures					
Supplies	61,000	19,000	13,000	14,000	107,000
Rent	—	—	—	—	—
Utilities	—	—	—	—	—
Repairs/Maintenance	—	—	—	—	—
Professional Services	—	—	—	—	—
Dues/Subscriptions	—	—	—	—	—
Travel	—	—	—	—	—
Printing	—	—	—	—	—
Fuel	—	—	—	—	—
Drugs/Chemicals	—	—	—	—	—
Total Operating Expenditures					
Capital Outlays	16,000	5,000	110,000	-0-	131,000
Debt Service	—	—	—	—	—
Total Expenditures	—	—	—	—	—
Other Financing Sources (Uses):					
Operating transfers	2,000	(15,000)	-0-	-0-	(13,000)
Total Expenditures and Other Financing Sources	—	—	—	—	—

All long-term liabilities, whether related to the purchase of fixed assets, claims, judgments, pensions, or compensated absences, are recorded in the general long-term debt account group. This convention requires calculation of long- and short-term components of such liabilities as compensated absences, pensions, and claims and judgments.

Recording only current assets and liabilities in the governmental funds also means that the expenditure for long-term assets is shown when current financial resources are affected. That is, the expenditure is recorded when the asset is acquired instead of as depreciation expense as the asset is used.

Debt Service Payments, Capital Outlays, and Operating Transfers
Debt service payments and capital outlays can occur in the general or special revenue funds. Alternatively, and depending upon the complexity of the payments, they may be reported in the debt service fund and capital projects funds. A single capital outlay, such as the purchase of equipment, normally would be made in the general fund. Similarly, if a governmental unit has only

one long-term debt issue, servicing of that debt will probably occur in the general fund. Complex debt transactions, on the other hand, would require a separate debt service fund.

Recording the transactions depends upon where they occur. If a capital outlay or debt service payment is made from the general fund, an expenditure is debited. If the capital outlay or debt service payment is made from the capital projects or debt service funds respectively, but financed by the general fund, a transfer is shown in the general fund and the receiving fund, after which the receiving fund debits an expenditure and credits cash. For example, if the general fund transferred $10,000 to the debt service fund to make principal and interest payments, the entries are:

GF	Operating Transfer	10,000	
	Cash		10,000
DS	Cash	10,000	
	Operating Transfer		10,000
DS	Expenditures	10,000	
	Cash		10,000

debt service payments when due

Governmental units are allowed to depart from GAAP when they record debt service payments. The expenditure is recognized when the principal or interest payment is due. Thus, if an interest payment to be paid from the general fund was due on January 15, 19X2, and covered the period July 15, 19X1, through January 15, 19X2, the expenditure and related liability would not be accrued on December 31, 19X1.

A governmental unit's operating statement distinguishes between debt service and capital expenditures on the one hand and transfers on the other. Debt service and capital expenditures are listed below operating expenditures in a separate section of the statement. Operating transfers are classified as other financing sources and uses, and as Exhibit 4-2 illustrates, they are shown in a separate section after total expenditures.

Accounting for Pensions   Pension accounting is a difficult and an unresolved issue. Usually governmental entity contributions are set by state statute and those amounts may or may not reflect the amount necessary to fully fund the actuarial present value of the defined benefit plan. Nonetheless, governmental entities are reluctant to recognize a pension asset or liability on their balance sheet for differences between the statutory funding requirement and the actuarially required contribution.

At one time the GASB seemed likely to adopt pension accounting standards closely paralleling those used by business entities. A portion of a preliminary views document containing that thrust and labeled as the "majority view" was resoundingly criticized by practitioners and those board members holding the "minority view." Subsequently, the GASB agreed to establish a standard reflecting the minority view. The minority view basically holds that within broad limits, governmental entities should be able to use the amount funded as the pension expenditure for the period:

As long as governmental employers are contributing to pension plans that are being funded in a *systematic and rational manner,* the actuarially determined pension contribution requirements should be used to measure the employer pension expenditure/expense.[3]

Until the GASB issues a definitive standard, several actuarial funding methods are currently being used, and the expenditure amount reported in any given period varies depending on which one is used. Actuarially determined benefit information, including any unfunded actuarial accrued liability, is expected to be reported in the schedule of funding progress, not in the balance sheet as it is in the private sector.

The employer's contribution/expenditure is an outflow from the general fund and an inflow to the pension trust fund. Transactions between the employer (general fund) and its plan (pension trust fund) are considered quasi-external transactions; the transaction is recognized as an expenditure by the general fund and as a contribution (revenue) by the trust fund. Thus, these items *are not* treated as transfers.

Under current accounting, if the governmental entity does not actually fund the amount actuarially determined, a liability results. Since it is long-term, any such liability is reported in the general long-term debt account group. Thus, only the amount actually funded is reported as an expenditure in the current year. The remainder is recognized as an expenditure in the year in which the long-term liability is liquidated.

Compensated Absences   Employee absences for which payment is made, such as vacation and sick leave, are compensated absences. GASB *Statement No. 16*[4] provides guidance for recognizing the expenditure and liability related to various types of compensated absences. For example, for vacation and related types of leave, a liability is recognized when:

1. the obligation is for service already rendered
2. it is probable that the employer will compensate the employee for the benefits earned

The recognition criteria are similar for sick leave. However, in this case, the governmental entity accrues the liability using one of two methodologies. One methodology calculates the liability based on the governmental entity's past experience of making termination payments for sick leave, adjusted for the effect of changes in its termination payment policy and other relevant factors. Under the other methodology, the sick-leave liability is accrued based on the sick leave accumulated by eligible employees at the balance sheet date.

[3]Governmental Accounting Standards Board, *Preliminary Views, State and Local Governmental Employers' Accounting for Pensions* (Norwalk, Conn.: GASB, 1988), v. Pension accounting is discussed further in Chapter 9 in connection with the pension trust fund, and in Chapter 13 as an issue in governmental accounting.

[4]Governmental Accounting Standards Board, *Statement No. 16, Accounting for Compensated Absences* (Norwalk, Conn.: GASB, 1992). In addition to the information provided here, the standard also gives examples of the detailed calculations necessary to accrue the liability.

Sabbatical leave, another compensated absence, is also discussed in the standard. Whether a liability is accrued for this type of leave depends upon its specific qualities. If the leave is merely a reassignment, such as from teaching to administration, it does not meet the definition of a compensated absence. However, if compensation will be paid for unrestricted time off, the salary paid during the leave is compensation for past service and a liability should be accrued.

Statement No. 16 also clarifies the Board's position on two related issues. Although the standard addresses specific types of compensated absences, it also makes clear that if similar types of employee benefit packages are developed, they should be treated similarly. Also, whenever a liability is accrued, any related salary payments such as social security and medicare should be accrued.

Some governmental entities allow employees the option of taking annual or sick leave when it is earned or accumulating some portion and receiving a cash settlement when they resign or retire. Under such a program, the leave expected to be taken in the current or subsequent period is classified as a current liability and is shown in the general or special revenue fund. The remainder, the portion not expected to be taken until retirement or resignation, is treated as a long-term liability and shown in the long-term debt account group.

Including only the current liabilities in the fund means that current-year expenditures relate only to short-term obligations. The long-term portion of the compensated absence liability is recognized as an expenditure in the year in which the long-term liability is liquidated. The following example illustrates the accounting for compensated absences.

Balance of current liability in the general fund, 19X0	$ 35,000
Balance of long-term liabilities in the general long-term debt account group, 19X0	280,000
Expenditures incurred for compensated absences (actually used) during 19X1	150,000
Balance of 19X0 current liability not expected to be used until retirement or resignation	5,000
Compensated absences earned in 19X1 but not taken then; expected to be taken in 19X2	11,000
Calculation of 19X1 Short-Term Liability:	
Balance 19X0	35,000
Less:	
Amount of 19X0 balance that is now considered long-term	(5,000)
Add:	
Amount earned in 19X1 but not expected to be taken until 19X2 (with current available resources)	11,000
Balance, as adjusted, December 31, 19X1	$ 41,000

The $150,000 is recorded as an expenditure throughout the year as employees' salaries are paid. At the end of the year, an adjustment is made to the current liability in the general fund and to the long-term liability in the general long-term debt account group. To continue the example, the balance in the current liability account is $35,000. It should be $41,000, so an adjusting entry is required:

| Expenditures | 6,000 | |
| Compensated Absence Liability | | 6,000 |

The long-term liability would be increased by $5,000 in the general long-term debt account group. When the employees later retire or resign, the expenditure is recorded in the debt service fund and the long-term liability is eliminated in the general long-term debt account group.

Claims and Judgments   Governmental entities recognize an expenditure and a liability in the governmental funds for claims and judgments that satisfy both of the following conditions:

a. Information available before the financial statements are issued indicates that it is *probable* that an asset had been impaired or a liability had been incurred at the date of the financial statements. It is implicit in this condition that it must be probable that one or more future events will also occur confirming the fact of the loss (emphasis added).
b. The amount of the loss can be reasonably estimated.[5]

Probable as defined in this section means the same as in the private sector, namely that the future event or events are likely to occur. Sometimes the reasonable estimate cited in the second condition is a range. If one amount within the range seems to be a better estimate than any other, it should be used as the amount to be recognized. Additional note disclosure is required if there is a reasonable possibility that the loss will exceed the amount recognized.

Other Accounting Considerations   Only a few accounting transactions have been discussed specifically under the flow of current financial resources model. No mention was made, for example, of leases, contingencies, debt defeasance, and a host of other transactions. Omitted as well was any discussion of prior period corrections, and the effects of a change in accounting principle. These accounting transactions do exist in governmental entities, just as in business.

Some transactions, such as leases, will be discussed later in connection with the specific fund in which the effects of these transactions are most obvious. Leases are discussed both in the chapter on capital projects funds and in the one describing the general long-term debt account group. Debt defeasance is discussed in the chapter on debt service funds.

Other accounting issues, such as corrections of errors and changes in accounting principle, are not addressed. The GASB's attention has been devoted, in large part, to such key issues as the measurement focus/basis of accounting, pensions, and financial reporting. If these issues were resolved, the accounting for many other transactions would follow naturally. Until they are resolved, the codification of governmental accounting financial reporting standards typically refers the reader to industry standards.

---

[5]GASB, *Codification*, sec. C50.110.

Subsidiary Ledgers

One control account is typically used for all expenditures and one for all revenues. Each major revenue and expenditure is recorded in a subsidiary ledger. Major revenue sources include property taxes, sales taxes, income taxes, fines and fees, intergovernmental revenue, licenses and permits, investment income, charges for services, and other specialized taxes. What subsidiary accounts are used for expenditures depends upon the scheme being used. If a functional scheme is utilized, each function would have a subsidiary account.

Subsidiary ledgers for balance sheet accounts follow the pattern used in business. They are established in areas in which details for individual accounts are necessary. Accounts receivable and accounts payable are two examples where additional detail is necessary. If substantial interfund lending and borrowing is prevalent, the due to and due from control accounts might require subsidiary ledgers for each fund.

GENERAL FUND AND SPECIAL REVENUE FUND REPORTING

Similar to business concerns, both the general fund and the special revenue funds have an operating statement and a balance sheet. In addition, they have a statement that helps oversight boards monitor compliance — a statement of revenues and expenditures, budget and actual.

The three basic statements are required for the general fund and all special revenue funds. Because the data in these financial statements are in summary form, for example, by object code or function, supplementary schedules are used to provide more detail. Sometimes supplementary schedules are also prepared to reconcile the financial information presented on a non-GAAP basis with GAAP. Non-GAAP statements may be required to conform to state or other mandates. Like business entities, governmental units may make use of statistical tables to present trend data, sometimes for ten years or more.

The Operating Statement

The statement of revenues, expenditures, and changes in fund balance shows revenues and expenditures with perhaps as many as three classification schemes for the general fund. Because a special revenue fund is typically established for every major earmarked revenue source, only the object classification is used.

The Balance Sheet

With one major exception, the balance sheet for both funds would look much like a balance sheet for a business. It has current assets and liabilities. Within the current asset and liability sections, the most liquid items would appear first, followed by those that are less liquid. It also has an equity section, although the term *fund balance* is used instead of *equity.*

Governmental balance sheets differ from their industrial counterparts in one major respect: No long-term assets or liabilities appear in the fund. General long-term assets are shown in the general fixed asset account group, and general long-term liabilities are placed in the general long-term debt account group.

Comparative Statement

The third required financial statement shows a comparison between actual and budgeted revenues and expenditures, and the resulting variances. As the following illustrates, budgets may be revised during the year, and more than one budget column may be presented:

	Original Budget	Final Budget	Actual	Variance (Actual to Final)
Revenues:				
Taxes				
Fees and Fines				
—				
—				
Total Revenues				
Expenditures:				
General Government				
Health and Welfare				
—				
—				
Total Operating Expenditures				
Capital Outlays				
Debt Service Payments				

If budget and accounting records are based on generally accepted accounting principles, the data in the statement of revenues, expenditures, and changes in fund balance, budget and actual, would be comparable. However, some state laws or local ordinances require a cash-basis budget, rendering the budget and actual columns incomparable. The GASB requires that the financial statement notes explain the differences and provide information necessary to reconcile the GAAP and non-GAAP information.

Statement Presentation for Special Revenue Funds

The same statements are prepared for special revenue funds as for the general fund. The fact that there is one general fund but potentially several special revenue funds may require additional presentations. For example, with several special revenue funds, there would be both a statement of revenues, expenditures, and changes in fund balance for each fund and a combining statement of revenues, expenditures, and changes in fund balance; one column is used for each fund:

	Cigarette Tax Fund	State Revenue Sharing Fund	Bed Tax Revenue Fund	Total
Revenues:				
Intergovernmental				
Fees				
Other				
Expenditures:				
Salaries and Wages				
Supplies				
Rent				
	—			
	—			
	—			

The same general format is typically used for the combining balance sheet for special revenue funds. Each fund's assets and liabilities are shown in a separate column with a total column at the far right.

A statement of revenues and expenditures, budget and actual, cannot be prepared in this same format. A budget is prepared for each separate fund, not the combined funds. Therefore, a comparative statement is prepared for each separate fund.

Interim Financial Statements

Interim financial reports are commonly prepared for the general fund and special revenue funds. They do not resemble the annual financial statements. Used primarily for managerial purposes, they usually compare actual results to date with budgeted amounts. Other interim reports included projected cash flows and capital construction progress reports.

If a governmental unit uses a non-GAAP basis for its budget, interim statements typically will be prepared according to the non-GAAP basis. This eliminates the necessity for reconciliation tables and notes. Because GASB does not require audited interim reports and because they usually are not issued externally, the primary criterion is usefulness rather than conformance to GAAP.

ILLUSTRATED FINANCIAL TRANSACTIONS

Although the accounting practices of the two funds are identical, a general fund has a broader variety of transactions. Therefore, selected financial transactions are presented for the general fund of Mineral County during 19X1. The county operates on a fiscal year ending December 31, and its budget is prepared on a GAAP basis.

The journal entries are shown for the control accounts with an occasional reference to subsidiary ledgers in order to increase the realism of the illustrations. Mineral County maintains revenue subsidiary ledgers by type of revenue, and expenditure subsidiary ledgers by object code and function. Enough detail is shown that subsidiary ledgers could be completed for object code expenditures.

Mineral County's commissioners approved the budget for Fiscal 19X1, which included estimated revenues of $610,000 and appropriations of $697,800. With the exception of capital outlays, managers are not required to adhere to line-item appropriations, only to the total for a particular function. Therefore, more could be spent in salaries, for example, than was budgeted as long as less was spent for some other line-item expenditure.

1.	Estimated Revenues	610,000	
	Budgetary Fund Balance	87,800	
	Appropriations		697,800

The $87,800 difference between the estimated revenues and appropriations is debited to an account called "budgetary fund balance." Ordinarily, three component parts of the fund balance would be displayed in the fund balance section of the balance sheet. The budgetary fund balance is one component. The difference between GAAP and the budget basis, if any, is another. If, for example, Mineral County's budget had been prepared on a non-GAAP basis, the budgetary-to-GAAP differences component would be the reconciling amount. The third component is the "unreserved fund balance," which is the difference between revenues and expenditures, on a GAAP basis, for the prior and current periods.

The budget detail shows the following breakdown of Mineral County's estimated revenues and appropriations:

SUBSIDIARY ESTIMATED REVENUE ACCOUNTS:

Property Taxes	$495,000
Intergovernmental Revenue	12,000
Fines and Fees	15,000
Licenses	16,000
Sales Taxes	68,000
Miscellaneous	4,000
Total	$610,000

SUBSIDIARY APPROPRIATIONS ACCOUNTS:

General Government Function		Public Safety Function	
Salaries and Wages	$182,000	Salaries and Wages	$ 95,000
Supplies	16,000	Supplies	20,000
Utilities	21,000	Insurance	7,000
Insurance	5,500	Communications	2,200
Repairs/Maintenance	26,000	Other Operating	1,100
Other Operating	4,700	Capital Outlays	55,000
Capital Outlays	22,000		
Debt Service	9,000	Total	$180,300
Total	$286,200		

(continued)

(continued)

SUBSIDIARY APPROPRIATIONS ACCOUNTS:

Health and Welfare Function		Highways and Roads	
Salaries and Wages	$ 76,000	Salaries and Wages	$ 78,900
Supplies	8,000	Supplies	6,000
Rent	6,800	Repairs/Maintenance	17,000
Outside Services	3,500	Other Operating	9,000
Miscellaneous	4,000	Capital Outlays	15,000
Other Operating	3,100		
Capital Outlays	4,000	Total	$125,900
Total	$105,400		

Ordinarily each governmental function would have the full range of object codes in its budget. For example, utilities would be budgeted by function, rather than as shown here under the general government function. A limited number of line items were shown under each function to simplify the presentation.

The Mineral County commissioners levied property taxes of $500,000 for the current fiscal period (the taxes are due before year end), estimating that 1.5 percent of the levy would be uncollectible.

2.	Taxes Receivable Current	500,000	
	Allowance for Uncollectible Current Taxes		7,500
	Revenues		492,500

A portion of the state sales tax is apportioned to the county in which it is collected. The amount collected by merchants and due during the first quarter totaled $34,200. The intergovernmental revenue is general revenue sharing from the state; it will be available to pay liabilities during the current period. Fines and fees of $2,970 and licenses of $5,500 were collected during the first quarter.

3.	Receivable from State Government	12,000	
	Cash (2,970 + 5,500 + 34,200)	42,670	
	Revenues		54,670

The revenue from the state is measurable and will be available during the current period; it is not a specific grant or contract, and therefore can be recognized now rather than when the qualifying expenditures are made.

Mineral County placed an equipment order totaling $89,000.

4.	Encumbrances	89,000	
	Reserve for Encumbrances		89,000

The liability was incurred for the debt service payment of $9,000 that came due during the quarter. This payment is made on a recurring basis.

5.	Operating Transfers	9,000	
	Due to Debt Service Fund		9,000

The receivable from the state was collected, as was $295,000 in property taxes.

6. Cash (295,000 + 12,000)   307,000
      Receivable from State Government   12,000
      Taxes Receivable Current   295,000

The following expenditures were paid or commitments incurred; the insurance covers only the current period:

Salaries	$250,000
Rent	3,400
Supplies Ordered	44,000
Insurance	12,500
Repairs Authorized	37,000
Communications	1,800
Other Operating	15,000
Total	$363,700

7. Expenditures   282,700
   Encumbrances (37,000 + 44,000)   81,000
      Cash   282,700
      Reserve for Encumbrances   81,000

Although not illustrated here, the expenditures and encumbrances would be reflected in subsidiary ledgers.

The equipment order was received; it cost $91,000 rather than $89,000 as previously encumbered.

8. Reserve for Encumbrances   89,000
   Expenditures   91,000
      Encumbrances   89,000
      Accounts Payable   91,000

As discussed earlier, capital outlays are recorded as expenditures in the general fund. Although not illustrated in this chapter, the equipment purchase would be recorded simultaneously in the general fixed asset account group.

The second installment on the property taxes, yielding cash of $200,000, was received, as were miscellaneous revenues of $3,000, sales taxes, $6,000, fines and fees, $5,000, and licenses, $4,900.

9. Cash   218,900
      Taxes Receivable Current   200,000
      Revenues   18,900

The county finance officer decided that $2,000 of taxes receivable current would not be paid and wrote this amount off.

10. Allowance for Uncollectible
    Current Taxes   2,000
        Taxes Receivable Current   2,000   *(reversal)*

If a receivable is written off and later collected, the receivable balance should be restored, along with the allowance amount, and then the cash recorded. Using this method helps to maintain accurate subsidiary records.

Because the timing of expenditures was estimated to occur before sufficient cash was available, tax anticipation notes payable totaling $165,000 were issued. These notes carry an interest rate of 7 percent and are due 30 days from issuance.

11. Cash   165,000
        Tax Anticipation Notes Payable   165,000

The supplies order was received and the repair work completed; they are recorded on account. Of the $44,000 supplies ordered and received, only $41,000 was consumed during the year, and Mineral County uses the "when consumed" method. These supply orders and other expenditures incurred during the remainder of the fiscal period are summarized below:

	Appropriated	Incurred Earlier	Incurred (Used) Now	Balance
Salaries and Wages	$431,900	$250,000	$190,500	$(8,600)
Insurance	12,500	12,500	-0-	-0-
Communications	2,200	1,800	400	-0-
Utilities	21,000	-0-	27,700	(6,700)
Outside Services	3,500	-0-	4,000	(500)
Miscellaneous	4,000	-0-	3,100	900
Other Operating	17,900	15,000	3,000	(100)
Rent	6,800	3,400	3,400	-0-
Repairs/Maintenance	43,000	-0-	37,000	6,000
Supplies	50,000	-0-	41,000	9,000
	$592,800	$282,700	$310,100	$ -0-

Combining these expenditures with those made earlier in the year reveals that, although close, the total for many line items is different from amounts originally appropriated. For example, $21,000 was appropriated for utilities and $27,700 is being spent. Although Mineral County is not required to adhere to line-item appropriations (except equipment), the amount in each subsidiary ledger for appropriations would be changed at this point. A change cannot be made in a subsidiary ledger without a control-account entry. Therefore, even though the total appropriations have not changed, entry 12 is necessary to make the subsidiary ledger changes.

12. Appropriations (9,000 + 6,000 + 900) ↓   15,900
        Appropriations (8,600 + 6,700 + 500 + 100)   15,900

The expenditures in the "Incurred (Used) Now" column are recorded in entries 13 and 14; entry 15 reverses the earlier encumbrances for supplies and repairs.

13.	Supplies Inventory	44,000	
	Accounts Payable		44,000
14.	Expenditures	310,100	
	Accounts Payable (310,000 − 41,000)		269,100
	Supplies Inventory		41,000
15.	Reserve for Encumbrances		
	(37,000 + 44,000)	81,000	
	Encumbrances		81,000

Ordinarily some of the remaining expenditures, such as outside services and utilities, would be encumbered; the encumbrance step was omitted to simplify the presentation.

The final equipment order was submitted. Since Mineral County cannot exceed this specific line-item appropriation, the amount must be $5,000 or less ($96,000 budgeted less $91,000 already spent). The equipment was not received by year end.

16.	Encumbrances	5,000	
	Reserve for Encumbrances		5,000

Accounts payable totaling $316,000 were paid.

17.	Accounts Payable	316,000	
	Cash		316,000

Third and fourth quarter receipts and expenditures are combined in the remainder of the entries. Following is a breakdown of the revenues.

	Received in Cash	**Accrued**
Property Taxes	$ -0-	$ -0-
Intergovernmental Revenue	-0-	1,000
Fines and Fees	12,200	-0-
Licenses	10,500	-0-
Miscellaneous	1,000	-0-
Sales Taxes	33,280	-0-
Total	$56,980	$1,000

18.	Cash	56,980	
	Receivable from State	1,000	
	Revenues		57,980

Had the revenue estimates been adjusted during the year, an entry would have been made debiting the control account "estimated revenues" and crediting the control account "estimated revenues," and debiting or crediting budgetary fund balance for any net increase or decrease in estimated revenues. This adjusting entry was omitted to simplify the presentation.

The tax anticipation notes, along with interest of $2,800, were paid.

19.	Expenditures	2,800	
	Tax Anticipation Notes Payable	165,000	
	Cash		167,800

As would be the case in business, an allowance for uncollectibles cannot exceed the related receivable. The balance in taxes receivable current is $3,000, and the allowance for uncollectible taxes shows a balance of $5,500. Therefore, an adjustment is needed.

| 20. | Allowance for Uncollectible Current Taxes | 2,500 | |
| | Revenue | | 2,500 |

Depending on when the $3,000 becomes delinquent, the taxes receivable current and the related allowance account would have to be reclassified as delinquent. Typically, this entry is made at the end of the fiscal period in which the taxes were levied or at the beginning of the next year. This illustration assumes the taxes are not delinquent until the beginning of the next period. Had they become delinquent this period, the following entry would have been made:

Taxes Receivable Delinquent	3,000	
Allowance for Uncollectible Taxes—Current	3,000	
Taxes Receivable Current		3,000
Allowance for Uncollectible Taxes—Delinquent		3,000

Since the ending fund balance for governmental entities is intended to represent the amount that can be budgeted in a succeeding year, another adjusting entry is necessary. Not all of the supplies were used and therefore a balance of $3,000 appears in the inventory account. To assure that financial statement readers understand that inventories and other prepaids are not "spendable assets," the fund balance is reserved for any such amounts, as illustrated in entry 21.

| 21. | Unreserved Fund Balance | 3,000 | |
| | Reserve for Inventories | | 3,000 |

Entries 22 and 23 close the nominal accounts for Mineral County. The budgetary accounts are closed separately from revenues, expenditures, and encumbrances in order to maintan the accuracy of the three component parts of the fund balance. The T-accounts in Exhibit 4-3 provide a summary of all transactions; they are helpful in tracing the amounts shown in the closing entries.

Exhibit 4-3

T-Accounts for Illustrated Transactions
Mineral County General Fund

Estimated Revenues			
(1)	610,000	610,000	(22)

Appropriation			
(12)	15,900	697,800	(1)
(22)	697,800	15,900	(12)

Budgetary Fund Balance			
(1)	87,800	87,800	(22)

Cash			
BAL 1/1	30,000	282,700	(7)
(3)	42,670	316,000	(17)
(6)	307,000	167,800	(19)
(9)	218,900		
(11)	165,000		
(18)	56,980		

Supplies Inventory			
(13)	44,000	41,000	(14)

Taxes Receivable Current			
(2)	500,000	295,000	(6)
		200,000	(9)
		2,000	(10)

Allowance for Uncollectible Current Taxes			
(10)	2,000	7,500	(2)
(20)	2,500		

Receivable from State			
(3)	12,000	12,000	(6)
(18)	1,000		

Tax Anticipation Notes			
(19)	165,000	165,000	(11)

Accounts Payable			
(17)	316,000	91,000	(8)
		44,000	(13)
		269,100	(14)

Reserve for Inventories			
		3,000	(21)

Due to Debt Service Fund			
		9,000	(5)

Operating Transfers			
(5)	9,000	9,000	(23)

Encumbrances			
(4)	89,000	89,000	(8)
(7)	81,000	81,000	(15)
(16)	5,000	5,000	(23)

Reserve for Encumbrances			
(8)	89,000	89,000	(4)
(15)	81,000	81,000	(7)
		5,000	(16)

Expenditures			
(7)	282,700		
(8)	91,000		
(14)	310,100		
(19)	2,800	686,600	(23)

Revenues			
(23)	626,550	492,500	(2)
		54,670	(3)
		18,900	(9)
		57,980	(18)
		2,500	(20)

Unreserved Fund Balance			
(22)	3,000	30,000	BAL 1/1
(23)	74,050		

22.	Appropriations	697,800	
	Estimated Revenues		610,000
	Budgetary Fund Balance		87,800
23.	Revenues	626,550	
	Unreserved Fund Balance	74,050	
	Encumbrances		5,000
	Expenditures		686,600
	Operating Transfers		9,000

ILLUSTRATED FINANCIAL STATEMENTS

The financial statements for Mineral County are shown in Exhibits 4-4 through 4-6. Exhibit 4-4 shows the statement of revenues, expenditures, and

Exhibit 4-4

Mineral County General Fund
Statement of Revenues, Expenditures, and Changes in Fund
Balance by Function and Object
For the Year Ending December 31, 19X1

	General Government	Highway and Roads	Public Safety	Health and Welfare	Total
Revenues:					
Property Taxes					$495,000
Sales Taxes					73,480
Intergovernmental	(Revenues are not normally broken down by function)				13,000
Fines and Fees					20,170
Licenses					20,900
Miscellaneous					4,000
Total Revenues					$626,550
Expenditures and Other Uses of Financial Resources:					
Salaries	$186,000	$ 76,100	$ 92,000	$ 86,400	$440,500
Supplies	13,000	14,000	7,000	7,000	41,000
Insurance	5,500	-0-	7,000	-0-	12,500
Communications	-0-	-0-	2,200	-0-	2,200
Utilities	27,700	-0-	-0-	-0-	27,700
Repairs	21,000	16,000	-0-	-0-	37,000
Rent	-0-	-0-	-0-	6,800	6,800
Interest	2,800	-0-	-0-	-0-	2,800
Outside Services	-0-	-0-	-0-	4,000	4,000
Miscellaneous	-0-	-0-	-0-	3,100	3,100
Other Operating	4,500	9,400	1,100	3,000	18,000
Total Operating Expenditures	$260,500	$115,500	$109,300	$110,300	$595,600
Debt Service	9,000	-0-	-0-	-0-	9,000
Capital Outlays	22,000	15,000	50,000	4,000	91,000
Total Expenditures and Other Uses	$291,500	$130,500	$159,300	$114,300	$695,600
Excess of Expenditures and Other Uses Over Revenues	—	—	—	—	(69,050)
Less: Reserve for Inventories, 12/31/X1	—	—	—	—	(3,000)
Reserve for Encumbrances, 12/31/X1	—	—	—	—	(5,000)
Fund Balance, January 1	—	—	—	—	30,000
Unreserved Fund Balance, December 31	—	—	—	—	$ (47,050)

Exhibit 4-5

Mineral County General Fund
Statement of Revenues, Expenditures, and Changes in Fund Balance, Budget and Actual
For the Fiscal Year Ending December 31, 19X1

	Budget	Actual	Variance Favorable (Unfavorable)
Revenues:			
Property Taxes	$495,000	$495,000	$ -0-
Sales Taxes	68,000	73,480	5,480
Licenses	16,000	20,900	4,900
Fines and Fees	15,000	20,170	5,170
Intergovernmental	12,000	13,000	1,000
Miscellaneous	4,000	4,000	-0-
Total Revenues	$610,000	$626,550	$16,550
Expenditures:			
General Government	$277,200	$282,500	$ (5,300)
Public Safety	180,300	159,300	21,000
Health and Welfare	105,400	114,300	(8,900)
Highways and Roads	125,900	130,500	(4,600)
Total Expenditures	$688,800	$686,600	$ 2,200
Excess of Expenditures Over Revenues	$ (78,800)	$ (60,050)	$18,750
Other Financing Uses:			
Operating Transfers:			
Debt Service Fund	$ (9,000)	$ (9,000)	$ -0-
Deficiency of Revenues under Expenditures and Other Financing Uses	(87,800)	(69,050)	18,750
Less: Reserve for Encumbrances, 12/31/X1		(5,000)	(5,000)
Reserve for Inventories, 12/31/X1		(3,000)	(3,000)
Fund Balance, January 1	30,000	30,000	-0-
Unreserved Fund Balance, December 31	$ (57,800)	$ (47,050)	$10,750

changes in fund balance. Exhibit 4-5 shows the statement of revenues, expenditures, and changes in fund balance, budget and actual; the balance sheet is shown in Exhibit 4-6.

Different formats were used for Exhibits 4-4 and 4-5 to illustrate the possible dimensions of the statements. The statement of revenues, expenditures, and changes in fund balance shows both the object and functional classifications. The statement of revenues, expenditures, and changes in fund balance, budget and actual, is presented in the more traditional format, by type and function.

The amounts budgeted for each function were shown at the beginning of the illustrated transactions. Subsequent subsidiary transactions were illustrated only for the object code classification. However, Mineral County would have to maintain subsidiary ledgers for both classifications in order to prepare the financial statement illustrated in Exhibit 4-4.

Several attributes of these statements should be emphasized:

Exhibit 4-6

Mineral County General Fund
Balance Sheet
December 31, 19X1

Assets

Current Assets:

Cash		$ 54,050
Inventories		3,000
Taxes Receivable—Current	$ 3,000	
Less: Allowances for Uncollectible Accounts	3,000	-0-
Receivable from State		1,000
Total Current Assets		$ 58,050
Total Assets		$ 58,050

Liabilities and Fund Balance

Current Liabilities:

Accounts Payable	$ 88,100	
Due to Debt Service Fund	9,000	
Total Current Liabilities		$ 97,100
Total Liabilities		$ 97,100
Fund Balance:		
Reserve for Encumbrances	$ 5,000	
Reserve for Inventories	3,000	
Unreserved Fund Balance	(47,050)	(39,050)
Total Liabilities and Fund Balance		$ 58,050

- While the capital outlays and debt service are shown as expenditures or other financing uses by the general fund, they are separated from operating expenditures. Frequently, they are not controlled by program managers, or in the case of capital outlays, budgeted separately. Therefore, they are not relevant to some aspects of evaluating performance or compliance.

- If Exhibit 4-4 was presented as part of the financial statements for all funds and account groups, the line "debt service" should be further described as an operating transfer, as it is in Exhibit 4-5. The caption might be "Operating Transfers Out—Debt Service." Then the debt service fund would show a line "Operating Transfers In—Debt Service," making it easy for readers to see where the debt service money came from and in which fund it was spent.

- Encumbrances are closed at the end of the year to the fund balance. However, they are not included in the expenditures portion of the statement. This is as it should be because an obligation has not been incurred. Therefore, in order to achieve the appropriate unreserved fund balance, the reserve for encumbrances at year end must be deducted from the net excess of expenditures and other uses over revenues. The same is true for the reserve for inventories.

- As Exhibit 4-5 shows, revenue collections exceeded projections, and expenditures also were under budget. However, not all programs complied with the budget limitations. For example, expenditures on public safety exceeded the budget, and the managers should be prepared to explain why this occurred. Favorable expenditure variances may also have to be explained, particularly if the managers of those areas expect to receive the same or increased authorization for the next period.

Since the illustrated entries were depicted for a general fund, only one fund is involved. Had the illustrations been prepared for a special revenue fund, the financial statements would have included combining statements.

SUMMARY

The accounting cycle for governmental funds begins with the budgeting process. Revenues are estimated by the chief executive or the oversight board. Each department head proposes a budget for his or her area of responsibility. If the sum of the departmental budgets is greater than total estimated revenues, additional taxes are levied or expenditures reduced. Various techniques have been used to force department heads to make realistic projections.

Budgets represent a plan of action for everyone in the governmental unit. They also are very important in evaluating performance of those responsible for managing the entity. Because there is no profit motive, how well management performed must be determined almost entirely by how closely it adhered to the budget.

The accounting system incorporates major budget decisions. The authorized budget is integrated into the general and subsidiary ledgers for both the general and the special revenue funds. Any budget amendment is reflected in the accounting records as well. Interim reports emphasize the relationship between actual revenues and expenditures and estimated revenues and appropriations.

The modified accrual basis of accounting is used for governmental funds. Generally, revenues are accrued when the resources are measurable and available. Most expenditures are recognized when incurred. The GASB made exceptions in the expenditure recognition basis for debt service payments on long-term debt. Recognition principles for pensions are not yet defined.

General and special revenue funds have the same accounting and reporting basis. The general fund is used to account for all of the general operating resources and expenditures of the governmental unit. A special revenue fund is established for each earmarked revenue source that the governmental entity wants to account for and report on separately.

Financial statements used for general and special revenue funds include the balance sheet; statement of revenues, expenditures, and changes in fund balance; and statement of revenues, expenditures, and changes in fund balance—budget and actual. In addition, combining operating statements and balance sheets are prepared for special revenue funds.

APPENDIX A

THE ACCRUAL BASIS OF ACCOUNTING

Presumably the GASB will eventually establish an effective date for implementing *Statement No. 11,* which requires accrual basis accounting for all governmental funds. This same standard also requires a measurement focus of **total** financial resources, rather than **current** financial resources. Understanding the accounting methodology under the new measurement focus/basis of accounting will be necessary for preparing financial statements after the effective date. The purpose of this appendix is to explain the rudiments of *Statement No. 11.*

The new basis of accounting does not alter the recognition criterion for expenditures. That is, under both the accrual and modified accrual bases of accounting, expenditures are recognized when the related liability is incurred. Consequently the following sections concentrate on the recognition criteria for revenues and the treatment of assets and liabilities.

Accounting for Revenues

The GASB struggled with the unique nature of some revenue transactions. Whether reliable bases exist for measuring the amounts that should be recognized was a key concern of the Board. It classified revenue sources as exchange or nonexchange transactions. **Exchange transactions** are like those encountered in business when each party to the transaction receives something of value. Revenue is recognized when the earnings process is complete. For such transactions, the GASB relies on the revenue recognition principles common to business. For example, if a user fee is charged by a general or special revenue fund, the revenue is recognized when the service or good for which the fee is charged has been provided—that is, when earned.

Most revenue sources for general and special revenue funds are of the **nonexchange** type in which no direct relationship exists between the value received and given. The taxpayer pays the tax bill, for example, and the government uses that money to provide a variety of services. The property tax bill is not based on the extent to which a particular taxpayer will use the services; it is based on the amount of real or personal property owned.

Statement No. 11 generally requires revenues from nonexchange transactions to be recognized when the transactions or events that increase net financial resources take place, regardless of when cash is received and when the government has demanded the revenue by setting a due date that falls within the current period. However, for such taxpayer-assessed taxes as income and sales taxes, administration lead time is considered not to offset the due date.[6] To assure some consistency among governmental units, the GASB had to devise estimation procedures for accruing some nonexchange revenues, such as sales and income taxes, property taxes, and fines and fees.

---

[6]Governmental Accounting Standards Board, *Statement No. 11, Measurement Focus and Basis of Accounting—Governmental Fund Operating Statements* (Norwalk, Conn.: GASB, 1990), ¶40.

Sales and Income Taxes Sales tax revenues are collected by merchants making the sale and are paid to the governmental unit at regular intervals. These revenues are recognized when the sale takes place, not when the merchant pays the governmental unit, provided the government has demanded the taxes before the end of the year, or within two months after the close of the period to allow for administration lead time. Any expected refunds to the merchant should be reported as liabilities, with a corresponding reduction in revenue. In other words, the estimated refunds should not be reported as expenditures. The estimates are based on historical trends, economic conditions, changes in tax laws, and similar data.

Both individual and corporate income taxes should generally be recognized when the taxpayer earns the revenue causing the tax liability. However, the GASB requires that the government must demand the tax. Again, the "demand" takes the form of a due date within the current period or two months after the end of the period. Estimated payments are deducted from the total tax due at the end of the tax year, at which time the taxpayer owes additional taxes or receives a refund, depending upon the accuracy of the estimates. According to *Statement No. 11,* income tax revenues, receivables, and refund liabilities should include not only amounts that are received when due but also those amounts that are delinquent:

1. Delinquent withholdings and estimated payments should be based on known data and historical trends adjusted for tax law and other changes that would distort those trends.
2. Current settlements should be recognized in revenue and should be calculated based on additional payments and refunds (1) received or paid before financial statements are issued, (2) reported but not received or paid before financial statements are issued, and (3) expected to be reported after financial statements are issued based on the history of delinquent final settlements filings that "trickle in" after financial statements are issued. Current final settlements are those that relate to a taxable period ending on or before the government's current fiscal year end and that are due within two months after that year end.
3. Revenue from income taxes that are subject to a future final settlement should be reduced to the extent the government has structured an over-demand for tax payments, for example, through an excess-payment requirement built into the income tax withholding or estimated payments system.
4. Other audit adjustments (billings) should be recognized during the period assessed, as well as those assessed before the financial statements are issued if the amounts meet the other recognition criteria stated above.
5. Interest should be accrued on unpaid taxes as earned over time and penalties as assessed.
6. Income tax revenue and receivables should be reduced by appropriate allowances for uncollectible amounts.[7]

---

[7]Adapted from GASB, *Statement No. 11,* ¶49.

Assume, for example, that employers and taxpayers are required to remit withholdings and estimated payments on a quarterly basis, and settlements are made on April 15 following the end of the calendar year. If the governmental unit has a fiscal year end of June 30, it would base its year-end accrual on withholdings to date, any reported but unpaid tax liabilities as of April 15, any unpaid liabilities (refunds owed) as of June 30, and any audit adjustments. The revenue earned during the period would be calculated as follows:

Withholdings Received During the Period for the Current Period	$1,200,000
Amounts Received During the Period for Prior Periods	(100,000)
Withholdings Receivable for Reporting Period and Due by June 30 but Not Yet Received	500,000
Historical Experience of Delinquent Payments after 2-month Cutoff	100,000
Total Gross Revenue	$1,700,000
Payments and Refunds Applicable to Tax Periods Ending on or Before the Balance Sheet Date:	
Additional Payments Received	300,000
Additional Liabilities Reported	100,000
Refunds Paid	(260,000)
Refunds Acknowledged	(50,000)
Structural Overwithholding	(25,000)
Net Revenue for the Period	$1,765,000

Property Taxes   Revenue from property taxes is recognized in the budgetary (fiscal) year for which the taxes are levied, provided the government has demanded the taxes on or before the end of the period. The demand date is the due date. Since property tax levies are a nonexchange transaction, the matching occurs between the levy and the expenditures the levy is intended to finance. If the property taxes are due before the period in which they will be used to cover expenditures, the receipt should be recorded as a deferred revenue, a liability. Property taxes that are due after the budgetary period for which levied should be recognized as revenue in the period due.

As mentioned earlier, even though property taxes constitute a lien on the property, a governmental unit rarely receives 100 percent of the levy. The revenue should be reduced by the expected uncollectible amount. For example, if the levy is $800,000 and the unit expects to collect 99 percent of the taxes, the entry would be:

Taxes Receivable Current	800,000	
Allowance for Uncollectible Current Taxes		8,000
Revenues		792,000

Interest on overdue taxes should be recognized as revenue as it accrues over time, and penalties should be recognized when assessed. The entry would be:

Interest Receivable	2,000	
Penalties Receivable	3,000	
Revenue		5,000

The revenue is reduced by any expected uncollectible amounts just as in the case of the initial levy.

Intergovernmental Revenue   The GASB does not specifically mention intergovernmental revenues except to say that other nonexchange revenues should be recognized when the underlying event takes place. Some accounting procedures currently used for intergovernmental revenues may be inconsistent with the adopted model. For example, under pronouncements preceding *Statement No. 11,* the GASB requires that entitlements or shared revenues from other levels of government should be recognized as revenue when "they are susceptible to accrual"; usually this means when the amount is known and measurable, which may not be the same recognition criteria as "when earned."

For such intergovernmental revenues as grants and contracts, a governmental entity has not performed its side of the transaction until expenditures are incurred. Therefore, revenue is recognized when the expenditure is made. If a governmental unit was, for example, awarded a $1,000,000 contract in 19X1, and it spent only $200,000 in that year, revenue would be $200,000, not $1,000,000.[8]

Fines and Fees   Fines are usually levied for violations of law or administrative procedure (for example, parking fines). Lengthy administrative or legal proceedings may be necessary before the fine is collected. The revenue is recognized when the entity has a legally enforceable claim against the violator. A governmental entity has a legally enforceable claim when:

- The date by which an individual may contest a court summons expires, and the fine is automatically imposed
- The offender pays the fine before the court date
- A court imposes the fine[9]

An allowance for uncollectible fines is established for fines that are imposed at the point of violation but expected to be waived through the appeals process. Speeding tickets are issued when the violation occurs, but some will not be paid or the payment will be reduced when the violation is appealed.

Permits and licenses can be either exchange or nonexchange transactions. User fees are exchange transactions and are recognized when earned, just as in business. Fees for permits or privileges related to administrative processes are nonexchange transactions. Even if the person later chooses to forgo the privilege, the fee is not refunded. Such fees are recognized as revenue when the entity has an "enforceable legal claim . . . provided the government has no obligation to refund amounts paid."[10]

---

[8]The GASB is reexamining the entire issue of intergovernmental revenue; no doubt when its work is finished, different standards will apply to each type of intergovernmental revenue.

[9]GASB, *Statement No. 11,* ¶55.

[10]GASB, *Statement No. 11,* ¶57.

Other nonexchange fees are for privileges extending over a period of time, such as a business license or a driver's license. The entity may recognize revenue from these fees ratably over the period covered by the fee, or when received.

Investment Earnings   With few exceptions, investment earnings are recognized just as they would be in a business enterprise. Dividends and interest on investments are recognized when earned. Gains or losses on investments generally are recognized when realized, that is, when the investment is sold.

Governmental entities treat losses from marketable equity securities differently than do businesses. Because the GASB does not distinguish between short-term and long-term investments in marketable equity securities, only permanent market declines are recognized in the financial statements. In contrast, business entities report losses differently depending upon whether the security is in the hold-to-maturity, trading, or available-for-sale categories.

The GASB made a few exceptions to the rule of recognizing only permanent declines. If temporary losses will be sustained because the entity will be forced to sell during a period of decline, the decrease in value would be promptly reported as a loss with a corresponding reduction in the carrying value of the investment.

Another exception relates to situations where several funds pool their investments to maximize return and minimize administrative costs. Investment pools are normally valued at market for purposes of determining each fund's share of the pool. In such circumstances, gains and losses will be recognized as market values change.

Accounting for Expenditures

Governmental units do not distinguish among operating, capital, and debt service payments. All three are reported as expenditures. Expenditures incurred for operating expenses are reported only in the fund making the expenditure. Capital and debt service payments are reported as expenditures in the fund making the disbursement or commitment. Simultaneously they are reported as assets or as a reduction to the principal amount of the debt in the general fixed asset or long-term debt account group respectively. As previously noted, these accounting conventions result from following the total financial resources rather than the total economic resources model.

Recognition Principles   Expenditures are generally recognized when transactions or events that result in claims against financial resources take place. Operating expenditures are recognized when incurred. For example, salaries and wages should be reported as expenditures during the period in which the employees perform the work. Insurance, supplies inventory, and other prepaid items are recognized over the period benefited by the expenditure. For supplies, this means that only the "when consumed" method will constitute GAAP.

Accounting for Assets and Liabilities

When governmental entities change to a measurement basis that focuses on total financial resources, both current assets and non-capital long-term assets will be recorded in the governmental fund types, including the general and special revenue funds. Both current and non-capital-related long-term liabilities also should be reported in these funds.

Capital assets and capital-related debt refer to fixed assets and the debt used to finance those fixed assets. After the effective date of *Statement No. 11,* the two account groups will pertain solely to capital assets. Accordingly, one issue the GASB is considering before it announces the effective date is whether these two account groups could be combined.

The implications for the liability section of the general fund in particular and, to a limited extent, the special revenue fund are far reaching. As explained in Chapter 3, any long-term liabilities not related to the acquisition of fixed assets should be reported in the fund incurring the liability. All long-term liabilities related to pensions, compensated absences, or general debt issued to finance operations should be reported in the governmental funds. The term *should* rather than *will* is used here intentionally. Conceptually, application of the total financial resources model means that all non-capital long-term liabilities would be reported in the governmental funds. However, in subsequent discussions, the GASB has indicated that those related to pensions, compensated absences, and contingencies may continue to be reported in the general long-term debt account group.

QUESTIONS

4-1 What does it mean if a revenue is a nonexchange transaction? Give some examples of nonexchange transactions in governmental units.

4-2 A governmental unit has asked for advice concerning the expenditure classification scheme(s) that it should use. Explain in general terms each scheme and its applicability to particular reporting objectives.

4-3 Under what circumstances would a governmental unit open a special revenue fund? Could more than one special revenue fund be required? Explain.

4-4 Describe the budgeting process for governmental funds.

4-5 Contrast incremental with zero-based budgeting.

4-6 What is the difference between an expenditure and an encumbrance? What effect does an encumbrance have on the financial statements?

4-7 What does it mean if the budgetary entry of a governmental unit shows a debit to the budgetary fund balance? Could a governmental unit remain viable with a debit to budgetary fund balance during several periods? Explain.

4-8 Explain the rationale for reporting such revenues as property taxes on a net basis.

4-9 The general fund has invested in short-term marketable securities, and at year end the market price was $52,000; original cost was $55,000. What entry would be made? Would your answer be the same if the unit had invested in long-term securities and the decline from $55,000 to $52,000 was considered permanent?

4-10 Under a flow of total financial resources model, what factors should be taken into consideration in accruing revenue from income taxes?

4-11 If accrual accounting is applied in governmental units as it is in industry, what treatment would be accorded to claims and judgments (claims and judgments are contingent liabilities of governmental entities)?

4-12 Contrast the "when consumed" and "when purchased" methods of accounting for inventories.

4-13 Give the entries necessary for a transfer from the general fund to the debt service fund for principal and interest payments on a debt issue.

4-14 Briefly describe the differences accorded property taxes under the accrual and modified accrual bases of accounting.

4-15 If an oversight board decided to generate net property taxes of $1,000,000, and the collection rate was 99 percent, what is the amount of the levy?

4-16 What incentives does a manager of a governmental program have to reduce expenditures or reexamine program offerings to determine if they could be operated more efficiently or effectively?

4-17 A city finance clerk sees no reason to establish subsidiary ledgers for expenditures. After all, he reasons, the oversight board only controls the overall budget and not each line item. Is the finance clerk correct? Explain.

4-18 How would the financial statements of a general fund and a special revenue fund differ? Be specific.

CASES

4-1 The state budget director has been asked to prepare a preliminary budget proposal for the next fiscal year. The budget will be submitted to a legislative finance committee before the next session with a goal of bipartisan support for the governor's proposal. The budget director has certain guidelines within which the projections will be made; she also has actual revenues and expenditures for the first ten months of the current fiscal year.

Budget Parameters:

1. Eighty-seven percent of the budgeted revenues and 83 percent of budgeted expenditures for the current year have been generated or expended.

	Current Fiscal Period (000)
Revenues:	
Income Taxes	$ 211,000
Sales Taxes	151,300
Cigarette and Beverage Taxes	364,900
Bed Tax	45,100
Licenses and Permits	60,000
Charges for Services, Fines	35,600
Federal Contracts and Grants	418,500
Investment Income	73,600
Miscellaneous	51,400
Total Revenues	$1,411,400
Expenditures:	
General Administration	$ 70,200
State Lands	60,000
Health and Welfare	320,000
Education and Cultural	238,600
Local Governmental Services	32,000
Commerce	210,000
Transportation	306,400
State Institutions	109,000
Total Expenditures	$1,346,200

With the exception of income taxes, revenues are expected to be collected as projected for the remainder of the year. No additional income taxes are anticipated; in fact, that division tells the budget director to plan for additional rebates of $10,000. The transportation and education budgets each will be reduced by $42,000,000 to compensate for the shortfall.

2. With two exceptions, next year's revenues are expected to increase by 5 percent over this year's actual. One exception is the bed tax, which should increase by 7 percent because it was instituted during the current year. The second exception is intergovernmental revenue; an additional grant of $100,000 is expected from the federal government and earmarked for the prison, which is administered through the Division of State Institutions.

3. With the exception of program modifications or new programs, the state uses incremental budgeting. The parameters for incremental increases are based on an object of expenditure. For the next year, the following increases are used for budgetary purposes:

Salaries and Employee Benefits	4 percent
Supplies	5 percent
Equipment	3 percent

The general administration budget for next year also will increase by a debt service payment of $10,000,000.

With the exception of education and welfare divisions, division budgets average 70 percent in salaries and benefits, 23 percent in supplies, and the remainder in equipment. The education and welfare divisions show 80 percent in salaries and employee benefits, 15 percent in supplies, and 5 percent in equipment.

4. Two program modifications are being proposed for next year. One is the federal grant (see Item 2), which will be spent all in the Division of State Institutions. The second modification is $400,000 allocated to the Education and Cultural Division for equipment.

5. Any additional revenues for next year will be placed in the Governor's Reserve, which is carried in the Division of General Administration, and any shortfall will be absorbed within the same division.

REQUIRED

Prepare a budget proposal for the next year that could be submitted to the Legislative Finance Committee. Make sure that the historical data are provided in enough detail to allow members of the committee to derive alternative proposals (round all calculations to the nearest $100,000).

4-2 After reviewing the budgeting information provided in Case 4-1, the Legislative Finance Committee wants to consider the possibility of changing its approach to budgeting. One member has recently attended a conference on zero-based budgeting. She raises the following questions:

1. How would the state's budgeting process change? (Use the process as implied in Case 4-1 as a basis for comparison.)
2. Could the state use the same administrative organization if it adopted zero-based budgeting, or would the divisions have to be changed?
3. From a budget director's perspective, what are the advantages and disadvantages of changing to zero-based budgeting? From the legislature's perspective?

REQUIRED

Prepare a report that responds to these questions.

4-3 Under the GASB's accrual basis of accounting, recognition rules for corporate and individual income taxes include a demand criterion.

REQUIRED

1. Explain why the GASB might have decided to include a demand criterion in the recognition procedures for corporate and individual income taxes.
2. In applying this demand criterion, will the governmental entity have accrued all revenue as the taxpayer owes it? Explain.

4-4 Chickory County adopted GASB *Statement No. 11* for its fiscal year ending June 30, 19X4. The following selected transactions pertain to Chickory's fiscal year, ending June 30, 19X4:

7/1	Encumbered $1,000 for supplies ordered
7/2	Billed other departments $880 for services rendered
7/15	Levied property taxes, $100,000, with a 1 percent allowance for uncollectible taxes
8/2	Merchants had collected $5,000 in sales taxes; demand criterion is met
9/25	Sales taxes were received
10/2	Supplies ordered were received; previously the county used the "when purchased" method
11/30	Property taxes of $45,000 were collected
1/17	A truck was purchased for $15,000
2/17	County paid for the truck
4/17	A restrictive grant for $50,000 was received from the state

REQUIRED

Set up a schedule showing the journal entries that should be made under the modified accrual and accrual bases of accounting as applicable to governmental units. Use the following format:

Date	Accounts	Modified Accrual		Accrual Basis	
		Dr.	Cr.	Dr.	Cr.

4-5 The Translvania City Council has several different sources of earmarked revenues, including:

Type of Tax	Projected Income
Cigarette Tax	$180,000
Hotel/Motel Bed Tax	33,000
Beer/Wine Tax	10,000
Special Property Tax Levy	125,000
State Revenue Sharing	66,000
Federal Reserve Sharing	265,000

Translvania's finance officer is unsure of how many special revenue funds should be established. He is trying to balance clear reporting and accountability. The more funds reported in the financial statements, the more the report might confuse the readers. The fewer the funds, the less likely it is that the city council and other financial statement users will be able to tell exactly how each earmarked revenue source was spent. In examining the documentation for each earmarked revenue, the finance officer offers the following additional information:

1. All of the hotel/motel bed tax is allocated to tourism projects, as is one-fourth of the special property tax levy. The remainder of the special property tax levy will be earmarked for road improvements, which enhance access to the community.

2. The wine and beer tax is used exclusively to support welfare and health programs aimed at alcohol and drug rebabilitation. The state collects the tax for the city but does not require any formal reporting on expenditures.

3. Both the federal and state revenue sharing programs support property tax relief—that is, the city replaces mill levies with these revenues.

4. The cigarette tax is used to finance the operation of local cultural and recreational events. If the city expends any of these funds on unallowable expenditures, the amount so spent must be rebated to the state. In addition, the state may assess a fine for the misappropriation.

REQUIRED

Draft a report to Translvania's finance officer containing recommendations for the number of special revenue funds that should be established by the city. Justify the recommendations in the report.

4-6 Boglona, a small community in a southeastern state, will adopt the GASB's total financial resources concept for its measurement focus and basis of accounting sometime in the future. A long-time member of Boglona's city council complains that this basis of accounting is confusing. He says that previously he could almost project the cash balance by year end, a figure he considers important in determining whether Boglona officials have complied with the budget. Now, he maintains, with all these "accrual" processes, he will have no idea how well-off the city is. Further, he says the fund balance will no longer represent the amount that can be considered excess at the end of the year and budgeted for the next year.

REQUIRED

1. Contrast the flow of current financial resources (modified accrual) with the flow of total financial resources (accrual except for depreciation) approach to accounting.

2. Under the flow of total financial resources, what is the significance of the fund balance? How does the significance of the fund balance differ under the modified accrual basis of accounting? Comment specifically on the significance with respect to budgeting.

EXERCISES

passages/scene

4-1 Appendix A of the textbook contains excerpts from comprehensive financial reports for the City of Raleigh, North Carolina. After reviewing the statements pertinent to the general fund and the special revenue funds, answer the following questions:

1. What primary financial statements are shown for the general fund? In what respects do those statements appear consistent with those presented in the textbook? How are they different? What notes or supporting schedules pertain specifically to the general fund? Explain why they are necessary.

2. Has the city of Raleigh acknowledged the future transition to the flow of total financial resources model? Analyze the explanation in terms of the average citizen who will read the reports. Is it clear and understandable? What additional information would be helpful to statement users? Should some information have been omitted? Explain.

3. Examine the financial statement presentations for the special revenue funds and determine in what respects they are consistent with generally accepted accounting principles. What statements are presented? Do the headings, format, and information seem consistent with the descriptions in the chapter? Are there specific examples of presentations that are not in accordance with GAAP?

4. What notes pertain specifically to special revenue funds? Do the additional notes help the readers to understand better the financial statements? What specific notes are most helpful?

5. With the information provided, is it clear how many special revenue funds are operated by Raleigh? Do the funds appear to be operated within budgetary constraints? What evidence is there to substantiate your observations?

4-2 Select the best answer for each question.

1. The reserve for encumbrances account of a governmental unit is decreased when:
   a. supplies previously ordered are received
   b. a purchase order is approved
   c. the vouchers are paid
   d. appropriations are recorded
   (Adapted from the May 1988 CPA Exam, Practice #52)

2. The following items were among Wood Township's expenditures from the general fund during the year ended June 30, 19X1:

Furniture for Township Hall	$10,000
Minicomputer for Tax Collector's Office	15,000

   The amount that should be classified as fixed assets in Wood's general fund balance sheet at June 30, 19X1, is:
   a. $25,000
   b. $15,000
   c. $10,000
   d. $0
   (Adapted from the May 1988 CPA Exam, Practice #41)

3. Timber County has total assessed property of $15,800,000. The total includes governmental property of $1,500,000 and $500,000 of property owned by charitable organizations. If the rate was 90 mills per $1,000 of assessed valuation, what would the collection rate have to be before at least $1,200,000 of revenue would be generated?
   a. 93 percent
   b. 97 percent

    c. 85 percent

    d. 94 percent

4. Possible budgeting techniques for governmental entities *do not* include which one of the following?

    a. planning-programming-budgeting systems

    b. incremental budgeting

    c. fixed-rate development system

    d. zero-based budgeting

5. Classifying expenditures by function and program would eliminate the need for which of the following subsidiary ledgers?

    a. health and welfare

    b. day-care program

    c. salaries and wages

    d. streets and highways

6. Legal authority to expend amounts budgeted is referred to as:

    a. budget development

    b. oversight board consensus

    c. allotment

    d. appropriation

7. If governmental GAAP follows business GAAP, a correction of a prior period error would be treated as:

    a. a revenue or expense in the year discovered

    b. an adjustment to beginning fund balance

    c. an adjustment to the excess of revenues over expenditures

    d. none of the above

8. Morey County has the following long-term debt:

Long-term debt issued to finance expansion of county offices	$1,200,000
Short-term tax anticipation notes payable	650,000
Long-term debt issued to finance general operations	110,000

Under the flow of total financial resources model, how much debt would Morey County show as a liability of its general fund?

    a. $1,200,000

    b. $650,000

    c. $0

    d. $760,000

9. The Pine Valley Township sold computer equipment that had been used in the mayor's office. The equipment cost $165,000, and Pine Valley showed accumulated depreciation in the general fixed asset account group of $120,000. When the equipment was sold for $15,000, what entry was made in the general fund?

a. cash	15,000	
miscellaneous revenues		15,000

b. cash	15,000	
loss on sale	30,000	
other financing sources		45,000
c. cash	15,000	
accumulated depreciation	120,000	
loss on sale	30,000	
equipment		165,000
d. cash	15,000	
other financing sources		15,000

10. An exchange transaction is one in which:
    a. both parties receive something of value
    b. one party receives something of value
    c. neither party receives something of value
    d. either (b) or (c)

4-3 Select the best answer for each question.

Items 1 through 6 are based on the following information:

Maple Township uses encumbrance accounting, and formally integrates its budget into the accounting records for its general fund. For the year ending June 30, 19X1, the Township Council adopted a budget comprising estimated revenues of $10,000,000, appropriations of $9,000,000, and an estimated transfer of $300,000 to the debt service fund. The following additional information is provided:

- For the month of April 19X1, a salary and wage expense of $200,000 was incurred.
- On June 10, 19X1, an approved $1,500 purchase order was issued for supplies. The supplies were not received by year end.
- Appropriations for Maple Township lapse at year end, and there is no obligation to pay for supplies received after year end.

1. On adoption of the budget, the journal entry to record the charge to the budgetary fund balance would be a:
   a. debit of $700,000
   b. credit of $700,000
   c. debit of $1,000,000
   d. credit of $1,000,000
2. Budgeted revenues would be recorded by a:
   a. debit to estimated revenues, $10,000,000
   b. debit to estimated revenues receivable, $10,000,000
   c. credit to estimated revenues, $10,000,000
   d. credit to other financing sources, $10,000,000
3. Budgeted appropriations would be recorded by a:
   a. debit to estimated expenditures, $9,300,000
   b. credit to appropriations, $9,300,000
   c. debit to estimated expenditures, $9,000,000
   d. credit to appropriations, $9,000,000
4. What journal entry would be made on June 10, 19X1, to record the approved purchase order?

a. expenditures	1,500	
encumbrances		1,500
b. encumbrances	1,500	
expenditures		1,500
c. encumbrances	1,500	
reserve for encumbrances		1,500
d. encumbrances	1,500	
appropriations		1,500

5. What journal entry should be made on June 30, 19X1, to reflect the fact that Maple did not receive the supplies order?

a. reserve for encumbrances	1,500	
encumbrances		1,500
b. reserve for encumbrances	1,500	
reserve for encumbrances—		
prior year		1,500
c. no entry		
d. appropriations	1,500	
encumbrances		1,500

6. What journal entry should be made to record the salaries and wages expense incurred for April?

a. salaries and wages		
expense	200,000	
vouchers payable		200,000
b. appropriations	200,000	
vouchers payable		200,000
c. encumbrances	200,000	
vouchers payable		200,000
d. expenditures	200,000	
vouchers payable		200,000

7. When a debt service payment is made by the debt service fund but funded by the general fund, the entry recording the receipt of money by the debt service fund for the payment would be:
   a. an operating transfer in the debt service fund
   b. an equity transfer in the general fund
   c. an operating transfer in the general fund
   d. an equity transfer in the debt service fund
8. Subsidiary ledgers usually would be established for:
   a. sales tax
   b. expenditures
   c. revenues
   d. revenues and expenditures
9. For general and special revenue funds using the flow of total financial resources model, revenue from nonexchange transactions is recognized when:

    a. an exchange finally takes place

    b. when title passes

    c. when the earnings process is complete

    d. when the underlying event takes place

10. Restricted intergovernmental revenues are recognized when:

    a. notification of the grant revenue is received

    b. an exchange takes place

    c. when the earnings process is complete

    d. cash is received

4-4 The City of Fairlane was recently incorporated. The following transactions relate to its general fund and occurred during its second year of operations.

1. The city council authorized a budget that included appropriations of $11,500,000 and estimated revenues of $12,100,000. This budget covered an order for supplies that had not been received by the end of the prior period. Local ordinance specifies that appropriations lapse at the end of the year, but the city has an obligation to pay for orders placed in the prior period. The city has a $4,600 reserve for encumbrances on the books.

2. Property taxes totaling $8,000,000 were levied. The city expects 1 percent of the taxes to be uncollectible.

3. Fairlane's other sources of revenue include a sales tax, fines and fees, revenue sharing from the state's income tax collections, a flat-fee license charge, and miscellaneous permits. Budgeted collections for the first half of the year are as follows:

Sales Taxes	$1,870,000
Revenue Sharing	110,000
Fines and Fees	23,000
Licenses	10,000
Miscellaneous Permits	3,000
	$2,016,000

    The revenue-sharing notice has been received by Fairlane and payment will be received before year end.

4. Delinquent taxes of $300,000 were collected; the balance of delinquent taxes amounting to $4,300 was written off (the city correctly accounted for these taxes in prior periods).

5. The general fund transferred $100,000 for principal and interest payments on debt issued in the prior year for construction of a city hall.

6. Tax and other revenue collections for the first half of the year totaled $9,833,200.

Property Taxes	$7,800,000
Sales Taxes	1,890,000
Revenue Sharing	110,000
Fines and Fees	21,000
Licenses	9,000
Miscellaneous Permits	3,200

7. An equipment order of $500,000 was placed, along with supplies orders totaling $110,000. The order placed in the prior fiscal year was received at a cost of $4,400. Fairlane uses the "when consumed" method.

8. Operating expenditures totaling $6,300,000 were incurred; $5,700,000 was paid in cash and the remainder were on account. .

9. Fairlane's internal service fund purchased miscellaneous supplies for all departments; the general fund's share of the supply order was $2,200. The amount owed was not paid.

10. Budgeted collections on non-property tax revenues for the second half of the year were:

Sales Taxes	$1,710,000
Revenue Sharing	350,000
Fines and Fees	32,000
Licenses	40,000
Miscellaneous Permits	5,000
	$2,137,000

11. The equipment order was received at the price estimated. One-half of the supplies order was received, but because the city did not get the order in before a price increase, an additional 4 percent was charged. Both orders were paid after being vouchered.

12. Under city ordinance, all money not spend on authorized projects is returned to the general fund. After completion of the city hall, $5,000 was transferred from the capital projects fund.

13. Cash received for revenues during the second half of the year were:

Property Taxes	$ 50,000
Intergovernmental	350,000
Sales Taxes	1,600,000
Fines and Fees	30,000
Licenses	42,000
Miscellaneous Permits	5,000
	$2,077,000

14. Fairlane invested $1,000,000 in short-term securities.

15. The remainder of the vouchers for Item 8 were paid. In addition, expenditures totaling $4,500,000 were incurred. Of the total $4,500,000, $3,800,000 was paid in cash. The remainder was for accrued wages at year end.

16. All of the supplies received during the year were consumed before year end.

REQUIRED

Prepare the transaction and closing entries under the modified accrual basis of accounting.

4-5   The following information relates to a state's historical collections of sales and income taxes.

Year	Sales Tax	Income Tax
19X1	$15,700,000	$43,800,000
19X2	12,900,000	44,500,000
19X3	16,000,000	44,700,000

The sales tax is 4 percent of all nonessential goods and services and has been in existence for many years. Sales tax revenue from in-state residents has been fairly constant at $10,000,000 for the past several years (it is earned evenly throughout the year). Fluctuations above that depend primarily on tourism. With the exception of 19X2, in which there was a severe drought and numerous forest fires, tourism receipts appear to be growing at 3 percent per year. About 75 percent of the tourism receipts are received in the second quarter; the remainder is received equally throughout the other three quarters.

The state income tax was initiated 5 years ago and is based on a sliding scale: The first $40,000 of income is taxed at 5 percent; the next $50,000 at 7 percent; anything over $90,000 is taxed at 10 percent. Total taxable corporate and personal income for 19X4 is estimated at $760,000,000. On average, one-half of personal and corporate income is taxed at the first tier, 25 percent at the second, and 25 percent at the third. However, recently there is some indication that the amount collected in the third tier shows a 1 percent decrease and the amount collected in the second shows a 1 percent increase.

Withholding is required for all salaried individuals. Also, self-employed persons and corporations must pay estimated income taxes on a quarterly basis. The withholding and estimated tax tables provide for excess withholding of approximately 10 percent. A total of $25,000,000 of income is subject to excess withholding. Withholding and estimated income tax payments seem to be constant over the four quarters. Payments are due April 15, July 15, October 15, and January 15.

REQUIRED

Prepare a quarterly and an annual projection of the state's revenue for income and sales taxes under the flow of total financial resources model.

4-6 The following information was abstracted from the accounts of the general fund of the city of Rom after the books had been closed for the fiscal year ended June 30, 19X1.

	POST-CLOSING TRIAL BALANCE June 30, 19X0	TRANSACTIONS Dr.	TRANSACTIONS Cr.	POST-CLOSING TRIAL BALANCE June 30, 19X1
Cash	$700,000	$1,820,000	$1,852,000	$668,000
Taxes Receivable	40,000	1,870,000	1,828,000	82,000
	$740,000			$750,000

(continued)

(continued)

Allowance for Uncollectible Taxes	$ 8,000	8,000	10,000	$ 10,000
Accounts Payable	132,000	1,852,000	1,840,000	120,000
Fund Balance:				
Reserve for Encumbrances	—	1,000,000	1,070,000	70,000
Unreserved Balance	600,000	140,000	60,000	
			30,000	550,000
	$740,000			$750,000

The budget for the fiscal year ended June 30, 19X1, provided for estimated revenues of $2,000,000 and appropriations of $1,940,000.

REQUIRED

Prepare journal entries under current GAAP to record the budgeted and actual transactions for the fiscal year ended June 30, 19X1.

(Adapted from the May 1981 CPA Exam, Practice II.)

4-7 The general fund trial balance of the city of Solna at December 31, 19X2, was as follows:

	Dr.	Cr.
Cash	$ 62,000	
Taxes Receivable—Delinquent	46,000	
Estimated Uncollectible Taxes—Delinquent		$ 8,000
Stores Inventory—Program Operations	18,000	
Vouchers Payable		28,000
Fund Balance Reserved for Stores Inventory		18,000
Fund Balance Reserved for Encumbrances		12,000
Unreserved Fund Balance		60,000
	$126,000	$126,000

Collectible delinquent taxes are thought to be correctly estimated. Solna uses the "when consumed" method to account for stores inventory. Appropriations lapse at year end, but Solna is expected to pay for goods ordered out of the subsequent appropriation. The following data pertain to 19X3 general fund operations:

1. Budget adopted:

Revenues and Other Financing Sources:	
Taxes	$220,000
Fines, Forfeits, and Penalties	80,000
Intergovernmental Revenue	30,000
Miscellaneous Revenue	70,000
Share of Bond Issue Proceeds	200,000
	$600,000

Expenditures and Other Financing Uses:	
Program Operations	$300,000
General Administration	120,000
Stores—Program Operations	60,000
Capital Outlay	80,000
Periodic Transfer to Debt Service Fund	20,000
	$580,000

2. Taxes were assessed at an amount that would result in revenues of \$220,800, after a deduction of 4 percent of the tax levy as uncollectible.

3. Orders placed:

Program Operations	\$176,000
General Administration	80,000
Capital Outlay	60,000
	\$316,000

4. The city council designated \$20,000 of the unreserved fund balance for possible future appropriations for capital outlays.

5. Based on historical trend data and the state's economic forecast, the city estimates the following revenues from sources other than property taxes (assume intergovernmental revenue amount is not assured):

Fines, Forfeits, and Penalties	\$ 87,000
Intergovernmental Revenue	30,000
Miscellaneous Revenues	69,000
	\$186,000

6. Cash collections and transfers:

Delinquent Taxes	\$ 38,000
Current Taxes	226,000
Refund on Overpayment of Invoice for Purchase of Equipment, Prior Year	4,000
Fines, Forfeits, and Penalties	88,000
Intergovernmental Revenue	30,000
Miscellaneous Revenues	60,000
Share of Bond Proceeds for Operations	200,000
Transfer of Remaining Fund Balance of a Discontinued Fund	18,000
	\$664,000

7. Canceled encumbrances and recorded expenditures:

	Estimated	Actual
Program Operations	\$156,000	\$166,000
General Administration	84,000	80,000
Capital Outlay	62,000	62,000
	\$302,000	\$308,000

8. Additional vouchers:

Program Operations	\$188,000
General Administration	38,000
Capital Outlay	18,000
Transfer to Debt Service Fund	20,000
	\$264,000

9. Albert, a taxpayer, overpaid his 19X3 taxes by $2,000. He applied for a $2,000 credit against his 19X4 taxes. The city council granted his request.
10. Vouchers paid amounted to $580,000.
11. Stores inventory on December 31, 19X3, amounted to $12,000.

REQUIRED

1. Complete a worksheet for Solna for the year ending December 31, 19X3. Begin with the general fund trial balance at December 31, 19X2; use one set of columns for transactions and adjusting entries, one for a pre-closing trial balance, one for the operating statement, and one for the balance sheet. Assume that Solna uses the modified accrual basis of accounting.
2. Prepare a statement of revenues, expenditures, and changes in fund balance, by program, for the period ending December 31, 19X3.
(Adapted from the November 1984 CPA Exam, Practice II, #4)

4-8 Delvona County voted several years ago to implement an income tax on all income generated in the county. Its estimates have proven very inaccurate and the commissioners decided to obtain outside assistance in calculating the income tax revenues and receivables (liabilities) for income taxes. The county's finance officer provides the following information (all amounts are in $000):

1. Delvona's fiscal year ends June 30. The tax year ends December 31.
2. Employers are required to remit withholdings for each calendar quarter; the withholdings are due 15 days after the end of each calendar quarter.
3. Taxpayers' final tax returns and all remaining payments are due April 15 following the end of the tax year.
4. Delvona's June 30, 19X4, balance sheet reported income taxes receivable of $10,000, and income tax refunds (a liability) of $1,000; these amounts have not been adjusted since 6/30/X3.
5. Cash receipts and payments during the 19X4 fiscal year:
    Tax withholdings (amounts increased by 10 percent in 19X5 as a result of a 10 percent surtax applied first during calendar 19X5):

For Quarter Ending	Date Received	Amount
9/30/X4	10/15/X4	$11,500
12/31/X4	1/15/X5	11,500
3/31/X5	4/15/X5	12,650
6/30/X5	7/15/X5	12,650
Total Withholdings		$48,300

Note: When calculating revenue, note that even though the last payment was not received during the fiscal period, it pertains to income earned in that period.
    April 15, 19X5, settlement data:

Refunds Paid	(1,100)
Additional Payments Received	300
Amounts Reported as Due but	
Unpaid by Taxpayers	150
Refunds Reported but Not Paid	100

6. The $10,000 in Item 4 was received and the $1,000 liability (see Item 5) was paid.
7. Assume Delvona uses the flow of total financial resources model.

REQUIRED

Calculate Delvona's income tax revenue, receivables, and liabilities at June 30, 19X5, using the following format:

Description of Item	Amount	Revenue	Receivable	Liability

4-9 The city of Sitterville earmarks part of its property tax levy for general recreation programs. The city's general fund also contributes to the effort.

1. The Sitterville City Council adopted the following budget for its special revenue fund:

Estimated Revenues	$57,000
Estimated Transfers In	7,000
Appropriations	60,000

2. Following a statewide revaluation of property, estimated revenues were increased by $5,200. Spiraling inflation also led the council to increase the appropriations by $7,000.
3. The general fund contributed $8,000 to the fund's activities.
4. Projected revenues were accurate, and the amounts were received.
5. Expenditures, all previously encumbered, totaled $59,000. In addition, $1,000 of encumbered supply orders were not received before year end. The expenditures were paid.
6. The budgetary and nominal accounts were closed.

REQUIRED

Assuming Sitterville uses a budgetary fund balance, prepare the journal entries for the transactions described above under the modified accrual basis of accounting.

4-10 The pre-closing trial balance for Noxon County is as follows:

Noxon County
Pre-Closing Trial Balance
As of January 1, 19X6

Cash	$	11,190	
Taxes Receivable Current		19,800	
Less: Allowance for Uncollectible Taxes			$ 1,400
Interfund Loans Receivable		7,000	
Due from Other Governments		10,000	
Due from Other Funds		33,200	

(continued)

(continued)

Inventories	1,800	
Other Financial Assets	17,250	
Accounts Payable		15,150
Due to Other Funds		10,100
Fund Balance:		
Reserved for:		
Encumbrances		10,000
Inventories		1,800
Unreserved		55,090
Appropriations		678,000
Estimated Revenues	632,000	
Encumbrances	10,000	
Estimated Other Financing Sources	80,600	
Revenues:		
Licenses and Permits		25,800
Property Taxes		330,000
Federal Indirect Costs		105,000
Local Sales Tax		116,600
Other Revenues		15,600
Expenditures:		
General Government	139,400	
Public Safety and Corrections	133,100	
Transportation	1,800	
Health and Social Services	118,100	
Education and Cultural	48,000	
Resource Development and Recreation	113,700	
Economic Development and Assistance	8,800	
Debt Service	5,900	
Capital Outlay	3,200	
Other Financing Sources—Capital Lease		79,200
Operating Transfers Out	50,300	
Equity Transfers In		1,400
Totals	$1,445,140	$1,445,140

Noxon had a prior-period adjustment of a negative $2,300; before this adjustment the fund balance on January 1, 19X6, was $24,590.

REQUIRED

Prepare a statement of revenues, expenditures, and changes in fund balance, and a balance sheet for Noxon's general fund. The operating statement should be prepared by function.

4-11 A condensed pre-closing trial balance for the city of Salina Falls is shown here. The books have been maintained by an inexperienced accountant.

Salina Falls
Pre-Closing Trial Balance
December 31, 19X1

Cash	$ 16,300	
Receivables (net)	26,000	
Fixed assets	16,000	
Bonds payable	6,000	
Interest payable	900	
Unearned reveue		$ 11,000
Accounts payable		1,500
Due to other funds		9,100

(continued)

(continued)

Lease payable		16,000
Fund balance		22,300
Revenues		22,000
Estimated revenues	25,000	
Appropriations		27,800
Expenditures	20,000	
Encumbrances	2,000	
Reserve for Encumbrances		2,500
Totals	$112,200	$112,200

In talking with the bookkeeper, you learn the following additional information:

1. The receivables include current taxes receivable of $15,000 for which there is an allowance for uncollectible accounts of $1,200. The remainder of the receivable is a receivable from another fund for a short-term loan.
2. The general fund is responsible for making interest and principal payments on the one long-term serial bond Salina Falls has outstanding. The principal amount was $6,000 and the interest payment was $900.
3. The general fund received $11,000 from a restricted intergovernmental grant at the beginning of the year. During the year, qualifying expenditures totaled $5,000; the expenditures were recorded correctly.
4. Salina Falls entered into a long-term capital lease in order to purchase needed equipment.
5. A $500 order that had not been received at the end of last year was received in the current year. The remainder of the reserve for encumbrances pertain to the current year.

REQUIRED
1. Prepare the necessary adjusting journal entries for the Salina Falls general fund assuming the modified accrual basis of accounting is used.
2. Prepare the closing journal entries for Salina Falls.

4-12 Rafner County commissioners are uncertain about the impact on the county's financial statements with the adoption of the GASB accrual basis accounting. Selected county transactions for calendar year 19X8 are described below:

1. On July 1, the county's finance officer secured $10,000 of financing through a three-year note. The proceeds would be used to augment general fund cash depleted by deficits incurred during the past three years.
2. Property taxes totaling $300,000 were levied on January 15, 19X8. To absorb the cash flow shortage until June 1, the county borrows $100,000 through 10 percent tax anticipation notes on January 15. The notes are due June 15.
3. Other county revenues include sales taxes, fines and fees, and charges for services rendered. Pertinent dates and amounts appear below:
   Sales Taxes—merchant report showing amount due of $29,600 received on 2/29/X8; payment received on 3/30/X9.

Fines and Fees — various cash payments received throughout the year of $2,000 and fines enforceable on December 31, 19X8, of $680. These latter fines are expected to be paid by June 30, 19X9.

Charges for Services — A total of $60,000 was earned by December 31, 19X8, one-half of which will be paid to the county by March 1, 19X9.

4. On June 1, 19X8, a truck costing $57,000 was purchased by issuing a four-year, 10 percent note. Interest is due annually on June 1 (assume debt service payments are made by the general fund).

REQUIRED

Prepare the journal entries for these transactions under the accrual and the modified accrual bases of accounting. Explain why the entries are different under each basis of accounting.

4-13   One Horse County has always prepared its budgets and financial reports on the cash basis. Recently the decision has been made to modernize the accouting system. All budgets and reports will use the modified accrual basis of accounting and be prepared according to current GAAP. Last year's cash basis operating statement follows:

One Horse County
General Fund
Statement of Revenues, Expenditures,
and Changes in Fund Balance (Cash Basis)
For the Year Ended 12/31/X1

Revenues:		
Property Taxes	$24,000	
Sales Taxes	10,800	
Intergovernmental Revenue	6,000	
Fines and Fees	4,000	
Interest Revenue	1,000	
Total Revenues		$45,800
Expenditures:		
Salaries and Wages	$16,200	
Rent	5,800	
Insurance	3,000	
Supplies	1,400	
Miscellaneous	4,000	
Total Expenditures		30,400
Excess of Revenues over Expenditures		15,400
Debt Service		12,000
Excess of Revenues over Expenditures and Other Financing Uses		3,400
Fund Balance, January 1		(2,100)
Fund Balance, December 31		$ 1,300

ADDITIONAL INFORMATION

1. Property taxes levied in 19X1 totaled $27,000. They are due in equal installments on November 31, 19X1, and February 1, 19X2.
2. It is estimated that sales taxes collected by merchants in 19X1 were $12,000.

3. The intergovernmental revenue consists of two $3,000 grants—one can be used for any purpose, and the other is restricted to use for improving the local rodeo grounds. No expenditures have been made related to either grant.

4. The interest revenue relates to interest received on delinquent property tax payments. The amount was collected in January 19X1, and was expected.

5. At year end 19X0, employees had earned a total of $1,500 for which they had not yet been paid. At year end 19X1, that amount was $800.

6. The county has decided to use the "when consumed" method of recording supplies. The supplies inventory has increased by $700 during 19X1. All supplies are paid for in cash.

7. Annual rent has been the same for the last 10 years. The insurance policy was purchased on July 1, 19X1. It is a one-year policy.

8. Accounts payable related to miscellaneous expenses were $300 in 19X0 and $700 in 19X1.

9. One Horse has only one long-term debt issue. Payments are made through the general fund, and are due every January 31. During 19X0 $6,000 of interest was due; during 19X1, the amount was $5,500. Payments on the principal are $6,500 annually.

10. The net change from prior period adjustments is a positive $500.

REQUIRED

Convert the cash basis statement to modified accrual basis.

CHAPTER 5

Capital Projects Funds

In business, fixed assets are capitalized when they are put into service. If they are constructed by the firm, the costs are accumulated in a construction work-in-progress account and transferred to the fixed asset account when construction has been completed.

In government, costs of capital assets constructed by the entity are accumulated in a capital projects fund. When construction is completed, the fund is closed and the asset is transferred to the general fixed asset account group. Governmental entities also use capital projects funds to account for the purchase of some fixed assets. Bond proceeds, capital grants, or operating funds related to the acquisition or construction of land, buildings, and equipment are recorded in the fund. Any long-term debt associated with the construction or acquisition is recorded in the general long-term debt account group.

Accounting for the acquisition and construction of fixed assets is discussed in this chapter, which covers the basis of accounting and reporting for capital projects funds. As in Chapter 4, generally accepted accounting principles (GAAP) currently in effect are discussed in the body of the chapter; an appendix discusses GAAP after *Statement No. 11* becomes effective.

Also discussed are specific accounting applications, such as capitalizing interest on constructed assets; recording premiums, discounts, and accrued interest on bonds; investment practices; and special assessments. The chapter concludes with illustrative entries and financial statements for capital projects funds.

NATURE OF PROJECTS ACCOUNTED FOR IN CAPITAL PROJECTS FUNDS

A governmental entity has two types of fixed assets: those available for use by the entire entity (general fixed assets) and those available for use by the proprietary or fiduciary funds (specific purpose assets). General fixed assets can be acquired through the general fund, special revenue funds, or capital projects funds. Once acquired or constructed, these assets are recorded in the general fixed asset account group. Associated long-term debt is shown in the general long-term debt account group.

Specific and General Purpose Assets

Specific purpose assets are acquired by proprietary or fiduciary funds and are treated just like capital assets in a business. They are used only for the

141

express purpose of the acquiring fund, and their costs — in the form of depreciation — are charged to the operations of that fund. The construction and financing as well as the fixed assets and the long-term debt are recorded in the fund making the capital outlay.

Expenditures related to general purpose assets can occur in the general or special revenue funds or capital projects funds. The capital purchases made in the general fund or special revenue funds usually involve a lump-sum payment of operating funds for assets with limited lives, such as equipment. In other words, capital purchases whose cost is easily traced to a single invoice and a single payment that do not involve debt financing are generally recorded in these funds. The cost of these assets is recorded as an expenditure in the fund making the payment, and the asset's cost is capitalized in the general fixed asset account group.

Capital Projects Fund Acquisitions

All general purpose fixed assets whose expenditures are not recorded in the general fund or special revenue funds are recorded in the capital projects funds. Although capital projects funds are not required by GAAP, local laws or regulations usually mandate establishing such funds for **major** capital acquisitions. Accounting for all sources of financing and expenditures for a given capital asset in a single fund facilitates the calculation of the asset's total cost. *Major* refers not only to the relative size of a project but also to those acquisitions involving long-term financing and/or requiring several periods to complete.

Like capital acquisitions procured by the general fund or special revenue funds, the fixed asset is recorded in the fixed asset account group. The cash received from debt financing is shown in the capital projects funds, but the long-term liability is entered into the long-term debt account group. Exhibit 5-1 summarizes the relationships among the funds and account groups.

Budgeting and Financing Capital Projects

Capital purchases made through a general or special revenue fund are budgeted as part of the operating budget as a "capital outlay." For capital acquisitions accounted for in a capital projects fund, the governmental unit usually establishes a separate capital budget. Most commonly the budget for the total cost of the project is approved at the beginning of the project, in which case appropriations do not lapse until the project is completed.

Most large capital acquisitions are financed by debt, or by a combination of debt, intergovernmental grants, and operating transfers. Debt financing usually involves issuing long-term bonds. Short-term financing may also be used, for example, while the entity is waiting for the best time to issue long-term debt.

Exhibit 5-1

Relationship Between Capital Projects Funds and Other Funds/Account Groups

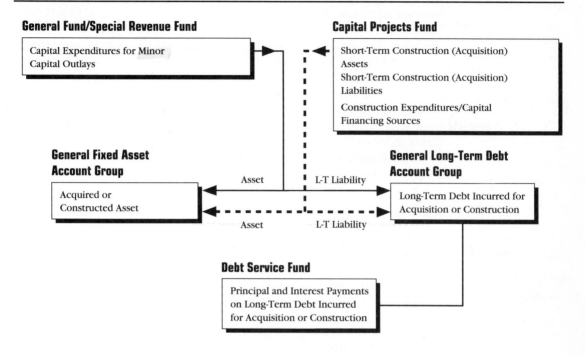

GENERALLY ACCEPTED ACCOUNTING PRACTICES

Capital projects funds use modified accrual accounting. Project expenditures are accrued when the related liability is incurred and revenues are recognized when measurable and available. When a project is financed by intergovernmental revenues restricted for capital purposes, the revenue is assumed to be measurable and available when the related expenditures are made. For example, if a governmental unit provided $500,000 for financing a project covering 19X1 and 19X2, and the expenditures on that grant totaled $200,000 in 19X1 and $300,000 in 19X2, $200,000 of revenue would be recognized in 19X1 and $300,000 in 19X2.

"Other financing sources," such as bond proceeds and transfers from other funds, have different recognition rules. Bond proceeds are recognized when the bonds are sold. Transfers from other funds are recognized when the transferring fund has the obligation to make the transfer. Neither bond proceeds nor transfers are considered revenues; they are shown in an "other financing sources" subsection of the operating statement following the excess of revenues over expenditures.

Budgetary accounts usually are integrated into the accounting system. If so, when the project is approved, estimated revenue is debited for the

[handwritten margin notes: restricted revenue]

[handwritten margin notes: OFS / bond proceeds / transfers]

est revenue xx
est fin sources xx
  Appropriations xx
  ↓
For est. expend.
or operating trf out

(opposite of
normal balances)

amount of intergovernmental or other revenue. The "estimated financing sources" account is debited for any anticipated bond proceeds or operating transfers. Appropriations are credited for the estimated expenditures or any operating transfers out. What amounts are debited or credited depends upon whether the oversight board approval covers the entire project or a single operating period. Subsidiary accounts are maintained for each type of revenue and expenditure. For example, the control account for estimated other financing sources probably would have one subsidiary account for bond proceeds and one for operating transfers.

Encumbrance accounting may be used for capital projects funds. When the contract is signed for the construction, for example, encumbrances and budgetary fund balance — reserve for encumbrances are debited and credited respectively for the entire amount of the contract. If a governmental entity constructs its own facility, encumbrances are debited as purchase orders are issued.

Accounting Issues

Mod accrual
Budgetary accts
encumbrance accts

Use of modified accrual accounting, integration of the budgetary accounts, and encumbrance accounting make the accounting for capital projects funds similar to other governmental funds. Nevertheless, accounting issues unique to these funds arise regarding temporary financing, interest capitalization, premiums and discounts, and investment of idle funds.

Short-Term Borrowing A governmental entity may use short-term debt to finance the early construction phases. The debt is usually described as bond anticipation notes because it is issued to provide the flexibility necessary to secure better rates on long-term issues. For example, in a declining market, the entity might issue bond anticipation notes rather than delay construction until long-term rates fall to the lowest level anticipated. The notes are repaid from the proceeds of the long-term debt.

BANs

Governmental entities may report bond anticipation notes as "other financing sources" in the capital projects fund and long-term debt in the general long-term debt account group when:

> (1) all legal steps have been taken to refinance the bond anticipation notes and (2) the intent is supported by an ability to consummate refinancing the short-term note on a long-term basis in accordance with the criteria set forth in FASB *Statement No. 6, Classification of Short-Term Obligations Expected to Be Refinanced*.[1]

Governmental entities try to meet the conditions necessary to classify bond anticipation notes as long-term debt. Those that do not qualify as general long-term debt are reported as a liability in the capital projects fund. Because they are reported as a liability rather than as "other financing sources," any construction expenditures made during the period will create a deficit

---

[1]Governmental Accounting Standards Board, *Codification of Governmental Accounting and Financial Reporting Standards* (Norwalk, Conn.: GASB, 1993), sec. B50.101.

fund balance. The deficit is temporary, but does occasionally cause concern among financial statement users who may not understand that the deficit will be eliminated when the long-term debt is issued.

Interest on bond anticipation notes and other short-term borrowings is reported in and paid by the capital projects fund. It is included as part of the project cost.

Interest Capitalization   Business entities capitalize interest costs incurred during the construction phase of certain assets. Financial Accounting Standards Board *Statement No. 34* indicates that interest costs that could have been avoided by not constructing the asset should be capitalized.

The amount of interest capitalized is based on the rate of interest times the average construction expenditures during the period. If the project is not financed specifically by one debt issue, but rather parts of the total are from several different debt issues, the interest rate used is the weighted average rate of interest on all borrowings. To illustrate the principles involved, assume that construction expenditures were as follows:

financed by one debt issue

*interest rate
× avg construction expenditures*

financed by several debt issues

*weighted-average interest rate on all borrowings
× avg construction expenditures*

	Construction Expenditures
January–April	$ 850,000
May–August	900,000
September–October	400,000
November–December	150,000
Total	$2,300,000

Calculation of Average Construction Expenditures:

January–April	$ 850,000 × 4 = $ 3,400,000
May–August	900,000
	$1,750,000 × 4 = 7,000,000
September–October	400,000
	$2,150,000 × 2 = 4,300,000
November–December	150,000
	$2,300,000 × 2 = 4,600,000
Total	$19,300,000

Average Construction Expenditures = $19,300,000/12 = $1,608,333

If the interest rate on the loan used to finance this construction is 9 percent, the amount capitalized is $144,750 ($1,608,333 × .09). On the other hand, if the construction expenditures could not be traced to a specific debt issue, the weighted average interest rate is used:

Loan 1	$1,000,000		10.0 percent
Loan 2	3,000,000		8.5 percent
$1,000,000 × .10	=	$100,000	
3,000,000 × .085	=	255,000	
Total	=	$355,000	
$355,000/$4,000,000	=	.0888	

Under these circumstances, the interest capitalized would total $142,820 ($1,608,333 × .0888).

Added Complexities for Governmental Entities. When constructing general purpose assets, governmental entities can either capitalize or expense interest costs during construction. The option selected must be described completely in the financial statements and applied consistently. In proprietary funds where the goal is to break even, however, the GASB requires interest capitalization.

Giving governmental entities the option to expense or capitalize interest costs in capital projects funds has created considerable controversy. Some argue that only by capitalizing interest costs can construction efficiencies of business and governmental entities be compared. Proponents also argue that capitalizing interest in one type of fund while not in the other does not make sense; the cost of an asset should not be determined by the fund responsible for its construction.

Those who support not capitalizing interest costs for general purpose assets and capitalization for proprietary fund assets maintain that the goals are not the same. The "break-even" goal of proprietary funds makes full costing important in those funds. Otherwise, comparison between similar governmental and business activities is impossible. The only purpose of capital projects funds is to account for the construction and acquisition of general purpose fixed assets; since comparison to businesses is irrelevant, full costing of assets is unnecessary.

▲   **OBSERVATION**

As long as governmental entities take depreciation only in proprietary funds, the controversy surrounding capitalization in the capital projects funds seems unimportant. Interest capitalization and subsequent depreciation assures proper matching of revenues and expenses. If depreciation is not taken, the matching principle is violated unless debt payments are used as a surrogate. If debt payments are a good surrogate, then the interest expense already has been matched with appropriate revenues.

Treatment of Interest Earnings. If a governmental entity decides to capitalize interest costs for assets constructed through the capital projects fund, it should follow *SFAS No. 34.* The FASB statement requires the entity to offset any interest earned from investing bond proceeds prior to construction against the interest costs. Continuing with the earlier example, the total interest to be capitalized was $142,820. Had the entity invested the proceeds of the $1,000,000 loan for three months prior to construction at 7 percent, it would have earned $17,500 ($1,000,000 × .07 × .25). The $17,500 would be offset against the $142,820, and only $132,320 would be capitalized.

▲   **OBSERVATION**

Under *Statement No. 34,* this offsetting of interest earnings and interest expense is appropriate only for tax-exempt borrowings. Most bonds issued for capital projects and accounted for in capital projects funds are tax exempt.

Recording Capitalized Interest Costs. Any interest capitalized as part of the asset cost should not be reflected in the capital projects fund. When the debt service fund makes an interest payment, expenditures are debited and cash credited for the amount of the interest. Upon completion of the construction, the portion of the interest capitalized is added to the asset's cost when it is recorded in the general fixed asset account group.

add. capitalized interest to asset's cost in GFAAG, at completion

Premiums and Discounts on Long-Term Debt Issues   Unlike the for-profit treatment, governmental units do not amortize discounts or premiums on debt issued by a capital projects fund. Instead, premiums or discounts are reported as other financing sources or uses under a caption of "issuance premium or discount." Issuance costs, such as underwriter fees, are reported as expenditures when the debt is issued. For example, if $1,000,000 of bonds are issued at 101, and underwriter fees total $67,000, the entry in the capital projects fund is:

Cash	943,000	*⎱ 1,100,000*
Expenditures	67,000	*⎰*
Other Financing Sources—		
Bond Proceeds		1,000,000
Other Financing Sources—		
Issuance Premium		10,000 *→ DSF transfer*

As suggested by this example, premiums could increase the resources available for a capital project, and discounts could decrease the total amount spent on the project. Whether the bond premium or discount is allowed to affect the project's budget depends on local regulations. Frequently, governmental units will establish a budget excluding the effects of any premiums or discounts. If the bonds are sold at a premium, the premium will be deposited directly in or transferred to the debt service fund for purposes of paying interest or principal amounts on the debt. Under such a policy, any discount is offset by an operating transfer in for the same amount. Transferring the $10,000 premium shown in the previous example would be recorded as follows:

Operating Transfers Out	10,000	
Cash		10,000

Accrued Interest on Debt   If a governmental unit issues debt between interest dates, the purchase price includes the interest accrued to date. For example, on $1,000,000 of 9 percent bonds sold two months after the last interest payment, the accrued interest totals $15,000 ($1,000,000 $\times$ .09 $\times$ 2/12). Ignoring any premium or discount, the bond price would be $1,015,000. Because the accrued interest will be paid on the next interest payment date, the $15,000 cannot be spent on the project. It would be transferred to the debt service fund, or recorded in that fund directly. The latter option is preferable as it will not clutter the capital projects fund.

Investing Idle Cash   Normally bonds approved for a capital project will be issued in one lump sum, not as the money is needed for the project. Because

*interest
earnings on
idle cash go
to DSF*

construction may take several months or years to complete, the governmental entity may have idle cash during the early phases of construction. This idle cash is invested. Any interest earnings on idle funds usually cannot be used for project expenditures; instead, the interest earnings are recorded directly in the debt service fund or transferred to that fund for making principal and interest payments.

The practice of investing idle cash at rates higher than those paid on the debt is called **arbitrage.** Internal Revenue Service requirements generally preclude arbitrage by governmental entities. Any governmental unit violating the Internal Revenue's arbitrage rulings runs the risk of having the interest payments taxable to bondholders. Bondholders would pay income taxes on the interest received from bonds purchased from the governmental entity. Because one reason for investing in governmental debt is to avoid federal income taxes on the interest income, the Internal Revenue Service regulations effectively preclude most arbitrage.

Installment Purchases When title passes, an installment purchase is reported as a capital expenditure and other financing source. Purchase of general fixed assets in this manner could take place in the general fund, special revenue funds, or capital projects funds. Under such circumstances, the rate reflected on any related debt must be "fair and adequate." If the rate is not fair and adequate, the expenditure should be reported at its fair market value or at the market value of the note, whichever is more clearly determinable.

Any difference between market value and the face amount of the debt should be reported as an issuance discount or premium and classified as an other financing source or use. Stated differently, discounts or premiums are not amortized over the life of the debt as they are in for-profit entities.

Operating Considerations

Generally accepted accounting principles do not fully address some operating issues, such as the number of funds to establish and the appropriate treatment for multiperiod projects. Making these managerial decisions requires a good understanding of the options available to governmental entities as well as an ability to analyze an entity's legal constraints.

Establishing the Proper Number of Funds Governmental entities often approve more than one major capital project for a single year. They must determine whether to establish a separate fund for each capital project. The Governmental Accounting Standards Board (GASB) guidance on this issue is limited. One accounting principle directs the entities to "maintain those funds required by law and sound financial administration."[2] Compliance with legal constraints is easy; if the law says one fund for each capital project, that practice must be followed. If the law is silent, however, and the number must be consistent with operating requirements, the decision is far more difficult.

[2]GASB, *Codification,* sec. 1100.104 and sec. 1300.108.

Criteria for determining the number of funds needed include necessary control over expenditures, type of financing, and the needs of financial statement users. Large projects involving several contractors or subcontractors, in which control over expenditures may be difficult, are prime candidates for separate funds.

Bond indentures frequently require the governmental entity to demonstrate that the proceeds were spent in accordance with its provisions. This demonstration is easier if each debt issue, and therefore each capital project, is accounted for in a separate fund.

The needs of statement users should be taken into consideration when determining the number of funds. Whether information on individual projects or groups of projects is more relevant to users depends, in part, on how the projects are budgeted. If a separate budget is prepared for each one, users probably intend to have each reported separately. Establishing a separate fund facilitates separate reporting. The sophistication of the users also affects the level of detail provided for each project.

A common practice is to establish a separate fund for each major project and a single fund for all minor projects. This resembles the treatment for construction work in progress for businesses, except that in business the accounts are subaccounts, not separate funds.

Accounting for Multiyear Projects   Governmental operating activities are planned and evaluated on an annual basis. For example, most budget-to-actual comparisons, as well as the results of operations, are geared to an annual operating cycle. Nonetheless, capital outlays for major capital projects are planned and evaluated on a project basis. The governmental entity has to develop some reporting practice that facilitates both annual and project reporting.

GAAP requires reporting the project's financial resources and expenditures for the current period as well as for total transactions to date. Fund administrators must decide how best to comply with GAAP. One option is to close the books each period and prepare a summary statement using the current-year and prior-period(s) statements in order to show the transactions to date. The major advantage of this method is the amounts shown in the general ledger will correspond to those in the financial statements. However, it is time-consuming.

Another option is to leave the accounts open and prepare a worksheet as though the books had been closed. In other words, although no entries would be made in the accounting records, closing entries would be performed on a worksheet. This option saves time; the accountant does not have to reopen encumbrance records or make any reversing entries. The disadvantage is that the financial statements and the general ledger amounts are not the same at the end of each period. Both methods are demonstrated later in connection with the illustrative transactions and financial statements.

A Single Debt Issue for Several Capital Projects   Selling one bond issue to finance several capital projects does not eliminate the need to report financial information by project. Administrators allocate the debt proceeds to several capital projects funds according to the amount approved for each project. This approach assures reporting by project; a note clarifies the fact that a single debt issue covers these separately reported projects.

Another approach is to account for all projects covered by a single debt issue in one fund. Adopting this option requires that expenditures and revenues related to the individual projects be separately identified. For example, if one bond issue covered both a street paving and a building project, each project should have separate expenditure and encumbrance control and subsidiary accounts. Construction expenditures of $500,000—$100,000 on the paving project and $400,000 on the building project—would be recorded as:

Expenditures—Paving	100,000	
Expenditures—Building	400,000	
Vouchers Payable		500,000

The budgetary, encumbrance, financing sources, and expenditure accounts would be identified separately, as would the fund balance, in the balance sheet. Other balance sheet accounts, such as cash or due from other funds, may not be identified by project.

ILLUSTRATED FINANCIAL TRANSACTIONS

Governmental entities conduct a number of different types of capital outlay activities—leases, installment purchases, outright acquisitions, and construction—in capital projects funds. They have considerable latitude in terms of the number of funds established and the way in which multiperiod projects are treated.

The diversity of projects and accounting approaches is illustrated by showing the transactions for a single construction project spanning two years. Other types of capital projects also are discussed and illustrated.

Comprehensive Capital Project

On January 1, 19X1, the Arkon City Council approved a capital project involving the construction of a new wing on city hall. The project is financed by a bond issue, a contribution from the general fund, and a grant from state government.

Year 1: Arkon City Council approves a total budget of $2,100,000, of which an estimated $1,500,000 will come from issuing bonds, $400,000 from a state grant, and $200,000 from the general fund.

1.	Estimated Other Financing Sources	1,700,000	
	Estimated Revenues—Intergovernmental Grant	400,000	
	Appropriations—Capital Outlay		2,100,000

Although not illustrated here, Arkon could open a separate subsidiary account for each type of other financing source — one for bond proceeds and one for operating transfers.

· OBSERVATION   ▲

Whether the transfer from the general fund is an operating or an equity transfer is debatable. A governmental unit that consistently finances part of its capital outlay program from operating resources probably would classify the transfer as operating.

The 7 percent 20-year bonds are issued on July 2 at 101. Bond premiums cannot be spent on the project, and Arkon capitalizes appropriate interest costs. The bonds issued are tax-exempt.

2.	Cash	1,515,000	
	Other Financing Sources — Bond		
	Proceeds		1,500,000
	Due to Debt Service Fund		15,000

Simultaneously, the debt service fund would debit due from other funds and credit revenues. The bond premium can be treated in any of several ways as long as the transaction does not increase the amount available to be spent on the project. For example, the $15,000 could have been reported directly by the debt service fund; if this option is followed, the debit to cash and the credit to proceeds in the capital projects fund would be for $1,500,000. The $15,000 would be reported as a debit to cash and a credit to revenues in the debt service fund.

Alternatively, the capital projects fund could report debt proceeds for the entire amount of the cash received. Under this option a second entry would be necessary: a debit to operating transfers and a credit to cash. The option shown in entry 2 or the option of reporting the $15,000 directly in the debt service fund seem preferable to recording the full proceeds in the capital projects fund and then transferring the premium to the debt service fund. These options require fewer entries, and therefore simplify the process.

Arkon receives an advance of $125,000 on the state grant, and the interfund receivable is established for the amount contributed by the general fund.

3.	Due from Other Funds	200,000	
	Cash	125,000	
	Other Financing Sources — Operating		
	Transfers		200,000
	Deferred Revenues — Intergovernmental		
	Grant		125,000

Because the intergovernmental revenue is restricted to capital outlays, revenue can be recognized only when the revenue is earned — that is, when the related expenditures are made.

With the cash advance from the state, Arkon calculates that it has enough cash to begin the project. It invests the bond proceeds (except for the amount due to the debt service fund) in a three-month 6 percent certificate of deposit.

4. Investments	1,500,000	
Cash		1,500,000

The contract for a $2,000,000 project is awarded to a local contractor. The remaining $100,000 budgeted ($2,100,000 − $2,000,000) involves costs incurred directly by Arkon. Such costs include architectural and other professional fees. Under the terms of the agreement, contract payments are based on submission of invoices showing costs incurred to date. Five percent of all contract payments is withheld until completion of the entire project. Just as in business, some percentage is withheld to cover any costs associated with the contractor's failure to comply with the contract.

5. Encumbrances	2,000,000	
Budgetary Fund Balance—Reserve for		
Encumbrances		2,000,000

An architect is selected and paid an advance of $3,000 toward the total contract price of $68,000. Advances to contractors are just like advances to employees; they do not represent expenditures until the contractor has accomplished the work.

6. Advance on Contract	3,000	
Encumbrances	68,000	
Cash		3,000
Budgetary Fund Balance—Reserve for		
Encumbrances		68,000

The architect completes the drawings; they are approved by Arkon's city planners, and the entire architectural fee is paid.

7. Budgetary Fund Balance—Reserve for		
Encumbrances	68,000	
Expenditures	68,000	
Encumbrances		68,000
Cash		65,000
Advance on Contract		3,000

A budgetary fund balance—reserve for encumbrances account is used in this chapter rather than simply reserve for encumbrances to allow for maintaining these reserves from one period to the next. As will be illustrated later in the chapter, the unreserved fund balance—reserve for encumbrances will be established at the end of the period. In other chapters, all budgetary accounts are closed at period end, making it unnecessary to add the qualifier of "budgetary fund balance" to each entry establishing a reserve for encumbrances.

The city pays legal and other miscellaneous expenses related to the project of $32,000.

actual *pay it one check* *write one check*

8.	Expenditures	32,000	
	Cash		32,000

The general fund transfers its share of project costs to the capital projects fund.

(3)

9.	Cash	200,000	
	Due from Other Funds		200,000

A progress billing received from the contractor shows total expenditures on the project of $230,000, or $20,000 less than anticipated for this portion of the project. The progress billing is paid.

5% withheld

10.	Budgetary Fund Balance—Reserve for		
	Encumbrances	250,000	
	Expenditures	230,000	
	Encumbrances		250,000
	Contracts Payable		218,500
	Contracts Payable—Retained		
	Percentage (230,000 × .05)		11,500
11.	Contracts Payable *(record actual payment)*	218,500	
	Cash		218,500

230,000 *11,500*

The certificate of deposit matures; $1,000,000 is reinvested in another certificate of deposit. Just as with premiums, the capital projects fund does not retain any of the interest earnings to increase the scope of the project. Even though the interest earnings may be used to calculate the total cost of the project recorded in the general fixed asset account group, the cash related to such earnings is recorded directly by the debt service fund and held for interest and principal payments on the bonds.

12.	Cash	500,000	
	Investments		500,000

The debt service fund records the $22,500 (1,500,000 × .06 × 3/12). Entry 12 shows the net effect of rolling over part of the money into another certificate of deposit. Alternatively, an entry could be made showing the receipt of the entire $1,500,000, followed by an entry reinvesting the $1,000,000.

The second progress billing is received for $310,000, the exact amount estimated for this portion of the contract. The contractor is paid.

13.	Expenditures	310,000	
	Budgetary Fund Balance—Reserve for		
	Encumbrances		310,000

(continued)

Encumbrances	310,000
Contracts Payable—Retained	
Percentage (310,000 × .05)	15,500
Cash	294,500

The debt service fund is responsible for making debt service payments and it receives the interest on any investments made by the capital projects fund. Therefore, no entry pertaining to these items is made in the capital projects fund.

Expenditures pertaining to the intergovernmental grant are calculated in the same ratio as the total grant bears to the total project (rounded to the nearest whole percent):

Intergovernmental Proportion: $400,000/$2,100,000 = 19 percent
Intergovernmental Revenue Earned in First Year = Intergovernmental
    Proportion × Total Expenditures:
.19 × ($68,000 + $32,000 + $310,000 + $230,000) = $121,600

14.	Deferred Revenue—Intergovernmental Grant	121,600
	Intergovernmental Revenue	121,600

No receivable is recorded because the advance of $125,000 (see entry 3) still exceeds the amount earned.

Closing the Books at the End of the First Year   Arkon closes its books annually even though budgetary authority is given for the entire project. Other than the $20,000 underbudget for expenditures (see entry 10), the amounts budgeted for the first year equal amounts expended or received. The pre-closing trial balance is as follows:

City of Arkon
Pre-Closing Trial Balance
December 31, 19X1

	Dr.	Cr.
Cash	$ 227,000	
Investments	1,000,000	
Contracts Payable—Retained Percentage		$ 27,000
Deferred Revenue		3,400
Due to Other Funds		15,000
Estimated Other Financing Sources—Bond Proceeds	1,500,000	
Estimated Other Financing Sources—Operating Transfers	200,000	
Estimated Revenues	400,000	
Appropriations		2,100,000
Other Financing Sources—Operating Transfers		200,000
Other Financing Sources—Bonds		1,500,000
Intergovernmental Revenue		121,600
Expenditures	640,000	
Encumbrances	1,440,000	
Budgetary Fund Balance—Reserve for Encumbrances		1,440,000
	$5,407,000	$5,407,000

As illustrated in entry 15, appropriations and estimated revenues have balances after the closing. Budgetary accounts established at the beginning of the project are closed only for amounts related to the first year's revenues and expenditures because the budgetary authority carries over into the second year. The unreserved budgetary fund balance is debited for the difference between the "expended" appropriations authority and "actual" revenues and other financing sources. Differences between budgetary amounts do not affect the **fund balance,** only the **budgetary fund balance.**

15.	Appropriations—Capital Outlay	640,000	
	(68,000 + 32,000 + 310,000 + 230,000)		
	Budgetary Fund Balance—Unreserved	1,181,600	
	Estimated Other Financing Sources—		
	Bond Proceeds		1,500,000
	Estimated Other Financing Sources—		
	Operating Transfers		200,000
	Estimated Revenues—		
	Intergovernmental		121,600

The nonbudgetary nominal accounts are closed.

16.	Revenues	121,600	
	Other Financing Sources—Bond Proceeds	1,500,000	
	Other Financing Sources—Operating Transfers	200,000	
	Expenditures		640,000
	Unreserved Fund Balance		1,181,600

In contrast to the closing of budgetary accounts, the difference between actual revenues and expenditures affects the **unreserved fund balance.**

Accounts not yet affected by these closing entries are encumbrances and budgetary fund balance—reserve for encumbrances. Because the project is incomplete, these two accounts remain open. Both show the unexpended but committed portion of the contract.

Because they are budgetary accounts, neither the encumbrances nor the budgetary fund balance are shown on the financial statements. Therefore, one additional entry is required: the unreserved fund balance (which was credited with the difference between the actual revenues and expenditures) must be reserved for the remaining commitment on the contract.

17.	Unreserved Fund Balance	1,440,000	
	Unreserved Fund Balance—Reserve		
	for Encumbrances		1,440,000

Because the budgetary accounts carry the appropriated reserve, entry 17 would be reversed at the beginning of the next year.

After these closing entries the unreserved fund balance shows a deficit of $258,400 (composed of a credit of $1,181,600 from entry 16 and a debit of $1,440,000 from entry 17). The deficit traces to the fact that not all of the revenue was received in the first year, but the entire project was encumbered.

400,000
- 121,600
278,400

The $258,400 represents the remaining amount to be collected from the state grant of $278,400 less the underexpenditure of $20,000 (see entry 10).

▲ **OBSERVATION**

The amount of the deficit is meaningless because presumably the remaining revenue from a state grant will be collected. It confuses statement users who may be unaware of accounting practices and presume that any deficit is bad.

Worksheet Approach to Closing Entries   Arkon could produce the same information without actually closing its books. Exhibit 5-2 shows a worksheet approach for preparing financial statements. The entries in the "closing entries" column form the basis of the operating statement, and the post-closing trial balance provides the information necessary for the balance sheet.

Exhibit 5-2

City of Arkon Worksheet for Preparing Financial Statements
Capital Projects Fund
First Fiscal Year Ending December 31, 19X1

ACCOUNTS	PRE-CLOSING TRIAL BALANCE		CLOSING ENTRIES* (WORKSHEET ONLY)		POST-CLOSING TRIAL BALANCE	
	Dr.	Cr.	Dr.	Cr.	Dr.	Cr.
Cash	227,000				227,000	
Investments	1,000,000				1,000,000	
Contracts Payable—Retained Percentage		27,000				27,000
Deferred Revenue		3,400				3,400
Due to Other Funds		15,000				15,000
Estimated Other Financing Sources— Bond Proceeds	1,500,000			1,500,000[1]		
Estimated Other Financing Sources— Operating Transfers	200,000			200,000[1]		
Estimated Revenue	400,000			121,600[1]	278,400	
Appropriations		2,100,000	640,000[1]			1,460,000
Other Financing Sources—Operating Transfers		200,000	200,000[2]			
Other Financing Sources—Bonds		1,500,000	1,500,000[2]			
Intergovernmental Revenue		121,600	121,600[2]			
Expenditures	640,000			640,000[2]		
Encumbrances	1,440,000				1,440,000	
Budgetary Fund Balance—Reserve for Encumbrances		1,440,000				1,440,000
	5,407,000	5,407,000				
Reserve for Encumbrances				1,440,000[3]		1,440,000
Budgetary Fund Balance—Unreserved			1,181,600[1]		1,181,600	
Unreserved Fund Balance			1,440,000[3]	1,181,600[2]	258,400	
			5,083,200	5,083,200	4,385,400	4,385,400

*Closing entries 1, 2, and 3 correspond to closing entries in text numbered 15, 16, and 17, respectively.

Year 2: Entry 17 is reversed before any transactions are recorded.

| 18. | Unreserved Fund Balance—Reserve for Encumbrances | 1,440,000 | |
| | Unreserved Fund Balance | | 1,440,000 |

The certificate of deposit matures; no further investments are made.

| 19. | Cash | 1,000,000 | |
| | Investments | | 1,000,000 |

The remaining portion of the intergovernmental grant is received, and the capital projects fund transfers the amount due to the debt service fund.

20.	Cash (400,000 − 125,000)	275,000	
	Deferred Revenue		275,000	— liability
21.	Due to Debt Service Fund	15,000	
	Cash		15,000

Arkon agrees to a $5,000 change order, after which the contractor submits the last progress billing for $1,445,000. The project is reviewed and determined satisfactorily completed; the contractor is paid the final billing and the retained percentage.

22.	Encumbrances	5,000	
	Budgetary Fund Balance—Reserve for Encumbrances		5,000
23.	Budgetary Fund Balance—Reserve for Encumbrances	1,445,000	
	Expenditures	1,445,000	
	Contracts Payable—Retained Percentage	27,000	
	Encumbrances		1,445,000
	Cash		1,472,000

The reserve for encumbrances debit includes the amount encumbered in the prior year ($1,440,000) plus the change order of $5,000. Once the completed construction is approved, the contractor is paid the amount retained throughout the contract period. If the construction is not satisfactory, a portion of the retained percentage is not paid to the contractor.

Now that the total project is complete, the remaining revenue on the intergovernmental grant can be recognized.

| 24. | Deferred Revenue (400,000 − 121,600) | 278,400 | |
| | Revenue | | 278,400 |

Because the project did not cost the exact amount budgeted and depending upon the nature of the grant from the state, a portion of the grant may have to be returned. For simplicity, this consequence is ignored in the illustration.

Closing the Books in Year 2   Regardless of the approach taken to prepare financial statements at the end of year 1, the books must be closed at the end of year 2. The project is complete and the appropriation authority lapses.

The encumbrance and budgetary fund balance — reserve for encumbrance accounts have zero balances, so closing involves only the balances in the budgetary accounts and the expenditures and revenues for the period.

25.	Appropriations	1,460,000	
	Estimated Revenues—Intergovernmental		278,400
	Budgetary Fund Balance—Unreserved		1,181,600
26.	Revenues	278,400	
	Unreserved Fund Balance	1,166,600	
	Expenditures		1,445,000

(handwritten in margin: #15   2,100,000 − 640,000 = 1460,000)
(handwritten: 400,000 − 121,600 = 278,400)

Expenditures for the period exceeded the amount anticipated, but as shown in Exhibit 5-5, the entire project is still under budget. In the first year, $20,000 less than expected was expended; $5,000 more than anticipated was expended during the second year. Thus, the unreserved fund balance and the cash account both carry the $15,000 difference.

Closing a Capital Projects Fund   Any unexpended funds are transferred to either the general fund or the debt service fund. When long-term debt is associated with the project, the transfer is usually to the debt service fund. Because the transfer is permanent and is not considered a recurring event, the transaction is classified as an equity transfer.

27.	Equity Transfer Out	15,000	
	Cash		15,000

The debt service fund records a debit to cash and a credit to equity transfers. The final entry in the capital projects fund closes the unreserved fund balance.

28.	Unreserved Fund Balance	15,000	
	Equity Transfer Out		15,000

All accounts now show a zero balance. Consequently, only operating statements are prepared for the Arkon capital projects fund at the end of the second year. Once the capital project is completed, the asset is recorded in the general fixed asset account group.

Capitalizing Interest Costs   If Arkon follows the practice of capitalizing interest, the asset's cost must include the interest incurred during construction. The computations are shown in Exhibit 5-3, and the entry to record the total project cost of $2,116,158 would be made in the general fixed asset account group. Interest is capitalized during the period in which the asset is being constructed. To simplify the computations, the expenditures were assumed to occur all in the first quarter in year 2 and throughout the first year (see Exhibit 5-3).

Exhibit 5-3

City of Arkon
Computation of Capitalized Interest Costs
City Hall Project

ASSUMED PATTERN OF CAPITAL EXPENDITURES:

	Year 1	Year 2
January 1–March 31	$100,000	$1,445,000
April 1–July 31	400,000	-0-
August 1–September 30	100,000	-0-
October 1–December 31	40,000	-0-
Total	$640,000	$1,445,000

AVERAGE CONSTRUCTION EXPENDITURES—YEAR 1

January–March	$100,000 × 3 =	$ 300,000
April–July	400,000	
	$500,000 × 4 =	2,000,000
August–September	100,000	
	$600,000 × 2 =	1,200,000
October–December	40,000	
	$640,000 × 3 =	1,920,000
		$5,420,000

Average Construction Expenditures: $5,420,000/12 = $451,667
Capitalized Interest: $451,667 × .07 = 31,617

AVERAGE CONSTRUCTION EXPENDITURES—YEAR 2

January–March		$2,116,617 × 3/12 = $ 529,154[a]
Interest Expense:		
Year 1—$451,667 × .07	=	$ 31,617
Year 2—$529,154 × .07	=	37,041
Total Interest Expense		$ 68,658
Interest Earnings:		
$1,500,000 × .06 × .25	=	$ 22,500
$1,000,000 × .06 × .25	=	15,000
Total Interest Earnings		(37,500)
Net Interest Expense to Capitalize		$31,158
Total Cost of Asset:		
Construction Costs		$2,085,000
Interest Capitalized		31,158
Total Cost		$2,116,158

[a]The $2,116,617 includes the carryover from year 1 of $640,000 plus the capitalized interest of $31,617. The investment earnings were not netted until the end of construction.

Handwritten annotations: 640,000 / 31,617 / 1,445,000 / 2,116,617

Handwritten: on CDs

Handwritten: in ✗ 68+32+230 + 310+1445

OTHER TYPES OF CAPITAL PROJECTS

Special Assessment Projects

Governmental entities sometimes construct facilities benefiting only a select group of constituents. Examples of such projects include street lighting, sewers, and gutters. If the constituents approve the project, a special improvement district encompassing the affected taxpayers is established. Those within the district are responsible for paying the project costs. Usually, long-term bonds are issued; each year the special improvement district (SID) residents pay their proportionate share for servicing the debt. The payment is referred to as a "special assessment"; it is added to the property tax bill.

Accounting for Special Assessment Projects   SID projects are accounted for through a capital projects fund and treated as any other project when the entity is obligated in some manner for the debt. The governmental entity may be **obligated** if it explicitly assumes that responsibility. For example, if a statement in the bond indenture requires payment by the governmental entity in the event of default by the assessed property owner, the governmental unit is obligated to repay the debt. The GASB also noted that "obligated in some manner"

> is intended to include all situations *other than those* in which (a) the government is *prohibited* (by constitution, charter, statute, ordinance, or contract) from assuming the debt in the event of default by the property owner or (b) the government is not legally liable for assuming the debt and *makes no statement, or gives no indication that it will, or may, honor the debt in the event of default*[3] (emphasis added).

When a governmental entity is obligated, the project is like any other capital project involving general fixed assets. The long-term debt is shown in the long-term debt account group. The only difference between a SID and other capital projects is that the affected taxpayers are primarily liable for the project's cost.

When a governmental entity has no obligation for the debt, the project is handled differently. Although the construction phase is accounted for in the capital projects fund, the proceeds from selling the bonds are clearly earmarked as derived from special assessment bonds. The resulting long-term debt is not accounted for in the general long-term debt account group. The asset is shown as a general fixed asset. Debt service payments on bonds for which the government has no explicit or implied obligation are accounted for through the agency fund, and will be discussed in the chapter on fiduciary funds.

The property owners within the SID rarely are expected to pay for the project in a single year. Therefore, the governmental unit issues long-term debt to finance the project, and the property owners incur a lien against their property until the debt is repaid. The total SID installments are set at the level necessary to make the interest and principal payments on the debt.

Because of the special nature of SID projects, a major accounting issue involves appropriate disclosure. Account titles and financial statement depictions should clearly distinguish this type of project from capital outlays that are the complete responsibility of the governmental entity. In the capital projects fund, for example, proceeds from issuing debt must be clearly noted.

[3]GASB, *Codification*, sec. S40.116.

In the general long-term debt account group, special assessment debt usually carries the title "special assessment debt with governmental commitment."

Illustrated Transactions   The illustrative entries for Arkon's special assessment project are based on a SID covering property owned by individual residents and the city. Further, under state statute, Arkon is secondarily liable for all special assessment debt. Because the city owns some of the property in the SID, it is solely liable for a portion of the debt and secondarily liable for the remainder.

The project involves curbs and gutters for a new development within the city. The project is estimated to cost $2,200,000; Arkon's share of the project is $200,000. Debt totaling $2,000,000 will be issued. The city's share of the project will be financed by an operating transfer from the general fund.

On July 1, the project was approved and the bonds were sold at par.

1.	Estimated Other Financing Sources—Special Assessment Debt	2,000,000	
	Estimated Other Financing Sources—Operating Transfers	200,000	
	Appropriations		2,200,000
2.	Cash	2,000,000	
	Other Financing Sources—Proceeds from Special Assessment Bonds		2,000,000

Had the bonds involved a premium, it would have been treated just as it was for the capital project illustrated earlier in this chapter. Any premium would be available for debt repayment and not for adding to the amount spent on the project. If the bonds are sold at a discount, the general fund may absorb the entire deficit by a transfer to the capital projects fund. Alternatively, it could be assessed against the property owners and the city in proportion to their contributions to the total project.

The contract is awarded for $2,200,000, followed by a transfer from the general fund for one-half of its obligation.

3.	Encumbrances—Special Assessment	2,200,000	
	Budgetary Fund Balance—Reserve for Encumbrances—Special Assessment		2,200,000
4.	Cash	100,000	
	Operating Transfers—Special Assessment		100,000

As these entries indicate, the basic accounting for special assessment projects involving governmental guarantees is like any other capital outlay. In fact, if the special assessment project was isolated in a single fund, the extensive descriptions for each account would be unnecessary. By clearly titling the fund as the one reflecting the special assessment project, the accountant could use "bond proceeds," "encumbrances," and so on, without the descriptors.

The capital projects fund is used to account for only the construction phase of a special assessment project. Nothing in that phase, except clear disclosure of the project's nature, is distinguishable from other capital projects. The unique aspect of special assessments — accounting for long-term receivable from the SID owners — surfaces in the debt service fund.

Capital Leases

Governmental units may find leasing of capital assets an attractive alternative to ownership. The cash requirements are spread over a number of years, which may be far easier to budget than one large lump sum in a single year. Also, for such capital items as duplicating machines or data processing and other office equipment involving rapidly changing technology, leases offer the benefit of ownership without the difficulties normally encountered in disposing of obsolete equipment.

Generally Accepted Accounting Principles Circumstances under which governmental units record a lease as a capital lease are the same as those in business. In deciding whether a lease is a capital lease, governmental units follow the guidelines developed by the Financial Accounting Standards Board (FASB) in *Statement No. 13*. If any one of the following conditions are met, a lease qualifies as a capital lease:

1. The lease transfers ownership.
2. The lease contains a bargain purchase option.
3. The lease term is equal to 75 percent or more of the remaining economic life of the property.
4. The present value of the minimum lease payments is greater than or equal to 90 percent of the fair market value of the leased asset at the inception of the lease.

Accounting principles for governmental units differ in two respects from those used in business entities:

1. The lease liability and the leased asset are reported in the long-term debt account group and the general fixed asset account group, respectively, rather than in the fund undertaking the lease.
2. No depreciation is taken on the asset.

Most governmental units account for leases in the general fund. However, some laws or regulations mandate separate accounting for *any* capital asset purchased or constructed. Under such circumstances, a capital projects fund is opened to record the initial lease. Thereafter, the debt servicing occurs in the debt service fund. Governmental units also may decide to use a capital projects fund for leases if they intend to spend material amounts in start-up costs related to the leased asset. Accounting for the lease in a separate fund enables financial statement users to evaluate the total "project" cost, not just the lease expenditures.

Illustrated Financial Transactions   Arkon leases data processing equipment from the manufacturer; a local ordinance requires that all capital acquisitions be accounted for in a capital projects fund. The lease period is five years and the annual lease payments, beginning the first day of the lease period, are $27,000. Title is transferred at the end of the lease period, and Arkon's borrowing rate is 9 percent. Arkon anticipates spending $50,000 for freight, preparing the system for use, and altering the space to accommodate the new equipment.

The lease meets the requirement for a capital lease, and the amount of the expenditure is $114,472 ($27,000 × present value of an annuity due for five years at 9 percent = $27,000 × 4.23972). Thus the total cost of the project is expected to be $164,472 ($114,472 + $50,000). The project's budget is approved. The general fund will transfer enough to make the initial lease payment and pay for the start-up costs.

$$1 + \frac{1 - (1+k)^{n-1}}{k}$$

1. Estimated Other Financing Sources—
    Capital Lease   87,472
    Estimated Other Financing Sources—
    Operating Transfers ($50,000 + $27,000)   77,000
        Appropriations   164,472

The general fund transfers the $50,000 for the start-up costs, as well as the amount for the first lease payment, to the capital projects fund and the city enters into the lease agreement.

2. Cash   77,000
    Operating Transfers —in   77,000

3. Expenditures   114,472
    Other Financing Sources—Capital Lease   87,472
    Cash   27,000

Arkon pays transportation, remodeling, and other start-up costs totaling $50,000.

4. Expenditures   50,000
    Cash   50,000

Unlike the case in business, the entire amount of the lease is shown as an expenditure when the lease agreement is signed. However, other financing sources offset the portion of the expenditure payment that is deferred ($114,472 − $27,000 or $87,472) with a net effect of $27,000, the current debt service amount, on the fund balance. Later, as the remaining interest and principal payments are made in the debt service fund, expenditures are debited and cash is credited. Again, these debt service payments act as a surrogate for depreciation in their effect on the fund balance.

The capital projects fund is closed.

5. Appropriations	164,472	
Estimated Other Financing Sources— Operating Transfers		77,000
Estimated Other Financing Sources— Capital Lease		87,472

6. Other Financing Sources—Capital Lease	87,472	
Other Financing Sources—Operating Transfers	77,000	
Expenditures		164,472

closing entries

The total cost of the leased asset, $164,472 ($114,472 + $50,000), is recorded in the general fixed asset account group. The lease liability of $87,472 is recorded in the general long-term debt account group.

Several Projects in a Single Fund

Small capital projects and those with joint financing are examples of situations in which a governmental unit uses a single fund to account for more than one capital project. Sometimes a capital outlay budget includes several outlays, all of which are small relative to the total budget. The accounting is less complex, particularly when the outlays occur at different times during the year or involve only a few entries, if a single fund is used. In other circumstances, one large debt issue may finance more than one acquisition. Rather than splitting the debt among several funds, all projects covered by the debt are accounted for in a single fund.

Accounting for the Projects in a Single Fund When several projects are accounted for in a single fund and the oversight board wants reports for individual projects, nominal and real accounts are opened for each project. The combining balance sheet and the statement of revenues, expenditures, and changes in fund balance includes a column for each separate project.

Illustrative Transactions Arkon's administrators decide to use one fund to account for a park improvement and an air conditioning project. The projects will be financed from internally generated funds. Improving the park is estimated to cost $120,000 and the air conditioning project will cost $80,000.

The total project budget is approved on July 1, and the transfers made from the general fund on that same date.

1. Estimated Other Financing Sources— Operating Transfers, Improvement	120,000	
Estimated Other Financing Sources— Operating Transfers, Air Conditioning	80,000	
Appropriations—Improvement		120,000
Appropriations—Air Conditioning		80,000

2. Cash	200,000		
Other Financing Sources—Transfers—			
Air Conditioning		80,000	*In*
Other Financing Sources—Transfers—			
Improvement		120,000	*In*

A governmental unit frequently only separates the cash for financial statement purposes. If this approach is used, cash is debited for $200,000 as illustrated. If the budgetary accounts and all nominal accounts are separately identified, the proper division of cash between the two projects is a simple matter at the end of the year.

A contract is let for each project, and the contractors <u>submit the first invoice</u>. The contractors' reimbursement requests total $105,000; $30,000 pertains to the improvement project and the remainder to the air conditioning project.

30 k
75 k

3. Encumbrances—Improvement	120,000	
Encumbrances—Air Conditioning	80,000	
Budgetary Fund Balance—Reserve for		
Encumbrances—Improvement		120,000
Budgetary Fund Balance—Reserve for		
Encumbrances—Air Conditioning		80,000

4. Budgetary Fund Balance—Reserve for		
Encumbrances—Improvement	30,000	
Expenditures—Improvement	30,000	
Encumbrances—Improvement		30,000
Contracts Payable—Improvement		30,000

invoice submitted

5. Budgetary Fund Balance—Reserve for		
Encumbrances—Air Conditioning	75,000	
Expenditures—Air Conditioning	75,000	
Encumbrances—Air Conditioning		75,000
Contracts Payable—Air Conditioning		75,000

invoice submitted

The remaining entries for both projects are similar to those illustrated. Control accounts are maintained for each project, and both the individual and combining statements portray each project.

FINANCIAL REPORTING PRACTICES

Three financial statements are prepared for capital projects funds: a balance sheet; a statement of revenues, expenditures, and changes in fund balance; and a statement of revenues, expenditures, and changes in fund balance — budget and actual. These statements are combined statements — that is, all the funds of a given type are combined in a single column.

If several capital projects funds are maintained, a combining balance sheet and a combining statement of revenues, expenditures, and changes in fund balance must be prepared. Each individual fund (or project, if several projects are included in one fund) is shown in a single column with the combined total at the far right. The combining statements typically include comparative amounts for the prior period, as illustrated in Exhibit 5-4 for XYC city.

What financial statements are required depends upon the initial project authorization. If the budgetary authority spans the entire project, a statement of revenues, expenditures, and changes in fund balance — budget and actual is not prepared. The GASB does, however, require budgetary comparisons for annually budgeted governmental funds. A balance sheet and an operating statement are prepared for all capital projects funds regardless of budgetary practices. Budgetary comparisons for Arkon's project are illustrated in Exhibit 5-5.

Exhibit 5-6 shows the operating statement for the entire project period. Ordinarily, an operating statement would be prepared annually, but the illustrated entries are easier to depict with a statement covering both years of the

---

Exhibit 5-4

XYC City
Capital Projects Funds
Combining Balance Sheet
December 31, 19X9
(with comparative totals for December 31, 19X8)
($000)

	Sewer Construction	Jail Improvement	19X9 Total	19X8 Total
Assets				
Cash	$150	$ 22	$172	$135
Short-term Investments	300	100	400	100
Interest Receivable	9	2	11	-0-
Intergovernmental Receivable	30	-0-	30	-0-
Receivable from Other Funds	-0-	10	10	50
Total Assets	$489	$134	$623	$285
Liabilities and Fund Balances				
Liabilities:				
Accounts Payable	$250	$ 40	$290	$110
Retained Percentages	50	20	70	100
Due to Other Funds	-0-	5	5	15
Total Liabilities	$300	$ 65	$365	$225
Fund Balances:				
Reserved for Encumbrances	$181	$ 70	$251	$ 60
Unreserved	8	(1)	7	-0-
Total Fund Balances	$189	$ 69	$258	$ 60
Total Liabilities and Fund Balances	$489	$134	$623	$285

Exhibit 5-5

City of Arkon
Capital Projects Fund
Statement of Revenues, Expenditures,
and Changes in Fund Balance — Budget and Actual
For the Project Period Ending December 31, 19X2

	Budget	Actual	Variance
Revenues and Other Financing Sources:			
Intergovernmental Revenue	$ 400,000	$ 400,000	$ -0-
Other Financing Sources—Bond Proceeds	1,500,000	1,500,000	-0-
Other Financing Sources—Operating Transfers	200,000	200,000	-0-
Total Revenue and Other Financing Sources	$2,100,000	$2,100,000	$ -0-
Expenditures and Other Financing Uses:			
Construction Contract	$2,000,000	$1,985,000	$15,000
Architectural Services	68,000	68,000	-0-
Legal Fees and Other Professional Services	32,000	32,000	-0-
Total Expenditures and Other Financing Uses	$2,100,000	$2,085,000	$15,000
Excess of Revenues and Other Financing			
Sources over Expenditures	$ -0-	$ 15,000	$15,000
Fund Balance—January 1, 19X2	-0-	-0-	-0-
Residual Equity Transfer to Debt Service Fund	-0-	15,000	15,000
Fund Balance—December 31, 19X2	$ -0-	$ -0-	$ -0-

Exhibit 5-6

City of Arkon
Capital Projects Fund
Statement of Revenues, Expenditures,
and Changes in Fund Balance
For the Project Period Ending December 31, 19X2

Revenues:		
Intergovernmental Revenue	$ 400,000	
Total Revenue		$ 400,000
Expenditures:		
Construction Contract	$1,985,000	
Architectural Services	68,000	
Legal Services and Other Professional Fees	32,000	2,085,000
Excess of Revenues over (under) Expenditures		$(1,685,000)
Other Financing Sources:		
Bonds	$1,500,000	
Operating Transfers	200,000	1,700,000
Excess of Revenues and Other Financing Sources		
over (under) Expenditures		$ 15,000
Fund Balance, January 1, 19X1		-0-
Equity Transfer to Debt Service		15,000
Fund Balance, December 31, 19X2		$ -0-

| Exhibit 5-7 | |

City of Arkon
Capital Projects Fund
Balance Sheet
(Project Incomplete)
As of December 31, 19X1

Assets		
Cash	$ 227,000	
Investments	1,000,000	
Total Assets		$1,227,000
Liabilities and Fund Balance		
Liabilities:		
Contracts Payable—Retained Percentage	$ 27,000	
Deferred Revenue	3,400	
Due to Other Funds	15,000	
Total Liabilities		$ 45,400
Fund Balance:		
Appropriated—Reserve for Encumbrances	$1,440,000	
Unencumbered	20,000	
	$1,460,000	
Unappropriated—Unreserved FB	(278,400)	1,181,600
Total Liabilities and Fund Balance		$1,227,000

[handwritten margin notes: "Spent less than anticipated"; "Intergov't Rev. 400,000 − 121,600 = 278,400"]

project. This particular format shows the revenues and expenditures first, with the other financing sources in a separate section after an excess of revenues over (under) expenditures. Since most capital projects are financed primarily by debt, this format is not very helpful. It emphasizes the relationship between revenues and expenditures instead of the relationship between total inflows and outflows. Depending upon local preferences and requirements, the statement is easily changed to group revenues and other financing sources together and to compare those total resources with total expenditures and other financing uses (see Exhibit 5-5).

Exhibit 5-7 shows a balance sheet for Arkon's comprehensive capital project at the end of the first year. With one exception, it is similar to balance sheets for other governmental funds. As the exhibit shows, the appropriated and unappropriated components of the fund balance should be displayed.

A balance sheet would not be prepared at the end of year 2 because the fund has been closed and the balance transferred to another fund. A statement of revenues, expenditures, and changes in fund balance would be sufficient to indicate the operating results and the disposition of any remaining balance or the funding of any deficit.

SUMMARY

The acquisition and construction of general fixed assets are accounted for in capital projects funds, special revenue funds, or general funds. Using a capital projects fund for this purpose is advisable whenever a governmental entity wants to report specific operating figures for major capital outlays.

General fixed assets are acquired in a variety of ways. Some are purchased; others are constructed. Still others are leased in a manner qualifying as a capital lease. All acquisition types can be accommodated in a capital projects fund. Special assessment projects also are accounted for in a capital projects fund.

Expenditure authority for major capital construction projects usually covers the entire project rather than a single operating period. Interim financial statements are prepared for continuing projects; however, budgetary comparisons are not required for such projects. When a project has been completed and any excess transferred, the balance sheet is not prepared.

Budgetary accounts usually are integrated into the accounting system. For continuing projects, the estimated revenues or other financing sources and appropriations are closed only for the actual amounts during the interim periods. Further, the fund balance shows the appropriated and unappropriated amounts.

Dealing with interest expenses and interest earnings is a major issue in capital acquisitions. Interest expense on short-term financing is reported as a project cost; the related debt frequently is a fund liability. Governmental entities may capitalize interest on long-term debt during the construction period. If they do capitalize interest, the computations are the same as for businesses, except that any interest earnings must be offset against the amount capitalized.

Capital projects budgets are not usually affected by premiums or discounts on long-term debt. Premiums are transferred to the debt service fund for later use in making principal and interest payments. Discounts usually are absorbed by the general fund through a transfer to the capital projects fund.

Governmental accounting practices make it difficult to visualize all aspects of accounting for capital outlays. The acquisition or construction is in one fund, and the debt repayment in another. The asset and liability balances are reported in the general fixed asset and long-term debt account groups respectively. For that reason, chapters on each of these funds or account groups follow the discussion of capital projects.

APPENDIX A

APPLYING THE ACCRUAL BASIS OF ACCOUNTING TO CAPITAL PROJECTS FUNDS

Until the effective date of *Statement No. 11,* the modified accrual basis of accounting is used for governmental-type funds, including capital projects funds. Because of the special provisions for capital assets and related debt, the change from the modified accrual basis to the accrual basis will have little impact on accounting in capital projects funds.

Capital asset accounting and reporting are currently envisioned as the same under the accrual or modified accrual basis of accounting. Long-term debt is recorded as an "other financing source" in the capital projects fund.

The liability is reported in the general long-term debt account group, and the asset in the general fixed asset account group. Interest and principal payments are accounted for in the debt service fund; they are recognized as expenditures "when due." None of these accounting practices is expected to change with the adoption of the new measurement focus/basis of accounting statement.

Because of the types of revenue received by capital projects funds, recognition criteria also remain largely unchanged. As the chapter pointed out, capital asset acquisitions are most often financed by long-term debt or transfers from the general fund. Recognition criteria for other financing sources—whether from transfers or issuance of long-term debt—occur when the related liability is incurred under the GASB's accrual and modified accrual bases of accounting.

If a capital project is financed by a restrictive intergovernmental grant, the accounting also would be the same. Under either method, revenue is recognized when the grant restrictions have been satisfied, namely, when the appropriate expenditures have occurred.

Revenues from nonrestrictive grants or temporary investments might be recognized differently under the two bases of accounting. Under the modified accrual basis of accounting, the revenue must be "measurable and available," whereas it must be earned before it can be recognized under the accrual basis. For example, notice of a nonrestrictive grant award might be received in year 1 and payable late in year 2. In these circumstances it could qualify as "earned" in year 1 under the accrual basis. Because of the delay in receipt it would not be "available" to meet current expenditures and therefore not recognized as revenue in year 1 under the modified accrual basis.

The same difference might apply to earnings on temporary investments. If, for example, a governmental unit invested in a 180-day certificate of deposit on November 1 of year 1, interest for one month would be accrued on December 31 under the accrual basis of accounting. Earnings from the investment normally would not be accrued under the modified accrual basis because, although "susceptible to accrual," the interest would not be available within the 60 days following the close of the fiscal period.

Both the accrual and modified accrual bases of accounting generally dictate expenditure/expense recognition when the related liability is incurred. Certain exceptions to the general recognition criteria are permitted under both GASB defined bases of accounting. However, none of the exceptions pertains to the type of expenditures recognized in a capital projects fund. Construction expenditures are recognized when incurred—that is, when the related liability is incurred. Any interest charges related to short-term financing also are recognized when incurred under both methodologies.

The new measurement focus/basis of accounting model portends few accounting changes for capital projects funds. Other GASB projects may, however, lead to accounting and reporting changes for all capital assets and any related debt. One possible scenario would combine the capital projects and debt service funds with the two account groups. Another would combine the two account groups. These accounting and reporting possibilities are discussed further in Chapter 13.

QUESTIONS

5-1 What capital outlays are accounted for in a capital projects fund? Explain why a governmental unit may choose to show the acquisition of a capital asset in the general fund.

5-2 Explain the process for recording the acquisition or construction of a fixed asset and contrast this process with the recording of the constructed or acquired asset.

5-3 What is the primary difference between general-purpose and specific-purpose assets of a governmental entity?

5-4 How does the accounting related to capitalizing interest costs for governmental entities differ from that of for-profit entities? Explain.

5-5 What funds or account groups are affected by a capital acquisition financed by a long-term lease? Explain the specific purpose served by each fund or account group.

5-6 Contrast the treatment of debt proceeds and interest payments related to short-term and long-term debt used to finance construction expenditures in a capital projects fund.

5-7 Identify the circumstances under which a lease is treated as a capital lease. What impact does a capital lease have on the financial statements of a governmental entity?

5-8 Some governmental units close the books for a capital project at the end of each fiscal period, whereas others wait until the project is complete. Which procedure is preferable? Why?

5-9 Explain the treatment of outstanding encumbrances for incomplete projects when a governmental unit approves a project rather than a period budget for capital outlays.

5-10 Describe the format and use of combining financial statements for capital projects.

5-11 Describe the treatment of premiums or discounts on the sale of long-term debt used to finance capital assets of a governmental unit.

5-12 In the context of capital projects fund investments, what is meant by the term *arbitrage*? What must a governmental unit do to avoid arbitrage?

5-13 A city comptroller lacks experience and wants advice on the number of capital projects funds to establish. Identify general guidelines that she should use in determining the proper number of funds.

5-14 Explain special assessments and their accounting treatment in a capital projects fund. Special assessments represent unique relationships between the affected taxpayers and governmental units. Explain a possible alternative accounting treatment during the construction or acquisition phase.

5-15 Explain the treatment of budgetary accounts at the end of the first year if budgetary authority spans the entire project.

5-16 What accounting treatment is accorded the issuance discount or premium on installment purchases of capital assets?

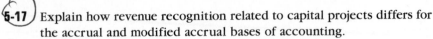

5-17 Explain how revenue recognition related to capital projects differs for the accrual and modified accrual bases of accounting.

5-18 Will there be any expenditure recognition changes in the capital projects fund with a shift from the modified accrual to the accrual basis of accounting? Explain.

CASES

5-1 The commissioners of Delvone County have received year-end financial statements. Several commissioners are confused by the reporting of capital outlays. Capital outlays appear in the general fund and special revenue funds. In addition, two capital projects funds were opened during the year—one for remodeling the courthouse, and one for constructing a paved road to one section of the county. They also note that a transfer for capital construction appears in the general fund. The commissioners want to know why capital outlays appear in several different funds. They also want to know if they are overlapping—that is, are the expenditures in the general fund and special revenue fund part of the two larger projects? Finally, if the projects do not overlap, why, ask the commissioners, did the general fund transfer funds to one of the capital projects funds?

REQUIRED

1. Prepare a concise report addressing the commissioners' concerns.
2. Explain how the county could avoid the confusion with regard to capital projects.

5-2 The city of Delphia undertook a major capital expansion project in Fiscal 19X3. The construction is planned for the next three years, and the city council provided budgetary authority for the entire project. Delphia closes its books annually; its post-closing trial balance for Fiscal 19X3 is displayed below:

City of Delphia
Capital Projects Fund
Post-Closing Trial Balance
Fiscal 19X3
($000)

Cash	50	
Investments	5,600	
Accrued Interest Receivable	180	
Due from Other Funds	500	
Accounts Payable		100
Contracts Payable—Retained Percentage		69
Deferred Revenue		2,100
Due to Other Funds		150
Unreserved Fund Balance	2,089	
Fund Balance Reserved for Encumbrances		6,000
	8,419	8,419

REQUIRED

1. The post-closing trial balance might raise concerns if it was reviewed without explanation. Explain those concerns.
2. Explain whether you think this project is in danger of going over budget. What specific factors in the trial balance led to your conclusions?

5-3   On a vote of the affected residents, Linnings Township has decided to replace the curbs and gutters in its Region Heights District. Linnings is issuing long-term serial bonds to finance the project, and the affected citizens will repay the debt plus interest over a ten-year period. The project costs $9,000,000. The 9 percent serial bonds mature ratably over the ten-year period. The bond indentures indicate that the township is not liable for the debt. Shortly before the bonds were issued, the mayor issued a press release in which he outlined the general nature of the project. In responding to a reporter's question about the impact of additional debt on the township, the mayor indicates, "Unless the property owners default, there is no effect on the township's financial statements. Technically, the township is not even liable for the debt in the event of default. However, the township would not permit its credit rating to be marred by default."

REQUIRED

What type of capital project is Linnings undertaking? Explain the appropriate accounting practices for the project, including the accounting treatment of the long-term debt and the resulting asset.

5-4   The city of Lorkin is contemplating several different capital outlays:
1. A paving project in a recently annexed section of the city. The total cost is $500,000, and it will be financed by money from the special revenue fund that accounts for the road tax.
2. Purchase of computer equipment costing $167,000. The payment will be made when the equipment is installed.
3. A new jail costing $3,500,000 that will involve county general property tax funds, and federal and state grants. The project is expected to take two years. Budgetary authority would span the entire two years.
4. Five photocopy machines will be leased under terms qualifying as a capital lease. The lease period is five years, and the financing of $20,000 per year is expected to come from annual operating funds.
5. Extension of the sewer line to a new development. The developers and eventually the property owners will be responsible for repaying the long-term debt issued to finance the project. The indentures carry the city's full faith and credit in the event of default by the taxpayers.

REQUIRED

1. How many, if any, capital projects funds should the city establish for these capital projects? Explain.
2. For what projects, if any, does the city have an option to establish a separate fund? Explain.

5-5 Burgundy Township is buying a teleprocessing system over time. The original contract called for a down payment of $150,000, and three succeeding installments of the same amount. The payments are made on July 1 each year. The note payable is carried by the vendor. Because he hopes this contract will lead to others with Burgundy, he has set the rate at 4 percent. The township's borrowing rate is 6 percent, which when applied to the contract yields a fair value of $550,952. The contract liability was recorded as $566,264 (present value of an annuity due at 4 percent for four years).

REQUIRED

Discuss the proper accounting and reporting procedures related to this installment purchase, including the appropriate amount to record as an asset and liability, the fund and/or account groups involved, and the treatment of any issuance discount or premium.

EXERCISES

5-1 The appendix at the end of this text contains excerpts from the comprehensive financial report for Raleigh, North Carolina. After reviewing the statements pertinent to capital projects funds, answer the following questions:

1. What primary financial statements are shown for capital projects funds? In what respects do those statements appear consistent with those presented in the text? How are they different? What notes, or supporting schedules, pertain specifically to capital projects funds?
2. Does the supporting material provide a description of capital projects funds? Is it clear which capital outlays occur in operating funds and which ones are accounted for in separate capital projects funds?
3. Does the Park Bond Fund appear to be over budget? How do you know? In general, are the capital projects financed by a single source or several sources? What are some of the financing sources?
4. Does the auditors' opinion contain any qualifications related to capital projects funds? If so, describe the qualifications.
5. Are any special assessment projects accounted for in capital projects funds? If so, is the related debt, if any, reported in the general long-term debt account group?

5-2 Select the best answer for each question.

1. Capital outlays normally accounted for in separate capital projects funds do not include which of the following?
   a. major capital outlays
   b. outlays occurring over several periods
   c. outlays for proprietary funds
   d. outlays financed by several different sources
2. Bond anticipation notes used to finance the initial phases of a capital project:

a. would be classified as long-term debt

b. appear as debt in the capital projects fund if classified as short-term

c. appear as debt in the capital projects fund if classified as long-term

d. would be classified as short-term debt in the general fund

3. Bond proceeds from debt issued to finance capital projects are shown:

a. as other financing sources in the fund reporting the capital outlay

b. as revenue in the fund reporting the capital outlay

c. as a net decrease in long-term liabilities

d. as a source of debt repayment in the debt service fund

4. The major difference between interest capitalization for governmental and for-profit entities is:

a. governmental entities use a weighted average of construction expenditures

b. governmental entities offset interest earnings against interest expense for tax-exempt debt

c. for-profit entities can choose whether to capitalize interest

d. none of the above

5. The following information pertains to a computer that Pine Township leased from Karl Supply Co. on July 1, 19X8, for general township use:

Karl's Cost	$5,000
Fair Value, at July 1, 19X8	$5,000
Estimated Economic Life	5 years
Fixed Noncancelable Term	30 months
Rental at Beginning of Each Month	$135
Guaranteed Residual Value	$2,000
Present Value of Minimum Lease Payments at July 1, 19X8, using Pine's Incremental Borrowing Rate of 10.5%	$5,120
Karl's Implicit Interest Rate of 12.04%	$5,000

On July 1, 19X8, what amount should Pine capitalize in its general fixed assets account group for this leased asset?

a. $0

b. $3,000

c. $5,000

d. $5,120

(Adapted from the November 3, 1988, CPA Exam, Practice #49)

6. If it cannot be used to expand the scope of a project, which of the following is not an appropriate treatment for a discount or premium on long-term debt used to finance a capital projects fund?

a. an other financing source and an operating transfer out of the capital projects fund

b. a revenue of the debt service fund

c. a revenue of the capital projects fund

d. none of the above

7. In the context of municipal financing, *arbitrage* refers to the investment of bond proceeds:

a. at rates more than paid on the bonds

b. at rates less than paid on the bonds

      c. without first getting a letter ruling on the investment strategy from the IRS

      d. in a municipality's pooled investment fund

8. Budgetary comparisons for capital projects funds are not required:

      a. for incomplete projects

      b. for projects financed by more than one debt issue

      c. for a capital projects fund used to account for more than one project

      d. for incomplete projects where budgetary authority spans the length of the project

9. When $1,000,000 of bonds are issued at 101 to finance a capital outlay and any premium is used for principal and interest payments, the following entry is made in the capital projects fund:

	Dr.	Cr.
a. Cash	1,010,000	
Bonds Payable		1,010,000
b. Cash	1,000,000	
Bonds Payable		1,000,000
c. Cash	1,010,000	
Other Financing Sources		1,000,000
Due to Debt Service Fund		10,000
d. Cash	1,010,000	
Revenue		10,000
Other Financing Sources		1,000,000

10. A combining financial statement for capital projects funds would:

      a. show all capital projects funds as a single column

      b. show each capital projects fund as a single column

      c. show balance sheet totals only for each capital projects fund as a single column

      d. none of the above

5-3 Select the best answer for each question.

1. If at the end of two years for a three-year capital project, the unreserved fund balance shows a deficit, it means:

      a. the project is over budget

      b. the revenues and financing sources exceed the expenditures and transfers out for the period

      c. the amount budgeted to be earned or received is less to date than the budgeted appropriations committed

      d. the expenditures, transfers out, and encumbrances to date exceed revenues and financing sources recognized

Items 2 and 3 are based on the following information:

On December 31, 19X7, Vane City paid a contractor $3,000,000 for the total cost of a new municipal annex built in 19X7 on city-owned land. Financing was provided by a $2,000,000 general obligation bond issue sold at face amount on December 31, 19X7, with the remaining $1,000,000 transferred from the general fund.

2. What account and amount should be reported in Vane's 19X7 financial statements for the general fund?
   a. other financing uses, $1,000,000
   b. other financing sources, $2,000,000
   c. expenditures, $3,000,000
   d. other financing sources, $3,000,000

3. What accounts and amounts should be reported in Vane's 19X7 financial statements for the capital projects fund?
   a. other financing sources, $2,000,000; general long-term debt, $2,000,000
   b. revenues, $2,000,000; expenditures, $2,000,000
   c. other financing sources, $3,000,000; expenditures, $3,000,000
   d. revenues, $3,000,000; expenditures, $3,000,000

(Adapted from the November 3, 1988, CPA Exam, Practices #41 and #42)

4. General purpose fixed assets appear in:
   a. the fixed asset account group
   b. the fund making the expenditure
   c. either the fixed asset account group or the fund making the expenditure, depending upon the financing sources
   d. proprietary funds

Items 5, 6, and 7 are based on the following information:

Sitville County issued $10,000,000 in bonds to finance two capital projects during Fiscal 19X8 and Fiscal 19X9. A state grant of $500,000 will also be applied equally to each project. One project with a total cost of $6,250,000 involves resurfacing a major portion of the streets in Sitville. The remaining funds will be spent on constructing a new city hall. Each project is accounted for in a separate fund, and budget authority is granted for the entire project.

5. If the bonds are sold at par, the amount of debt shown in the fund accounting for the resurfacing project should be:
   a. $10,000,000
   b. $6,000,000
   c. $4,000,000
   d. $0

6. If the bonds are sold on an interest date at 102, and the premium can be applied to the projects, the other financing sources—bond proceeds account, in the city hall fund would be debited for:
   a. $0
   b. $4,080,000
   c. $4,000,000
   d. $80,000

7. At the beginning of the project, the estimated revenues—state grant account in the fund accounting for the paving project would be credited for:

　　　a. $6,000,000
　　　b. $250,000
　　　c. $500,000
　　　d. $0

　8. Construction activity pertaining to special assessment projects for which a governmental entity has no legal responsibility is accounted for in:

　　　a. general fund
　　　b. general long-term debt account group
　　　c. agency fund
　　　d. capital projects fund

　9. Which one of the following is not a condition of capitalizing a leased asset and recording a long-term lease liability?

　　　a. the lease contains a bargain purchase option
　　　b. the lease transfers ownership
　　　c. the lease specifies that the full faith and credit of the governmental entity is backing the lease
　　　d. the lease term is equal to 75 percent or more of the remaining economic life of the property

　10. A $125,000 contribution from the general fund was used to finance part of a construction project accounted for in a capital projects fund. The general fund would report:

　　　a. $125,000 in expenditures—capital outlay
　　　b. $125,000 in operating transfers
　　　c. no entry at the time of the transfer
　　　d. none of the above

5-4　Wakerville Township undertook a three-year capital project two years ago. The project involves razing and rebuilding the township's fire station; the budget for the entire project was approved on July 1, 19X0. The preclosing trial balance at the end of June 30, 19X2 appears below:

Wakerville Township
Capital Projects Fund
Pre-Closing Trial Balance
June 30, 19X2

Cash	$ 80,000	
Investments	490,000	
Interest Receivable	11,295	
Due from General Fund	160,000	
Accounts Payable		$ 121,000
Contracts Payable—Retained Percentage		319,000
Deferred Revenue		90,000
Appropriations		1,700,000
Estimated Other Financing Sources—Operating Transfers	1,200,000	
Estimated Revenues—Intergovernmental Grant	200,000	
Expenditures	1,200,000	
Other Financing Sources—Operating Transfers		1,000,000
Interest Revenues		11,295
Revenues—Intergovernmental Grant		110,000

(continued)

(continued)

Budgetary Fund Balance—Unreserved	300,000	
Encumbrances	500,000	
Budgetary Fund Balance—Reserve for Encumbrances		500,000
Unreserved Fund Balance		290,000
Totals	$4,141,295	$4,141,295

REQUIRED

Answer each of the following questions. If the questions cannot be answered based on information provided, explain why.

1. Were the interest revenues anticipated, and are they being applied to the construction project?
2. Was the entire operating transfer for this project received during the year? What amount was anticipated for the last two years?
3. Why might the intergovernmental grant revenue amount differ from the amount expected?
4. Is the project likely to be over budget for the three-year period?
5. Assuming a portion of the project is financed by debt, why was the estimated other financing sources—bond proceeds account, omitted from the pre-closing trial balance?
6. What is the total authorization for this project? The total uncommitted authorization remaining on the project?

5-5   Using the information provided in exercise 5-4, and assuming Wakerville closes its accounts each year, prepare the closing entries for the fiscal period ending June 30, 19X2.

5-6   Assuming the rest of the project goes as projected, make summary transactions and closing entries for the Wakerville Township project explained in exercise 5-4 (exercise 5-5 should be completed first).

5-7   Danzig County opened a capital projects fund for a bridge construction project expected to take two years to complete. The project will cost $5,000,000, and be financed by a general fund transfer of $100,000 each year, a federal grant of $820,000, and bonds for the remaining costs. The following transactions occurred during the first year.

1. The budget was approved on July 1, 19X0.
2. The general fund transferred the first year's contribution, and the state acknowledged approval of the grant. The grant funds will be paid at each year end; the amount paid will be based on federal governmental proportional share of construction expenditures.
3. Seven percent bond anticipation notes totaling $500,000 were issued on August 1; they do not qualify as long-term debt.
4. On August 10, a contract for the entire project was awarded to a contractor who received a $100,000 advance. The advance will be repaid when the last billing is received.

5. On September 1, the remaining cash on hand was invested in the investment pool at 6 percent.

6. The first progress billing was received on November 1 for $505,000; the funds were withdrawn from the investment pool to make the payment. No retainage was held on this first payment. Interest earnings are recognized on invested funds as they are withdrawn, and they can be used to expand the project. The change in appropriations is made each time interest earnings are recognized as income.

7. Bonds were sold on January 1, 19X1; the bonds sold at 99 and the stated rate of interest was 7 percent. Interest is payable on January 1 and July 1 of each year. Bond discounts must be absorbed by the project, and the adjustment to the budgetary accounts was made when the bonds were sold.

8. After repaying the bond anticipation notes with interest to January 1, excess funds were invested in the investment pool at 6 percent.

9. A progress billing of $890,000 was received from the contractor on February 1; all but the 5 percent retainage was paid, and the appropriate adjustments made to the investment pool and the budgetary accounts.

10. The contractor requested a $7,000 change order to the contract; the amount was approved and it will be paid for by the general fund in its second installment. The appropriate adjustments were made to appropriations and funding sources.

11. A third progress billing of $630,000 was received on June 30; except for the retainage, the bill was paid and investments and the budgetary accounts adjusted accordingly.

12. Danzig County made adjusting entries and closed its books on June 30, 19X1. On that date, $50,000 interest had accrued on the pooled investments and it will be available for paying current liabilities. The state paid its share of the expenditures for the year.

REQUIRED

Prepare the journal entries for Fiscal 19X1 for Danzig's capital projects fund. Round all amounts to the nearest dollar. Adjust the budgetary amounts and recognize interest earnings only on the cash withdrawn from the investment pool in Items 9 and 11 as in Item 6.

5-8 Prepare the financial statements for the Danzig County capital projects fund as of June 30, 19X1 (see exercise 5-7). Hint: If exercise 5-7 was not required, prepare T-accounts for the transactions ending June 30, 19X1.

5-9 The city of Plentywood capitalizes interest on assets constructed for its own use. Currently, the city is constructing a facility for juvenile delinquents. Construction expenditures for the calendar years ending December 31, 19X0 and 19X1, are:

	19X0	**19X1**
January–March	$ 150,000	$ 100,000
April–June	380,000	350,000
July–September	1,200,000	600,000
October–December	670,000	250,000
Total	$2,400,000	$1,300,000

To finance the project, $3,700,000 of 7 percent, 20-year bonds were issued on January 1, 19X0. The funds were invested immediately in Plentywood's pooled investment fund, which yielded 6 percent throughout the construction period. Any withdrawals from the fund must be made on the first day of each quarter.

REQUIRED

Assuming Plentywood's capital projects manager invests as much as possible each quarter, what amount should be capitalized on its juvenile delinquent facility?

5-10   The city of Oleandar issued $7,000,000 of 6 percent long-term bonds to finance capital construction. The bonds were issued on January 1, 19X0, at 101, when the budget for the entire project was approved. Any premium was transferred to the debt service fund for purposes of making principal and interest payments, which are due on January 1 and July 1 of each year. Any balance required to pay interest and $117,000 to provide for the retirement of bond principal are transferred from the general fund to the debt service fund on July 1 of each year.

The contract for construction was signed on January 1, 19X0. Construction costs of $5,000,000 were incurred during 19X0; the remaining construction was completed during 19X1.

REQUIRED

Make the necessary journal entries for Oleandar's capital projects and general funds during 19X0 and 19X1. (Entries for the debt service fund and the account groups will be made in subsequent chapters.)

5-11   On January 2, 19X5, Pine City's Council officially approved a three-year special assessment project for a street-improvement program. Approval of this project was based on the following information:

• Issuance of $9,000,000 serial bonds at face amount on January 2, 19X5, as follows:

Amount	**Rate**	**Maturity Date**
$2,000,000	6%	December 31, 19X5
3,000,000	8%	December 31, 19X6
4,000,000	9%	December 31, 19X7

- Interest expense on the serial bonds for 19X5, 19X6, and 19X7 is estimated at $720,000, $600,000, and $360,000, respectively.
- Assessments of $9,000,000 will be levied, payable over a three-year period by property owners benefiting from the project, with $3,000,000 due on June 30, 19X5, 19X6, and 19X7, respectively. Interest, to be charged at the simple rate of 10 percent on deferred installments, from June 30, 19X5, to the due dates, is expected to be as follows:

Due Dates	Interest
January 2, 19X6	$300,000
June 30, 19X6	300,000
January 2, 19X7	150,000
June 30, 19X7	150,000

- Signing of a construction contract for a fixed fee with the following payment schedule: $1,500,000 in advance on January 15, 19X5; progress billing based on the percentage of completion to be computed every November 30, payable on December 31; and $2,000,000 on completion. Completion estimates are 30 percent on November 30, 19X5, an additional 40 percent on November 30, 19X6, and the final 30 percent on November 30, 19X7.
- Investment of temporary funds in six-month certificates of deposit, at an estimated rate of 7 percent; interest revenue on the certificates of deposit for 19X5, 19X6, and 19X7 is estimated at $500,000, $400,000, and $200,000, respectively. Of the total certificate of deposit earnings, $120,000 in 19X6 and $200,000 in 19X7 are not needed for debt repayment and are used to expand the scope of the project. These excess earnings are contemplated in the original budget.
- Project to be accounted for by integration of formal budgetary accounting entries and control accounts.

REQUIRED

1. Make the budgetary entries for the special assessment capital project, assuming Pine City is backing the issue with its full faith and credit. (Hint: Calculate the total project cost.) More information than necessary may be provided.
2. Calculate the total revenues/other financing sources and total expenditures for the capital projects fund in 19X6.
   (Adapted from the November 1986 CPA Exam, Practice #4)

5-12   Each transaction described below pertains to the Haley School District's capital projects fund. The school district is renovating the gymnasium. It operates on a calendar year.

1. On July 2, 19X1, $150,000 in bond anticipation notes were sold. The notes were outstanding on December 31, 19X1, and they carry an interest rate of 10 percent.
2. Only $100,000 of the money from transaction no. 1 was needed before the bond issue was sold; the remaining $50,000 was invested on October 1, 19X1, in a six-month certificate of deposit yielding 6 percent.

3. On October 1, 19X1, Haley was notified of a $400,000 federal grant award. The grant could be used for any purpose, and Haley decided to apply the money to this project. The cash payment is received on March 15, 19X2.
4. On January 1, 19X2, $500,000 in 8 percent general obligation long-term bonds were issued at par.

REQUIRED

1. Make the journal entries that would be required under the modified accrual basis of accounting.
2. Make the journal entries for those transactions that require different entries under the accrual basis of accounting.

5-13   Etacude School District is building a new administration complex. The project is expected to take two years, and budgetary authority was provided for the full project. At the end of the first year, the capital projects fund had the following adjusted trial balance:

Etacude School District
Capital Projects Fund
Pre-Closing Trial Balance
December 31, 19X3

Cash	$ 27,500	
Interest Receivable	25,250	
Grants Receivable	250,000	
Investments	260,000	
Due to Debt Service Fund		$ 45,250
Contracts Payable—Retained Percentage		67,500
Deferred Revenue		125,000
Estimated Other Financing Sources—Operating Transfers	300,000	
Estimated Other Financing Sources—Bond Proceeds	1,000,000	
Estimated Revenues—Intergovernmental Grant	500,000	
Appropriations		1,800,000
Other Financing Sources—Operating Transfer		300,000
Other Financing Sources—Bond Proceeds		1,000,000
Revenues—Intergovernmental Grant		375,000
Expenditures	1,350,000	
Encumbrances	450,000	
Budgetary Fund Balance—Reserve for Encumbrances		450,000
	$4,162,750	$4,162,750

REQUIRED

1. Use the worksheet method to close Etacude's capital projects fund for the first year.
2. Prepare summary entries to show the completion of the project.
3. Prepare final closing entries.

CHAPTER 6

Debt Service Funds

Payment of interest and principal on debt owed by the governmental entity is called debt service. Payments on **general purpose long-term debt** are generally accounted for in a separate fund. Servicing of specific-purpose debt held in individual funds, such as the proprietary funds, is accounted for in the fund carrying the liability.

Generally accepted accounting principles (GAAP) for governmental entities do not require setting up a special fund for servicing general purpose long-term debt. Although such activities may be accounted for in a debt service fund, they may also be accounted for in the general fund, or possibly even a special revenue fund if the revenue is earned for that purpose. Nonetheless, many governmental entities use a separate debt service fund for reflecting interest and principal payments on long-term debt. Governmental policy, state statutes, or bond indentures may require separation. In other cases, a governmental entity may choose to establish a separate fund to facilitate accounting and reporting.

Lease payments on capital leases, serial debt installments, term debt (including sinking fund requirements), special assessment installments, and most other types of long-term borrowing are commonly made through debt service funds. Also, if a governmental unit extinguishes debt early, either by retirement or refunding, the transactions are accounted for in a debt service fund.

This chapter explains the general uses of debt service funds. General accounting and reporting practices are discussed and illustrated. Emphasis is placed on the more difficult issues, such as accounting for sinking funds, special assessments, and advance refundings.

DETERMINING THE NUMBER OF DEBT SERVICE FUNDS

At one time, governmental entities opened a separate debt service fund for almost every debt issue. Technological developments have made segregation possible without establishing a separate fund. Modern accounting systems allow complete reporting by debt issue even when cash, investments, and other assets are commingled for effective management. Thus, several debt issues may be accounted for in a single fund.

Some circumstances still make separate accounting desirable or mandatory. Bond indentures may require sinking funds. The investments and accruals related to such sinking funds are easier for financial statement users to grasp if maintained separately. Some state statutes or local ordinances also require separate funds for certain or all debt issues.

GENERAL BUDGETING AND ACCOUNTING PRACTICES

Budgetary Considerations

Principal and interest payments frequently represent a substantial portion of a governmental entity's annual obligations. They are included in the operating budget along with other operating expenditures. Whether the budgetary amounts are integrated into the accounting records depends upon legal requirements and local preferences. Generally accepted accounting principles do not require budgetary integration, especially when debt servicing is derived from operating transfers. The necessary amounts already have been budgeted and integrated into the general fund's accounting system. Both because the budgeting is clear from the general fund budget and because variations from budgeted amounts are unlikely, repeating the entries in the debt service fund is unnecessary.

Not necessary

When the source of financing involves direct deposits to the debt service fund, integration may be advisable. For example, some governmental units earmark a portion of property tax revenues for debt repayment. The earmarked revenue would be deposited directly in the debt service fund, and the amount may differ from that budgeted. In this case, budget integration helps decision makers assess how accurate the estimates were and whether supplemental appropriations may be necessary. Integrating the budget is also beneficial for special assessments when the governmental entity is "obligated in some manner." It improves accountability for the revenue sources and debt payment expenditures.

General Accounting Practices

Only payments on general purpose long-term debt are recorded in a debt service fund. (Servicing of short- or specific-purpose long-term debt is recorded in the fund that has the liability.) Payments of both principal and interest are classified as expenditures. For example, if a $10,000 principal and $60,000 interest payment is due on long-term bonds, the following entry is made:

making payments

Expenditures	70,000	
Bonds Payable		10,000
Interest Payable		60,000

When the payments are made, the liabilities are debited and cash is credited. As will be discussed in Chapter 7, when the liability for the bonds is recorded in the debt service fund, another entry is made removing the liability from the general long-term debt account group.

Payments made on interest and principal in the debt service fund usually are derived from transfers from the general fund or earmarked taxes. Interest revenues on investments or earmarked taxes are recorded as revenues of the debt service fund. Transfers from other funds are classified as operating or equity transfers. If a transfer is made to pay the principal and interest payment discussed above, the entry in the debt service fund is:

GF
SRF

Cash	70,000	
Operating Transfers ~ In		70,000

At the same time this entry is made, an entry is made in the general fund showing the transfer out. If, on the other hand, earmarked taxes were deposited in the debt service fund directly to make the principal and interest payments, the entries in the debt service fund are:

Taxes Receivable Current	70,000	
Revenues		70,000
Cash	70,000	
Taxes Receivable Current		70,000

Recognition Principles   Revenue recognition generally follows the modified accrual basis of accounting. Tax revenues deposited directly to the debt service fund are recognized in the year levied, provided the taxes will be received in the period or within two months thereafter. Interest income on fund investments is recognized when it is measurable and available.

Special recognition principles apply to debt service expenditures. Both principal and interest payments on general long-term debt are classified as expenditures. Further, matured debt and interest on such debt are recognized as expenditures "when due." For example, if interest of $50,000 and term bond principal of $560,000 are due on January 10, 19X2, the total $610,000 is recognized as an expenditure on *January 10, 19X2, when the payments are due.* No accrual is made for the interest on December 31, 19X1.

The Governmental Accounting Standards Board (GASB) has made one exception to the "when due" recognition principle. If the funds are budgeted and transferred in the previous period, normal accrual procedures are used. Continuing the example, if the funds were budgeted and transferred to the debt service fund in 19X1, the expenditures should also be recognized in that year.

This departure from modified accrual practices was originally justified because it provided a better matching between fund inflows and outflows. If a principal and interest payment is due January 10, 19X2, resources are not usually transferred to the debt service fund until 19X2. Recognizing the expenditures at year end 19X1 would, assuming no other transactions, result in a deficit debt service fund balance at year-end 19X1 (a debit to an expenditure, but no credit for transfers or revenues). Although the deficit fund balance would be meaningless because of the anticipated transfer in early 19X2, it might unnecessarily concern readers of the financial statements.

The "when due" principle was adopted to avoid concern over the deficit. It ensures that the budgetary authority, transfer, and expenditure all will be reported in the same year—that is, matching is achieved. Although the requirement ensures matching, it may mean inconsistent reporting from one period to the next. Depending upon budgetary cycles, entities could skew reporting by showing two years of payments as expenditures in one year and none in the next. If the payment due in early 19X1 was transferred when due and the payment due in early 19X2 was transferred in late 19X1, two interest/principal payments would be reflected in 19X1 and none in 19X2.

OBSERVATION ▲

Since the "when due" practice was first adopted, new debt instruments have been developed by governmental entities. One such instrument, deep discount debt bonds, demonstrates the misleading nature of the "when due" practice. Recognizing the expenditure when the debt is due means that no expenditure is recognized until the deep discount issue reaches maturity, not as the value is increasing. Current practices distort the matching concept.

Accounting Entries   Three basic types of entries appear in debt service funds. Receipt of resources to make the debt payments is one such entry:

Cash	xxx	
Operating Transfers In		xxx
or		
Revenues		xxx
or		
Equity Transfers		xxx

Operating transfers usually are budgeted in and transferred from the general fund. Whenever the amount is classified as an operating transfer by the general fund, it must be classified the same way in the debt service fund.

Revenues are credited for interest on investments held by the debt service fund or taxes or other revenue sources deposited directly to the debt service fund. Premiums on bond issues that cannot be applied to a project and are received directly by the debt service fund are also classified as debt service fund revenue. Residual equity transfers usually result from closing out a capital projects fund and transferring the balance to a debt service fund.

The second common entry is recording the principal and interest expenditures on general long-term debt.

Expenditures	xxx	
Matured Bonds Payable		xxx
or/and		
Matured Interest Payable		xxx

The third entry records the payment of principal and interest when the debt matures.

Matured Bonds Payable	xxx	
or/and		
Matured Interest Payable	xxx	
Cash		xxx

▲ | **OBSERVATION**

> If the matured bonds or interest payments are not all liquidated in a given pe-
> riod, bonds payable may be carried in the financial statements of a debt service
> fund. This is the only circumstance in which long-term debt is classified as a
> **fund** liability.

Use of Subsidiary Accounts   Normally, all revenues are credited to a
single control account; all transfers are credited to another. Similarly, all expenditures are debited to a single control account. If control accounts are
used in this manner, subsidiary accounts are established for each different
source and use. For example, a subsidiary account is established for each
type of revenue, such as interest revenue, issuance premiums, and so forth.
Likewise, interest and principal payments are debited to separate subsidiary
accounts. In addition, if more than one debt issue is accounted for in a single
fund, subsidiary accounts should be established for inflows and outflows pertaining to each debt issue.

Specific Accounting Conventions

Sinking funds for term debt and advance refundings or extinguishments represent the major accounting issues pertaining to debt service funds. These issues, as well as those related to delinquent taxes and investment losses, are
discussed in the following sections.

Sinking Fund Requirements for Term Debt   Debt servicing of term
bonds is complicated by the fact that although interest is due annually, the
entire bond issue matures at the end of the term. Rarely do governmental entities wait until the end of the term to budget resources sufficient to pay off
the bonds. They set aside a portion of the issue each year into a **sinking
fund.**[1] The amount set aside each period is invested, and the interest earnings are added to the sinking fund. Together, the set-aside amounts and the
interest are sufficient to pay off the term bonds at maturity.

Calculating the annual contribution to the sinking fund is a matter of
applying present value concepts to an entity's particular circumstances. For
example, if a governmental entity issued $5,000,000 of 8 percent, 20-year
bonds, the object is to determine how much would have to be set aside annually to accumulate the $5,000,000 at the end of 20 years. If the sinking fund
contribution is made at the beginning of the year and investments are expected to earn 6 percent on average, the annual payment required is:

---

[1]The term *sinking fund* does not mean a fund as the term is used in governmental entities.
Rather, it means restricting the use of the cash to only one function: to repay the debt. This
money may be sent to a third-party fiscal agent who invests it for the governmental entity.

Exhibit 6-1

Sinking Fund Requirements for a Term Bond Issue

	COLUMN 1	COLUMN 2	COLUMN 3
Year	Set-Aside Payment[1]	Investment Earnings[2]	Fund Balance
1	$128,300	$ 7,698	$ 135,998
2	128,300	15,858	280,156
3	128,300	24,507	432,963
4	128,300	33,676	594,939
5	128,300	43,394	766,633
.	.	.	.
.	.	.	.
.	.	.	.
20	125,690	283,019	5,000,000

[1]FVAD $\int_{20}^{6\%}$ x = 5,000,000

       x = 128,300 (rounded to the nearest $100)

[2]In year 1, $128,300 × .06 = $7,698. Thereafter, Column 3 + Column 1 for the next year × 6%, for example, for year 2: .06(135,998 + 128,300) = $15,858.

Future Value of an Annuity Due at 6%, 20 years = $5,000,000

FVAD$\int_{20}^{6\%}$ X = 5,000,000
          X = 5,000,000/38.99273
          X = $128,300 (rounded to nearest $100)

Aside from rounding differences, an annual payment of $128,300, when invested at a yield of 6 percent, will total $5,000,000 by the beginning of the 20th year when the bonds mature. Exhibit 6-1 shows the required installments and earnings for the first several years.

The governmental entity will annually transfer the sinking fund payment and the current interest payment to the debt service fund. The sinking fund manager invests the money or sends it to the fiscal agent who invests it. The fund balance of the debt service fund should be reserved for the amount deposited, plus accrued interest.[2] For example, in year 1, the following entries would be made in the debt service fund:

Cash (128,300 + [5,000,000 × .08])	528,300	
Operating Transfers		528,300
(To record transfer from general fund)		
Expenditures (5,000,000 × .08)	400,000	
Cash		400,000
(To record current interest expense)		
Investments with Fiscal Agent	128,300	
Cash		128,300
(To record investment of annual installment)		

[2]In this case, the interest earnings meet the definition of measurable and available.

Investment with Fiscal Agent
    (128,300 × .06)   7,698
    Interest Revenue   7,698
    (To record earnings on first year's installment)

▲   **OBSERVATION**

The principles governing the calculation of the amounts necessary to repay the debt are identical to those explained for sinking funds for businesses. The only difference is that governmental entities usually account for the accumulations in a separate fund.

At year end, the nominal accounts would be closed; the operating transfers and interest earnings would exceed expenditures by $135,998, the amount reserved at year end.

Operating Transfers   528,300
Interest Revenue   7,698
    Expenditures   400,000
    Unreserved Fund Balance   135,998
    (To close the accounts)
Unreserved Fund Balance
    (7,698 + 128,300)   135,998
    Fund Balance Reserved for Term Bond
        Sinking Fund   135,998
    (To record reservation of fund balance for first
    installment and earnings on first installment)

Establishing a sinking fund for term bond payments necessitates a change in the budgetary accounts used in the debt service fund. To avoid confusion with current appropriations and financing sources, account titles are changed to reflect the notion of a sinking fund. The budgetary account for an annual installment is termed *required operating transfers,* and the earnings on each installment are referred to as *required earnings.* Only the portion of the transfer pertaining to current interest payments is credited to appropriations. Continuing with the preceding example, the correct budgetary entry for year 1 is:

Required Operating Transfers   528,300
Required Interest Earnings   7,698
    Appropriations   400,000
    Budgetary Fund Balance   135,998
    (To record the budget for the first year)

Advance Refundings and Defeasance   Governmental entities sometimes sell one debt issue to retire another. In profit-making entities, the practice is referred to as *advance refunding.* Advance refundings are used to lower the total interest costs, improve the payment schedule, modify indenture restrictions, and/or extend the maturity date. In an advance refunding, new debt is issued to provide monies to pay interest on old, outstanding debt as it becomes due, and to pay the principal on the old debt either as it matures or at an earlier call date....The proceeds of the new debt are invested until the maturity or call date of the old debt.[3]

If the proceeds of the new debt are used to retire the old debt, the transaction is called a **legal defeasance.** Under a legal defeasance, bond holders surrender their holdings in the old debt issue for bonds of the new issue, or are paid off from the proceeds of the new issue. Just as in profit-making firms, a governmental entity may sometimes arrange an in-substance rather than a legal defeasance.

With an **in-substance defeasance,** the governmental entity places cash or low-risk securities on deposit with a trustee. The securities, plus interest on the securities, must be sufficient to make all interim interest payments and the principal payment to retire the bonds upon maturity or call. If the restrictions for in-substance defeasance are met, the old debt issue is removed from the general long-term debt account group. Only the new debt is shown as a long-term liability.

Measuring the Economic Impact of Refundings and Defeasance. When debt is refunded or defeased, oversight boards and other interested parties must be able to assess the impact on the governmental entity. A simple comparison of the total cash flows related to the new and old debt issues provides some indication of the impact. However, this comparison does not take into account the time value of money. GASB *Statement No. 7* requires governmental entities to calculate the gain or loss on the transaction in the same manner as is required of businesses.

Calculating the Economic Gain or Loss. The GASB's guidance on measuring the economic gain or loss parallels the FASB's *Statement No. 76* on early extinguishment of debt. Although the measurement of the gain or loss is basically the same for governmental and for-profit entities, the GASB guidance requires only note disclosure of the gain or loss. *Thus, the gain or loss does not impact the entity's financial position or operating results.*

The economic gain or loss is defined as the difference between the present value of the old and new debt service requirements. The discount factor is the rate that makes the present value of the new debt equal to the net proceeds from issuing the debt. *Net proceeds* refers to the amount remaining after unrecoverable issuance costs and any related discount or premium adjustment are subtracted from the sales proceeds. Other attributes of the methodology include the following:

- If the new debt issue involves both refunding and new projects, only the amount pertaining to the refunding should be used in the calculations.
- If new debt at variable interest rates is being issued to defease old debt carrying a fixed interest rate, the entity must make sure that the economic gain or loss is not based solely on the current interest rate of the new variable

[3]Governmental Accounting Standards Board, *Statement No. 7, Advance Refunds Resulting in Defeasance of Debt* (Stamford, Conn.: GASB, 1987), ¶3.

rate bonds; additional disclosures are necessary, for example, at both the maximum and minimum rates.

- Accrued interest received at the bond issuance date should be excluded from the new debt cash flows.
- If part of the issuance costs are recoverable by escrow account earnings, they are ignored in computing the effective interest rate.
- The economic gain must be reduced or the economic loss increased by additional cash paid.

The following example demonstrates the principles involved:

Old Debt: $100 of 10% term bonds, interest paid annually on 12/31
Issued 1/1/X1, callable date 12/31/X2, due 12/31/X3

Debt Service Requirements after 12/31/X1

To Call:			To Maturity:		
12/31/X2	10.00	(interest)	12/31/X2	10.00	(interest)
12/31/X2	100.00	(principal)	12/31/X3	10.00	(interest)
			12/31/X3	100.00	(principal)
Total	110.00				
			Total	120.00	

New Debt:
Escrow Yield: 6 percent (also rate on new bonds)
Issuance Costs: $5.00
Issue Date: 1/1/X2

The object in measuring the economic gain or loss is to compare the present value of the old debt service requirements with the present value of the new debt service requirements. The following three-step procedure results in the comparison for the circumstances described above:

Step 1. Calculate the amount of debt to be issued:
New debt required to be issued is an amount that can be invested on 1/1/X2 at 6 percent to yield $110.00 on 12/31/X2:

$$\$110.00 \times PV \int_1^{6\%} = 110.00 \times .94340 = \$103.77$$

But since there are issuance costs, sufficient new debt must be issued to cover those costs plus enough, when invested at 6 percent, to call the old debt issue:

New debt amount $103.77 + 5.00 = $108.77

Step 2. Calculate the new debt service requirements:

12/31/X2	$ 6.53	(interest)	[108.77 × .06]
12/31/X3	6.53	(interest)	
12/31/X3	108.77	(principal)	
	$121.83		

The problem is to find by trial and error the interest rate that will discount this payment stream back to the net amount of 103.77. Exhibit 6-2 shows the calculation; the interpolated rate is 8.61.

Step 3. Calculate the economic gain or loss:

Using the present value factors derived from extrapolation, the present values of the old and new debt service are:

	Old Debt Service			New Debt Service	
12/31/X2	10.00 × .92075 =	9.21		6.53 × .92075 =	6.01
12/31/X3	10.00 × .84779 =	8.48		6.53 × .84779 =	5.54
12/31/X3	100.00 × .84779 =	84.78		108.77 × .84779 =	92.21
Totals	120.00	102.47		121.83	103.76*

*Difference is due to rounding.

Comparing the difference in cash flow with the economic gain or loss demonstrates how markedly different the impact is if the time value of

---

Exhibit 6-2

Calculation of Effective Interest Rate

Trial and error suggests that the interest rate that will discount the given cash flows to $103.77 is between 8 and 9 percent:

8 PERCENT			**9 PERCENT**		
12/31/X2	6.53 × .92593 =	6.05	12/31/X2	6.53 × .91743 =	5.99
12/31/X3	6.53 × .85734 =	5.60	12/31/X3	6.53 × .84168 =	5.50
12/31/X3	108.77 × .85734 =	93.25	12/31/X3	108.77 × .84168 =	91.55
Total		$104.90			$103.04

$$\frac{\text{Difference between present value at 8\% and net amount}}{\text{Difference between present value at 8\% and present value at 9\%}} =$$

$$\frac{104.90 - 103.77}{104.90 - 103.04} = \frac{1.13}{1.86} = .61 \text{ so the rate is } 8.61\%$$

Calculation of present value factors based on an interpolated rate of 8.61%:

1 year = .92593 − .61[.92593 − .91743] = .92075
2 year = .85734 − .61[.85734 − .84168] = .84779

Proof of calculation:

12/31/X2	6.53 × .92075 =	6.01
12/31/X3	6.53 × .84779 =	5.54
12/31/X3	108.77 × .84779 =	92.21
Total		103.76 ($.01 difference is due to rounding.)

Difference in cash flow is $1.83 (121.83 − 120.00)
Economic loss is $1.29 (103.76 − 102.47)

money is taken into consideration. Although the difference in cash flow is $1.83 ($121.83 − $120.00), the economic loss is only $1.29 ($102.47 − $103.76).

In this example, both the difference in cash flows and the economic consequences are negative. Despite the negative results, a governmental unit might still undertake refunding because the annual debt servicing for 19X2 is less than it was for the old debt issue. Further, the governmental entity might have gained some advantage in the terms of the indenture; certainly, the interest rate is less under the new issue.

Making the Entries. The entries for the refunded or defeased debt are made in the debt service fund. Presuming the above example had been correctly anticipated in the original budget adoption, and the governmental entity directly receives the proceeds from the advance refunding, the following entries would be made in the debt service fund:

Cash	103.77		
Other Financing Uses—Refunding			
Bond Issuance Costs		5.00	
Other Financing Sources—Proceeds of			
Refunding Bonds			108.77
Other Financing Uses—Payment to Refunded Bond			
Escrow Agent		103.77	
Cash			103.77

If the governmental entity does not receive the proceeds from the new debt, the two debt service fund entries should be combined and the net cash received or paid reflected in the entry. In this example, no net cash is received or paid, so the entries are simply combined by eliminating the debit and credit to cash.

In the example, the amount of the new bond issue was determined exactly by calculating the present value of the payments due on December 31, 19X2. However, in a more realistic situation, movements in the bond markets generally preclude selling the bonds for precisely the amount calculated. Consequently, cash proceeds from the sale are less than or more than the amount needed. For example, if the proceeds were $101.00 instead of $103.77, the entry recording the payment to the escrow agent would be:

Expenditures—Advance Refunding	2.77	
Other Financing Uses—Payment to Refunded Bond		
Escrow Agent	101.00	
Cash		103.77

As the entries illustrate, the inflow or outflow of bond proceeds is always classified as other financing sources or uses. Because the transfer to the trustee is simply a matter of substituting new debt service requirements for old ones, the Board concluded that the outflow and inflow should be reported as other financing uses and sources. Reporting both the inflow and the outflow the same way makes the transaction symmetrical. It also enables statement users to distinguish between transfers to the trustee and debt servicing amounts.

Costs associated with the refunding and/or money spent in addition to the proceeds are termed *expenditures,* for example, $2.77 in the preceding example. They represent outflows of financial resources not provided by another source.

Disclosure Requirements. As the preceding entries indicate, only the amount of the issuance costs and any additional cash required above the proceeds of the debt issue are recorded as expenditures. The economic loss of $1.29 is not reflected in any of the entries. *The GASB requires the governmental entity to calculate and disclose the economic gain or loss in the notes; the entity does not have to recognize it.* Accordingly, although the calculations are similar for governmental and for-profit entities, the impact on the financial statements is far different. For governmental entities, only net cash requirements and issuance costs, and not the full economic gain or loss, impact the operating statement. For-profit entities must recognize the gain or loss in the financial statements when it is incurred.

In addition to the economic gain or loss, governmental entities must disclose the general nature of the transaction and whether the refunding qualified as a **legal** or an **in-substance defeasance.** If the transaction resulted in an in-substance defeasance, disclosure of the amount defeased must continue until the original issue matures. The following is one possible note disclosure for the example:

> On January 1, 19X2, the City issued $108.77 in general obligation two-year bonds with an interest rate of 6 percent to advance refund $100.00 of outstanding 19X1 bonds with an interest rate of 10 percent. The net proceeds of $103.77 (after payment of $5.00 in underwriting fees and other issuance costs) were used to purchase U.S. government securities. Those securities were deposited in an irrevocable trust with an escrow agent to provide debt servicing on the 19X1 term bonds. As a result, the 19X1 term bonds were considered defeased and the liability for those bonds has been removed from the general long-term debt account group.
>
> The City's advance refunding of the 19X1 term bonds resulted in favorable changes in the bond indenture requirements for sinking fund and maintenance reserves. It increased the debt service payments over the life of the new issue by $1.83 and resulted in an economic loss (difference between the present values of the debt service payments on the old and new debt) of $1.29.

OBSERVATION ▲

Considerable effort is devoted to calculating a "gain or loss" that is never reflected in the operating statement of governmental entities. The Board also went to great lengths to distinguish "expenditures" from "other financing uses" when accounting for debt extinguishment. The distinction is not always that clear in other areas of governmental accounting. Both practices probably trace to the sensitivity of the public to long-term debt and related financing issues.

Considerations at Maturity   Regardless of the type of debt issued, best estimates sometimes are inaccurate. Earnings on sinking fund investments may be less than anticipated. The investment values sometimes decline near the maturity date of the bonds. If specific taxes are earmarked to pay the debt, some taxpayers may default, resulting in a shortage of money to pay principal or interest. Events can be favorable, too, resulting in a balance in the debt service fund after all principal and interest payments have been made. Governmental entities must plan for these situations.

Shortfalls in Sinking Fund Earnings. A governmental entity usually increases the budgeted transfer from the general fund during the last period when earnings are less than anticipated. Of course, if the shortfall is obvious before the last period, the present value calculations should be redone with more realistic interest rates, and annual transfers to the sinking fund adjusted accordingly.

A Decline in Investment Values. The proper handling of investment-value declines depends upon the market outlook. If the decline is temporary, the best solution probably is a short-term loan to the debt service fund. When the market rebounds, investments can be sold and the loan repaid. If the decline is considered permanent, investments should be sold and the difference between the proceeds and the debt service requirements transferred from another fund. For general obligation bonds, the transfer usually is made from the general fund.

Delinquent Taxes. When governmental entities earmark certain taxes for debt servicing, any delinquencies mean insufficient resources for principal or interest payments. For general obligation debt, the simplest solution is to transfer the delinquent tax collection function to the general fund in exchange for cash. If, for example, the debt service fund had delinquent taxes of $1,000 and penalties of $60, it could exchange those receivables for cash:

Debt Service	Cash	1,060	
	Taxes Receivable—Delinquent		1,000
	Penalties Receivable		60
General Fund	Taxes Receivable—Delinquent	1,000	
	Penalties Receivable	60	
	Cash		1,060

Since the general fund is responsible for general tax collection and general obligation debt, this approach is better than lending money to the debt service fund. It also avoids cluttering the debt service fund with transactions no longer relevant to its primary function.

Delinquent special assessment taxes, especially amounts in excess of that anticipated in the initial mill levy, may pose a difficult problem. All taxpayers are not expected to pay for the special improvement; any transfer from the general fund means a general sharing of the shortfall caused by one or more delinquencies. On the other hand, the governmental entity pledged its full faith and credit when the bonds were issued and is therefore indirectly liable for any delinquencies. Typically, borrowing from another debt service fund or the general fund is the best solution: it makes the necessary cash available without imposing an immediate burden on unaffected taxpayers. If the law prohibits interfund borrowings, the entity may be forced to borrow externally.

Remaining Fund Balances. Most state statutes and some bond indentures allow residual equity transfers of any remaining funds. Usually those transfers are made to other debt service funds first; when no other debt service funds exist, the transfer is usually made to the general fund.

ILLUSTRATED FINANCIAL TRANSACTIONS

Chance County has three debt service funds. One accounts for a term bond issue funded by a sinking fund. Another is used for a special assessment project undertaken to extend underground utility services to a new subdivision. Servicing of two other debt issues, one a lease and one a serial bond, is combined in the third fund. Financial transactions for all three debt service funds are illustrated in the following sections.

Term Bond Issue with Sinking Fund

On March 1, 19X1, Chance County commissioners sold $1,500,000 of 8 percent, 20-year bonds at 102 to finance a capital project. The indenture required Chance to establish a sinking fund; fund investments earn an average of 7 percent. The general fund transfers annual sinking fund contributions from general tax revenues at each year end. Budgetary accounts are fully integrated into the general accounting records.

The sinking fund requirements must be calculated before making the budgetary or transaction entries. Annual sinking fund payments total $36,590; the calculations appear below:

$$FVOA \int_{20}^{7\%} X = 1,500,000$$
$$X = 1,500,000/FVOA \int_{20}^{7\%}$$
$$X = 1,500,000/40.99549$$
$$X = 36,590 \text{ (rounded to the nearest \$10)}$$

In addition to the sinking fund payment, the general fund transfers the annual interest payments that are due on January 1 and July 1 of each year. The July interest payment is transferred at that time, and the January 1 payment is budgeted and transferred the preceding December 31, along with the contribution to the sinking fund.

19X1 The budgetary amounts for 19X1 exclude any required earnings because the first transfer is made at year end. Further, because the bonds are sold between interest dates, interest for two months is accrued. Only one interest period falls within the first budgetary cycle, but because the January 1, 19X2, payment is transferred in 19X1, it must be budgeted in 19X1.

1/1	Required Contributions [(1,500,000 × .08)		
	+ 36,590]	156,590	
	Appropriations		120,000
	Budgetary Fund Balance		36,590

Technically, the amount transferred from the general fund is an operating transfer. However, the term *required contributions* or *required earnings* is a more explicit description of the transfer; the amount transferred is the amount *required* by the indenture and the future value calculation. The general fund classifies the amount as an operating transfer, perhaps with a descriptor of sinking fund payment or required contribution to sinking fund.

The premium is not contemplated when the original budgetary entries are made; it constitutes "extra" resources and can be used to reduce the required transfer for the 19X1 annual interest payment or the sinking fund amount. Since the amount of the premium is not known until after the budget is approved, a budgetary amendment is necessary. Appropriations can be reduced by the amount of the accrued interest and revenues increased by the amount of the premium. Required transfers are reduced by the combined total of the premium and the accrued interest.

3/1	Estimated Revenues—Bond Premium		
	(1,500,000 × 1.02 − 1,500,000)	30,000	
	Appropriations (1,500,000 × .08 × 2/12)	20,000	
	Required Contributions		50,000

The premium and accrued interest are deposited directly into the debt service fund.

3/1	Cash (30,000 + 20,000)	50,000	
	Accrued Interest Payable		20,000
	Revenues—Bond Premium		30,000

Instead of crediting accrued interest payable for two months of interest *expenditures—interest* could have been credited. To avoid distorting the future value computations, the premium is applied to the first interest payment and therefore no investment occurs until year end when the general fund makes its sinking fund transfer.

7/1	Cash (60,000 − [20,000 + 30,000])	10,000	
	Operating Transfers		10,000
	Expenditures—Interest	40,000	
	Accrued Interest Payable	20,000	
	Cash		60,000

At year end, the second transfer is received and the January 1, 19X2, interest accrued. The sinking fund contribution is invested; securities with a par value of $37,000 are purchased for $36,590.

12/31	Cash (60,000 + 36,590)	96,590	
	Operating Transfers		96,590
	Expenditures	60,000	
	Accrued Interest Payable		60,000

Investments	37,000	
Unamortized Discount		410
Cash		36,590

The budgetary and nominal accounts are closed. Because the $36,590 is committed to the sinking fund, the unreserved fund balance also must be reserved.

12/31	Appropriations (120,000 − 20,000)	100,000	
	Budgetary Fund Balance	36,590	
	Required Contributions (156,590 − [20,000 + 30,000])		106,590
	Estimated Revenues—Bond Premium		30,000
	Revenues—Bond Premium	30,000	
	Operating Transfers In	106,590	
	Expenditures (40,000 + 60,000)		100,000
	Unreserved Fund Balance		36,590
	Unreserved Fund Balance	36,590	
	Reserve for Term Bond Principal		36,590

19X2 During the second year, the previous year's deposit is estimated to earn 7 percent. On January 1, 19X2, the 19X2 budget is approved and the accrued interest paid.

OBSERVATION ▲

If the $37,000 investment earns the average rate of 7 percent, actual earnings will be slightly more than 7 percent because the investments were purchased at a discount. Unless significant, the discount probably would not be reflected in the budgetary accounts. Instead, the budget would be maintained at the levels indicated by the future value computation.

1/1	Required Earnings (36,590 × .07)	2,560	
	Required Contributions (36,590 + 120,000)	156,590	
	Appropriations		120,000
	Budgetary Fund Balance		39,150
	Accrued Interest Payable	60,000	
	Cash		60,000

The operating transfer is received from the general fund, and the July 1, 19X2, interest payment is made.

7/1	Cash	60,000	
	Operating Transfers		60,000
	Expenditures	60,000	
	Cash		60,000

At year end, the general fund transfers the required sinking fund contribution, along with the interest payment due January 1, 19X3. Interest on the bonds is accrued.

12/31	Cash (36,590 + 60,000)	96,590	
	Operating Transfers		96,590
	Expenditures	60,000	
	Accrued Interest Payable		60,000

The trust agent notifies Chance that the investments earned $2,500 during 19X2.

12/31	Investments	2,500	
	Revenues—Investment Earnings		2,500

The Governmental Accounting Standards Board makes no mention of using the effective interest method for amortizing discounts and premiums on debt service investments. Accordingly, any systematic and rational basis is acceptable. For purposes of these illustrations, the straight-line method is used. The investments purchased in 19X1 have a ten-year life, so the annual amortization is $40 ($410/10 to the nearest $10).

12/31	Unamortized Bond Discount	40	
	Miscellaneous Earnings—Bond Discount		40

▲ **OBSERVATION**

The GASB has mentioned or utilized discounting and other present value concepts in numerous statements. Accordingly, one might anticipate that at some future time premiums and discounts will be amortized using the effective interest method if they are material.

The budgetary and nominal accounts are closed, and the reserve is established for the current-year contribution to the sinking fund.

12/31	Appropriations	120,000	
	Budgetary Fund Balance	39,150	
	Required Earnings		2,560
	Required Contributions		156,590
	Operating Transfers	156,590	
	Revenues—Investment Earnings	2,500	
	Miscellaneous Earnings—Bond Discount	40	
	Expenditures		120,000
	Unreserved Fund Balance		39,130

As illustrated, investment earnings fell short of the estimate by $60, but the amortization of bond discount made up for some of the shortfall. The credit to the unreserved fund balance is $39,130 compared to the $39,150 anticipated in the budget.

```
12/31   Unreserved Fund Balance                    39,150
            Reserve for Term Bond Principal                     39,150
```

The fund balance reservation pertaining to the sinking fund is based on future value computations. This practice enables statement users to assess the overall performance of the investments. If the reservation exceeds the amount in the unreserved fund balance, the unreserved fund balance will show a deficit, signaling something is wrong with the assumptions or the trustee's investment practices. Although not a major difference, Chance's sinking fund is underfunded by $20 ($39,150 − 39,130), the amount of the deficit in the unreserved fund balance.

Special Assessment Debt Service Fund

Prior to 1987, special assessment projects were accounted for in separate funds; entries for the construction, debt, assessment levies, and debt servicing all were made in a special assessment fund. This approach was judged inadequate, even misleading. It did not distinguish appropriately between assessment projects that were the responsibility of the governmental entity and those that were not. Also, accounting practices applied to the special assessment fund led to a deficit fund balance during the early years of the project.

For these reasons, special assessment funds have been eliminated for reporting purposes. Now, special assessment capital projects for which the governmental entity is obligated in some manner are treated like any other capital project. The interest and principal payments on the long-term debt are made in the debt service fund. The only difference is that specific taxpayers are responsible for those payments. Annually or semiannually, they pay an assessment that is sufficient to cover the interest and principal payments on the debt.

Accounting issues related to financial reporting for capital improvement special assessments are being considered in the GASB's capital reporting project. In the meantime, under the modified accrual basis of accounting, tax levies are recognized as revenues when measurable and available. Installments from property owners frequently are due shortly before the related debt service payments will be made. If a taxpayer elected to pay the entire assessment at the beginning of the project, the amount would be recorded as revenue at that time.

To demonstrate these principles, on January 1, 19X1, Chance issues $3,000,000 in 10 percent bonds at 102 to finance the extension of underground utilities to a new subdivision. One million dollars of the bonds matures in each succeeding year, and interest on the bonds is to be paid annually on December 31. Bond proceeds are invested during the period preceding construction; together with the bond premium, earnings were sufficient to pay the first interest installment. Subdivision residents approved the project and agreed to pay special assessment taxes of $1,125,000 on December 31,

19X1, 19X2, and 19X3. Chance invests any balance in the debt service fund at 8 percent.

Payments, interest earnings, and amounts invested related to the special assessment debt service fund are shown below; these amounts form the basis for the entries during the three-year period.

Date 12/31	Debt Service Payments*	Tax Assessments	Amount Invested	8% Investment Earnings	Projected Balance in Debt Service
19X1	300,000	1,125,000	-0-	-0-	$1,125,000
		300,000**		-0-	
19X2	1,300,000	1,125,000	1,125,000	90,000	1,040,000
19X3	1,200,000	1,125,000	1,040,000	83,200	1,048,200
19X4	1,100,000	-0-	1,048,200	83,856	32,056

*Interest and principal payments.

**The premium and interest earned on bond proceeds before construction starts (3,000,000 × .08 + [3,000,000 × 1.02 − 3,000,000]).

Because state law precludes borrowing from other funds, Chance County commissioners budgeted a cushion of $32,056 when determining the annual assessments. If no delinquencies or foreclosures are necessary, the $32,056 will be proportionally credited on future tax levies.

Only control accounts are illustrated in this example. With only one debt service activity being accounted for in the fund, subsidiary accounts probably are unnecessary. Nonetheless, Chance could use them if management felt that subsidiary ledgers facilitated the accounting or reporting functions.

The illustrated journal entries reflecting each year's debt service transactions follow.

19X1 On January 1, 19X1, the bonds are sold at 102 and the money invested at 8 percent. The debt service fund receives the premium directly. The construction contract is approved, but the first progress payment is not due until construction is completed, which is expected to occur on December 31, 19X1.

1/1	Estimated Revenues—Special Assessments	1,125,000	
	Estimated Revenues—Bond Premium (3,060,000 − 3,000,000)	60,000	
	Estimated Revenues—Interest Revenues (.08 × 3,000,000)	240,000	
	Appropriations		300,000
	Budgetary Fund Balance		1,125,000
	Cash	60,000	
	Revenues—Bond Premium		60,000

If the premium is not known when the initial budgetary entries are made, a budgetary amendment must be approved and the budgetary accounts adjusted accordingly when the bonds are sold.

Interest earnings on the $3,000,000 bond issue that is invested until the contractor is paid are earned on a quarterly basis and paid directly to the debt service fund.

3/30	Cash	60,000	
	Interest Revenues (3,000,000 × .08/4)		60,000
6/30	Cash	60,000	
	Interest Revenues		60,000
9/30	Cash	60,000	
	Interest Revenues		60,000

The project is completed on December 31, 19X1; the special assessment taxes are levied upon completion, and interest accrues at 8 percent on any amounts unpaid 30 days after the due date.

12/31	Special Assessments Receivable—Current	1,125,000	
	Revenues—Special Assessments		1,125,000

On December 31, the last quarter's interest earnings are received and the debt service payment made. Not everyone paid the first assessment; only $1,000,000 of the total $1,125,000 due is received by year end.

12/31	Cash	60,000	
	Interest Revenues		60,000
	Expenditures—Interest	300,000	
	Cash		300,000
	Cash	1,000,000	
	Special Assessments Receivable—Current		1,000,000

The cash balance is invested and the budgetary and nominal accounts closed.

12/31	Investments	1,000,000	
	Cash		1,000,000
	Appropriations	300,000	
	Budgetary Fund Balance	1,125,000	
	Estimated Revenues—Bond Premium		60,000
	Estimated Revenues—Interest		240,000
	Estimated Revenues—Special Assessments		1,125,000
	Revenues—Special Assessments	1,125,000	
	Revenues—Bond Premium	60,000	
	Revenues—Interest	240,000	
	Expenditures		300,000
	Unreserved Fund Balance		1,125,000

Delinquent assessments are reclassed and the reserve for future debt service payments is established for the amount of the debt service payments that is available in the debt service fund.

12/31	Special Assessments Receivable—Delinquent	125,000	
	Special Assessments Receivable—		
	Current		125,000
	Unreserved Fund Balance	1,000,000	
	Reserve for Special Assessment		
	Debt Service Payments		1,000,000

The assessments cover both interest and principal. Because they are based on a level-payment plan, part of the revenue recognized in 19X1 relates to future principal *and* interest payments. Consequently, the reserve must be established for the total amount available in the debt service fund.

19X2   The 19X2 budget is approved. Even though the delinquent taxpayers may not make the assessment payment and regardless of the amount of interest accruing on those delinquencies, budgetary entries are typically based on the *plan* initially established, not the experience to date.

1/1	Estimated Revenues ([1,125,000 × .08]		
	+ 1,125,000)	1,215,000	
	Budgetary Fund Balance	85,000	
	Appropriations		1,300,000

The 19X2 tax levy is recorded.

| | Special Assessment Receivable—Current | 1,125,000 | |
| | Revenues—Special Assessments | | 1,125,000 |

On February 1, $100,000 of delinquent installments are received, along with accrued interest. The receipts are immediately invested.

2/1	Cash (100,000 + [100,000 × .08 × 1/12])	100,667	
	Special Assessments Receivable—		
	Delinquent		100,000
	Revenues—Interest		667
2/1	Investments	100,667	
	Cash		100,667

Each quarter, one-fourth of the interest earnings are accrued. Interest for the first quarter is accrued for three months on the $1,000,000 invested by year end 19X1 and for two months on the $100,667 invested on February 1 (and rounded to the nearest $10). Thereafter, the interest is accrued for a full three months on $1,100,667. To simplify the presentation, compounding of interest was ignored.

3/30	Accrued Interest Receivable ([1,000,000 ×		
	.08 × 1/4] + [100,667 × .08 × 2/12])	21,340	
	Revenues—Interest		21,340

6/30	Accrued Interest Receivable (1,100,667 × .08 × 1/4)	22,010	
	Revenues—Interest		22,010
9/30	Accrued Interest Receivable	22,010	
	Revenues—Interest		22,010

Assessments of $1,100,000 are received by December 31. Interest earnings are received, debt service payments made, and accounts reclassified.

12/31	Cash (1,100,000 + 22,010 + 22,010 + 22,010 + 21,340)	1,187,370	
	Special Assessments Receivable— Current		1,100,000
	Accrued Interest Receivable (22,010 + 22,010 + 21,340)		65,360
	Revenues—Interest (1,100,667 × .08/4)		22,010

Some investments are sold because the current installment plus 19X2 earnings is insufficient to make the debt service payments (1,300,000 − 1,187,370 = 112,630).

Cash	112,630	
Investments		112,630
Expenditures—Serial Bonds	1,000,000	
Expenditures—Interest	300,000	
Matured Interest and Bonds Payable		1,300,000
Matured Interest and Bonds Payable	1,300,000	
Cash		1,300,000
Sepcial Assessments Receivable—Delinquent	25,000	
Special Assessments Receivable—Current		25,000

Whether interest is accrued on delinquent installments is a matter of judgment. The GASB pronouncement on special assessments is silent on the matter so the accountant should apply the general rules of the modified accrual basis of accounting. The accountant must judge whether the interest will be available to meet current liabilities. The same is true of any penalties assessed against the property owners who did not pay the 19X1 installment. In this instance, the interest is assumed to be available to meet current liabilities in 19X3. No penalties are assessed in this example.

Accrued Interest Receivable—Delinquent (25,000 × .08)	2,000	
Revenues—Interest		2,000
Appropriations	1,300,000	
Budgetary Fund Balance		85,000
Estimated Revenues		1,215,000

Revenues—Interest (22,010 + 22,010 + 22,010 + 21,340 + 667 + 2,000)	90,037	
Revenues—Assessments	1,125,000	
Unreserved Fund Balance	84,963	
Expenditures—Interest		300,000
Expenditures—Serial Bonds		1,000,000

The reserve for special assessment debt service payments must be adjusted at year end. At the end of 19X1 it was credited for the amount remaining in the debt service fund, or $1,000,000. After the payments by the assessed taxpayers and debt service payments, the fund has a balance of $988,037 (1,000,000 + 100,667 + 1,187,370 − 1,300,000). Therefore, the reserve needs to be reduced by $11,963 (1,000,000 − 988,037).

Reserve for Special Assessment Debt Service Payments	11,963	
Unreserved Fund Balance		11,963

The unreserved fund balance shows a credit at year end 19X2—that is, revenues have exceeded expenditures and reservations of fund balance.

Unreserved Fund Balance

12/31/X1	1,000,000	1,125,000	12/31/X1
12/31/X2	84,963	11,963	12/31/X2
		52,000	12/31/X2 Balance

If the estimates for the entire project are valid, the ending balance on 12/31/X4 will be $32,056. To date, the earnings projections appear appropriate, but the positive fund balance may be misleading. The entire amount of revenue has been accrued each year, but the delinquent assessments are in doubt. Neither the unreserved fund balance nor the reserve account balance signals this potential problem. Only by looking at delinquent accounts on the balance sheet do readers begin to get a feeling for the potential problem.[4]

Combined Debt Service Fund

Chance enters into a long-term capital lease arrangement in which it acquires a fixed asset and lease liability of $268,000. The implicit rate used in calculating the lease and asset value is 7 percent, and the annual debt service payments total $28,000. The annual payment is funded by a transfer from the general fund.

Another debt service requirement involves a $2,000,000, 8 percent, serial bond issue; $500,000 matures each year and is funded by an annual tax as-

[4]This example assumed that the special assessments bonds matured evenly over the period. Not all special assessment bonds mature in this way. Some have a period of deferral before they begin maturing. Others mature in unequal amounts over the term.

sessment (for the principal) and an operating transfer (for the interest) from the general fund. In addition, the serial bond indenture requires a general fund transfer of $16,000, which will be invested for potential contingencies related to tax collections. If the contingency amount is not used, it is transferred back to the general fund after all debt installments are paid.

With two unrelated debt servicing activities accounted for in a single fund, subsidiary ledgers are advisable and therefore illustrated. Particularly critical for statement users is the ability to relate any reserves or unreserved fund balances to the appropriate debt issue.

19X1 is the first year for both debt issues. The 19X1 budget is established for both debt issues on January 1, 19X1. It assumes all transfers, tax collections, and payments occur at year end.

1/1	Estimated Other Financing Sources		
	(28,000 + 16,000 + [.08 × 2,000,000])	204,000	
	Estimated Revenues	500,000	
	Appropriations		
	(500,000 + 28,000 + 160,000)		688,000
	Budgetary Fund Balance		16,000

Subsidiary Estimated Revenues and Revenues Accounts:

Property Taxes—Serial Bond	500,000 Dr.

In subsequent years, a second subsidiary account would be necessary for interest earnings on the annual exigency transfer from the general fund.

Subsidiary Other Financing Sources Accounts:

Operating Transfers—Serial Bond	
(160,000 + 16,000)	176,000 Dr.
Operating Transfers—Lease	28,000 Dr.

Subsidiary Appropriations and Expenditures Accounts:

Bond Principal—Serial Bond	500,000 Cr.
Bond Interest—Serial Bond	160,000 Cr.
Lease Interest (268,000 × .07)	18,760 Cr.
Lease Principal (28,000 − 18,760)	9,240 Cr.

The tax levy is made on January 1 of each year; 1 percent of the levy is expected to be uncollectible.

1/1	Taxes Receivable Current	500,000	
	Allowance for Uncollectible Taxes		5,000
	Revenues		495,000

Subsidiary Revenue Account:

Property Taxes—Serial Bond	495,000 Cr.

At year end, the general fund transfers the contingency amount ($16,000), the annual lease payment ($28,000), and the interest on the serial debt ($160,000). Earmarked taxes totaling $497,000 also are collected.

12/31	Cash	701,000	
	Operating Transfers		204,000
	Taxes Receivable Current		497,000

Subsidiary Other Financing Sources Accounts:

Operating Transfers—Serial Bond	176,999 Cr.
Operating Transfers—Lease	28,000 Cr.

As these illustrated entries suggest, the subsidiary accounts serve two purposes: (1) to show the composition of various control accounts, such as revenues and appropriations, and (2) to identify the debt service activity to which the various debits and credits relate.

Projected collections on taxes totaled $495,000; $497,000 was actually collected. Consequently, the allowance is too high and must be adjusted.

12/31	Allowance for Uncollectible Taxes	2,000	
	Revenue		2,000

Subsidiary Revenue Account:

Property Taxes—Serial Bond	2,000 Cr.

The matured bond and interest payments and lease payment are paid at year end.

12/31	Expenditures	688,000	
	Matured Bond Principal Payable		500,000
	Matured Bond Interest Payable		160,000
	Matured Lease Principal Payable		9,240
	Matured Lease Interest Payable		18,760

Subsidiary Expenditures Accounts:

Bond Principal—Serial Bond	500,000 Dr.
Bond Interest—Serial Bond	160,000 Dr.
Lease Interest	18,760 Dr.
Lease Principal	9,240 Dr.

Establishing the payables—bond interest, lease interest, lease principal, and lease interest—might be unnecessary in this particular illustration because the payment entry follows immediately after this entry. However, in practice, matured long-term debt accounts always are established because a delay is likely between recognition of the expenditure and the actual payment.

Matured Bond Principal Payable	500,000
Matured Bond Interest Payable	160,000

Matured Lease Principal Payable	9,240	
Matured Lease Interest Payable	18,760	
Cash		688,000
Investments (16,000 − 3,000 shortfall on taxes)	13,000	
Cash		13,000

Although not illustrated, the budgetary and nominal accounts are closed. Also, an entry reserving the fund balance pertaining to the serial bond exigency balance is necessary.

Unreserved Fund Balance—Serial Bonds	13,000	
Reserve for Exigencies—Serial Bonds		13,000

Only the unused amount of the transfer for exigencies is reserved; it matches the amount that will be shown as investments in the asset section of the balance sheet. As the entry illustrates, identifying the debt service activity to which the reserve relates, namely the serial bonds, is absolutely critical. The GASB requires separate fund balances and reserves whenever two activities are accounted for in a single fund. Had the serial bond debt servicing been maintained in a separate fund, the term *serial bonds* could have been eliminated from the account title.

DEBT SERVICE REPORTING PRACTICES

Generally accepted accounting principles require a balance sheet and a statement of revenues, expenditures, and changes in fund balance. A statement of revenues, expenditures, and changes in fund balance—budget and actual also is required if the budgetary accounts are integrated into the accounting system. For debt service funds involving annual transfers for current debt service, the budgetary comparisons are not very revealing or meaningful to statement users. The budget rarely differs from the actual figures, resulting in a very simplistic statement. However, when sinking funds are required, the statement takes on considerable meaning. Careful monitoring of the statement on an annual basis should eliminate any surprises at maturity. The governmental entity should be able to adjust the annual transfers to compensate for investment declines or earnings shortfalls.

Combining and Comparative Financial Statements

For comprehensive financial reports, governmental entities usually include comparative data for the three primary financial statements. These statements provide relevant data as long as they pertain to a single debt service fund. If more than one debt service activity is accounted for in a single fund or the entity has several debt service funds, only the more sophisticated readers derive any relevant information from comparative data for combined financial statements.

Since most governmental entities open more than one debt service fund, they prepare combining financial statements for the comprehensive annual financial report (CAFR). Each debt service fund is placed in a separate column with a combined total in the far right-hand column. Applying this standard to the funds illustrated here, the term bond issue would be in one column and the special assessment project in another. Chance's debt service fund accounting for two activities would be shown in a third column; however, a separate fund balance would be shown for each activity.

Illustrated Financial Statements

All three of Chance's debt service funds are used as a basis for the illustrated financial statements. Exhibit 6-3 depicts a balance sheet as of December 31, 19X1, for the term bond debt service fund. A combining statement of revenues, expenditures, and changes in fund balance for all three funds is illustrated in Exhibit 6-4. Finally, in Exhibit 6-5, the serial bond and lease debt service fund is used to illustrate a traditional format for a statement of revenues, expenditures, and changes in fund balance — budget and actual.

The format used for each statement portrays some aspects of financial statements that go beyond the illustrated debt service funds. For example, both Exhibits 6-3 and 6-5 include account titles common to debt service funds that were not used in the illustration.

Exhibit 6-3

County of Chance
Term Bond Debt Service Fund
Balance Sheet
December 31, 19X1

Assets		
Cash		$60,000
Investments	$37,000	
Less: Unamortized Discount	410	36,590
Interest Receivable on Investments		—
Due from Other Funds		—
TOTAL ASSETS		$96,590
Liabilities and Fund Balance		
Accrued Interest Payable	$60,000	
Matured Bonds Payable	—	
Total Liabilities		$60,000
Unreserved Fund Balance	$ -0-	
Reserve for Term Bond Principal	36,590	
Total Fund Balance		36,590
TOTAL LIABILITIES AND FUND BALANCE		$96,590

Exhibit 6-4

County of Chance
Debt Service Funds
Combining Statement of Revenues, Expenditures,
and Changes in Fund Balance
For the Year Ending December 31, 19X1

	Term Bond	Special Assessment	Lease/ Serial	Total
Revenues:				
Bond Premium	$ 30,000	$ 60,000	—	$ 90,000
Special Assessment Taxes	—	1,125,000	—	1,125,000
Interest Revenues	—	240,000	—	240,000
Property Taxes	—	—	$497,000	497,000
Total Revenues	$ 30,000	$1,425,000	$497,000	$1,952,000
Other Financing Sources:				
Operating Transfers	106,590	—	204,000	310,590
Total Revenues and Other Financing Sources	$136,590	$1,425,000	$701,000	$2,262,590
Expenditures:				
Bond Principal	—	—	$500,000	$ 500,000
Bond Interest	$100,000	$ 300,000	160,000	560,000
Lease Interest	—	—	18,760	18,760
Lease Principal	—	—	9,240	9,240
Total Expenditures	$100,000	$ 300,000	$688,000	$1,088,000
Excess of Revenues and Other Financing Sources Over Expenditures	$ 36,590	$1,125,000	$ 13,000	$1,174,590
Fund Balance, January 1	-0-	-0-	-0-	-0-
Fund Balance, December 31	$ 36,590	$1,125,000	$ 13,000	$1,174,590

Exhibit 6-5

County of Chance
Serial Bond and Lease Debt Service Fund
Statement of Revenues, Expenditures,
and Changes in Fund Balance — Budget and Actual
For the Year Ending December 31, 19X1

	Budget	Actual	Variance Favorable (Unfavorable)
Revenues:			
Property Taxes	$ 500,000	$ 497,000	$(3,000)
Special Assessment Taxes	—	—	—
Interest	—	—	—
Total Revenues	$ 500,000	$ 497,000	$(3,000)

(continued)

(continued)

	Budget	Actual	Variance Favorable (Unfavorable)
Expenditures:			
Bond Principal	$ 509,240	$ 509,240	$ -0-
Interest	178,760	178,760	-0-
Total Expenditures	$ 688,000	$ 688,000	$ -0-
Deficiency of Revenues Under Expenditures	$(188,000)	$(191,000)	$(3,000)
Other Financing Sources:			
Operating Transfers	204,000	204,000	-0-
Excess of Revenues and Other Financing Sources Over Expenditures and Other Financing Uses	$ 16,000	$ 13,000	$(3,000)
Fund Balance, January 1	-0-	-0-	-0-
Fund Balance, December 31	$ 16,000	$ 13,000	$(3,000)

The operating statement can be prepared to emphasize the difference between revenues and expenditures. It also can be constructed to compare total financial resources with total financial payments. Exhibit 6-5 is an example of a statement emphasizing the difference between revenues and expenditures. Exhibit 6-4 highlights the net increase. For most debt service activities, the latter presentation emphasizes the salient financial information.

SUMMARY

Governmental entities use debt service funds for activities related to servicing general long-term debt. Unless required by law or regulation, governmental entities have the option of opening separate funds for each debt service activity or combining several in a single fund. For immaterial debt servicing, such as one term bond, or isolated payments, such as lease payments, most entities make the payments through the general fund. Beyond these limited activities, governmental units use debt service funds to accumulate and pay resources earmarked for servicing debt.

Modified accrual accounting is applied to transactions in debt service funds. Interest earnings, property taxes, and other revenue are recorded when measurable and available. Because property taxes are susceptible to accrual, they are recorded as revenue when levied. Principal and interest payments generally are recognized as expenditures when due. Only when debt payments are budgeted in the year in which accrual recognition would occur is the accrual principle followed.

Special assessment debt for which the governmental entity is liable is serviced in the same manner as other general long-term debt.

Debt service funds are especially useful for reflecting sinking fund activities related to term bonds. The sinking fund contribution generally is transferred from the general fund annually or semiannually. Either the entity or a third-party trustee invests the annual deposit. The debt service fund balance is reserved for the accumulated amount in the sinking fund. Budgetary account titles include reference to required earnings or required contributions to reflect clearly the nature of the debt service activity.

Defeasance or early refundings are handled in debt service funds. Governmental entities must calculate and disclose the economic consequences of the refundings, but the gain or loss does not impact the operating statement. Payments to the escrow agent out of bond proceeds are other financing uses, just as bond proceeds are classified as other financing sources. However, any payments made to the escrow agent above the amount of the proceeds are classified as expenditures.

Estimates of debt service requirements rarely materialize. The longer the term of servicing, the more likely it is that actual amounts and estimates will differ. Local regulation and state law must be examined carefully to see what options are available if a debt service fund experiences a shortfall or an excess. Borrowing from other funds, transfers from general government operating funds, and external borrowing are possible options for offsetting a shortfall.

The three financial statements common to most governmental funds are prepared for debt service funds. A balance sheet, a statement of revenues, expenditures, and changes in fund balance, and a statement of revenues, expenditures, and changes in fund balance—budget and actual—are required under GAAP.

APPENDIX A

APPLYING THE ACCRUAL BASIS OF ACCOUNTING TO DEBT SERVICE FUNDS

Under either the flow of current financial resources or total financial resources model, only debt carried in the general long-term debt account group is serviced in the debt service funds. Under the flow of current financial resources, current GAAP, all general-purpose long-term debt is reflected in the account group. Therefore, all principal and interest payments on long-term debt are shown in debt service funds. In contrast, after the accrual/total financial resources model is adopted, only long-term debt issued to finance capital acquisitions will be serviced in the debt service funds.[5]

Revenue recognition criteria will change after the new model is adopted. Under the new model, revenues will be recognized when earned. Currently, they are recognized when measurable and available. Because of the type of revenue received by debt service funds, the change in accounting basis has far less impact on the debt service funds than might be anticipated.

As explained in the chapter, debt service funds generally receive funding from operating transfers from the general fund or earmarked tax revenues.

[5]Although the decision probably will not affect this statement, the GASB has tentatively concluded that the long-term portion of pension and related liabilities will be in the general long-term debt account group.

Under either basis of accounting, operating transfers are not classified as revenues, and therefore the change in accounting basis has no effect on accounting entries made for these transfers. Earmarked tax sources usually involve property taxes, and under the modified accrual basis, property taxes are *susceptible to accrual* and recognized just as they will be under the accrual basis of accounting. Thus, the bulk of the inflows are recognized and treated the same before and after the change in accounting practice.

Some revenues might be accounted for differently after the adoption of the accrual basis of accounting. Debt service funds sometimes obtain their money, particularly when sinking funds are required, from interest earnings or shared revenue from other governmental units. In such cases, applying the modified accrual criteria of measurable and available might result in recognition at times other than the "when earned" criterion for the accrual basis. For example, suppose that $100,000 was collected by the state November 1, 19X1, and that the state notified the county that its share of the revenue was $40,000, which will be paid in April 19X2. If the recipient unit, the county, has a calendar year reporting period, the revenue would be recognized in 19X1 under the accrual basis and in 19X2 under the modified accrual basis of accounting. Under the latter basis, the money is not *available* for 19X1 expenditures. It is received more than 60 days after the close of the period. Similar differences might apply to investment earnings.

One accounting issue related to revenue recognition has yet to be determined under the new model. This issue relates to special assessment taxes. Since taxpayers have agreed to the assessments, are they "earned" when the entire levy is approved or as annual (semiannual) installments are levied? The answer depends upon one's perspective of the assessments. If the assessments are to pay for construction costs, revenue is earned when construction is completed. If the purpose of the payments is to service the debt, the earnings process is really not complete until the related debt payment is due.

When the GASB adopted the accrual basis of accounting, no specific reference was made to special assessment levies. In the exposure draft, the Board noted:

> Certain requirements of this [special assessment] section are not necessarily consistent with the flow of financial resources measurement focus.... Issues related to financial reporting for capital improvement special assessments are currently being considered by the GASB in its capital reporting project.[6]

Because a lien is filed in conjunction with the levy, consistency with the accrual basis of accounting suggests that the entire assessment is revenue when the levy is approved. The extended payment arrangement simply represents a convenience to the taxpayers.

Referring to the special assessment example in the chapter, the recording would change if the levy was recorded consistent with the accrual basis of

---

[6]Governmental Accounting Standards Board, *Exposure Draft: Proposed Statement on Measurement Focus and Basis of Accounting — Governmental Funds* (Norwalk, Conn.: GASB, 1987), Appendix D, section S40.

accounting. In 19X1, the budgetary entry for estimated revenues would show $3,375,000 rather than $1,125,000. On December 31, when the first installment was levied, the entry would be:

Special Assessments Receivable—Current	1,125,000	
Special Assessments Receivable—Deferred	2,250,000	
Revenues—Assessments		3,375,000

Expenditure recognition in the debt service fund is the same before and after the new standard. Under both accounting bases, principal and interest payments are recognized when due rather than when the related liability is incurred. A departure from generally accepted accounting principles is permitted under both the accrual and the modified accrual bases of accounting for debt servicing. As previously noted, the only difference after the effective date of *Statement No. 11* is in which debt will be serviced in debt service funds.

The Governmental Accounting Standards Board is continuing its research and investigation of accounting issues related to debt servicing. These deliberations were not completed by the time the measurement focus/basis of accounting statement was issued. Rather than adopt some new basis of accounting for debt servicing prematurely, recognition methods applicable to debt payments under the earlier model were retained. This does not mean, however, that the basis of accounting currently applied to debt payments will remain unchanged.

QUESTIONS

6-1 What is the purpose of debt service funds? How does a municipality determine whether a debt service fund is necessary?

6-2 What type of debt servicing activity should not be accounted for in a debt service fund under *Statement No. 11*? Why?

6-3 Describe the possible sources of debt service resources. Explain how each one is treated in debt service funds.

6-4 A municipality operating on a calendar-year basis opened a debt service fund to account for accumulating resources and making principal and interest payments on a term bond. Interest is due on July 1 and January 1. When are the expenditures recognized for these interest payments? For the principal payment due 10 years from the current January 1?

6-5 What accounts likely would be found in a debt service fund used to account for a sinking fund and payment of principal and interest on term debt?

6-6 A state is selling debt service fund investments to retire a term bond issue. How is the gain on those investments treated? Is it the same if the sale results in a loss?

6-7 Why might a governmental unit choose to refund a debt issue?

6-8 Under what circumstances would the account "matured bonds payable" appear in a debt service fund?

6-9 Explain the circumstances under which debt service subsidiary accounts facilitate accounting and reporting practices.

6-10 Is the "when due" convention used by debt service funds consistent with accrual accounting? Explain why it is used.

6-11 Describe how accounting for special assessment debt changed in 1987. How does a governmental entity determine whether the debt should be serviced in a debt service fund?

6-12 What recognition options are justifiable for special assessment levies under the accrual basis of accounting? Explain.

6-13 How are debt payment transfers from the general fund treated in the debt service fund? Is the same treatment accorded tax levies deposited directly in the debt service fund? Explain.

6-14 Explain the difference between a legal and an in-substance defeasance.

6-15 What happens if tax collections for the period are insufficient to pay the related principal or interest payments?

6-16 A governmental and a for-profit entity both calculated a $10,000 economic loss on defeased debt. How is the loss treated on the financial statements of the two entities? What is the significant difference?

6-17 What treatment is accorded to debt service fund balances remaining after all servicing is completed?

6-18 What is the significance of the call versus the maturity date for defeased debt issues?

6-19 Explain how the accounting for debt service funds changes with the new pronouncement on measurement focus/basis of accounting.

CASES

6-1 Piltzville needs assistance in determining whether it should defease a bond issue maturing in five years and callable two years from now. Piltzville's treasurer indicates that an in-substance defeasance would net the city $820,000 in cash flow. The economic loss is $150,000. If the debt is defeased, the debt service requirements will be spread over seven instead of five years. Accordingly, the annual payments are less, but the new debt reduces the amount of debt the city could issue for two additional years.

REQUIRED
Prepare a report to explain how the decision on defeasance should be evaluated.

6-2 Lewis and Clark County has a number of debt servicing activities:

- Lease payments on a 5-year capital lease for computer equipment
- A serial bond issue pertaining to a special improvement district for which Lewis and Clark is not liable for the debt

- A term bond issue for which a sinking fund is being established; the interest on the debt is paid semiannually, and the sinking fund amounts are set aside annually. Money placed in the sinking fund is derived from the annual operating budget
- A long-term note payable pertaining to operating funds for the general fund
- Interest and principal payments on a mortgage covering several private residences purchased by the county for extra office space
- Bond anticipation notes qualifying as general long-term debt on which annual interest and principal payments are made

REQUIRED

Identify each debt service activity that could be accounted for in a separate debt service fund. Within the group of those that could be accounted for in a separate fund, which debt servicing activities are most likely to be accounted for in a separate fund?

6-3 The liability and fund balance sections of Mendon's combined balance sheet for its debt service funds appears below:

County of Mendon
Excerpts from the Combined Balance Sheet
December 31, 19X1

Liabilities:	
Matured Serial Bonds Payable	$120,000
Matured Interest Payable	56,000
Due to General Fund	11,000
Unamortized Bond Discount	1,400
Total Liabilities	$188,400
Fund Balance:	
Unreserved Fund Balance	$ (5,000)
Reserve for Term Bond Principal	37,000
Total Fund Balance	$ 32,000

REQUIRED

Draft a report to Mendon's county commissioners explaining as much as possible from the information provided. Include an explanation of the types of debt, and how they are being financed. Explain why each account might be present and the reason for its current balance.

6-4 The city of Clayer issued long-term debt to finance construction of gutters and sewer lines to the north side of the city. Clayer's full faith and credit is pledged to servicing the debt. City council members have been thoroughly briefed and agree that the city will adopt the accrual basis of accounting for its governmental funds whenever the method is made effective by the GASB. However, council members are deeply divided over the question of accounting for the special assessment levy under the accrual basis.

REQUIRED

1. Will the city have an option in treating the special assessment tax levy? Explain.
2. If the city will have an option, which basis should the city use? Justify your answer.

6-5 A local accounting firm is auditing the city of Bellwood. During the audit, the firm raised a number of issues concerning transactions and entries related to Bellwood's debt service funds. The questionable transactions and, when appropriate, the entries are explained below:

1. Included in Bellwood's budgetary entries is one to reflect a planned transfer from the general fund to the debt service funds for paying principal and interest on serial bonds, and interest and a sinking fund contribution related to term debt:

Required Contributions	1,000,000	
Required Earnings	62,000	
Appropriations		1,062,000

2. The sinking fund transfer has been made for a number of years. The balance with the trustee is $878,000 (includes interest earnings from prior years, all of which is invested); the current year's addition is $107,000. Interest on the term debt for the current year totals $320,000. Bellwood's records show a reserve of the fund balance of $1,305,000.

3. When the final installment of a special assessment bond issue (for which Bellwood had assumed responsibility) matured, cash in the debt service fund was insufficient to make the payment. Two taxpayers in the special assessment district had not paid all assessments, and the debt service fund showed the following account balances:

	Dr.	Cr.
Taxes Receivable Delinquent	$27,100	
Allowance for Uncollectible Delinquent		
Taxes		$4,200
Penalties and Interest on Taxes		
Receivable Delinquent	2,380	

To cover the shortfall, the city's finance officer recorded a loan from the general fund to the debt service fund:

Cash	25,280	
Due to General Fund		25,280

4. A Bellwood capital projects fund issued bonds to cover construction costs related to renovation of the city hall. The bonds were sold in a favorable market yielding a premium of $20,000. The premium was received by the capital projects fund and transferred to the debt service fund, resulting in the following entry for the debt service fund:

Cash		20,000	
Revenues			20,000

REQUIRED

Identify what, if anything, is wrong with the accounting treatment of each item. If applicable, explain what Bellwood should have done in reflecting the transaction.

EXERCISES

6-1 Appendix A of the textbook contains excerpts from the comprehensive financial report for Raleigh, North Carolina. After reviewing the statements pertaining to the debt service funds, answer the following questions:

1. What primary financial statements are shown for the debt service funds? What notes or supporting schedules pertain to debt service?
2. Is the manner in which Raleigh handles debt service consistent with the presentation in the text? Is it in accordance with GAAP? Explain why Raleigh may have chosen this method.
3. Is it possible to determine whether a bond sinking fund has been established for any term debt? Explain.
4. Is it possible to determine whether any special assessment debt is being serviced? If so, have the revenues been recognized for the whole levy, or only for the current installment?
5. Does the auditors' opinion make any reference to qualifications related to debt service funds? If so, describe the qualification.

6-2 Select the best answer for each question.

1. Ariel Village issued the following bonds during the year ended June 30, 19X3:

For installation of street lights, to be assessed against properties benefited and without any obligation of the governmental unit	$300,000
For construction of public swimming pool; the activity is accounted for in an enterprise fund and the bonds repaid by fees collected from pool users	400,000

How much should be accounted for through the debt service funds for payments of principal over the life of the bonds?
   a. $0
   b. $300,000
   c. $400,000
   d. $700,000
   (Adapted from the May 1984 CPA Exam, Practice #58)

2. A debt service fund of a municipality is an example of which of the following types of fund?

   a. fiduciary
   b. governmental
   c. proprietary
   d. internal service
   (Adapted from the November 1982 CPA Exam, Theory #54)

Items 3 and 4 are based on the following information:
   The following events related to the city of Albury's debt service funds occurred during the year ended December 31, 19X1:

Debt Principal Matured	$2,000,000
Unmatured (accrued) Interest on Outstanding Debt at	
Jan. 1, 19X1	50,000
Interest on Matured Debt	900,000
Unmatured (accrued) Interest on Outstanding Debt at	
Dec. 31, 19X1	100,000
Interest Revenue from Investments	600,000
Cash Transferred from the General Fund for Retirement	
of Debt Principal	1,000,000
Cash Transferred from the General Fund for Payment of	
Matured Interest	900,000

All principal and interest due in 19X1 was paid on time.

   3. What is the total amount of expenditures that Albury's debt service funds should record for the year ended December 31, 19X1?
      a. $900,000
      b. $950,000
      c. $2,900,000
      d. $2,950,000
   4. How much revenue should Albury's debt service funds record for the year ended December 31, 19X1?
      a. $600,000
      b. $1,600,000
      c. $1,900,000
      d. $2,500,000
      (Adapted from the May 1982 CPA Exam, Practice #26 and #27)
   5. During the fiscal year ended June 30, 19X8, Lake County financed the following projects by special assessments:

Capital Improvements	$2,000,000
Service-Type Projects	800,000

   For financial reporting purposes, what amount of debt should be serviced by special assessment funds?
      a. $2,800,000
      b. $2,000,000
      c. $800,000
      d. $0
      (Adapted from the November 1988 CPA Exam, Practice #46)
   6. Under current GAAP, which of the following types of debt is not serviced through a debt service fund?

a. special assessment bonds carrying the full faith and credit of the governmental unit

b. operating debt for general fund expenditures

c. serial debt financing a city hall improvement

d. none of the above

7. A premium received on a bond issue that cannot be used as part of the project's financing is classified as:

a. revenue if received directly by a debt service fund

b. revenue if received directly by a capital projects fund

c. always as an other financing source

d. an operating transfer if received directly by a debt service fund

8. The "when due" convention for recognizing principal and interest payments as expenditures can be justified:

a. for deep discount debt issues

b. as appropriate for the accrual basis of accounting

c. under the matching principle when the modified accrual basis of accounting is used

d. for debt issued for operating purposes

9. The required contributions and required earnings budgetary accounts are used for:

a. any bond issue involving transfers from the general fund and debt service investments

b. bond issues involving contributions from other funds

c. debt for which a sinking fund has been established

d. bond issues for which transfers are made to a third-party trustee

10. Which of the following is not true of an in-substance defeasance?

a. the economic impact of the decision must be disclosed

b. the payment to the trustee from refunding debt is classified as an other financing use

c. the old debt is retired

d. risk-free securities are deposited with a trustee

6-3 Select the best answer for each question.

1. Proceeds from a refunding issue total $1,300,000; payments to the third-party trustee total $1,310,000. The additional $10,000 is treated as:

a. an expense

b. an operating transfer

c. an expenditure

d. an other financing use

2. Amounts remaining in a debt service fund after all principal and interest payments have been made are treated as:

a. an operating transfer

b. a reserve of fund balance

c. miscellaneous revenue

d. none of the above

3. A debenture for a term bond requires periodic transfers from the general fund to the debt service fund: $52,800 addition to the sinking

fund; $13,000 for a contingency reserve; and $108,100 for annual interest payments. At the end of the first year, the reserve for term bonds would total:

   a. $65,800

   b. $173,100

   c. $52,000

   d. $108,100

4. Interest and principal payments on short-term term debt:

   a. are reflected in either the fund carrying the liability or a debt service fund

   b. are reflected in the fund carrying the liability

   c. are recorded in a debt service fund

   d. none of the above

5. Drummond Township provides for the retirement of term bonds by setting aside a portion of general property taxes and investing those proceeds. The investment activity should be reflected in:

   a. a special revenue fund

   b. the general fund

   c. a trust fund

   d. a debt service fund

6. The entry in the debt service fund to record the maturity of a serial bond is:

a. Expenditures	xxx	
Matured Bonds Payable		xxx
b. Matured Bonds Payable	xxx	
Cash		xxx
c. Expenditures	xxx	
Cash		xxx
d. Cash	xxx	
Matured Bonds Payable		xxx

7. Earnings on investments carried in a debt service fund are recognized as revenue when earned under the:

   a. modified accrual basis of accounting

   b. cash basis

   c. accrual basis

   d. accrual or modified accrual basis depending upon the circumstances

8. Premiums on long-term debt issues generally are transferred to what fund or account group?

   a. general fund

   b. capital projects fund

   c. debt service fund

   d. general long-term debt account group

9. The annual contribution to a sinking fund beginning on the first day of the year would be calculated using:

   a. future value of an ordinary annuity

   b. future value of $1

    c. future value of an annuity due

    d. present value of $1

  10. Which of the following factors is not taken into consideration in calculating the economic gain or loss on an in-substance defeasance?

    a. the cash received from the new debt

    b. debt service requirements to maturity for the old debt issue

    c. the potential yield on escrowed amounts

    d. the accrued interest received from the issuance of the new debt

6-4 Delair County decides that it ought to investigate possible refunding of $400,000, 20 percent term bonds. The interest is paid annually on December 31. The bonds were issued on January 1, 19X1; they are due on December 31, 19X3, and callable on December 31, 19X2, at par. No issuance costs would be incurred, and the escrow fund yield is 10 percent.

REQUIRED

  1. Assuming the new 10 percent debt is issued on January 1, 19X2, calculate the amount of the new debt proceeds that is necessary to refund the bonds on the call date.

  2. Calculate the economic gain or loss on the refunding, assuming the new debt is due on 12/31/X3.

Present Value Factors:

Period 1	10%	.90909
Period 2	10%	.82645

6-5 The city of Arcadia has a serial debt service fund financed by transfers from other funds, sales tax revenue, and interest earnings. Debt service principal payments are made on September 30 of each year; interest is due then and on March 31. Arcadia's fiscal year ends on June 30, and it integrates the budgetary accounts into the general accounting records. A post-closing trial balance for June 30, 19X3, follows:

City of Arcadia
Post-Closing Trial Balance
Serial Bond Debt Service Fund
June 30, 19X3

	Dr.	Cr.
Cash	$125,000	
Investments	300,000	
Accrued Interest Receivable	2,100	
Receivable from State	10,100	
Due from General Fund	7,900	
Matured Bonds Payable		$100,000
Matured Interest Payable		17,000
Reserve for Serial Bond Payments		266,100
Unreserved Fund Balance		62,000
Total	$445,100	$445,100

appropriation for that year

The debt service fund is notified of its share of sales tax proceeds to be paid from the state's general fund when the proceeds are received by the state. Because the revenue is earmarked for debt service, the payments do not necessarily bear any relationship to the current serial bond interest and principal payments. Debt service payments are budgeted in the fiscal years paid.

The following transactions occurred during fiscal 19X4:

1. The budget was established for 19X4:

Serial Bonds Maturing	$300,000
Interest on Bonds	400,000
Scheduled Transfers from Other Funds:	
General Fund	100,000
Special Revenue Fund	50,000
Share of Sales Taxes	710,000
Interest Earnings	26,000

2. Fiscal year-end receivables were collected; the payables were liquidated.
3. The state notified Arcadia that its share of sales tax revenue for 19X4 totaled $706,000. The amount will be collected by the end of the fiscal period.
4. General fund and special revenue fund transfers were received; the debt service fund invests any cash balances above $15,000.
5. One-half of the current year's sales taxes was received, as was 7 percent interest on the investment balance at the end of Fiscal 19X3. This amount was invested.
6. All but $10,000 of the principal due on serial bonds and $1,000 of interest payments due were made for the current year. The fund liquidated investments necessary to make the payment and leave the required cash balance.
7. Accrued interest receivable at year end was $5,400. It will be received in January. The remaining sales taxes were received.
8. The reserve for serial bonds was increased by the excess of total revenues and other financing sources over current-year expenditures.
9. Nominal and budgetary accounts were closed.

REQUIRED

Prepare the necessary journal entries for Arcadia's debt service fund for Fiscal 19X4. Subsidiary accounts are not required.

6-6 Using the information provided in exercise 6-5, prepare a statement of revenues, expenditures, and changes in fund balance, as well as a balance sheet for Arcadia for Fiscal 19X4.

6-7 Felda County established a sinking fund to retire its 20-year, 7 percent bond issue. On January 1, 19X1, $1,000,000 of the term bonds were issued at par. All sinking fund contributions have been made at year end, beginning on December 31, 19X1.

REQUIRED

1. If the bond sinking fund earns 6 percent, what is the annual contribution made by Felda's general fund?

2. Assume that ten years have elapsed and it is determined that sinking fund investments have yielded 5 percent rather than the 6 percent originally contemplated. To avoid a serious financial shortfall upon maturity of the bonds, Felda County commissioners decide to adjust the annual contribution. What amount must be contributed annually?

Future Value Factors:

	5%	6%
Amount of an Ordinary Annuity, 10 years	12.57789	13.18079
Amount of an Ordinary Annuity, 20 years	33.06595	36.78559
Amount of $1, 10 years	1.62889	1.79085
Amount of $1, 20 years	2.65330	3.20714

6-8 Pine Ridge is a growing suburban community that previously has been accounting for all debt service activities in a single fund. The city manager believes separate funds and combining financial statements should be used in the future. The post-closing trial balance for the combined debt service fund on December 31, 19X2, is as shown:

The City of Pine Ridge
Debt Service Fund
Post-Closing Trial Balance
December 31, 19X2

	Dr.	Cr.
Cash	$ 150,100	
Receivable from State	97,000	
Due from General Fund	200,000	
Investments	564,000	
Interest and Penalties Receivable	19,000	
Special Assessments Receivable—Current	154,470	
Allowance for Uncollectible Assessments		$ 3,100
Matured Serial Bonds Payable		100,000
Matured Interest Payable		96,000
Reserve for Serial Bond Payments		360,000
Reserve for Term Bond Payments		614,470
Unreserved Fund Balance		11,000
Total	$1,184,570	$1,184,570

Investigation reveals the following additional information:

1. A sinking fund for the term bond retirement fund involves an operating transfer from the general fund; the amount for 19X2 has not been received yet. The total transferred annually is $200,000, and 19X2 is the third year of the transfer. Sinking fund contributions are invested on January 1 of the year following the transfer. The investments earn 6 percent and the earnings are added to the investment account.
2. Revenue sharing from the state helps finance the serial bond retirement; Pine Ridge's annual share is accrued at year end, but not received until February 1 of the following year.

3. The serial bond fund has cash on hand sufficient to pay liabilities; the rest of its idle cash is invested.
4. The matured interest relates to special assessment debt.
5. The special assessment fund has no cash or investments.

REQUIRED

Prepare a spreadsheet allocating the combined post-closing balance sheet amounts to the appropriate debt service fund.

6-9 On January 1, 19X0, Waukon City issued special assessment serial debt of $300,000 to complete a sewer and gutter project in a new suburb. Construction was completed by December 31, 19X0. Residents agreed to retire the 9 percent bond issue over three years, with annual assessments of $110,000 beginning January 3, 19X0. Interest on the bonds is due annually on January 1, beginning January 1, 19X1, when one-third of the bonds also is due. Waukon officials believe that .5 of 1 percent of the assessments will not be collected, and any shortfall will be covered by an interest-free loan from the general fund. Any excess cash on hand can be invested at 8 percent; any interest earnings are received on December 31.

REQUIRED

Ignoring budgetary entries and assuming the projected default rates, make the journal entries required for 19X1. (Hint: Note the dates cash is expended and received.) Cash received three days after the first of the year can be assumed to yield interest for a full year.

6-10 This problem is a continuation of exercise 5-10 involving Oleandar's issuance of $7,000,000, 6 percent term bonds to finance capital construction. The bonds were issued on January 1, 19X0, at 101; any premium is received by the debt service fund for purposes of making principal and interest payments due on January 1 and July 1 of each year. Any balance required to pay interest is transferred on January 1 and July 1 from the general fund. The $117,000 required annually to provide for the retirement of bond principal is transferred on July 1 of each year. All premiums and the sinking fund resources are invested immediately at 5 percent; amounts earned on sinking fund assets are added to the investments by the trustee. Oleander integrates its budgetary data into its general accounting records.

REQUIRED

Make the necessary journal entries for Oleandar's debt service fund for 19X0.

6-11 The New Crowford city council is interested in understanding the specific changes that occur in accounting for debt service funds under *Statement No. 11*. The members ask the city finance officer to demonstrate the differences in recognition by taking 19X3 revenues and expenditures and showing what would be recognized under the new standard. The following revenues, transfers, and expenditures are taken from New Crowford's general ledger for 19X3:

Earmarked Sales Tax Revenue	$125,000
Property Tax Revenue	97,000
Transfers from the General Fund	100,000
Earnings on Temporary Investments	8,000
Equity Transfer from Capital Projects Fund	2,000
Principal Payments	110,000
Interest Payments	200,000

The records of New Crowford reveal the following additional information:

1. The sales tax revenue represents the amount actually received. New Crowford received notification on December 31, 19X3, that an additional $51,000 had been collected for the city but would not be forwarded until April 1, 19X4.
2. Property tax revenues represent those earmarked for debt service payments and levied during 19X3, less $5,100 estimated to be uncollectible.
3. Investment earnings reflect cash received of $5,000 and accruals of $3,000, which were earned in November and would be received by February 1, 19X4. Another $3,000 was earned in December but would not be received until April 1, 19X4.
4. Of the principal and interest payments shown above, $40,000 of principal payments and $60,000 of interest payments were for non-capital-related debt.

REQUIRED

Prepare a comparative statement of revenues, transfers, and expenditures for 19X3 under current GAAP and under the new standard.

6-12   In 19X2, Old City built a new park. The purchase of the land and the improvements were to be made with the proceeds of a bond issue. The purchase and construction were accounted for in a capital projects fund. On January 1, 19X2, $500,000 of 8 percent, 10-year bonds were sold at 102. The premium was received directly by the debt service fund. Interest payments were due annually on January 1. The bond indenture required a sinking fund with contributions to be made at the first of every year. The fund is expected to earn 5 percent. Interest payments and the sinking fund contribution are to be transferred from the general fund every January 1.

In 19X4, when the present value of the old debt was $575,943, the city decided to refund those bonds by issuing new 6 percent bonds and depositing the proceeds with an agent, where they will earn 5 percent. The bonds were issued on January 2 at 98. Issuance costs were $25,000.

Future Value of an Annuity Due:

Years	5%	6%	8%
1	1.05000	1.06000	1.08000
2	2.15250	2.18360	2.24640
3	3.31012	3.37462	3.50611
—	—	—	—
—	—	—	—
10	13.20679	13.97164	15.64549
20	34.71925	38.99273	49.42292

REQUIRED

1. Calculate the total transfers that were made from the general fund to the debt service fund for the first bond issue.
2. Make the required entries to show the refunding.
3. Assuming a sinking fund is required for the new bond issue, and that the amount in the old fund can be used for that purpose, calculate the new annual contribution required from the general fund.

CHAPTER 7

General Fixed Asset and Long-Term Debt Account Groups

An account group is a self-balancing set of accounts. Governmental entities use two account groups: the general fixed asset account group (GFAAG) and the general long-term debt account group (GLTDAG). Both account groups reflect transactions recorded in other governmental funds. General purpose fixed assets — those used by the entire entity — are recorded as expenditures in the governmental funds when purchased and as assets in the general fixed asset account group. General long-term debt issues are recorded as other financing sources in the funds and as liabilities in the general long-term debt account group.

Assets acquired by proprietary funds and some fiduciary funds are not "general purpose" and therefore not accounted for in the general fixed asset account group. Similarly, long-term debt issued by these funds is accounted for in the specific fund, not in the account group.

An account group is basically a single-entry accounting system. When assets are acquired, for example, the asset account is debited. The credit is simply an account that explains the source of the asset. Issuance of long-term debt is similar. The debt account is credited; the debit is an account describing the resources needed to retire the debt. Such debits and credits are self-balancing.

This chapter explains the nature of the two account groups by contrasting governmental and for-profit approaches to fixed-asset and long-term debt accounting. Entries in the two account groups are related to those made earlier in governmental funds pertaining to asset acquisition and debt issuance. Because the Governmental Accounting Standards Board is examining fixed-asset accounting and reporting, possible alternative accounting methodologies are explained. Illustrative entries, financial statements, and supporting schedules are also shown.

ACCOUNTING FOR FIXED ASSETS AND LONG-TERM DEBT

Expenditures for long-lived tangible assets can be accounted for in two ways: (1) charge the cost as an expense (expenditure) in the year the asset is acquired, or (2) maintain the acquisition cost as an asset until the date of disposition. Without any adaptation, the second option would never show an expense associated with the asset. However, an asset does not last forever; eventually it wears out or becomes obsolete. The accounting convention of

taking depreciation rectifies the situation; a portion of the asset's cost is expensed each year of its expected life.

Annual operating statements vary significantly depending upon which option is selected. Under the first option, the entire expense (expenditure) is recognized in the year the asset is acquired. The second option recognizes the total expense gradually over the asset's life. The net income for the entire period is the same under either option, but the excess of revenue over expenses differs for each period.

The For-Profit Approach

How fixed assets and their related debt are reflected in the accounts depends upon the measurement focus. As discussed in previous chapters, the measurement focus defines what is being expressed in an entity's financial statements. If the focus is total economic resources, as it is in business, the operating statement measures the net change in total economic resources, and the balance sheet depicts all economic resources. Fixed assets increase economic resources; long-term debt to finance those assets decreases economic resources. Thus, when an entity acquires a fixed asset with debt, the net change in total economic resources is zero. Total economic resources decline as depreciation charges are made, but presumably the entity is earning money with the asset utilization that offsets or exceeds the depreciation charge. The repayment of debt principal has no effect on net economic resources; debt and cash both decrease.

The Governmental Entity Model

For **governmental funds**, governmental entities use a current financial resources measurement focus. Only transactions affecting current financial resources (cash or claims to cash) and claims against those current financial resources are reflected in individual funds. The current financial resources model differs from the economic resources model in terms of when resource outflows are recognized in the financial statements. Under a current financial resources model, for example, when an asset is acquired with cash, the decrease in cash reduces current financial resources so an expenditure is debited. Under an economic resources model, the debit to the asset has no effect on expenses. Similarly, issuing debt increases cash, a current financial resource, but it is not a revenue, so the account "other financing sources" is credited. Under an economic resources model, a liability is credited. Because the current financial resources model dictates recording an increase in financial resources when issuing debt and a decrease when purchasing an asset, the net effect on financial resources is zero. Thus, although the operating statements look different, these initial transactions yield a zero change in the operating statement under either the current financial or economic resources models.

The similarity between asset acquisitions in for-profit and governmental entities ends with the initial acquisition. Depreciation is not taken in governmental funds; as shown above, the entire cost of the asset is expended in the year of acquisition (offset, of course, by an equal increase in financial resources). However, the process does not end with the acquisition. Since the focus for governmental funds is current financial resources, the debt repayment must be addressed. Repayment of the principal and interest constitutes a use of financial resources: an expenditure is debited and cash is credited. Taking the governmental entity as a whole, financial resources decrease by the cash expended. The principal portion of the payment can be considered a surrogate for depreciation if it follows the same general pattern as the using up of the physical asset.

If a governmental entity focused only on current financial resources, entries depicting the decrease (purchase of the asset and repayment of debt) and increase in financial resources (issuance of debt) would be sufficient. However, governmental entities also need to know how much debt is outstanding, when it matures, and what the debt servicing requirements are. Also, without some permanent record of the assets acquired, governmental entities would not know the amount of fixed assets available for providing services, nor would they be able to maintain adequate control over the assets.

OBSERVATION ▲

Most financial statement users are more familiar with for-profit than nonprofit financial statements. Therefore, this practice of showing the full acquisition cost of the asset as an expenditure and **also** recording the cost in this "thing" called an account group is very difficult to understand. Not surprisingly, the GASB is receiving considerable pressure to change the accounting to enable readers to more easily understand governmental financial statements.

Options for Handling General Purpose Fixed Assets and Related Debt   To limit accounting transactions in governmental funds to current financial resources, asset and related long-term debt records cannot be maintained in the operating fund. One option is to maintain those records external to the accounting system. With a simple listing of fixed assets and long-term debt, governmental officials could answer specific questions regarding future financial requirements and available assets. The disadvantage is that financial statement users would not necessarily have access to this information.

Given a current financial resources model, a second option is to establish a single fund to account for construction activities, debt servicing, fixed assets, and related debt. Some nongovernment nonprofits, such as colleges and universities, use this option. The fund typically is referred to as a **plant fund**; it contains fixed assets and any related debt (mortgages, bonds, capital lease obligations, and so forth). Debt servicing activities are reflected in the same fund. (The amount required to service the debt is transferred from the general fund.) Any net difference between total assets and debt represents the entity's net investment in fixed assets.

Under the current financial resources model, a third option is used. The listing identified with the first option is incorporated into the financial accounting system by using two account groups. In order to mesh with other attributes of the accounting system, a double-entry convention is forced onto the listing. Assets are debited in the general fixed asset account group and an

investment in fixed assets is credited. Long-term capital debt is credited in the general long-term debt account group, and the **amount to be provided** is debited.

Since a listing with a forced debit or credit does not constitute a financial entity, the resulting accounting record cannot be referred to as a fund; hence, the term *account group* is used. The only advantage of this option over the simple listing is an ability to incorporate the assets into the entity's financial statements. The assets and liabilities can be easily displayed in a combined balance sheet. The offsetting credits or debits appear in the fund balance section of the balance sheet but provide little information.

Not a financial entity

Environment for Change   A change in the account groups is imminent. As long as governmental funds use the modified accrual basis of accounting, not much impetus for change exists. All long-term liabilities are excluded from the individual governmental funds and included in the debt account group. If another alternative was contemplated, such as a plant fund, standard setters would have to decide where to put the noncapital liabilities. However, once the total financial resources model becomes effective and fund liabilities are moved to the funds, a number of possible options become available.

A change in the account groups would eliminate considerable confusion. Statement users typically are unfamiliar with account groups; they are not used in business accounting or in other nonprofit organizations. Adopting some option closer to either type of entity would no doubt eliminate transition problems for many lay boards and some government officials.

Future Direction from the GASB   Recently, the GASB examined these three options as well as one that would absorb the general fixed assets into the capital projects fund and the general long-term debt into the debt service fund. What option will be adopted is unclear, but more than likely the Board will discard the current option. Since the only long-term debt in the general long-term debt account group will be that related to fixed assets, the Board might either combine the two account groups into a single account group or combine all capital asset activities into a separate fund. Possible changes in accounting for fixed assets and related debt are discussed again at the end of the chapter when these other options can be placed in the context of the current methodology.

THE GENERAL FIXED ASSET ACCOUNT GROUP

General fixed assets are all assets used for general governmental purposes, including land, equipment, buildings and improvements, and infrastructure assets. **Infrastructure assets** are improvements other than buildings that add value to land. Examples of infrastructure assets include curbs, gutters, sidewalks, bridges, streets, dams, ditches, and canals.

With the exception of fixed assets purchased by the proprietary or some fiduciary funds, all fixed assets are recorded in the general fixed asset account group. These general purpose fixed assets also are recorded as expenditures in the governmental funds. The expenditure entry impacts the operating statement. The entry in the general fixed asset account group simply helps the entity account for and control its fixed assets.

Governmental fixed assets are generally defined as they are by other types of entities: tangible items that will be used for more than a year or operating cycle. Governmental entities usually establish a materiality threshold to distinguish between fixed assets and repairs or supplies. The threshold differs from one entity to the next, but generally ranges from $200 to $1,000. The threshold often is set by statute and may remain long after inflation outdates it.

Acquisition, Use, and Disposal

Acquisition Unless acquired by gift, fixed assets are recorded at cost, which includes all set-up and transportation charges. If acquired by gift, the fair market value is used as the basis. The entry recording a purchased asset is made when the expenditure occurs in a governmental fund. For example, if the general fund expends $100,000 on equipment, the entries are:

```
GF     Expenditures                              100,000
             Cash (Accounts Payable)                         100,000

GFAAG  Equipment                                 100,000
             Investment in General Fixed Assets—
                  General Fund                                100,000
```

The credit side of the general fixed asset account group entry not only explains the character of the debit, that is, an investment, but also the source of the funds—in this case, the general fund. Of course, if the asset is a gift, no expenditure entry would be made in the general fund.

For constructed assets, the amounts expended are initially recorded in the capital projects fund. At the end of each period or when construction is completed, an entry is made in the general fixed asset account group. If the entry is made annually, the account title used during construction is construction in progress; when construction is completed, the cost is transferred to an asset account. If, for example, a building is constructed over two years with $100,000 expended the first year and $185,000 the second year, the following entries are made in the GFAAG:

```
Year 1   Construction in Progress                100,000
               Investment in General Fixed Assets—
                    Capital Projects Fund                    100,000

Year 2   Buildings                               285,000
               Investment in General Fixed Assets—
                    Capital Projects Fund                    185,000
               Construction in Progress                      100,000
```

The net result of these transactions is to report an asset costing $285,000 and a net investment in fixed assets for the same amount. The construction in progress account remains in the GFAAG only until construction is completed, when the amount is transferred to the appropriate asset item.

If an entry is made when construction is completed, the only entry made in the general fixed asset account group is:

Year 2	Buildings	285,000	
	Investment in General Fixed Assets—		
	Capital Projects Fund		285,000

Sometimes several fixed assets will be purchased for a lump sum. Allocation of the total cost is made to the individual asset accounts in the same manner as in for-profit entities. The purchase price is allocated among the assets in relation to each one's proportional share of the total market value.

Use of Fixed Assets   As mentioned previously, the gradual use of general fixed assets does not decrease financial resources and consequently has no relevance in the accounting for governmental funds that use the current financial resources model. Nonetheless, depreciation is a hotly contested issue in government circles.

Research undertaken by the GASB in 1985 suggested that most users consider recognizing depreciation in the general fund to be of little or no use. Grouping all users together, only 40 percent of those surveyed felt that a depreciation charge would provide relevant information.[1] Some of those favoring depreciation may be overestimating its informational value by mistakenly equating depreciation with a decline in market value or evidence of maintenance requirements. Some respondents may have recognized that debt service principal, which is an expenditure of the debt service fund, is similar to depreciation. To include depreciation as well would constitute double counting. Also, if minor expenditures of roughly the same magnitude are made from the general fund annually, the overall effect is the same as recording depreciation.

An important consideration is whether interperiod equity (the relationship between current services and current payment for those services), and service costs and accomplishments—objectives of the GASB—can be adequately measured without some reflection of the using up of assets. Perhaps one reason the GASB is considering alternative accounting and reporting models for fixed assets is to develop an accounting system that would accommodate a depreciation charge without recording it in the governmental funds.

Whether a depreciation charge for governmental general fixed assets makes sense depends upon one's perspective. If one's perspective is the usefulness of the resulting information and the relevance of nonfinancial charges in a current financial resources model, the charge cannot be supported. Users have proclaimed its limited usefulness. Depreciation does not require financial resources and therefore is alien to the measurement focus used by governmental entities.

---

[1] Governmental Accounting Standards Board Research Report, *The Needs of Users of Governmental Financial Reports* (Stamford, Conn.: GASB, 1985), 40.

Shifting the focus to the assets changes the answer. Few could argue that general governmental fixed assets do not deteriorate or lose productive capacity. Therefore, the assets should be depreciated; the accounting and reporting system should disclose this gradual using up of the assets.

OBSERVATION ▲

Regardless of the position taken on the depreciation of assets purchased with operating funds or debt, few argue for taking depreciation on gifted assets or those purchased with contributed funds. The entity has no obligation to replace the gifted asset. No useful purpose is served by affecting an entity's operating performance by such a charge.

Some argue that both perspectives can be accommodated by simply showing the **accumulated depreciation** in the general fixed asset account group (or a plant fund if the GASB adopts another alternative). Currently, governmental entities may disclose accumulated depreciation in the GFAAG. If a building depreciated $67,000 during the current period, the following entry can be made:

Investment in General Fixed Assets—Source	67,000	
Accumulated Depreciation—Building		67,000

Many governmental entities use this option. Just as in business, statement users can assess the decline in productive capacity of the assets by observing how much of the total cost has been written off. This option does not affect operating performance, however, and unless debt principal service payments are used as a surrogate for depreciation, the cost of providing services is overstated in the year of acquisition and understated in all subsequent periods.

Disposal   Under the flow of financial resources model, disposal of fixed assets for cash increases financial resources. The fund receiving the cash—usually the general fund—debits cash and credits miscellaneous revenues or other financing sources. The gain or loss on disposition does not change financial resources; consequently, it is ignored. For example, if an asset costing $100,000 and showing accumulated depreciation of $80,000 was sold for $25,000, the entry made in the general fixed asset account group would be:

[handwritten margin note: Don't recognize gain or loss]

Investment in General Fixed Assets—General Fund	20,000	
Accumulated Depreciation	80,000	
Equipment		100,000

[handwritten margin note: Sales]

If the entity had not used the option of showing accumulated depreciation, the entry changes slightly:

Investment in General Fixed Assets—General Fund	100,000	
Equipment		100,000

[handwritten margin note: reversed]

Increasingly, some assets, such as computer hardware, are not sold outright but traded in for newer models. Until the GASB issues specific guidelines for trade-ins, governmental entities may follow the authoritative guidance provided by the Financial Accounting Standards Board for "like-kind" exchanges. The FASB rules provide that, if similar assets are exchanged, the new asset should be recorded at the fair value of the assets exchanged. Thus, the governmental entity removes the book value of the old asset from the GFAAG and enters the market value of the trade-in plus any cash paid in a "like-kind" exchange transaction.

How to record the transaction in the fund making the expenditure is unclear. Two options seem acceptable: record the cash payment as an expenditure (the net method), or record the expenditure for the value of the asset acquired and recognize another financing source for the fair value of the trade-in (the gross method).[2]

The following details relate to a purchase involving a trade-in:

Book Value of Old Asset	$ 75,000
Cash Paid from General Fund	305,000
Invoice Price of New Asset	450,000

Under the net method, the value of the asset is recorded in the GFAAG and the amount of the expenditure in the general fund.

GFAAG	Investment in General Fixed Assets—		
	General Fund	75,000	
	Equipment		75,000
	Equipment	450,000	
	Investment in General Fixed		
	Assets—General Fund		450,000
GF	Expenditures	305,000	
	Cash		305,000

The net method is most common in practice, but as the following entry indicates, the substance of the transaction is better reflected under the gross method:

GF	Expenditures	450,000	
	Cash		305,000
	Other Financing Sources—Trade-In		
	Proceeds		145,000

The entries in the general fixed asset account group are the same regardless of which option is used.

Additions and Betterments Additions and betterments add to existing fixed assets by extending their lives, enhancing their value, or improving

[2]Based on the professional guidance provided in a technical inquiry response printed in *GAAFR Review* (March 1986): 2.

their efficiency. Accordingly, such expenditures should increase the book value of the assets reported in the GFAAG. Like other entities, governmental units have difficulty distinguishing between these capital outlays and repair and maintenance items.

The prescribed distinction between repairs/maintenance and additions/betterments should be adhered to in the budgeting and accounting processes. Most governmental units use the same threshold for determining additions/betterments as they do for determining assets — $200 to $1,000. Explicit guidelines for enhancing the value, extending the life, or improving the efficiency should be developed and made available to all responsible for budgeting. If the expenditure is incorrectly classified in the budgeting process, chances are that it will remain misclassified in the accounting system and financial statements. Additions and betterments should be classified as capital outlays in the budget of the fund making the expenditure.

Managing Investments in Fixed Assets

Maintaining interperiod equity is nowhere more important than in connection with fixed assets. Fixed assets represent the one clear benefit that is passed from one generation to another. Proper internal control over and maintenance of these assets is therefore critical. Otherwise, future generations inherit the debt related to the assets without the assets necessary to generate money to service the debt. Fixed assets are preserved by appropriate: (1) internal controls, (2) accounting and reporting, and (3) repair and maintenance.

Internal Controls   Controlling fixed assets involves establishing and maintaining adequate files, developing standardized purchasing and disposal policies, and conducting periodic audits. The internal control system is designed to take into account the volume of assets, the number of transactions likely to occur each year, and the effect of various purchasing and screening procedures on maintaining the system.

Establishing and Maintaining the Files. Setting the threshold for capitalizing assets is a key element of any fixed asset policy. If it is set too low, managers spend an inordinate amount of time controlling insignificant items. Also, the lower the number, the more transactions and paperwork. With limited resources, a governmental unit is well advised to concentrate on controlling large-ticket items well rather than all possible assets poorly. Setting the threshold too high understates interperiod equity. As in many other accounting issues, the cost associated with maintaining a system with a given threshold must be balanced against the benefits derived from the system.

The first step in developing a fixed asset system is to establish standardized descriptive files and documentation supporting the valuation bases. The asset file should be maintained for the life of the asset in chronological order to facilitate retrieval. Minimal information and documentation include:

- Type of asset and identifying characteristics, such as serial numbers, color, model numbers, and brands

- Purchase date, vendor invoice, and cost basis, if appropriate; for example, invoice price plus freight, installation costs, and so forth
- Location, use, and responsible department or program

Asset file

Some entities also record the replacement cost of important assets; this amount is needed for insurance purposes.

Updating the information is as important as the initial documentation. Internal control procedures should provide for asset reassignments. Records should be updated simultaneously with the reassignment. All updating cannot be accomplished by examining paper flows. Periodic inventories are an important attribute of any internal control system. Depending upon the volume of assets, the periodic inventory may be done on a revolving basis: health and welfare one year, public safety the next, and so on.

Tagging assets helps identify them during the inventory process. A number or color code identification usually relates directly to the master file. Tagging also is a constant reminder that the asset belongs to the governmental entity. Systematic procedures should be developed so that an asset purchase triggers the coding and the physical tagging; the tag should be affixed as soon after the asset is purchased as possible.

Developing First-Time Fixed Asset Records. Some governmental entities operate for years without fixed asset records. They may eventually adopt generally accepted accounting practices, and therefore have to develop asset records long after the documentation has been destroyed or misplaced. In such circumstances, the first step is a physical inventory. A search of the records to locate invoices, construction records, and financing sources follows. An attempt must then be made to match the physical inventory and the documentation.

Typically not all asset bases can be traced to formal documents; therefore, some assets may have to be appraised. The financing source also may be difficult to trace, in which case one credit entry is "net investment in general fixed assets — source unknown." To avoid misleading statement readers, the entity should disclose its general procedures for developing its fixed asset records, the date first developed, and any anomalies encountered.

Standardized Purchasing and Disposal Policies. Adequate purchasing policies begin with the budgeting process. All proposed fixed asset purchases should be identified as capital outlays in the budget. Authority to make the purchase should be keyed to budget authorization.

A formal review and approval process is important to the integrity of the system. The person reviewing the purchase order should cross-check the specifications and cost against the budget request and authorization. Also, for expensive items, surplus warehouses and vendor lists should be examined to determine whether alternative purchase avenues might be more cost effective. Sometimes fixed assets are purchased through open bidding from the lowest bidder. Violation of bidding constraints may result in fines or other costly penalties so they must be reviewed carefully by those with purchasing authority.

Disposal is another important property management function. Obtaining approval and completing the required paperwork is as important when disposing of as when purchasing a fixed asset. The paperwork should include a description of the asset, the person or department responsible for disposition, the method of disposal (sale, scrap, destruction, and so on), and the proceeds, if any. Final approval for disposal should be given only after the proper forms and notifications are completed.

OBSERVATION ▲

Alternative sources, such as surplus warehouses, do not always yield lower costs. The same is true for the "lowest bidder" system. Specialized equipment needs filled by the "next best" asset often mean costly delays, invalid test results, or frustrated users. The best way to avoid these problems is to define the equipment needs thoroughly and precisely.

The federal government, many state governments, and some local governmental entities have surplus property warehouses. Governmental entities should make every effort to ensure that assets with unused productive capacity are transferred to these warehouses. Assets purchased with public funds should be available for public use as long as possible.

Accounting and Reporting   As in for-profit entities, the entire cost of fixed assets, including the following, should be recorded in the GFAAG:

- Legal and title fees
- Appraisal fees
- Site preparation, including demolition
- Freight
- Closing costs
- Installation costs
- Interest costs during construction (optional)
- Insurance during construction

Unlike for-profit entities, governmental entities have an option of reporting infrastructure assets (canals, dams, ditches, streets, sidewalks, gutters, bridges, and lighting systems, among others). Attached to the land and useful only to the governmental entity, these assets are easy to control. Since control is not a problem and depreciation is not taken on general fixed assets, many argue that it is immaterial whether they are included in the formal accounting and reporting system. Others maintain that exclusion understates an entity's service capacity. While the option remains, recent articles and public commentaries urge governmental entities to report all assets. The GASB is examining this question in connection with its capital reporting project.

Governmental entities must establish consistent policies for the treatment of all fixed assets. For example, the entity must decide whether accumulated depreciation will be shown. Either all or none of the depreciable assets should reflect the depreciation accumulated to date. As another example, governmental entities have two choices for recording capital outlays involving a trade-in. The method selected should be applied consistently. The same is true of infrastructure assets; all should be included or none included.

Transfers Between a Fund and the GFAAG. General purpose assets sometimes are transferred to proprietary funds for a specific purpose. If, for example, a governmental entity centralized copying services, copiers used by individual departments may be transferred to the internal service fund. Conversely, when proprietary funds are closed, any remaining fixed assets are transferred to the GFAAG.

A transfer should be reported at the lower of book value (depreciated cost) or market value. If the transfer is made from the GFAAG to a proprietary fund and the governmental entity does not show accumulated depreciation, the proprietary fund should capitalize the fixed asset at original cost less an amount equivalent to the depreciation that would have been recorded had the asset always belonged to the proprietary fund. Any asset transferred from a proprietary fund will show accumulated depreciation. For example, a $50,000 asset with accumulated depreciation of $20,000 and market value of $35,000 that was transferred from a proprietary fund to the GFAAG is reported in the GFAAG as:

Asset Type	50,000	
Accumulated Depreciation—Asset Type		20,000
Net Investment in Fixed Assets—Proprietary Fund		30,000

If the governmental entity does not reflect accumulated depreciation, the net book value is recorded in the asset and investment accounts.

Financial Statement Presentations. Supporting schedules and note disclosures provide much more information about general fixed assets than do the formal statements. In terms of formal statements, the only one relevant to the GFAAG is the balance sheet. It shows the total investment in fixed assets by type and source; if accumulated depreciation is reflected, it also will be shown in the balance sheet.

Governmental entities should include supporting schedules showing the individual types of assets, the amount of accumulated depreciation, and the depreciation policies by class of asset. Probably the most helpful supporting schedule recommended for governmental entities is the schedule of changes in general fixed assets. As Exhibit 7-1 shows, the schedule starts with the beginning year balances; additions, transfers, and deletions also are shown along with an ending balance. The negative sign on some transfers means those assets have been assigned to some other function, such as a proprietary fund. Transfers with positive signs are reassignments to the general operating purposes of the entity.

▲   **OBSERVATION**

> Some governmental entities refer to these supporting schedules as statements of changes in general fixed assets. Technically, however, they are schedules because the GASB has not defined them as one of the required financial statements.

Repair and Maintenance   Physical repair and maintenance is the least glamorous aspect of preserving fixed assets. Oversight boards, the general

Exhibit 7-1

Governmental Entity
Schedule of Changes in General Fixed Assets
For the Period Ending June 30, 19X1
($000)

Type of Asset	Balance June 30, 19X0	Additions	Transfers	Deletions	Balance June 30, 19X1
Land	$ 22,000	$ 1,200	$ 129	$ (2)	$ 23,327
Buildings	32,500	2,200	1,600	—	36,300
Streets and Sidewalks	59,600	7,400	2,300	—	69,300
Improvements	16,200	610	938	(900)	16,848
Bridges, Canals, Dams	9,600	—	—	—	9,600
Furniture and Fixtures	2,000	120	—	(5)	2,115
Construction in Progress	8,600	12,200	(5,000)	—	15,800
Total	$150,500	$23,730	$ (33)	$(907)	$173,290

public, and managers get far more excited about spending another $5 million on new parks, roads, equipment, or office facilities than they do about budgeting that same amount for repairing and maintaining existing structures or infrastructure assets. Deferring normal repairs and maintenance is, however, a costly decision in the long run. Unless properly maintained, capital assets deteriorate more rapidly and the replacement cycle is shortened. Also, unnecessarily costly repairs may be incurred.

Unlike current services, maintenance can be deferred several years, even decades, before the full effect is obvious to the general public. Bridges collapse or water mains break before citizens recognize the full impact of deferred maintenance. National commentaries and local press reports gradually have raised the level of awareness, but a tremendous gap remains between needed maintenance and annual appropriations. Most governmental entities could allocate their entire operating budgets to deferred maintenance for several years without restoring all their facilities to good condition.

Solving the deferred maintenance problem is a critical public policy issue. Because most taxpayers are interested in immediate benefits from their tax dollars and many politicians are more interested in reelection than in preserving public assets, maintenance is a budget item that is easily postponed as pressures for public services mount. Even when oversight boards are aware of maintenance needs, determining the deferred amount and accounting for it are tough problems.

Calculating deferred maintenance costs is expensive. It involves estimating the condition of the assets had regularly recurring repair work been done. The more accurate the estimate, the more costly it is to develop. The costs of obtaining the information may even exceed the benefit of having it.

Once estimated, deferred maintenance costs must be brought to the attention of the public and oversight boards. No one has determined how best to reveal the information. Some would simply disclose the current cost of maintenance in the notes to the financial statements, as a supplemental schedule.

Others propose charging current maintenance costs to operations and showing the resulting amount as a fund liability.

▲ **OBSERVATION**

Although a noble idea for keeping the issue before boards and citizens, deferred maintenance meets the definition of a liability only if it is the result of a past transaction or event. Deferring something, taking no action, is not an event. Only if the entity commits resources, that is, makes the expenditure, is a liability present. Once a commitment has been made, however, it is no longer deferred! Further, deferred maintenance costs, by definition, do not require current financial resources and therefore are not a *fund liability.*

In summary, several unresolved management issues relate to governmental fixed assets. Some issues relate to the accounting methodology; a plant fund, for example, would enable managers to consolidate all fixed asset transactions in a single location and therefore improve control over and management of fixed assets. Other issues require broad changes in public policy for resolution. Until it becomes fashionable (or necessary) to maintain public facilities adequately, deferred maintenance will continue to pose accounting and reporting dilemmas.

GENERAL LONG-TERM DEBT ACCOUNT GROUP

Under the current financial resources model, a clear distinction is made between long-term and short-term liabilities. Short-term liabilities are financial resources and therefore shown in the fund incurring the liability. Long-term liabilities, whether used to finance operating needs or the acquisition of capital, are shown in the general long-term debt account group. Ordinarily, mortgages, bonds, and notes relate to the acquisition of capital assets while other long-term liabilities, including compensated absences, pensions, and judgments and claims, relate to other long-term financing of the governmental entity.[3]

Debt Issuance and Repayment

Entries to record debt issuance already have been discussed in connection with the capital projects fund. The general long-term debt account group entries mirror those earlier ones. To review and as one example, when debt is issued for capital acquisitions, an entry is made in the capital projects fund:

---

[3]Effective with the new basis of accounting, GASB also makes a clear distinction between fund long-term liabilities and general capital-related long-term debt. If *Statement No. 11* provisions are followed, fund long-term liabilities will include (1) *any* long-term debt of proprietary and trust funds, and (2) long-term liabilities related to operating needs, such as compensated absences, pensions, judgments and claims, or bonds or notes issued to finance operating deficits.

```
CPF    Cash                                           xxx
            Other Financing Sources—
                Proceeds from Bonds                              xxx
```

An entry is made simultaneously in the GLTDAG:

```
GLTDAG    Amount to Be Provided for Term Bonds        xxx
                Term Bonds Payable                              xxx
```

As has been mentioned, the debit account is simply there to assure a self-balancing set of accounts. It is neither an asset nor an expenditure, and it adds no additional information; the reader already knows how much is due by looking at the credit side of the entry.

The debit part of the entry changes if a governmental entity sets aside money to repay the debt. For example, if the term bond reflected in the preceding entry was sold at a premium and the premium was transferred to the debt service for **principal repayment**, an entry is made in the GLTDAG:

```
GLTDAG    Amount Available to Repay Term Bonds    (amount of
                                                   premium)

                Amount to Be Provided for Term
                    Bonds                                  (amount of
                                                           premium)
```

If a sinking fund is established, the amount available would increase and the amount to be provided would decrease as the sinking fund amounts are set aside in the debt service fund.

OBSERVATION ▲

Without the *amount available account*, financial statement users would have to compare the amount of the debt in the GLTDAG and the amount reserved for the sinking fund in the debt service fund. This way, the amount set aside is apparent without looking at two different statements. Although helpful, a better way to enable users to examine debt would be to consolidate all debt activities in a single fund.

When general long-term debt matures, it is transferred to the debt service fund and paid. The entry sequence begins in the GLTDAG:

```
GLTDAG    Debt Payable                                xxx
                Amount to Be Provided for...                    xxx
                Amount Available for...                         xxx
```

The type of debt is specified in both the debit and credit sides of the entry. If, for example, the preceding entry was for term bonds, the debit would be to term bonds payable, and the amount to be provided or available for term bonds would be credited.

The debt service fund records the receipt of the matured bonds and payment thereof:

```
DSF    Expenditures                              xxx
            Matured Bonds Payable                        xxx
       Matured Bonds Payable                     xxx
            Cash                                         xxx
```

Selected Debt Issues

Long-term debt associated with operating activities, claims and judgments, and compensated absences has been discussed in earlier chapters. Therefore, this section focuses on the types of debt associated with capital acquisitions.

Governmental entities use several types of debt to finance capital acquisitions. Although long-term or serial bonds may be the most common, governmental units also use capital leases, mortgages, notes, or special assessment bonds. Under some circumstances, demand bonds also may be classified as general long-term debt.

Government debt issues are generally accounted for on the same basis as comparable debt in a for-profit entity. Any accounting or reporting differences relate to the basis of accounting and not to any intrinsic differences in governmental and for-profit debt issues. A mortgage is a mortgage regardless of the nature of the mortgagee. Accounting for deep discount debt and premiums and discounts has special applications in governmental entities. Another debt issue, demand bonds, is confined almost entirely to governmental entities, so the only accounting guidance pertains to those entities.

Deep Discount Debt A popular financing mechanism during the late 1980s, deep discount bonds have a zero interest rate, or a rate considerably below current market rates. Under GASB pronouncements, the debt qualifies as deep discount if the stated rate is less than 75 percent of the effective interest rate. The purchaser buys the bond at a large discount and receives full par value at maturity. For example, a $1,000 bond sold for $400 with no stated rate of interest would be a deep discount bond. At maturity it would be worth $1,000; the $600 discount encompasses both the implied interest and the discount on the issue. Similarly, if the effective interest rate was 10 percent, a $1,000 bond yielding 4 percent and selling for $800 would be a deep discount bond. The yield of 4 percent is less than 75 percent of the effective interest rate.

Insofar as accounting issues are concerned, the question is whether interest should be recognized as an expenditure (expense) as it accrues or in total upon maturity. A 0 percent, 20-year, $1,000 bond sold for $350 in 19X0 will be worth $1,000 at maturity. The operating statements for each year will differ markedly under the modified accrual and "when due" recognition criteria. If all the interest was recognized at maturity, in the 20th year, interest expense would total $650. If it was accrued as incurred, assuming straight-line amortization, the annual interest expense would be $32.50 ($650/20).

After examining the impact of accruing the interest expense on governmental entities, the GASB decided that the recognition criteria should be "when due." However, the Board recommended that the principal amount of the debt reported in the general long-term debt account group should gradually be increased as the interest accrues. Using the preceding example, the following entry would be made in the GLTDAG each year:

GLTDAG	Amount to Be Provided...	32.50	
	Bonds Payable		32.50

Because the Board was silent on the methodology, presumably accounting standards related to interest expenditures should be applied and the effective-interest method used unless there is no material difference between that and the straight-line method. The stated interest and the effective interest rates, along with the face amount of the deep discount debt, must be disclosed in the notes to the financial statements.

Premiums and Discounts on General Long-Term Debt   Other than deep discount debt, general long-term debt is recorded at its face amount. The difference between the face amount and the proceeds should be recorded as an issuance premium or discount in the year the debt is issued. Premiums and discounts *are not* amortized over the life of the issue as they are in for-profit entities. Suppose that to finance a capital construction project, $100,000 in serial bonds was issued at 102. The entries in the GLTDAG, the debt service fund, and the capital projects fund would be:

Debt recorded at face amount

GLTDAG	Amount to Be Provided for Serial Bonds	100,000	
	Serial Bonds Payable		100,000
DSF	Cash	2,000	
	Revenue		2,000
CPF	Cash	100,000	
	Other Financing Sources—		
	Serial Bonds Proceeds		100,000

Demand Bonds   Governmental units occasionally have difficulty issuing long-term debt at favorable rates or repayment provisions. Because the purchase or construction of capital assets cannot be delayed indefinitely waiting for more favorable conditions, entities may issue interim financing instruments. When market conditions improve, they issue long-term financing to pay off the interim issue.

One method of interim financing is through demand bonds. Frequently issued at variable interest rates, demand bonds contain provisions giving bondholders the right to redeem the bonds within a certain period after giving notice of this intent. The redemption period is usually 1 to 30 days; the exercise option may begin immediately after the bond is issued or after a period of time, say five years after issuance. The redemption price is face value plus any accrued interest.

Since the governmental entity cannot predict when bonds will be redeemed, it must make financing arrangements for eventual redemptions. The governmental entity usually hires an agent to sell redeemed bonds. Through agreements called *letters of credit,* local financial institutions provide financing between the redemption and the resale date. To cover the possibility that the agent will be unable to resell redeemed bonds, governmental entities also secure long-term alternative financing. Called a **take-out agreement**, this financing may be provided by the local financial institution or through separate agreements with other institutions or financiers. Take-out agreements usually convert the debt to a long-term installment note.

From an accounting standpoint, the issue is whether demand bonds are classified as short-term or long-term debt. If short term, the debt will appear as a liability in the fund issuing the debt—even if used to finance capital acquisitions. If long term, the liability will appear in the GLTDAG.

In *Interpretation 1,* the GASB allows governmental units to classify demand bonds as general long-term debt if the following conditions are met:

1. Before the financial statements are issued, the issuer has entered into a take-out agreement to convert demand bonds not resold into some form of long-term obligation. The take-out agreement cannot expire within one year from the date of the balance sheet.
2. The take-out agreement cannot be cancelled by the lender during that year, and obligations incurred under the agreement cannot be cancelled during that year.
3. The lender, prospective lender, or investor must be financially capable of honoring the take-out agreement.[4]

Regarding Item 2, the take-out agreement frequently allows the lender to cancel the arrangement if certain conditions are violated. If the governmental entity has not violated any of the conditions, the agreement is not considered cancellable, and therefore the debt is still classified as long term.

▲   **OBSERVATION**

The third condition places an additional burden on the entity's auditors. Not only must they examine the entity's compliance with the three conditions, but they also must attest to the lender's or investor's financial capability of honoring the take-out agreement.

In addition to general disclosures required of all general long-term debt, governmental entities with demand bonds outstanding must describe the demand bond program, explain the terms of the letters of credit and take-out agreements, and disclose any commitment fees paid and amounts drawn on letters of credit. They also should describe the nature of the debt service requirements if the take-out agreement is exercised.

---

[4]Governmental Accounting Standards Board, *Codification of Governmental Accounting and Financial Reporting Standards* (Norwalk, Conn.: GASB, 1992), sec. D30.108.

Accounting for Long-Term Obligations During the Transition

Changing from the modified accrual to the accrual basis of accounting will significantly affect placement of long-term liabilities. Under the modified accrual basis of accounting, all unmatured long-term debt appears in the long-term debt account group. Under the total financial resources model, only long-term debt used to finance capital acquisitions will belong in the general long-term debt account group. Without some transition mechanism, the new accounting basis will force governmental entities to suddenly show huge deficits in governmental funds, especially the general fund. As an example, if a governmental entity has $1 million in long-term debt issued to cover a deficit when the accounting basis changes, the following entries will be made when first adopting the financial resources model:

GLTDAG	Operating Debt—Long-Term	1,000,000	
	Amount to Be Provided—		
	Operating Debt		1,000,000
GF	Fund Balance	1,000,000	
	Operating Debt		1,000,000

Many governmental officials are worried that suddenly showing a deficit will lead the public to conclude that the entity is suddenly in danger of insolvency. They are, therefore, opposed to the new basis of accounting.

OBSERVATION ▲

Moving debt from a single-entry system where the debit balance had no significance to a double-entry system where the debit reduces the fund balance demonstrates how misleading it is to use an account group.

The GASB concluded that the potential deficit created by the change in the basis of accounting presented a serious problem for governmental entities. The Board also realized that until the problem was addressed, the total financial resources model would not receive a fair hearing. Some governmental officials opposed its adoption solely on the basis of the impact on the fund balance. Late in the review process for the measurement focus/basis of accounting project, the Board removed the subject of compensated absences from the project. More important, it assured practitioners that the outcome of any future decision about compensated absences would not negatively impact governmental fund balances. If nothing else, this assurance certainly limits future accounting options related to compensated absences. More recently, the GASB has tentatively concluded that long-term liabilities related to pensions, contingencies, and compensated absences will remain in the general long-term debt account group. Therefore, only long-term debt related to operations would be moved to the funds incurring the debt.

About the same time, the GASB began exploring financial statement presentations. One option would display an accrual basis operating statement and a balance sheet showing both a budgetary (current) basis and a nonbudgetary (noncurrent) basis. Presumably, the dual reporting would enable governmental entities to report "a balanced budget for the current period" in the current column and a deficit (because of the transfer of long-term liabilities) in the noncurrent column.

Records for and Reporting of General Long-Term Debt

Record keeping for general long-term obligations begins when the debt is issued. A file should be established for each debt issue. It should provide a general description of the debt, the covenants, if applicable, debt service requirements, call provisions, if any, and pertinent dates, such as maturity, issuance, or call dates. All correspondence related to the issue — including attorneys' opinions, local restrictions or resolutions, and letters of agreement with agents or trustees — should be retained in the file.

The file should be maintained and updated until the debt matures and the obligation is paid in full. Any redeemed interest coupons and bonds should be carefully controlled and destroyed once the payment has been made. Internal control over documentation is a major area reviewed during audits. Special control procedures should be developed for debt that is frequently resold, such as demand bonds.

Most standard financial statements have little relevance to the general long-term debt account group. The GLTDAG is included in the combined balance sheet, but that statement provides information only about broad classes of debt and the total amounts to be provided for payment or available in the debt service fund. Other than increasing or decreasing the obligation balances, no transactions are reported in the account group; therefore, no operating statement is prepared.

Supplementary schedules are far more useful than the balance sheet to financial statement users. One such schedule shows the changes in general long-term obligations. As shown in Exhibit 7-2, changes in each type of debt and the related debits are displayed for an entire fiscal period. GASB standards require that changes in a given type of debt not be netted. For example, if $100,000 of 8 percent bonds were issued, and $400,000 of 8 percent bonds matured, the two transactions could not be netted for a net decrease of $300,000.

Another useful schedule is one showing comparative data for two consecutive periods. Debit and credit balances are displayed for each type of debt. This schedule helps statement users assess at a glance the total change in debt and comparative amounts available, or to be provided, to pay the entity's total obligations. The comparative statement is like Exhibit 7-2 without the change columns. The column for debt service operations indicates items no longer available in the debt service fund. Using the figures in Exhibit 7-2, $4.5 million was used to repay long-term serial bonds; the debt has been retired, and the amount available for debt retirement has decreased by the same amount.

Governmental entities also provide schedules showing the debt limit and debt margin. Most states establish debt limits as a percentage of the assessed

Suppl. Schedules very important

Exhibit 7-2

Governmental Entity
Schedule of Changes in Long-Term Obligations
For the Period Ending June 30, 19X1
($000)

	Balance June 30, 19X0	General Long-Term Obligations Incurred	General Long-Term Obligations Retired	Debt Service Fund Operations	Balance June 30, 19X1
Amount Available in Debt Service Fund	$ 5,700	$ —	$ —	$(4,500)	$ 1,200
Resources to Be Provided for:					
Retirement of Bond Anticipation Notes	—	3,900	—	—	3,900
Long-Term Serial Bonds	25,500	1,080	5,095	4,500	25,985
Special Assessment Serial Bonds	1,595	609	43	—	2,161
Other Installment Obligations	595	513	—	—	1,108
Capital Leases	2,730	23	57	—	2,696
Total Available and to Be Provided	$36,120	$6,125	$5,195	$ —	$37,050
General Long-Term Obligations Payable:					
Bond Anticipation Notes	$ —	$3,900	$ —	$ —	$ 3,900
Long-Term Serial Bonds	30,895	1,080	5,095	—	26,880
Other Installment Obligations	595	513	—	—	1,108
Special Assessment Bonds	1,900	609	43	—	2,466
Capital Leases	2,730	23	57	—	2,696
Total General Long-Term Obligations Payable	$36,120	$6,125	$5,195	$ —	$37,050

value of real and personal property, typically from 4 to 20 percent. The legal debt margin represents the amount of debt that could be issued without exceeding the debt limit. As Exhibit 7-3 shows, the amount of any sinking funds is offset against outstanding debt, and therefore increases the debt margin. Also, the state statute establishing the debt limit may exclude the assessed values of certain types of property or certain types of debt from the calculation.

Schedules detailing debt service requirements to maturity round out the reporting for the general long-term debt account group. Like the schedule prepared by for-profit entities, it simply lists the principal and interest payments for each succeeding year (see Exhibit 7-4 for a schedule of debt payments). For-profit entities generally list the individual amounts for the succeeding five years and summarize the remaining payments in one lump sum. Governmental entities frequently show individual amounts for the entire period covered by current debt issues.

Exhibit 7-3

City of Marysville
Schedule of Legal Debt Limit and Margin
September 30, 19X9
($000,000)

Appraised Valuation of Real and Personal Property			$7,800
Less Excluded Property:			
Religious Organization Real Property		$ 27	
City-Owned Real Property		152	179
Net Assessed Valuation			$7,621
Debt Limit, 7 Percent of Appraised Valuation			$ 533
Gross Debt:			
Outstanding General Obligation Bond Debt:			
General Obligation Bonds	$ 28		
Water Bonds	36		
Sewer Bonds	16		
Parking Facility Bonds	4	$ 84	
Authorized but Unissued General Bond Obligation Debt:			
General Obligation Bonds		105	
Bond Anticipation Notes		4	
Other:			
Installment Notes	$ 1		
Mortgage	3		
Lease Purchase Obligation	2	6	
Gross Debt		$199	
Less Statutory Deductions:			
Bond Sinking Funds	$116		
Uncollected Special Assessments Levied for Sewer			
Development	8	(124)	75
Legal Debt Margin			$458

Exhibit 7-4

City of Anywhere
Schedule of Long-Term Obligation Maturities and Debt Service Requirements
June 30, 19X1

	ENTERPRISE							
	Water and Sewer		Parking Deck		General Government		Total	

Maturities on All Long-Term Obligations:
General Obligation Bonded Debt:

Fiscal Year Ended June 30	Principal	Principal & Interest	Principal	Principal & Interest	Principal	Principal & Interest	Principal	Principal & Interest
19X2	$ 4,510,000	$ 6,116,948	$ 215,000	$ 415,711	$ 2,630,000	$ 3,754,641	$ 7,355,000	$10,287,300
19X3	4,460,000	5,844,180	225,000	411,961	2,620,000	3,593,342	7,305,000	9,849,483
19X4	4,430,000	5,586,763	240,000	412,430	2,585,000	3,407,848	7,255,000	9,407,041
19X5	4,365,000	5,290,823	260,000	416,805	2,575,000	3,250,597	7,200,000	8,958,225
19X6	4,305,000	4,994,202	285,000	424,702	2,560,000	3,088,008	7,150,000	8,506,912
19X7	3,540,000	4,001,053	310,000	430,960	2,320,000	2,714,050	6,170,000	7,146,063
19X8	2,380,000	2,643,166	335,000	435,643	1,210,000	1,475,454	3,925,000	4,554,263
19X9	1,005,000	1,156,987	350,000	429,065	1,145,000	1,336,385	2,500,000	2,922,437
20X0	980,000	1,069,460	385,000	440,912	610,000	745,765	1,975,000	2,256,137
20X1	930,000	959,295	410,000	440,870	610,000	707,335	1,950,000	2,107,500
20X2	—	—	285,000	293,977	590,000	649,535	875,000	943,512
20X3	—	—	—	—	650,000	670,475	650,000	670,475

(continued)

Exhibit 7-4   (continued)

| | ENTERPRISE | | | | | | | |
| | Water and Sewer | | Parking Deck | | General Government | | Total | |

Maturities on All Long-Term Obligations:
General Obligation Bonded Debt:

Fiscal Year Ended June 30	Principal	Principal & Interest	Principal	Principal & Interest	Principal	Principal & Interest	Principal	Principal & Interest
Total General Obligation Bonded Debt	30,905,000	37,662,877	3,300,000	4,553,036	20,105,000	25,393,435	54,310,000	67,609,348
Other Long Term Obligations:								
Lease Purchase and Other Installment Obligations:								
19X2-X6	1,588,497	1,706,667	114,316	307,173	—	—	1,702,813	2,013,840
19X7-X1	—	—	242,684	348,849	—	—	242,684	348,849
20X2-X3	—	—	96,900	104,116	—	—	96,900	104,116
	1,588,497	1,706,667	453,900	760,138	—	—	2,042,397	2,466,805
Reimbursement Contracts	48,292	48,292[1]	—	—	342,315	342,315[1]	390,607	390,607[1]
Earned Vacation Pay	—	—	—	—	2,247,744	2,247,744[2]	2,247,744	2,247,744[2]
Total Other Long-Term Obligations	1,636,789	1,754,959	453,900	760,138	2,590,059	2,590,059	4,680,748	5,105,156
Total Long-Term Obligations	$32,541,789	$39,417,836	$3,753,900	$5,313,174	$22,695,059	$27,983,494	$58,990,748	$72,714,504

[1] Interest to be paid in future periods not determinable in advance

[2] Interest not applicable

RELATIONSHIPS AMONG THE CAPITAL FUNDS AND ACCOUNT GROUPS

Because both account groups are basically single-entry listings, their transactions are always triggered by an entry in one or more funds. The acquisition of assets, for example, requires an entry in the general fixed asset account group. If long-term debt is issued to finance the purchase, an entry also is made in the general long-term debt account group.

Sometimes a single transaction triggers entries in more than one fund and both account groups. Each entry was explained in the appropriate chapter, but depicting them all in one location helps visualize the interrelationships among the various funds and account groups. Construction of a fixed asset with the proceeds of a long-term debt issue is used to demonstrate the various entries.

OBSERVATION ▲

Interfund transactions and interfund relationships are not the same. In an interfund transaction, a reciprocal of the entry made in the initiating fund is made in a second fund, for example, money transferred by one fund is received by another fund. An interfund relationship simply means that entries in the various funds or account groups reflect a common event, for example, when debt proceeds are reported in a fund and the debt in an account group.

Larkin County's commissioners approved construction of a modern jail facility costing $6,200,000. The construction is financed by $6,000,000,

6 percent term bonds and $200,000 from the general fund. The bonds were issued at 101 and the premium cannot be used to expand the project size. Encumbrances are omitted; budgetary entries are included for some funds and not for others. A sinking fund requiring an annual contribution of $260,000 is required. The amount is transferred from the general fund, as are the interest payments. One-half of the construction activity was completed in 19X1 and the remainder in 19X2.

19X1 Entries

Capital Projects Fund   The capital projects fund budgets the project, receives the bond proceeds, transfers the premium to the debt service fund, and undertakes the construction activity. If encumbrances were incorporated, the capital projects fund would also encumber the fund balance for the amount of the project.

Estimated Other Financing Sources—Bond Proceeds	6,000,000	
Estimated Other Financing Sources—Operating		
Transfers	200,000	
Appropriations		6,200,000
(To establish the project budget)		
Cash	6,060,000	
Due to Debt Service Fund		60,000
Other Financing Sources—Bond Proceeds		6,000,000
(To record the sale of bonds at a premium of ($60,000)		
Cash	100,000	
Operating Transfers		100,000
(To reflect the transfer from the general fund)		
Due to Debt Service Fund	60,000	
Cash		60,000
(To transfer the premium to the debt service fund)		
Expenditures	3,100,000	
Cash		3,100,000
(To record the construction expenditures)		
Appropriations	3,100,000	
Budgetary Fund Balance	3,000,000	
Estimated Other Financing Sources—Bond		
Proceeds		6,000,000
Estimated Other Financing Sources—		
Operating Transfers		100,000
(To close the budgetary accounts)		
Other Financing Sources—Bond Proceeds	6,000,000	
Other Financing Sources—		
Operating Transfers	100,000	
Expenditures		3,100,000
Unreserved Fund Balance		3,000,000
(To close the nominal accounts)		

Unreserved Fund Balance	3,100,000	
Reserve for Construction		3,100,000

(To establish a reserve for the remainder of the project)

General Fund The transfers to the debt service fund and to the capital projects fund are included as part of the general fund's budget; the interest and sinking fund transfers would be budgeted as other financing uses — debt service, and the $100,000 per year would be budgeted as a capital outlay. Because these items represent only a portion of the general fund's budget, the budgetary entries are omitted for this fund.

Operating Transfers — Debt Service	560,000	
Operating Transfers — Capital Outlays	100,000	
Cash		660,000

(To record the transfer for the sinking fund, the interest, and the capital outlay; the entire interest payment is not required because of the $60,000 premium on the bonds sold)

Debt Service Fund Although omitted here, the debt service fund budget would show both the operating transfer from the general fund and any projected earnings on the amount transferred. Its budget probably would not reflect the premium because the amount, if any, would be unknown when the budget is set. In addition, the debt service fund's entries would reflect the receipt of the premium and the transfer from the general fund.

Due from Other Funds	60,000	
Revenues		60,000

(To record the premium on capital projects bonds)

Cash	60,000	
Due from Other Funds		60,000

(To record receipt of the premium on capital projects bonds)

Cash (300,000 + 260,000)	560,000	
Operating Transfers		560,000

(To record the transfer for interest and the sinking fund)

Investments	260,000	
Cash		260,000

(To reflect the investment of sinking fund assets)

Expenditures	360,000	
Cash		360,000

(To record the payment of interest on term bonds)

Operating Transfers	560,000	
Revenues	60,000	
Expenditures		360,000
Unreserved Fund Balance		260,000

(To close the nominal accounts)

Unreserved Fund Balance	260,000	
Reserve for Term Bond Sinking Fund		260,000
(To establish a reserve for the sinking fund contribution)		

General Long-Term Debt Account Group   Entries in the general long-term debt account group for the first year reflect incurring the liability for the term bonds and receipt of the sinking fund cash. Because only the principal is recorded in the general long-term debt account group, receipt of money by the debt service fund for interest payments has no effect on its accounts.

Amount to Be Provided for Term Bonds	6,000,000	
Term Bonds Payable		6,000,000
(To record the issuance of term bonds by the capital projects fund)		
Amount Available in Debt Service Fund—Term Bonds	260,000	
Amount to Be Provided for Term Bonds		260,000
(To record the sinking fund contribution from the general fund)		

General Fixed Asset Account Group   Governmental units usually record construction in progress at the end of each period. Larkin's project is partially complete at the end of the first year; it would record the portion completed in its general fixed asset account group.

Construction in Progress—Buildings	3,100,000	
Investment in General Fixed Assets— Capital Projects		3,100,000
(To record the partially completed construction of the jail facility)		

19X2 Entries

Capital Projects Fund   The total budget was approved and entered in the first year, so the only budgetary entry required is that which will reverse the reserve for the remainder of the project. The other capital projects fund entries for 19X2 include receipt of the general fund contribution and completion of the construction.

Reserve for Construction	3,100,000	
Unreserved Fund Balance		3,100,000
(To reverse the reserve for the construction project)		
Cash	100,000	
Operating Transfers		100,000
(To record the operating transfer from the general fund)		
Expenditures	3,100,000	
Cash		3,100,000
(To record the remaining construction costs)		

Appropriations	3,100,000	
Estimated Other Financing Sources—		
Operating Transfers		100,000
Budgetary Fund Balance		3,000,000
(To close the remaining budgetary balances)		

Operating Transfers	100,000	
Unreserved Fund Balance	3,000,000	
Expenditures		3,100,000
(To close the nominal accounts)		

Because the project costs did not vary from those budgeted, these closing entries zero out the capital projects fund. Had the proceeds and transfers exceeded the construction costs, a residual equity transfer would have been used to close out the fund.

General Fund   Just as in 19X1, the general fund's 19X2 budget includes interest payments due on the bonds ($6,000,000 \times .06 = $360,000$), the amount set aside for the sinking fund ($260,000), and the general fund's share of the project cost ($100,000). In the second year, the full amount of the interest payment must be transferred because the bond premium was already used in 19X1 to offset interest costs.

Operating Transfers—Debt Service	620,000	
Operating Transfers—Capital Outlays	100,000	
Cash		720,000
(To record the transfer of the interest costs and the contribution to the debt service and capital projects funds)		

Debt Service Fund   The entire transfer relating to debt service and sinking fund payments ($360,000 + 260,000$) is reflected as an operating transfer to the debt service fund. No distinction is made between the amount for the interest payment and the amount for the sinking fund. Only the transferring fund distinguishes between debt service payments and capital outlays. A less simplistic example would include budgetary entries and recognition of investment earnings on the prior year's sinking fund contribution.

Cash	620,000	
Operating Transfers		620,000
(To record the transfer from the general fund)		

Expenditures	360,000	
Cash		360,000
(To reflect the interest payment on term bonds)		

Investments	260,000	
Cash		260,000
(To invest the sinking fund assets)		

Operating Transfers	620,000	
Expenditures		360,000
Unreserved Fund Balance		260,000
(To close the nominal accounts)		
Unreserved Fund Balance	260,000	
Reserve for Term Bond Sinking Fund		260,000
(To establish a reserve for the term bond sinking fund)		

General Long-Term Debt Account Group   Since no bonds have matured and interest payments appear only in the debt service fund, the only change in the GLTDAG is the addition to the sinking fund.

Amount Available in Debt Service Fund	260,000	
Amount to Be Provided for Term Bonds		260,000
(To reflect the addition to the term bond sinking fund)		

General Fixed Asset Account Group   With the project completed, the construction in progress account is eliminated and the fixed asset is recorded at cost.

Buildings	6,200,000	
Investment in General Fixed Assets—Capital		
Projects		3,100,000
Construction in Progress—Buildings		3,100,000
(To reflect completion of the jail construction)		

If Larkin had chosen to capitalize interest costs, the entry changes slightly:

Buildings (6,200,000 + 720,000)	6,920,000	
Investment in General Fixed Assets—Capital		
Projects		3,820,000
Construction in Progress—Buildings		3,100,000

FUTURE ACCOUNTING POSSIBILITIES FOR ACCOUNT GROUPS

As the illustration for Larkin County demonstrates, the two account groups, the capital projects fund, and the debt service fund are clearly interrelated. When the GASB embarked on the measurement focus/basis of accounting project, some board members and reviewers suggested that the Board also address the whole area of capital reporting.

Numerous suggestions for alternative reporting were proposed, but three primary approaches are being investigated by the GASB: (1) retain the current reporting—that is, two account groups, a debt service fund, and a capital projects fund; (2) establish a capital account group that would combine the two account groups; or (3) combine the current operations of the two account groups and the debt service and capital projects funds into a plant fund. Under the second approach, if total assets exceeded total liabilities, the governmental entity would report the difference as the net investment in plant. One variation of the third option would require a separate debt service fund with both account groups and the capital projects fund combined into one fund.

One key issue in determining the best approach is the extent to which the capital reporting will be consistent with the total financial resources model. For example, under the third option and its possible variations, the capital fund would contain both financial and capital resources. If this option is selected, the reporting must be structured to report the financial flows separately. In the discussion memorandum describing this option, the Board notes:

> Financial resources transactions that occur with the capital fund have an opposite effect on its capital resources. Accordingly, a dual accounting entry is required within the capital fund to record the decrease in financial resources when, for example, cash is expended for capital assets.[5]

Capital reporting is in the process of evolution. Although the ultimate choice of the GASB is unclear, the difficulties inherent in changing the basis of accounting are evident. A change in the basis of accounting for governmental funds led to a reexamination of capital reporting. This latter review may (and perhaps should) lead to a reconsideration of when to recognize debt payments and, more fundamentally, of whether such payments really ought to be recognized as expenditures. To design an accounting system that is internally consistent and meets users' and managers' reporting needs is indeed difficult.

SUMMARY

Governmental entities use two self-balancing sets of accounts called account groups, in which they record general purpose capital assets and long-term liabilities. These account groups are basically lists of assets and liabilities with matching credits and debits that describe the items on the list. Capital assets and long-term liabilities are segregated in these account groups to permit a *financial resources* focus in the governmental funds.

Capital or fixed assets are usually defined as tangible assets whose cost exceeds a set limit and which will last more than one year. Infrastructure assets—those representing improvements to the land, such as bridges, roads, and sewers—do not have to be recorded in the general fixed asset account group. However, for full disclosure and a basis for charging use of those assets on government contracts, many governmental units include all capital assets in the account group.

---

[5]Governmental Accounting Standards Board, *Discussion Memorandum, An Analysis of Issues Related to Capital Reporting* (Norwalk, Conn.: GASB, 1989), ¶11.

Governmental entities do not record depreciation in the operating statements. Entities wanting to show the effect of depreciation may do so by recording the accumulated depreciation as a reduction in the investment in fixed assets. If they opt to show accumulated depreciation, governmental units must disclose the basis of their calculations in the notes to financial statements.

Managing capital assets involves proper controls, accounting and reporting, and maintenance. Historically, governmental entities have done a poor job of property management. For example, far more attention was paid to controlling cash than fixed assets. Reporting was nonexistent for the bulk of the infrastructure assets, and maintenance was something that could be postponed in times of fiscal stress. Internal controls have been improved with the adoption of computerized property management systems developed first in profit-making entities. Reporting has improved, too, although the GASB is in the midst of reexamining the accounting and reporting options. The issue of measuring, reporting, and funding regular repair and maintenance still has not been addressed adequately. Although extremely important, adequate maintenance has few supporters in periods of limited funding.

Under the current financial resources model, the general long-term debt account group includes all long-term obligations. When the debt is issued, the liability is recorded in the account group. As resources are set aside to repay the debt, the offsetting debit entry is changed from resources to be provided to resources available. Otherwise, the only entries in the account group occur when the debt is issued and again when it is repaid.

Principal and interest payments are recognized as expenditures when due. Accordingly, interest expense accruing on deep discount debt is not reported in the operating statements. However, the balance reflected in the general longterm debt account group is increased as the interest accrues.

Demand bonds are reported as long-term debt when alternative financing is assured through the succeeding year and the long-term lender is financially capable of assuming the debt. Otherwise, demand bonds, even if they finance capital acquisitions, would be reported in the governmental fund issuing the debt.

Financial statements or schedules are prepared for both account groups. Such schedules show the current balances, by type, and the changes in those balances for the period. Financing requirements for debt issues also are detailed either in the notes or supporting schedules. Since no transactions are reported in these account groups, operating statements are not prepared.

QUESTIONS

7-1　Describe the nature of an account group and explain the use of account groups in governmental entities.

7-2　Capital outlays may be made through the general fund, special revenue fund, or capital projects fund. Does the fund through which the acquisition is made affect the reporting in the general fixed asset account group? Explain.

7-3 The GASB is considering a number of accounting options related to capital outlays and the related debt. Explain three such options. Which one best reflects the substance of these transactions?

7-4 What is the nature of the account entitled "investment in general fixed assets"? What information does it provide to the users of financial statements.

7-5 Should depreciation be taken by governmental entities? Should it appear in the operating statement? Explain.

7-6 Why is deferred maintenance a critical issue in governmental accounting?

7-7 If a governmental entity had $1,000,000 of 9 percent bonds outstanding and a sinking fund of $380,000 to repay these bonds, what are the account balances in the general long-term debt account group?

7-8 Why are fixed assets and long-term debt of proprietary funds excluded from the two account groups?

7-9 What financial statements or schedules are prepared for the two account groups?

7-10 Governmental entities are not required to include infrastructure assets in the general fixed asset account group. Why is this accounting optional? Is it appropriate?

7-11 An asset originally financed through a capital projects fund is sold. What are the required entries?

7-12 Discuss the differences between an improvement/betterment and repairs/maintenance.

7-13 At what point is an asset recorded in the general fixed asset account group? A liability in the general long-term debt account group?

7-14 What options are available to account for an asset acquisition involving a trade-in of a similar asset?

7-15 What advantages would there be to reporting capital outlays, debt service, and fixed assets and the related debt in a single capital fund?

7-16 Explain the relationship between interperiod equity and general fixed assets.

7-17 How is the cost of a capital asset defined? What items are considered in determining the cost?

7-18 What information does the account "amount available for..." impart to users of financial statements? If this account were eliminated, how could governmental entities provide the same information?

7-19 What effect will the change from the current financial resources model to the total financial resources model have on the fund balance of the general fund?

7-20 A governmental entity received a gift of three acres of land for a public playground. What valuation basis should be used in recording the asset? What is the credit entry?

CASES

7-1 The mayor is requesting advice on the appropriate response to an exposure draft issued by the GASB. She explains that the exposure draft proposes a capital fund for governmental entities. It would include the traditional debt service activities, capital projects funds, and the two account groups. The following display characteristics for the fund balance are included in the proposal:

> Fund Balance:
> Current Financial Resources:
>   Unreserved
>   Reserved for Bonds Payable
>   Reserved for Construction in Progress
> Capital Resources:
>   Net Investment in General Fixed Assets
> Total Fund Balance

The mayor does not understand why the fund balance has two distinct parts. She also wants to know how the fund balance total would affect the budgeting process: can that amount be included in the budget for a succeeding year as resources available for expenditures?

REQUIRED
1. Discuss the general implications of the proposed consolidation of the account groups and the two funds.
2. Prepare a response to the mayor's specific questions.

7-2 Each year Chilo receives a qualified audit report because it has never had a property management system. The city council has voted to develop one and to include infrastructure assets. Local architects and appraisers have been selected and soon will begin the valuation of the city's fixed assets. Chilo's finance director has no previous experience in managing a system and he wants assistance in developing policies for acquiring, disposing of, and using the city's fixed assets.

REQUIRED
Develop a policy statement for each of the following areas related to a property management system: (1) depreciation, (2) acquisition costs, (3) trade-ins, and (4) interfund transfers.

7-3 In preparing for a final exam, Delmita University's nonprofit accounting class recently reviewed past CPA exams; they found one that appears to have an incorrect answer. The problem posed on the exam was stated as follows:

A local government shows the following long-term liabilities and related accounts on its books as of June 30, 19X1:

Term Bonds, 6/30/X1 Maturity	$ 400,000
Accumulated Sick and Annual Leave	1,200,000

Special Assessment Bonds for which the City Is	
Liable, $100,000 Matures each July 1	800,000
Pension Liability, Long-Term	1,800,000
Mortgage Payable	50,000
Special Assessment Sinking Fund	280,000

What amount should appear in the general long-term debt account group under the total financial resources model?

The answer given in the CPA exam problem was $3,750,000.

REQUIRED

1. Explain the circumstances under which the answer is correct.
2. What assumption(s) must be made in order to classify the answer as correct, even under existing accounting standards?

7-4 A small community in a rural area, Troy Township, is having difficulty selling bonds to finance major renovation of the city's administrative offices. Interest rates are high and Troy's bond rating is only a B. The $1,000,000 of bonds would have to carry a 9 percent effective rate in order to sell; average rates for municipal bonds are around 7.5 percent. The finance director asks the township's administrators to consider issuing demand bonds until Troy's rating improves or rates, in general, fall. He explains that the demand bonds can be issued for 8 percent. A local institution is willing to provide a letter of credit with a one-half of 1 percent guarantee fee (paid whether or not the Township draws on the letter of credit), and a regional insurance company has agreed to a long-term, take-out agreement at 8.75 percent.

REQUIRED

1. Explain what demand bonds are and how they might benefit a township such as Troy.
2. Would you recommend that Troy issue the demand bonds? Explain.

7-5 A sparsely populated midwestern state engages your CPA firm to consult with it on the question of deferred maintenance. With the aid of appraisers, engineers, and state officials, the state's budget director has put together the following list of deferred maintenance by major capital asset category:

Buildings	$57,000,000
Land Improvements	26,400,000
Structures Other Than Buildings	28,360,000
Major Equipment	16,000,000

The state's total budget for the general and special revenue funds for the next fiscal period is $1.1 billion. Projected capital outlays for the same funds total $22 million, including a major new prison facility required to meet federal standards, a fine arts building for one university, and a state highway department facility (partial financing from the federal government). The state has no constitutional limit on its power to issue obligations or incur debt other than a provision that no debt may be created to cover deficits incurred because appropriations exceed anticipated revenues. The state's general long-term obligations total $244,700,000 and an additional $16 million is contemplated for the capital outlays in the next fiscal period.

REQUIRED

1. Prepare a report advising the state how to proceed in addressing its deferred maintenance problems, including additional information needed to prepare public education statements.
2. The budget director is planning to address a joint session of the legislature to explain the problem. What key points should she make?

EXERCISES

7-1   Using the information pertaining to the city of Raleigh, North Carolina, contained in Appendix A of the textbook, answer the following questions:

1. Does Raleigh have both account groups? If so, what kind of description appears in the materials for each one? What basic statements or schedules are provided for each account group?
2. In terms of the fixed asset account group, what categories of fixed assets are shown in the statements? What evidence is provided that all infrastructure assets are included or excluded from the fixed asset account group? Is accumulated depreciation shown for depreciable fixed assets? Is there any explanation of the depreciation practices in the notes?
3. How were the bulk of Raleigh's fixed assets financed? Are all sources listed in the statements/schedules, or is part of the information found in the notes to the financial statements? Explain. Which sources account for over 50 percent of all fixed assets?
4. In terms of the general long-term debt account group, are general obligations shown separately from fund obligations? How is that distinction made in the statements or schedules? What is the total financing requirement for all general obligations during the upcoming fiscal period? Could the display be clearer? If so, how?
5. Does Raleigh have any special assessment debt for which the city is obligated? If so, is it clearly distinguished from other general obligation debt?
6. Does the report contain information about the allowable level of debt financing? If so, what is the debt margin? The debt limit? Any overlapping debt?

7-2   Select the best answer for each question.

1. Which of the following debt types might appear in the general long-term debt account group under the current financial resources model?
   a. long-term pension liability
   b. long-term compensated absence balances
   c. special assessment bonds
   d. all of the above
2. Ridge City issued the following bonds during the year ended July 31, 19X1:

General obligation bonds issued for the Ridge City
water and sewer enterprise fund that will service
the debt $700,000
Revenue bonds to be repaid from admission fees
collected by the Ridge City municipal swimming
pool fund   290,000

The amount of these bonds that should be accounted for in Ridge City's general long-term debt account group is:

a. $990,000
b. $700,000
c. $290,000
d. $0

(Adapted from the November 1988 CPA Exam, Practice #50)

3. The amount to be provided for retirement of general long-term debt is an account of a governmental unit that would be included in the:
a. asset section of the general long-term debt account group
b. asset section of the debt service fund
c. liability section of the general long-term debt account group
d. fund balance section of the general long-term debt account group

(Adapted from the May 1984 CPA Exam, Theory #56)

4. Which of the following accounts would be included in the fund equity section of the combined balance sheet of a governmental unit for the general fixed asset account group?

	Investment in General Fixed Assets	Fund Balance Reserved for Encumbrances
a.	yes	yes
b.	yes	no
c.	no	yes
d.	no	no

(Adapted from the May 1987 CPA Exam, Practice #56)

5. Fred Bosin donated a building to Palma City in 19X3. Bosin's original cost was $100,000. Accumulated depreciation at the date of the gift amounted to $60,000. Fair market value at the date of the gift was $300,000. At what amount should Palma City record this donated fixed asset in the general fixed asset account group?

a. $300,000
b. $100,000
c. $40,000
d. $0

6. Fixed assets used by a governmental unit should be accounted for in the:

	Capital Projects Fund	General Fund
a.	no	yes
b.	no	no

c.	yes	no
d.	yes	yes

(Adapted from the May 1986 CPA Exam, Theory #54)

7. The comprehensive annual financial report (CAFR) of a governmental unit should contain a combined statement of revenues, expenses, and changes in fund balance for:

	General Fixed Asset Account Group	**General Long-Term Debt Account Group**
a.	yes	yes
b.	yes	no
c.	no	no
d.	no	yes

(Adapted from the May 1988 CPA Exam, Theory #58)

8. If construction and debt service activities as well as general-purpose fixed assets and related long-term debt are consolidated into a single reporting entity, the entity is a(an):
   a. general fixed asset account group
   b. capital account group
   c. capital fund
   d. operating fund

9. Which of the following correctly reflects governmental entities' options for accounting and reporting of general fixed assets?
   a. infrastructure assets are reported in the general fixed asset account group, but other assets are in the operating funds
   b. depreciation is taken on all general fixed assets, but reported in the account group instead of in the operating funds
   c. all general fixed assets exceeding the entity's threshold amount are reported in the general fixed asset account group
   d. general-purpose fixed assets are generally reported in the fund incurring the expenditure, but infrastructure assets are reported in the general fixed asset account group

10. Which of the following conditions must be met before demand bonds issued by a governmental entity can be classified as general long-term debt?
    a. a letter of credit must be available for an unlimited period of time
    b. the lender providing the take-out credit must be financially able to carry the demand bond debt
    c. the governmental entity must have no other outstanding demand debt
    d. the governmental entity must use the proceeds of the debt to finance capital acquisitions

7-3   Select the best answer for each question.

1. Property management systems are maintained for general-purpose fixed assets to:

a. improve internal control
b. determine depreciation charges for operating statements
c. determine the reserve for sinking funds
d. develop budgets for capital outlays

2. Under the total financial resources model, capital-related long-term debt would be reported in the:
   a. capital projects fund
   b. general long-term debt account group
   c. fund making the capital outlay
   d. general fund

3. General long-term debt is transferred to the capital projects fund when:
   a. due
   b. adequate resources have been accumulated to repay the debt
   c. interest payments are accrued
   d. none of the above

4. Interest accruing on deep discount debt issues is accounted for by:
   a. the effective interest method in the general fund
   b. the effective interest method in the general long-term debt account group without any charge in the debt service fund
   c. the effective interest method in the debt service fund
   d. the general fund as the amount accrues

5. Under the current financial resources model, the long-term portion of compensated absences is accounted for in:
   a. general long-term debt account group
   b. any fund in which the employees earn the compensation
   c. general fund
   d. none of the above

6. Chancey issued $800,000 general long-term debt at par to finance construction of a sewer line; entries would be made in:
   a. general fund, debt service fund, capital projects fund, and general long-term debt account group
   b. debt service fund, capital projects fund, and general long-term debt account group
   c. capital projects fund and general long-term debt account group
   d. capital projects fund and general fixed asset account group

7. Which of the following does not describe an appropriate transaction for a capital outlay?
   a. a debit to expenditures and a credit to cash in the general fund
   b. a debit to expense and a credit to cash in a proprietary fund
   c. a debit to expenditures and a credit to cash in a capital projects fund
   d. a debit to expenditures and a credit to cash in a special revenue fund

8. A statement/schedule required for the general fixed asset account group is:
   a. statement of changes in financial resources
   b. statement of revenues, expenses, and changes in fund balance
   c. statement of changes in fund balance
   d. statement of changes in general fixed assets

9. Under current accounting principles, which statement best describes a general long-term debt account group?
   a. a self-balancing set of accounts that shows total general long-term debt of a governmental entity
   b. a capital fund for long-term debt related to the acquisition of general fixed assets
   c. a self-balancing set of accounts for reporting the acquisition of general fixed assets
   d. a single-entry listing of long-term debt and amounts available or to be provided for debt relating to the acquisition of general fixed assets

10. What fixed asset outlays are reported as expenditures in the general fixed asset account group?
    a. all those exceeding a particular threshold amount, usually $200 to $1,000
    b. only those financed by general long-term debt
    c. all except infrastructure assets
    d. none of the above

7-4   Due to continuing audit criticisms, the city of Wildwood has decided to develop a property management system encompassing all its general fixed assets. The information presented below has been drawn from property acquisition and construction records, past budget documents, and expenditure records. The city finance director knows the information is incomplete; he needs advice on how to continue.

General Fixed Assets Located:	
Land	$ 260,000
Buildings	4,750,000
Equipment	1,200,000
Improvements Other Than Buildings	2,490,000
Construction in Progress	165,000
Infrastructure Assets	22,400,000
	$31,265,000

Financing Sources Determined:	
Gifts	$ 112,000
General Fund	4,660,000
Special Revenue Fund	1,715,000
Capital Projects Fund	21,300,000
Special Assessments	3,250,000
Federal Grants	900,000
	$31,937,000

ADDITIONAL INFORMATION

1. Certain assets for which records were available could not be located (they could have been torn down, sold, or destroyed): buildings, $180,000; improvements other than buildings, $89,000; equipment, $600,000; infrastructure assets, $1,980,000.
2. Certain assets were located and appraised for which there is no documentation relating to acquisition: equipment, $150,000; land, $83,000; buildings, $1,000,000; infrastructure assets, $2,100,000.

3. Of the federal grant sources, $35,000 could not be related to any general fixed asset included in the inventory. The same was true for $18,000 of assets gifted to Wildwood, $960,000 of special revenue sources, and $1,060,000 of general fund sources.

4. Of the total fixed assets derived from special assessments, $680,000 related to infrastructure assets for which Wildwood had no legal liability to pay the special assessment debt. These assessments related to improvements other than buildings.

5. Construction in progress excluded from the above inventory totals $916,000 and pertains to work undertaken this year in the capital projects fund.

REQUIRED

1. Can Wildwood establish a general fixed asset account group with this incomplete information? Explain.

2. Without prejudicing your answer to part 1, make the necessary journal entry to establish a general fixed asset account group. Show all computations.

7-5 You have been engaged by the town of Rego to examine its June 30, 19X8, balance sheet. You are the first CPA to be engaged by the town and find that acceptable methods of municipal accounting have not been used. The town clerk states that the books have not been closed and presents the following pre-closing trial balance of the general fund as of June 30, 19X8:

	Debit	Credit
Cash	$150,000	
Taxes Receivable—Current	59,200	
Estimated Losses—Current Year Taxes		$ 18,000
Taxes Receivable—Prior Year	8,000	
Estimated Losses—Prior Year Taxes		10,200
Estimated Revenues	310,000	
Appropriations		348,000
Donated Land	27,000	
Building Addition	50,000	
Serial Bonds Paid	16,000	
Other Expenditures	280,000	
Special Assessment Bonds Payable		100,000
Revenues		354,000
Accounts Payable		26,000
Fund Balance		44,000
	$900,200	$900,200

ADDITIONAL INFORMATION

1. The estimated losses of $18,000 for current year taxes receivable were determined to be a reasonable estimate.

2. Included in the revenues account is a credit of $27,000 representing the value of land donated by the state as a grant-in-aid for construction of a municipal park.

3. The building addition account balance is the cost of an addition to the town hall. This addition was constructed and completed in June 19X8. The general fund recorded the payment as authorized.

4. The serial bonds paid account reflects the annual retirement of general obligation bonds issued to finance the construction of the town hall. Interest payments of $7,000 for this bond issue are included in expenditures.

5. Operating supplies ordered in the prior fiscal year and chargeable to that year were received, recorded, and consumed in July 19X7. The outstanding purchase orders for these supplies, which were not recorded in the accounts at June 30, 19X7, amounted to $8,800. The vendors' invoices for these supplies totaled $9,400. Appropriations lapse one year after the end of the fiscal year for which they are made.

6. The special assessment bonds were sold in June 19X8 to finance a street paving project for which the town is liable. No contracts have been signed for this project and no expenditures have been made.

7. The balance in the revenues account includes credits of $20,000 for a note issued to a bank to obtain cash in anticipation of current tax collections. The tax anticipation note was still outstanding on June 30, 19X8.

8. Included in the other expenditures account was a capital outlay for general purpose equipment totaling $34,000.

REQUIRED

1. Prepare the formal adjusting and closing entries for the general fund for the fiscal year ended June 30, 19X8. Assume that capital projects and debt service may be accounted for legally in the general fund.

2. The foregoing information disclosed by your examination was recorded only in the general fund even though other funds or account groups may have been involved. Prepare the formal adjusting journal entries for any other funds or account groups.
   (Adapted from the AICPA Exam)

7-6 Sublett County has embarked on a major capital acquisition effort. The following transactions related to capital acquisitions and occurred during the period ending June 30, 19X2.

1. Seven percent term bonds with a par value of $14,000,000 were issued on July 2, 19X1, at 101 to finance administrative offices for the county government. Interest is due on January 1 and July 1 of each year; both payments were budgeted in Fiscal 19X2.

2. The general fund expended $187,000 for computer equipment on July 27, 19X1.

3. The contract for the construction project was let for $13,800,000, and expenditures of $7,900,000 were incurred during the first year; the remainder of the money was invested at 6 percent on February 1, 19X2.

4. A local philanthropist donated 5 acres valued at $160,000 to the county for a park near the new administrative complex.

5. A special revenue fund received $30,000 earmarked for equipment; a total of $28,900 was spent for the equipment purchases authorized.

6. On October 1, 19X1, the county commissioners established a sinking fund for the term bonds; the first transfer of $280,000 from the general fund was made on April 1, 19X2, and invested at 6 percent.

7. Sublett leased equipment for general fund departments through the general fund under a capital lease. The value of lease to be capitalized is $610,000; an initial payment of $87,000 was made.

[handwritten margin note:] april, May, June 3 months

[handwritten margin note:] —PV of lease payments

REQUIRED

Make all the necessary journal entries to record these transactions (ignore budgetary accounts and closing entries). Identify the fund or account group in which the entries are being made.

7-7   The West Derry municipality upgraded its computer hardware, trading in several items for newer technology. The municipality's governing board authorized the transactions through the general fund. Pertinent information is summarized below:

Book Value of Equipment Traded In	$260,000
Accumulated Depreciation on Equipment Traded In	112,000
Market Value of Equipment Traded In	88,000
Invoice Price of New Equipment	390,000
Cash Paid from General Fund	122,000
Market Value of New Asset	210,000

REQUIRED

1. Prepare the necessary entries in the appropriate funds/account groups to reflect the equipment trade-in and acquisition. Assume West Derry uses the gross method.

2. Using the preceding information but assuming a three-year note was issued for the balance due instead of cash, prepare the necessary entries in the appropriate funds/account groups to reflect the equipment trade-in and acquisition. Use the net method.

7-8   The Rice independent school district shows the following information as its beginning balance of general fixed assets on January 1, 19X2:

Land	$ 260,000
Buildings	1,100,000
Buildings Under Construction	360,000
Equipment	440,000
Improvements Other Than Buildings	180,000
	$2,340,000

During the year, the Rice school district undertook other capital acquisition and construction projects.

1. Term bonds of $235,000 were issued at par to construct a playground and to purchase equipment for it. The equipment cost $116,000 and was all purchased in 19X2. The playground construction cost $119,000 and was completed in 19X2.

2. Additional costs of $480,000 were incurred related to the construction project that was in progress on January 1, 19X2.
3. A donor contributed land for a playing field; the land cost the donor $25,000 and it had a fair market value of $18,000.
4. Equipment costing $11,000 (purchased eight years earlier) was replaced by similar equipment having a market value of $22,000. The school district paid $16,000 on the exchange.
5. Equipment with a total cost of $30,000, accumulated depreciation of $12,857, was transferred to an internal service fund during the year.

ADDITIONAL INFORMATION

1. Effective January 1, 19X1, Rice's school board decided to show accumulated depreciation for its facilities (for buildings, the depreciation will begin the year following completion or acquisition); estimated useful lives are shown below:

Buildings	40 years	The facilities existing on 1/1/X2 were completed ten years earlier.
Equipment	7 years	$100,000 of the beginning balance is fully depreciated. $200,000 was five years old at the beginning of the year. The remainder of equipment is three years old.
Improvements Other Than Buildings	15 years	Improvements all were made four years ago.

Rice uses straight-line depreciation.

2. The land was donated ten years earlier, and it was recorded at the donor's cost. Fair market value today is $300,000; it was $175,000 on the date of the gift.

REQUIRED

Make any necessary adjustments to the beginning balances, and then prepare a statement of changes in general fixed assets for the Rice school district on December 31, 19X2.

7-9 Operating within the state framework, Monroe County has a debt limit of 20 percent of the assessed value of all real and personal property. According to the state regulations, all property of religious organizations is exempt from property taxation and, therefore, cannot be included in determining the debt limit. Any special assessment debt for which Monroe is not obligated is excluded from the legal debt limit, as is any debt backed by sinking funds. Monroe reports the following information on July 1, 19X3:

Assessed Value of Real Property*		$784,140,000
Assessed Value of Personal Property		53,012,000
Church Property		1,189,000
Total Outstanding Debt, All Types		127,316,000
General Obligation Bonds	$120,000,000	
Special Assessment Debt	890,000	
Leases and Other	6,426,000	
Sinking Fund Balance, General Obligation		10,933,000
Special Assessment Debt Without the Backing of Monroe County		561,000

*including church property

REQUIRED

Prepare a statement showing the legal debt limit and margin for Monroe County.

7-10 This exercise is a continuation of exercises 5-10 and 6-10. Oleandar issued long-term bonds to finance capital construction; entries for the capital projects and general fund were made in Chapter 5, and the entries for the debt service fund were made in Chapter 6.

REQUIRED

Referring to the information in exercise 5-10, make the necessary entries for Oleandar's general fixed asset and general long-term debt account groups for 19X0 and 19X1.

7-11 On July 1, 19X1, the city of Kayenta issued $800,000 of 3 percent, 30-year bonds; proceeds from the bonds totaled $385,000. Kayenta follows generally accepted accounting principles in recording the debt proceeds and the accrual of interest expenditures. The proceeds were used to construct a municipal golf course operated by the general fund; construction was completed by June 30, 19X2. Interest payments are due July 1 of each year.

REQUIRED

Make the general journal entries for the appropriate funds and account groups for the year ending June 30, 19X2.

7-12 The following events relate to the city of Green Flats:

1. On January 1, 19X2, $900,000 in 8 percent term bonds were issued. The 10-year bonds sold at 99, and the proceeds will be used to provide new computers to all departments within the city. Interest payments are due on July 1 and January 1. The bond indenture requires a sinking fund to be established. The $65,000 annual contribution is to be made by the general fund each December 31.

2. On March 1, most of the new computers were purchased. The invoice price was $645,000. Shipping costs were $42,000, and installation charges were $23,000. The city paid a private consultant $18,000 to test the computers to make sure they were working properly. Insurance on the computers was purchased at a cost of $33,000. The three-year policy covers all possible casualties.

3. On April 1, the remaining funds from the sale of the bonds were used to purchase a computer for the city transit system. The transit system is operated in an enterprise fund.

4. On January 1, 19X3, a wealthy resident donated a computer to the city. The system had cost her $50,000, and she had taken depreciation of $20,000. Fair market value on the date of the gift was $20,000.

5. On July 1, a new hard drive, a new disk drive, and a new memory board were purchased for the donated computer. Total cost was $16,000. The expected useful life of the computer was not increased.

6. On September 1, one of the original computers broke down. The local computer consultant charged the city $8,000 to fix it. He told the city's

finance manager that the computers were not being properly maintained. He estimated that the amount required to bring all computers owned by the city up to proper condition would be $25,000.

7. On January 1, 19X4, one of the computers was traded in on a newer model. The computer had been part of the 19X2 bulk purchase and had originally cost $80,000. The dealer offered the city $18,000 as a trade-in allowance, and is willing to take a $71,000 note for the rest of the purchase price. The note carries an interest rate of 10 percent and is to be paid in four equal annual installments of $22,400 beginning on January 1, 19X5.

8. Green Flats shows the effect of depreciation for all its fixed assets. The useful life for all computers is five years. Depreciation is calculated to the nearest month.

REQUIRED

What amounts related to the above transactions will be shown on Green Flats' 19X4 balance sheet in the columns for the two account groups? Be sure to state where on the balance sheet each account will appear.

CHAPTER 8
Proprietary Funds

As discussed in earlier chapters, governmental funds relate to operating activities of governmental units—raising and expending taxes and other revenues to provide a government's constituents with services and facilities. A primary accounting and reporting issue for governmental funds is the extent to which interperiod equity is maintained—that is, current-year revenues are sufficient to pay for current-year services.

Proprietary funds, in contrast to governmental funds, are established to account for goods or services provided to the public or to other departments within the governmental unit for a fee. Like for-profit entities, proprietary funds focus on capital maintenance. Current-year revenues should be sufficient to cover all costs of operation, including depreciation.

Both types of proprietary funds—internal service and enterprise funds— are discussed in this chapter. Included in the discussion are important operating characteristics, similarities to private industry, and selected accounting peculiarities. Detailed accounting and financial statement illustrations for each fund follow the general overview.

Capital maintenance

1 Internal Service
2 Enterprise

OVERVIEW OF PROPRIETARY FUNDS

Proprietary funds were added to the governmental fund structure to increase the operating efficiency of certain activities. For example, managers recognized that economies of scale could be achieved by centralizing the purchasing function. Accounting for stores' activities separately and billing departments for requisitioned supplies enables managers to determine the total cost of all purchasing activities. Establishing a separate proprietary fund usually increases the efficiency of the overall governmental unit and the accountability of individual departments.

Governmental units also need to increase the operating efficiency of and accountability for services or facilities provided through user fees. Governing boards may provide certain facilities (for example, swimming pools) or services (sewage disposal) by methods other than taxation. To assure that only those residents benefiting from the facility or service pay for it, managers need to assess charges sufficient to cover all operating costs. Until these facilities or services were accounted for separately, managers had no way of measuring their self-sufficiency.

Proprietary funds account for many internal and external activities when the intent is to cover all costs or to maintain initial capital. If the purpose is to provide goods or services to the *general public* and to recover the costs

increase operating efficiency

economies of scale

↑ operating efficiency

primarily through user charges, an enterprise fund is established. Internal service funds, on the other hand, are used to account for financing and cost recovery of goods or services provided by one department or agency to *other departments or agencies within the governmental unit.*

Operating Characteristics

not required by GAAP

Proprietary funds are not required under GAAP. Official pronouncements reference the optional nature of these funds and their use in accounting for activities operated similar to businesses. Thus, one governmental unit could decide to operate a repair shop on a cost reimbursable basis while another could account for all repair work out of the general fund. Once a unit decides on an accounting approach, however, it should operate consistently from year to year.

Obtaining Fund Approval   Governing board action is usually required to establish proprietary funds. Justification for the action should be included in the documentation provided to the governing board by departmental managers.

The governing board usually determines how the operations should be financed. Will some general fund assets be transferred to the proprietary fund? Will long-term debt be issued to finance initial operations? Will the startup costs be financed by a temporary loan from the general fund? By a permanent contribution? Answers to these questions determine not only the accounting entries but also the operating philosophy. For example, if governmental fund assets are transferred to the new fund, the governing board must decide whether prices should be high enough to provide a return on the unit's use of those assets. (As a minimum, these assets could be earning interest if invested in securities owned by the general fund.)

Staffing the Operation   Once general operating policies are determined, staffing is usually the next issue. Specialized proprietary activities, such as the operation of a public utility plant, require hiring personnel with the requisite skills. For other activities personnel may be reassigned. For example, if a centralized copy service is established, a clerical employee may be transferred from a user department to manage the new fund.

Accounting Characteristics

The accounting system for proprietary funds must provide data for managerial decision making, general purpose financial statements, and comprehensive annual financial reports.

A proprietary fund uses accrual accounting, including the depreciation of fixed assets. Revenues are recognized when earned and expenses when incurred and net income or loss is the difference between them. Revenue and expense classifications parallel those used in business. Fixed assets and total liabilities are reported in the fund. In short, proprietary fund accounting is the same as that for any profit-seeking enterprise operating in the private sector.

Even with the eventual adoption of the accrual basis of accounting for governmental funds, governmental entities will have two measurement focuses: total financial resources for governmental funds and total economic resources for proprietary and some other funds. The GASB is addressing this problem and might, at some point, change the measurement focus of the proprietary funds to be consistent with the governmental funds. Some argue strenuously against this possibility because it would eliminate financial statement comparability between governments and similar types of activities carried out by businesses.

A GASB statement, which is effective for years beginning after December 15, 1993, allows governmental entities two options in applying business-type accounting and financial reporting to proprietary fund activities:[1]

a. The first approach applies GASB pronouncements and FASB or its predecessors' statements issued before November 30, 1989 — provided they do not conflict with GASB statements — to proprietary fund accounting and reporting.

b. The second approach applies GASB pronouncements and FASB or its predecessors' statements — provided they do not conflict with GASB statements — to proprietary fund accounting and reporting.

The options are similar except that the first has a cut-off date of November 30, 1989. This cut-off date was used because it was the date on which the Financial Accounting Foundation reaffirmed the GASB's purview over all governmental entities. This statement provides interim guidance while the GASB is studying the entire issue of the appropriate accounting and financial reporting model for proprietary funds.

Budgeting As pointed out in the 1988 *Governmental Accounting, Auditing, and Financial Reporting* guide, flexible budgets should be prepared for proprietary funds.[2] A flexible budget shows estimated costs for various levels of production or service. Actual results can be compared to the flexible budget at the actual activity level. Because of either legal requirements or limited possible variations in service levels, most governmental unitsuse a fixed budget (projected costs and revenues for a given level of service).

Ordinarily the budgetary accounts are not integrated into the accounting system. Budgetary comparisons are also excluded from the general purpose financial statements. However, many government units include supplementary data showing budget and actual comparisons in the comprehensive annual financial report.

Legal constraints may require governmental units to prepare proprietary fund budgets on a cash basis, for example, and actual results on the accrual

---

[1] Governmental Accounting Standards Board, *Statement No. 26, Accounting and Financial Reporting for Proprietary Funds and other Governmental Entities that use Proprietary Fund Accounting* (Norwalk, Conn.: GASB, 1993).

[2] Government Finance Officers Association, *Governmental Accounting, Auditing, and Financial Reporting* (Chicago: GFOA, 1988), 62.

basis. In such circumstances, the non-GAAP budgetary basis is reconciled to the full accrual basis and the reconciliation is presented in the statements.

Cost Accounting   Like their private business counterparts, proprietary fund managers use cost accounting systems. Only by understanding how various costs are affected by changes in the level of activity can a manager budget and plan self-supporting services. Depending upon the complexity of the activity and the sophistication of the governmental unit, a detailed analysis of fixed and variable costs (or controllable and uncontrollable costs) is generated by the cost accounting system.

Cost accounting systems used in business are applicable to proprietary funds. **Job order costing** is typically used by proprietary funds offering discrete services, such as repair work. **Process costing** best fits those services characterized by repetition, such as garbage disposal. A **standard cost system** may be used for a manufacturing activity; the financial statements would show the same work-in-progress and finished-goods inventory accounts as a business manufacturing the same product.

Pricing   Cost accounting systems are used not only to plan operations and control the activity, but also to set prices. Most proprietary fund activities involve providing either a continuous service, such as a central repair shop for all county departments, or a service for specified times, such as a swimming pool operated during the summer months. Consequently, the per unit pricing models discussed in cost accounting are rarely used. The governmental entity would likely determine total operation costs, assume certain usage rates by other departments or the public, and fix prices accordingly. If the cost to maintain and staff the swimming pool during the summer months is estimated at $85,000 and 112,500 swimmers are expected, each swimmer would be charged approximately $0.75.

The price charged should generate revenue sufficient to cover *total costs.* Defining that price depends upon the type of fund. If a governmental unit establishes a central supplies store, the price necessary to cover total costs is the invoice amount plus a surcharge to cover procurement and storage costs. For most other internal service funds, the price should recover full costs, but not exceed the price that would be paid if a department purchased the same goods or services from an external supplier. Whether the price generates a *return on investment* for the governmental unit is a matter of public policy.

For enterprise funds, the prices ordinarily are set to recover total direct costs and some indirect costs. The cost of allocating some overhead items—administrative salaries, insurance, interest, and so on—is high and, therefore, frequently ignored. Only when the enterprise fund is in direct competition with private businesses are governing boards inclined to insist upon full costing. To make the comparison with private industry more realistic, some enterprise funds pay a cost *in lieu of taxes.* Some governmental units that operate public utilities demand a return on invested capital. When the payment bears a reasonable relationship to the utility service provided, courts have generally allowed such payments in the pricing structure.[3]

[3]Andre C. Dasent and George J. Whelan, "Governmentally Owned Utilities: A Rationale for Payments Made to Government Owners," *Government Finance Review* (February 1988): 18–20.

No pricing system is perfect and proprietary funds are apt to over- or underprice their services or products. Theoretically, if the price is too high in one period, the excess should be returned to the purchasing departments or users. If it is too low, additional charges should be billed. Because this is not an efficient way to operate, prices charged in subsequent periods are generally adjusted to "even out" the over- or undercharge.

OBSERVATION ▲

Because many services provided by a government are monopolistic, price setting is not nearly as complicated as in business. If the price is too high in one period, demand may drop some but not enough to jeopardize the activity.

Allocating overhead is a major problem in determining total costs for any business-type activity. Some governmental employees work on several different activities and often do not keep detailed records of how they spend their time, particularly at the supervisory and administrative levels. Therefore, it may be necessary to estimate some of the personnel costs associated with proprietary fund operations. Other overhead costs requiring allocation include utilities, rent, insurance, and general support services.

Capitalizing Interest Costs

Proprietary funds that receive little or no subsidy from the governmental unit rely extensively on debt financing. FASB pronouncements require capitalization of *material* interest costs during the construction of fixed assets.[4] The amount of interest capitalized is the weighted average of accumulated expenditures times either the specific new borrowing rate or the weighted average rate on other borrowings if no specific debt was incurred to construct the asset. For example, if $1,000,000 of 7 percent debt was issued on July 1 to construct a new building, and the weighted average expenditures from July 1 to December 31 were $820,000, the maximum interest capitalized would be $28,700 ($820,000 $\times$ .07 $\times$ 6/12).

Adjustments made to the basic calculation depend on the type of debt and the circumstances surrounding issuance. The following rules summarize the adjustments:

1. If the debt is tax-exempt (the bond purchasers do not pay federal income tax on the interest income), interest income earned by the governmental unit is offset against the interest expense incurred and only the net amount, if any, is capitalized. The calculation could result in negative interest expense. However, the IRS enforces rules prohibiting a governmental unit from investing the debt proceeds at a rate higher than the cost incurred on the debt. A governmental unit could not, for example, issue 6 percent bonds and invest the proceeds at 9 percent.

---

[4]Financial Accounting Standards Board, *Statement No. 34, Capitalization of Interest Cost* (Stamford, Conn.: FASB, 1979), and *Statement No. 62, Capitalization of Interest Cost in Situations Involving Certain Tax Exempt Borrowings and Certain Gifts and Grants* (Stamford, Conn.: FASB, 1982).

2. If interest on the debt is taxable, interest income is not offset against interest expense, and the gross amount of interest expense is capitalized.[5]
3. If the asset is acquired or constructed by grant or gift funds, no interest expense is capitalized.
4. Interest capitalization begins when the debt is issued and construction is underway. It ends when the construction is completed.
5. The amount of interest capitalized cannot exceed the actual interest for the period.

To demonstrate the principles involved, assume that $1,000,000 of 7 percent debt was issued on June 1 to finance construction of proprietary fund assets. Construction began on July 1, and between June 1 and July 1, the proceeds were invested at 6 percent. Construction expenditures and the weighted average computation follows:

	Expenditure	Time	Weighted Average
July 1	$200,000	3/12	$ 50,000
October 1	100,000		
Subtotal	300,000	2/12	50,000
December 1	500,000		
Subtotal	800,000	1/12	66,667
Total			$166,667

If interest on the debt was taxable, interest expense of $11,667 ($166,667 × .07) would be capitalized. If the debt was tax exempt, the capitalized interest would total $6,667 ($11,667 − [1,000,000 × .06 × 1/12]).

Interest capitalization is a complex accounting issue. Capitalizing interest costs complicates comparison between units using debt financing and those using financing from internal sources. Asset cost comparison would be facilitated by imputing interest costs when internal financing was used, but overall performance measures would then have less relevance and the "make-or-buy" decision would be meaningless.

INTERNAL SERVICE FUNDS

Governmental units use internal service funds for various purposes. Examples include copy or repair shops, motor pools, printing, data processing, purchasing, and central stores. More recently, as the liability for compensated absences has escalated, some governmental units have established inter-

---

[5] Although governmental units continue to finance the majority of their assets with tax-exempt debt, the Tax Reform Act of 1986 restricted the amount of tax-exempt debt that state and local governments may issue.

nal service funds for handling these costs. The fund serves as an accounting vehicle for determining what portion of the total cost applies to other departments or agencies within the governmental entity.

Another use of internal service funds is for self-insurance. The governmental unit establishes the total amount necessary to be set aside annually. The internal service fund accounts for the total and charges individual departments for their share of the self-insurance program.

Self-insurance

A separate fund is used to account for each service. Accounting for more than one service in a single fund defeats the purpose of internal service funds. If more than one activity were included in a single fund, total costs of any one service would be difficult to determine and the resources generated by one service could be improperly used to subsidize another.

Operating and Accounting Procedures

Because the impetus for internal service funds is to increase efficiency—primarily by economy of scale purchases or by eliminating duplication—all assets used by the fund must be included in establishing prices. Within the constraint of cost-benefit analysis, all costs associated with the internal service fund should be properly allocated to it. Otherwise, assessing the benefits accruing to the governmental unit becomes very difficult. Similar to the make-or-buy decision in business, a governmental unit should determine if efficiency is improved by centralizing services or production.

Establishing the Internal Service Fund As mentioned previously, assets or money are usually transferred to the internal service fund at its inception. Entries reflecting the transfer must distinguish between permanent and temporary advances. Permanent transfers are subsidies and should be labeled as such. As an example, if the general fund provides permanent financing, the necessary entries would be:

GF	Equity Transfer	XX	
	Cash		XX
ISF	Cash	XX	
	Contributed Capital		XX

The contributed capital is a part of the fund's equity. The fund is not expected to generate sufficient revenue to repay it or to earn a return for the general fund. The internal service fund is being subsidized by the government's general tax base, just as if each department had individually purchased its own service or produced its own product. In this case, the equity transfers out will not agree with equity transfers in within the financial statements; note disclosure is recommended to explain the difference.

General purpose fixed assets transferred to an internal service fund are treated similarly. The internal service fund credits contributed capital. Governmental entities have an option of closing depreciation expense on these assets directly to the contributed capital account. If this option is selected, depreciation expense on transferred assets does not affect the operating performance for the period.

If, on the other hand, the internal service fund is expected to repay the initial capital contribution, the general fund and the internal service fund would make the following entries:

GF	Advance to Internal Service Fund	xx	
	Cash		xx
ISF	Cash	xx	
	Advance from General Fund		xx

Usually the general fund does not require any return on its advance, only a repayment of the principal at some specified time.

Estimating a Budget   Internal service fund sales depend on the demand from other departments, which, in turn, depends on the funding level and management flexibility within those departments. If user departments must use the internal service fund, the internal service fund's budget is fixed by authorized expenditure levels in user departments. For example, if a line item for repair work in the highway (user) department budget is only $1,000, no additional expenditures could be made without a budget amendment. A centralized repair shop could count on sales of only $1,000 to the highway department regardless of the price charged per hour or per job. A critical issue in developing the internal service fund budget is whether the government's departments are *required* to use the internal service fund. The greater the flexibility of user departments, the more flexible budgeting makes sense for internal service funds.

If user department budgets are fixed, internal service fund managers typically estimate total costs and calculate predetermined use rates that, given expected demand, will cover all costs. Significant budget errors are usually corrected by adjusting prices in subsequent periods.

Because of user departments' timing, an internal service fund cannot always meet their demands, and user departments may be forced to use outside services. Timing considerations should be incorporated when developing the budget. Also, certain downtimes for equipment repair or replacement could have important budget implications. Insofar as possible, those implications should be estimated and reflected in the budget.

Interfund Transactions   When a user department buys an internal service fund's product or uses its service, the buying department has incurred an expenditure. The internal service fund has generated revenue. The basis of accounting determines when the expense/expenditure and revenue are recognized in the respective funds.

Transfers among funds also occur when the general fund provides the initial capital for an internal service fund. If general governmental assets are transferred to the internal service fund, the asset should be recorded at book value. If book value exceeds market value, the asset should be recorded at market. If the governmental unit did not record accumulated depreciation on the asset prior to its transfer, those calculations need to be made to determine the appropriate transfer value.

Illustrated Transactions

For purposes of illustrating the transactions for internal service funds, assume that Jasper County officials decided early in 19X9 to centralize all duplicating and printing services. Previously, each department used outside printing and duplication services or had their own copy machines. The largest in-house copier, with a book value of $65,000, was transferred to the internal service fund; the others were sold and the proceeds of $150,000 were contributed to the fund. Revenue bonds totaling $550,000 at 7 percent are sold (at par) to finance the remodeling of several offices assigned to the new department and to augment the resources available for purchasing additional equipment. The contribution, asset transfer, and bond issuance were recorded in the printing fund as:

1.	Cash	150,000	
	Equipment	65,000	
	Contributed Capital		215,000
2.	Cash	550,000	
	Bonds Payable		550,000

The state has a special grant program to encourage efficiency in local governments; efficiencies achieved by the printing fund qualified and Jasper County received $60,000 from the state. Under the terms of the grant, $30,000 was a permanent contribution for equipment and the remaining $30,000 amounted to an interest-free loan and was to be repaid annually at a rate of 1 percent of gross billings. Entry 3 reflects the receipt of the grant:

3.	Cash	60,000	
	Contributed Capital		30,000
	Long-Term Grant Liability		30,000

Because not all of the cash was needed immediately, the manager invested $70,000. Investment earnings totaled $5,000 for the year. These transactions are illustrated in entries 4 and 5.

4.	Investments	70,000	
	Cash		70,000
5.	Cash	5,000	
	Nonoperating Revenue		5,000

OBSERVATION ▲

Rather than describe its character, as is done in business, revenue not related directly to operations is referred to as nonoperating revenue.

Equipment necessary for printing was purchased, and the remodeling was completed (the fund will rent the basic structure from the county):

6.	Building Improvements	100,000	
	Equipment	450,000	
	Cash		550,000

Supplies purchases of $70,000 are entered as:

| 7. | Supplies Inventory | 70,000 | |
| | Accounts Payable | | 70,000 |

Departments are billed for the actual cost of direct materials and labor for all printing jobs. Printing overhead charges (for example, indirect materials and labor, rent, insurance, repairs and maintenance, and depreciation) are *estimated* to run 115 percent of direct labor and materials. For copying services, the departmental charge is set at $.09 per copy, which includes direct and indirect costs.

Actual printing costs incurred by the printing department for the period were:

	Direct	Indirect	Total
Labor	$70,000	$15,000	$ 85,000
Materials	20,000	7,000	27,000
Other Overhead		64,000	64,000
Total	$90,000	$86,000	$176,000

Entry 8 records the billings to departments and is based on the actual direct expenses and estimated overhead amounts. As shown in entry 9, $160,000 was received on account by year end:

8.	Due from Other Funds	193,500	
	Departmental Billings		193,500
	($90,000 + [1.15 × $90,000])		

| 9. | Cash | 160,000 | |
| | Due from Other Funds | | 160,000 |

In addition to printing services, user departments made 700,000 copies for total billings of $63,000; $50,000 was paid by year end.

| 10. | Due from Other Funds | 63,000 | |
| | Departmental Billings | | 63,000 |

| 11. | Cash | 50,000 | |
| | Due from Other Funds | | 50,000 |

A breakdown of the actual expenses for both printing (as shown above) and copying during the year follows:

	Printing	Copying
Direct Labor	$70,000	$18,000
Indirect Labor	15,000	8,000
Direct Materials	20,000	6,000
Indirect Materials	7,000	3,000
Rent	10,400	2,200
Repairs/Maintenance	8,000	300
Interest Expense	35,000	3,500
Other Operating Expenses	10,600	700

(To simplify the presentation, the labor accounts include payroll taxes and fringe benefits. In practice, separate accounts would be maintained for these items.)

The expenses are recorded in entries 12 and 13.

12.	Direct Labor	88,000	
	Indirect Labor	23,000	
	Interest Expense ($550,000 × .07)	38,500	
	Cash		149,500
13.	Direct Materials	26,000	
	Indirect Materials	10,000	
	Repairs/Maintenance	8,300	
	Rent	12,600	
	Other Operating Expenses	11,300	
	Supplies Inventory (D + I materials)		36,000
	Accounts Payable		19,600
	Due to Other Funds		12,600

OBSERVATION ▲

A cost of services or cost of supplies account could have been used to combine the production costs related to printing and copying, in which case only interest, other operating costs, rent, and so on, would appear in the operating expenses section of the income statement. See Exhibit 8-1.

The used copier is depreciated over 8 years and the remaining equipment over 15 years; the building improvements have a useful life of 25 years and the straight-line method is used for all fixed assets.

14.	Depreciation Expense	42,125	
	Accumulated Depreciation—Building Improvements		4,000
	Accumulated Depreciation—Equipment		38,125
	($100,000/25 = $4,000; $65,000/8 = $8,125; and $450,000/15 = $30,000)		

Entry 15 records the payment made to the state on the long-term grant liability.

15.	Long-Term Grant Liability	2,565	
	Cash		2,565
	(.01 × [193,500 + 63,000])		

At year end, accounts payable are reduced to $5,000; the payment is shown in entry 16.

| 16. | Accounts Payable | 84,600 | |
| | Cash | | 84,600 |

Closing entries are as follows:

17.	Departmental Billings	256,500	
	Nonoperating Revenue	5,000	
	Direct Labor		88,000
	Indirect Labor		23,000
	Direct Materials		26,000
	Indirect Materials		10,000
	Rent		12,600
	Depreciation		42,125
	Repairs and Maintenance		8,300
	Other Operating Expenses		11,300
	Interest Expense		38,500
	Excess of Net Billings over Costs		1,675
18.	Excess of Net Billings over Costs	1,675	
	Retained Earnings		1,675

▲   **OBSERVATION**

Because the illustration represented a hypothetical situation, the results of operations were contrived very close to break even. In an actual situation, initial price setting may not be that accurate. Further, investment earnings will not continue, so prices must be increased in succeeding years.

Illustrated Financial Statements

The statement of revenues and expenses for Jasper County's printing fund during its first year is shown in Exhibit 8-1. Ordinarily, the operating statement would include a section on the changes in retained earnings. However, because the statement is illustrated for the fund's first operating year, that section of the statement is omitted. Exhibit 8-2 presents the printing fund's balance sheet for December 31, 19X9. A cash flow statement is not shown, but it would be similar in format and content to the cash flow statement for an enterprise fund depicted later in the chapter.

Without assumptions regarding asset replacement, it is difficult to determine whether the $1,675 net "excess" for the period is adequate. For example, if depreciation accurately reflects fixed asset replacement costs, the prices charged during the first year will be sufficient to replace the fund's assets as they wear out or become obsolete. Of course, a cash amount equivalent to

Exhibit 8-1

Jasper County
Printing and Copying Fund (Internal Service Fund)
Statement of Revenues and Expenses
For the Year Ended December 31, 19X9

Departmental Billings		$256,500
Less: Cost of Services Provided		147,000
Gross Margin		$109,500
Other Operating Expenses:		
Depreciation	$42,125	
Rent	12,600	
Interest Expense	38,500	
Repairs and Maintenance	8,300	
Other Operating Expenses	11,300	
Total Operating Expenses		112,825
Operating Loss		$ (3,325)
Nonoperating Revenue		5,000
Net Excess of Revenue over Expenses		$ 1,675

Exhibit 8-2

Jasper County
Printing and Copying Fund (Internal Service Fund)
Balance Sheet
As of December 31, 19X9

Assets

Current Assets:			
Cash	$118,335		
Due from Other Funds	46,500		
Investments	70,000		
Supplies Inventory	34,000		
Total Current Assets			$268,835
Property, Plant, and Equipment:			
Equipment	$515,000		
Less: Accumulated Depreciation	38,125	$476,875	
Building Improvements	$100,000		
Less: Accumulated Depreciation	4,000	96,000	
Total Property, Plant, and Equipment			572,875
TOTAL ASSETS			$841,710

Liabilities and Fund Equity

Current Liabilities:			
Due to Other Funds	$ 12,600		
Accounts Payable	5,000		
Total Current Liabilities			$ 17,600
Long-Term Liabilities:			
Grant Liability	$ 27,435		
Bonds Payable	550,000		
Total Long-Term Liabilities			577,435
Fund Equity:			
Contributed Capital	$245,000		
Retained Earnings	1,675		
Total Fund Equity			246,675
TOTAL LIABILITIES AND FUND EQUITY			$841,710

depreciation would have to be set aside each year to assure funding. On the other hand, the nonoperating revenue ($5,000 interest earnings) may have been a one-year boon; if so, the prices charged probably are too low to sustain the fund's operation.

From another perspective, the fund should generate enough money to repay debt principal and interest. If the debt term and the asset life are similar, the debt would be paid off by the time the retiring assets need to be replaced. Long-term debt could be issued to finance the purchase of replacement assets. Neither depreciation nor debt payments may accurately reflect the replacement cost for fixed assets. Fund managers need to carefully monitor replacement prices to adequately provide for asset replacement.

ENTERPRISE FUNDS

The other proprietary fund, the enterprise fund, is established to account for goods or services sold to the general public. NCGA *Statement 1* also permits governments to use enterprise fund accounting for any service that has a *significant potential* for financing operations through user charges. Parking facilities, recreational facilities (swimming pools, golf courses, amusement parks), public utilities (garbage, water, sewer), airports, hospitals, public housing, and dock and wharf facilities are common examples of enterprise fund operations. Governments may provide these services in the public interest, or because private enterprise cannot provide the same service as economically or as efficiently.

One of the more recent uses of the enterprise fund is to account for entity risk pools, a cooperative group of governmental entities joining together to finance an exposure, liability, or risk.

A pool may be a stand-alone entity or be included as part of a larger governmental entity that acts as a pool's sponsor.... All public entity risk pools should account for their activities in an enterprise fund regardless of whether there is a transfer or pooling (sharing) of risk.[6]

Budgeting

Service levels of enterprise funds are determined by consumer demand, and revenues and expenses fluctuate with changing service levels. Therefore, flexible budgeting is generally used for planning and evaluating enterprise fund spending levels. Budgetary data are not required in the financial reports of enterprise funds, but the information is sometimes provided in supplementary schedules of comprehensive annual financial reports.

[6]Governmental Accounting Standards Board, *Codification of Governmental Accounting and Financial Reporting Standards* (Norwalk, Conn.: GASB, 1993), sec. Po20.110 and Po20.114.

Accounting Practices

Enterprise funds generally use business accounting practices—that is, accrual accounting. Revenues are recognized when earned, and expenses are recognized when incurred. All assets and liabilities relating to enterprise fund operations are reported in the fund's balance sheet. Fixed assets are depreciated over their useful lives.

Most account classifications are similar to business. Income statement accounts include revenues and expenses. The revenues typically are referred to as "customer billings" rather than as sales. To enhance the comparability between financial statements for enterprise funds and businesses offering similar services, parallel account classifications are encouraged.

An enterprise fund may earn revenues incidental to its primary activity. A public utility fund, for example, may earn rent from facilities not used in its operations or water tap fees from customers. Another peripheral revenue source is an operating grant from the state or federal government. These **non-operating** revenues are reported below the operating section of the statement of revenues, expenses, and changes in fund equity.

Interfund Transactions   As explained in earlier chapters, transactions between two *governmental* funds affect "other financing sources or uses;" they do not involve recognizing revenues or expenses. Those interfund transactions were described as operating transfers, equity transfers, or reimbursements. In contrast, when other funds use enterprise fund services, such as utilities used by governmental departments, the buying department recognizes an expenditure and the enterprise fund recognizes revenue.

The enterprise fund also may incur expenses that result from charges by other funds. Remittance of payments in lieu of taxes to the general fund is a common example. The fee is revenue to the "taxing fund" and an expense to the enterprise fund.

Intergovernmental Support   Enterprise funds may receive grants, entitlements, or shared revenues from state or federal governments. This support should be reported as nonoperating revenue. Support restricted to the acquisition or construction of capital assets should be recorded as **contributed capital.** Depreciation taken on the assets acquired or constructed from intergovernmental support may be shown in the operating statement and closed to the excess of revenues over expenses account. As an option, depreciation may be closed to the contributed capital account. Accumulated depreciation is shown as an offset to the asset account, but the operating statement is unaffected by depreciation expense. For example, if an enterprise fund received a $1,000,000 grant for facility construction from the federal government, and the constructed asset has an expected life of 40 years, the entries in the first year would be:

Cash	1,000,000	
Contributed Capital		1,000,000

Depreciation Expense	25,000	
Accumulated Depreciation		25,000
Contributed Capital	25,000	
Depreciation Expense		25,000

▲ **OBSERVATION**

NCGA, the GASB's predecessor, reasoned that because the intergovernmental resources did not have to be repaid, the enterprise fund's operating performance should not be affected by depreciation on assets acquired or constructed from such support. Accumulated depreciation is still shown to reflect the asset's undepreciated cost.

Accounting for Entity Risk Pools

Risk pools provide one way for governmental entities to manage certain types of risk exposure. Several governmental entities may use a risk pool to **self-insure** their risks on an individual entity basis. "Premiums" are charged in advance, but each entity is billed for the amount by which its losses for the period exceeded its "premiums." The self-insurance risk pool may also treat activities in the aggregate, rather than on an individual insured entity basis. It will make additional assessments on all participants if the loss experience of all participants exceeds the premiums; refunds will be made to all, or future premiums adjusted downward, if the loss experience of all entities is less than anticipated.

The primary accounting issue related to entity risk pools is the recognition of revenues and liabilities. Ordinarily, premiums are recognized over the contract period in relation to the amount of risk protection provided. For example, if a governmental entity paid the entity risk pool $100,000 for level risk protection over a two-year period, $50,000 would be recorded as revenue each period unless the amount of risk protection changes according to a predetermined schedule.

Claim liabilities are recognized when the insured event occurs. Such liabilities include costs related to incurred but not reported claims as long as it is probable that a loss has incurred and the amount is reasonably estimable. The amount is based on the estimated ultimate cost of settling the claim. Usually this estimate is based on past experience adjusted for any current trends, such as inflation, and other societal and economic factors. Claim adjustment expenses, such as legal and adjuster fees, should be accrued when the related claim liability is accrued.

Unlike the accrual in the private sector, discounting of governmental entity risk pool liabilities is allowed but not required. However, if a governmental entity enters into a structured settlement in which an initial cash payment is made to satisfy a claim and annuity payments used to satisfy the remainder, the claim liability should be discounted.

Accounting for Restricted Assets

Because enterprise-type activities, such as public utilities, transportation systems, and amusement parks, require huge capital outlays, debt financing is common. Revenue bond indentures typically restrict the proceeds to construction costs. They also require a systematic accumulation of money to make interest and principal payments and to meet emergency capital needs. In businesses, these restrictions would be referred to as *funds* (for example, bond sinking fund). To avoid the obvious confusion with governmental entities, which are called funds, revenue bond indenture requirements are referred to as **restricted asset accounts.** The result is a fund within a fund.

Revenue bond restricted asset accounts are usually required for (1) construction proceeds, (2) current debt service, (3) future debt service, and (4) contingencies. When the bonds are issued, the cash is deposited into the account restricted for construction proceeds. Disbursements for authorized construction work or plant acquisitions are made from this account.

The bond indenture specifies the amounts to be deposited in the other three restricted asset accounts. For example, the indenture may require that one-twelfth of the annual debt service payment should be deposited into the current debt service account each month. During the initial operating phase of the enterprise — typically 60 months — a certain portion of total revenues will be set aside in the future debt service account to cover any deficiency in the current debt service account. Finally, the indenture may require a certain percentage of either total revenues or the total bond issue to be accumulated in the bond contingency account.

Just as in business, retained earnings are appropriated for any restricted long-term asset account. The 1980 GAAFR describes the requirement as follows:

> Amounts that should be accumulated in the . . . accounts should be recorded as a reservation of retained earnings. If amounts accumulated in these accounts are less than what is required, details of the shortage(s) should be disclosed in the notes to the financial statements. Required amounts for the Revenue Bond Current Debt Service Account are reduced by the amount of current liabilities for revenue bond principal and interest and related fiscal charges.[7]

If the enterprise fund accumulates more than is required by the indenture, the excess also is reported as a reservation of retained earnings.

OBSERVATION ▲

The term *reservation* is outdated and not used by business organizations. It was dropped from acceptable usage because it might imply a *cash reserve* and therefore confuse financial statement readers. No doubt the GASB will eventually change the title to *appropriation*. Segregating restricted cash or short-term investments from operating cash helps reduce confusion caused by the use of the term.

---

[7]MFOA, *Governmental Accounting, Auditing, and Financial Reporting,* 62. While the *1988 GAAFR* does not include this same reference, the concept is illustrated.

Some enterprise funds receive deposits from customers. Until the customer withdraws from the service arrangement, those deposits represent fund liabilities. Current GAAP requires these deposits to be shown in a restricted asset account.

Illustrated Transactions

Most enterprise fund accounting transactions are the same as those of businesses and internal service funds. To avoid duplication, the transactions shown here depict only the more difficult conceptual areas of enterprise accounting. Accounting for revenue bond proceeds and related restrictions, debt servicing, and asset acquisition and depreciation are emphasized.

The illustrated transactions pertain to an amusement park operated by a city. The city authorities issued $2,700,000 of 7 percent serial revenue bonds to finance a major renovation of the park. Among other restrictions, the bond indentures require one-half of 1 percent of gross revenues to be set aside for contingencies during the first three years. The bonds were issued on 7/1/X8 at par; a semiannual payment of $102,000 is due on January 1 and July 1 of each year. Current debt service payments must be accumulated monthly in a restricted account. In addition, beginning in 19X9, the equivalent of six semiannual principal payments must be ratably accumulated in a restricted asset account over the first five years for future debt service.

Revenue Bond Proceeds   Entry 1 reflects the issuance of the bonds; entries 2 through 5 summarize the construction process.

1.	7/1/X8	Cash	2,700,000	
		Revenue Bonds Payable		2,700,000
2.	7/1/X8	Revenue Bond		
		Construction Account	2,700,000	
		Cash		2,700,000
3.	Various	Construction in Progress	2,600,000	
		Construction Contracts Payable		2,600,000
4.	10/1/X8	Building Improvements	2,600,000	
		Construction in Progress		2,600,000
5.	10/1/X8	Construction Contracts Payable	2,600,000	
		Revenue Bond Construction		
		Account		2,600,000

Normally, any excess bond proceeds restricted for construction must be applied to reduce the amount set aside for current or future debt service amounts. Assuming that any excess (in this case $100,000) is used to reduce the amount that must be set aside for future debt service payments, the amusement park would make entry 6.

6.	10/1/X8	Revenue Bond Future Debt Service		
		Account	100,000	
		Revenue Bond Construction		
		Account		100,000

Asset Restrictions   Entry 7 shows the deposit made each month to accumulate amounts necessary for the first semiannual payment due January 1, 19X9.

7.	7/30/X8	Revenue Bond Current Debt Service		
		Account	17,000	
		Cash		17,000
		(102,000/6 = 17,000)		

By 12/31/X8 the total cash necessary to make the first semiannual payment would be accumulated in the revenue bond current debt service account.

Sometimes restricted resources are invested by the governmental unit's agent, in which case each of the debits would have been to the cash with fiscal agent account rather than to the revenue bond current debt service account. Investment earnings from restricted assets may be available for operations or may be restricted for the same purpose as the principal.

Assuming operating revenues of $1,500,000 for the second half of 19X8 (the period in which the bonds are outstanding), the amusement park makes entry 8 to establish the contingency fund.

8.	12/31/X8	Revenue Bond Contingency Account	7,500	
		Cash		7,500
		(1,500,000 × .005)		

Accruing Interest   Entry 9 accrues the interest at the end of the first year. Just as in business, the effective interest method is used to calculate the interest and principal portions of the total payment.

9.	12/31/X8	Interest Expense	94,500	
		Accrued Interest Payable		94,500 ✓
		(2,700,000 × .07 × .5)		

Reserving Retained Earnings   In entries 10 and 11, retained earnings are reserved for amounts accumulated in the future debt service and contingency accounts.

10.	12/31/X8	Retained Earnings	7,500	
		Retained Earnings Reserved for		
		Revenue Bond Contingencies		7,500
11.	12/31/X8	Retained Earnings	100,000	
		Retained Earnings Reserved for		
		Revenue Bond Future Debt		
		Service		100,000

No reservation is necessary for the revenue bond current debt service account because a current liability equal to the payment due January 1, 19X9, already reflects the obligation against current assets. However, if the amusement park deposits more than required in the revenue bond current debt service account, the excess would require a reservation.

Debt Servicing The amusement park makes the January 1, 19X9, payment as follows:

12.	1/1/X9	Accrued Interest Payable	94,500	
		Revenue Bonds Payable	7,500	
		Revenue Bond Current		
		Debt Service Account		102,000
		(102,000 − [(2,700,000		
		×.07) × .5] = 7,500)		

The amusement park would continue to place $17,000 per month in the revenue bond (RB) current debt service account throughout 19X9 and in future years. Calculations of interest and principal components pertaining to each semiannual payment would follow the effective interest schedule.

Either annually or monthly, the amusement park would also set aside the required amount in the revenue bond future debt service account (the equivalent of six semiannual principal payments ratably over five years). If the indenture requires an annual payment at the beginning of each year, the following entry would be made on January 1, 19X9:

13.	1/1/X9	Revenue Bond Future Debt Service		
		Account	22,400	
		Cash		22,400
		([102,000 × 6/5] = 122,400		
		− 100,000 = 22,400)		

The $100,000 was deducted for the 1/1/X9 annual payment because this amount was transferred from the construction account to the future debt service account.

Asset Acquisitions from Contributed Equity The 19X9 receipt of an intergovernmental grant to enhance the facility is shown by entry 14. The grant is restricted for purchasing equipment that will reduce energy consumption. Entry 15 transfers the funds to a restricted asset account, and entry 16 records the equipment acquisition.

14.	3/1/X9	Cash	200,000	
		Contributed Capital		200,000

15.	3/1/X9	Government Grant Construction		
		Account	200,000	
		Cash		200,000

16.	6/1/X9	Equipment	200,000	
		Government Grant		
		Construction Account		200,000

Assuming a ten-year life and a half-year convention for depreciation, the amusement park makes entry 17 to depreciate the asset in 19X9.

17.	12/31/X9	Depreciation Expense	10,000	
		Accumulated Depreciation—		
		Equipment		10,000
		(200,000/10 × .5) = 10,000		

Under the options provided by current GAAP, the depreciation expense can be closed to the operating summary account *or* to contributed capital as shown in entries 18(a) and 18(b), respectively.

18(a).	12/31/X9	Excess of Revenues over		
		Expenses	10,000	
		Depreciation Expense		10,000
18(b).	12/31/X9	Contributed Capital	10,000	
		Depreciation Expense		10,000

Illustrated Financial Statements

A balance sheet, a statement of revenues, expenses, and changes in retained earnings, and a cash flow statement are prepared for an enterprise fund. In addition, when more than one enterprise fund exists and general purpose financial statements are issued, a statement combining several funds into a single statement is prepared. General purpose financial statements contain a combined balance sheet for all funds, including the enterprise funds.

Based on the entries illustrated and other transactions, Exhibit 8-3 shows a balance sheet for the amusement park; Exhibit 8-4, the statement of revenues, expenses, and changes in retained earnings; and Exhibit 8-5, the cash flow statement.

Exhibit 8-3

Hypothetical City
Amusement Park Enterprise Fund
Balance Sheet
As of December 31, 19X8

Assets

Current Assets:			
Cash	$ 4,600		
Inventory of Supplies	60,000		
Due from General Fund	4,000		
Total Current Assets			$ 68,600
Property, Plant, and Equipment:			
Land		$ 200,000	
Buildings	$ 800,000		
Less Accumulated Depreciation	160,000	640,000	
Equipment	$2,900,000		
Less Accumulated Depreciation	420,000	2,480,000	
Total Property, Plant and Equipment			3,320,000

(continued)

Exhibit 8-3	*(continued)*		

Restricted Assets:

Revenue Bond Contingency	$ 7,500		
Revenue Bond Future Debt Service	122,400		
Revenue Bond Current Debt Service	102,000		
Total Restricted Assets			231,900
TOTAL ASSETS			$3,620,500

Liabilities and Equity

Current Liabilities:

Accounts Payable	$ 220,000		
Accrued Interest Payable	94,500		
Current Portion of Long-Term Debt	7,500		
Total Current Liabilities		$ 322,000	
Long-Term Liabilities:			
7% Bonds Payable		2,692,500	
Total Liabilities			$3,014,500
Equity:			
Contributed Capital		$ 376,500	
Retained Earnings:			
Reserved for RB Future Debt Service	$ 122,400		
Reserved for RB Contingencies	7,500		
Unreserved Retained Earnings	99,600	229,500	
Total Equity			606,000
TOTAL LIABILITIES AND EQUITY			$3,620,500

Exhibit 8-4		

Hypothetical City
Amusement Park Enterprise Fund
Statement of Revenues, Expenses, and Changes in Retained Earnings
For the Period Ending December 31,19X8

Operating Revenues:		
Public Ticket Sales	$1,950,000	
Concession Sales (net)	675,000	
Souvenirs and Miscellaneous (net)	125,000	
Total Operating Revenues		$2,750,000
Operating Expenses:		
Salaries, Wages, and Benefits	$1,220,000	
Supplies	506,000	
Utilities	350,000	
Repairs and Maintenance	204,000	
Depreciation	220,000	
Office Expenses	160,000	
Interest Expense	94,500	
Total Operating Expenses		2,754,500
Operating Loss		$ (4,500)
Nonoperating Income (net)		2,000
Excess of Expenses over Revenue		$ (2,500)
Retained Earnings, January 1, 19X8		232,000
Retained Earnings, December 31, 19X8		$ 229,500

Exhibit 8-5

Hypothetical City
Amusement Park Enterprise Fund
Cash Flow Statement
For the Period Ending December 31, 19X8

Differences

Cash Flows from Operating Activities:		
Net Operating Income	$ 90,000[a]	
Adjustments to Reconcile Net Income to		
Cash Provided by Operating Activities:		
Depreciation	220,000	
Decrease in Current Liabilities	(132,000)	
Net Increase in Current Receivables	(50,000)	
Net Cash Flows from Operating Activities		$ 128,000
Cash Flows from Noncapital Financing Activities:		
Net Repayments Under Operating Loan	$ (25,000)	
Operating Grants Received	83,000	
Interest on Operating Loan	(8,000)	
Net Cash Provided by Noncapital Financing Activities		50,000
Cash Flows from Capital Financing Activities:		
Proceeds of Sale of Revenue Bonds	$ 2,700,000	
Retirement of Long-Term Mortgage Payable	(60,000)	
Capital Contributed from General Fund	100,000	
Interest on Revenue Bonds and Mortgage	(94,500)	
Net Cash Provided by Capital Financing Activities		2,645,500
Cash Flows from Investing Activities:		
Renovation of Property and Equipment	$(2,600,000)	
Increase in Restricted Assets	(209,500)	
Net Cash Used by Investing Activities		(2,809,500)
NET INCREASE IN CASH		$ 14,000

[a][(4,500) + 94,500]

← exclude interest payments on debt

4 categories

As Exhibit 8-5 shows, the cash flow statement for the amusement park differs from that of a similar for-profit activity. The major differences between this cash flow statement and that of a for-profit enterprise are (1) four categories are used for classifying cash transactions instead of three, (2) the *operating* category is more narrowly focused, and (3) the "net cash provided by operations" is required to be reconciled to net operating income rather than net income for the year.

Defining Operating Cash Flows   Cash inflows from operating activities include cash flows from sales of goods and services and cash receipts from quasi-external transactions with other funds. Cash outflows include payments to acquire materials and other operating items, payments for taxes, duties, and fines, and payments for quasi-external transactions with other funds, including payments in lieu of taxes. The primary difference from the operating section of a for-profit cash flow statement is that the operating cash flows of a governmental entity exclude interest payments on amounts borrowed.

Distinguishing Between Capital and Noncapital Financing Activities
Capital financing is debt related to the purchase or acquisition of fixed assets.

The debt proceeds and repayments (both interest and principal) should be classified as capital financing activities.

Cash flows from noncapital financing activities are any proceeds or repayments (both interest and principal) related to all other debts. Usually noncapital debt represents money borrowed or repaid that pertains to operating activities. For example, money borrowed for short-term working capital needs would be classified as noncapital debt.

Reconciling Net Operating Income to Net Cash Flow from Operations

The cash flow statement for proprietary funds can be prepared according to the direct or indirect method. Using the direct method, the reconciliation of net operating income to net cash flow from operations should be presented as a separate schedule or in the notes to the financial statements. If prepared as a separate schedule, it can be placed on the same page or on a page following the statement of cash flows. For the indirect method, the reconciliation can be presented within the body of the statement or as a separate schedule.

The reconciliation is not shown for the amusement park, but it would be similar to the reconciliation prepared by for-profit companies. The only difference is that the amusement park schedule would reconcile **net operating income** rather than **net income.**

Regulatory Requirements and Utility Enterprise Funds

Local governments frequently operate public utilities (sewer, water, or electric power). Such utility operations are subject to regulatory requirements. Rates are approved at levels intended to recover incurred or estimated costs of providing utility products or services, including financing costs and a reasonable return to the stockholders. The costs included in the rate-making structure are referred to as *allowable costs.* Rate-making commissions would prefer financial statements designed with their needs in mind, and they might demand that public utilities submit numerous special purpose reports. However, the interest here is the content and format of general purpose financial statements that will provide meaningful information to governmental governing boards and creditors.

The GASB has not addressed accounting for utilities other than to note that they should be operated as enterprise funds and follow GAAP "applicable to similar businesses in the private sector."[8] Consequently, the FASB pronouncements apply to both privately and publicly owned utilities. Because regulatory requirements affect asset valuations and revenue and expense recognition, FASB pronouncements provide very specific guidance for certain utility accounting practices.

Revenue and Expense Recognition Regulatory commissions establish rates that will generate sufficient revenue to cover costs as they are incurred

---

[8]Governmental Accounting Standards Board, *Codification of Governmental Accounting and Financial Reporting Standards,* (Norwalk, Conn.: GASB, 1993), sec. UT5.

or *before they are incurred.* Regulators may also permit cost recovery in a period other than the one in which the costs would be charged to expense by an unregulated entity. For example, a public utility may be required to capitalize certain costs that under GAAP would be expensed immediately. These regulatory practices cannot be used for financial reporting. If rate structures generate revenues applicable to future expenses, the FASB requires creation of a liability for the "future" portion of the revenue stream. Also, if "allowable costs" are covered by future, not present, rates, and it

> is probable that future revenue in an amount at least equal to the capitalized cost will result from inclusion of that cost in allowable costs for rate-making purposes,[9]

the entity must capitalize all or part of an incurred cost that would otherwise be charged to expense.

Fixed Asset Accounting and Reporting   Fixed assets are by far the largest and most important assets of public utilities. Accordingly, regulatory commissions prefer that those assets be shown first in the balance sheet, followed by other property, current and accrued assets, and, finally, any deferred assets. Instead of referring to property, plant, and equipment, utilities use the notation *utility plant.*

The FASB permits these format and account title differences for utilities because they do not represent substantive differences between utilities and other businesses. A substantive difference is the effect of regulatory commission practices on fixed assets. If a commission excludes part of an asset's cost from the *allowable costs,* the asset has limited value to the utility. In such circumstances, FASB requires a write-down of the asset and recognition of a loss on its impairment.

When a public utility purchases its assets from others rather than constructing them, regulatory practices require reporting the acquisition at **original cost.** *Original cost* refers to the cost incurred when the asset was originally placed in "public" service. Forcing utilities to record puchased assets at original cost assures that the public will only pay once for a given asset through the rate-making process. If the utility pays more than original cost, the excess is placed in a **utility plant adjustment** account. Depreciation on the amount in the utility plant adjustment account is not one of the allowable costs for rate-making purposes. For example, if a utility paid $18,000,000 for a plant with an original cost of $22,000,000 and accumulated depreciation of $6,000,000, the acquiring utility would make the following entry:

Utility Plant	22,000,000	
Utility Plant Adjustment	2,000,000	
Accumulated Depreciation		6,000,000
Cash		18,000,000

[9]Financial Accounting Standards Board, *Accounting Standards, Current Text, Industry Standards* (Stamford, Conn.: McGraw-Hill, 1986), 67111. Two FASB statements, *Nos. 90* and *92,* provide detailed guidance for regulated operations. The coverage here is necessarily brief and the two FASB statements should be consulted for specific accounting practices.

Special purpose reports would include the utility plant (usually net) and the utility plant adjustment account as assets, but only the depreciation on the net utility plant ($16,000,000) would be recorded in allowable costs for rate-making purposes. The income statement, however, would include depreciation on $18,000,000 as a period expense.

High utility plant costs have created the most significant problems for financial reporting. Tremendous investments in utility plants have forced rate commissions to adopt *phase-in* plans in order to moderate initial rate increases when a new plant is completed. For example, assume that a utility completed a $40,000,000 plant expansion project with an expected useful life of 40 years. Even on a straight-line basis, depreciation included in allowable costs would increase by $1,000,000 per year. The increase in allowable costs may result in utility rate increases above that which is considered reasonable by regulatory commissions. Accordingly, they may rule that one-third of the increase will be phased in over the next three years. Under this plan, $333,000 would be included in allowable costs in year one, $666,000 in year two, and the full $1,000,000 in year three.

If the phase-in meets certain criteria, all allowable costs deferred under the regulatory plan are capitalized for financial reporting as a separate asset. In the preceding example, the $666,000 would be capitalized in the first year. The phase-in criteria are:

1. The allowable costs in question are deferred pursuant to a formal plan that has been agreed to by the regulator.
2. The plan specifies the timing of recovery of allowable costs that will be deferred under the plan.
3. All allowable costs deferred under the plan are scheduled for recovery within 10 years of the date when deferrals began.
4. The percentage increase in rates scheduled under the plan for each future year is no greater than the percentage increase in rates scheduled under the plan for each immediately preceding year. That is, the scheduled percentage increase in year two is no greater than the percentage increase granted in year one, the scheduled percentage increase in year three is no greater than the scheduled percentage increase in year two, and so forth.[10]

Exhibit 8-6 illustrates a balance sheet for a public utility enterprise fund. It reflects the anomalies of a regulated entity, as well as the special recognition issues related to public utilities. For example, the property, plant and equipment are shown first, followed by current assets and restricted assets. The unbilled receivables relate to the fact that billings are done on a cycle basis and therefore all revenue that is due may not be billed at the period end. The portion of the customer deposits that relate to earnings is shown as a reserve

---

[10] Financial Accounting Standards Board, *Statement No. 92, Regulated Enterprises — Accounting for Phase-in Plans* (Stamford, Conn.: FASB, 1987), 2.

Exhibit 8-6

Any County
Electric Utility Enterprise Fund
Balance Sheet
As of December 31, 19X1

Assets

Utility Plant:

Land	$ 500,000	
Buildings	800,000	
Improvements Other Than Buildings	1,300,000	
Machinery and Equipment	622,000	
Utility Plant Adjustment	200,000	
Total	$3,422,000	
Less: Accumulated Depreciation	1,400,000	
Total Property, Plant and Equipment		$2,022,000

Current Assets:

Cash	$ 70,000	
Accounts Receivable, net	132,000	
Unbilled Accounts Receivable	25,000	
Accrued Interest Receivable	2,000	
Supplies Inventory	47,000	
Prepaids	5,000	
Total Current Assets		281,000

Restricted Assets:

Customer Deposits	$ 15,000	
Debt Service	185,000	
Principal and Interest Reserve	560,000	
Contingencies	100,000	
Total Restricted Assets		860,000
TOTAL ASSETS		$3,163,000

Liabilities

Current Liabilities:

Accounts Payable	$ 175,000	
Due to General Fund	46,000	
Accrued Wages and Salaries Payable	102,000	
Other Accrued Liabilities	55,000	
Total Current Liabilities		$ 378,000

Liabilities Payable from Restricted Assets:

Customer Deposits	$ 14,000	
Debt Service, Accrued Interest	8,000	
Total Liabilities Payable from Restricted Assets		22,000

Long-Term Liabilities:

Bonds Payable	$1,620,000	
Unamortized Discount on Bonds	10,000	
Total Long-Term Liabilities		1,610,000
Total Liabilities		$2,010,000

Equity

Retained Earnings:

Reserve for Earnings on Customer Deposits	$ 1,000	
Reserve for Bond Principal and Interest	720,000	
Total Reserved		721,000
Unreserved		102,000
Total Retained Earnings		$ 823,000

Contributed Capital:

Contributed Capital, Governmental Unit		330,000
Total Fund Equity		1,153,000
TOTAL LIABILITIES AND FUND EQUITY		$3,163,000

of retained earnings. It is not a liability yet because it is not owed to the customers at the present time; in the exhibit, the $14,000 liability and the $1,000 reserve add up to the total of the restricted asset account.

Segment Reporting by Enterprise Funds

GAAP for governmental units requires segment disclosures for enterprise funds if:

1. Material long-term liabilities are outstanding
2. The disclosures are essential to assure the general purpose financial statements are not misleading
3. They are necessary to assure interperiod comparability.[11]

Because a fund is established for each separate activity, the term *segment* means an **individual enterprise fund** for governmental accounting purposes. Consequently, certain information about individual funds is disclosed that would otherwise be combined. For example, if a city had six enterprise funds, the combined statements would, in the absence of the segment reporting requirement, include only one column for all six.

The first condition is largely self-explanatory. The materiality criterion is evaluated in terms of each individual enterprise fund, not in terms of enterprise funds taken as a whole. The requirement of avoiding misleading financial statements is harder to interpret and requires considerable professional judgment. The intent is to avoid combining major nonhomogeneous activities, such as an airport and an amusement park, in the financial statements.

Interperiod comparability should be maintained. If segment information was shown for a particular fund in earlier years and likely will be required for later years, segment information should also be shown for the current period even if not required under the first two conditions.

Several separate items must be disclosed whenever segment data are presented. A description of the activity (often the fund title is sufficient) is required. Major operating figures, such as depreciation, operating revenues, operating income or loss, and tax revenues, must be disclosed. Disclosures also must include changes in property, plant, and equipment; bonds and other material long-term liabilities; and total assets and equity. The governmental unit may display some of the information in separate columns in the combined statements, but the preferred treatment is disclosure in the notes to the general purpose financial statements. Accountants must use judgment in determining what specific approach is best suited to the particular entity.

SUMMARY

Other than remembering that accounting and reporting take place within the overall structure of a fund, accounting for proprietary activities does not pose

---

[11]GASB, *Governmental Accounting and Financial Reporting Standards,* sec. 2500, ¶102.

any particular difficulties for accountants. Accrual accounting is used and the format of statements and the account classifications are similar to those used in business. A balance sheet, a statement of revenues, expenses, and changes in retained earnings, and a cash flow statement are prepared for each proprietary fund.

Governmental units use two different proprietary funds to distinguish between services or products offered to other governmental departments and those offered to the public. *In-house* services or products include supply warehouses, copy or data processing centers, repair shops, motor pools, and the like. These in-house services are operated as an internal service fund. Enterprise funds are used to account for *public* services ranging from amusement parks to airports. The most common enterprise funds are public utilities.

Public utilities operated by governmental units must adhere to GAAP as defined by the FASB because the GASB has not yet addressed their accounting. Because regulatory reporting requirements differ in several respects, public utilities prepare numerous special purpose reports. Regulatory requirements may even affect asset values and general purpose financial reporting.

Under certain circumstances, enterprise funds must disclose segment information. Interperiod comparability, material long-term debt, and nonhomogeneity of enterprise funds form the bases upon which the need for segmentation is determined.

QUESTIONS

8-1 What is the purpose of an internal service fund? An enterprise fund?

8-2 How is a transfer to an enterprise fund from the general fund treated by both funds? Explain why this treatment is appropriate.

8-3 What types of restricted assets is an enterprise fund using debt financing likely to show on its balance sheet? Explain why each is necessary.

8-4 Explain why cost accounting is used in managing enterprise funds.

8-5 How does the accounting for a utility enterprise fund differ from that for a nonutility enterprise fund? Be specific.

8-6 Under what circumstances might it be inappropriate for a proprietary fund to include depreciation as an operating expense in determining prices charged to the public or to other departments?

8-7 How is accounting for proprietary funds similar to that of business organizations? How is it different?

8-8 What is the difference between an advance and an equity transfer from the general fund to a proprietary fund? What are the accounting entries required for each transaction?

8-9 Lionel City is currently reporting compensated absence liabilities in each fund to which the absences pertain. Several city council members want to change this practice and establish an internal service fund for this purpose. What response would you make to this suggestion?

8-10 What is the meaning of "allowable costs" in the context of accounting for a public utility enterprise fund?

8-11 Why is it necessary for an enterprise fund to reserve retained earnings equivalent to restricted assets specified by the bond indenture?

8-12 Explain how budgeting is used for internal service funds. How is that different from budgeting for governmental funds?

8-13 An accountant hired by the mayor to conduct a performance review of the city's internal service fund argues that no matter what the process, the budget for the internal service fund is fixed. Explain the basis for the accountant's argument.

8-14 What is the essential difference between the accounting bases for proprietary and governmental funds?

8-15 During a recent orientation meeting for new county commissioners, the county's finance officer explained that the supplies warehouse operated by the county could be accounted for in an internal service fund, the general fund, or a special revenue fund. Under what circumstances would each of these funds appropriately be used for the supply function?

8-16 When should segment information be provided for an enterprise fund?

8-17 What are some reasons for establishing proprietary funds? Are they likely to serve their intended purpose?

8-18 Why must public utilities record asset acquisitions at "original cost"? What is the ultimate effect on consumers?

8-19 Why are accurate cost data important for proprietary funds? Explain.

8-20 Would the "when consumed" or "when purchased" method be used to account for the supplies inventory of a proprietary fund? Why?

8-21 What proprietary fund account is similar to the income summary used by business? Why do you think that particular title is used?

CASES

8-1 The city of Blaire operates an internal service fund that provides repair services to three departments. The space allocated for repairs is inadequate and Blaire's city council wants to expand the operation not only to better serve the three departments but also to provide service to other departments. The city's finance officer presents the following summary pertaining to the fund's operations:

City of Blaire
Internal Service Fund
Condensed Balance Sheet
As of December 31, 19X0

Assets		Liabilities and Equity	
Cash	$ 17,000	Current Liabilities	$ 33,000
Other Current Assets	26,000	Long-Term Debt	175,000
Fixed Assets (net)	320,000	Deferred Revenue	22,000
TOTAL ASSETS	$363,000	Total Liabilities	$230,000

(continued)

(continued)   ***Liabilities and Equity***

Contributed Capital	100,000
Retained Earnings	33,000
Total Equity	$133,000
TOTAL LIABILITIES AND EQUITY	$363,000

The excess of revenues over costs for the most recent period totaled $7,800; a breakdown of direct and indirect costs follows:

Direct Wages and Salaries	$350,000
Direct Materials and Supplies	110,000
General Overhead (interest, insurance, rent, depreciation, supplies, administration salaries)	92,100

The repair garage employs eight people who each work 2,020 hours per year.

The planned expansion requires hiring one additional employee, purchasing equipment costing $65,000, and adding space; the remodeling cost is estimated at $8,000.

Current rates are based on direct costs for labor ($22 per hour) and for materials, plus an overhead rate of 25 percent of direct labor and 5 percent of direct materials. The finance officer recommends funding the expansion by raising the labor rates to $25 per hour and by raising the overhead rates to 27 and 7 percent of labor and materials, respectively.

REQUIRED

1. Based on the information provided, reconstruct the operating statement for 19X0.
2. Assuming total billable hours and materials remain constant under the proposed rate structure, how long would it take Blaire's internal service fund to cover the cost of expansion? Explain.
3. What response would you make to the finance officer's proposal at the next city council meeting? What other alternatives might be considered?

8-2 You have just completed an audit for Broadwater County, and now the commissioners want to hire you as a consultant. The commissioners are trying to determine whether to establish an enterprise fund for a golf course recently completed and operated by the county. The centrally located course is open to the public and used by a large segment of the golfing population in both Broadwater and Stillman counties.

Acquisition of the land and construction of the facility cost $7,500,000; the project was financed by general fund contributions ($300,000), intergovernmental grants ($800,000), and debt ($6,400,000). One-half of the intergovernmental grant must be repaid out of revenues at the rate of 1 percent of gross revenues payable annually on January 1 of each year. The general fund also advanced $200,000 for working capital.

Greens fees and other charges were set competitively with other local golf courses, but some residents have complained that rates should be lower because tax dollars helped to finance the facility.

REQUIRED

1. Prepare a written response to the county evaluating whether an enterprise fund should be established. Be specific.
2. Assume that the county was satisfied with your work. Draft a response the commissioners can use when answering complaints about the rate structure.

8-3 Teton County operates a public utility that supplies water to local residents. About twenty years ago, the county constructed a purification plant near the water source, which it estimated to have a thirty-year life. Recently, the water at the county's access point has become contaminated by giardia, a parasitic condition arising from heavy concentrations of wild and domestic animals roaming near the stream. Effective control of the parasite requires relocation of the treatment facility. The current facility cannot be moved, so it will be abandoned and a new facility constructed.

Preliminary discussions with the Wyoming Public Service Commission indicate that at least one commissioner will vote to exclude the remaining depreciation costs on the old plant from allowable costs.

REQUIRED

1. Develop the rationale that the public service commissioner might be using to deny depreciation on the old facility as an allowable cost.
2. From an accounting standpoint, is the denial appropriate? If it is, give examples of similar circumstances in a nonutility business entity. If it is not appropriate, explain why.

8-4 Arkanaville operates a supplies inventory fund for all city departments. Selected data from the latest operating statement and balance sheet appear below:

Total Billings to Departments	$516,000
Total Assets	800,000
Short-Term Liabilities	50,000
Advance from General Fund	8,000
Net Excess of Expenses over Revenues	360

The fund is intended to be fully self-supporting, and it has no contributed equity.

Several departments have complained to Arkanaville's city council that they can buy certain supplies more cheaply through local suppliers. Departmental complaints lead the city council to review the fund's operation.

REQUIRED

1. In your opinion and based on the information provided, was the fund well managed? Defend your answer.
2. To make a comprehensive review, what additional information would you request? Explain why you need additional information.

8-5 New Oleans operates an amusement park through an enterprise fund. The fund has not been supervised closely and decision making has been left to the park's manager. The fund's December 31, 19X8, balance sheet appears below:

City of New Oleans
Amusement Park Enterprise Fund
Balance Sheet
As of December 31, 19X8

Assets

Current Assets:			
Cash		$ 10,000	
Supplies Inventory		4,000	
Prepaid Insurance		2,000	
Accrued Interest Receivable		2,500	
Total Current Assets			$ 18,500
Property, Plant, and Equipment:			
Equipment	$980,000		
Less: Accumulated Depreciation	850,000	$130,000	
Building and Improvements	$700,000		
Less: Accumulated Depreciation	620,000	80,000	
Total Property, Plant, and Equipment			210,000
Investments:			
U.S. Treasury Bills			100,000
TOTAL ASSETS			$328,500

Liabilities and Fund Equity

Current Liabilities:			
Accounts Payable		$ 16,500	
Due to Other Funds		8,000	
Total Current Liabilities			$ 24,500
Long-Term Liabilities:			
5% Term Bond Due 19X9			25,000
Fund Equity:			
Contributed Capital		$105,000	
Retained Earnings		174,000	
Total Fund Equity			279,000
TOTAL LIABILITIES AND FUND EQUITY			$328,500

The contributed capital reflects an equity transfer from the general fund when the amusement park fund was established. It was used to purchase fixed assets.

Recently a member of the city council observed, "Such large retained earnings suggest that the fund is over-pricing its services, and that the fund may be mismanaged." A group of citizens have banded together and petitioned the New Oleans mayor to refund any overcharges by reducing property taxes.

You have been retained as an independent party to examine the situation and to make recommendations to the city council.

REQUIRED

1. Is the fund overcharging its patrons? Develop a rationale and document your answer.
2. Is there evidence of mismanagement? Explain.
3. What course of action do you recommend the city council take regarding the allegations of over-charging and mismanagement?

EXERCISES

8-1 Refer to the selected financial statements for the city of Raleigh, North Carolina, that are presented in Appendix A, and answer the following questions:

1. Does the city of Raleigh have internal service funds? Enterprise funds? If so, identify each fund and its purposes.
2. Does the report state what basis of accounting is used for each fund, and is the presentation consistent with GAAP? With the stated basis? Is the same basis used for reporting and budgetary purposes? Explain.
3. Are the required financial statements presented for the proprietary funds? Is the format consistent with that shown in the chapter? Are current assets, fixed assets, and other assets properly distinguished in the balance sheet? Are current and long-term debt separated and properly disclosed?
4. Is contributed capital presented separately from retained earnings? Are there appropriations of retained earnings? If so, are their purposes clear?
5. What information do the notes to the financial statements contain about the proprietary funds?
6. Is a cash flow statement presented for the enterprise funds? If so, how do the sources of funds shown in this statement relate to the sources of revenues shown in the statement of revenues, expenses, and changes in fund balance? Is the statement broken down by type of activity? Are there any differences between the format of this statement and the one presented in the chapter? Explain.

8-2 Select the best answer for each question.

1. How would customers' security deposits be classified in the balance sheet of a governmental unit's enterprise fund?
   a. as a liability and restricted asset
   b. as a liability and other asset
   c. as a restricted asset and deferred revenue
   d. none of the above
   (Adapted from the May 1984 CPA Exam, Theory #57)
2. Fixed assets used in a city-owned utility are accounted for in which of the following?

	Enterprise Fund	General Fixed Asset Account Group
a.	no	no
b.	no	yes
c.	yes	no
d.	yes	yes

(Adapted from the May 1982 CPA Exam, Theory #51)

3. Which of the following is an appropriate basis of accounting for a proprietary fund of a governmental unit?

	Cash Basis	Modified Accrual Basis
a.	yes	yes
b.	yes	no
c.	no	no
d.	no	yes

4. Which of the following would not be a purpose of a proprietary fund?
   a. to increase efficiency of an operating unit
   b. to measure performance and maintain capital
   c. to provide services through user charges
   d. to develop vehicles through which nontax revenues can be generated
5. The entry in an internal service fund to record an equity transfer from the general fund would be:
   a. debit cash, credit retained earnings
   b. debit cash, credit contributed capital
   c. debit equity transfer, credit contributed capital
   d. debit cash, credit advance from general fund
6. The FASB pronouncements are used for enterprise fund accounting because:
   a. they are more appropriate than those of the GASB
   b. under the order of GAAP importance, the FASB pronouncements take precedence
   c. the GASB has not issued pronouncements specifically on enterprise funds
   d. the GASB standards cannot be used for audit purposes
7. Which of the following accounts would not appear in the balance sheet of an internal service fund?
   a. equipment
   b. due to other funds
   c. revenue bond future debt service
   d. retained earnings
8. Segment information for enterprise funds cannot be shown:
   a. in the notes to financial statements
   b. in a separate report attached to the financial statements
   c. in separate columns of the combined statements
   d. none of the above

9. If the current debt service requirement under an enterprise fund bond indenture is $42,000 per year, and the total set aside in 19X1 was $47,000, what entry would be necessary at year end?
   a. no entry is required for current debt service amounts
   b. debit retained earnings $47,000, credit reserve for RB current debt service $47,000
   c. debit retained earnings $42,000, credit reserve for RB current debt service $42,000
   d. debit retained earnings $5,000, credit reserve for RB current debt service $5,000

10. Revenues not centrally related to the purpose of an internal service fund would:
   a. be reported as nonoperating revenue
   b. not be reported in the internal service fund
   c. be reported as other operating revenue
   d. be offset against operating expenses

8-3 The city of Darnington decided to establish an internal service fund to provide computer services to all city offices and departments. The internal service fund was established by a transfer of cash and property from the city's general fund, and facilities were leased in a building adjoining City Hall but owned by a local business. During its first year of operations, the internal service fund had the following transactions:

1. 1/1/X9: equipment of $3,500,000, furniture and fixtures of $60,000, and a cash advance of $85,000 were received from the city's general fund. The fund is not required to generate income to replace the equipment and furniture.
2. 3/1/X9: $21,000 was used by the fund to provide leasehold enhancements for security and humidity control.
3. 3/1/X9: as required in the lease agreement (noncapital lease), the $30,000 lease payment covering two years was made.
4. 4/1/X9: the fund purchased computer supplies for $30,000 and paid a three-year insurance policy of $9,000.
5. Various: departments were billed $340,000 for services rendered; cash received from departments totaled $300,000.
6. Various: the following expenses were incurred:

Wages and Salaries	$180,000
Payroll Taxes	37,800
Repairs and Maintenance	16,000
Payments in Lieu of Taxes to General Fund	6,000
Other Operating Expenses	22,000

The payroll taxes and salaries and wages were paid entirely; $38,000 of the remaining expenses were paid.
7. 10/1/X9: $10,000 of the city's advance was repaid.
8. 10/15/X9: the fund applied for an intergovernmental grant to upgrade its computer facilities. On 11/1, the state notified the manager that Darnington had an excellent chance of receiving the grant.

9. One department contested its billing and, after careful investigation, the internal service fund notified the contesting department that $300 could not be documented and therefore would not need to be paid.

10. The following useful lives are being used by the fund (straight-line depreciation is used):
    a. equipment, 7 years
    b. leasehold improvements, 3 years (assume a full year's depreciation for Item 2 above)
    c. furniture and fixtures, 5 years

11. Year-end supplies on hand totaled $3,200.

12. Accrued salaries were $4,100, and payroll taxes owed on these salaries totaled $875.

REQUIRED

1. Prepare all necessary transactions, adjusting, and closing journal entries for the internal service fund during 19X9.

2. Make the journal entry required for the general fund or other funds (or account groups) for the transfer of equipment, other fixed assets, and cash to the internal service fund.

8-4 Bucrane County is exploring the possibility of establishing a centralized motor pool. Before the commissioners approve the plan, they want to know whether a centralized motor pool will save money. The commissioners ask the internal audit staff to examine what is now being spent and to compare that with proposed charges to departments that would use the service. Any vehicles now owned by Bucrane would be transferred to the motor pool as a contribution; the pool would replace those vehicles as they wear out. The following information was obtained by the audit staff:

1. Four departments currently have one automobile each available for their use; the rest pay individual employees for use of their own automobiles.

Total mileage costs paid by departments without autos	$ 44,000
Total miles driven by departments without autos	200,000
Book value of autos assigned to four departments (Each auto cost $16,000 and had a projected useful life of four years.)	$ 32,000
Mileage traveled by the four departments with autos	60,000
Gas, oil, and maintenance costs for city-owned autos	$ 6,800

2. Annual operating costs projected for the internal service fund:

Salaries and Wages, Maintenance and Dispatching Person	$25,000
Supplies	1,000
Bulk Gasoline	17,500
Other Operating Costs	3,000

3. Two additional cars at a cost of $17,500 each would be needed immediately; these would be financed by an interest-free advance from the

general fund that would be repaid in equal annual installments over the next five years. The automobiles would be replaced every five years.

REQUIRED

1. Assuming automobile replacement is the sole responsibility of the central motor pool, what mileage rate would have to be charged in the first year? (Also assume that the same total mileage is driven in the first year as was driven under the current arrangements.) How does that compare with average mileage cost without a motor pool? (Hint: Depreciation should be included in calculating costs per mile.)
2. Based on your answer in Item 1, would you recommend a long-term decision to establish an internal service fund? Explain.

8-5 The July 1, 19X0, trial balance for Lacey's water utility enterprise fund appears below:

	Debit	Credit
Utility Plant	$7,500,000	
Accumulated Depreciation—Utility Plant		$2,200,000
Utility Plant Adjustment	100,000	
Accumulated Depreciation—Utility Plant Adjustment		25,000
Construction Work in Progress	150,000	
Cash Restricted for Construction	50,000	
Cash Restricted for Future Debt Service	200,000	
Cash Restricted for Contingencies	90,000	
Cash	200,000	
Accounts Receivable	240,000	
Allowance for Uncollectible Accounts		12,000
Materials and Supplies	150,000	
Revenue Bonds Payable		5,200,000
Vouchers Payable		160,000
Accrued Expenses		92,000
Contributed Capital		208,000
Retained Earnings—Reserved		290,000
Retained Earnings—Unreserved		493,000
Total	$8,680,000	$8,680,000

The following transactions took place for Lacey's public utility from 7/1/X0 to 6/30/X1:

1. The construction in progress was completed at a cost of $50,000.
2. Accrued expenses on 7/1/X0 were paid in full.
3. Uncollectible accounts totaling $3,200 were written off.
4. Billings to public customers totaled $1,560,000; the general fund bill was $69,000. The general fund paid all of its bill and $1,700,000 was received from public customers. The fund manager estimated that 2.5 percent of the public billings would never be paid.
5. $100,000 was set aside for eventual debt repayment, and $45,000 was set aside for contingencies.
6. The following expenses were incurred and paid during the year:

Salaries and Wages	$480,000
Supplies Inventory Purchased	390,000
Interest Expense	400,000
Miscellaneous Office Supplies	10,000
Other Operating Expenses	250,000

7. $120,000 was paid on vouchers outstanding on 7/1/X0.
8. Accrued expenses for salaries totaled $22,600 on 6/30/X1.
9. The supplies inventory on 6/30/X1 amounted to $110,000.
10. All utility plant assets are being depreciated over 40 years, and the half-year convention is used for all assets completed during a period.
11. The facility requiring the plant adjustment account was acquired 10 years ago.

REQUIRED

Prepare and complete a worksheet with the following headings:

Trial Balance (7/1/X0)

Transactions for Fiscal 19X1

Pre-Closing Trial Balance (6/30/X1)

Income Statement

Balance Sheet

8-6 The Eaton town council opened a public fitness center on October 1, 19X0. The center has proven to be a financial success. All the 2,000 budgeted subscriptions were sold by opening day and, to date, all patrons have been making installment payments promptly. Eaton does have one problem, however. The bookkeeper assigned to the project is not trained in accounting. He prepared an unadjusted trial balance, after which the town council hired your firm to prepare the necessary adjustments and train the bookkeeper. The bookkeeper's trial balance is presented here:

Eaton Fitness Center
Unadjusted Trial Balance
As of June 30, 19X1

	Debit	Credit
Cash	$127,000	
Restricted Cash	50,000	
Supplies Inventory	20,000	
Investments	100,000	
Accounts Payable		$ 7,000
Due to Other Funds		60,000
Customer Billings		330,000
Other Operating Revenues		50,000
Equipment Expenditures	95,000	
Operating Expenses	162,000	
Other Income		7,000
Other Financing Sources		100,000
Totals	$554,000	$554,000

Additional information developed during the review:

1. The annual subscription is $180, of which one-twelfth is due upon enrolling, two-twelfths is due by the end of the first month, and one-twelfth is due each month thereafter until the subscription for the year is paid in full.
2. $100,000 of bonds were issued to finance the purchase of equipment. The 7 percent bonds were issued at par on October 1, 19X0; the first semiannual interest payment was paid on March 1, 19X1, and is included in operating expenses. The next is due on October 1, 19X1.
3. Because of the unexpected success of the fitness center and the delayed billing on the equipment, the bond proceeds were invested long enough to earn $7,000. Then $95,000 was used to purchase equipment.
4. A $25 deposit is required upon enrolling in a fitness program. When a member in good standing drops the program, the deposit, less any payments owing, is returned to the member.
5. The general fund advanced $60,000 in working capital. The advance must be repaid at a rate of $10,000 per year at the end of each operating period. The payment has been made but not recorded because the bookkeeper did not know how to make the entry.
6. At the end of the year, $18,000 of supplies were on hand.
7. Facilities were contributed by a group of local businesses. Because the facilities were contributed, the bookkeeper made no entry. The fair market value of the facilities approximated $218,000 on October 1, 19X0.
8. The equipment has a useful life of 5 years and was installed right before the center opened. The facilities have a useful life of 20 years. A full year's depreciation is appropriate for the fiscal year ending June 30, 19X1.
9. Other than the adjustments necessitated by the preceding items, the operating expenses were checked and found accurate.

REQUIRED

Prepare a worksheet showing the unadjusted trial balance, the adjustments, and an adjusted pre-closing trial balance.

8-7 Crater County issued revenue bonds to construct a new sewage treatment plant. $6,800,000 in 7 percent revenue bonds were issued at 100 on October 1, 19X1. The revenue bonds were taxable. Construction costs were incurred as follows:

November 1, 19X1	$ 800,000
December 1, 19X1	2,000,000
December 31, 19X1	500,000

During the period from October 1 to October 31, the bond proceeds were invested at 7.1 percent.

Crater County operates on a calendar year. The first semiannual interest payment is due April 1, 19X2.

REQUIRED

1. How much interest should be capitalized during 19X1?
2. What is the amount of interest expense charged as a period cost for 19X1?

8-8 Select the best answer for each question.

1. Payments in lieu of taxes by an enterprise fund would be reported as:
   a. operating transfers
   b. equity transfers
   c. expenses
   d. expenditures

2. Capitalization of interest on proprietary fund debt used for construction stops when the:
   a. bonds are repaid
   b. construction is complete
   c. interest earnings equal the interest expense
   d. first construction payment is made

3. One characteristic of financial reporting for public utilities is:
   a. restricted cash can be shown as a short-term or long-term asset depending on the nature of the restriction
   b. current liabilities are combined with long-term liabilities
   c. fixed assets are shown before current assets
   d. contributed equity is not distinguished from other equity

4. Which of the following would not likely be a note disclosure for an internal service fund?
   a. employee compensated absences
   b. segment disclosures
   c. basis of accounting
   d. valuation basis for fixed assets

5. If partial or no return on investment is likely to be provided through the regulatory rate-making process, a public utility shall:
   a. recognize the abandonment as a loss
   b. recognize the abandonment as a loss if it is probable and reasonably estimable
   c. exclude the abandonment from rate requests but make no changes in the financial statement
   d. recognize the abandonment loss ratably over the useful life of the asset

6. Which of the following statements does not describe budgeting for proprietary funds?
   a. flexible budgets are prepared for proprietary funds
   b. budgets are incorporated into the accounting system
   c. comparative data showing budgeted and actual figures are included in the comprehensive financial report
   d. the budgetary basis may be different from the accounting basis

7. For regulated utilities, a phase-in plan is not:
   a. a method of recognizing allowable costs under certain conditions
   b. a method of rate making intended to moderate a sudden increase in rates caused by additional investments
   c. an order given by regulators to defer a portion of the costs for future recovery
   d. a way in which investment costs are reported for general purpose financial reporting

8. Which of the following proprietary activities would be most likely to use a process-costing system?
   a. a copy shop
   b. a sewage treatment plant
   c. a repair shop
   d. none of the above

9. The Emeryville city council has decided to open an internal service fund to account for self-insurance. If all accidents are covered by the self-insurance program, a reasonable basis for allocating the costs among the various departments would be:
   a. historical data covering accident experience for each department
   b. total assets pertaining to each department
   c. payroll costs
   d. number of departments covered by the program

10. Resources loaned by the general fund to a proprietary fund would be classified as:
    a. contributed equity by the proprietary fund
    b. an equity transfer by the general fund
    c. an operating transfer by the general fund
    d. a liability by the proprietary fund

8-9   The bookkeeper for Brodus County's repair shop prepared a pre-closing trial balance. This is the fund's first operating year and a permanent accountant has not yet been hired. Not entirely familiar with the accounting and reporting requirements for these funds, the bookkeeper asks for your assistance in preparing the balance sheet and statement of revenues, expenses, and changes in equity. Here is the unadjusted trial balance:

Brodus County
Repair Shop (Internal Service Fund)
Unadjusted Pre-Closing Trial Balance
June 30, 19X1

	Debits	Credits
Cash	$ 14,000	
Due from Other Funds	83,000	
Inventory Purchases	69,000	
Possible Bad Debts		$ 10,000
Interest Received		8,000
Treasury Cash Investments	97,000	
Buildings	200,000	
Equipment	150,000	
Furniture and Fixtures	20,000	
Departmental Revenue		310,000
Uncollected Interest	1,500	
Depreciation Taken	32,750	
Salaries and Wages Expense	90,000	
General Fund Contributions		200,000
Debt Financing from Bonds		215,000
Other Expenses	22,220	
Vouchers Owed		5,200
Interest Paid	8,000	
Other Credits		39,270
Total	$787,470	$787,470

During your discussions, you learn several additional facts from the book-keeper:

1. Other credits is an account in which the bookkeeper placed items with which she was unfamiliar.
2. All fixed assets were purchased at the beginning of the year. The building has a useful life of 20 years, the equipment, 8 years, and the furniture and fixtures, 5 years.
3. The $8,000 of interest expense includes both that paid during the year and the $1,020 accrued interest payable at year end.
4. Inventory at year end was $1,000.
5. A general fund advance of $4,000 was not repaid by year end.

REQUIRED

Prepare a statement of revenues, expenses, and changes in equity, and a balance sheet for the Brodus County repair shop for the year ending June 30, 19X1. (Hint: T-accounts or a spread sheet should be used to establish the correct balances before preparing the statements.)

8-10 The following cash flow statement for Alhambra's electric utility fund was prepared for audit staff review:

City of Alhambra
Enterprise Fund
As of December 31, 19X2

Net Operating Income	$ 34,800	
Adjustments to Reconcile Net Operating Income to		
Cash Provided by Operating Activities:		
Depreciation of Facilities	35,000	
Net Increase in Current Liabilities	67,800	
Amortization of Bond Premium on Investments	(200)	
Net Increase in Interest Earned but not Received	(300)	
Net Decrease in Current Receivables		
(Other than Interest Receivable)	(55,000)	
Net Cash Flow		$ 82,100
Acquisition of Property, Plant, and Equipment	$ 815,000	
Increase in Restricted Net Assets	(21,300)	
Net Cash Flow		793,700
Residual Equity Transfers from General Fund	$ 310,000	
Retirement of Bond Principal	50,000	
Issuance of Bonds	(100,000)	
Net Cash Flow		260,000
Total Cash Flow		$1,135,800

ADDITIONAL INFORMATION

1. Bond retirements pertained to bonds originally issued to cover an operating deficit.
2. Bonds issued during the period pertain to capital increases as did the residual equity transfers from the general fund.
3. Interest on bonds retired totaled $3,000.
4. Interest on newly issued debt totaled $6,000.
5. The interest expense (Items 3 and 4) is reflected in net operating income.

REQUIRED

The electric utility fund's cash flow statement contains numerous errors. Prepare a corrected cash flow statement.

8-11   The following transactions relate to the city of Carloney's general fund and its internal service fund. The transactions are unrelated unless otherwise noted.

1. The general fund transferred general fixed assets with a book value of $220,000 and a market value of $306,000 to the internal service fund.
2. The general fund advanced $180,000 to the internal service fund for operating purposes; the internal service fund must repay the general fund at the rate of $20,000 per year.
3. The internal service fund issued $700,000 of 6 percent long-term bonds at 105. Of the proceeds, $650,000 was used to remodel a building the fund is renting from the general fund for $8,000 per year.
4. Department billings, all paid in cash, totaled $675,000 for the year. Later in the year, one department that was dissatisfied with the work was given a refund of $280.
5. The annual advance repayment referred to in Item 2 was paid.
6. The building improvements are being depreciated over 40 years, and the other fixed assets over 10 years.
7. The internal service fund manager decided that fixed assets with a value of $32,000 when transferred to the internal service fund should be transferred back to the general fund because they were no longer needed. The transfer was made after depreciation for the year was recorded. Equipment costing $8,000 was sold for $2,200. Accumulated depreciation on the equipment totaled $5,200.
8. Interest on the bonds issued in Item 3 is due the first day of the next fiscal period and, therefore, accrued at year end (assume the bonds were issued the first day of the second quarter and, for simplicity, the premium is amortized over 30 years using the straight-line method).
9. Because of heavy debt commitments and a good operating year, the manager established a restricted cash account for bond repayment; $100,000 was deposited in the restricted account during the year. It was, in turn, invested with the county's fiscal agent, and yielded $3,200 in earnings.

REQUIRED

1. Make the journal entries reflecting the transactions for Carloney's internal service fund (you may assume that entries 1 and 2 occurred the first day of the fiscal period).
2. Make any necessary entries in the general fund or other funds or account groups.

CHAPTER 9

Fiduciary Funds

The fiduciary fund classification of governmental entities encompasses trust funds and agency funds. Trust funds account for those assets held in a trustee capacity for the benefit of the governmental entity, while agency funds account for assets held for others. Governmental entities typically have three types of trust funds: (1) nonexpendable, (2) expendable, and (3) pension.

Nonexpendable and expendable trust funds usually involve donations, which have restricted use. In the case of the nonexpendable funds, the donor requires that the amount donated (principal or corpus) be held in perpetuity. The word *endowment* is used to describe principal sums that must be held in perpetuity by the donee. The income generated by the corpus can be either restricted or unrestricted; that is, the income may be spent for specific purposes (restricted) or spent for any lawful purpose (unrestricted). In the case of expendable trust funds, the donor allows expenditure of both income and principal; however, both must be spent for a specific purpose. These funds resemble special revenue funds except that the source is a gift rather than earmarked taxes or intergovernmental revenue.

Pension trusts account for the assets and liabilities related to public employee retirement systems (PERS). Through these funds, a governmental entity acts as its own trustee for its pension program. In industry, the trustee is usually a third party.

An agency fund is used to account for resources held for another governmental entity, another fund, or an individual. For example, when a state government collects taxes on behalf of a local government, the state acts as an agent for the local government and uses an agency fund.

The nature and purpose of each fiduciary fund is discussed in this chapter. The chapter also explores current accounting and reporting issues related to each fund type. Illustrated transactions and financial statements are presented, along with disclosure requirements for pension trust funds.

NONEXPENDABLE AND EXPENDABLE TRUSTS

Externally restricted gifts are accounted for in a nonexpendable or an expendable trust fund. If the principal must be retained indefinitely, it is accounted for in a nonexpendable trust fund. Such trusts include land trusts and cemetery perpetual care funds. Sometimes neither principal nor interest can be spent; money given for purposes of making loans is one example. The interest earned from lending the principal is added to the principal so that the entity can make additional loans.

If the principal must be spent for a specific purpose, the accounting records are maintained through an expendable trust fund. A single gift may involve characteristics of both an expendable and a nonexpendable trust. For example, a donor may give money for enhancing a public park and specify that the principal must be maintained intact and any income generated by investing the principal must be used to enhance public parks. In this circumstance, many governmental entities establish a nonexpendable trust fund to account for the principal and an expendable trust fund to account for the earnings on the assets of the nonexpendable trust fund. However, establishing an expendable trust fund for this purpose is not required unless mandated by law; the earnings and expenditure of those earnings can be accounted for in the nonexpendable trust fund.

Guidance for the accounting and reporting of expendable and nonexpendable trust funds is limited. The Governmental Accounting Standards Board has not issued specific pronouncements. Its predecessor, the National Committee on Governmental Accounting, did little more than describe the nature and purpose of these funds. This void traces to the fact that nonexpendable trust funds are similar to proprietary funds, and expendable trust funds are like governmental funds. The accounting and reporting standards applicable to these other funds generally are applied to the nonexpendable and expendable trust funds.

Accounting for Nonexpendable Trust Funds

Authoritative literature does not require the use of nonexpendable trust funds. Governmental entities using this fund classification always have the option of accounting for trust assets in another fund, as long as the restriction on the assets is clearly indicated. Even though it is optional, most governmental entities use nonexpendable trust funds for assets that must be held in perpetuity.

A formal trust document is normally written by the donor for any assets given to an entity when the assets must be held "in perpetuity." The nature of the assets and the donor's intent regarding expenditures is defined in the trust document. Thus, trust law governs the treatment of such assets. Legal counsel or insurance experts may be consulted to interpret the provisions. Regardless of the specific provisions contained in the document, the nature of these gifts indicates that a major accounting problem exists in determining the extent to which the governmental entity adhered to the trust's provisions. Compliance with any budgetary provisions is secondary to compliance with trust provisions. Further, since the principal must be retained, capital maintenance is a primary goal.

Nonexpendable trust funds use the flow of total economic resources measurement focus and the accrual basis of accounting. Accordingly, depreciation is taken on fixed assets. All revenues and expenses are accrued, and prepaid and deferred items are accounted for just as they would be in a business.

Accounting and Valuation Issues Related to Assets   When the trust is established, assets transferred to it are recorded at their **fair market value**

on the date of the gift. Following the capital maintenance focus, the basis of a fixed asset would be cost less any accumulated depreciation, or amortized cost in the case of debt securities.

The treatment of marketable equity securities, particularly if held for the short run, is unclear. Although accounting for nonexpendable trust funds follows the guidance established for proprietary funds, proprietary funds normally do not have these investments. Without guidance from the GASB, governmental entities would appear to have a choice of looking to trust laws or to standards set by the Financial Accounting Standards Board.

Under trust law, the securities are valued at cost. Realized gains and losses on the sale of securities would be regarded as changes in principal; therefore, gains or losses affect the fund balance, not the investment revenue for the period. For example, if investments sold during the period yielded a gain of $5,000, the gain would be shown as a change in the fund balance under trust law. The $5,000 would be credited directly to fund balance without being reported in the income statement.

Experts disagree on the appropriate valuation of securities and the recognition criteria. The 1988 edition of *Governmental Accounting, Auditing and Financial Reporting* (GAAFR) shows realized gains or losses on the sale of securities as **nonoperating** gains or losses.[1] Therefore, the gain or loss would be added to or subtracted from the amount that could be spent from the trust in any one year. Some textbooks show realized gains or losses as adjustments to fund balance and, therefore, such gains or losses do not affect the amount that can be spent in a given period. Most authoritative sources ignore the valuation issue, but in practice governmental entities appear to carry securities at cost. When the GASB completes its project on financial reporting, the guidance in this area should become clearer.

Accounting ambiguities can be avoided by spelling out the intent in the trust document. For example, if the trust document directs the trustee to charge gains or losses against the principal or the income, the governmental entity must comply with the instructions. This avoids the accounting argument about which approach is appropriate.

Segregation of Fund Balances   Some governmental entities feel that the accounting is simplified by using a nonexpendable trust to account for the principal and an expendable trust for the earnings. However, both the corpus and income may be accounted for in a nonexpendable trust fund. The principal amount that cannot be spent should be reserved for the intended purpose, and the earnings, if not spent during the year, closed to fund balance—**unreserved, undesignated.**

Illustrated Transactions of Nonexpendable Trust Funds   Carter County has a nonexpendable trust fund that is used to account for the principal and earnings of a trust providing for the care and maintenance of a public

---

[1]Government Finance Officers Association, *Governmental Accounting, Auditing and Financial Reporting* (Chicago: GFOA, 1988), 83.

park honoring an important public figure. The terms of the trust make it clear that security gains and losses affect earnings, not principal.

The donor gave an apartment building, equity securities, and cash to provide for the perpetual care and maintenance of the park. Carter County officials had the apartment building and the securities appraised at the date of the gift. The apartment building was valued at $280,000; its expected useful life was 35 years. The securities were valued at $22,000, and the cash totaled $5,000. The entry to record the gift in the nonexpendable trust fund is:

1.	Cash	5,000	
	Equity Securities	22,000	
	Fixed Assets	280,000	
	Fund Balance—Reserved for Perpetual		
	Care		307,000

Rentals received during the year totaled $32,400; maintenance and other costs associated with operating the rental unit were $6,000. Carter County uses straight-line depreciation.

2.	Cash (32,400 − 6,000)	26,400	
	Operating Expenses	6,000	
	Depreciation Expense ($280,000/35)	8,000	
	Operating Revenues		32,400
	Accumulated Depreciation		8,000

Midway through the year, Carter County sold $8,000 of the equity securities at a gain of $500 and reinvested the proceeds, along with the initial $5,000 cash, in bonds with a par value of $13,050 — that is, the trust paid a premium for the bonds. They mature in three years.

3.	Cash	8,500	
	Equity Securities		8,000
	Nonoperating Revenues		500
4.	Investment in Bonds	13,500	
	Cash		13,500

The unamortized premium could be established in a separate account but it is normally included in the investment account, just as it would be in a business entity. Amortization of the premium occurs at year end.

The trust incurred costs of $7,600 for landscaping and other operational expenses of the park.

5.	Operating Expenses	7,600	
	Accounts Payable		7,600

Interest earnings of $2,000 were received during the year.

6.	Cash	2,000	
	Nonoperating Revenues		2,000

The trust reimbursed the county $1,100 for labor expenses in maintaining the park.

7.	Operating Expenses	1,100	
	Cash		1,100

The reimbursement is not a transfer because work done by the general fund is treated as an arms-length transaction, just as if it had been done for a proprietary fund. Carter's general fund would treat the $1,100 as a revenue.

At year end, interest earned but not yet received amounted to $3,200, and the trust fund amortized the bond premium.

8.	Accrued Interest Receivable	3,200	
	Nonoperating Revenues		3,200
9.	Nonoperating Expenses [(13,500 − 13,050)/3 × 6/12]	75	
	Investment in Bonds		75

The premium is written off over the three years until maturity, but the bonds were held for only six months during the current year.

The trust fund paid $6,000 on its accounts payable.

10.	Accounts Payable	6,000	
	Cash		6,000

Nominal accounts were closed.

11.	Operating Revenues	32,400	
	Nonoperating Revenues	5,700	
	Operating Expenses ($6,000 + $8,000 + $7,600 + $1,100)		22,700
	Nonoperating Expenses		75
	Fund Balance—Unreserved, Undesignated		15,325

As explained earlier, any income not used for the intended purpose is placed in a fund balance that is clearly distinguished from the fund balance pertaining to the corpus. If Carter County had used an expendable trust fund to account for the earnings and expenses, the income from the nonexpendable trust would have been reported directly in the expendable trust fund. Under this alternative, the only entries made in the nonexpendable trust relate to the initial receipt by Carter County and the transaction showing the sale and the reinvestment. Even the gain or loss on the security sale and the amortization of the bond premium would have been shown in the expendable trust fund.

Expendable Trust Funds

Expendable trust funds can be used to account for money held in a trustee relationship whenever there is no prohibition against spending the trust principal. The trustee relationship may be established either by statute or a formal trust document. An expendable trust fund is clearly appropriate if a donor specifies the nature of the expenditures but permits spending of both income and principal. An expendable trust fund also would be established whenever state law or local ordinance requires a separate fund to account for assets entrusted to an entity for specific use. General practice also suggests that expendable trust funds may be used to account for the income of a nonexpendable trust.

An expendable trust fund *should not be used* to account for an entity's own restrictions on its assets. For example, if the county commissioners pass a resolution reserving $80,000 for a specific purpose, a trust fund is not appropriate. An entity cannot establish a fiduciary relationship with itself. A better way to note the resolution is by showing a portion of the general fund's balance as reserved or designated.

A number of activities, such as federal grants, self-insurance funds, and employee benefit plans (excluding pensions and deferred compensation plans), can be accounted for in any one of several different funds. Although treatment varies, federal grants are better suited to a special revenue than to an expendable trust fund. The money belongs to the governmental entity provided it follows the granting agency's rules. Accordingly, a trustee relationship is unlikely.

NCGA *Statement 4* recommends that self-insurance activities be accounted for in an internal service fund. Most governmental entities have now adopted the NCGA recommendation.

In the employee benefits area, one interpretation issued by NCGA specifically provided that state unemployment compensation benefit plans should be accounted for in an expendable trust fund. This pronouncement led many entities to presume that all employee benefit programs not specifically addressed by some authoritative pronouncement should be accounted for in expendable trust funds. However, because most benefits are paid directly by the employing fund, a trustee relationship does not seem to exist.

Expendable trust funds also may be used for escheat property. An escheat is the reversion of property to the governmental entity in the absence of legal claimants or heirs. Examples include real property, stocks and bonds, and other abandoned property for which the governmental entity is unable to locate the legal owner or heir. A property account would be debited upon receipt; a liability would be credited. Ultimately, and if it is unlikely that the governmental entity can find the rightful owner, the asset would be transferred to the general fund and used for operating purposes. Some state laws require that, if the owner cannot be located, such property be held in perpetuity, in which case the asset would still remain in the expendable trust fund forever.

▲   **OBSERVATION**

If the law requires holding escheat property indefinitely, it makes sense to eventually transfer the property to a nonexpendable trust fund. The standard would allow such treatment because it requires that escheat property be reported in *either* an expendable trust fund or *the fund to which the property ultimately escheats.*

Unemployment Programs   State governments and the federal government have developed unemployment assistance programs. Employers are taxed a certain amount based on gross wages paid. When workers meet certain employment requirements and are terminated, they may apply for unemployment assistance. If the state has insufficient funds, it may apply to the federal government for an advance.

NCGA *Interpretation 9* allows governments to account for state unemployment programs in expendable trust funds. The reasoning behind the interpretation was that states are collecting taxes and administering the unemployment compensation plans in a trustee capacity for the federal government. Taxes collected from employers are deposited in the fund. Liabilities are established when the fund owes a qualified applicant or when the federal government advances funds to pay claims.

Other Uses of Expendable Trust Funds   Some special district activities— parks, libraries, schools, and so forth—have never been addressed directly or indirectly by NCGA or GASB. As long as the district is not part of the governmental entity performing the accounting and reporting functions, a trustee relationship may exist. Without official guidance on trust fund inclusions and only limited guidance on determining the reporting unit, treatment varies among governmental entities. In many entities, expendable trust funds have become a haven for any accounting activity that does not clearly pertain to some other fund.

General Accounting Practices of Expendable Trust Funds   Most references to the accounting for expendable trust funds are very general; official pronouncements simply state that the accounting practices applied to governmental funds should also be applied to expendable trust funds. Thus, the focus is on current financial resources and the accounting basis is modified accrual. Income is recognized when measurable and available, and expenditures are recognized when the related liability is incurred. Although the pronouncements do not spell out such details, presumably any debt expenditures are recognized when due. An expendable trust fund may use the "when consumed" or "when purchased" basis for inventory.

Accounting for Assets and Liabilities of Expendable Trust Funds
Although expendable trust funds use the same basis of accounting as governmental funds, some ambiguities exist concerning the general application of this principle. Specifically, long-term assets and liabilities related to such trust funds should be accounted for within these funds.[2] This provision seems inconsistent with the basis of accounting. Under a current financial resources model, fixed assets and long-term debt would not be accounted for within the fund. On the other hand, a trustee relationship suggests that all assets and liabilities pertaining to the trust ought to be accounted for in the trust fund.

---

[2] National Council on Governmental Accounting, *Statement 1, Governmental Accounting and Financial Reporting Principles* (Chicago: Municipal Finance Officers Association of the United States and Canada, 1979).

Many governmental entities do not interpret the *Statement 1* provisions literally, and instead rely on basic principles found elsewhere in the same document. The primary principle relied upon is the requirement that expendable trust funds and governmental funds be accounted for similarly. Accordingly, these entities report fixed assets and long-term liabilities in the two account groups. If a governmental entity chooses this approach, those assets associated with an expendable trust fund should be separately identified.

Recognizing Pledges The largest source of revenue for some expendable trust funds comes from donations. Sometimes donations are pledged in one year and the cash received in another. Without definitive guidelines from the GASB, entities must turn to other authoritative literature to determine how to account for these pledges. The FASB requires nonprofit organizations under its purview to record unconditional pledges as revenue at the time the pledge is made.

▲ **OBSERVATION**

Although the treatment is inconsistent with the current financial resources model, the distortion to financial statements probably is minimal. Pledge programs usually are regular and recurring, so after the first year, revenue reporting would be the same as if the entity used the modified accrual basis.

In-Kind Contributions Citizens often contribute their time to worthwhile community projects. The accounting question is, should the value of that contributed time be shown as a revenue? If it is shown as a revenue, the contributed time also would be an expenditure because without the contribution, an expenditure would have been incurred to do the work. The GASB has not addressed the issue of in-kind contributions, so governmental entities must search other authoritative literature to determine appropriate accounting practices. Nonprofits under the FASB purview report contributed services as revenues/expenses if the services received (1) create or enhance nonfinancial assets or (2) require specialized skills, are provided by individuals possessing those skills, and would typically need to be purchased if not provided by donation.[3] In the absence of GASB guidance on the matter, governmental entities could debit an expenditure and credit revenues when these conditions were met.

Illustrated Transactions of Expendable Trust Funds Carter County established an expendable trust fund to account for contributions related to its meals-on-wheels program for senior citizens confined to their homes. The program is funded entirely from gifts, interest earnings from a nonexpend-

---

[3]Financial Accounting Standards Board, *Statement of Financial Accounting Standards No. 116, Accounting for Contributions Received and Contributions Made* (Norwalk, Conn.: FASB, 1993), ¶9. The standard mentions that services requiring specialized skills include those of accountants, architects, carpenters, doctors, electricians, lawyers, nurses, plumbers, teachers, and other professionals.

able trust fund, and contributed time and supplies from local merchants and charity organizations.

The county finance director establishes an annual budget. However, because the budget does not require approval by the county commissioners, the budgetary accounts are not integrated into the accounting system.

A trial balance for the previous year end follows:

Carter County
Senior Citizens Meals-on-Wheels Expendable Trust Fund
Trial Balance
December 31, 19X1

Cash	$ 2,100	
Investments	10,800	
Interest Receivable	610	
Accounts Payable		$ 1,960
Fund Balance—Unreserved		11,550
	$13,510	$13,510

A fund-raising drive began in early 19X2, yielding $16,100 in cash and pledges of $11,000. The pledges are expected to be received before year end or shortly thereafter.

1.	Cash	16,100	
	Pledges Receivable	11,000	
	Revenues		27,100

In addition to these donations, several community service groups volunteered their time to make deliveries and to prepare the meals. Volunteer services are an important part of any meals-on-wheels program, but the in-kind contributed services for Carter County will be judged immaterial in order to simplify the illustrated transactions.

During 19X2, food purchases totaled $5,200, and other operating costs totaling $3,000 were incurred. Carter County uses the "when consumed" method of accounting for inventory.

2.	Inventories	5,200	
	Expenditures	3,000	
	Accounts Payable		8,200

The interest receivable was collected, and $4,000 was paid on accounts payable.

3.	Cash	610	
	Interest Receivable		610
4.	Accounts Payable	4,000	
	Cash		4,000

Investments with a cost basis of $1,200 were sold for $1,350; the proceeds were reinvested in a certificate of deposit.

5.	Cash	1,350	
	Investments		1,200
	Revenues		150
6.	Investments	1,350	
	Cash		1,350

Because this is an expendable trust fund, the gain on the sale is shown as a revenue, just like other sources of income. The entire amount in the fund is expendable, so segregating those gains or losses related to principal and those related to income is unnecessary. Some governmental entities would credit a "gain" account rather than revenues so that various sources can be identified in the operating statement.

Additional operating expenses of $8,000 were incurred; cash was disbursed to pay for these expenses and all but $800 of the remaining accounts payable.

7.	Expenditures	8,000	
	Accounts Payable	5,360	
	Cash		13,360

Interest of $750 was earned (and measurable and available) on investments; of that total, $600 was received in cash.

8.	Cash	600	
	Interest Receivable	150	
	Revenues		750

At year end, the fund purchased a used van for $8,000, using $5,200 cash on hand for the down payment and incurring a three-year note for the balance. Carter County elects to put long-term liabilities and fixed assets in the account groups.

9.	Expenditures	8,000	
	Cash		5,200
	Other Financing Sources—Notes Payable		2,800

The adjusting and closing entries for 19X2 are shown below. No depreciation is taken on the fixed assets. Of the inventory purchased, only $300 remained on hand.

Expenditures	4,900	
Inventories		4,900
Revenues	28,000	
Expenditures		23,900
Fund Balance—Unreserved		4,100

AGENCY FUNDS

Funds held *on behalf of* another entity are accounted for in an agency fund. Authoritative literature requires the use of agency funds in two circumstances: (1) Section 457 deferred compensation programs, and (2) debt service transactions of a special assessment issue for which the government is not obligated in some manner. In addition, agency funds often are used for some pass-through grants, and when the government acts as the tax collection agent for other levels of government.

OBSERVATION ▲

Entity is used in the literal sense of the term. Therefore, "funds held on behalf of another entity" includes funds held on behalf of other funds of the governmental unit. A typical example is when an agency fund is used to account for pooled investments, a use described later in the chapter.

Required Uses of Agency Funds

As mentioned previously, agency funds are used for Section 457 deferred compensation programs and special assessment collections when the governmental entity has no obligation for the special assessment debt. In the case of the deferred compensation programs, the assets are being held until employees draw upon them. Special assessment collections are being held awaiting disbursement to bondholders. In both cases, the assets are being held for the benefit of outsiders, so a trust fund is not used.

def comp
(retirement plan)

Section 457 Plans   Section 457 of the Internal Revenue Code permits governmental entities to establish deferred compensation programs for their employees. Under a deferred compensation plan, employees may place a certain portion of their pretax salary in an approved investment program. Salary amounts placed in the deferred compensation programs are not taxable to the employee until the funds are withdrawn by the employee or beneficiary, usually after retirement. In order to establish such plans,

- all amounts of compensation deferred under the plan,
- all property and rights purchased with such amounts, and
- all income attributable to such amounts, property, or rights shall remain . . . solely the property and rights of the state . . . subject only to the claims of the state's general creditors.[4]

---

[4]Governmental Accounting Standards Board, *Statement No. 2, Financial Reporting of Deferred Compensation Plans Adopted under the Provisions of Internal Revenue Code Section 457* (Stamford, Conn.: GASB, 1986), 1. The term *state* in this context is defined as a state, a political subdivision of a state, or any agency or instrumentality of a state or political subdivision of a state.

The accounting for these plans has been hotly contested. As the Code citation makes clear, employees' contributions to the deferred compensation plans must be treated as *assets of the governmental entity.* Many argue that the governmental entity has no claim against these assets. After all, employees' salaries, not governmental assets, are invested in the plan. Others maintain that even though the salary has been earned by the employee, legal ownership does not vest until the salary amounts become due and payable to the employee under the terms of the plan.

Both sides of the issue seem reasonable. The fact is, however, that in order to qualify under Section 457, employees and governmental entities must agree to treat plan assets as governmental assets. Since these assets would be tapped by creditors only if a governmental entity was insolvent, the treatment of the assets may be a mere technicality.

▲   **OBSERVATION**

As a practical matter, an entity's insolvency is a gradual process. With some forewarning, the governmental entity and the employees would have time to cancel the program and withdraw the funds. Paying tax on a lump-sum distribution from the plan would be preferable under these circumstances to losing the money to general creditors.

Special Assessment Collections   When the governmental entity is not obligated to pay special assessment debt, it acts as an agent for the assessed taxpayers and the bondholders. As the assessments mature, the taxpayers forward their money to the governmental entity. The governmental entity forwards the money to the bondholders. If time elapses between the payment and the disbursement, the governmental entity usually invests the money.

An agency fund reports the cash collected and any interest receivable as assets and amounts due the bondholders as liabilities. The amount of taxes receivable from the taxpayers is also reported in the agency fund. The total receivables always equal the liability to the bondholders, so there is no fund balance.

Other Uses of Agency Funds

Consolidation of Liabilities   Governmental entities use agency funds to consolidate and simplify the accounting for certain liabilities. For example, payroll deductions for income tax withholdings or health insurance programs may be accounted for and reported in the fund paying the salary or the insurance premium. These payments also may be consolidated in an agency fund. Under consolidation, each fund transfers its liability for these payments to the agency fund. The agency fund pays the entire amount due with one check, greatly simplifying the accounting for payroll deductions and other liabilities involving a number of funds.

Deciding when to use an agency fund for these transactions is a matter of judgment. In general, the larger the government, the more likely an agency fund will simplify the accounting process. A large governmental unit is apt to have the volume of transactions necessary to justify the additional accounting and reporting. Also, the magnitude of the transactions should be used to judge the advisability of establishing a separate fund. An agency fund provides a single place where all the separate fund liabilities can be balanced and compared against the labor and tax reports filed by the governmental entity.

Tax Collection Services   Agency funds are used when one governmental entity is the tax collection agent for another. For example, county governments may collect the property taxes for a school district. When the tax is levied, taxes receivable current and due to other governments would be debited and credited, respectively, in an agency fund. As the levy is collected, cash is debited and the receivable is reduced. The liability is debited when the cash is sent to the school district.

Grants and Entitlements   GASB guidelines also allow the use of agency funds for certain grant and entitlement programs. Resources received by one governmental unit on behalf of a secondary recipient may be accounted for through an agency fund, as one example. An agency fund allows the governmental entity to keep a record of the funds that have "passed through" the entity. In some cases, however, the governmental entity has some discretion about the amount that is passed through. If the governmental entity can vary the amount, the funds should be accounted for in the general fund or a special revenue fund.

A second permitted use involves grants and entitlements that may be used in more than one fund at the discretion of the recipient entity. While the entity is deciding where to account for the activity, it can deposit the funds in an agency fund.

Finally, agency funds can be used when the grant or entitlement program uses an accounting basis or fiscal period different from the entity's. The receiving entity must have a way to report revenues and expenditures according to the granting agency's recognition principles or fiscal period. Using memorandum entries in an agency fund simplifies the accounting process. The transactions are recorded as they occur using memorandum revenue and expenditure accounts based on the granting agency's basis of accounting. The same transactions are recorded as revenue and expenditures/expenses in the appropriate fund according to the governmental entity's basis of accounting. According to the GASB's *Codification,*

> this "dual" recording approach may be especially helpful where the grant accounting period is different from that of the fund(s) financed, that is, multiyear or different operating year awards. This "dual" recording approach is suggested only when a beneficial purpose is served.[5]

The dual accounting approach sounds more complex than it is in practice. As an example, assume a governmental entity is awarded a two-year $100,000

[5]Governmental Accounting Standards Board, *Codification of Governmental Accounting and Financial Reporting Standards* (Norwalk, Conn.: GASB, 1993), sec. G60, ¶108.

grant by an agency that has an October 1 through September 30 fiscal year. The governmental entity uses a special revenue fund and calendar year for financial reporting. Both the agency and the recipient recognize expenditures and revenues, respectively, when earned. For the recipient "when earned" means when expended. The recipient spent $33,000 by September 30 of 19X1; by December 31, the recipient had spent $77,000. Cash was received 30 days after filing the expenditure report.

Agency Fund Entries—19X1:

1/1	Memo Grant Receivable	100,000	
	Memo Deferred Revenue		100,000
9/30	Memo Expenditures	33,000	
	Memo Accounts Payable		33,000
9/30	Memo Deferred Revenue	33,000	
	Memo Revenue		33,000

The report filed to the granting agency for the period ending September 30, 19X1, would show total expenditures of $33,000 and no receipt of cash. The cash received and remaining expenditures would be reported in 19X2. Because no cash was received in 19X1, the receivable would be $100,000 at year end.

Special Revenue Fund Entries—19X1:

1/1	Grant Receivable	100,000	
	Deferred Revenue		100,000
Various	Expenditures	77,000	
	Payables		77,000
Various	Deferred Revenue	77,000	
	Revenue		77,000
10/30	Cash	33,000	
	Grant Receivable		33,000

For the governmental entity, revenues and expenditures during 19X1 would total $77,000. At year end, the grant receivable would be $67,000 ($100,000 − $33,000), and deferred revenue would be $23,000 ($100,000 − $77,000). None of the memo accounts shown in the agency fund would be reported on the financial statements of the governmental entity.

The GASB is reexamining the accounting and financial reporting issues related to grants and other forms of financial assistance. Motivated in part by the eventual change to accrual accounting for governmental funds, the GASB issued a discussion memorandum on the subject in 1992. The following year the GASB agreed that it should start with a reexamination of the issues related to pass-through grants. Issues involving expenditure-driven grants and nonreimbursed grants will be dealt with later.

Pooled Investments   Agency funds are frequently used to account for pooled investments. Pooled investments exist when the idle cash of several different funds is pooled and invested.

An agency fund used for this purpose records the cash deposits from each fund, the investments purchased with those funds, and the distribution of earnings to each fund. For example, if the general fund and capital projects fund contributed $15,000 and $65,000, respectively, to a pooled investment fund, the entry in the agency fund would be:

```
Cash                                            80,000
        Due to General Fund                               15,000
        Due to Capital Projects Fund                      65,000
```

The agency fund personnel invest the cash, and as earnings are received, they are prorated to each fund. Earnings of $7,000 would be recorded as:

```
Cash                                            7,000
        Due to General Fund
            (15,000/80,000 × 7,000)                        1,312
        Due to Capital Projects Fund
            (65,000/80,000 × 7,000)                        5,688
```

Although used for this purpose in practice, it is difficult to argue that a governmental unit can be an agent for itself. A better approach might be to account for the pooled investments in the general fund. A special line item would depict the pooled investments and the liability accounts. In this case, the "due to" both funds would be clearly designated as related to the pooled investments.

Accounting Practices and Financial Reporting for Agency Funds

Accounting for agency funds is relatively easy. Because they are used for *holding* assets that belong to another entity, total assets equal total liabilities. Revenues or expenditures related to assets that belong to another entity or fund are not shown, eliminating nominal accounts or a fund balance. Usually assets held on behalf of another entity are disbursed in the short run. Consequently, no valuation issues arise.

Financial reporting is also relatively easy. Budgets are not prepared. Since the fund is simply a pass-through for assets held for another entity or fund, the amounts in the fund are budgeted elsewhere. The principal financial statement prepared for agency funds is a balance sheet. Nonetheless, governmental entities are required to report a combining statement of changes in agency fund assets and liabilities in the comprehensive annual financial report.

Oftentimes the fund has been closed before year end. For example, if a fund were used for a grant and the grant is complete, no balances would remain in the fund. Similarly, most tax collection services for other entities are finished and the cash disbursed by year end. On the other hand, deferred compensation programs are continuing programs; a balance sheet shows the extent to which money has been accumulated to pay future liabilities.

Illustrated Transactions for Deferred Compensation Agency Funds
As required by the GASB, Carter County accounts for its deferred compensation program in an agency fund. Amounts withheld from employees are deposited in and invested by the fund. Payments are made to retired employees and to those who terminate their employment with Carter County. The trial balance for the previous year shows investments of $267,000 and deferred compensation benefits payable for the same amount.

Amounts withheld are deposited each month, but to simplify the illustration, the entire annual amount is recorded in one entry.

1.	Cash	115,000	
	Deferred Compensation Benefits Payable		115,000

Three employees terminated their employment; they had $16,000 invested in the program.

2.	Deferred Compensation Benefits Payable	16,000	
	Cash		16,000

Two employees retired during the year and elected to receive their deferred compensation in a lump sum. One employee had $6,100 in the program, and the other had $2,600.

3.	Deferred Compensation Benefits Payable (2,600 + 6,100)	8,700	
	Cash		8,700

Interest of $21,360 was earned on investments; of that total, $18,000 was received in cash.

4.	Cash	18,000	
	Accrued Interest Receivable	3,360	
	Deferred Compensation Benefits Payable		21,360

Carter County charges 1 percent of the total withholding each year to administer the program. The revenue would be recorded in the general fund, but because this fee is a charge against employees, it reduces the employees' net investment.

5.	Deferred Compensation Benefits Payable (.01 × 115,000)	1,150	
	Cash		1,150

Excess cash was invested.

6.	Investments (115,000 + 18,000 − [16,000 + 8,700 + 1,150])	107,150	
	Cash		107,150

Because no revenues or expenditures are reported in the fund, closing entries are unneccessary. The year-end balance sheet shows investments of $374,150 and accrued interest receivable of $3,360. At the same date, liabilities total $377,510.

Illustrated Transactions for Special Assessment Project   A special assessment project for curbs and gutters was approved. Under the terms of the assessment, affected taxpayers owe $867,000, payable in three equal annual installments. Carter County is not liable for the underlying debt. Because this is a new project, the fund has no carry forward amounts. Each year's installment is levied on January 1; one-half of the annual tax levy is due on May 31 and one-half on November 30. Interest of 8 percent is earned on any late payments and temporary investments. The interest earnings are assumed when calculating the amounts due to bondholders, and an annual payment to bondholders of $280,000 is made annually on January 1, beginning in 19X2. The total amount due to bondholders of $840,000 ($280,000 × 3) is different from the total amount assessed of $867,000 because some taxpayers may not pay their assessment. If they all pay the entire amount due, the excess is refunded to the property owners or used to reduce their future assessments.

The tax assessment for 19X1 was levied.

1/1/X1	Taxes Receivable Current (867,000/3)	289,000	
	Due to Special Assessment		
	Bondholders		289,000

To conform to the GASB requirement that "special assessment debt for which the government is not obligated in some manner should not be displayed in the government's financial statements,"[6] only the current year's assessment is reflected as a receivable.

By May 1, the entire first-half installment was collected and invested in short-term securities.

Various	Cash	144,500	
	Taxes Receivable Current		144,500
Various	Investments	144,500	
	Cash		144,500

All but $8,000 of the second-half installment was received and invested by December 1.

Various	Cash	136,500	
	Taxes Receivable Current		136,500
Various	Investments	136,500	
	Cash		136,500

[6]GASB, *1993 Codification*, sec. S40, ¶117.

On December 31, investment earnings were accrued, and the interest charged on past due taxes was also accrued (amounts of interest on investments and delinquent taxes are assumed in order to simplify the calculations). The amounts are accrued because they are assumed to be measurable and available. Current taxes receivable are reclassified as delinquent.

12/31	Interest Receivable	5,000	
	Due to Special Assessment		
	Bondholders		5,000
	Taxes Receivable Delinquent	8,000	
	Taxes Receivable Current		8,000

Carter County's balance sheet would include this agency fund. Assets of the fund include the taxes receivable delinquent of $8,000, investments of $281,000, and miscellaneous receivables of $5,000. The only liability is the amount owed to special assessment bondholders, $294,000.

On January 1, 19X2, the investments are sold, and the proceeds disbursed to the bondholders. Also, the second year's assessment is levied. For the sake of simplicity, the investments are assumed to be sold at par. Only the amount needed is taken out of the investments.

1/1/X1	Cash	280,000	
	Investments		280,000
	Due to Special Assessment Bondholders	280,000	
	Cash		280,000
	Taxes Receivable Current	289,000	
	Due to Special Assessment		
	Bondholders		289,000

The remainder of the second and third years' entries would follow the same general pattern. Unless the delinquency rate is higher than projected when the assessment was initially calculated, sufficient resources will be available to make the annual payments to bondholders. If a shortfall exists, an additional assessment will be levied, or the proceeds from the sale of the taxpayers' property will be used to make any remaining payments to bondholders. Excess cash usually is prorated to the affected taxpayers and credited to their future property tax bills.

ACCOUNTING AND REPORTING FOR PENSION TRUST FUNDS

Following the practices of industry, most governmental entities provide a pension program for their employees. Governmental pension programs are generally referred to as public employee retirement systems (PERS). Accounting for the employer's expenses and liabilities was discussed in Chapter 4. The pension plan is accounted for and reported in a pension trust fund.

A PERS may be structured in several ways. In some states, each individual unit of government may establish its own program. The governmental unit decides what type of pension plan it wants (for example, contributory, non-contributory, funded, unfunded) and collects and/or makes the contributions to the plan. The unit also invests the funds and pays retired or terminated employees, as appropriate. A separate board or the finance director usually manages the fund and supervises the pension activities.

In other states, statewide pension programs are established. Each type of employee—teachers, firefighters, police officers, and so on—may be included in a separate statewide pension program. Or, governmental units of a given type (counties, cities) may develop a statewide pension program. In these latter types, the investments typically are managed by one agent, and one oversight board supervises the plan for all employees or governmental units included.

A PERS may cover employees of only one employer (single-employer plans) or employees of several employers (multiple-employer plans). Under the typical multiple-employer plan, the risks, investments, and all administrative functions are pooled. Each employer uses the same actuarial schedule to determine employer/employee contributions, and each shares in the administrative and benefit costs. A single-employer plan is just the opposite. Each employer has its own management, actuarial valuations, and investment account, although they may all be under a common board or administrator.

If several single-employer plans are aggregated, they also are referred to as multiple-employer plans. In this type of multiple-employer plan, the investment and administrative duties are pooled, but each entity receives its own actuarial valuations necessary to determine employer contributions.

Historical Perspective of PERS Accounting and Reporting

Pension accounting and reporting practices for governmental entities have been laden with the same controversy and indecision as in the private sector. Acceptable cost methods, asset valuation standards, and the relationship between the entity and the plan pose significant theoretical and practical problems. The practices adopted in any of these three problem areas significantly affect the financial statements and, consequently, much is at stake in settling the issues.

The GASB placed pensions as a high priority on its initial agenda. Its pension project was divided into two parts: disclosure requirements, and accounting and reporting requirements. The latter part includes issues related to measurement and recognition.

The GASB chose to address the disclosure requirements first, culminating with *Statement No. 5* in 1986. The statement does not address accounting and reporting of pension plans; it only adds to the disclosure requirements contained in FASB *Statement No. 35.*

Current Authoritative Guidance for Pension Plan Accounting and Reporting

The only significant guidance is found in the *Codification*. It gives governmental entities three options in accounting for pension programs. The second paragraph in the pension fund section states:

> When it began operations, the GASB concluded that, pending issuance by GASB of a Statement or Statements concerning pension accounting and reporting, the following pronouncements are considered as sources of acceptable accounting and reporting principles for public employee retirement systems (PERS) and state and local governmental employers...: (a) NCGA Statement 1; (b) NCGA Statement 6 (as interpreted by NCGA Interpretation 8); and (c) FASB Statement 35.[7]

All three pronouncements discuss pension plans, although *Statement No. 35* is the only one that deals specifically with this subject. The NCGA pronouncements cover both the employer's and the plan's accounting and financial reporting. As was pointed out in Chapter 4, the two NCGA pronouncements also are used as a basis for determining the employer's pension costs.

NCGA Statement 1   The accrual basis of accounting and the flow of total economic resources are required for pension trusts under the first NCGA pronouncement on pensions. Although asset valuation is not mentioned specifically, the accrual basis would suggest a cost/amortized cost basis. Illustrations in the *1968 Governmental Accounting, Auditing and Financial Reporting*[8] support this interpretation.

NCGA's intent regarding the measurement of liabilities is unclear in *Statement 1*. In practice, entities using this statement for guidance usually show current liabilities payable to retirees (or those terminated but vested). The difference between plan assets and these current liabilities is shown as a reserve for employees' retirement. In other words, the amount needed to provide the retirement benefits is not calculated independently of the actual funding method. For example, if the actuarial present value of the benefit obligation is $32,000,000 and the employer has funded only $26,000,000, the reserve would be the difference between any current liabilities and the $26,000,000. If current liabilities were $1,000,000, the reserve would be $25,000,000. The rest of the liability, $6,000,000, is ignored under NCGA *Statement 1*.

Nonetheless, the *Codification* depiction of *Statement No. 1* accounting shows both the reserve described above *and* an unfunded actuarial deficit. This seems to suggest something beyond the scope of *Statement 1:* showing (1) the difference between plan assets and current liabilities as a reserve for employees' retirement, and (2) the difference between the actuarial present value of the obligation and the reserve for employees' retirement as an "unfunded deficit." Using the earlier example, the unfunded deficit totals

[7]GASB, *1993 Codification*, sec. P20, ¶102.

[8]Municipal Finance Officers Association of the United States and Canada, *Governmental Accounting, Auditing and Financial Reporting* (Chicago: MFOA, 1968), 70–73.

$7,000,000 ($32,000,000 − $25,000,000). Because the *Codification* represents acceptable accounting practice, governmental employers presumably could use either the NCGA pronouncement or the GASB interpretaton of *Statement 1*. Exhibit 9-1 depicts the NCGA *Statement 1* format.

The NCGA Statement 6 Alternative As optional guidance, NCGA *Statement 6* specifically discusses both plan assets and liabilities. Accrual-based accounting is applied under this alternative, and the focus is on the flow of total economic resources. Unlike the earlier NCGA statement, valuation procedures for assets and liabilities are defined.

Valuing Assets and Recognizing Gains and Losses. The cost principle is used, except when market declines appear to be permanent. Permanent declines should be recognized as a loss, thereby reducing the cost basis to market. Fixed-income securities should be reported at amortized cost, subject to appropriate adjustments for market value declines that are judged to be permanent. If a governmental entity intends holding the security until maturity, all market value declines should be judged temporary. In amortizing premiums or discounts, the effective interest method (not the straight-line method) should be used.

Treatment of gains and losses of fixed-income securities has long been an issue in governmental accounting. Under NCGA *Statement 1,* gains or losses

---

Exhibit 9-1

Any Governmental Unit
Statement 1 Presentation
Pension Trust Fund
Balance Sheet
As of December 31, 19X1

Assets

Cash	$ 5,000	
Investments	4,860,000	
Receivables	210,000	
TOTAL ASSETS		$5,075,000

Liabilities

Annuities Payable	$ 11,800	
Due to Terminated Employees	3,200	
Total Liabilities		$ 15,000

Fund Balance

Reserve for Employee Contributions	$ 2,650,000	
Reserve for Employer Contributions	1,980,000	
Actuarial Deficiency—Reserve for Employer Contributions	3,450,000	
Reserve for Retiree Annuities	430,000	
Unreserved Fund Balance (Deficit)	(3,450,000)	
Total Fund Balances		5,060,000
TOTAL LIABILITIES AND FUND BALANCE		$5,075,000

are recognized using the completed transaction method. However, the *Codification* permits governmental units to use the deferral-and-amortization method when the transaction can be described as an exchange. An exchange is defined as follows:

(a) Both the sale and the purchase must be planned simultaneously; that is, each half undertaken in contemplation of the other and each half executed conditioned upon execution of the other;

(b) Both the sale and the purchase must be made on the same day, although settlement of the two transactions may occur on different dates;

(c) The sale and purchase must result in an increase in the net yield to maturity and/or an improvement in the quality of the bond held; and

(d) The purchase must involve an investment-grade bond that is better rated, equally rated, or rated no worse than one investment grade lower than the bond sold.[9]

When *all* these conditions are met, the gain or loss is deferred and amortized over the remaining life of the security sold or purchased, whichever is shorter. The option—recognition or deferral—selected must be applied consistently from one period to the next.

Presentation of Liabilities and Fund Balances. The character of a PERS balance sheet changes under the NCGA *Statement 6* option. The difference between assets, valued according to the preceding principles, and current liabilities to retirees and terminated employees is reported as **net assets available for benefits.** Rather than depict assets equal to liabilities plus fund balance, the liabilities are shown as a reduction in the assets available for payment of benefits.

Exhibit 9-2 shows a summarized version of a PERS balance sheet under *Statement 6.* In this example, the actuarial present value of the obligation plus the current liabilities exceed total assets; therefore, there is an unfunded deficit fund balance. If total assets available for benefits exceed the present value of the projected benefit obligation, the difference is entitled net assets available for future benefits and is added to calculate the total fund balance.

▲   **OBSERVATION**

Despite the GASB's repeated references to the fact that governmental entities may use optional reporting formats, no substantive differences exist between the *Statement 1* and the *Statement 6* presentations. The total of the four reserves in Exhibit 9-1 equals $8,510,000, the exact amount of the total actuarial present value of projected benefits in Exhibit 9-2. The unfunded actuarial present value of $3,450,000 in Exhibit 9-2 equals the unreserved fund balance deficit in Exhibit 9-1.

Measurement and Presentation Under FASB Statement No. 35   Major differences exist between the two NCGA statements and the FASB statement.

[9]GASB, *1993 Codification*, sec. Pe5, ¶118.

Exhibit 9-2

Any Governmental Unit
Statement 6 Presentation
Pension Trust Fund Balance Sheet
As of December 31, 19X1

Assets

Cash	$ 5,000	
Investments	4,860,000	
Receivables	210,000	
Total Assets		$ 5,075,000

Liabilities

Annuities Payable	$ 11,800	
Due to Terminated Employees	3,200	
Total Liabilities		15,000
NET ASSETS AVAILABLE FOR BENEFITS		$ 5,060,000

Fund Balance

Actuarial Present Value of Projected Benefits Payable to—		
Current Retirees and Beneficiaries	$3,900,000	
Terminated Vested Employees	110,000	
Active Employees:		
Member Contributions	1,500,000	
Employer Portion	3,000,000	
Total Actuarial Present Value of Projected Benefits		$ 8,510,000
Unfunded Actuarial Present Value of Credited Projected Benefits		(3,450,000)
TOTAL FUND BALANCE		$ 5,060,000

No balance sheet is required for pension trust funds using the FASB guidance. Instead such plans should report a statement of net assets available for benefits that resembles the top half of a balance sheet prepared in conformity with NCGA *Statement 6.* The FASB statement requires a market value approach to asset valuation. It also provides a different basis for calculating the actuarial present value of projected benefit payments. Under the two NCGA pronouncements, future salary increases are taken into consideration. In contrast, the FASB statement uses current salaries. Other factors being equal, the projected benefit obligation will be larger under the NCGA than under the FASB approach.

Some disclosure requirements differ as well. However, as the following section makes clear, GASB *Statement No. 5* tends to standardize the disclosure requirements regardless of which of the three options is used in accounting for the pension trust.

Effect of GASB Statement No. 5   Issued in 1986, GASB *Statement No. 5* details the disclosure requirements for **pension plans** and **employers.**

Although it does not address the accounting issues, it does, by determining the items to be disclosed, force governmental entities to depict pension obligations as though they had used the accounting methodologies described in the earlier sections.

The disclosure requirements vary by type of plan and character of the financial statements. They vary depending upon whether the employer participates in:

- a single-employer PERS or a multiple-employer agent
- a multiple-employer cost-sharing PERS
- a defined contribution plan

Also, the format for separately issued statements differs from that for statements included in an employer's comprehensive annual financial report.

The detailed disclosure requirements are beyond the scope of this textbook. They are exceedingly complex, and a simple overview is likely to lead to more questions than answers. Additionally, an in-depth analysis is clearer in the context of preparing financial statements and related notes than in the type of display possible in a textbook. However, selected reporting techniques for all types of plans are important to a basic understanding.

One key requirement of GASB *Statement No. 5* is disclosure of the actuarial basis. Regardless of which accounting and reporting option is followed, a standardized measure of the pension obligation must be disclosed in the notes to the financial statements. Previously, the basis used for calculations was also used for disclosure. With the exception of single-employer plans for very small employers, *Statement No. 5* requires disclosure based on a calculation that takes future salaries into consideration even if it is not used for computing the pension obligation.

▲ **OBSERVATION**

Statement No. 5 deals only with disclosure requirements. However, if a unit has to report the calculations using a specific methodology, such reporting might tend over time to also result in standardized accounting practices. Whether this was the GASB's intent is unclear.

A second requirement for all types of pension plans is that all governmental units must recalculate their actuarial values every two years. In the off year, updates are mandated. An update "refers to an estimate or projection of the pension benefit obligation developed by using techniques and procedures considered necessary by the actuary."[10] The *Codification* goes on to explain that if economic conditions (return on assets, population covered, and so forth) are relatively stable, only minor adjustments may be necessary.

The Board felt strongly that whatever accounting methodology is used, the financial statements alone do not provide sufficient information. Therefore, *Statement No. 5* also requires disclosure of ten-year trend data in the statisti-

---

[10] GASB, *1993 Codification*, sec. Pe6, Supplemental Glossary.

cal section. Although they are not included in the auditor's opinion, they are subject to certain prescribed audit procedures. In certain circumstances three-year trend data must be disclosed in the notes to the financial statements. The three-year trend data, when required, are included within the auditor's opinion. Other *Statement No. 5* disclosures are more traditional. They involve an explanation of the pension plan characteristics, such as the type of plan, whether the unit is involved in a cost-sharing arrangement, the period over which any unfunded liability is being amortized, and whether the plan is single- or multiple-employer. Most of these disclosures are considered primary and therefore subject to the auditor's opinion. Exhibit 9-6 contains the basic plan and accounting disclosures for a statewide PERS plan.

Even though the pronouncement relates only to disclosure, the GASB indicated that governmental employers should not "change their pension accounting and reporting to comply with FASB *Statement No. 87* pending issuance of relevant GASB statements."[11]

OBSERVATION ▲

To most employers and plans, the disclosure requirements involve added costs to prepare financial statements. In fact, the GASB deleted some disclosure requirements contained in the exposure draft because of preparers' objections to the costs. However, many statement users may benefit from the additional information.

Although a statement has not been issued, the GASB has selected a framework for the financial reports of pension plans. A portion of that framework was explained in Chapter 4 in connection with the employer accounting requirements. Also, more of the background and the basis for that framework is discussed in Chapter 13. Some of the provisions pertain to pension plan reporting.

Under the framework, and presumably in the final statement, defined benefit pension plans would present a balance sheet, a statement of changes in net assets available for benefits, and two schedules pertaining to required supplementary information.

The balance sheet would include assets, current liabilities, and reserves equal to the net assets. Assets would be valued at market, except for fixed assets used in plan operations, which would be reported at depreciated cost. Because the framework refers only to *current* liabilities, the actuarial benefit obligation will be reported in one of the schedules and not on the balance sheet.

Increases and decreases in net assets during the year would be reported in the statement of changes in net assets. Reporting of depreciation, asset appreciation, or realized gains and losses has not yet been determined.

One of the required schedules would compare the employer's actual contribution rates, as a percentage of payroll, with the actuarially determined

---

[11]Governmental Accounting Standards Board, *Statement No. 5, Disclosure of Pension Information by Public Employee Retirement Systems and State and Local Governmental Employers* (GASB, Stamford, Conn.: 1986), ¶76.

5.	Accounts Payable	21,000	
	Operating Expenses—Benefits	47,000	
	Cash		68,000

Administrative expenses of $150,000 were incurred during the year; $110,000 of that amount was paid.

6.	Operating Expenses—Administration	150,000	
	Accounts Payable		40,000
	Cash		110,000

Several employees retired. Employee and employer contributions plus earnings during the employment period were $180,000 and $259,000, respectively. Carter County adds actual interest to the two reserves so additional investment earnings need not be reclassified.

7.	Fund Balance—Employer Contributions Reserve	259,000	
	Fund Balance—Employee Contributions Reserve	180,000	
	Fund Balance—Benefit Reserve		439,000

Two employees who were vested in the program terminated their employment. An acknowledged amount of $5,600 was owed to these two employees.

| 8. | Operating Expenses—Refunds | 5,600 | |
| | Payable to Terminated Employees | | 5,600 |

At year end, Carter County had a cash balance of $204,150. Officials estimated that only $10,000 of that would be needed before additional cash amounts were received.

| 9. | Investments | 194,150 | |
| | Cash | | 194,150 |

Interest earnings of $151,000 were accrued.

| 10. | Accrued Interest Receivable | 151,000 | |
| | Operating Revenues—Interest | | 151,000 |

Nominal accounts were closed, and the reserve adjusted for current-year contributions.

11.	Operating Revenues—Employer Contributions	1,020,000	
	Operating Revenues—Employee Contributions	860,000	
	Operating Revenues—Interest	325,590	
	Operating Revenues—Gain	880	
	Operating Expenses—Refunds		5,600
	Operating Expenses—Benefits		47,000
	Operating Expenses—Administration		150,000
	Fund Balance—Unreserved, Undesignated		2,003,870

Classifying employer and employee contributions as revenues and benefits payments and refunds as expenses seems contrary to accounting practices for most entities. Pension expense already has been recognized in the fund employing the individuals. To incur another expense when paying the employee seems like double counting. However, the plan is a separate entity. Consequently, inflows to the plan (contributions and earnings) are revenues, and outflows (refunds and benefits) are expenses.

Reserves were established for employer and employee contributions.

12.	Fund Balance—Unreserved, Undesignated	1,880,000	
	Fund Balance—Employer		
	Contributions Reserve		1,020,000
	Fund Balance—Employee		
	Contributions Reserve		860,000

Interest earnings were allocated to the respective reserves, as were the total expenses. After the expenses and earnings are allocated, the fund balance — unreserved, undesignated account reflects only the *unfunded* actuarial deficiency. To simplify the illustration, amounts allocated to each reserve are in proportion to the percentage each beginning reserve bears to the total of all reserves. The net amount to be allocated is $123,870 (325,590 + 880 − [5,600 + 47,000 + 150,000]).

13.	Fund Balance—Unreserved, Undesignated	123,870	
	Fund Balance—Employee Contributions		
	Reserve		47,070
	Fund Balance—Employer		
	Contributions Reserve		68,130
	Fund Balance—Benefits		8,670

The remaining element of accounting for Carter County's pension plan is to recalculate the actuarial present value of the benefit obligation and update the deficiency reserve. The information necessary for this updating comes from the actuary; the actuary indicates that the actuarial present value is $17,014,000. The adjustment to the deficiency reserve is calculated as follows:

Beginning of Year Reserves—	
Employee	$ 5,210,000
Employer	7,516,000
Benefits	928,000
Total Beginning Balance	$13,654,000
Adjustments:	
Employee Contributions	860,000
Employer Contributions	1,020,000
Net Earnings	123,870
Total Year-End Balance	$15,657,870
Actuarial Present Value of Benefit	
Obligation	17,014,000
Year-End Deficiency	$ 1,356,130

14.	Fund Balance—Unreserved,		
	Undesignated ($1,356,130 − $914,000)	442,130	
	Fund Balance—Actuarial		
	Deficiency Reserve		442,130

As shown from the calculations and the resulting balance in the deficiency reserve ($914,000 + $442,130 = $1,356,130), the gap is widening between the actuarial present value and the contributions and earnings. This is vital information both for management and external users of the financial statements.

FINANCIAL STATEMENT PRESENTATIONS FOR FIDUCIARY FUNDS

With one exception, the same financial statements are prepared for nonexpendable trust funds and pension plans. A balance sheet and a statement of revenues, expenses, and changes in fund balance are prepared for both fund types. A cash flow statement is required for nonexpendable trust funds but not for pension plans. A balance sheet and a statement of revenues, expenditures, and changes in fund balance are prepared for an expendable trust fund. The first two fiduciary funds use the flow of total economic resources while the expendable trust uses the flow of current financial resources. This accounts for the differences in the types of financial statements prepared for each fund type.

A balance sheet and a statement of changes in assets are prepared for an agency fund. Because agency funds have no revenues or expenditures, an operating statement is irrelevant.

With the exception of the statement of changes in assets for an agency fund and the disclosure requirements for pension trust funds, the format of the statements for fiduciary funds is similar to those illustrated in other chapters. Therefore, each fund's entire set of financial statements will not be illustrated here.

A balance sheet is illustrated (see Exhibit 9-3) for a nonexpendable trust fund. As Exhibit 9-3 illustrates, the "equity" account is entitled fund balance even though the fund uses full accrual accounting. Perhaps the authoritative literature uses this notation because typically no earnings are retained. If the earnings are distributed to other funds or beneficiaries, only the corpus remains. If under the trust document earnings are added to the corpus, they become part of it. Therefore, no retained earnings exist.

An expendable trust fund's statement of revenues, expenditures, and changes in fund balance is depicted in Exhibit 9-4.

If the comprehensive annual report included an expendable trust fund's operating statement, it would probably be a comparative statement. Whereas comparative statements for several years are common inclusions in annual reports for private businesses, comparative data for only two years are most frequently included for governmental entities.

Exhibit 9-3

Name of Govenmental Entity
Nonexpendable Trust Fund
Balance Sheet
As of December 31, 19X1

Assets

Cash	$ 3,000
Investments	59,000
Interest Receivable	1,000
TOTAL ASSETS	$63,000

Liabilities and Fund Balances

Liabilities:

Accounts Payable	$ 900
Due to Other Funds	1,100
Total Liabilities	$ 2,000

Fund Balances:

Reserved for...	$ 3,000
Unreserved, Undesignated	58,000
Total Fund Balances	$61,000
TOTAL LIABILITIES AND FUND BALANCES	$63,000

Exhibit 9-4

Name of Governmental Entity
Expendable Trust Fund
Statement of Revenues, Expenditures, and Changes in Fund Balance
For the Period Ending December 31, 19X1

Revenues:		
Interest Earnings	$ 1,400	
Contributions	11,200	
Total Revenues		$12,600
Expenditures:		
Operating Expenditures	$ 5,000	
Capital Outlays	2,200	
Total Expenditures	$ 7,200	
Transfers:		
Distribution to General Fund	4,000	
Total Expenditures and Transfers		11,200
Excess of Revenues Over Expenditures and Transfers		$ 1,400
Fund Balance, January 1		2,000
Fund Balance, December 31		$ 3,400

A cash flow statement for a nonexpendable trust fund would be just like the one illustrated earlier for enterprise funds with four sections: noncapital financing, operating, capital and related financing, and investing. Therefore, no illustration is presented here.

A statement of changes in assets and liabilities for agency funds shows the beginning balance, any additions or deletions, and an ending balance. Some agency funds, such as those used to record tax collections for other entities, may have zero beginning and ending balances. If so, the statement would be omitted. Others, such as a deferred compensation agency fund, would have beginning and ending balances. Exhibit 9-5 shows the format of a statement for a deferred compensation program.

Exhibit 9-6 provides note disclosures for a pension trust fund. They are patterned after those contained in the authoritative literature but insofar as possible reflective of the Carter County pension described earlier in the chapter. As Exhibit 9-6 makes clear, only excerpts from the specific notes pertaining to the pension trust fund are included. Bracketed phrases within the notes describe lengthy portions that are excluded to simplify the illustration.

Exhibit 9-5

Name of Governmental Entity
Deferred Compensation Agency Fund
Statement of Changes in Assets and Liabilities
For the Period Ending December 31, 19X1

	Balance January 1, 19X0	Additions	Deletions	Balance December 31, 19X1
Assets				
Cash	$ 1,000	$348,000	$346,000	$ 3,000
Investments	910,000	300,000	-0-	1,210,000
Due from Other Funds	6,200	-0-	6,200	-0-
Interest Receivable	17,160	21,400	17,160	21,400
TOTAL ASSETS	$934,360	$669,400	$369,360	$1,234,400
Liabilities				
Deferred Compensation Benefits Payable	$934,360	$346,000	$ 45,960	$1,234,400

Exhibit 9-6

Carter County
Notes to Financial Statements
December 31, 19X2

Note 1. Summary of Significant Accounting Policies

Included Within the Reporting Entity:

Carter County Public Employees Retirement System. Carter County's public employees participate in the Public Employees Retirement System (PERS). PERS functions for the benefit of these employees and is governed by a five-member pension board of trustees. The trustees are authorized to establish

(continued)

Exhibit 9-6	*(continued)*

benefit levels and to approve actuarial assumptions used in determining contribution levels by employees and Carter County. Funding is established separately from the actuarial present value determinations.

Note 2. Employee Retirement Systems

Full-time employees participate in the PERS, a single-employer, defined benefit pension plan. [A description of the number of active, retired, and terminated but vested employees would follow.]

Employees attaining the age of 55 who have completed 25 or more years of continuous service are entitled to pension benefits of 2.5 percent of their average monthly earnings of the last three years of continuous employment. Early retirement with reduced benefits is permitted if the employee has completed 20 years of continuous service. [Any special provisions, such as disability arrangements, would be disclosed, as would arrangements with beneficiaries.]

If an employee terminates employment before retiring, he or she is entitled to a detailed description of vesting provisions and the amount contributed, if any, by the employee toward the pension program.

The actuarial present value of pension benefits, adjusted for effects of projected salary increases, is disclosed below. This information helps users assess the funding status on a going-concern basis and make comparisons with other public employee retirement plans possible. This measure of the obligation is independent of the basis used for funding purposes. [The actuarial assumptions used in estimating the obligation, including the assumed rate of salary increases, and the return on assets invested in the plan are detailed.]

The unfunded pension obligation totals $_____ . [A schedule showing the composition of the pension obligation by type of employee would be detailed. The total for all employees compared to the net assets available for benefits shows the derivation of the unfunded pension obligation.]

In accordance with contribution requirements, employer contributions totaled $1,020,000 for the year ended December 31, 19X2; employees contributed $860,000. The employer contribution consisted of $_____ for normal costs. No significant changes were made in the actuarial assumptions during the year ended December 31, 19X2. Ten-year historical trend data are presented in the statistical section of this report.

SUMMARY

Governmental entities have four types of fiduciary funds: (1) agency, (2) expendable trust, (3) nonexpendable trust, and (4) pension trust. Agency funds are used when a governmental entity is acting as a custodian for another entity. Tax collections for other governmental units are often accounted for in agency funds, as are deferred compensation programs and special assessment collections when the governmental entity has no obligation for the underlying debt.

If both the interest and principal can be spent, an expendable trust fund is used. Whenever the principal must be maintained in perpetuity, the gift is placed in a nonexpendable trust fund. One common use of an expendable trust fund is for unemployment compensation programs. Public employee retirement systems are accounted for in pension trust funds.

Full accrual accounting is used for both nonexpendable and pension trust funds. The flow of current financial resources model and modified accrual basis are used for expendable trust funds. Because agency funds are used for recording custodial assets, no revenues or expenditures (expenses) are reported in the funds. Accordingly, an accounting basis is not relevant for these funds.

The greatest accounting complexities are associated with the pension trust fund. Although the GASB has ruled on the disclosure requirements, it has not issued a statement on the accounting issues. Preparers have three options for the reporting methodology: NCGA *Statement 1*, NCGA *Statement 6*, or FASB *Statement No. 35*. Regardless of the option chosen, the GASB requires governmental entities to disclose the actuarial present value of the pension obligation and the unfunded portion. The actuarial present value must be calculated using future rather than current salaries. A governmental entity using some other basis for funding must therefore make two sets of calculations and disclose the methodologies used for costing and funding. Preparing the financial statements on one basis and the notes on another will no doubt cause some confusion for financial statement users until the GASB completes its project on pensions.

Selecting the NCGA *Statement 6* option changes the character of the pension plan's balance sheet. It is constructed in a fashion that highlights the net assets available for paying the pension obligation. Under either of the other two options, the traditional "assets = liabilities plus fund balance" format is used. In all three cases, reservations of fund balance are separately identified for employer and employee contributions and benefits for retirees. Any difference between the funding and actuarial present value of the total obligation (under whichever accounting methodology the entity chooses) results in a deficit fund balance.

A balance sheet is prepared for all fiduciary funds. A statement of revenues, expenses, and changes in fund balance is prepared for the pension trust and the nonexpendable trust funds. An operating statement also is prepared for the expendable trust, but because the accounting methodology is different, the title refers to expenditures rather than to expenses. A cash flow statement is prepared for nonexpendable trust funds. A balance sheet and a statement of changes in assets are prepared for agency funds.

QUESTIONS

9-1 What types of fiduciary funds do governmental entities establish? How do they differ?

9-2 What are some of the uses for an agency fund? How would you determine when an agency fund is being used improperly?

9-3 Describe circumstances under which a governmental entity might open an expendable and a nonexpendable trust fund for related purposes.

9-4 Distinguish between a pension plan and the employer. Describe where the activities of each are accounted for in a governmental entity.

9-5 What options are available to governmental entities in accounting for public employee retirement plans?

9-6 Explain the relationship(s) between display/reporting and accounting aspects of public employee retirement systems. How does one influence the other?

9-7 Explain precisely the difference(s) between accounting and reporting under NCGA's *Statement 6* and NCGA's *Statement 1*.

9-8 How are gains or losses on fixed-income securities recognized under NCGA *Statement 6?*

9-9 Should pension accounting be the same for governmental and business entities? Explain.

9-10 What are the key differences between FASB *Statement No. 35* and the two NCGA statements, *Statement 1* and *Statement 6,* on pension accounting/reporting?

9-11 Explain the effect of GASB *Statement No. 5* on the accounting/reporting of pensions for governmental entities.

9-12 In what fund would the accounting for a governmental grant for distribution to local school districts occur? Explain your selection.

9-13 What focus and basis of accounting are used for nonexpendable trust funds? Why?

9-14 A city received a gift that ultimately will be used to restore a historical painting in the courthouse. For the first ten years, the gift is to remain inviolate, and any earnings added to the principal. After the first ten years, subsequent earnings are to be used to restore and maintain the painting. What fund should the city use? Does the type of fund change after the first ten years? Explain.

9-15 What accounting practices apply to expendable trust funds? Why do they differ from those used for nonexpendable trust funds?

9-16 What is a deferred compensation program? What accounting issues relate to these programs?

9-17 Explain the circumstances under which the collection aspects of a special assessment bond issue would be handled in an agency fund.

9-18 What financial statements are prepared for an agency fund? Explain.

9-19 A donor established a scholarship fund in which both the principal gift and any earnings can be awarded as scholarships. What fund should the county use to record the gift, earnings, and scholarships?

CASES

9-1 A governmental entity decides to establish an investment pool to which several funds will contribute their idle cash. Some of the participating funds may invest through the pool for a lengthy period. Others will be in and out of the fund on a short-term basis. The city treasurer will manage the funds, giving each fund its proportional share of net earnings (interest and dividends less administrative costs).

REQUIRED

1. In what fund should the accounting for the investment pool be handled? Does the city have any options in terms of the fund used? Explain.
2. Without prejudicing your answer, what would your response be to the city finance director who wants to account for the pool in an agency fund?

9-2   Several years ago, a wealthy benefactor gave $400,000 to the city with the understanding that the earnings on the principal amount would be used to provide access for the handicapped. The trust specified that the principal was to be maintained in perpetuity. The city has not violated the intent of the trust document, and it has not been revised. However, the principal amount in the fund is now $260,000. One member of the city council wants an explanation of how this decline could have occurred without violation of the trust.

REQUIRED

Draft a report to the city council member explaining how this decrease might have occurred.

9-3   On January 1, 19X1, Drexal Township began a pension program for its employees. The township manager must decide what accounting and reporting options will be adopted by Drexal before year end. She reports to you that with all the options available for accounting and portraying financial information, she cannot decide which option is best for the pension trust fund. The manager indicates that the main objectives are clarity of presentation and avoidance of duplicate information. Also, she thinks investments should be reported at cost, lower of cost or market, or amortized cost.

REQUIRED

1. Analyze the options available to Drexal with the township manager's objectives in mind.
2. Is it possible to satisfy all her objectives with a single methodology? Why or why not?

9-4   Belarmey County is reassessing its fund structure. In particular, the county finance officer is trying to decide how many agency and expendable and nonexpendable trust funds should be maintained for its current activities. Activities related to the question are described below:

1. The county has 8,000 employees representing several different unions and personnel classifications. Over half of the employees are paid through the general fund; some of them are paid through the capital projects fund when the county undertakes its own construction activities. The remaining 4,000 are employed by all other funds, including proprietary, fiduciary, and special revenue.
2. The county manages a life estate for a previous county council member. It is a large estate, and during her life, the spouse receives 50 percent of the earnings with the remaining 50 percent going to the county. When the spouse dies, the principal will revert to the county. However, only earnings can be spent in the first ten years after her death.
3. State revenue sharing programs are funneled through Belarmey to its school districts and other quasi-governmental agencies located in the county. The amount distributed to each one depends upon the programs it undertakes and the quality of its work. Any money not distributed can be used by the county through an application process to the state revenue sharing offices.

4. The county has established a loan and scholarship program for those enrolling in the local vocational-technical school. Several years ago, the county commissioners set aside $100,000 for this purpose. The motion approving the program suggested that loans and scholarships be limited to earnings on the principal unless the recipient's circumstances represented a true hardship case.

5. Each year the county solicits contributions from local businesses to fund its economic development agency. The agency funds organizational costs, provides property-tax relief, and prepares marketing information for new and prospective businesses.

REQUIRED

Explain which fiduciary funds, and how many of each, Belarmey needs for the activities described above. If a particular activity should not be operated out of a fiduciary fund, indicate in which fund the accounting should be reflected.

9-5 A western state uses generally accepted accounting and financial reporting standards for its fiduciary funds. Recently it published comprehensive financial statements in which statements for individual fiduciary funds appeared. A legislator on an oversight committee writes that the financial statements are confusing in a number of regards. His concerns are:

1. The balance sheet for an expendable trust fund contains fixed assets but the operating statement for the same fund shows no depreciation.

2. Collection activities for one special assessment activity appear in an agency fund, while those for another special assessment project are reflected in a debt service fund.

3. Figures reflecting the actuarial present value for the pension obligation appearing in the financial statement do not agree with those in the notes to the financial statement.

4. The deferred compensation program established for employees appears in the financial statements. The legislator points out that the state has not contributed to that program, and yet the investments show as assets of the state.

REQUIRED

Bearing in mind that the legislator is not an accountant, prepare a report responding to his concerns.

EXERCISES

9-1 Using the information pertaining to Raleigh, North Carolina, contained in Appendix A of the textbook, answer the following questions:

1. What fiduciary funds does Raleigh have? What financial statements are shown (for example, for individual funds, combining, combined) for these funds?

2. Are the various fiduciary funds defined and explained in the notes to the financial statements? Why or why not?

3. Is the pension program for the bulk of Raleigh's employees fully funded?

9-2 Select the best answer for each question.

1. Which of the following funds of a governmental unit currently uses the same accounting as a special revenue fund?

   a. nonexpendable trust fund

   b. pension trust fund

   c. expendable trust fund

   d. none of the above

2. A gift received from donors who have stipulated that the principal is nonexpendable but the income generated may be expended for maintaining public facilities would be accounted for in:

   a. an endowment fund

   b. a nonexpendable trust fund

   c. an expendable trust fund

   d. a nonexpendable and expendable trust funds

3. The following proceeds received and spent by Grove City in 19X7 were legally restricted for specific purposes:

Donation by a benefactor mandated to provide meals for the needy	$300,000
Sales taxes to finance the maintenance of tourist facilities in a shopping district	$900,000

What amounts should be accounted for in Grove City's expendable trust funds?

   a. $0

   b. $300,000

   c. $900,000

   d. $1,200,000

(Adapted from the November 1988 CPA Exam, Practice, Part II, #44)

4. Which of the following funds would include retained earnings in its balance sheet?

   a. agency

   b. nonexpendable trust fund

   c. expendable trust fund

   d. none of the above

5. Which of the following statements would not be prepared for an expendable trust fund?

   a. balance sheet

   b. statement of revenues, expenditures, and changes in fund balance

   c. cash flow statement

   d. none of the above

6. To qualify as an exchange transaction for purposes of determining the treatment of gains and losses on fixed-income securities:

   a. the sale and purchase must be made on the same day

   b. both the sale and the purchase must be planned simultaneously

    c. the sale and purchase must increase the net yield or improve the quality of the bond held

    d. all of the above

7. Which of the following is not an option for accounting and reporting practices of pension funds in governmental units?

    a. FASB *Statement No. 35*

    b. NCGA *Statement 6*

    c. NCGA *Statement 1*

    d. APB *Opinion No. 8*

8. A primary purpose of GASB *Statement No. 5* is:

    a. to change the accounting methodology for pensions

    b. to expand the display requirements beyond those in *Statement No. 35*

    c. to require disclosure of the actuarial present value of the benefit obligation using a particular methodology

    d. to require one-year valuation and update periods

9. Grant entitlement programs in which the governmental unit has no discretion in distributing should be accounted for in:

    a. a nonexpendable trust fund

    b. an agency fund

    c. a special revenue fund

    d. none of the above

10. If the general fund billed a nonexpendable trust fund for work done on its behalf, the payment would be recorded by the trust fund as:

    a. an expenditure

    b. a transfer

    c. an expense

    d. a reduction of income

9-3 Select the best answer for each question.

1. "Dual" reporting of a grant or entitlement program typically would involve:

    a. showing memo entries in an agency fund and revenue/expenditure entries in the fund responsible for the activity

    b. showing memo entries in the fund responsible for the activity and revenue/expenditure entries in an agency fund

    c. showing revenue/expenditure entries in an agency fund and in the fund responsible for the activity

    d. showing memo entries in an agency fund and in the fund responsible for the activity

2. If the actuarial present value of a government pension program is $3,800,000, any unfunded liability will be determined by:

    a. comparing $3,800,000 and the amounts contributed thus far by employees and employer

    b. comparing $3,800,000 to the pension cost since inception of the plan

    c. comparing $3,800,000 with the benefits paid to date and those recognized during the current year

      d. comparing $3,800,000 with the total assets available for benefit payments

3. What basis of accounting is used for a nonexpendable trust fund?
    a. full accrual accounting
    b. flow of total financial resources
    c. modified accrual
    d. cash basis

4. In accounting for a nonexpendable trust fund, the difference between assets and liabilities is:
    a. retained earnings
    b. net assets available for trust use
    c. fund balance
    d. none of the above

5. Under an unemployment assistance program, a $5,000 advance from the federal to the state government would be recorded as:

	Dr.	Cr.
a. Cash	5,000	
Due to Federal Government		5,000
b. Advance from Federal Government	5,000	
Due to Federal Government		5,000
c. Cash	5,000	
Contributed Capital		5,000
d. Cash	5,000	
Due to Beneficiary		5,000

6. Expendable trust funds probably would recognize pledges as revenue when:
    a. cash is received
    b. the money is spent
    c. the pledge is legally enforceable
    d. the pledge is made

7. One required use of agency funds is:
    a. investment pools
    b. special assessment collection and disbursement when the government is liable for the underlying debt
    c. Section 457 deferred compensation plans
    d. money set aside for special purposes by oversight board

8. A special assessment annual levy is $500,000; the total tax levy related to the same special assessment project for which the government is not liable totals $5,000,000. In the first year, the tax levy entry would be recorded as:

	Dr.	Cr.
a. Special Assessment Taxes		
Receivable	500,000	
Due to Bondholders		500,000
b. Special Assessment Taxes		
Receivable	500,000	
Revenue—Taxes		500,000

	Dr.	Cr.
c. Special Assessment Taxes		
Receivable	5,000,000	
Deferred Taxes		4,500,000
Due to Bondholders		500,000
d. Special Assessment Taxes		
Receivable	5,000,000	
Due to Bondholders		5,000,000

9. A PERS must be one of the following types:
   a. a noncontributory defined benefit program
   b. a noncontributory defined contribution program
   c. a defined benefit program
   d. none of the above

10. A pension trust fund with assets of $15,000,000, current liabilities of $2,000,000, and an unfunded actuarial present value of projected benefits of $3,000,000 has assets available for benefits of:
    a. $15,000,000
    b. $13,000,000
    c. $10,000,000
    d. $0

9-4 A number of governmental activities are described below. Identify the type of fund to be established by the local government for each activity. If more than one fund could be used to account for the activity, explain all possibilities.

1. A donor contributed $50,000 to establish a loan fund for employees. Both the principal and interest can be used to make loans.
2. A state has a defined benefit pension program, and all state and local governmental employees participate in the program. The local governments do not contribute to the program, but employees at the local level contribute 1 percent of their annual salary to the pension program.
3. Local governments participate in an entitlement program from the federal government. The entitlements may be used for any lawful purpose, as long as the annual reports pertaining to the federal program are received by the federal agency within one month after the close of its fiscal period. The federal and local governments have different fiscal-year ends but use the same basis of accounting.
4. Local businesses raised money for a governmental economic development program. One member of the group was a banker who is responsible for controlling the funds. He established a trust account in the bank and disburses the money to the governmental entity when he receives vouchers from the entity.
5. The local government issued a challenge to its aging-services division. It agreed to match every dollar raised from private sources. During the year, $80,000 was raised from private sources for transporting senior citizens.

9-5 Dooley's city swimming pool is maintained and staffed in part by the earnings from a nonexpendable trust fund. The trust corpus must remain inviolate, but gains and losses on securities represent adjustments to principal. The trust's assets include a rental unit, marketable securities, and cash. On the first day of Fiscal 19X1 the corpus totaled $560,000. The following transactions occurred during Fiscal 19X1.

1. Interest earnings of $18,600 were collected; of that total, $2,200 had been accrued at the end of 19X0.
2. Securities costing $3,100 were sold for $3,900; the proceeds were reinvested.
3. Rental revenues totaled $46,000; related expenses amounted to $13,600, of which $12,000 was paid in cash.
4. Depreciation on the rental facility was $21,200.
5. Interest on investments of $1,800 was accrued at year end.
6. Net earnings were transferred to Dooley's expendable trust fund for use in maintaining and staffing the city's swimming pool.
7. Nominal accounts were closed.
8. $1,000 cash was retained for paying bills; the rest was invested.

REQUIRED

1. Prepare the journal entries for Dooley's nonexpendable trust fund.
2. Prepare the journal entry for Dooley's expendable trust fund.

9-6 The state of Alahoma has a defined benefit pension program in which all state and local government employees participate. A statewide Board of Investments manages the pension program. During 19X3, employees contributed $713,000, and employers contributed $1,300,000. Interest earnings, all received in cash, totaled $410,000, and investments costing $427,000 were sold for $345,000. Retiring employees had accumulated $235,000 in the pension program; employer contributions for the same employees were $410,000. Two employees with vested rights in the pension program terminated during the year; employee and employer contributions totaled $67,000 and $83,000, respectively. Benefits of $162,000 were paid to retired employees. Idle cash of $3,500,000 was invested.

The various reserves had the following balances on January 1, 19X3:

Employee Contributions Reserve	$17,532,000
Employer Contributions Reserve	21,960,000
Benefit Reserve	2,480,000
Fund Balance—Actuarial Deficiency Reserve	1,890,000

The actuary informed Alahoma that the actuarial present value of the pension obligation was $46,195,000 at year end.

REQUIRED

1. Prepare the journal entries for Alahoma's pension trust fund for 19X3. Closing entries and earnings distributions to reserves may be ignored.
2. Calculate the balance in the actuarial deficiency reserve on December 31, 19X3.

9-7 The 19X1 trial balance for a Duval County trust fund appears below:

Duval County
Trust Fund Trial Balance
As of December 31, 19X1

	Dr.	Cr.
Cash	$ 13,000	
Accrued Interest Receivable	5,200	
Rent Receivable	1,100	
Investments	190,000	
Fixed Assets	280,000	
Accumulated Depreciation		$ 42,000
Accounts Payable		3,100
Due to Other Funds		1,700
Operating Expenses	31,000	
Operating Transfers	29,510	
Nonoperating Revenues		6,310
Operating Revenues		56,000
Nonoperating Expenses	1,800	
Fund Balance—Unreserved, Undesignated		14,900
Fund Balance—Reserved for Services to the Handicapped		427,600
Totals	$551,610	$551,610

REQUIRED

1. To what type of trust does the trial balance pertain? Explain.
2. Prepare an appropriate operating statement for the trust for the year ending December 31, 19X1.

9-8 Pooley County has established a deferred compensation program for its employees. A trial balance for the year ending December 31, 19X1, follows:

Pooley County
Deferred Compensation Program
Agency Fund
Post-Closing Trial Balance
As of December 31, 19X1

Cash	$ 10,000	
Investments	482,000	
Accrued Interest Receivable	1,200	
Due from Other Funds	7,600	
Deferred Compensation Liabilities		$500,800
Totals	$500,800	$500,800

Transactions occurring during 19X2 included:

1. Employees set aside a total of $268,000 from their salaries as part of the deferred compensation program.
2. The deferred compensation fund collected the amount withheld during the current year plus $2,000 of the amount owing at year end 19X1.

3. Accrued interest receivable was collected, as was $43,380 additional interest on the fund's investments.
4. Investments costing $9,100 were sold for $9,400.
5. One employee retired and withdrew the entire $13,100 she had in the deferred compensation program.
6. The general fund charges one-half of 1 percent for investing the funds. The charge is applied to the investment balance as of December 31 of the prior year. The charge was recongnized but not paid.
7. Any excess cash above $10,000 was invested.

REQUIRED

1. Prepare the journal entries for the fund accounting for deferred compensation programs for the year ending December 31, 19X2.
2. Prepare any related journal entries in any other fund(s) affected by the transactions recorded in part 1.

9-9   Using the data from exercise 9-8, prepare a statement of changes in assets and liabilities for Pooley's deferred compensation agency fund.

9-10   The city of Trowbridge has several fiduciary funds. The city's bookkeeper is new and inexperienced. He prepared a combined trial balance for all three funds: a group insurance agency fund, an expendable trust fund, and a nonexpendable trust fund. The combined trial balance appears below:

City of Trowbridge
Fiduciary Funds
Combined Trial Balance
As of December 31, 19X7

Assets		
Cash	$ 80,000	
Short-Term Investments	740,000	
Receivables:		
Accrued Interest	7,400	
Other	1,100	
Due from Other Entities	14,650	
Due from Other Funds	147,000	
Liabilities and Fund Balance		
Accounts Payable		$151,820
Premiums Withheld		25,070
Due to Other Funds		11,900
Fund Balance:		
Unreserved		706,580
Reserved		94,780
Totals	$990,150	$990,150

ADDITIONAL INFORMATION

1. The total fund balance for the expendable trust is $94,780.
2. The expendable trust fund owes external suppliers a total of $15,120.
3. The nonexpendable trust fund has investments of $700,000 and $10,680 in cash.

4. The group insurance agency fund has $9,320 in cash and total assets of $161,770.
5. The federal government owes Trowbridge $14,650 for its group insurance program.
6. The group insurance fund owes external agencies a total of $136,700 for insurance coverage.
7. Earnings on the nonexpendable trust fund, which are initially recorded in the nonexpendable trust fund and later accounted for in the expendable trust fund, totaled $10,300.
8. Accrued interest on endowed assets held by the nonexpendable trust fund is $6,200.

REQUIRED

Prepare a working paper showing the combined totals and the allocations to each type of fiduciary fund.

9-11 River County has two school districts—Upper Hills and Lower Hills. The board of each district determines the amount of its mill levy, but the property owners are billed by the county along with a county property tax. The county collects all taxes and then sends the proper amount to each district. An agency fund was established to account for the property tax. The accountant in charge understands that some fiduciary funds use full accrual accounting, so he has kept the records on that basis. The year-end trial balance follows:

River County
Agency Fund
Trial Balance
December 31, 19X2

	Dr.	Cr.
Cash	$ 23,500	
Taxes Receivable—Current	493,000	
Allowance for Uncollectible Taxes—Current		$ 17,890
Taxes Receivable—Delinquent	6,400	
Allowance for Uncollectible Taxes—Delinquent		1,290
Due to General Fund		4,700
Revenues—Upper Hills		615,600
Revenues—Lower Hills		334,620
Expenses—Upper Hills	3,030	
Expenses—Lower Hills	1,670	
Fund Balance—Upper Hills	287,850	
Fund Balance—Lower Hills	158,650	
	$974,100	$974,100

ADDITIONAL INFORMATION

1. Property taxes are levied in two equal installments due on December 31 and June 30. When the second installment is levied, any receivable remaining from the first is reclassified as delinquent.

2. The general fund charges a 1 percent administrative fee on all cash collected. The general fund properly records this as a revenue.

3. On August 31, any cash that has been collected, less a 5 percent reserve, is remitted to the school districts. (The accountant debited fund balance.)

4. Upper Hills levies a total of $648,000 annually.

5. The percentage of uncollectible taxes has been stable over the past few years. The amount applicable to Lower Hills is 1 percent.

6. No cash has yet been collected from the December 31 levy.

7. During the year, $15,000 in uncollectible taxes was written off for Upper Hills.

REQUIRED

1. Prepare the necessary entries to adjust the agency fund trial balance.

2. Determine how much of the accounts that would appear on a corrected trial balance pertains to each school district.

CHAPTER 10

Financial Reporting for
Governmental Units

Financial reporting is the systematic arrangement of accounting data to satisfy specific informational needs. It encompasses financial statements, internal (management) reports, and specific purpose external reports. Compared to that of businesses, financial reporting for governmental units is complicated by the existence of separate funds within a unit and the practice of displaying each fund separately without consolidation. Because of the proliferation of entities receiving financial or operating support from a number of governmental units, preparers also have difficulty determining what peripheral entities should be included in each unit's report.

In its initial concepts statement, the Governmental Accounting Standards Board listed three reporting objectives for governmental entities: (1) to demonstrate and assess accountability, (2) to enable financial statement users to evaluate operating results, and (3) to enable users to judge a unit's financial position and productive resources. The GASB is gradually issuing accounting pronouncements that will improve governments' reporting to users. However, the clarity of a financial report is dependent, in large part, on the precision and specificity of the principles defining the underlying accounting practices. Consequently, until the GASB establishes accounting principles in all areas that materially affect financial reports, these reports might not be comparable among units. Display and disclosure elements also will be improved as overall consistency among accounting principles is achieved.

This chapter focuses primarily on the *financial statements,* which are one type of financial report. Some internal and special purpose reports are discussed, but the emphasis is on the financial statements. Common display and disclosure elements are discussed, as are some specific notes required by GASB pronouncements. The chapter also includes a discussion of the reporting unit.

FINANCIAL REPORTING WITHIN GOVERNMENT

Financial reporting within government differs from business financial reporting. In business, the principal characteristics of the financial statements are described briefly and presented in an annual report, which also includes an auditor's opinion and certain note disclosures. In government, annual reports include a myriad of statements, beginning with highly summarized statements and ending with detailed data about each fund. The GASB describes in some detail the form and content of financial statements for each level of detail.

Interest in financial reporting is much broader for governmental units than for private business. Investors and creditors are the principal interested parties in the private sector. In contrast, governmental financial reports are of interest to a wide variety of users. Those interested in governmental financial reporting can be grouped in three main categories: (1) citizen groups (for example, taxpayers, service consumers, and voters); (2) oversight bodies (for example, legislators, county commissioners, and city councils); and (3) investors/creditors (for example, bondholders, suppliers, and joint venture partners). Not only are the interested parties diverse, but their specific interests cover almost every aspect of a governmental entity. With a wide range of people having broad interests, some common elements of interest must be identified. Otherwise, a governmental entity would be providing an individual report to each group.

As the GASB's concepts statement makes clear, financial reports should allow users to assess accountability and examine interperiod equity. In assessing accountability the report user wants to know, for example, if the unit operated within its budget, what service levels were maintained, and what was accomplished. Examining interperiod equity is more narrowly focused: to what extent did the current generation pay for the services it received during the year?

The broad goals of assessing accountability and interperiod equity translate into three reporting objectives:

1. To enable users to assess an entity's accountability, including its ability to maintain interperiod equity
2. To enable users to assess the entity's operating results, including its ability to finance activities and meet cash requirements
3. To assist users in assessing the level of services that can be provided by the governmental entity and its ability to meet obligations as they become due.

The GASB-defined objectives were developed long after governmental financial reporting practices. Many of the new concepts and requirements are being superimposed on existing formats and accounting systems. This freqently means that preparers must develop information from sources outside the accounting system to meet reporting requirements. It also means that data disclosed in notes are not always consistent with that in the financial statements. Pension accounting and reporting is probably the best example: one accounting principle may be used in the financial statements, while another is disclosed in the notes.

Types and Nature of Financial Reporting in Government

Types of Financial Reports   Financial reporting can be defined in terms of the reports' content. Financial statements, special-purpose external reports, and internal (management) reports constitute the most common types of governmental financial reports. As Exhibit 10-1 shows, financial statements encompass an operating statement, a balance sheet, and, for some activities, a cash flow statement or a statement of changes in assets. As explained in more detail later in the chapter, governmental financial statements can be prepared for each individual fund, for all funds of a given type, or for all funds and account groups combined.

Special purpose reports are prepared for specific types of users, for example, bondholders. They also report on a specific aspect of the government for all users, such as a detailed narrative/financial report on a large construction project. They typically are patterned after, but show more detail than, one of the financial statements. For example, a governmental entity might prepare an operating statement showing the revenues and expenses associated with all grant/entitlement programs, but it also might prepare a separate report on each program. Nonfinancial special purpose reports are common to larger governmental entities. Providing special reports on procurement activities is one example. Such a report would cover purchase orders issued and contracts entered into during the reporting period. It might include dollar volume or efficiency measures, such as the average length of time between placement of the order and receipt of the merchandise or service.

Internal or management reports usually are of three types: (1) statements showing individual revenue and expense items, or assets and liabilities; (2) projections for specific activities under various taxing or funding assumptions; and (3) narrative reports analyzing accounting information. Reports showing

[handwritten margin notes: "Special purpose → external reports" and "Internal or mgmt reports"]

Exhibit 10-1

Types and Nature of Financial Reports for Governmental Entities

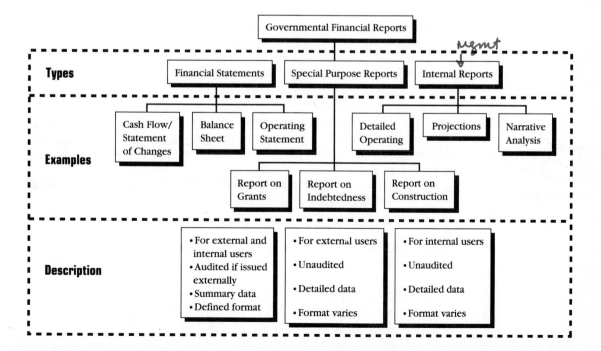

functional expenses, without regard to fund, is an example of the first type of report. Managers often project operating statements under various assumptions before the budget is presented to an oversight board, an example of the second type of internal report. Narrative reports take the form of feasibility studies or comparative analyses of specific years or administrative units.

interim reports / mangers / compliance → w/ oversight intent

Reporting Patterns   Financial reports can be classified in terms of timing—that is, some are interim and others are annual. Annual reports are distributed broadly to all external users, but interim reports usually are given only to internal users and perhaps key members of oversight boards.

Interim Reports. The primary purpose of interim reports is to determine how well managers are complying with oversight intent. Thus, most interim reports provide budgetary comparisons or progress reports on the amount or percentage of revenues earned and expenditures/expenses incurred. Comparisons between actual revenues for the current and prior years also provide useful information to oversight boards. Balance sheets may be included but are not as important for management and compliance reporting during the interim periods as are operating statements.

Because interim reports are used to measure performance, they do not always reflect generally accepted accounting principles (GAAP). For example, if the governmental unit does not follow GAAP in preparing its budget (if it uses a cash basis), it prepares interim reports on the budgetary rather than on the GAAP accounting basis.

The fact that interim reports are prepared almost entirely for internal use does not diminish their importance. One of GASB's accounting principles is devoted to interim reporting. The principle allows non-GAAP reporting and refers to the management focus:

> Interim reports typically are prepared primarily for internal use. Thus, they usually are prepared on the budgetary basis and often do not include statements reporting general fixed assets or general long-term debt. Further, they may properly contain budgetary or cash flow projections and other information deemed pertinent to effective management control during the year.[1]

The frequency of interim reporting varies among governmental entities. Some prepare monthly reports, while others provide semiannual or quarterly reports. Most authoritative sources suggest preparing operating statements and budget and actual comparisons on a monthly basis. Balance sheets, however, could be prepared on a quarterly or semiannual basis.

annual reports / managerial performan

Annual Reports. Annual reports represent an entity's performance for the fiscal period and its financial status at the end of the period. Oversight boards use them to judge managerial performance. Service recipients use them to evaluate actual and budgeted service levels. Taxpayers and most other report readers examine the extent to which the unit stayed within budgetary constraints and taxing limitations. Bond rating agencies and current and pro-

---

[1]Governmental Accounting Standards Board, *1993 Codification* (Norwalk, Conn.: GASB, 1993), sec. 2900, ¶101.

spective bondholders use annual reports to verify the unit's ability to meet interest and principal payments.

A government's annual report is referred to as a **Comprehensive Annual Financial Report (CAFR)**. Like annual reports for businesses, it contains some narrative as well as financial data. Primary financial statements are included, as are note disclosures and summary statistical information. Unlike annual business reports, however, information on individual fund types is included. Consolidated financial statements are not prepared when more than one governmental unit is included within the operating unit, as they often are for businesses.

COMPREHENSIVE ANNUAL FINANCIAL REPORT

The content of the comprehensive annual financial report is complicated by the fund structure and accounting basis used by governmental units. Requiring a balance sheet, operating statement, and statement of changes in assets or cash flow statement does not provide adequate guidance: Are the statements for each fund, for each fund type, or for the entity as a whole included? Since some funds integrate the budget into the accounting records, should the budgetary data be included as well? Some funds use the economic resources model while others use the current financial resources model; how are the differences among funds reflected?

The GASB and its predecessor, the NCGA, use a pyramid concept to explain what ought to be included in a comprehensive annual financial report. As Exhibit 10-2 shows, the "pyramid" begins with highly aggregated summary data and ends with the individual transactions taken from the accounting records. Between these two extremes are the combined, combining, and individual fund/account group financial statements.

As the bracket to the left of the chart indicates, neither the extreme detail nor the highly summarized data are necessarily included in the CAFR. Rather, the CAFR includes combined and combining statements, and perhaps individual fund and account group statements and selected schedules. In summarizing the information contained in the pyramid, the GASB notes:

> The governmental unit need go only as far down the reporting pyramid—in terms of increasing levels of detail—as necessary to report the financial position and operating results of its individual funds and account groups, to demonstrate compliance with financial-related legal and contractual requirements, and to assure adequate disclosure at the individual fund entity level. Those statements and schedules necessary for these purposes are required; others are optional.[2]

Governmental units must exercise judgment to determine which statements are included in the CAFR. As indicated above, the key is to provide enough

[2]Ibid., sec. 1900, ¶114.

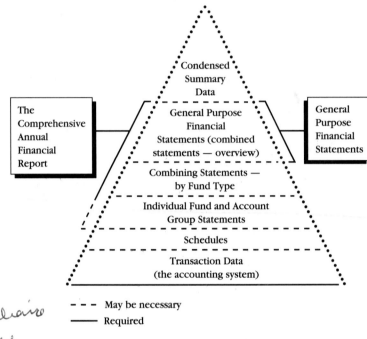

Exhibit 10-2

The Financial Reporting Pyramid

Condensed
Summary
Data

The Comprehensive Annual Financial Report

General Purpose Financial Statements (combined statements — overview)

General Purpose Financial Statements

Combining Statements — by Fund Type

Individual Fund and Account Group Statements

Schedules

Transaction Data (the accounting system)

- - - - May be necessary
———— Required

[handwritten margin notes:]

P
A
R

Key
① demonstrate compliance
② adequate disclosure
③ report financial position & operating results

detail to demonstrate compliance, to ensure adequate disclosure, and to report financial position and operating results.

This brief statement not only addresses what statements ought to be included but also what form they should take. For example, for those funds where budgetary information is integrated into the accounting records, the budgetary/actual comparisons should be included in the CAFR. Otherwise, the governmental unit would not be demonstrating compliance — in this case, compliance with budgetary constraints.

Combined Financial Statements

Combined financial statements present summary data for each fund type. As the combined balance sheet shown in Exhibit 10-3 (p. 370–371) illustrates, these statements provide an overview of the more detailed statements and schedules that follow. In a combined financial statement, data for all funds of a given type are shown in a single column. For example, regardless of how many special revenue funds this unit had, the assets of all of them are combined into a single column on this balance sheet.

Combined financial statements allow governmental entities to show their entire operations or financial position on a single page (or facing pages). The far right column shows a total for all funds and account groups. Because the statements are *combined* and not *consolidated*, the column total is referred to as "Memo Only." The reference to Memo Only also is necessary because the summation includes fund totals with different accounting bases. For example, the assets of proprietary funds in which the full accrual basis is applied are added to those of governmental funds in which the current financial resources model is used. As a result, the total column has little meaning.

Combined financial statements may be difficult for some to understand. Preparers should make every effort to make them as readable as possible. To improve the readability of the statements, governmental entities should precede the statements with a divider page explaining their nature and purpose. Also, if the asset side of the combined balance sheet includes "amounts to be provided" from the account groups, the column should be entitled "assets and other debits." The fund equity section of the combined balance sheet includes equity of a number of types. Therefore, it should be clearly segregated into the various types: fund balances, contributed capital, retained earnings, and the self-balancing figure "investment in general fixed assets," from the general fixed asset account group.

Combining Financial Statements

The next level of detail included in the CAFR is the combining statements. In contrast to combined financial statements, **combining statements** show a separate column for each fund of a particular type or account group. A combining operating statement for debt service funds is shown in Exhibit 10-4 (p. 372). Although only an operating statement is shown here, the same general principles apply to the combining balance sheet and statement of cash flow or changes in assets.

The fourth column shows the total for all three debt service funds. Because the interfund transactions have not been eliminated, the total column is entitled "Memo Only." The total column for a given fund type in the combining statements should agree with the total shown for that fund type in the combined statement.

Combining and *combined* statements usually differ in terms of the detail provided. For example, a governmental unit's combined balance sheet might have five asset classifications: cash, investments, receivables, fixed assets, and other. More detail might be provided in a combining statement, for example, cash, several investment classes, two or more receivables classes, and so forth.

The combining statements should not be quite as confusing to readers as the combined statements. These statements do not combine funds with different accounting practices, but titling should be carefully considered to avoid any possible confusion. For example, the term *reimbursement* should not be used as a title for any revenue source. Reimbursements reduce expenditures rather than increase revenues. Governments may include the capital outlays of governmental funds as a current expenditure; if so, this should be clear to statements users and used consistently for all governmental funds.

When financial data for several funds are shown on the same page, one source of confusion pertains to the transfers among funds. The transfers in and transfers out should never be netted for a single fund or for the total column. Further, to make sure readers distinguish between equity and operating transfers, each should be clearly labeled. Similarly, principal and interest

*ex —
one for
Debt Service
Funds*

Exhibit 10-3

Governmental Unit
Combined Balance Sheet
All Fund Types and Account Groups
June 30, 19X2
($000)

	GOVERNMENTAL FUND TYPES				PROPRIETARY FUND TYPES		FIDUCIARY FUND TYPES	ACCOUNT GROUPS		TOTALS (MEMO ONLY)	
	General	Special Revenue	Debt Service	Capital Projects	Enterprise	Internal Service	Trust and Agency	General Fixed Assets	General Long-Term Obliga-tions	June 30, 19X2	June 30, 19X1
Assets and Other Debits											
Cash and Cash Equivalents	$11,200	$133,100	$43,000	$17,600	$ 2,500	$12,900	$ 518,200	$	$	$ 738,500	$ 775,800
Cash with Fiscal Agent	—	1,500	2,300	—	1,900	2,900	—	—	—	8,600	18,100
Receivables (Net)	19,800	22,700	3,400	900	9,900	800	62,100	—	—	119,600	135,600
Interfund Loans Receivable	7,000	36,100	—	—	—	200	3,200	—	—	46,500	36,000
Due from Other Governments	2,800	27,400	—	—	—	—	300	—	—	30,500	48,300
Due from Other Funds	43,300	38,000	200	100	700	7,300	38,700	—	—	128,300	154,600
Inventories	1,800	17,400	—	—	6,600	2,700	—	—	—	28,500	33,100
Advances to Investment Pool	—	24,500	4,000	11,100	9,700	1,900	372,300	—	—	423,500	418,500
Long-Term Notes/Loans Receivable	400	10,400	13,900	100	494,800	100	15,300	—	—	535,000	471,600
Investments	—	8,300	12,800	1,100	185,100	3,400	1,454,800	—	—	1,665,500	1,451,300
Deferred Gains (Losses)	—	—	—	—	—	—	21,600	—	—	21,600	27,400
Restricted Assets	—	—	—	—	77,400	—	—	—	—	77,400	57,900
Land	—	—	—	—	—	900	49,500	38,400	—	88,800	94,700
Buildings and Improvements	—	—	—	—	2,100	1,200	300	156,700	—	160,300	351,900
Equipment	—	—	—	—	1,500	68,100	200	59,200	—	129,000	203,100
Other Fixed Assets	—	—	—	—	—	—	—	1,000	—	1,000	29,700
Construction in Progress	—	—	—	—	—	100	—	17,800	—	17,900	33,300
Accumulated Depreciation	—	—	—	—	(1,200)	(27,800)	(200)	—	—	(29,200)	(27,900)
Intangible Assets	—	—	—	—	—	—	—	—	—	—	100
Amount Available—Debt Service Fund	—	—	—	—	—	—	—	—	73,200	73,200	24,700
Resources to Be Provided in Future Years	—	—	—	—	—	—	—	—	197,400	197,400	217,000
Other Assets	1,600	2,100	—	—	100	—	22,000	—	—	25,800	29,200
TOTAL ASSETS AND OTHER DEBITS	$87,900	$321,500	$79,600	$30,900	$791,100	$74,700	$2,558,300	$273,100	$270,600	$4,487,700	$4,584,000

Liabilities and Fund Equity

Liabilities:											
Accounts Payable and Accruals	$15,200	$46,300	$2,900	$400	$10,100	$2,100	$4,400	$—	$—	$81,400	$99,400
Interfund Loans Payable	24,400	21,600	—	—	300	300	—	—	—	46,600	36,000
Due to Other Governments	—	1,800	—	—	—	—	20,100	—	—	21,900	42,600
Due to Other Funds	10,100	52,500	1,800	800	1,000	4,400	56,500	—	—	127,100	154,600
Deferred Revenue	19,400	16,300	1,700	200	500	100	2,400	—	—	40,600	42,100
Installment Purchase/Lease Payable	—	—	—	—	12,600	—	—	—	700	13,300	13,500
Long-Term Notes/Bonds Payable (Net)	—	—	—	—	711,700	—	—	—	244,700	956,400	821,800
Property Held in Trust	100	800	—	—	—	—	555,400	—	—	556,400	600,800
Compensated Absences Payable	—	—	—	—	1,500	100	400	—	25,200	27,200	38,500
Allowance for Realized Gains (Losses)	—	—	—	—	—	—	13,700	—	—	13,700	2,900
Estimated Insurance Claims	—	—	—	—	—	3,200	—	—	—	3,200	—
Other Liabilities	—	1,900	—	—	—	—	24,700	—	—	26,600	20,200
Total Liabilities	$69,200	$141,200	$6,400	$1,400	$727,200	$21,100	$677,300	$—	$270,600	$1,914,400	$1,872,400
Fund Equity:											
Investment in Fixed/Plant Assets	$—	$—	$—	$—	$—	$—	$—	$273,100	$—	$273,100	$561,700
Contributed Capital	—	—	—	—	3,400	—	—	—	—	3,400	2,900
Fund Balances/Retained Earnings:											
Reserved for:											
Encumbrances	900	9,000	—	—	—	—	—	—	—	9,900	15,900
Inventories	1,800	17,400	—	—	—	—	—	—	—	19,200	18,400
Long-Term Assets	—	7,500	13,900	—	—	—	1,700	—	—	23,100	13,700
Debt Service	—	—	59,300	—	—	—	38,800	—	—	98,100	76,200
Employee Benefits	—	—	—	—	—	—	14,400	—	—	14,400	14,400
Insurance Claims	—	—	—	—	—	10,200	—	—	—	10,200	9,000
Student Loans/Trust/ Principal/Endowment	—	—	—	—	—	—	688,100	—	—	688,100	631,500
Retirement Systems	—	—	—	—	—	—	1,100,400	—	—	1,100,400	960,800
Unreserved	16,000	146,400	—	29,500	60,500	43,400	37,600	—	—	333,400	407,100
Total Fund Equity	$18,700	$180,300	$73,200	$29,500	$63,900	$53,600	$1,881,000	$273,100	$—	$2,573,300	$2,711,600
Commitments/Contingencies											
TOTAL LIABILITIES AND FUND EQUITY	$87,900	$321,500	$79,600	$30,900	$791,100	$74,700	$2,558,300	$273,100	$270,600	$4,487,700	$4,584,000

Exhibit 10-4

Governmental Unit
Combining Statement of Revenues,
Expenditures, and Changes in Fund Balances
Debt Service Funds
For the Period Ending June 30, 19X2

	Airport Bonds	Highway Revenue Bonds	Water Development	Total (Memo Only)
Revenues:				
Taxes:				
Natural Resources	$—	$ —	$ 530	$ 530
Individual Income Tax	10	—	160	170
Tobacco	16	—	—	16
Charges for Fines and Forfeits	50	—	—	50
Investment Earnings	20	600	512	1,132
Grants and Contracts	—	—	19	19
Other Revenues	—	—	2	2
Total Revenues	$ 96	$ 600	$1,223	$ 1,919
Expenditures:				
Debt Service:				
Principal Payments	$—	$ 4,975	$ 140	$ 5,115
Interest Charges	—	741	572	1,313
Total Expenditures	$—	$ 5,716	$ 712	$ 6,428
Excess of Revenues Over (Under) Expenditures	$ 96	$(5,116)	$ 511	$(4,509)
Other Financing Sources (Uses)				
Operating Transfers In	$—	$ 5,200	$ 190	$ 5,390
Operating Transfers Out	(80)	—	(185)	(265)
Total Other Financing Sources	$ (80)	$ 5,200	$ 5	$ 5,125
Excess of Revenues and Other Financing Sources Over (Under) Expenditures	$ 16	$ 84	$ 516	$ 616
Fund Balance, July 1	$200	$ 120	$ 19	$ 339
Fund Balance, June 30	$216	$ 204	$ 535	$ 955

expenditures for debt service funds should be shown separately. If debt service retirements include both bonds and leases, the bond retirements should be shown separately from lease payments.

Individual Fund and Account Group Statements

Individual fund statements show the financial information for a single fund on one page. Because only one fund or account group is presented on a single page, there is no total column. Individual financial statements have been illustrated in earlier chapters.

Under most circumstances individual statements are discretionary. They usually are included whenever a governmental entity has only one fund of a particular type, for example, one debt service fund, or when the entity wishes to focus attention on a particular activity. Since every governmental unit has only one general fund, at least one individual fund set of statements will be included in each CAFR.

Individual fund statements are also included when a governmental unit cannot meet the GASB disclosure requirements with combining statements. For example, depending upon the accounting methodology used for pension trust funds, disclosure requirements may not be satisfied by combining the pension trust fund with all other fiduciary funds. If not, an individual statement must be included in the CAFR. Sometimes a governmental unit may find it useful to present comparative data for a particular activity. Individual fund statements would be used for this purpose, too. Exhibit 10-5 illustrates the format of a statement of revenues, expenditures, and changes in fund balance for a governmental entity's general fund.

Exhibit 10-5

Governmental Unit
General Fund
Statement of Revenues, Expenditures, and Changes in Fund Balance
For the Fiscal Year Ended June 30, 19X3
($000)

	TOTALS YEAR ENDED JUNE 30	
	19X2	**19X3**
Revenues:		
Licenses/Permits	$ 27,700	$ 25,800
Taxes:		
Gas/Oil/Coal Production	30,500	46,000
Individual Income	121,500	110,200
Corporate Income	19,700	33,900
Other Taxes	20,900	19,900
Charges for Services/Fines/Forfeits	16,600	16,600
Investment Earnings	15,200	15,300
Sale of Documents/Merchandise/Property	3,500	100
Rentals/Leases/Royalties	100	200
Grants/Contracts/Donations	—	—
Federal	400	200
Federal Indirect Cost Recoveries	600	600
Other Revenues	2,900	5,600
Total Revenues	$ 259,600	$ 274,400
Expenditures:		
Current:		
General Government	$ 33,700	$ 39,400
Public Safety/Corrections	30,700	33,200
Transportation	1,600	1,900
Health/Social Services	134,500	118,400
Education/Cultural	45,300	47,600
Resource Development/Recreation	11,300	13,900
Economic Development/Assistance	15,500	8,900
Debt Service		
Principal Retirement	100	100
Interest/Fiscal Charges	4,300	2,100
Capital Outlay	1,700	3,700
Total Expenditures	$ 278,700	$ 269,200
Excess of Revenues Over (Under) Expenditures	$ (19,100)	$ 5,200

(continued)

Exhibit 10-5   (continued)

	TOTALS YEAR ENDED JUNE 30	
	19X2	**19X3**
Other Financing Sources (Uses):		
Bonds Proceeds	100	100
Inception of Lease/Installment Contract	100	—
Operating Transfers In	85,000	79,200
Operating Transfers Out	(106,800)	(102,700)
Total Other Financing Sources (Uses)	$ (21,600)	$ (23,400)
Excess of Revenues/Other Sources Over (Under) Expenditures/Other Uses	$ (40,700)	$ (18,200)
Fund Balance—July 1—As Previously Reported	18,700	19,300
Prior Period Adjustments	—	—
Fund Balance—July 1—As Restated	$ 18,700	$ 19,300
Increases (Decreases) in Inventories	—	(300)
Residual Equity Transfers	41,300	4,200
Fund Balance—June 30	$ 19,300	$ 5,000

Supporting Schedules

The GASB clearly distinguishes between financial statements and schedules:

> Data presented in schedules are not necessary for fair presentation in conformity with GAAP unless referenced in the notes to the financial statements.[3]

Because schedules are optional, governmental entities should include only those that will be helpful to financial statement users. The GASB *Codification* mentions three circumstances that may require supporting schedules. One demonstrates compliance with legal or regulatory mandates that are not obvious from reviewing the financial statements. A grant or entitlement program may require certain presentations, for example.

A second use of supporting schedules is to provide additional detail. If individual fund statements are not required and combining statements do not adequately present operational characteristics of a specific fund, a supporting schedule may be appropriate. One example would be an itemization of cash receipts and disbursements for an agency fund used for special assessment collections.

Supporting schedules may also be used for information omitted from all financial statements. For example, no financial statement adequately presents debt servicing requirements over time. Such information is best depicted in a supporting schedule.

Budgetary Reporting

The GASB *Codification* makes it clear that although budgetary practices are outside the scope of reporting standards, guidance on budgetary compari-

[3]Ibid., sec. 1900, ¶118.

sons included in financial reports are within that scope. In general, budgetary comparisons should be included for all funds for which an annual budget is prepared.

At a minimum, the presentation should include a combined statement of revenues, expenditures, and changes in fund balances—budget and actual for general and special revenue fund types. Exhibit 10-6 depicts budgetary comparisons for special revenue funds as adapted from a State of Montana CAFR. Based on the general guidance, if the debt service funds also were budgeted, a combined operating statement—budget and actual—would be prepared for those funds.

Determining what budget figures to include is complicated by budgetary amendments and by some governmental units' practice of preparing budgets on a non-GAAP basis. The budget figures are those formally adopted by the oversight board—the appropriated budget. It includes all reserves, transfers, allocations, supplemental appropriations, and other legally authorized changes. If the budget is amended during the year, the amended budget figures should be used in the financial statement presentation.

When budgets are prepared on a non-GAAP basis, the actual data should be on the same basis as the budget. This means the data presented in the combined financial statements and those presented in any comparative statements will not agree. Differences between the GAAP and the non-GAAP basis should be explained in the notes to the financial statements. Also, the notes should include a reconciliation schedule.

The GASB also requires governmental entities to prepare individual fund and account group presentations of prior year and budgetary comparisons. For example, if special revenue funds were budgeted and the CAFR included individual fund statements for special revenue funds, comparative statements would be necessary. However, if the budgetary basis differs from GAAP, the individual fund statement should not include budgetary data. Rather, a supporting schedule is used to show the budgetary and actual data on the budget basis.

OBSERVATION ▲

The importance placed on budget presentations is obvious from this discussion. This importance traces to the fact that budget presentations are one means of demonstrating accountability and compliance.

THE FORMAT OF THE COMPREHENSIVE ANNUAL FINANCIAL REPORT

The financial reporting pyramid displayed in Exhibit 10-2 describes the *financial* statements or data included in the CAFR. In preparing a CAFR, the order of the financial statements is important, as is the additional information that should be included. Exhibit 10-7 (p. 378) outlines the order and contents of a comprehensive annual financial report. The appendix to this text provides

Exhibit 10-6

State of Montana
Schedule of Revenues, Expenditures, and Other Financing Sources (Uses) —
Budget and Actual with Reconciliation of Expenditures/Other Financing Uses per the Statewide
Budgeting and Accounting System to Budget Basis Statement in the GPFS —
Special Revenue Funds for the Fiscal Year Ended June 30, 19X7
($000)

	STATE SPECIAL REVENUE FUND			FEDERAL SPECIAL REVENUE FUND			TOTALS YEAR ENDED JUNE 30		
	Budget	Actual	Variance — Over (Under)	Budget	Actual	Variance — Over (Under)	Budget	Actual	Variance — Over (Under)
Revenue/Other financing Sources:									
Licenses/Permits	$ 50,900	$ 52,500	$ 1,600	$ —	$ —	$ —	$ 50,900	$ 52,500	$ 1,600
Taxes:									
Gas/Oil/Coal Production	27,800	25,800	(2,000)	—	—	—	27,800	25,800	(2,000)
Individual Income	48,400	52,300	3,900	—	—	—	48,400	52,300	3,900
Corporate Income	15,500	11,500	(4,000)	—	—	—	15,500	11,500	(4,000)
Other Taxes	133,100	137,800	4,700	1,100	1,000	(100)	134,200	138,800	4,600
Charges for Services/ Fines/Forfeits	23,900	20,600	(3,300)	600	1,000	400	24,500	21,600	(2,900)
Investment Earnings	38,500	40,000	1,500	800	900	100	39,300	40,900	1,600
Sale of Documents/ Merchandise/Property	1,100	1,300	200	—	—	—	1,100	1,300	200
Rentals/Leases/Royalties	500	600	100	—	—	—	500	600	100
Contributions/Premiums	300	500	200	—	—	—	300	500	200
Grants/Contracts/Donations	2,300	1,100	(1,200)	1,300	700	(600)	3,600	1,800	(1,800)
Federal	20,200	23,500	3,300	387,400	388,100	700	407,600	411,600	4,000
Federal Indirect Cost Recoveries	—	—	—	1,400	1,400	—	1,400	1,400	—
Other Revenues	400	900	500	—	2,100	2,100	400	3,000	2,600
Bond Proceeds	96,100	78,400	(17,700)	—	—	—	96,100	78,400	(17,700)
Operating Transfers In	99,300	80,600	(18,700)	1,700	1,700	—	101,000	82,300	(18,700)
Total Revenues/Other Financing Sources	$558,300	$527,400	$(30,900)	$394,300	$396,900	$ 2,600	$ 952,600	$924,300	$ (28,300)

	1	2	3	4	5	6	7	8	9
Expenditures/Other Financing Uses:									
Appropriated Expenditures	506,700	428,300	78,400	415,800	390,000	25,800	922,500	818,300	104,200
Appropriated Transfers Out	84,000	72,500	11,500	3,600	3,400	200	87,600	75,900	11,700
Total Expenditures/Other Financing Uses (SBAS)	$590,700	$500,800	$ 89,900	$419,400	$393,400	$26,000	$1,010,100	$894,200	$115,900
Net Adjustments for Rounding/Accruals	—	$ (1,700)	$ (1,700)	$ —	$ 1,600	$ 1,600	$ —	$ (100)	$ (100)
Excess of Revenues/Other Sources Over (Under) Expenditures/Other Uses—Budget Basis	$ (32,400)	24,900	57,300	$ (25,100)	5,100	30,200	$ (57,500)	$ 30,000	$ 87,500
Reconciliation of Budgetary/GAAP Reporting:									
1. Adjust Expenditures for Encumbrances	—	7,900	7,900	—	(800)	(800)	—	7,100	7,100
2. Adjustments for Appropriated Loans and Other Nonbudgeted Activity	—	15,200	15,200	—	(3,000)	(3,000)	—	12,200	12,200
Excess of Revenues/Other Sources Over (Under) Expenditures/Other Uses—GAAP Basis	$ (32,400)	$ 48,000	$ 80,400	$ (25,100)	$ 1,300	$26,400	$ (57,500)	$ 49,300	$106,800
Unreserved Fund Balances—July 1	129,000	128,900	140,900	12,000	12,000	—	141,000	140,900	(100)
Residual Equity Transfers	(4,500)	(4,500)	—	—	—	—	(4,500)	(4,500)	—
Increase Encumbrances Reserve	—	(5,900)	(5,900)	—	—	—	—	(6,600)	(6,600)
Increase Debt Service Reserve	—	(19,100)	(19,100)	—	(700)	(700)	—	(19,100)	(19,100)
Decrease Long-Term Loans and Reserve	—	200	200	—	—	—	—	200	200
Prior Period Adjustments	—	6,700	6,700	—	—	—	—	6,700	6,700
Unreserved Fund Balances—June 30	$ 92,100	$154,300	$ 62,200	$ (13,100)	$ 12,600	$25,700	$ 79,000	$166,900	$ 87,900

Exhibit 10-7

Contents of a Comprehensive Annual Financial Report

I.   Introductory Section
   A.   Letter of Transmittal and Other Highlights
   B.   Certificate of Excellence
   C.   General Description of Organization/Names of Key Individuals

II.   Financial Section
   A.   Auditor's Report
   B.   Combined Financial Statements
   C.   Notes
      1.   Summary of Significant Accounting Policies
      2.   Other Types of Notes
   D.   Individual/Combining Statements
   E.   Individual Statement for General Fund—Usually Comparative

III.   Statistical Section
   A.   Supporting Schedules
   B.   Single Audit Reports*
   C.   Auditor's Opinion on Supplementary Information Contained in Schedule of Federal Financial Assistance*
   D.   Auditor's Report on Compliance, Major/Nonmajor Financial Assistance Programs, and Internal Accounting Controls*

*These are not always included in the statistical section; these may appear in a single audit section of the GAFR.

excerpts from the city of Raleigh, North Carolina, Comprehensive Annual Financial Report for the year ended June 30, 1992; it is helpful in visualizing the overall contents of a CAFR.

Introductory Section

The introductory section includes the letter of transmittal from the unit's chief officer, the Certificate of Achievement for Excellence in Financial Reporting information, and general information about the organization. The **letter of transmittal** may be one of the most important parts of the CAFR. It should explain the overall nature of the CAFR, give a definition of the reporting entity, and add other highlights about the governmental unit.

The other highlights explain key characteristics of the governmental entity and the environment in which it operates, including a brief overview of economic conditions. Comments about the major objectives and achievements also help financial statement users put the year's financial results in perspective. A brief overview of future plans is helpful as well.

The letter of transmittal should also provide a summary of the financial data included later in the CAFR, including the administrative and accounting controls used to maintain the integrity of the financial information. General government functions should be explained with a recap of total revenues and expenditures. Debt administration, cash and risk management, and an explanation of any proprietary or fiduciary activities should be cited and discussed briefly.

The introductory section contains information about the **Certificate of Achievement program**. The Government Finance Officers Association has a formal program to judge the quality of CAFRs submitted for review. If a governmental unit's CAFR is prepared using generally accepted accounting principles and is independently audited, it is eligible for consideration under the program guidelines. Governmental entities whose reports are judged excellent receive national publicity and a certificate that can be reproduced for inclusion in the following year's CAFR. The Certificate of Achievement is a prestigious award and represents a significant accomplishment for the governmental entity. Consequently, most units receiving recognition do publish the certificate in their annual CAFR.

Cert of Achievement

OBSERVATION ▲

The Certificate of Achievement program was at one time called the Certificate of Excellence. It was initiated as a way of encouraging governmental entities to obtain financial audits and to use generally accepted accounting principles. Governmental entities do not have nearly as strong a reason to follow GAAP or to obtain audits as do businesses. Therefore, they need special impetus, which the Certificate Program was meant to provide.

Descriptor of Orgn.

A **general description** of the unit's organization should be included in the introductory section. Governmental units typically publish an organizational chart or simply list key officials and department heads. The description should be detailed enough so that statement users can determine areas of primary responsibility and distinguish persons charged with oversight responsibility.

Financial Section

The auditor's report, financial statements, and notes are included in the financial section. The various financial statements have been discussed previously, so this section focuses on the other two items.

Auditor's Report   The auditor's opinion precedes all financial statements and notes, just as it does in a business annual financial report. The scope of the audit engagement is clearly defined in the opinion statement (see Exhibit 10-8 pertaining to an audit of a state). The audit was made to form an opinion on the general purpose financial statements.[4] In this particular audit the combining statements were excluded from the scope.

This audit was completed by the Legislative Auditor, a branch of the legislature. In many states, the audit is completed by private firms working under contract with the state. As the scope paragraph indicates, the Legislative Auditor relied on other auditors for one enterprise fund, the Board of Housing.

Any reporting exceptions with respect to generally accepted accounting principles are included in the opinion statement. Apparently, the general purpose financial statements were prepared according to GAAP.

---

[4]General purpose financial statements are discussed in a later section.

Exhibit 10-8

Auditor's Opinion Letter

To the Legislative Audit Committee of the State Legislature:

We have examined the general purpose financial statements of the State as of and for the year ended June 30, 19X7, as listed in the Table of Contents. Our examination was made in accordance with generally accepted auditing standards and, accordingly, included such tests of the accounting records and such other auditing procedures as we considered necessary in the circumstances. We did not examine the financial statements of the Board of Housing which statements reflect total assets, liabilities, revenues, and expenses of 87 percent, 91 percent, 42 percent, and 46 percent, respectively, of the related Enterprise Fund Type. These statements were examined by other auditors whose report thereon was furnished to us, and our opinion expressed herein, insofar as it relates to the amounts included for the Board of Housing, is based solely upon the report of other auditors.

In our opinion, based upon our examination and the report of other auditors, the general purpose financial statements referred to in the Table of Contents present fairly the financial position of the State at June 30, 19X7, and the results of operation and the changes in financial position of its proprietary fund types for the year then ended, in conformity with generally accepted accounting principles applied on a basis consistent with that of the preceding year.

Our examination was made for the purpose of forming an opinion on the general purpose financial statements taken as a whole. The combining financial statements listed in the Table of Contents are presented for the purposes of additional analysis and are not a required part of the general purpose financial statements of the State. Such information has been subjected to the auditing procedures applied in the examination of the general purpose financial statements and, in our opinion, is fairly stated in all material respects in relation to the general purpose financial statements taken as a whole.

Respectfully submitted,
Deputy Legislative Auditor

October 30, 19X7

Notes   As in business, a key section of governmental annual reports is the notes. Well-written explanations of important accounting information lead to a level of comprehension that is almost impossible to achieve solely with financial statements, graphs, or supporting schedules. Such explanations usually cover items that are not readily apparent or cannot be included in the body of the statements.

What information should be included in governmental annual reports is an unsettled issue. A 1985 survey by the GASB reported that the diversity of statement users makes it difficult to determine what information should be included in the notes.[5] Of the three primary user groups — citizen groups, oversight bodies, and investors/creditors — the citizen groups are probably the least informed about government accounting and reporting practices. They may need much of the voluminous information currently disclosed in notes to governmental reports, although many observers have argued that the level of detail and complexity of note disclosures is excessive.

Note disclosures for governmental entities can be grouped into three general areas: (1) accounting policies, (2) financial detail, and (3) additional information.

Accounting Policy Notes. Like notes for business entities, the first note in most governmental annual reports is the summary of significant accounting

Note disclosures:

---

[5]Governmental Accounting Standards Board, *The Needs of Users of Governmental Financial Reports* (Stamford, Conn.: GASB, 1985).

policies. Authoritative guidance suggests that all accounting principles materially affecting the financial data reported should be disclosed in this note. These policies might involve unusual or unique accounting applications of GAAP, practices peculiar to governmental entities, such as fund accounting, and areas in which the governmental entity had a choice of acceptable accounting principles.

The basis of accounting and the fund structure should be described in this note. Disclosure is complicated by the fact that different funds use different accounting bases and by the multitude of funds and account groups that need to be explained. A basis of accounting note might be written as follows:

> The accounting and reporting treatment applied to a fund is determined by its measurement focus. All governmental funds, expendable trust funds, and agency funds are accounted for on a flow of current financial resources measurement focus. Modified accrual accounting is used.
>
> All proprietary funds, pension trust funds, and nonexpendable trust funds are accounted for on a flow of economic resources focus. This means that the full accrual basis of accounting is used, including the depreciation of fixed assets.

Other disclosures included in the first note describe the budgeting basis (and sometimes the budgeting process), encumbrances, fixed assets and depreciation method (for proprietary funds), the basis for calculating any estimates of uncollectible receivables, and the methodology for reporting inventory expenditures.

What is excluded is as important as what is disclosed. If a particular type of note does not pertain to the entity, no reference should be made to that item. For example, if the entity does not have proprietary funds, the preparer should say nothing. As another example, the basis of accounting for inventories should not be described if the entity has no beginning or ending inventory.

Notes on Financial Detail. Notes are also used to provide the financial detail necessary to substantiate the summary data presented in the financial statements. A single financial statement should fit on one page or on facing pages. This limits the number of individual items that can be portrayed on the statements. Rather than list all interfund transactions in an operating statement, for example, a note could be used to provide this detail by fund. The summary total for this detail should be keyed to the related figure in the financial statements.

Also, information of interest only to selected users should be reserved for the notes. Item-by-item listings of prior period adjustments, bond refundings, and defeased debt are examples of financial detail reserved for note disclosure. Exhibit 10-9 provides an example of the financial detail necessary for a note showing prior period adjustments. Some readers need this level of detail; others do not, and for them, the information only clutters up the statements and makes them more difficult to understand.

Notes on Additional Information. A note of additional information is usually a narrative description of some aspect of the financial statements. An example is note disclosures for pension funds. The pension cost would be

Exhibit 10-9

Sample Note Disclosures for Financial Detail
Prior Period Adjustments

| Fund Type: | TYPE OF PRIOR PERIOD ADJUSTMENT | | | | Total |
| | A | B | C | D | |
			[Increase (Decrease)]		
General Fund	$(1,099)				$(1,099)
Special Revenue	8,500		$ 700		9,200
Enterprise		$(1,300)			(1,300)
Internal Service		2,100		$1,100	3,200
Expendable Trust			(781)		(781)
Nonexpendable Trust	(8,200)				(8,200)
Totals	$(799)	$ 800	$(81)	$1,100	$ 1,020

reported in the fund(s) accounting for employee compensation, and the pension plan assets and liabilities would be reported in the pension trust. As discussed in Chapter 9, GASB requires numerous disclosures about pensions. The nature of the pension program must be described as well as employees included in the system, the actuarial basis for calculating liabilities, and the method for determining pension costs.

Contingencies also are described in the additional information type of disclosure. Any pending lawsuits qualifying as contingencies should be explained, for example. One such contingency is described in the following sample note:

> The Supreme Court has recently ruled against the Division of Workers' Compensation in a suit questioning the constitutionality of a law allowing discounting of workers' compensation benefits. The statute was amended during the 19X7 legislature requiring lump-sum payments of permanent benefits to be discounted by 7 percent, compounded annually. The amended statute was intended to apply to all cases not yet settled or awarded in a lump-sum as determined by court order. The Supreme Court's ruling states that discounting of lump-sum payments can only be made for cases in which the injury occurred after the effective date of the amendment, June 1, 19X7. The state actuary estimates that the Supreme Court ruling could result in additional costs of $20 million to $30 million.

Additional information notes may be the most difficult to draft. The preparer must decide whether the information is really necessary and, if necessary, how much detail to include. Preparers should spend considerable time determining key factors related to the item before attempting to draft a note. The note on the workers' compensation case cited above was distilled from a report of over ten pages. The important facts are: (1) what created the contingency, (2) the key facts of the case, and (3) the financial impact on the entity.

In drafting such notes, there is no substitute for concise and clear writing. Any additional information that cannot be described in a single paragraph should be reevaluated.

Statistical Section

The statistical section includes supporting schedules, results of the single audit, supplementary audit opinions about federal financial assistance, and the auditor's report on internal controls. The single audit is a special audit conducted for governmental entities that receive a certain level of federal contracts and grants. Because it and related opinions and reports are described in more detail in a later chapter, only the supporting schedules and the report on internal controls will be discussed here.

Supporting Schedules   Supporting schedules are graphs or tables that provide background information to the financial statements, the entity in general, or the environment in which it operates. The distinction between a supporting schedule and a financial detail note is not always clear. Typically, supporting schedules are longer than the related type of note. They also tend to cover several periods, whereas a financial detail note pertains only to the current year. For example, the taxable value of various types of property for the current year probably is explained in a note, but historical trends in such values would be included in a supporting schedule. As another example, the debt margin and debt limit for a single year would be explained in a note, but analyses of these relationships over time would be included in the statistical section as a supporting schedule.

Unlike the financial detail note, supporting schedule totals may not relate to a specific number in the financial statements. They are sometimes used to provide a context in which to assess the financial results of a governmental entity. For example, time series data on employment, per capita income, and other economic factors highlighted in the introductory section may be shown in detail in the statistical section. Other examples of trend data include:

1. property tax levies and collections—ten-year trend data
2. property values, construction activity, and bank deposits—last ten years
3. property tax rates—last ten years
4. population figures, by area or age categories—last ten years
5. telephone or electrical hookups—ten-year trends
6. principal source of revenues—last ten years

Report on Internal Controls   One requirement of a single audit is a report on internal controls. Some entities that do not need a single audit will ask their auditors to report on internal controls in connection with their financial activities.

An examination of internal controls involves reviewing the significant internal accounting controls to determine the nature, timing, and extent of the audit procedures necessary for expressing an opinion on the financial statements. The more weaknesses found in the internal control procedures, the more the auditor extends the necessary audit tests. The AICPA Audit Guide gives several different ways in which to classify the major internal accounting controls.

The report on internal controls explains the major weaknesses found during the examination. Usually the report indicates that it is intended only for management or perhaps the oversight board. Weaknesses disclosed in the report are those resulting in some risk that material errors or irregularities in relation to the financial statements may occur and not be detected in a timely manner. The auditor describes the existing conditions, the criteria used in making the judgment that the condition warranted a "material weakness" classification, the effect of the weakness, and its cause.

▲   **OBSERVATION**

Auditors prepare other reports in connection with a single audit. As pointed out earlier, they may not be included in the statistical section; sometimes, the comprehensive annual report contains an additional section devoted to reports related to the single audit, if one is required.

In summary, the CAFR is a complex document. It includes an introductory, a financial, and a statistical section. Several different levels of financial statements may be included: combined, combining, and individual. In addition, budgetary comparisons are provided for those funds requiring budgets. The notes and explanatory materials generally are more involved and confusing than would be the case for business annual reports. The added complexity and detail traces primarily to governmental use of fund accounting and to different accounting bases for different funds. A CAFR also appears bulkier and more difficult to follow than a business annual report because it frequently includes not only the financial statement audit but also the single audit and its related reports.

GENERAL PURPOSE FINANCIAL STATEMENTS

The GASB and its predecessor, the NCGA, recognized that many statement users are overwhelmed by the level of detail included in the CAFR. *Statement 1* issued by the NCGA suggested that governmental entities present the combined financial statements and notes to the financial statements preceding the combining and individual fund statements. The combined statements, together with the notes, auditor's opinion, and general narrative, could be lifted from the CAFR and used for broad general distribution. This report is referred to as the general purpose financial statements (GPFS).

General purpose financial statements may be issued separately from the CAFR. They may be included in official statements for security offerings or for broad distribution to the general public. People who do not require detailed reports get an overview of a governmental entity without wading through the CAFR. Many units publish a CAFR with the general purpose financial statements as a distinct part. Some governments publish only general purpose financial statements even though the standard-setting bodies recommend publishing a comprehensive annual financial report. General purpose financial statements meet the GAAP requirements of fair presentation and full disclosure.

Whether issued separately or as part of the CAFR, the general purpose financial statements must include all disclosures necessary for fair presentation. Such disclosures include:

a. summary of significant accounting policies
b. cash deposits with financial institutions
c. investments, including repurchase agreements
d. significant contingent liabilities
e. encumbrances outstanding
f. significant effects of subsequent events
g. pension plan obligations
h. material violations with compliance requirements
i. debt service requirements to maturity
j. commitments under noncapitalized leases
k. construction and other significant commitments
l. changes in fixed assets
m. changes in long-term debt
n. any excess of expenditures over appropriations
o. deficit funds balance or retained earnings of individual funds
p. interfund receivables and payables[6]

The length of this list suggests that most CAFR notes apply as well to general purpose financial statements. The *Codification* goes on to point out that this list is not all-inclusive. Other notes should be included, as required. Twenty-five other possible areas requiring note disclosure are listed as suggestions to preparers. Most are common to business and governmental units, but the ones on segment information and investments have special applications in government.

OBSERVATION ▲

The lengthy list of disclosures for governmental entities might lead one to the conclusion that every possible subject is covered in the notes. However, preparers must exercise professional judgment in determining which subjects are appropriate disclosures for a particular entity. No note should be included *just to check off items on a list of possible disclosures.*

Enterprise Fund Segment Information

General purpose financial statements must include segment information for certain individual enterprise funds. Although the general reference to the

---

[6]GASB, 1993 *Codification*, sec. 2300, ¶106.

term *segment* has the same meaning as it does for businesses, defining the precise nature of a segment has differences due to fund accounting. A *segment* refers to an individual enterprise fund of a state or local government. Additional disclosures are required for each enterprise fund if:

> (a) material long-term liabilities are outstanding, (b) the disclosures are essential to assure the GPFS are not misleading, or (c) they are necessary to assure interperiod comparability.[7]

When considering the materiality of long-term liabilities, the comparison is the amount of debt to the total assets of the *individual enterprise fund,* not the total assets of all enterprise funds.

Whether the disclosures are *essential to avoid misleading GPFS* is a matter of judgment. Operating results or balance sheet items of one fund should not obscure important characteristics of another fund or all funds combined. The GASB *Codification* indicates factors to consider when determining whether disclosure is required:

- material intergovernmental or intragovernmental operating subsidies to an enterprise fund
- material enterprise fund tax revenues
- material enterprise fund *operating* or *net* income or loss[8]

Preparers must also make sure that the financial statements are comparable from one period to the next. Thus, once segment data have been included, they should be presented in subsequent years, even if otherwise not required.

The specific segment data to be disclosed are extensive, but can easily be obtained from the individual fund statements. The disclosures range from a description of the types of goods or services provided by the fund to total assets and net income or loss. Several data elements relate to fixed assets, depreciation, and operating results. As expected, material long-term liabilities and interunit or interfund transfers also are important disclosures.

Governmental entities have two options for reporting segment information: in the financial statements or in the notes to the financial statements. Most use the option of reporting the required data in the notes.

If the first option is selected, the combined statements would include a column for each individual fund that qualifies as a segment. This option is not preferred because it is apt to confuse the reader. Especially if combining statements are included in the CAFR, the individual columns in the combined statements may lead readers to wonder why only some of the individual funds are shown in the combined statements. Governmental entities also present individual fund statements for segment funds in the general purpose financial statements. In addition to causing confusion, this presentation tends to clutter up the general purpose financial statements.

---

[7] Ibid., sec. 2500, ¶102.

[8] Ibid., sec. 2500, ¶105 (emphasis added).

Cash Deposits with Financial Institutions and Selected Investments

Governmental entities try to earn the highest return possible on idle cash. They deposit their cash in certificates of deposit and invest in other high-yielding short-term investments, such as repurchase agreements. GASB *Statement No. 3* establishes special note disclosures for deposits with financial institutions and certain investments. *Statement No. 3* was issued because several fraudulent schemes resulted in substantial losses for governmental entities. Certain security transactions, such as repurchase agreements and reverse repurchase agreements, entail unusual risks to governmental entities. The GASB felt that these risks should be acknowledged in the notes.

Nature of the Risks   *Statement No. 3* requires special disclosures for three types of investment arrangements: cash deposits, repurchase agreements, and reverse repurchase agreements. All three involve using investment securities as collateral. Accordingly, in all three, the governmental entity faces the risk that the actual investment securities do not exist or that declines in their market prices have eroded the investment quality of the collateral.

disclose
1. Cash deposits
2. RPO
3. Reverse RPO

Governmental entities frequently deposit excess cash in interest-bearing *uninsured deposits with financial institutions*. Many state laws require the financial institution to designate specific government securities or "pools" of securities to guarantee the safety of the deposit. In some states, the financial institution must place this collateral in the name of the governmental entity making the deposit. In others, the collateral is held in the name of the financial institution or the institution's trust department. If the institution fails and the collateral is not in the name of the governmental unit, the risks associated with collection of the deposit may be very high. Even if the collateral is in the depositor's name, market value declines may mean recovering less than the full amount of the deposit.

Investments in *repurchase and reverse repurchase agreements* also may have high credit risks. Repurchase agreements involve short-term loans in a national market. The borrower transfers securities to the lender and promises to repay the cash with interest. Many of these investments are for overnight or for two or three days. In a reverse repurchase agreement, the borrowing and lending parties are just reversed. If the governmental entity is the lender under a repurchase agreement, it is a borrower under a reverse repurchase agreement.

The level of risk depends upon who holds the securities. If the investors (lenders) hold the securities themselves, they can judge their quality and force repayment before release of the securities. If the securities are held by a broker/dealer, its agent, or an independent third party, the risk increases. Were the securities actually transferred to the lender? Are the same securities being held as collateral for more than one loan? Are the securities of the quality and market value represented by the borrower? Opportunities for fraudulent schemes abound any time a third party holds the securities.

In a reverse repurchase agreement, risk arises when the borrower repays the loan but the lender fails to return the securities. The best security for the borrower is to have some third party hold the securities. When the borrower can prove repayment, the securities should be automatically transferred back to that entity.

▲   **OBSERVATION**

With the obvious risks associated with these transactions, it seems clear that a governmental entity would always insist upon actual custody of the collateral, or putting the securities in its name and depositing them with an independent third party. However, such transactions involve millions of dollars daily, and the investment period may be for a single night. Transferring the securities is complicated and would frequently involve more time than the period of the investment.

GASB Guidance on Investments   *Statement No. 3* provides considerable guidance to governmental entities who want to become involved in these investments. For example, the statement indicates that governmental entities may protect themselves by:

1. Establishing the rights and responsibilities of the parties by entering into a written repurchase agreement
2. Using the bank serving the governmental entity as the custodian for securities involved in repurchase or reverse repurchase agreements
3. Structuring a repurchase or reverse repurchase agreement so that the underlying securities can be quickly liquidated under the Federal Bankruptcy Code
4. Reviewing audited financial statements and other information furnished to regulatory agencies of the banks in which the deposits are made
5. Establishing the entity's unconditional rights to the collateral through a written contract with the financial institution
6. Making sure that all written agreements give the depositor/lender the right to demand additional securities for collateral whenever the market value of the existing securities falls below the required level[9]

Disclosure Requirements   The GASB is insistent that the nature and extent of the risks associated with these deposits or investments be clearly identified in the notes to the financial statements. In general, the disclosure requirements involve revealing the extent to which there is adequate collateral or insurance to enable the entity to recover its investments and the amount of risk being assumed by the entity. Specifically, disclosures pertain to defining authorized investments and the nature of these investments, revealing the individual types of deposits and investments, and providing various listings of the amounts of each type of investment at the balance sheet date. The disclosures are made for the entity as a whole, but additional disclosures

---

[9]Adapted from the Governmental Accounting Standards Board, *Statement No. 3, Deposits with Financial Institutions, Investments (including Repurchase Agreements), and Reverse Repurchase Agreements* (Stamford, Conn.: GASB, 1986).

for specific funds — such as a pension trust fund — are required in certain circumstances.

OBSERVATION ▲

Statement No. 3 discusses only the risks associated with investments that are most common to governmental portfolios. As governments become more sophisticated in investing idle resources, the disclosure requirements and procedures necessary to reduce risk exposure should be applied to additional investment vehicles.

To enable users to evaluate a governmental entity's compliance with related laws and regulations, a description of authorized types of investments should precede any notes related to these deposits. Of particular importance is disclosure of any significant violations of the authorizations.

Deposits with Financial Institutions. The level of disclosure depends on whether the deposits are insured. If they are insured, the entity only needs to disclose that fact. Otherwise, the carrying amount of the total deposits classified by type of credit risk must be disclosed. According to the GASB, the three types of credit risk are:

1. Insured deposits held in the entity's name
2. Collateralized deposits held by the pledging institution's trust department or agent in the entity's name
3. Uncollateralized[10]

Uncollateralized deposits include bank balances backed by securities held by the pledging institution or its trust department but not in the entity's name.

Repurchase Agreements. The carrying and market values of investments, including repurchases, should be disclosed. Each type of investment should be listed separately, classified according to the type of credit risk. The three risk classes for investments are: (1) insured or held by the entity in its own name, (2) uninsured and unregistered but held in the entity's own name, and (3) uninsured and unregistered but not held in the entity's own name. Whenever the aggregate listing of investments in a particular risk class obscures unrealized losses of individual funds, the carrying and market values should be listed for each fund.

Reverse Repurchase Agreements. The requirements for reverse repurchase agreements affect the balance sheet, operating statement, and the notes. The GASB requires that the assets being held to back repurchase agreements should not be netted against the related liabilities. A fund liability entitled "obligations under reverse repurchase agreements" should be reported; the underlying securities should be reported as investments. Losses and gains from such activities should not be reported as interest income, nor should the gains and losses be netted. The notes should include the credit risk related to reverse repurchase agreements.

---

[10]Ibid., ¶67.

FINANCIAL REPORTING AND THE USER

The sheer size of the comprehensive annual financial report, together with the numerous specialized reporting requirements, sometimes overshadows the primary purpose of the CAFR: to present usable and understandable financial information to users. Therefore, preparers must constantly ask themselves whether the information is meaningful and whether different displays or reporting formats would be helpful to those analyzing the information.

Typical display formats were used for the illustrations presented in this chapter. Nonetheless, they undoubtedly could be improved. For example, a critical evaluation of Exhibit 10-6, a comparison of budget and actual for Montana's special revenue funds, might elicit some changes. Is the level of aggregation or disaggregation appropriate? Do the column headings clearly define the content? Should all variances be illustrated individually or just those that are significant—the others aggregated? Is it appropriate to further explain some significant variances in the notes? Should the reconciliation be reported on a separate page or as an integral part of the statement? These are all valid points to raise with regard to the most useful display. How they are answered depends upon the primary purpose of the statement. They also must be answered in the context of the user's level of sophistication.

Because users' ability to assimilate the material varies, preparers may have difficulty assessing appropriate presentations. For example, and using the information in Exhibit 10-6, an unsophisticated reader may simply look at the net excess of revenues and other sources over expenditures and other uses and decide that all is well with the special revenue funds. A more sophisticated reader may well calculate the excess of revenues over expenditures to see if the special revenue funds are generating sufficient revenue to pay current obligations. For those readers, a statement that used subtotals between revenues and other sources and expenditures and other uses would facilitate the analysis. Those same users probably understand the significance of the indirect costs generated by federal contracts and grants, so separating out that revenue item is most helpful. For others, simply knowing that this revenue source was part of the federal money received is sufficient. No formula nor reporting standard resolves the preparers' dilemmas about the level of detail and preferred format. In general, however, preparers should concentrate on communicating the general knowledge in the general purpose financial statements and provide more detailed information in the remaining statements and schedules.

THE REPORTING UNIT

Users must be able to determine what activities, organizations, and functions are being represented in the comprehensive annual financial report or the general purpose financial statements. Without such knowledge, users could not identify the entities for which their elected officials ought to be held accountable. They also would not know whether the information for one period was comparable to that for another period; the reporting unit could change from one period to the next and render comparative data meaningless.

Sometimes the organizations, functions, or activities that should be included with a certain reporting unit are obvious. Peripheral entities are under the control of and funded by a single county, city, or state. Accordingly, their operating results and financial position are included within the comprehensive annual financial report or general purpose financial statements of the primary unit.

For other governmental entities, affiliations between peripheral and primary entities are unclear. The oversight board of a particular activity or organization may be elected independently of the governing board of the reporting unit. Some organizations receive funding from several different reporting units. Others may operate independently except for certain broad oversight responsibilities or fiscal control by the reporting entity.

Determining the affiliation among organizations is complicated by the lack of a single criterion to measure control. In business organizations, control is measured by ownership. If Entity A owns more than 50 percent of the stock of Entity B, Entity A controls the board of directors and consequently all management functions and policies of Entity B. No similar criterion exists in government. One reporting unit may fund more than 50 percent of another, but the oversight board may be elected independently of the funding organization. Similary, the board may be selected by one reporting unit while most of the funding comes from another source. In this case, the reporting unit has control of management, but because it has no control over funding, it has little influence over the entity's operations. Both GASB and its predecessor, the NCGA, have struggled with the problem of defining the reporting unit.

Defining the Reporting Unit

The primary unit covered by a CAFR or GPFS is the *reporting entity*. Affiliated units included with the primary unit are called *component units*. Those being considered for inclusion are referred to as *potential component units*.

Defining the primary and component units is especially difficult in the governmental sector. No stock ownership exists in this sector; as a result, a standard on inclusion of potential component units cannot reference control, for example, 51 percent, as does the comparable standard in the private sector. In 1991, when the GASB issued *Statement No. 14, The Financial Reporting Entity,* it said that **accountability** is the primary determinant of whether a potential component unit is declared a component unit. Nonetheless elements of control are evident in the criteria.

According to *Statement No. 14,* the reporting unit shall include the primary unit, any unit for which the primary unit is accountable, and *any other units whose exclusion would make reports misleading.* The primary governmental unit is accountable if:

it appoints a voting majority of the organization's governing body and (1) it is able to **impose its will** on that organization or (2) there is a potential for the organization to provide specific financial benefits to, or impose specific financial burdens on, the primary government.[11]

The statement also indicates that financial accountability may exist if a potential component unit is fiscally dependent on the primary unit regardless of the nature of the appointment or election process of the oversight board. A potential component unit would be fiscally dependent if its budget must be approved by the primary unit and it does not have the power to set rates or charges without approval of the primary unit, or if it cannot issue debt without that approval. If a potential component unit had part of its board appointed by the boards of different primary units but was fiscally dependent on only one of those units, it should become a component unit of the primary unit on which it is fiscally dependent.

 Interpretations of the various criteria for judging whether a potential unit is a component unit are necessary. For example, the criteria state that a voting majority must be appointed; if a two-thirds vote is necessary, appointment of two-thirds of the board would be necessary. Also, the appointment process must include substantive powers; selecting two names from a list of three cannot be described as substantive.

 The primary unit has the ability to impose its will on a potential component unit if it can significantly affect its operations. The following are given as examples of the ability to significantly influence operations:

a. The ability to remove appointed members of the board at will
b. The ability to modify the organization's budget
c. The ability to modify, approve, or change fee charges affecting revenues
d. The ability to veto, modify, or overrule decisions (other than those in b and c)
e. The ability to appoint, reassign, or dismiss managers.[12]

Financial benefits or burdens may result from statutory provisions related to entitlements or obligations. Such benefits or burdens may also result simply because the primary unit appoints the majority of the component unit's board. If any of the following conditions exist, a financial benefit or burden exists:

a. The primary unit is legally entitled to or can otherwise access the component unit's resources.
b. The primary unit is responsible for or assumes responsibility for financing deficits.
c. The primary unit is obligated in some manner for the debt of the organization.[13]

---

[11]Governmental Accounting Standards Board, *Statement No. 14, The Financial Reporting Entity* (Norwalk, Conn.: GASB, 1991), ¶21.

[12]Ibid., 26.

[13]Ibid., 27.

Reporting Component Units   The GASB developed reporting standards for component units that provide an overview of the reporting entity while allowing users to distinguish between the primary unit and its component unit(s). Depending on the relationship between the primary unit and its component units, two types of reporting are prescribed: **blending** or **discrete reporting**.

Blending involves combining component unit fund types with the similar fund types of the primary unit. For example, a component unit's capital projects funds would be included in a primary unit's capital projects fund column on a combined balance sheet of a primary unit. Under blending, a component unit's general fund becomes a special revenue fund of a reporting entity. Thus, by looking only at the combined statements, a user would not realize that the primary unit had any component units. Exhibit 10-10 shows a

2 types of reporting CUs
① blending
② discrete

Exhibit 10-10

Presentation by Measurement Focus
**Combining Statement of Revenues, Expenditures, and Changes in
Fund Balances**
All Governmental Fund Types and Expendable Trust Fund
For the Fiscal Year Ended December 31, 19X0

Different Fund Types

	Totals Primary Government (Memorandum Only)	Component Unit	Totals Reporting Entity (Memorandum Only)
Revenues:			
Taxes	$28,181	$ 3,763	$31,944
Licenses and Permits	2,041	-0-	2,041
Intergovernmental	6,332	24,069	30,401
Charges for Services	2,300	-0-	2,300
Other Revenues	3,723	-0-	3,723
Total Revenues	$42,577	$27,832	$70,409
Expenditures:			
Current:			
General Government	$ 4,330	$ -0-	$ 4,330
Public Safety	13,438	-0-	13,438
Highways and Streets	4,477	-0-	4,477
Sanitation	3,726	-0-	3,726
Culture and Recreation	6,883	-0-	6,883
Instruction Programs and Staff Support	-0-	16,978	16,978
Administrative and Operating Support	-0-	9,209	9,209
Community Services	-0-	91	91
Central Support	-0-	30	30

(continued)

Exhibit 10-10 _(continued)_			
	Totals Primary Government (Memorandum Only)	**Component Unit**	**Totals Reporting Entity (Memorandum Only)**
Capital Outlay	5,461	1,548	7,009
Debt Service	5,203	-0-	5,203
Total Expenditures	$43,518	$27,856	$71,374
Excess (Deficiency) of Revenues Over (Under) Expenditures	(941)	(24)	(965)
Other Financing Sources (Uses):			
Operating Transfers In	$ 5,383	$ -0-	$ 5,383
Operating Transfers Out	(5,383)	-0-	(5,383)
Special Assessment Bond Proceeds	4,690	-0-	4,690
Proceeds of Refunding Bonds	3,365	-0-	3,365
Payment to Refunded Bond Escrow Agent	(3,300)	-0-	(3,300)
Other	145	-0-	145
Total Other Financing Sources (Uses)	$ 4,900	$ -0-	$ 4,900
Excess of Revenues and Other Financing Sources Over Expenditures and Other Financing Uses	$ 3,959	$ (24)	$ 3,935
Fund Balances, January 1	13,955	2,813	16,768
Residual Equity Transfers Out	(45)	-0-	(45)
Fund Balances, December 31	$17,869	$ 2,789	$20,658

Source: Adapted from Government Finance Officers Association, _GAAFR Review_ (Chicago, Ill.: GFOA, 1991), vol. 8, no. 8.

combining statement under the blended format. This exhibit begins with the memo only column for the primary unit. If this were an actual statement, one would see a column for each fund type preceding that memo only column as depicted earlier in this chapter.

Discrete reporting involves using a separate column or columns for component unit financial information. Three different discrete options are available under the standard. A reporting entity may report all funds of all component units in a single column, in which case the reporting entity should probably show separate equity lines so that users can tell whether the component units have different fund types. Another option is to report all fund types of each component unit in a column, for example, one column for each component unit. Finally, a reportng entity may use one column for each fund type of all component units. Under this format and using the combined balance sheet as an example, the memo total for the primary unit would be followed by a column for governmental funds, all component units, and one for proprietary funds for all component units, and finally, a grand total—memo only—for the reporting unit. Exhibits 10-11, 10-12, and 10-13 illustrate the three display options for discrete reporting.

Selecting a particular display option should take into consideration the nature of the component units. For example, if one component unit is dominated by proprietary fund activities while the other component units have all fund types, the display option showing each fund type in a separate column might be preferable. On the other hand, if one component unit is relatively

Exhibit 10-11

Single Column Presentation (With Optional Equity Presentations)
Combined Balance Sheet
All Fund Types and Account Groups
December 31, 19XX

	Totals Primary Government (Memorandum Only)	Component Units	Totals Reporting Entity (Memorandum Only)
Assets and Other Debits			
Assets:			
Cash	$ 37,082	$ 19,298	$ 56,380
Receivables (Net)	6,665	4,639	11,304
Due from Other Funds	479	-0-	479
Due from Primary Government	-0-	39	39
Due from Component Units	87	-0-	87
Advances to Other Funds	78	-0-	78
Restricted Assets	-0-	27,454	27,454
Other Assets	205	1,009	1,214
Fixed Assets (Net)	65,227	145,870	211,097
Other Debits	42,857	724	43,581
TOTAL ASSETS AND OTHER DEBITS	$152,680	$199,033	$351,713
Liabilities, Equity, and Other Credits			
Liabilities:			
Vouchers and Accounts Payable	$ 2,100	$ 2,890	$ 4,990
Compensated Absences	2,291	374	2,665
Other Payables	569	564	1,133
Due to Other Funds	479	-0-	479
Due to Primary Government	-0-	87	87
Due to Component Units	39	-0-	39
Debt Principal and Interest (Current)	325	2,671	2,996
Deferred Revenue	4,480	102	4,582
Payable from Restricted Assets	-0-	4,358	4,358
Advances from Other Funds	78	-0-	78
Debt (Noncurrent)	45,387	63,011	108,398
Total Liabilities	$ 55,748	$ 74,057	$129,805
[Equity Presentation—Option 1]			
Equity and Other Credits:			
Investment in General Fixed Assets	$ 58,912	$ 29,000	$ 87,912
Contributed Capital	2,957	58,924	61,881
Retained Earnings	445	34,263	34,708
Fund Balance	34,618	2,789	37,407
Total Equity and Other Credits	$ 96,932	$124,976	$221,908
TOTAL LIABILITIES, EQUITY, AND OTHER CREDITS	$152,680	$199,033	$351,713
[Equity Presentation—Option 2]			
Equity and Other Credits:			
Investment in General Fixed Assets	$ 58,912		$ 58,912
Contributed Capital	2,957		2,957
Retained Earnings	445		445
Fund Balance	34,618		34,618
Investment in General Fixed Assets—			
Governmental Component Units		$ 29,000	29,000
Contributed Capital—			
Proprietary Component Units		58,924	58,924

(continued)

Exhibit 10-11   (continued)

	Totals Primary Government (Memorandum Only)	Component Units	Totals Reporting Entity (Memorandum Only)
Retained Earnings—			
Proprietary Component Units		34,263	34,263
Fund Balance—			
Governmental Component Units		2,789	2,789
Total Equity and Other Credits	$ 96,932	$124,976	$221,908
TOTAL LIABILITIES, EQUITY, AND OTHER CREDITS	$152,680	$199,033	$351,713
[Equity Presentation—Option 3]			
Equity and Other Credits:			
Investment in General Fixed Assets	$ 58,912		$ 58,912
Contributed Capital	2,957		2,957
Retained Earnings	445		445
Fund Balance	34,618		34,618
Equity and Other Credits—Component Units		$124,976	124,976
Total Equity and Other Credits	96,932	124,976	221,908
TOTAL LIABILITIES, EQUITY, AND OTHER CREDITS	$152,680	$199,033	$351,713

Source: Adapted from Government Finance Officers Association, *GAAFR Review* (Chicago, Ill.: GFOA, 1991), vol. 8, no. 8.

Exhibit 10-12

Separate Columns for Each Component Unit
Combined Balance Sheet
All Fund Types and Account Groups
December 31, 19XX

	TOTALS PRIMARY GOVERNMENT (MEMORANDUM ONLY)	COMPONENT UNITS		TOTALS REPORTING ENTITY (MEMORANDUM ONLY)
		School District	Water & Sewer	
Assets and Other Debits				
Assets:				
Cash and Investments	$ 37,082	$ 3,549	$ 15,749	$ 56,380
Receivables (Net)	6,665	1,609	3,030	11,304
Due from Other Funds	479	-0-	-0-	479
Due from Primary Government	-0-	-0-	39	39
Due from Component Units	87	-0-	-0-	87
Advances to Other Funds	78	-0-	-0-	78
Restricted Assets	-0-	-0-	27,454	27,454
Other Assets	205	155	854	1,214
Fixed Assets (Net)	65,227	29,228	116,642	211,097
Other Debits	42,857	724	-0-	43,581
TOTAL ASSETS AND OTHER DEBITS	$152,680	$35,265	$163,768	$351,713
Liabilities, Equity, and Other Credits				
Liabilities:				
Vouchers and Accounts Payable	$ 2,100	$ 1,653	$ 1,237	$ 4,990
Compensated Absences	2,291	-0-	374	2,665
Other Payables	569	28	536	1,133

(continued)

Exhibit 10-12　*(continued)*

	TOTALS PRIMARY GOVERNMENT (MEMORANDUM ONLY)	COMPONENT UNITS		TOTALS REPORTING ENTITY (MEMORANDUM ONLY)
		School District	Water & Sewer	
Due to Other Funds	479	-0-	-0-	479
Due to Primary Government	-0-	-0-	87	87
Due to Component Units	39	-0-	-0-	39
Debt Principal and Interest (Current)	325	-0-	2,671	2,996
Deferred Revenue	4,480	102	-0-	4,582
Payable from Restricted Assets	-0-	-0-	4,358	4,358
Advances from Other Funds	78	-0-	-0-	78
Debt (Noncurrent)	45,387	727	62,284	108,398
Total Liabilities	$ 55,748	$ 2,510	$ 71,547	$129,805
Equity and Other Credits:				
Investment in General Fixed Assets	$ 58,912	$29,000	$ -0-	$ 87,912
Contributed Capital	2,957	-0-	58,924	61,881
Retained Earnings	445	966	33,297	34,708
Fund Balance	34,618	2,789	-0-	37,407
Total Equity and Other Credits	$ 96,932	$32,755	$ 92,221	$221,908
TOTAL LIABILITIES, EQUITY, AND OTHER CREDITS	$152,680	$35,265	$163,768	$351,713

Source: Adapted from Government Finance Officers Association, *GAAFR Review* (Chicago, Ill.: GFOA, 1991), vol. 8, no. 8.

Exhibit 10-13

Separate Columns for Each Measurement Focus
Combined Balance Sheet
All Fund Types and Account Groups
December 31, 19XX

	TOTALS PRIMARY GOVERNMENT (MEMORANDUM ONLY)	COMPONENT UNITS		TOTALS REPORTING ENTITY (MEMORANDUM ONLY)
		Governmental	Proprietary	
Assets and Other Debits				
Assets:				
Cash and Investments	$ 37,082	$ 2,908	$ 16,390	$ 56,380
Receivables (Net)	6,665	1,597	3,042	11,304
Due from Other Funds	479	-0-	-0-	479
Due from Primary Government	-0-	-0-	39	39
Due from Component Units	87	-0-	-0-	87
Advances to Other Funds	78	-0-	-0-	78
Restricted Assets	-0-	-0-	27,454	27,454
Other Assets	205	-0-	1,009	1,214
Fixed Assets (Net)	65,227	29,000	116,870	211,097
Other Debits	42,857	724	-0-	43,581
TOTAL ASSETS AND OTHER DEBITS	$152,680	$34,229	$164,804	$351,713
Liabilities, Equity, and Other Credits				
Liabilities:				
Vouchers and Accounts Payable	$ 2,100	$ 1,643	$ 1,247	$ 4,990
Compensated Absences	2,291	-0-	374	2,665
Other Payables	569	-0-	564	1,133

(continued)

Exhibit 10-13   *(continued)*

	TOTALS PRIMARY GOVERNMENT (MEMORANDUM ONLY)	COMPONENT UNITS		TOTALS REPORTING ENTITY (MEMORANDUM ONLY)
		Governmental	Proprietary	
Due to Other Funds	479	-0-	-0-	479
Due to Primary Government	-0-	-0-	87	87
Due to Component Units	39	-0-	-0-	39
Debt Principal and Interest (Current)	325	-0-	2,671	2,996
Deferred Revenue	4,480	73	29	4,582
Payable from Restricted Assets	-0-	-0-	4,358	4,358
Advances from Other Funds	78	-0-	-0-	78
Debt (Noncurrent)	45,387	724	62,287	108,398
Total Liabilities	$ 55,748	$ 2,440	$ 71,617	$129,805
Equity and Other Credits:				
Investment in General Fixed Assets	$ 58,912	$29,000	$ -0-	$ 87,912
Contributed Capital	2,957	-0-	58,924	61,881
Retained Earnings	445	-0-	34,263	34,708
Fund Balance	34,618	2,789	-0-	37,407
Total Equity and Other Credits	$ 96,932	$31,789	$ 93,187	$221,908
TOTAL LIABILITIES, EQUITY, AND OTHER CREDITS	$152,680	$34,229	$164,804	$351,713

Source: Adapted from Government Finance Officers Association, *GAAFR Review* (Chicago, Ill.: GFOA, 1991), vol. 8, no. 8.

large, the option showing each component unit in a separate column might provide readers with a better understanding of the component units. When all the component units are insignificant, a single column for all of them might suffice.

If the primary unit has complete control over its component units, blending is required. In all other situations, primary units should use discrete reporting. Although additional information is reported in the notes to the financial statements, reporting all information pertaining to component units only in the notes is not permitted, regardless of the significance of the component unit.

▲ **OBSERVATION**

> Some accountants were unhappy about the limited options for reporting component units. They felt that reporting should vary depending on the significance of the component unit to the primary unit. For example, a component unit that had little significance would be reported in the notes to the financial statements. The units falling into the next level of importance would be blended. The most significant ones would be reported discretely.

Other Display Features   A number of reporting requirements are described in the standard, some of which relate to the financial statement display or notes. Others relate to the requirements for the component unit financial statements.

Whenever a reporting entity shows several different fund types and component units in a single column, it has to consider the possibility of confusing the reader. For that reason, several different display options are available for the equity section. As illustrated in Exhibit 10-11, those options are: (1) each type of equity account on a separate line, (2) one lump sum for the equity of the component unit, or (3) one line for each fund type equity.

Because of the additional reporting burden related to component units, the GASB does allow the omission of some things from the CAFR. For example, financial data for individual funds is not required as long as it is available in the separate financial statements of the component units. Also, budgetary data for discretely presented component units need not be reported in the reporting entity's combined statement of revenues, expenditures, and changes in fund balance—budget and actual.

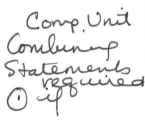

Combining statements related to component units are required in two situations. If fund types are disaggregated in the combined financial statements, combining statements should be prepared for each column in the combined statement. For example, if the reporting entity shows proprietary funds in one column and government funds in another, a combining statement for each fund type should be included in the CAFR. Governments also should present combining statements to support discrete columns that include data for more than one component unit.

Additional disclosures are required for **major** component units. A major component unit is one that is significant in relation to other component units and the primary unit. Although *significant* is not defined specifically in the standard, normal standards of materiality ought to apply in making the judgment. The additional disclosures may be made in the form of either note disclosure or condensed financial statements.

SUMMARY

The systematic arrangement of financial data for specific informational needs is known as financial reporting. It includes reports issued to management, special purpose external reports, and financial statements. For external reporting, the primary focus is the interest of citizen groups, oversight bodies, and investors/creditors. Many of these interested parties need information about specific governmental activities as well as information about the overall performance of the governmental unit.

In developing reporting standards, the GASB has been guided by the practical needs of the various user groups. It has adopted reporting objectives that enable users to assess: (1) an entity's accountability, (2) the entity's operating results, and (3) the level of services that can be provided by the governmental entity and its ability to meet obligations as they become due. Developing reporting standards that meet these objectives is a major agenda item for the GASB. With the exception of those for pensions, the GASB has yet to issue comprehensive reporting guidelines.

Governmental entities issue interim and annual reports. Annual reports are termed *comprehensive annual financial reports*. They include combined and combining financial statements as well as introductory material, an auditor's report, and notes. Budgetary comparisons should be included for all funds for which an annual budget is prepared and approved. Many governmental units also include a statistical section for more detailed reporting of specific trends or activities. Individual statements for the general fund are included in the comprehensive annual financial report. Individual statements for other fund or account groups are optional and usually excluded from the comprehensive annual financial report.

Note disclosure tends to be very detailed. Some notes provide information about the accounting policies used by the reporting entity. Others provide additional information about individual transactions. Still others explain or discuss major events transpiring during the year. This latter type is usually in narrative form.

Governmental entities are allowed to "lift" a portion of the comprehensive annual financial report and use it for broad distribution. The liftable portion of the CAFR is called general purpose financial statements (GPFS). General purpose financial statements include combined financial statements, notes, the auditor's opinion, and general narratives. GPFS are less likely to confuse the lay reader; they provide a general overview of the entity, leaving the detailed CAFR for the more knowledgeable user.

Specific note disclosures are required for enterprise funds qualifying as segments and for cash deposits and selected investments. Segment information is required if the enterprise fund has material long-term liabilities outstanding, if failure to disclose these funds separately would be misleading, or in order to maintain interperiod comparability. Disclosure requirements for segments include descriptive information about the fund as well as financial data used to assess performance and financial solvency.

Deposits with financial institutions and certain investments may entail unusual risks to governmental entities. These risks must be disclosed in the notes. The level of risk depends upon who holds the collateral for deposits or investments, such as repurchase or reverse repurchase agreements. The governmental entity must disclose this information as well as the value of the collateral in relation to the deposit or investment.

A comprehensive annual financial report is issued for each reporting unit. Trying to decide which potential component units should be included within a reporting unit is a difficult issue in the governmental sector. Although accountability determines exclusion or inclusion, the fact that one unit *does not own another* makes accountability an elusive criterion.

Under current GASB standards, a primary unit is accountable for a potential component unit if it appoints the majority of the board and either imposes its will on that unit or assumes a financial burden for or provides financial benefits to the component unit. These criteria need to be interpreted carefully, and accountants need to exercise professional judgment in applying them.

Professional judgment is particularly critical in making the decision about how to display the component units. Users' needs and the nature of the component unit should be considered when selecting the type of discrete display to use.

QUESTIONS

10-1 What is a comprehensive annual financial report? What is included in such a report?

10-2 What types of reports are typically produced by governmental entities? Describe each type.

10-3 Who uses a governmental entity's financial statements? Are the users of governmental financial statements different from those found in the private sector?

10-4 Describe the types of notes common to governmental financial statements.

10-5 What disclosure requirements pertain to repurchase agreements?

10-6 Explain the circumstances in which segment information must be shown for enterprise funds. Why is it important to disclose segment information for some enterprise funds?

10-7 Explain several circumstances that might cause financial statements to lack comparability between periods or among governmental entities.

10-8 Explain the risks associated with governmental deposits in financial institutions. How could a governmental entity avoid these risks?

10-9 What are general purpose financial statements? What is their intended use?

10-10 What is the difference between combining and combined financial statements? Which ones are more useful to the users of financial statements?

10-11 Why is it important to define the reporting unit correctly and consistently?

10-12 What items might appear in the statistical section of a comprehensive annual financial report? How do items included in the statistical section differ from financial detail notes?

10-13 What is a report on internal controls? Why is it important to include the report in the comprehensive annual financial report?

10-14 What are reverse repurchase agreements? How would a governmental unit limit the risk associated with such a transaction?

10-15 Define the current reporting objectives for governmental units.

10-16 What are special purpose reports? Give examples and explain why they are important aspects of governmental financial reporting.

10-17 How might internal reports used in governmental entities differ from internal reports used in private industry? How are they similar?

10-18 How is the CAFR organized? What are the major organizational differences between the CAFR and the annual financial report for a business?

CASES

10-1 Auditors for the state of Texarkana are trying to determine the state's reporting entity. The University of Texarkana and other publicly supported institutions of higher education pose particular problems in this regard. All colleges and universities are governed by a Board of Regents, the chairperson of which is appointed by the governor. Other members are selected by the board. The Board of Regents is responsible for all aspects of governance: hiring and firing standards, admission requirements, salary scales and tuition charges, curriculum requirements, and degree-granting options for the various institutions.

Texarkana's institutions of higher education are heavily research-oriented, receiving approximately one-half of their support from federal and private sources. The other half is derived from a state appropriation and tuition and fees. Each institution has its own admission policy, but in general any student from an in-state high school who graduates in the top 30 percent of the graduating class is admitted. Admission requirements for out-of-state students are more rigorous. Total state funding for higher education is approximately 20 percent of the state's general fund expenditures.

Faculty and staff are members of several different unions. All contract negotiations are made between the unions and the Board of Regents. Contracts negotiated are not necessarily consistent with contracts bargained for by other state employees.

Appropriation requests are submitted to the state budget director, and the governor decides what request will be made to the legislature. Frequently, Board of Regents representatives are able to secure funding other than that requested by the governor. Once the budget is approved, the higher education institutions must abide by all state laws in spending the resources.

REQUIRED
1. Is the system of higher education a component unit of the state of Texarkana? Explain.
2. What additional information might make the decision easier?

10-2 Mudville uses a cash basis for budgeting while its accounting system and resulting financial statements adhere to generally accepted accounting principles. The primary difference between the cash budget and the accounting records is in the areas of accrued interest receivable, property taxes, and miscellaneous other revenues, such as revenue sharing.

City department heads prepare preliminary budget requests and submit the requests to the mayor, who forwards the city's entire budget request to the city council. The preliminary budgets must be submitted to the mayor by January 1; the budget request must be forwarded to the city council by February 1. The city's fiscal period is July 1 to June 30.

REQUIRED
1. What type(s) of note(s) would be used to present this information in a comprehensive annual financial report? Explain.

2. Draft the appropriate note(s) pertaining to this information. Leave blanks for any monetary amounts that should be disclosed.

10-3   An influential citizen has raised a number of questions about the operations and financial condition of the city of Tidewell:

1. What are the city's various special revenue sources, and how much of the total has been obtained from federal financial assistance programs?
2. How does the tax levy this year compare with prior years? Is the tax base shrinking? Is the levy increasing or decreasing? How do actual collections this year compare with those of earlier periods?
3. How many separate construction activities is the city involved in? What are they for? Taken as a whole, what is the financial status of these projects? Are they under budget? Over budget?

REQUIRED

Assuming Tidewell produces a comprehensive annual financial report that satisfies all reporting standards, indicate the section of the report to which the citizen would refer to obtain the information requested. Be specific. If the information cannot be found in the comprehensive annual financial report, describe the contents of the special report that would be necessary to provide the data.

10-4   Several reporting formats are possible for component units. Describe each format briefly, indicate when each is preferable, and explain why.

10-5   The following data were extracted from a comprehensive annual financial report of a governmental entity.
   Changes in the general fixed asset account group during the fiscal year are shown below:

	Balance 1/1/X8	Additions	Retirements	Completed Construction	Transfers	Balance 12/31/X8
Land	$38,000	$ 550	$—	$ —	$ —	$38,550
Buildings	7,800	31	—	472	(87)	8,216
Improvements Other Than Buildings	4,600	—	—	—	—	4,600
Equipment	7,400	1,200	(64)	—	(4,100)	4,436
Construction in Progress	700	2,058	—	(472)	—	2,286
Totals	$58,500	$3,839	$(64)	$(-0-)	$(4,187)	$58,088

REQUIRED

1. Should these data have been included in the statistical section of the comprehensive annual financial report or in a note on fixed assets? Explain.
2. How should the data be altered in order to place it in the section not selected in part 1?

EXERCISES

10-1 Using the information pertaining to Raleigh, North Carolina, contained in Appendix A of the textbook, answer the following questions:

1. What financial statements are presented for Raleigh? Is there an individual statement for the general fund? Do the statements appear to use the same format recommended in the chapter? For which funds are combining statements presented? Are any budgetary statements included? If so, to what funds do they apply?

2. Does Raleigh's comprehensive annual financial report reflect the same general format as recommended in the chapter? What differences are evident?

3. What topics are covered in the introductory narrative? What other topics might have been covered? Is the auditor's report included in the introductory section?

4. What items are covered by the significant accounting policies note? Are the notes clearly written and informative? What note was the most difficult to understand? The easiest?

5. What supporting schedules are included in the statistical section? Is this section clearly marked? Can you tell whether the auditor's opinion covers the statistical section? What other data might have been included in the statistical section?

10-2 Select the best answer for each question.

1. Which of the following is not a reporting objective for governmental financial reports?
   a. to enable users to evaluate a unit's financial position and productive resources
   b. to demonstrate and assess accountability
   c. to enable users to judge a unit's operating results
   d. to provide cash flow projections

2. A governmental entity's component unit is:
   a. one or more of the entity's separate funds
   b. any organization receiving funding from the entity
   c. a unit for which the entity is accountable
   d. none of the above

3. Which of the following statements would be prepared for a governmental entity's general fund?
   a. statement of revenues, expenditures, and changes in fund balance
   b. statement of revenues, expenditures, and changes in fund balance —budget and actual
   c. balance sheet
   d. all of the above

4. A financial report designed to present data relevant for a specific decision or type of user is called a(n):
   a. internal report
   b. financial statement

    c. special purpose report
    d. supporting schedule

5. Which of the following presentation schemes for component units is used most often under the GASB promulgation?
    a. discrete presentation
    b. consolidation
    c. blending
    d. combining statements

6. Segment information may be a required disclosure for:
    a. proprietary funds
    b. fiduciary funds
    c. enterprise funds
    d. nonexpendable trust funds

7. One user group for governmental financial statements is:
    a. taxing authorities
    b. regulatory agencies
    c. oversight board
    d. all of the above

8. General purpose financial statements:
    a. are required for all governmental entities
    b. may be prepared for smaller governmental entities that are not required to prepare a comprehensive annual financial report
    c. include selected portions of the CAFR for general distribution
    d. are prepared independently of the audited financial statements

9. The report on internal controls:
    a. is prepared in connection with the single audit
    b. is issued privately to management following an audit
    c. discusses the limitations of the audit scope
    d. all of the above

10. Combined financial statements show:
    a. each fund or account group in a separate column
    b. balance sheet data for an entity and its component unit
    c. the overall financial position or operating results for a governmental entity
    d. each governmental fund in a separate column with a memo total

10-3 Select the best answer for each question.

1. The comprehensive annual financial report (CAFR) of a governmental unit should contain a combined statement of revenues, expenses, and changes in retained earnings for:

	Governmental Funds	Proprietary Funds
a.	no	yes
b.	no	no
c.	yes	no
d.	yes	yes

(Adapted from the May 1986 CPA Exam, Theory #58)

2. The CAFR of a governmental unit should contain a combined balance sheet for:

	Governmental Funds	Proprietary Funds	Account Groups
a.	yes	yes	no
b.	yes	yes	yes
c.	yes	no	yes
d.	no	yes	no

(Adapted from the May 1985 CPA Exam, Theory #58)

3. Which of the following would be included in the combined statement of revenues, expenditures, and changes in fund balances — budget and actual in the CAFR of a governmental unit?

	Enterprise Fund	General Fixed Asset Account Group
a.	yes	yes
b.	yes	no
c.	no	yes
d.	no	no

(Adapted from the May 1984 CPA Exam, Theory #58)

4. The introductory section of a governmental CAFR would include:
   a. the auditor's report on internal controls
   b. the auditor's opinion statement on federal financial assistance programs
   c. the Certificate of Achievement
   d. the auditor's opinion on the general purpose financial statements
5. Which of the following is not the purpose of notes to governmental financial statements?
   a. to explain further data included in the financial statements
   b. to define significant accounting practices and policies followed by the governmental entity
   c. to highlight the environment in which the governmental entity operates
   d. to provide additional information that cannot be included on the face of the statement
6. The ending fund balance for a governmental fund type would appear on:
   a. combining statement of revenues, expenditures, and changes in fund balance
   b. combined statement of revenues, expenditures, and changes in fund balance
   c. statement of revenues, expenditures, and changes in fund balance — budget and actual
   d. all of the above

7. Under a discrete presentation, the component unit's financial results would be:
   a. shown in a separate column on the combined financial statements included in the comprehensive annual financial report
   b. consolidated with those of the reporting unit
   c. disclosed in the statistical section of the reporting unit's CAFR
   d. none of the above
8. General purpose financial statements include:
   a. combining financial statements, notes, auditor's opinion, and narrative
   b. combined financial statements, notes, auditor's opinion, and narrative
   c. combined and combining statements, notes, auditor's opinion, and narrative
   d. combined statements, statistical section, notes, and auditor's opinion
9. Segment information for enterprise funds must be:
   a. disclosed in the body of the financial statements
   b. disclosed in the statistical section of the financial statements
   c. shown either in the body of the financial statements or in the notes
   d. shown in either the body of the statements or the statistical section
10. A correct heading for a statement of financial position should show the date:
    a. as of the statement date
    b. for the period ending with the statement date
    c. for the two periods encompassing the changes shown in the statement
    d. none of the above

10-4 A pre-closing trial balance for Denville County's general fund follows (budgetary accounts have been ignored to simplify the presentation):

Denville County
General Fund
Pre-Closing Trial Balance
December 31, 19X9
($000)

Cash	$ 23,510	
Accounts Receivable	1,157	
Due from Other Funds	746	
Taxes Receivable—Current	177	
Due from Other Governments	1,140	
Inventories	460	
Advances to Other Funds	3,990	
Allowance for Uncollectible Current Taxes		$ 22
Allowance for Uncollectible Accounts Receivable		160
Accounts Payable		1,827
Accrued Liabilities		1,076
Compensated Absences		270
Due to Other Funds		47
Due to Other Governments		6,790

(continued)

(continued)

Deferred Revenues		248
Tax Anticipation Notes Payable		1,935
Reserve for Inventories		460
Reserve for Encumbrances		314
Reserve for Advances to Other Funds		3,990
Unreserved Fund Balance		263
Designated for Project Appropriations		12,277
Property Tax Revenues		18,110
Licenses and Fees		9,544
Intergovernmental Revenues		24,090
Fines and Forfeitures		1,098
Sales Tax Revenues		10,650
Other Revenues		5,350
Administrative Expenditures	2,485	
Planning and Development Expenditures	2,723	
Finance Expenditures	1,161	
Public Safety and Security Expenditures	30,500	
Social Services Expenditures	15,216	
Public Recreation and Entertainment Expenditures	8,600	
Other Current Operating Expenditures	4,167	
Capital Outlay Expenditures	122	
Debt Service Expenditures	6,774	
Operating Transfers In		15,000
Operating Transfers Out	10,593	
Totals	$113,521	$113,521

Denville's balance sheet for the year ending December 31, 19X8, follows:

Denville County
General Fund
Balance Sheet
December 31, 19X8
($000)

Assets

Cash	$18,200
Accounts Receivable	1,600
Allowance for Uncollectible Accounts Receivable	(115)
Due from Other Funds	200
Taxes Receivable—Current	521
Allowance for Uncollectible Taxes	(47)
Due from Other Governments	116
Inventories	375
Advances to Other Funds	4,120
TOTAL ASSETS	$24,970

Liabilities and Fund Balance

Liabilities:

Accounts Payable	$ 4,608
Accrued Liabilities	1,210
Compensated Absences	182
Due to Other Funds	16
Due to Other Governments	1,470
Deferred Revenues	180
Total Liabilities	$ 7,666

(continued)

(continued)

Fund Balance:	
Reserve for Inventories	$ 375
Reserve for Encumbrances	2,909
Reserve for Advances	4,120
Unreserved Fund Balance	900
Designated for Projects	9,000
Total Fund Balance	$17,304
TOTAL LIABILITIES AND FUND BALANCE	$24,970

REQUIRED

Prepare the balance sheet and the statement of revenues, expenditures, and changes in fund balance for Denville's general fund. The balance sheet should be in the comparative form.

10-5   Denville's general fund budget for the year ending December 31, 19X9, follows:

Denville County
General Fund Budget
For the Year Ending December 31, 19X9
($000)

Revenues:	
Property Taxes	$18,622
Licenses and Fees	9,536
Intergovernmental	24,901
Fines and Forfeitures	1,149
Sales Taxes	9,844
Other	5,211
Total Revenues	$69,263
Current Operating Expenditures:	
Administrative	$ 2,564
Planning and Development	2,168
Finance	1,162
Public Safety and Security	29,655
Social Services	15,337
Public Recreation and Entertainment	8,721
Other Current Operating Expenditures	4,239
Total Operating Expenditures	$63,846
Capital Outlays	123
Debt Service Expenditures	6,774
Total Expenditures	$70,743
Operating Transfers In	14,668
Operating Transfers Out	9,326
Total Operating Expenditures and Other Financing Sources and Uses	$65,401

REQUIRED

Using the information presented above and in exercise 10-4, prepare a statement of revenues, expenditures, and changes in fund balance — budget and actual, for Denvill's general fund for the year ending December 31, 19X9.

10-6   The statements prepared in exercises 10-4 and 10-5 were submitted to Denville's newest county commissioner. Never having been a commissioner before, he is unable to evaluate the performance and financial position of the county. He asks for assistance in addressing the major issues outlined below:

1. Did Denville spend as much as was budgeted to serve county residents? Which figures pertain to the services provided? How is it possible that the county budgeted expenditures in excess of revenues? Is that a poor practice?
2. Is the county solvent? Is its position improving or deteriorating? Is the unreserved fund balance adequate? What does it mean when there is an unreserved fund balance? Does that represent cash that can be budgeted for the succeeding year?
3. What key budgeting issues might the commissioner face based on past performance of the county's several departments?

REQUIRED

Draft a report that addresses the questions raised by the new commissioner. Justify all conclusions reached in the report and document the conclusions with figures from the financial statements.

10-7   Following are balance sheets and operating statements for the city of Crocket's three enterprise funds:

City of Crocket
Enterprise Funds
Condensed Balance Sheets
As of December 31,19X7

	Water Utility	Parking	Golf Course
Assets			
Current Assets:			
Cash and Investments	$ 110,470	$ 65,000	$ 4,390
Accounts Receivable	22,100	15,109	7,432
Allowance for Doubtful Accounts	(1,642)	(175)	(53)
Due from Other Governments	1,219	910	—
Due from Other Funds	17,600	—	—
Inventories	—	—	16,100
Prepaid Expenses	1,850	—	780
Total Current Assets	$ 151,597	$ 80,844	$ 28,649
Restricted Assets:			
Cash	$ 50,100	—	$ —
Due from Other Governments	—	—	1,600
Total Restricted Assets	$ 50,100	$ —	$ 1,600
Property, Plant, and Equipment:			
Land	$ 70,600	$ 30,900	$110,000
Buildings (Utility Plant)	890,000	260,000	16,900

(continued)

(continued)

	Water Utility	Parking	Golf Course
Equipment	680,000	106,000	69,320
Other	10,470	—	—
Total	$1,651,070	$ 396,900	$196,220
Less: Accumulated Depreciation	(495,320)	(119,070)	(58,866)
Net Property, Plant, and Equipment	$1,155,750	$ 277,830	$137,354
Unamortized Bond Discount	46,600	—	—
TOTAL ASSETS	$1,404,047	$ 358,674	$167,603

Liabilities and Fund Equity

	Water Utility	Parking	Golf Course
Current Liabilities:			
Accounts Payable	$ 106,200	$ 1,200	$ 600
Accrued Liabilities	10,800	4,110	1,900
Advance Payments	—	—	4,810
Accrued Interest	7,200	1,500	—
Due to Other Funds	—	—	960
Other Current Liabilities	1,040	690	—
Total Current Liabilities	$ 125,240	$ 7,500	$ 8,270
Long-Term Liabilities:			
Bonds Payable	$ 860,000	$ 300,000	$ —
Advances from Crocket General Fund	—	—	130,000
Advances from Other Funds	—	—	9,881
Leases Payable	—	12,000	—
Total Long-Term Liabilities	$ 860,000	312,000	$139,881
Fund Equity:			
Reserved for Debt Service	$ 260,000	$ 40,000	$ 14,430
Reserved for Capital Projects	75,000	—	—
Reserved for Renewal and Replacement	—	2,690	5,000
Unreserved	83,807	(3,516)	22
Total Fund Equity	$ 418,807	$ 39,174	$ 19,452
TOTAL LIABILITIES AND FUND EQUITY	$1,404,047	$ 358,674	$167,603

City of Crocket
Enterprise Funds
Statement of Revenue and Expenses
For the Year Ending December 31, 19X7

	Water Utility	Parking	Golf Course
Revenues:			
User Charges	$460,000	$ —	$ —
Fees	—	5,600	98,000
Rental Income	—	132,000	8,290
Parking Fines	—	1,200	—
Equipment Sales	—	—	15,400
Total Operating Revenues	$460,000	$138,800	$121,690

(continued)

(continued)

	Water Utility	Parking	Golf Course
Operating Expenses:			
Salaries and Wages	$160,000	$ 62,100	$ 51,940
Employee Benefits	21,220	13,040	10,907
Contractual Services	10,760	16,200	15,200
Depreciation	61,512	19,845	9,810
Material and Supplies	15,931	5,319	1,210
Insurance	4,910	1,720	6,200
Payments in Lieu of Taxes	—	—	9,230
Cost of Equipment Sold	—	—	9,230
Other Operating Expenses	16,940	19,136	6,763
Total Operating Expenses	$291,273	$137,360	$120,490
Operating Income	$168,727	$ 1,440	$ 1,200
Nonoperating Revenues (Expenses)			
Income on Investments	$ 8,000	$ 4,200	$ —
Interest Expense	(60,200)	(20,840)	—
Net Nonoperating Income (Expense)	$ (52,200)	$ (16,640)	$ —
Income (Loss) Before Other Sources and Uses	$116,527	$ (15,200)	$ 1,200
Other Sources and Uses:			
Operating Transfers In	—	12,400	—
Operating Transfers Out	(81,500)	—	—
Total Other Sources (Uses)	$ (81,500)	$ 12,400	$ —
Income Before Extraordinary Items	$ 35,027	$ (2,800)	$ 1,200
Extraordinary Gain on Advance Refunding	—	1,400	—
NET INCOME	$ 35,027	$ (1,400)	$ 1,200

ADDITIONAL INFORMATION

1. For the past several years, segment information has been shown for the water utility enterprise fund, largely based on the material amount of long-term debt that existed in those years. The utility fund provides electrical power for city residents.
2. The parking facility fund operates a downtown parking structure originally financed by issuing bonds. Those parking in the facility can rent spaces by the month or pay by the hour.
3. The golf course was initially developed by an advance from an internal service fund. Over the years, the golf course fund has been repaying that advance.

REQUIRED

1. Should segment information be shown for any of the enterprise funds? Explain and provide documentation for your answer.
2. If segment information should be disclosed, list some of the items that should be included in the notes or financial statements.

10-8 Revenue and expenditure data follow for Bally County and its one component unit. The data shown pertain to the special revenue funds of each entity.

Bally County
Special Revenue Funds
Condensed Statement of Revenue, Expenditures,
and Changes in Fund Balance
For the Period Ending June 10, 19X0   *sale to*
($000)

	Bally County	Component Unit
Revenues:		
Property Taxes	$2,511	$ 40
Sales Taxes		1,210
Other	—	52
Total Revenues	$2,511	$1,302
Expenditures:		
Salaries and Wages	$1,310	$ 341
Employee Benefits	56	22
Materials and Supplies Used	560	816
Equipment Rental	240	10
Other	160	36
Total Expenditures	$2,326	$1,225
Excess (Deficiency) of Revenues Over (Under) Expenditures	$ 185	$ 77
Fund Balance, Beginning of the Year	110	(10)
Fund Balance, End of the Year	$ 295	$ 67

REQUIRED

Assuming there are intercompany payables and receivables of $46,000 resulting from the sale of materials and supplies at cost from the component unit to Bally during the year (all materials and supplies were used), depict the component unit by: (a) blending, (b) consolidation, and (c) discrete presentations.

10-9   The bookkeeper for the Cade County school district is not versed in preparing financial statements for governmental units. She prepared the following balance sheet for combining all funds for the school district when instructed to prepare a combined balance sheet.

Cade County School District
Combined Balance Sheet
As of June 30, 19X1

Assets	
Cash	$321,132
Investments	31,000
Receivables—	
Taxes	58,398
Loans	62,000
Accrued Interest	1,800
Allowance for Uncollectible Taxes	(57,200)
Due from Other Funds	12,400
Due from Other Governments	116,000

(continued)

(continued)

Inventory	29,868
Prepaid Expenses	4,060
Equipment	110,000
Accumulated Depreciation	(46,120)
TOTAL ASSETS	**$643,338**

Liabilities and Fund Balance

Accounts Payable	$316,830
Vouchers Payable	27,940
Bonds Payable	62,790
Long-Term Loans Payable	62,000
Due to Other Funds	12,400
Deposits from Users	11,300
Total Liabilities	$493,260
Reserve for Inventory	29,868
Reserve for Encumbrances	18,520
Reserve for Loans	62,790
Unreserved	38,900
Total Fund Balance	$150,078
TOTAL LIABILITIES AND FUND BALANCE	$643,338

ADDITIONAL INFORMATION

1. The Cade County school district operates three funds: special revenue, general fund, and internal service.
2. The internal service fund is a copy center for all school district personnel. It was started by a loan from the general fund. All inventories and prepaid items relate to the internal service fund. It operates solely on user charges, of which $11,000 is due from the general fund and $1,400 from the special revenue fund.
3. The special revenue fund is supported, in part, by a special earmarked portion of the property tax levy. The fund is due $50,000 of current property taxes. The proportion of bad debts is the same for the entire property tax levy. The remaining support comes from intergovernmental grants.
4. The general fund's unreserved fund balance on June 30, 19X1, is $8,478. Sixty-five thousand dollars of the total cash and all of the total investments relate to general fund activities. It also has accounts payable of $162,000 and $20,000 of vouchers payable.
5. The general fund has a receivable of $60,000 from the state.
6. The special revenue fund has no accounts payable due, but does have vouchers due of $7,940. It has just enough cash to cover total liabilities.

REQUIRED

Prepare a spreadsheet in which the combined total is allocated to each fund. An adjustment column is not necessary. (Hint: Add up the column totals when the allocations based on the additional information have been completed.)

10-10   Selected balance sheet information for a component unit's general fund, special revenue fund, and all other funds are displayed below. Combined balance sheet data for the primary unit also are provided.

Selected Balance Sheet Information
For the Primary and Component Unit

	PRIMARY UNIT COMBINING DATA			COMPONENT UNIT INDIVIDUAL FUNDS		
	General Fund	Special Revenue	All Others	General Fund	Special Revenue	All Others
Assets						
Cash	$ 180	$56	$ 200	$40	$10	$ 60
Taxes Receivable (Net)	1,200	15	—	—	20	—
Due from Other Funds	10	—	10	20	—	—
Component Unit Receivables	30	—	—	—	—	—
Fixed Assets	—	—	42,500	—	—	2,110
Amount to Be Provided	—	—	27,400	—	—	1,000
TOTAL ASSETS	$1,420	$71	$70,110	$60	$30	$3,170
Liabilities and Fund Equity						
Due to Other Funds	$ —	$10	$ 10	$20	$—	$ —
Component Unit Payables	—	—	—	—	20	10
Accounts Payable	1,100	50	150	30	10	—
Long-Term Debt	—	—	27,400	—	—	1,000
Investment in Fixed Assets	—	—	42,500	—	—	2,110
Fund Equity	320	11	50	10	—	50
TOTAL LIABILITIES AND FUND EQUITY	$1,420	$71	$70,110	$60	$30	$3,170

REQUIRED

1. Prepare a combined balance sheet for the reporting entity, using the discrete format with a single column and appropriate "totals" columns.
2. Prepare a combined balance sheet for the reporting entity using the blending presentation style.

CHAPTER 11

State and Local Government Audits

Chapter 10 pointed out that taxpayers, oversight boards, and bonding agencies are demanding improved financial reporting by state and local governments. In response, more and more entities are preparing financial statements using generally accepted accounting principles (GAAP) and having financial statements audited in accordance with generally accepted auditing standards (GAAS). Many local government audits are conducted by public accountants. Therefore, accountants must be knowledgeable about governmental audit practices.

This chapter describes the types of audits conducted at the state and local levels, the audit standards applicable to these audits, and recent concerns over the quality of governmental audits performed by public accountants. More detailed information on compliance auditing is contained in Chapter 12.

AUDIT ENVIRONMENT OF STATE AND LOCAL GOVERNMENTS

Oversight boards have a fiduciary responsibility to taxpayers and other resource providers, the general public, and other interested parties. They need to explain how resources obtained during the period were used, whether interperiod equity was maintained, and what the entity's financial position was at year end. Most provide this information in the form of a comprehensive annual financial report, which includes general purpose financial statements. Increasingly, these financial statements are audited.

Accountability

One financial reporting objective for governmental entities is to ensure that information contained in financial reports enables users to assess accountability. As the GASB *Concepts Statement No. 1* phrases it:

> Accountability is the cornerstone of all financial reporting in government. . . . Accountability requires governments to answer to the citizenry—to justify raising public resources and the purposes for which they are used. Governmental accountability is based on the belief that the citizenry has a "right to know," a right to receive openly declared facts that may lead to public debate by the citizens and their elected representatives.[1]

[1]Governmental Accounting Standards Board, *Concepts Statement No. 1, Objectives of Financial Reporting* (Norwalk, Conn.: GASB, 1987), ¶56.

Accountability begins with full disclosure. In accounting, full disclosure means giving users a complete set of financial statements: an operating statement, a balance sheet, and a statement of changes in net assets/cash flow for the various funds. Users also need to understand the basis on which the financial reports were prepared. At the very least, the entity must state that the reports were prepared according to GAAP, or if not GAAP, what basis was used and why.

Audited financial statements provide a basis for users to assess an entity's accounting and reporting practices. Auditors are independent of the entity being audited. They not only disclose whether the statements were prepared according to GAAP, but also attest to the fairness of the presentation. Users need not rely solely on an entity's description of the accounting practices. The auditor's statement is like getting a second opinion in medicine.

Compliance

An entity's fiduciary responsibilities include compliance with fiscal requirements. Users must know whether an entity lived within its overall budget. They also examine actual and budgeted revenues and expenses to determine significant variances. When the federal government makes grants to or contracts with state and local units, it is interested in verifying that program funds were spent for the intended purpose and only on allowable costs. For example, if expenditures for certain types of equipment or modes of travel are unallowable, the federal agency will not pay for them.

Audited financial statements add credibility to an entity's claims, demonstrating compliance with the rules and regulations. Auditors examine, on a sample basis, individual transactions to determine if they were recorded correctly and if they were allowable. Although audits are not intended to discover fraud or other illegal acts, the auditor does examine the extent to which the entity complied with legal and regulatory mandates.

Other Pressures for Audited Financial Statements

Mounting pressure for greater accountability and compliance results from *users* demanding audited financial statements. However, users are not the only source of such pressure. Financial and accounting officers of governmental entities also push for audited financial statements.

The Governmental Finance Officers Association (GFOA) instituted a Certificate of Achievement Program that recognizes excellence in financial reporting. The entity may publish this award in its comprehensive annual financial report (CAFR) the year following receipt of the award, thereby enhancing its public image. To be eligible for a Certificate, the CAFR must include general purpose financial statements prepared in substantial conformance with GAAP that *have been independently examined in accordance with generally accepted auditing standards.*

An entity's bond rating may be enhanced by submitting audited financial statements. Two major credit-rating firms recommend that the financial statements be audited by public accounting firms or by qualified, independent state or local agencies as a condition for receiving a favorable rating.[2] A favorable rating may lower debt financing costs, a matter of considerable interest to all financial officers. For the same reasons that the public feels more comfortable with audited financial statements, bond rating agencies view audited financial statements as one indication that they did not miss something significant in their evaluation of the governmental unit. Also, generally accepted auditing standards require auditors to comment if the unit's future is uncertain (the going concern evaluation). In times of fiscal stress, the going concern evaluation may be far more than a cursory examination. Exhibit 11-1 depicts the pressures for audited financial statements.

AUDITS OF STATE AND LOCAL GOVERNMENTS

gov't audits
① financial
* (fed funding)*
② performance

All audits have objectives. Those objectives determine the type of audit to be conducted and the audit standards to be followed. Two broad types of governmental audits are performed: financial and performance audits. A financial audit usually is required whenever the governmental entity receives federal funding. Performance audits are done under special circumstances and also may be required when federal funding is provided to state and local governments.

Exhibit 11-1

Pressures for Audited Financial Statements

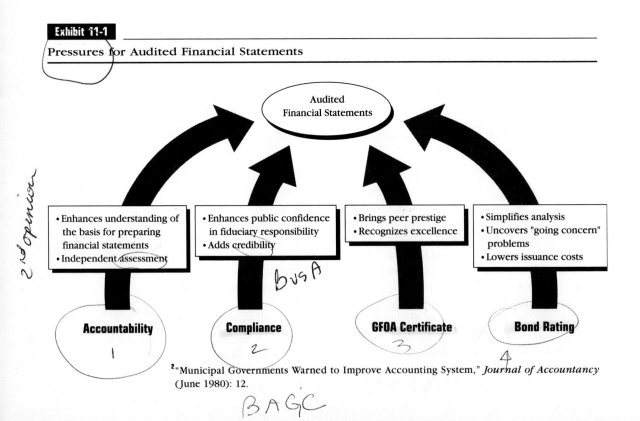

2nd opinion

| Accountability | Compliance | GFOA Certificate | Bond Rating |

- Enhances understanding of the basis for preparing financial statements
- Independent assessment

- Enhances public confidence in fiduciary responsibility
- Adds credibility

- Brings peer prestige
- Recognizes excellence

- Simplifies analysis
- Uncovers "going concern" problems
- Lowers issuance costs

B vs A

Accountability   1
Compliance   2
GFOA Certificate   3
Bond Rating   4

Audited Financial Statements

[2] "Municipal Governments Warned to Improve Accounting System," *Journal of Accountancy* (June 1980): 12.

BAGC

As Exhibit 11-2 indicates, the objective of **financial audits** (also called operational audits) is to determine the **fair presentation** of financial position, results of operations, and cash flows in accordance with generally accepted accounting principles, and to determine **compliance** with applicable laws and regulations relating to transactions and events. **Performance audits** include economy and efficiency, and effectiveness audits. **Economy and efficiency audits** focus on the efficient use of resources, while **effectiveness audits** examine program achievements. If a unit combined the objectives of all these audits, it would refer to the result as a **comprehensive audit.**

Because governments lack a profit motive, the audit criteria are broader than those for businesses. Governments operate in an environment in which compliance with legal requirements is a critical element of performance. Therefore, the audit scope for a financial audit is broadened to include both fair presentation and compliance. As with business, the auditor states an opinion about fair presentation, in conformity with GAAP, and in compliance with laws, regulations, and budgetary constraints.

The following sections describe financial and performance auditing, and discuss the auditor's responsibility for each type of audit.

Financial Audits

The fair presentation portion of the financial audit serves the same objective for a government as for a private firm—that is, as an expression of an opinion

---

Exhibit 11-2

Audits of State and Local Governments

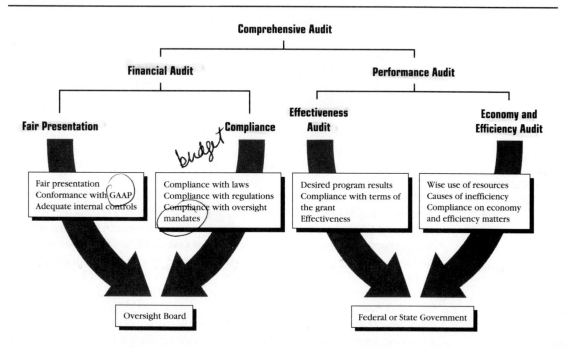

on the fairness of presentation in conformity with GAAP. Auditors examine the internal control procedures and test the accuracy of certain financial transactions and balances. Selected expenditure transactions are examined, and related liability and asset balances are verified. Similarly, selected revenue transactions are examined, along with the resulting asset and liability balances. The auditors also determine the adequacy of disclosure by examining the notes and supporting schedules.

The compliance aspect involves judging adherence to specific requirements. One aspect of compliance is related to the budget: whether the governmental unit limited its expenditures to the total authorized by the oversight board. A governmental entity must also comply with laws imposed by federal or state governments or by local ordinance. Specific mandates may be issued by the city council, county commissioners, or other governing board. For example, the board may require that general fund subsidies to an enterprise activity be limited to a certain sum. If the governing board adopted this limit, another aspect of compliance would be management's adherence to that mandate.

The Impact of Fund Accounting on Financial Audit Procedures   Although the presence of fund accounting does not change the overall purpose of a financial audit, it does add additional review work. Interfund transactions must be examined to determine if the appropriate payables and receivables have been recorded and properly classified in the affected funds. The funds and account groups must be reviewed to determine whether the appropriate liabilities and assets are reported. For example, the auditor must verify that the general long-term debt account group contains all long-term liabilities.

Fund accounting also complicates disclosure requirements. A comprehensive financial report must include the general purpose financial statements:

1. A combined balance sheet for all fund types and account groups
2. A combined statement of revenues, expenditures, and changes in fund balances — budget and actual for those funds using budgets
3. A combined statement of revenues, expenditures, and changes in fund balance
4. A combined statement of revenues, expenses, and changes in fund equity — all proprietary fund types
5. A combined statement of cash flows — all proprietary fund types

The number of required statements complicates disclosures. In addition, (and as indicated in earlier chapters) required supplementary information is more extensive than it would be without the fund structure. When a given transaction could be reported in more than one fund, statement users should be told which transactions are in what funds. A reader must understand, for example, the difference between debt reported in the general long-term debt account group and debt reported in the general fund.

Non-GAAP Presentations   Some state or local governments prescribe accounting bases, financial reports, and audit guidelines inconsistent with those prescribed by the GASB. For example, a state may require cash-basis accounting when GAAP requires the modified accrual basis of accounting. Consequently, the financial statements provided to the oversight body must conform to the governmental unit's requirements.

An auditor conducting a financial audit has two choices when non-GAAP reporting or accounting practices are required. One alternative is to write an opinion statement indicating that the financial statements are not in conformity with GAAP—that is, the governmental unit receives a qualified or adverse opinion. The other option is to issue the state or local statements as special purpose reports, and prepare another set of financial statements according to GAAP. A separate opinion statement would cover the GAAP statements. An opinion may be given on the extent to which the special purpose reports conform to state or local law.

[handwritten margin note: Non Gaap Used — give opinion or — prepare another set of fin. statem]

Performance Audits

If a state or local entity receives funds from the federal government, performance audits may be required. Performance audits are designed to assess the economy and efficiency of an entity's operations, or the effectiveness of the programs it offers. In an **economy and efficiency audit,** the auditor determines:

a. Whether the audited entity is managing and utilizing its resources.... economically and efficiently
b. The causes of inefficiencies or uneconomical practices and
c. Whether the entity has complied with laws and regulations concerning matters of economy and efficiency.[3]

Established during the late 1960s, when local and state governments relied heavily on federal funding, the **effectiveness audit** (also called a program audit) judges how well the unit carried out the program financed by the grantor (usually the federal government). Factors inhibiting satisfactory performance are detailed in the audit report.

[handwritten margin note: Performance audits]

Performance audits differ markedly from financial audits. Financial audits are done annually (or biannually), usually by CPAs. Performance audits are conducted infrequently and often by nonaccountants. If done by an accounting firm, performance audits are conducted by the consulting division of the firm, not the audit division. No opinion statement is provided with performance audits. The report issued contains constructive criticism. The federal government uses performance audits to make funding decisions about individual programs and funding choices among state and local entities.

[handwritten margin note: Conducted infrequently — No opinion given — used in funding decisions]

OBSERVATION ▲

A business could also have effectiveness or economy and efficiency audits performed, but they usually are conducted by the internal auditor rather than by the external auditor.

---

[3]United States General Accounting Office, *Government Auditing Standards* (Washington, D.C.: GAO, 1988), 2–3.

EC + Eff
audits

Competitive
bidding

Is it using / manage
its resources
wisely.

Scope of Economy and Efficiency Audits   Economy and efficiency audits are designed to determine whether the entity is managing and using its resources economically and efficiently. The audit report suggests probable causes of inefficiencies. Of particular importance is the extent to which the entity has complied with laws and regulations concerning efficiency. For example, competitive bidding is an accepted practice to decrease the cost of purchased goods and services. An auditor assesses the extent to which competitive bidding practices were followed by the entity. The auditor also recommends ways to improve the efficiency of the entity's operations.

The standards for governmental audits issued by the General Accounting Office (GAO) contain specific recommendations concerning which practices an auditor should review in assessing economy and efficiency. Auditors should, where appropriate, consider whether the entity:

1. Is following sound procurement practices
2. Is following proper procedures to ensure that the needed type, quality, and amount of items are available, and are properly used and maintained
3. Avoids duplication of effort by employees
4. Avoids work that serves little or no purpose
5. Avoids overstaffing
6. Uses efficient operating procedures
7. Uses assets, equipment, and facilities efficiently
8. Is complying with laws and regulations that could significantly affect the acquisition, management, and utilization of the entity's resources
9. Has an adequate system for measuring and reporting performance on economy and efficiency[4]

Items 7 and 8 were added in the 1988 revision of the GAO standards, presumably to reflect the government's growing interest in fixed assets and procurement policies. At the time of the revision, a major scandal was brewing in the Pentagon. Assets had been purchased for outlandish prices and, once purchased, were used inefficiently or discarded. Allegedly the agency had not complied with federal procurement requirements. State and local governments also have had a history of poor procurement and use practices.

Results
achieved

①

② *planned +*
realized
objectives

The Purpose of Effectiveness Audits   Although frequently referred to as program audits, effectiveness audits may be applied to entire organizations or to particular activities or functions. Regardless of the scope, an effectiveness audit focuses on the results achieved and on the relationship between the planned and realized objectives. If the objective is to improve employability through training (for example, the Job Corps), the accomplishment is how many trainees get and keep jobs. Estimating the additional employment is very difficult. Accomplishments are hard to measure, and therefore effectiveness audits are difficult to perform. The GAO standards indicate that an auditor should, where appropriate:

[4]Adapted from *Government Auditing Standards*, 2-3 and 2-4.

1. Assess whether the program objectives are proper, suitable, or relevant
2. Determine the extent to which a program achieves a desired level of program results
3. Assess the effectiveness of the program and/or of individual program components
4. Identify factors inhibiting satisfactory performance
5. Determine whether management has considered alternatives that might yield desired results more effectively or at a lower cost
6. Determine whether the program complements, duplicates, overlaps, or conflicts with other related programs
7. Identify ways of making programs work better
8. Assess compliance with laws and regulations applicable to the program
9. Assess the adequacy of management's system for measuring and reporting effectiveness[5]

As shown by this list of appropriate review areas, a program audit can be very extensive. However, not all possible areas of review need to be included in one audit. The audit may concentrate on only one or two of the areas listed. The written scope of the audit is extremely important because of the broad, all-encompassing nature of the possible review areas.

A Comparative Review of Financial and Performance Auditing

To some laypersons an "audit is an audit," but to professional accountants and oversight agencies, financial and performance auditing are different. The nature of the audit reports is different, as is their focus.

Nature of the Audit Report Perhaps the most significant difference between a financial and a performance audit is the absence of an auditor's opinion in a performance audit. No opinion is justified because, unlike financial auditing, performance auditing does not evaluate absolute states.

Financial audits relate to absolute conditions: the financial statements are presented fairly, the entity followed generally accepted accounting principles, and the principles were applied on a basis consistent with prior years' applications. Although an evaluation involves auditor judgment, conclusions about fairness, adherence, and consistency are based on agreed-upon criteria. Either the agency has achieved these states or it has not. As another example, by sampling certain transactions, an auditor can determine within a certain level of accuracy whether transactions or account balances are correctly stated. Another judgment is whether the transactions are correct or incorrect.

Performance auditing, on the other hand, involves relative assessments. Efficiency, economy, and effectiveness are not absolute terms, such as accuracy or consistency. When making judgments about relative terms, the assessment is always made relative to some standard. For example, an auditor would indicate that compared to some norm, the agency is overstaffed, duplicates the

---

[5]*Government Auditing Standards,* 2-5 and 2-6.

purposes of another, or has irrelevant objectives. An auditor cannot express an opinion about an entity having reached any maximum level of efficiency, economy, or effectiveness.

Differences in Focus   Financial and performance auditing also differ in focus. Financial auditing procedures, even the compliance aspects, concentrate on the financial consequences of certain actions — that is, the recording of accounting transactions and the issuance of financial statements. Performance auditing examines the policies and procedures surrounding the actions. Are the policies and procedures appropriate? Do they lead to effective decisions? Are they relevant to the particular program? Could they be designed to achieve greater efficiencies?

Basis for Auditor's Report   Financial audits rely primarily on financial data. Performance audits are much less quantitative. They emphasize nonmonetary information, and even qualitative, judgmental information. Nonetheless, both financial and performance audits rely on the same internal control system. If, for example, an auditor was evaluating the cost of delivering a particular service, the analysis would be based on the costs reported in the financial statements. Whether financial statements or performance measures accurately portray an entity's operations depends upon the effectiveness of its internal controls.

THE SINGLE AUDIT

Depending upon local requirements and the extent of federal funding, local governments and state agencies conceivably could be under constant audit. For example, an agency might be subject to an annual financial and compliance audit. Each federal program that provides funding may also require an occasional efficiency/economy and/or effectiveness audit. If a local government received funding from ten federal programs, an audit staff could be present constantly, and the audits could overlap. The presence of external auditors requires staff assistance to answer questions, retrieve documentation, and assist in audit procedures. This assistance is time consuming and costly to the governmental entity.

The growth in federal funding of state and local programs during the 1960s and 1970s both increased the audit load and heightened congressional interest in audit results. With a long history of federal agency independence related to auditing, little cooperation existed among the agencies. Sometimes audit staffs were even reluctant to share their audit reports with other agencies. Members of Congress had difficulty assessing the overall performance of a local agency's use of federal dollars when several federal programs provided financial assistance.

To address the problem of audit overload and poor coordination, Congress passed the Single Audit Act in 1984.[6] The law legislated what had been a set of

---

[6]Single Audit Act of 1984, Public Law 98–502.

widely ignored federal regulations suggesting single audits for state and local governments. An estimated 19,000 governmental entities were covered by the new law. The act sets the parameters for the single audit and instructs the Office of Management and Budget (OMB) to interpret and implement the act.

General Requirements of the Single Audit Act

OMB Circular A-128, the implementing regulation, requires all state and local governments to identify the federal funds received and expended in their accounts. If a governmental unit receives more than $100,000 in such funds, a single audit is performed covering all federal funds.

The single audit is conducted by one designated federal agency. Audit results are shared with the other federal agencies that provided funding to the governmental unit being audited. Unless programmatic or compliance violations surface as a result of the single audit, the nonauditing agencies are not supposed to conduct any audit of that governmental unit.

OBSERVATION ▲

Although the intent is a *single* audit, the OMB regulations are very specific about the right of federal agencies to conduct other audits necessary to meet their responsibilities under federal law and regulation.

Entities and Programs Covered by the Act

Any governmental unit receiving $100,000 or more in federal assistance for any one year is subject to a single audit. Those receiving more than $25,000 but less than $100,000 have the option of a single audit or of complying with any applicable audit requirements of the federal program under which the assistance is provided. Governmental units receiving less than $25,000 are exempt from these audit requirements. They must keep adequate records and permit grantor federal agencies and the Comptroller General access to their records.

Federal assistance includes grants, contracts, loans, interest subsidies, cooperative agreements, property, insurance, loan guarantees, or direct appropriations. For purposes of determining the total to any one governmental unit, both federal dollars received directly from the federal government and indirectly through another governmental unit are included.

Defining Local Governments   A local government is defined as any unit of government within a state, including a county, borough, municipality, city, town, township, parish, local public authority, special district, school district, intrastate district, council of governments, or any other instrumentality of local government.[7] The definition of *state* is equally broad, extending to the Commonwealth of Puerto Rico, the Virgin Islands, and other United States'

---

[7]Single Audit Act of 1984, ¶7501.

possessions. It also includes any multistate, regional, or interstate entity as well as Indian tribes that has governmental functions.[8]

The audit scope prescribed by Circular A-128 permits the exclusion of public hospitals and colleges and universities; however, the OMB subsequently issued Circular A-133, which applies to colleges and universities and certain other nonprofit organizations. This latter circular extends similar single audit requirements to these organizations.

Major Federal Assistance Programs   Under the Single Audit Act, the auditor must determine whether the governmental entity has complied with all laws having a material effect on each *major* federal financial assistance program. Compliance is required with both general regulations, such as following procurement standards, and program-specific regulations. The auditor must select and test a representative number of transactions to determine compliance.

A **major federal assistance program** is defined in terms of the relationship between federal assistance expenditures for a given program and total expenditures for all programs. When expenditures for all programs exceed $100,000 but are less than or equal to $100 million, the cutoff for a major program is the larger of $300,000 or 3 percent of total program expenditures. For governments with federal assistance expenditures in excess of $100 million, the act defines a major federal assistance program according to a sliding scale. The ranges and levels for the sliding scale are depicted in Exhibit 11-3. As indicated there, if expenditures for all programs exceed $100 million but are less than $1 billion, a major program is one with expenditures of at least $3 million. As another example, if expenditures for all programs exceed $7 billion, a major program is one incurring total expenditures of at least $20 million.

Exhibit 11-3

Defining Major Federal Assistance Programs
Single Audit Act

If expenditures for all federal programs are:	A major federal assistance program is one whose expenditures are greater than or equal to:
Greater than $100 million, less than or equal to $1 billion	$ 3 million
Greater than $1 billion, less than or equal to $2 billion	$ 4 million
Greater than $2 billion, less than or equal to $3 billion	$ 7 million
Greater than $3 billion, less than or equal to $4 billion	$10 million
Greater than $4 billion, less than or equal to $5 billion	$13 million
Greater than $5 billion, less than or equal to $6 billion	$16 million
Greater than $6 billion, less than or equal to $7 billion	$19 million
Greater than $7 billion	$20 million

---

[8]Ibid.

The internal control review is more extensive for major federal assistance programs. All such programs are subject to the type of in-depth study and evaluation that would be necessary if an auditor were relying on the internal control system to determine substantive testing.[9] Further, if there are no major programs, the review must be extended to the controls over the largest non-major programs until at least 50 percent of the federal financial assistance program expenditures have been reviewed and evaluated.

Responsibility for the Auditing

The Single Audit Act makes one federal agency responsible for overseeing the audit process in a given entity. The Office of Management and Budget assigns a lead agency for each state and large local government. This lead agency, the **cognizant** agency, has responsibility for implementing the act with respect to a particular state or local government. In less populated areas, one cognizant agency may be assigned to several state and local governments or even to all governmental units within a state.

Implementing the act does not mean conducting the audit. The cognizant agency ensures that (1) audits are made in a timely manner and in accordance with requirements of the act, and (2) audit reports and corrective action plans are transmitted to the appropriate federal agencies. To the extent practicable, the cognizant agency also coordinates audits made in addition to the single audit, using persuasive powers to ensure that such additional audits build upon rather than duplicate the single audit.

The audits are conducted by independent auditors. Independent auditor does not necessarily mean a public practitioner; a state or local governmental auditor who meets the independence tests specified by generally accepted auditing standards also could perform the audit. Normally the auditor who conducts the entity's financial and compliance audit will also do the single audit.

The single audit must be completed within one year of the end of the audit period. Copies of the audit report must be submitted to the cognizant agency and to all federal agencies providing assistance within thirty days after the audit is completed. Governmental units receiving more than $100,000 in federal assistance also must submit one copy of the report to the OMB's central clearinghouse. The auditor has responsibility for completing the audit in a timely fashion. The entity must ensure that the reports are submitted on a timely basis to the appropriate bodies.

Reports Required Under the Single Audit Act

The Single Audit Act and OMB Circular A-128 require preparation of two audit reports and two supplemental reports. Audit reports contain opinion statements while supplemental reports include general recommendations or assessments of various operating systems.

First, the auditor must provide a financial audit covering the examination of the general purpose financial statements of the auditee department, agency, or

[9]Substantive testing involves testing for dollar errors directly affecting the correctness of financial statement balances. It includes examining relationships and trends in financial data.

establishment. The financial audit must include an opinion regarding the fair presentation of financial position and the results of operations in accordance with generally accepted accounting principles. This audit report must include a supplementary schedule of federal assistance for each program.

Second, a compliance audit report is required. OMB Circular A-128 indicates specifically that the auditor shall determine whether the governmental unit has complied with laws and regulations that may have a material effect on the general purpose financial statements.

One supplemental report covers the entity's internal control system. It is designed to assess whether the governmental entity has an internal control system necessary to provide reasonable assurance that it is managing federal financial assistance programs in compliance with applicable laws and regulations. As part of the review, the auditor tests the functioning of the internal control system as well as examines the entity's system for monitoring any subrecipients.

The auditor must also prepare a second supplemental report that identifies all findings of noncompliance and questioned costs. This report should include an assessment of compliance with laws and regulations for each major assistance program, and is in addition to the entity's compliance audit report.

Reporting the Audit Results

The reporting structure is an important part of the regulations implementing the act. Typically, the report would begin with the financial audit report, including the auditor's opinion, the financial statements, supplementary information, and statistical tables. The supplemental reports, including compliance audit information, would follow the financial audit as a separate section. Each subpart of the audit—the financial and compliance audit reports, and the reports on internal control and federal assistance programs—should be clearly distinguishable.

The report on federal assistance programs should identify all questioned costs and any instances of noncompliance. It also should contain the auditor's recommendations for correcting any noncompliance procedures or practices. Guidelines developed by the Government Finance Officers Association (GFOA) suggest that auditor findings should be developed to include the following elements:

- relative frequency of the noncompliance
- criteria used to determine noncompliance
- significance of the problem
- cause of the problem
- recommendations concerning corrective action[10]

For all material weaknesses in internal control and any noncompliance, a governmental unit must submit a plan of corrective action to the cognizant agency. The unit should explain the noncompliance or weakness, what specific

---

[10]Government Finance Officers Association, *GAAFR Review* 2 (May 1985): 8.

action will be taken to correct the deficiency, when the action will be taken, and how similar deficiencies will be avoided in the future.

Requirements for Monitoring Subrecipients

The primary recipient has certain responsibilities related to subrecipients of federal funds. These responsibilities are in addition to those pertaining to the subrecipient's own responsibility to perform a single audit. State or local governments receiving federal financial assistance and providing $25,000 or more of it to a subrecipient within a fiscal period shall:

- Determine whether the subrecipient spent Federal assistance funds provided in accordance with applicable laws and regulations. This may be accomplished by reviewing an audit of the subrecipient made in accordance with the applicable federal requirements
- Ensure that appropriate corrective action is taken within six months after receiving the audit report in instances of noncompliance with Federal laws and regulations
- Consider whether subrecipient audits necessitate adjustment of the recipient's own records
- Require each subrecipient to permit independent auditors to have access to the records and financial statements as necessary to comply with the Single Audit Act[11]

As these requirements suggest, the primary recipient has a general responsibility to ensure that the subrecipient adheres to the same federal requirements as the primary recipient.

Other Significant Provisions of the Single Audit Act

Although the single audit is not necessarily intended to ensure discovery of illegal acts or irregularities,[12] the act prescribes treatment for any that may be uncovered. The auditor should report them immediately to recipient officials above the level of involvement. A recipient of federal funds must immediately notify the cognizant agency of the irregularities or illegal acts. The cognizant agency should also be informed of any proposed or actual actions necessary to correct and prevent recurrence of the problem. When the auditor makes the formal audit report, all fraud, abuse, illegal acts, or indications of such acts are normally included in a separate report.

The act provides for differences of opinion between the auditors and the unit. If the auditors report questioned costs and the governmental unit disagrees, the cognizant agency monitors the resolution of audit findings affecting the programs of more than one federal agency. Both the governmental unit

[11] Adapted from OMB Circular A-128, ¶9.

[12] Section 13 of OMB Circular A-128 defines illegal acts and irregularities to include such matters as conflicts of interest, falsification of records or reports, and misappropriations of funds or other assets.

and the federal agency have a responsibility to resolve all differences within six months after the audit.

The Single Audit Act can have a profound effect on state and local governments as well as on public accountants. Auditing of federal assistance programs must be better coordinated and more effective. Certainly one audit covering several federal programs ought to be cost effective and easily scheduled without disrupting the operations of the entity being audited. The ultimate success of the single audit depends, in part, on the extent to which several funding agencies accept the audit work of another. It also depends upon the strength of governmental audit standards. If the audit standards are poor, then the audit quality will suffer and federal agencies and the public alike will lose confidence in the process.

GENERALLY ACCEPTED AUDITING STANDARDS

GAAS

Set by the Auditing Standards Board (AICPA)

Audit standards establish the performance level for conducting an audit. Generally accepted auditing standards are set by the Auditing Standards Board, a board of the American Institute of Certified Public Accountants (AICPA). Under the accounting profession's standards of professional conduct, members departing from these standards in conducting an audit must be prepared to justify the departure.

Certified public accountants (CPAs) performing audits of state and local governments adhere to the generally accepted auditing standards regardless of the entity—business or governmental—being audited. In addition, several AICPA auditing standards have been promulgated since the Single Audit Act that refer specifically to compliance. For example, *Statement on Auditing Standards (SAS) No. 53* deals with the auditor's responsibility to detect and report errors and irregularities. *SAS No. 68* details the compliance auditing standards applicable to governmental entities and other recipients of federal assistance. It requires reporting on compliance at the major program level, which results in two reports. The first report is an opinion on compliance with applicable laws and regulations. The second report describes the internal control structure, the scope of the auditor's work, and the reportable conditions.

U.S. GAO

CPAs auditing governmental entities also are subject to auditing standards of the U.S. General Accounting Office (GAO). The GAO issues standards pertaining to audits of governmental organizations and programs. These standards apply to all audits involving an entity that receives federal assistance. In some cases these standards incorporate those issued by the AICPA but in others they go beyond the Institute's requirements.

Single Audit Act State gov'ts

Other audit standards originate from specific federal or state legislation. For example, some audit standards are referenced in the Single Audit Act. Some state societies or governments also have promulgated audit standards that may go beyond the AICPA's or the GAO's requirements. The following sections discuss the nature of auditing standards and the interrelationship among the various sets of standards.

Types of Generally Accepted Auditing Standards

The AICPA began issuing auditing standards long before formal auditing of governmental units was prevalent. Consequently, the general standards as well as the standards of field work and reporting refer primarily to business organizations. For example, almost all interpretations of these standards pertain to situations found in business entities. Nonetheless, they are broad enough to encompass auditing of state and local governments.

General Standards   As the Institute states, "standards deal with the measures of the quality of the performance."[13] The general standards relate to the characteristics of the auditor rather than to the quality of the work performed. Nonetheless, they are applicable whenever an auditor performs the field work or the reporting. The general standards are:

- The audit is to be performed by a person or persons having adequate training and proficiency as an auditor.
- In all matters relating to the assignment, an independence in mental attitude is to be maintained by the auditor or auditors.
- Due professional care is to be exercised in the performance of the audit and the preparation of the report.[14]

The first standard clearly indicates that education alone is not a sufficient condition for performing an audit. Auditors must also have experience; they get that experience by performing audit activities under the supervision of other skilled personnel.

Independence involves a person's state of mind as well as appearance to others. It implies an attitude of impartiality and fairness. If auditors have other relationships with an entity being audited, their impartiality is clouded, at least in appearance. Even if the auditors can maintain an unbiased attitude by being both an auditor and a consultant to the entity, the credibility of the audit may be reduced because the public may not view the auditor as independent.

The third general standard requires auditors to critically review every level of the audit. Auditors must recognize that when they offer to perform the work, they are holding themselves out to the public as possessing the skills and judgment to perform the work with the necessary diligence and proficiency.

Standards of Field Work   Field work standards pertain to the work that is performed when auditing an entity. These standards provide guidance in planning and supervising the audit, evaluating internal controls, and acquiring sufficient documentation. The standards are:

- The work is to be adequately planned and assistants, if any, are to be properly supervised.

[13]Committee on Auditing Procedure, American Institute of Certified Public Accountants, *Codification of Statements on Auditing Standards* (New York: AICPA, 1993), AU sec. 150.01.
[14]*Codification of Statements on Auditing Standards*, AU sec. 150.02.

- A sufficient understanding of the internal control structure is to be obtained to plan the audit and to determine the nature, timing, and extent of tests to be performed. *(for scope)*
- Sufficient competent evidential matter is to be obtained through inspection, observation, inquiries, and confirmations to afford a reasonable basis for an opinion regarding the financial statements under audit.[15] *(Supporting documentation)*

The first field work standard involves planning. Audit planning entails developing the scope and approach to the audit. An auditor should review the books and records before undertaking the audit. Only after such a review can preliminary judgments be made regarding the level of testing, the amount of adjustment work necessary, and any areas that may need special attention. The entity's particular industry, its accounting policies and procedures, and the adequacy of its internal control system all affect the strategy for conducting the audit.

An entity's internal control structure, the subject of the second field work standard, is a key factor in an auditor's attestation that the financial statements fairly present the entity's financial position and results of operations. The better the system, the more reliance the auditor can place on it in determining audit tests. An auditor is primarily interested in the accounting control structure. However, the administrative controls that affect the reliability of the financial statements, such as safeguarding assets, should also be examined. This audit standard also guides the auditor in assessing the risk associated with the attestation, as well as in establishing materiality levels.

The third field work standard concerns evidential matters. An auditor needs to review enough supporting documentation to verify that the transactions and balances reflected in the financial statements are complete, accurate, and properly disclosed. Supporting documentation covers information ranging from the accounting ledgers and journals to reconciliations, cost allocations, and memoranda describing financial matters.

Standards of Reporting   The four standards of reporting relate to the nature and form of the opinion rendered on the financial statements. As briefly and succinctly as possible, the opinion must reflect the scope of the auditor's work. The four standards are:

- The report shall state whether the financial statements are presented in accordance with generally accepted accounting principles.
- The report shall identify those circumstances in which such principles have not been consistently observed in the current period in relation to the preceding period.
- Informative disclosures in the financial statements are to be regarded as reasonably adequate unless otherwise stated in the report.
- The report shall either contain an expression of opinion regarding the financial statements, taken as a whole, or an assertion to the effect that an opinion cannot be expressed. When an overall opinion cannot be expressed, the

---

[15]Ibid.

reasons therefor should be stated. In all cases where an auditor's name is associated with financial statements, the report should contain a clear-cut indication of the character of the auditor's work, if any, and the degree of responsibility the auditor is taking.[16]

Presenting financial statements in accordance with generally accepted accounting standards is largely self-explanatory. The Institute's standards clarify that "generally accepted accounting principles" means not only the practices themselves but also the methods of applying them. Generally accepted accounting principles encompass the rules, the accounting procedures, and the conventions that define acceptable practice at a given point in time.

SAS No. 58 changed the second reporting standard. Before *SAS No. 58*, it referred to consistent application of accounting principles and was meant to ensure comparability among firms and between periods. The standard report no longer mentions consistent application of accounting principles. It must, however, explain the general nature of an audit, including judgments and estimates that are inherent in the audit process. It also emphasizes the fact that an audit focuses on achieving only reasonable assurance.

The third reporting standard makes clear that no relevant disclosure should be omitted from the financial statements. If it is, auditors may have to qualify their opinions. Full disclosure specifically requires disclosure of segment information that has particular relevance to the proprietary activities of a state or local governmental unit.

The public is affected most by the fourth reporting standard. Auditors' opinions must explain clearly what responsibility they are assuming when their names are associated with the financial statements. Accordingly, the standard contains detailed discussions of circumstances under which an auditor could not render an opinion, when the opinion must be qualified, and when an adverse opinion must be issued. Public understanding is enhanced if auditors issuing similar opinions use comparable language. The standard provides examples of how to phrase particular opinions. It also describes the auditor's responsibility when conditions preclude the application of necessary audit procedures. Some examples of audit opinion paragraphs that reflect these reporting standards are provided in Exhibit 11-4.

In summary, general, field work, and reporting standards guide auditors from the initial planning effort to the reporting phase. Auditors who fail to comply with these standards automatically violate the standards of professional conduct. Despite the comprehensive nature of these standards, auditors have additional responsibilities when auditing state and local governments.

American Institute Audit Guide

In addition to standards specifically applicable to governmental entities, the AICPA has published an audit guide that applies to state and local

---

[16]Ibid.

Exhibit 11-4

Sample Paragraphs of Auditor Reports

Introductory Paragraph

General Purpose Statements: We have examined the general purpose financial statements of the City of Noname, Any State, as of and for the year ended June 30, 19XX, as listed in the table of contents. Our examination was made in accordance with generally accepted auditing standards and, accordingly, included such tests of the accounting records and such other auditing procedures as we considered necessary under the circumstances.

Opinion Paragraph

General Purpose Statements: In our opinion, the general purpose financial statements referred to above present fairly the financial position of the City of Noname, Any State, at June 30, 19XX, and the results of its operations and cash flow of its proprietary funds for the year then ended, in conformity with generally accepted accounting principles applied on a basis consistent with that of the preceding year.

Extra Paragraph (basis of accounting differs from GAAP)

General Purpose Statements: As described in Note___, the city's policy is to prepare its financial statement on a prescribed basis of accounting that demonstrates compliance with the cash basis and budget laws of Any State. This practice differs from generally accepted accounting principles. Accordingly, the accompanying financial statements are not intended to present financial position and results of operations in conformity with generally accepted accounting principles.

Internal Control Report (as part of the audit of general purpose statements)

Introductory Paragraph: We have examined..., and have issued our report thereon dated September 21, 19XX. As part of our examination, we made a study and evaluation of the system of internal accounting control of the City of Noname, Any State, to the extent we considered necessary to evaluate the system as required by generally accepted auditing standards and the standards for financial compliance contained in the U.S. General Accounting Office *Standards for Audit of Governmental Organizations, Programs, Activities, and Functions.* For the purpose of this report, we have classified the significant internal accounting controls in the following categories.

Report on Compliance (no major federal programs)

Extra Paragraph: The management of the City of Noname, Any State, is responsible for the city's compliance with laws and regulations. In connection with the audit referred to above, we selected and tested transactions and records from nonmajor federal financial assistance programs to determine the city's compliance with laws and regulations that we believe could have a material effect on the allowability of program expenditures.

---

governments.[17] It is intended to assist auditors in applying generally accepted auditing standards to state and local government audits. It also includes descriptions and references to generally accepted accounting and reporting practices of state and local governments. For example, it describes the governmental entity, its fund structure, and types of audit engagements appropriate for state and local governments.

One specific engagement described in the Audit Guide is the single audit. As stated in the Audit Guide, the act requires auditors to express an opinion on "fair presentation in conformity with GAAP." If the financial statements are

---

[17]State and Local Government Committee, American Institute of Certified Public Accountants, *Audits of State and Local Governments,* Rev. Ed. (New York: AICPA, 1986), hereafter referred to in this chapter as the Audit Guide.

not prepared according to GAAP, auditors should follow auditing standards applicable to special purpose reports.[18]

The Audit Guide also refers to the auditing standards that should be applied in conducting state and local government audits:

> AICPA Statements on Auditing Standards (SASs) and related interpretations apply to the audits of financial statements of governments, except to the extent the underlying subject matter is not present in such statements.[19]

The Audit Guide goes on to explain that some states require prescribed audit procedures. If this is the case, auditors should follow both GAAS and the state requirements, even if it means issuing two different reports.

According to the Audit Guide, other audit standards are applicable as well:

> The GAO, the OMB, and other federal agencies have issued various audit guides and circulars and other publications that contain important guidance for audits of specific federal assistance programs. If applicable, the auditor should become knowledgeable with respect to their provisions.[20]

If auditors fail to follow the standards and procedures described in the Audit Guide, they violate the standards of professional conduct. The violation is considered an act discreditable to the profession.

Generally Accepted Governmental Auditing Standards

The General Accounting Office prescribes generally accepted auditing standards that auditors must follow when auditing federal organizations, programs, activities, functions, and funds received by contractors, nonprofit organizations, and other nonfederal organizations. Commonly referred to as the Yellow Book, these audit standards also apply to single audits of state and local governments receiving federal financial assistance.[21] However, the Single Audit Act and OMB Circular A-128 require adherence to specific audit standards that exceed the minimal audit standards imposed by the GAO.

The GAO audit standards are very comprehensive. They incorporate, by reference, generally accepted auditing standards issued by the AICPA as described previously. Several additional field work and reporting standards are identified, including: (1) expanded field work and reporting relating to the entity's compliance with laws and regulations, (2) an expanded report on the entity's internal control system, and (3) an auditor's awareness of situations

[18] Audit Guide, 152. In these cases the independent auditor should follow the guidance in *Statement on Auditing Standard No. 62.*

[19] Audit Guide, ¶1.10.

[20] Audit Guide, ¶1.14.

[21] United States General Accounting Office, *Government Auditing Standards* (Washington, D.C.: GAO, 1988).

or transactions that could be indicative of fraud, abuse, and illegal expenditures and acts.[22]

The GAO standards also list specific field work and reporting standards applicable to governmental audits. They differ typically in the level of detail required, not in substance. For example, under the field work standards for performance audits, one standard requires a review of the general and application controls in computer-based systems. No AICPA field work standard refers specifically to "general and application" controls, but a review of the computer-based systems is contemplated in the review of internal controls.

Standards Applicable to the Single Audit Act

[handwritten margin note: More emphasis on: ① Compliance ② internal controls related to federal assistance programs]

As mentioned previously, some auditing standards required for single audits and included in the Single Audit Act or OMB Circular A-128 exceed the GAO standards. Single audit standards place more emphasis on the compliance aspects. As an example, an auditor must report all instances of noncompliance with laws and regulations found during the audit. The standard says nothing about *material* instances of noncompliance, which is a common statement in most other audit standards. As another example, auditors must study and evaluate whether the entity has internal controls that provide reasonable assurance that it is managing federal financial assistance programs in compliance with laws and regulations. In most other audits, detailed examination of the internal controls would be required only if the controls are relied upon for selecting substantive tests.

Auditing state and local governments is a complex undertaking. Depending upon the type of audit, so many different standards apply that auditors have a difficult task meshing them together for a cohesive audit program. So many different bodies—AICPA, GAO, individual states—impose audit standards that conflicting and duplicative standards are possible. Thus far, conflicting standards have been avoided because the GAO and most state laws incorporate the AICPA audit standards as a starting point (see Exhibit 11-5). Duplication is not inherently bad, but it requires considerable review and experience to discern the exact requirements of a particular audit.

THE ISSUE OF AUDIT QUALITY

The quality of governmental audits has received considerable attention in recent years. At congressional request in the mid-1980s, the General Accounting Office reviewed audits performed by nonfederal auditors to determine the extent to which CPAs comply with professional auditing standards. The GAO documented what it described as serious and widespread deficiencies

---

[22]Appendix 11-1 summarizes the generally accepted governmental auditing standards contained in the 1988 revision of the Yellow Book.

Exhibit 11-5

Overview of Audit Standards

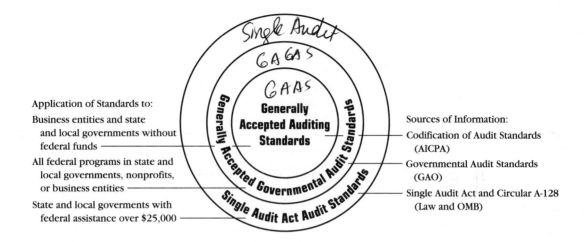

Application of Standards to:

Business entities and state
   and local governments without
   federal funds

All federal programs in state and
   local governments, nonprofits,
   or business entities

State and local goverments with
   federal assistance over $25,000

Sources of Information:

Codification of Audit Standards
   (AICPA)

Governmental Audit Standards
   (GAO)

Single Audit Act and Circular A-128
   (Law and OMB)

in CPA audits of federal assistance programs received by state and local governments.[23]

According to some reports, the public accounting profession would face a crisis situation if it could not improve audit quality. Based on the GAO sample, about 34 percent of the audit work done by CPAs was unsatisfactory. More than one-half of the unsatisfactory audits had "severe standards violations." Auditors failed most often to: (1) perform sufficient audit work in testing compliance with governmental laws and regulations, (2) properly evaluate internal accounting controls, including controls over federal expenditures, and (3) document the work performed or the conclusions reached.

As part of its review, the GAO suggested that the accounting profession take several actions. Better enforcement efforts, broadened continuing professional education programs (CPE) in the governmental area, and expansion of the college curricula to focus more attention on governmental entities were among the suggestions made by the GAO.

Reaction to GAO Study

The AICPA responded by establishing a task force on the quality of governmental audits. Among other duties, the task force was asked to prepare a comprehensive action plan that would substantially improve the quality of audit performance.

No easy solutions were found. The task force concluded that the problems of substandard work required broad-based effort from all segments of the

[23]United States General Accounting Office, *CPA Audit Quality: Many Governmental Audits Do Not Comply with Professional Standards* (Washington, D.C.: GAO, March 1986).

accounting profession. The task force's plan, known as the 5 E's, called for attention and change in five important areas:

(handwritten margin note: AICPA Task Force Plan)

- **Education of auditors:** governmental accounting and auditing courses should be mandatory for people who perform governmental audits; guidance provided to auditors should be improved; and a statement on auditing standards should be issued for compliance auditing.
- **Engagement of auditors:** the process by which auditors are selected should be improved to ensure their competence and to allow sufficient time to develop a credible audit proposal.
- **Evaluation of audit quality:** a comprehensive program to strengthen the audit evaluation process should be developed.
- **Enforcement of standards:** federal agencies and state societies should develop a simple, efficient way to refer substandard audit work to the appropriate enforcement bodies.
- **Exchange of information:** memberships of national and regional audit forums should be broadened to include public accounting practitioners; governing bodies and committees of government auditors and financial officers' associations should include public practitioners.[24]

(handwritten margin note: 5 E's   EDEN/EVEN/EX)

Corrective Actions

The profession responded promptly to the GAO report and the subsequent AICPA proposals. Many continuing education programs emphasizing governmental accounting and auditing have been added to state society professional education agendas. The GAO has issued a report on recommended practices for procuring audit services.[25] The report includes four attributes for an audit procurement process: competition among auditors, formal solicitation of audit proposals, technical evaluation of the audit proposal and completed audits, and a written agreement covering the audit scope and process. The GAO also revised its Yellow Book to expand and clarify the responsibilities of the auditor relative to certain standards.

The AICPA also has responded by issuing a statement on auditing standards related to compliance auditing.[26] A key attribute of the statement is its explanation of the relationship between the requirements of generally accepted auditing standards and generally accepted governmental accounting standards. It also provides guidance on testing compliance with federal laws and regulations when performing audits under the Single Audit Act. Other audit standards have been issued that affect governmental audits. For example, *SAS No. 55* on internal control broadens the term to embrace both accounting and administrative controls referred to in the Yellow Book.

[24]Joan Meinhardt, Joseph F. Moraglio, and Harold I. Steinberg provide a succinct summary of the task force work in "Governmental Audits: An Action Plan for Excellence," *Journal of Accountancy* (July 1987), 86–91.

[25]United States General Accounting Office, *CPA Audit Quality: A Framework for Procuring Audit Services* (Washington, D.C.: GAO, 1987).

[26]Accounting Standards Board, American Institute of Certified Public Accountants, *Compliance Auditing Applicable to Governmental Entities and Other Recipients of Governmental Financial Assistance* (New York: AICPA, 1989).

Although it is too soon to conclude that the quality of governmental audits has improved, the profession certainly responded promptly with a meaningful action plan for making the improvements. CPAs have taken the GAO admonishments seriously. Recent GAO audit reviews show some improvement in the quality of audit reports.

SUMMARY

Audits of governmental entities have become an important aspect of monitoring the stewardship of government. Audits are used to examine the extent to which the financial statements present fairly the position and results of operations of a governmental entity, compliance with laws and regulations, and performance. State or local oversight boards usually require a financial and compliance audit.

When a governmental entity receives federal assistance, additional audit requirements are mandated. Many federal programs require efficiency and economy audits as well as effectiveness audits. If both audits are combined, the entity has had a performance audit. The Single Audit Act also requires certain additional audit procedures for those entities receiving more than $25,000 in federal assistance.

The American Institute of Certified Public Accountants is responsible for issuing generally accepted auditing standards. These standards apply to any audit performed by a member of the accounting profession. The United States General Accounting Office issues generally accepted governmental auditing standards. In addition, the Single Audit Act and the Office of Management and Budget prescribe specific audit standards for governmental units required to have a single audit.

Substandard audit performance attracted congressional attention in the mid-1980s, and since then the profession has markedly increased its attention to the accounting and auditing of governmental entities. An AICPA task force developed a comprehensive plan for the long-run improvement of auditing practices. Several new audit standards have been issued to strengthen audit procedures. Also, the GAO has issued guidelines to governmental entities in procuring audit services. A coincidental revision of the Yellow Book helps tie together the various audit standards for governmental entities.

APPENDIX A

SUMMARY OF GENERALLY ACCEPTED GOVERNMENT AUDITING STANDARDS[1]

I. Introduction
   A. Purpose

---

[1] United States General Accounting Office, *Government Auditing Standards* (Washington, D.C.: GAO, 1988 Revision), Appendix A—Summary of Statement on Government Auditing Standards.

1. This statement contains standards for audits of government organizations, programs, activities, and functions, and of government funds received by contractors, nonprofit organizations, and other nongovernment organizations.

2. The standards are to be followed by auditors and audit organizations when required by law, regulation, agreement or contract, or policy.

II. **Types of Government Audits**

A. Purpose

1. This chapter describes the types of audits that government and nongovernment audit organizations conduct, and that government organizations arrange to have conducted. This description is not intended to limit or require the types of audits that may be conducted or arranged.

2. In conducting these types of audits, auditors should follow the applicable standards included and incorporated in this statement.

B. Financial Audits

1. Financial statement audits determine (a) whether the financial statements of an audited entity present fairly the financial position, results of operations, and cash flows or changes in financial position in accordance with generally accepted accounting principles, and (b) whether the entity has complied with laws and regulations for those transactions and events that may have a material effect on the financial statements.

2. Financial related audits include determining (a) whether financial reports and related items, such as elements, accounts, or funds, are fairly presented, (b) whether financial information is presented in accordance with established or stated criteria, and (c) whether the entity has adhered to specific financial compliance requirements.

C. Performance Audits

1. Economy and efficiency audits include determining (a) whether the entity is acquiring, protecting, and using its resources (such as personnel, property, and space) economically and efficiently, (b) the causes of inefficiencies or uneconomical practices, and (c) whether the entity has complied with laws and regulations concerning matters of economy and efficiency.

2. Program audits include determining (a) the extent to which the desired results or benefits established by the legislature or other authorizing body are being achieved, (b) the effectiveness of organizations, programs, activities, or functions, and (c) whether the entity has complied with laws and regulations applicable to the program.

D. Understanding the Audit Objectives and Scope

1. Audits may have a combination of financial and performance audit objectives, or may have objectives limited to only some aspects of one audit type.

2. Auditors should follow the appropriate standards in this statement that are applicable to the individual objectives of the audit.

E. Other Activities of an Audit Organization

1. Services other than audits: The head of the audit organization should establish policy on which audit standards from this statement should be followed by the auditors in performing such services. However, as a minimum, auditors should collectively possess adequate professional proficiency and exercise due professional care for the service being performed.

2. Investigative work: The head of the audit organization should establish policy on whether the audit standards in this statement, or some other appropriate standards, are to be followed by the employees performing this work.

3. Nonaudit activities: The head of the audit organization should establish policy on what standards in this statement are to be followed, or whether some other appropriate standards are to be followed, by the employees in performing this type of work.

III. **General Standards**

A. Qualifications: The staff assigned to conduct the audit should collectively possess adequate professional proficiency for the tasks required.

B. Independence: In all matters relating to the audit work, the audit organization and the individual auditors, whether government or public, should be free from personal and external impairments to independence, should be organizationally independent, and should maintain an independent attitude and appearance.

C. Due Professional Care: Due professional care should be used in conducting the audit and in preparing related reports.

D. Quality Control: Audit organizations conducting government audits should have an appropriate internal quality control system in place and participate in an external quality control review program.

IV. **Field Work Standards for Financial Audits**

A. Relationship to AICPA Standards

1. The standards of field work for government financial audits incorporate the AICPA standards of field work for financial audits, and prescribe supplemental standards of field work needed to satisfy the unique needs of government financial audits.

2. The field work standards of the AICPA and the supplemental standards of this statement apply to both financial statement audits and financial-related audits.

B. Planning

1. Supplemental planning field work standards for government financial audits are:

a. Audit Requirements for All Government Levels: Planning should include consideration of the audit requirements of all levels of government.

b. Legal and Regulatory Requirements: A test should be made of compliance with applicable laws and regulations.

(1) In determining compliance with laws and regulations:
 (a) The auditor should design steps and procedures to provide reasonable assurance of detecting errors, irregularities, and illegal acts that could have a direct and material effect on the financial statement amounts or the results of financial-related audits.
 (b) The auditor should also be aware of the possibility of illegal acts that could have an indirect and material effect on the financial statements or results of financial-related audits.

C. Evidence (Working Papers)
 1. The AICPA field work standards and this statement require that: A record of the auditors' work be retained in the form of working papers.
 2. Supplemental working paper requirements for financial audits are that working papers should:
 a. Contain a written audit program cross-referenced to the working papers.
 b. Contain the objective, scope, methodology and results of the audit.
 c. Contain sufficient information so that supplementary oral explanations are not required.
 d. Be legible with adequate indexing and cross-referencing, and include summaries and lead schedules, as appropriate.
 e. Restrict information included to matters that are materially important and relevant to the objectives of the audit.
 f. Contain evidence of supervisory reviews of the work conducted.

D. Internal Control
 1. The AICPA field work standards and this statement require that: A sufficient understanding of the internal control structure is to be obtained to plan the audit and to determine the nature, timing, and extent of tests to be performed.

V. **Reporting Standards for Financial Audits**
 A. Relationship to AICPA Standards
 1. The standards of reporting for government financial audits incorporate the AICPA standards of reporting for financial audits, and prescribe supplemental standards of reporting needed to satisfy the unique needs of government financial audits.
 2. The reporting standards of the AICPA and the supplemental standards in chapter 5 of this statement apply to both financial statement audits and financial-related audits.
 B. Supplemental reporting standards for government financial audits are:
 1. Statement on Auditing Standards: A Statement should be included in the auditors' report that the audit was made in accordance with generally accepted government auditing standards. (AICPA standards require that public accountants state that the audit was

made in accordance with generally accepted auditing standards. In conducting government audits, public accountants should also state that their audit was conducted in accordance with the standards set forth in chapters 3, 4, and 5.)

2. Report on Compliance: The auditors should prepare a written report on their tests of compliance with applicable laws and regulations. This report, which may be included in either the report on the financial audit or a separate report, should contain a statement of positive assurance on those items which were tested for compliance and negative assurance on those items not tested. It should include all material instances of noncompliance, and all instances or indications of illegal acts which could result in criminal prosecution.

3. Report on Internal Controls: The auditors should prepare a written report on their understanding of the entity's internal control structure and the assessment of control risk made as part of a financial statement audit, or a financial-related audit. This report may be included in either the auditor's report on the financial audit or a separate report. The auditor's report should include as a minimum: (a) the scope of the auditor's work in obtaining an understanding of the internal control structure and in assessing the control risk, (b) the entity's significant internal controls or control structure including the controls established to ensure compliance with laws and regulations that have a material impact on the financial statements and the results of the financial-related audit, and (c) the reportable conditions, including the identification of material weaknesses, identified as a result of the auditor's work in understanding and assessing the control risk.

4. Reporting on Financial-Related Audits: Written audit reports are to be prepared giving the results of each financial-related audit.

5. Privileged and Confidential Information: If certain information is prohibited from general disclosure, the report should state the nature of the information omitted and the requirement that makes the omission necessary.

6. Report Distribution: Written audit reports are to be submitted by the audit organization to the appropriate officials of the organization audited and to the appropriate officials of the organizations requiring or arranging for the audits, including external funding organizations, unless legal restrictions, ethical considerations, or other arrangements prevent it. Copies of the reports should also be sent to other officials who have legal oversight authority or who may be responsible for taking action and to others authorized to receive such reports. Unless restricted by law or regulation, copies should be made available for public inspection.

VI. **Field Work Standards for Performance Audits**

A. Planning: Work is to be adequately planned.

B. Supervision: Staff are to be properly supervised.

C. Legal and Regulatory Requirements: An assessment is to be made of compliance with applicable requirements of laws and regulations when necessary to satisfy the audit objectives.

1. Where an assessment of compliance with laws and regulations is required: Auditors should design the audit to provide reasonable assurance of detecting abuse or illegal acts that could significantly affect the audit objectives.

2. In all performance audits: Auditors should be alert to situations or transactions that could be indicative of abuse or illegal acts.

D. Internal Control: An assessment should be made of applicable internal controls when necessary to satisfy the audit objectives.

E. Evidence: Sufficient, competent, and relevant evidence is to be obtained to afford a reasonable basis for the auditor's judgments and conclusions regarding the organization, program, activity, or function under audit. A record of the auditor's work is to be retained in the form of working papers. Working papers may include tapes, films, and discs.

VII. **Reporting Standards for Performance Audits**

A. Form: Written audit reports are to be prepared communicating the results of each government audit.

B. Timeliness: Reports are to be issued promptly so as to make the information available for timely use by management and legislative officials, and by other interested parties.

C. Report Contents

1. Objectives, Scope, and Methodology: The report should include a statement of the audit objectives and a description of the audit scope and methodology.

2. Audit Findings and Conclusions: The report should include a full discussion of the audit findings, and where applicable, the auditor's conclusions.

3. Cause and Recommendations: The report should include the cause of problem areas noted in the audit, and recommendations for actions to correct the problem areas and to improve operations, when called for by the audit objectives.

4. Statement on Auditing Standards: The report should include a statement that the audit was made in accordance with generally accepted government auditing standards and disclose when applicable standards were not followed.

5. Internal Controls: The report should identify the significant internal controls that were assessed, the scope of the auditor's assessment work, and any significant weaknesses found during the audit.

6. Compliance with Laws and Regulations: The report should include all significant instances of noncompliance and abuse and all indications or instances of illegal acts that could result in criminal prosecution that were found during or in connection with the audit.

7. Views of Responsible Officials: The report should include the pertinent views of responsible officials of the organization, program, activity, or function audited concerning the auditors' findings, conclusions, and recommendations, and what corrective action is planned.

8. Noteworthy Accomplishments: The report should include a description of any significant noteworthy accomplishments, particularly when management improvements in one area may be applicable elsewhere.

9. Issues Needing Further Study: The report should include a listing of any significant issues needing further study and consideration.

10. Privileged and Confidential Information: The report should include a statement about any pertinent information that was omitted because it is deemed privileged or confidential. The nature of such information should be described, and the basis under which it is withheld should be stated.

D. Report Presentation: The report should be complete, accurate, objective, and convincing, and be as clear and concise as the subject matter permits.

E. Report Distribution: Written audit reports are to be submitted by the audit organization to the appropriate officials of the organization audited, and to the appropriate officials of the organizations requiring or arranging for the audits, including external funding organizations, unless legal restrictions, ethical considerations, or other arrangements prevent it. Copies of the reports should also be sent to other officials who may be responsible for taking action on audit findings and recommendations and to others authorized to receive such reports. Unless restricted by law or regulation, copies should be made available for public inspection.

VIII. **AICPA Generally Accepted Auditing Standards** *(GAAS)*

A. General Standards

1. The examination is to be performed by a person or persons having adequate technical training and proficiency as an auditor.

2. In all matters relating to the assignment, an independence in mental attitude is to be maintained by the auditor or auditors.

3. Due professional care is to be exercised in the performance of the examination and the preparation of the report.

B. Standards of Field Work

1. The work is to be adequately planned and assistants, if any, are to be properly supervised.

2. A sufficient understanding of the internal control structure is to be obtained to plan the audit and to determine the nature, timing, and extent of tests to be performed.

3. Sufficient competent evidential matter is to be obtained through inspection, observation, inquiries, and confirmations to afford a reasonable basis for an opinion regarding the financial statements under examination.

C. Standards of Reporting
1. The report shall state whether the financial statements are presented in accordance with generally accepted accounting principles.
2. The report shall identify those circumstances in which such principles have not been consistently observed in the current period in relation to the preceding period.
3. Informative disclosures in the financial statements are to be regarded as reasonably adequate unless otherwise stated in the report.
4. The report shall either contain an expression of opinion regarding the financial statements, taken as a whole, or an assertion to the effect that an opinion cannot be expressed. When an overall opinion cannot be expressed, the reasons therefor should be stated. In all cases where an auditor's name is associated with financial statements, the report should contain a clear-cut indication of the character of the auditor's examination, if any, and the degree of responsibility he is taking.

QUESTIONS

11-1 Why would a governmental unit be interested in having an audit performed if it is not required to do so?

11-2 Describe the types of audits that might be performed for state or local governments. How do they differ from those performed for business organizations?

11-3 Assume that the firm for which you work has been engaged to do an audit of a local governmental unit and that a close relative of yours works there. You indicate to the supervisor that you will not have any problem maintaining independence. She is still worried. Explain why.

11-4 Explain how generally accepted audit standards differ from generally accepted governmental auditing standards.

11-5 What does the term *questioned costs* mean in the context of a federal audit?

11-6 Describe the conditions under which a single audit is required.

11-7 Why was the Single Audit Act passed? If you were responsible for evaluating the effectiveness of the act, what factors would you assess?

11-8 Briefly describe each of the general auditing standards.

11-9 A junior member of your audit staff is confused. He cannot understand why, with the AICPA audit standards, the GAO audit standards, and the requirements of the Single Audit Act, the AICPA also has published an Audit Guide for State and Local Governments. Explain what purpose the Audit Guide serves.

11-10 What is the 5 E's plan of the American Institute of Certified Public Accountants?

11-11   Assume the State Society of CPAs in your state wants to improve the capabilities of its membership in the area of governmental reporting and auditing. As a member of the planning committee, what suggestions would you make?

11-12   What are the responsibilities of the cognizant agency under the Single Audit Act?

11-13   Explain how audits help fulfill the fiduciary responsibilities of a state or local oversight body.

11-14   Under the Single Audit Act, what is a major program? Describe the general conditions for identifying such programs.

11-15   Your firm has agreed to perform a financial audit for the local county. When you present a draft of your engagement letter, one county commissioner asks why it is necessary to review the county's internal controls. He points out that the internal auditor already has conducted such a review. How would you reply?

11-16   Explain how financial statement audits are complicated by fund accounting.

11-17   An audit of a local government revealed that it uses the modified accrual basis of accounting for all funds. Since modified accrual is not GAAP for some funds, can you complete the audit? What options do you have?

CASES

11-1   Members of the state legislature have received copies of the GAO report on the quality of CPA audits of state and local organizations receiving federal assistance. The state contracts with public CPAs to conduct all state and local government audits. Because substantial deficiencies were identified in the GAO report, some legislators want to pass legislation requiring all state and local audits to be conducted by CPAs who work full time for state government. These legislators argue that by having staff auditors, state government can maintain better control over the quality of audits.

REQUIRED

As a member of the State Society of CPAs Legislative Committee, you are required to testify before the legislature. What key points would you make?

11-2   Phil and John Cates, owners of a small CPA firm, were asked to conduct an audit of the local school district. The school district official explained that their brother, Bob Cates, who teaches in the district, had suggested a call to the Cates' CPA firm. The school district needs a financial audit, and quickly; the audit is required as part of the application for funds under a federal program. Phil and John discussed the matter, called the school district official back, and accepted the engagement. They promised to begin the work Monday morning.

Another client approached the firm later in the day with additional work that was also required within two weeks. Undaunted, the Cates brothers hired two accounting students to assist in the audit. Both had taken two semesters of auditing. Phil Cates spent two hours on Monday morning explaining the purpose of the audit, took them out to meet the coordinating school official, and told them to report back when they needed additional assistance. Because the audit was part of an application for federal funds, Phil explained that the students did not need to spend much time on internal control. Most of their time should be spent making sure that the financial transactions and resulting account balances were correct.

Two weeks later the students reported to the Cates brothers. They provided financial statements, a schedule of other financial assistance received by the school district, and a draft opinion. The students explained that no material errors were discovered. Accordingly, they did not prepare any notes. Their working papers included copies of original ledger sheets and adding machine tapes verifying the accuracy of the account balances.

Phil and John prepared an unqualified auditor's report without mentioning the basis upon which the financial statements were prepared or whether the same principles were used in earlier years.

REQUIRED

Explain which generally accepted auditing standards were violated, if any, and an alternative action that Phil and John Cates should have taken for each instance.

11-3 Georgetown is completing its budgeting process for the upcoming fiscal year. Projected expenditures exceed projected revenues by $3,500,000, and the city council is trying to determine what items could be eliminated from the budget. One council member proposed the following expenditure reductions:

Health and Welfare—Subsidized Day Care	$ 100,000
Transportation—Road Maintenance	1,240,000
Law Enforcement—Fewer Police Officers and Fewer Shifts	721,000
General Administrative Services:	
Internal Audit Staff	210,000
City Planning and Architectural Services	860,000
External Financial and Compliance Audit	89,000
Other	280,000
Total	$3,500,000

None of the cuts is pleasant, and many affect vital services to the city's constituency. One council member feels strongly about eliminating the external audit and the internal audit staff. She maintains that with such stringent budget reductions it is more important than ever to maintain an internal audit staff and the external audits. How else, she argues, will the city be assured that the council's mandates for program reductions are followed?

Others on the city council are outraged at her position. They argue that a time when vital services are being eliminated or severely curtailed is no time to argue for something as peripheral as external and internal audits. Besides, they continue, the city has had a financial audit for the past several years and always received an unqualified opinion. What harm would it cause to go without one for one year?

REQUIRED

1. Which argument ought to prevail? Is the proponent of maintaining the audit staff and retaining an external auditor right? If so, explain why and give further arguments to support her position. If not, explain why not.
2. How should the dilemma faced by Georgetown be resolved? Is there some compromise that would be better than either position? Explain.

11-4 Los Quitos, a California county, received financial assistance under a number of federal programs. Los Quitos' commissioners have requested some assistance in interpreting the requirements of the Single Audit Act. Each federal program is listed below:

Federal Program	Grant/Contract	19X1 Expenditures	Totals
Education	1	$ 150,000	
	2	310,000	
	3	60,000	$ 520,000
Transportation	1	800,000	800,000
Commerce	1	1,000,000	1,000,000
Human Services	1	42,500	
	2	500,000	
	3	225,600	
	4	165,000	933,100
Total, All Programs			$3,253,100

REQUIRED

1. Is Los Quitos subject to a single audit or can an alternative procedure be followed in lieu of this audit? Explain.
2. If it is subject to a single audit, which are major and which are nonmajor programs?
3. If Los Quitos contracts with Border City to conduct part of the commerce grant and pays $420,000 for this purpose, would Border City have to have a single audit? Does the subcontracting change the requirements for Los Quitos? Explain.

11-5 The following passages are from several different audit or special reports to state and local governments:

We have audited the general purpose financial statements of the city as of and for the year ended June 30, 19X1, and have issued our report thereon dated September 21, 19X1. These financial statements are the responsibility of the city's management. Our responsibility is to express an opinion on these financial statements based on our audit. The accompanying Schedule of Federal Financial Assistance is presented for purposes of additional analysis and is not a required part of the general purpose financial statements. The information in that schedule has been subjected to the auditing procedures applied in the audit of the general purpose financial statements, and in our opinion, is fairly stated in all material respects in relation to the general purpose financial statements taken as a whole.

Our study and evaluation was more limited than would be necessary to express an opinion on the internal control systems used in administering the federal financial assistance programs of the city. Accordingly, we do not express an opinion on the internal control systems used in administering federal financial assistance programs.... However, our study and evaluation and examination disclosed no condition that we believe to be a material weakness in relation to a federal financial assistance program of the city.

We have audited the general purpose financial statements of the city as of and for the year ended June 30, 19X1. Our audit was conducted in accordance with generally accepted auditing standards. Those standards require that we plan and perform the audit to obtain reasonable assurance about whether the financial statements are free of material misstatement. An audit includes examining, on a test basis, evidence supporting...

Having reviewed the extent of increased aid-to-foster-care expenditures, the analysis was designed to determine the causes of the increases and, thus, the city's need for budget amendments. In the analysis, the number of recipients, eligible persons, and total expenditures for each major category of service (drugs, dental care, physicians' services, and so on) were examined. The analysts concluded that the city should develop an improved information system for its medical assistance programs. They also encouraged the city to develop better criteria for awarding assistance in order to make sure that the program goals were being achieved.

REQUIRED

Examine each excerpt and determine the type of audit or special report that is being addressed. Be specific. For example, indicating that the excerpt is part of a single audit is not sufficient; explain what aspect of the single audit is being addressed.

11-6   The Nebraska legislature formed a legislative audit committee to review both state and local governmental audits completed each year. Nebraska has no legislative audit staff; it contracts all state and local audit work with public accounting firms. The legislative audit committee has received its first batch of audit reports to review. Since this is the committee's first experience, the chairperson believes the committee needs some background information before it begins its review. Several accounting firms with experience in state and local government auditing have been asked to present certain facets of governmental auditing to the committee. Your firm has been asked to address generally accepted auditing standards, with emphasis on the following issues:

1. The relationship between generally accepted auditing standards and generally accepted governmental auditing standards
2. The relationship between auditing standards related to a single audit and standards used to guide other types of governmental audits

3. The requirements of the AICPA's Audit Guide for state and local governments

REQUIRED

Prepare a statement to explain the major points outlined above for presentation to the legislative committee.

11-7 Smith and Jones, CPAs, have conducted a financial audit of Corvalli County. Smith has become concerned about some aspects of the audit. He believes that auditing standards may have been violated. Jones, who has 25 years of experience auditing business entities, assures him that no violations of the AICPA's generally accepted auditing standards have occurred. The situations under discussion are:

1. No audit procedures were specifically designed to detect violations of laws or regulations. However, the auditors maintained the proper degree of professional skepticism and were alert for possible irregularities that other audit tests might have brought to their attention.
2. The working papers are complete and show evidence that each portion of the audit was well planned and properly supervised. However, some of the schedules are not cross-referenced to the original plan.
3. Although there was an "except for" qualification included in the audit report, no recommendations for correction of the problem were included.
4. The second paragraph of the audit report begins: "We conducted our audit in accordance with generally accepted auditing standards."
5. The audit report states that nothing came to the auditors' attention that caused them to believe that the county had not complied, in all material respects, with provisions of related grants and contracts.

REQUIRED
1. For each of the situations above, determine whether a violation of generally accepted governmental auditing standards has occurred. Explain.
2. The accounting profession in the United States is determined to maintain its independence from governmental regulation. Do the existence of governmental auditing standards and the requirement that they be followed represent a loss of this independence?

EXERCISES

11-1 Appendix A of the textbook contains excerpts from the comprehensive financial reports for Raleigh, North Carolina. After reviewing the auditor's reports contained in those reports, answer the following questions:

1. What audits were conducted that related to Raleigh, North Carolina? Were some of those audits combined and covered in a single opinion statement? If so, which ones? Describe the scope of each audit.

2. Did Raleigh, North Carolina, receive unqualified or "clean" opinions on all audits? If not, describe which opinions were qualified. Are there other reports from the auditors? If so, describe them and the auditors' findings.

3. Did the audit of the general purpose financial statements include the statistical information published along with the statements? Provide evidence to substantiate your conclusion.

11-2 Select the best answer for the question.

1. The compliance report contained in a single audit should include:
   a. recommendations concerning corrective action
   b. extent of the problem
   c. cause of the problem
   d. all of the above

2. Responsibilities of a primary recipient include:
   a. determining that the federal funds received by the recipient were spent in accordance with applicable laws and regulations
   b. conducting an internal audit of the subrecipient
   c. considering whether subrecipient audits necessitate notification to the Justice Department
   d. none of the above

3. A comprehensive audit encompasses a:
   a. financial, compliance, effectiveness, and single audit
   b. financial and performance audit
   c. financial, efficiency and economy, and single audit
   d. performance and single audit

4. The GAO's response to the report on the substandard performance of CPAs conducting state and local government audits was to:
   a. require competitive bidding for all state and local audits
   b. revise the code of ethics for all CPAs performing these audits
   c. issue guidelines for state and local governments in procuring audit services
   d. mandate educational and experience requirements for CPAs performing governmental audits

5. A single audit is performed by:
   a. a public practitioner
   b. an internal auditor
   c. a state or local auditor who is independent
   d. a or c

6. A program audit would not address which of the following issues?
   a. the extent to which the objectives of the program are being achieved
   b. factors inhibiting satisfactory performance
   c. the suitability of the program objectives
   d. the extent to which sound procurement practices are being followed

7. Oversight boards are encouraged to obtain financial and compliance audits because:
   a. bond agencies refuse to provide bond ratings without a financial audit
   b. audits provide a way to preclude fraud or other illegal acts
   c. a financial audit is required to assure accountability
   d. none of the above
8. A primary difference between performance and financial auditing is:
   a. performance audits contain an opinion statement; financial audits do not
   b. financial audits contain an opinion statement; performance audits do not
   c. the testing procedures vary significantly
   d. performance auditing is done by internal auditors; financial audits are performed by public practitioners
9. The field work auditing standard that relates to planning and supervision implies:
   a. only one assistant should be taken on each audit so the person can be adequately supervised
   b. planning should be done at the end of the audit in anticipation of the next engagement
   c. the books and records should be reviewed to determine special areas of concern
   d. the audit should be performed by supervisory level personnel only
10. One general auditing standard relates to:
    a. planning
    b. informative disclosures
    c. conditions for a disclaimer
    d. independence

11-3 Select the best answer for the question.

1. Which of the following is not one of the solutions for an audit of a governmental unit that did not follow GAAP?
   a. prepare non-GAAP statements as special purpose reports
   b. qualified opinion
   c. issue a single opinion for the non-GAAP and the GAAP statements
   d. none of the above
2. An audit that examines whether the entity has complied with laws and regulations concerning matters of economy and efficiency is called a(an):
   a. program audit
   b. compliance audit
   c. effectiveness audit
   d. economy and efficiency audit
3. An opinion would not be required for a(an):
   a. single audit
   b. effectiveness audit

     c. financial and compliance audit

     d. none of the above

4. One difference between a financial and a performance audit is:

     a. performance auditing is concerned with only qualitative information while financial auditing deals only with quantitative information

     b. a performance audit would be required if federal funds are involved and a financial audit is required when state or local funding is involved

     c. performance audits deal with the financial consequences, whereas financial audits deal with policies and procedures surrounding the financial transactions

     d. none of the above

5. If a single audit has been performed:

     a. the governmental unit has met its obligations for federal financial assistance

     b. a performance audit is required

     c. an internal audit staff is unnecessary

     d. another auditor would have to complete the financial audit

6. Which of the following entities may be excluded under the Single Audit Act?

     a. an interstate development corporation funded by two states

     b. a governmental hospital

     c. a regional airport authority

     d. both a and b

7. Subrecipients of federal funds are required, under the Single Audit Act, to:

     a. have a single audit performed

     b. report expenditures through the primary recipient

     c. allow the primary recipient's internal audit staff to perform a single audit

     d. issue financial statements combined with the primary recipient

8. The federal agency responsible for implementing the Single Audit Act is:

     a. GAO

     b. OMB

     c. GAO and OMB

     d. none of the above

9. In all matters relating to an audit assignment, an independence in mental attitude is to be maintained by the auditor for:

     a. audits initiated by oversight bodies

     b. audits conducted under the Single Audit Act

     c. audits conducted under the GAO's Yellow Book

     d. all of the above

10. When an overall audit opinion cannot be stated:

     a. the auditor should withdraw from the engagement

     b. the auditor should state the reasons why an opinion cannot be stated

     c. the engagement should be expanded until an opinion can be stated

     d. the governmental entity should engage another auditor

CHAPTER 12

Compliance Auditing and Reporting

The basic types of governmental audits and their general requirements were discussed in Chapter 11. With increasing attention on performance measurement in the public sector and the absence of a bottom line to measure, compliance auditing, not surprisingly, is the focal point for much public sector auditing. The reasons for that importance, along with an in-depth look at current standards for compliance auditing and reporting, are discussed in this chapter.

DEVELOPMENT OF COMPLIANCE AUDITING

The concept of evaluating a governmental entity's compliance with laws and regulations has evolved gradually. Inclusion of the budget and actual comparisons for all budgeted fund types in the CAFR suggests that compliance with budget ceilings and other regulations has long been important to oversight bodies and other financial statement users. Compliance auditing, however, did not gain significance until the federal government began making grants and awards of federal financial assistance to state and local governments. Initially, compliance auditing referred to a grant-by-grant audit with each federal agency defining the areas to be covered. Gradually, with issuance of the Yellow Book by the General Accounting Office, the AICPA's Audit Guide for state and local governments, the Single Audit Act of 1984, and the OMB's Circular A-128, compliance audit requirements have become more standardized and comprehensive.

Refinement of compliance auditing continues. The Yellow Book was revised in 1988, and further revisions that would significantly affect reporting on compliance audits are currently being considered. Since 1988, the AICPA has issued five audit standards that have had a significant impact on compliance audits:

- *SAS No. 53, The Auditor's Responsibility to Detect and Report Errors and Irregularities*
- *SAS No. 54, Illegal Acts by Clients*
- *SAS No. 55, Consideration of the Internal Control Structure in a Financial Statement Audit*
- *SAS No. 60, Communication of Internal Control Structure Related Matters Noted in an Audit*
- *SAS No. 68, Compliance Auditing Applicable to Governmental Entities and Other Recipients of Governmental Financial Assistance*

The AICPA also has pending another revision of the governmental audit guide.

All these refinements tend to make the audit and reporting requirements for a compliance audit more explicit. Some also add to the auditor's responsibilities. For example, *SAS No. 53* and *SAS No. 54* require auditors to design the audit to provide reasonable assurance of detecting illegal acts that could have a direct and material effect on financial statement amounts. One section of the standard specifically refers to the added responsibilities associated with some engagements:

> An auditor may accept an engagement that entails a greater responsibility for detecting illegal acts than that specified in this section. For example, a governmental unit may engage an independent auditor to perform an audit in accordance with the Single Audit Act of 1984. In such an engagement, the independent auditor is responsible for testing and reporting on the governmental unit's compliance with certain laws and regulations applicable to Federal financial assistance programs.[1]

In planning a governmental audit, an auditor must become aware of the appropriate laws and regulations and design audit tests and procedures that, with proper assessment, will limit the risk of not detecting violations to an acceptable level. As another example, *SAS No. 68* confirms the standards contained in the 1988 revision of the Yellow Book and provides guidance on *actually conducting* an audit.[2]

NATURE OF COMPLIANCE AUDITING

The nature and full extent of compliance auditing depends on whether the audit is a financial and compliance audit, an audit conducted under GAO standards, or a single audit. In a financial and compliance audit conducted under generally accepted auditing standards (GAAS), management has a responsibility for ensuring that the entity it manages complies with the laws and regulations applicable to its activities. In a local government financial and compliance audit, applicable laws and regulations include those pertaining to (1) budget adoption and administrative procedures, (2) limits on types of activities or services that can be performed by local governments, and (3) debt ceiling limitations and debt issuance practices. Numerous other operating, procurement, and taxing practices could be governed by specific laws or regulations, all of which may have a direct and material effect on the financial statements. The governmental entity has a responsibility to make these laws and regulations known to auditors. Auditors need to understand those applicable specifically to the entity being audited.

For an audit conducted under generally accepted governmental auditing standards (GAGAS), compliance standards include all those associated with a GAAS audit plus some others related to federal laws and regulations. For example, revenue sharing and entitlement programs often require reporting and

---

[1]Committee on Auditing Procedure, American Institute of Certified Public Accountants, *Codification of Statements on Auditing Standards* (New York: AICPA, 1992), AU sec. 316.24.

[2]Although not relevant to this chapter, *SAS No. 68* also includes the effects of OMB Circular A-133, which applies the single audit concept to colleges and universities, hospitals, and other nonprofits receiving federal financial assistance.

operational parameters that must be followed by the state or local recipient governments. As another example, federal revenue sharing mandates public hearings; auditors would review the records to determine that those public hearings had been held prior to distribution of the funds. Under a GAGAS audit, the due professional care standard includes follow-up on known findings and recommendations from previous audits that could have an effect on current audit objectives. Granted, compliance with these laws and regulations might be tested during the course of a financial and compliance audit, but under a GAGAS audit, they are *specifically required.*

Two basic levels are added to the audit responsibility under a single audit: general requirements and specific requirements. The general requirements involve significant national policy. They may or may not be laws and regulations that have a direct and material effect on the financial statement amounts. It does not matter; they are subject to audit anyway.

The specific requirements encompass regulations or rulings that relate to the department or agency providing the federal financial assistance. For example, certain federal programs may disallow some types of services or expenditures. Other programs might require the recipient government to match the federal expenditures with its own resources or to earmark certain revenues for use in a program or grant. Sometimes program funds may be provided only to people meeting certain income or personal characteristics.

Because single audits place the greatest demands on the auditor in terms of compliance testing and because the most common GAGAS audit would also be a single audit, the remainder of the chapter focuses on compliance requirements under the Single Audit Act.

PLANNING AND CONDUCTING A SINGLE AUDIT[3]

Planning a Single Audit

Any well-planned audit begins with an engagement letter that clearly defines the scope of the audit, the general time frame, the fee structure for the audit services, and the responsibilities of parties involved in the audit.[4] These items are standard to most audit engagements. In addition, when planning a single audit, auditors should consider including a statement about following GAGAS, a list of the special reporting requirements associated with this type of audit, and an identification of the auditor's and entity's responsibilities in reporting illegal acts uncovered during the audit.

Because the cognizant agency is involved in a single audit, auditors frequently hold a planning meeting with the auditee and the cognizant agency. The important aspects of the engagement letter as well as the audit plan,

---

[3]This section is based largely on information contained in the AICPA's *Statement of Position 92-7, Audits of State and Local Governmental Entities Receiving Federal Financial Assistance* (New York: AICPA, 1992) and its *Audits of State and Local Governmental Units,* Rev. Ed. (New York: AICPA, 1986).

[4]The governmental entity may utilize a formal contract to define more clearly the specifics of each party's responsibilities and the scope of the work to be performed.

specific audit tests to be performed, the status of prior-year findings and questioned costs, and the scope of the consideration of the internal control structure, among other subjects, would be discussed at this planning meeting. Before any field work activities begin, disagreements about these matters should be resolved to the satisfaction of the auditor, the auditee, and the cognizant agency.

Resolution of any disagreements with the cognizant agency is exceedingly important in a single audit. Cognizant agencies are responsible for ensuring that the audits are conducted and completed in a timely fashion. In many cases, these agencies have as much interest, as well as broad authority, as the auditee in matters related to the audit. For example, under OMB Circular A-128, cognizant agencies are responsible for providing technical assistance and acting as liaison to state and local governments and independent auditors. They also are responsible for obtaining or making quality control reviews of selected independent and nonfederal audits.

Some planning activities are necessary before an engagement letter or contract can be fully completed. As in other types of audits, the independent auditor must obtain an understanding of the governmental unit's operations. Elements auditors should understand include:

- the accounting system
- the major sources of revenue
- the entity's status as a subrecipient or grantor of federal financial assistance
- how the various funds are used, for example, are internal service funds used? Does the general fund service general purpose debt? and so forth.
- whether the entity has component units, joint ventures, unusual investments
- the identification of and documentation related to federal financial assistance programs
- the nature of the services provided, for example, the governmental entity might include a hospital or college or university
- the number of employees in each major function[5]

Although most of these items pertain to most governmental audits, identifying and documenting federal financial assistance is specific to a single audit. The Single Audit Act and OMB Circular A-128 require the auditor to prepare a supplementary schedule of and report on federal financial assistance. Such a schedule should list, by federal grantor agency, all federal financial assistance programs administered by the governmental entity. Most federal assistance programs are identified in the *Catalog of Federal Domestic Assistance* (CFDA). If a program has not yet been identified in the CFDA, it should be captioned "other federal assistance." Exhibit 12-1 is an example of a supplementary schedule of federal financial assistance.

Planning also encompasses establishing the audit approach (types of audit tests), determining the general nature and content of the audit programs, and evaluating the factors affecting the scope of testing. These duties are also applied to other types of audits or auditing of other types of entities. The auditor

---

[5]Other factors to be considered are identified in the AICPA's *Audits of State and Local Governmental Units*, Rev. Ed. (New York: AICPA, 1986), sec. 5.7.

Exhibit 12-1

Illustrative Supplementary Schedule
Federal Financial Assistance
For the Year Ended June 30, 19X1
Minimum Data Required by OMB Circular A-128 Only

Federal Grantor/ Pass-Through Grantor Program Title*	Federal CFDA Number	Pass-Through Grantor's Number	Expenditures[†]
U.S. Department of Education Direct Programs:			
Impact Aid	84.041[‡]	N/A	$XXX
Bilingual Education	84.003	N/A	XXX
			XXX
Pass-Through State Department of Education:			
Chapter 1	84.011	XXXXX	$XXX
Chapter 2	84.151	XXXXX	XXX
Vocational Education—Basic Grants to States	84.048	XXXXX	XXX
			XXX
Total Department of Education			XXX
U.S. Department of Housing and Urban Development Direct Programs:			
Community Development Block Grant—Entitlement	14.218	N/A	XXX
Urban Development Action Grant	14.221	N/A	XXX
			XXX
Pass-Through State Department of Community Development:			
Community Development Block Grant— States Program	14.219	XXXXX	XXX
Total U.S. Department of Housing and Urban Development			XXX
Other Federal Assistance[§]			
Department of Defense Engineering Study Contract	—	—	XXX
TOTAL FEDERAL ASSISTANCE EXPENDED			$XXX

CFDA = Catalog of Federal Domestic Assistance

*All major and nonmajor programs should be individually identified, including those completed or terminated during the audit period.

[†] If the schedule is prepared on a basis of accounting other than GAAP, the basis should be disclosed. A reconciliation to the general purpose financial statements may be provided.

[‡] Major program as defined by OMB Circular A-128.

[§] Significant programs or grants that have not been assigned a CFDA number should be identified separately.

Source: Adapted from Government Accounting and Auditing Committee, American Institute of Certified Public Accountants, *Statement of Position 92-7, Audits of State and Local Governmental Entities Receiving Federal Financial Assistance* (New York: AICPA, 1992), Chapter 3, Exhibit 3.1.

must simply keep in mind the nature of the entity being audited and the type of audit being conducted as the precise nature of the duties is developed. For example, in evaluating the factors affecting the scope of testing, any audit would involve an assessment of the effectiveness of overall financial controls and the internal audit function, segregation of duties, and the qualifications and turnover of key personnel. In a single audit, an auditor also would be evaluating any reductions or eliminations of federal or state grant funds that fund key local programs as well as assessing federal requirements for expanded audit scope. When making these assessments, auditors also must remember that materiality is considered in relation to the fund type, major program, or individual fund, not to the entity as a whole as it would be in an audit of a business.

Internal Control Structure

A single audit results in a report on the internal control structure and a report on compliance with laws and regulations applicable to federal financial assistance. In order to report on the internal control structure, an auditor must determine whether the entity has internal control structure policies and procedures sufficient to provide reasonable assurance that it is managing its programs in compliance with federal requirements.

Components of the Internal Control Structure

To clarify the scope of the auditor's responsibility to gain an understanding of the internal control structure, *SAS No. 55* specifies three components of the control structure: (1) the control environment, (2) the accounting system, and (3) control procedures. Before an opinion can be issued on the financial statements of an entity, auditors must be satisfied with the adequacy of procedures affecting the accounting system. However, auditors engaged to test and report on compliance should also obtain an understanding of the control procedures and environment affecting the administrative requirements imposed on the entity.

The *control environment* encompasses all those factors that determine the effectiveness of specific policies and procedures. Personnel policies, management's philosophy, and the functioning of the oversight board and its various committees all have an impact. In other words, the control environment reflects the *overall* attitude, awareness, and actions of the oversight board.

The books and records and accounting methods that support the preparation of the financial statements constitute the *accounting system.* Auditors must gain an understanding not only of how transactions are initiated and processed but also of any actions affecting that processing, from original entry to financial statement presentation.

Control procedures are those policies and processes established by management to assure proper authorization of transactions, segregation of duties, safeguarding of assets, and independent checks on performance. Because these control procedures are integrated into the control environment and the accounting system, auditors obtain partial understanding of them when examining those two components.

In evaluating the three components of the control structure, the AICPA's *Statement of Position (SOP) 92-7* indicates that an auditor should:

a. perform tests of controls to evaluate the effectiveness of the design and operation of the policies and procedures in preventing or detecting material noncompliance

b. examine the organization's control system for monitoring its subrecepients and obtaining and acting on subrecipients' audit reports[6]

To satisfy the single audit internal control provisions, auditors need to understand the design of relevant internal control structure policies and procedures. A literal reading of the Single Audit Act would suggest that *each* control should be understood and tested regardless of the size of the federal program. After passage of the Single Audit Act, government representatives and members of the accounting profession agreed on an interpretation of the requirements. The agreed-upon approach included the understanding that auditors would perform tests according to *SAS No. 55,* and that the understanding would include all "significant" audit controls.

Auditors also need to make sure that the policies and procedures have been placed in operation. This information should be sufficient to plan the compliance aspects of the audit, enabling the auditors to:

a. identify the types of potential material noncompliance
b. consider matters that affect the risk of material noncompliance
c. design effective tests of compliance with requirements applicable to major federal financial assistance programs.[7]

Testing the Internal Control Structure

The extent of an auditor's testing is much greater for major than for nonmajor programs. In the case of major programs, an auditor must perform tests of controls to evaluate the effectiveness of the design and operation of the internal control structure and policies and procedures relevant to preventing or detecting material noncompliance. Preventing or detecting noncompliance relates to three aspects of a major federal program:

a. requirements specific to the type of federal program, such as the type of services allowed or not allowed, eligibility criteria for the recipients of the services, matching requirements, etc.
b. requirements which apply generally to all federal programs
c. requirements governing claims for advances and reimbursements, including claims for matching[8]

Specific requirements are associated with each type of federal assistance and are found in the award materials pertaining to the program. General requirements represent broad social or administrative concerns applicable to all federal programs; they are identified in the OMB Circular A-128 Compliance Supplement. Each is summarized here.

---

[6]Government Accounting and Auditing Committee, American Institute of Certified Public Accountants, *Statement of Position 92-7, Audits of State and Local Governmental Entities Receiving Federal Financial Assistance* (New York: AICPA, 1992), sec. 4.4.

[7]Ibid., sec. 4.35.

[8]Ibid., sec. 4.6.

- **Political Activity** Federal funds cannot be used for partisan political activity by anyone in the organization involved in the administration of federally assisted programs.
- **Davis-Bacon Act** Applicable only to programs involving construction activity, the act requires the wages of laborers and mechanics employed by contractors to be no lower than the prevailing regional wage rate.
- **Civil Rights** No persons may be discriminated against or excluded from involvement in federal assistance programs because of race, color, national origin, age, or handicap.
- **Cash Management** Consistent with the Federal Cash Management Improvement Act, recipients of federal financial assistance are supposed to minimize the time elapsed between the transfer of federal funds to the grantee and the disbursement of those funds.
- **Relocation Assistance and Real Property Acquisition** Whenever property acquisitions through federal financial assistance programs involve relocation of families or businesses, the grantee must follow certain procedures and make sure that it assists in the relocation.
- **Federal Financial Reports** Reports made to the granting agency must be supported by or traceable to the grantee's books and records — that is, reports cannot be based on estimates.
- **Allowable Costs/Cost Principles** Principles and standards for determining costs applicable to grants, contracts, and other agreements are described in OMB Circular A-87.[9] To be eligible for federal reimbursement, costs have to satisfy nine criteria, such as reasonable and necessary, allowable under state law or regulation, and documentable. Determining allowable indirect costs is an important part of this requirement. To be eligible for reimbursement under federal programs, indirect costs must be allocated in accordance with a pre-approved plan or by applying a negotiated indirect cost rate.
- **Drug-Free Workplace** Grantees receiving federal assistance directly from a federal agency are required to certify that they will have a drug-free workplace before they are eligible for federal financial assistance. The requirement is not applicable to those situations in which the grantee is simply a pass-through entity.
- **Administrative Requirements** Recipients of grants and cooperative agreements must adhere to a number of administrative requirements, such as cash management, financial reporting, and cost principles.

Audit procedures used in testing an organization's compliance with the general requirements are not usually suited to transactions testing. Inquiry and observation normally will be used instead, except for testing allowable costs/cost principles, which is accomplished by transactions testing during the compliance audit.

The actual testing of internal controls is done in accordance with generally accepted auditing standards, in particular *SAS No. 55*,[10] but some aspects

[9]Appendix D of the AICPA Guide, *Audits of State and Local Governmental Units*, Rev. Ed. (New York: AICPA, 1986) contains a synopsis.

[10]Auditing Standards Board, American Institute of Certified Public Accountants, *Codification of Statements on Auditing Standards* (New York: AICPA, 1992), sec. 319.

are expanded for a single audit. Testing of internal controls should be performed regardless of whether the auditor would otherwise choose to obtain evidence to support an assessment of control risk below the maximum amount. These tests may be omitted only when the internal control structure policies and procedures are likely to be ineffective in preventing or detecting fraud. In such circumstances the auditor should report the condition to the entity's audit committee or its equivalent. This is referred to as a **reportable condition.** A reportable condition may be so significant that it represents a **material weakness.** A material weakness is a situation in which the design or operation of one or more of the internal control structure elements does not reduce, to a relatively low level, the risk that noncompliance with laws and regulations that would be material to a federal financial assistance program may occur and not be detected in a timely fashion.

The tests conducted on the internal control structure are used in formulating an opinion on an entity's compliance with laws and regulations applicable to federal assistance programs. As pointed out in the previous chapter, if the major programs do not constitute 50 percent of total federal assistance expenditures, the tests appropriate to such programs must be applied to nonmajor programs until the 50 percent threshold is reached. If an entity has no major federal programs, the scope applicable to major programs should be applied to the nonmajor programs.

Presuming an entity does have major programs, testing related to the internal control structure for nonmajor federal financial assistance programs is less than that for major programs. As *SOP 92-7* points out:

> For all other [those not tested as necessary to reach the 50 percent threshold] federal nonmajor financial assistance programs, the auditor should, at a minimum, obtain an understanding of each of the three elements of the organization's internal control structure — the control environment, the accounting system, and control procedures — that he or she considers relevant to preventing or detecting material noncompliance.[11]

Compliance Testing

An auditor's reporting responsibilities vary depending on whether the program is a major or a nonmajor one. The auditor expresses an opinion related to major programs and provides only limited assurance on any of the transactions selected from nonmajor programs. As *SOP 92-7* makes clear:

> This limited assurance is positive concerning compliance for those items tested and negative for those items not tested. Instances of noncompliance, regardless of materiality, are reportable.[12]

Compliance testing involves both the general and specific program requirements previously discussed. OMB's A-128 Compliance Supplement not only describes the general requirements and some specific requirements related to the larger federal assistance programs, but also suggests procedures

[11]AICPA, *Statement of Position 92-7*, sec. 4.10.
[12]Ibid., sec. 4.25.

for testing compliance with the specific requirements. Because not all specific requirements are referenced in the Supplement, management may also identify these requirements by consulting with the Regional Inspector General for Audit for the various federal agencies. As identified in *SOP 92-7*, specific requirements pertain to the following aspects of the programs:

a. *Types of services allowed or unallowed:* specifies the types of goods or services entities may purchase with financial assistance
b. *Eligibility:* specifies the characteristics of individuals or groups to whom entities may give financial assistance
c. *Matching, level of effort, and/or earmarking:* specifies amounts entities should contribute from their own resources toward projects for which federal financial assistance is provided
d. *Reporting:* specifies reports entities must file in addition to those required by the general requirements
e. *Special tests and provisions:* other provisions for which federal agencies have determined noncompliance could materially affect the program (for example, some programs require recipients to hold public hearings on the proposed use of federal financial assistance; others set a deadline for the expenditure of federal financial assistance)[13]

In addition, two of the general requirements described earlier are also two of the specific requirements. First, federal financial reports and claims for advances and reimbursements must be supported by the books and records from which the financial statements have been prepared. Second, the cost principles must be applied to amounts used for matching (see the general requirement on administrative requirements).

An auditor must perform procedures to test *each* requirement. When considering noncompliance, an auditor must consider the effect of noncompliance on two levels of materiality. First, instances of noncompliance must be assessed relative to the materiality level set for the applicable program; that is, "the materiality of known and projected instances of noncompliance must be assessed relative to the affected program to determine if an audit report modification is necessary."[14] If the affected program is material to the financial statements being audited, instances of noncompliance (known and projected) must be assessed relative to the financial statements as a whole — that is, "relative to the materiality level set for the combined or individual financial statements being reported on."[15]

Statistical sampling is not required by the Single Audit Act or the supplementary OMB materials. Nonetheless, and based on professional judgment, a representative number of transactions should be selected from each major federal program. Auditors generally concede that, although not required, a separate sample from each federal program provides the best evidentiary base. The sample size is whatever is necessary for the auditor to express an opinion concerning compliance.

---

[13]Ibid., sec. 4.30.
[14]Ibid., sec. 4.33.
[15]Ibid., sec. 4.33.

Naturally, the audit requirements are less for nonmajor programs. Those transactions involving nonmajor programs that were selected as part of the sample will be tested for compliance with the laws and regulations governing that federal program. The primary focus in these tests is on whether the program expenditure is allowable and whether the individuals or groups receiving the assistance are eligible under the federal program. Unlike the tests for controls, auditors are not required to test the selected transactions relating to nonmajor programs for compliance with the general requirements. *SOP 92-7* gives one example that is particularly helpful in understanding these testing requirements:

> If the auditor selected a travel claim that was charged to a nonmajor program, he or she should examine evidence indicating whether the person who performed the travel worked on the program, whether the purpose of the travel was related to the program, whether administrative travel was an allowable charge to the program, and whether travel allowances were within administratively prescribed limits. The auditor is not required to test the transactions for compliance with the general requirements, including compliance with relocation or cash management limitations.[16]

Another example might involve the selection of a transaction related to an equipment purchase. The auditor would examine whether equipment purchases were permitted on the grant, whether the purchase was necessary to the program, and whether procurement was consistent with the grant requirements (for example, some grants require that such items be purchased through the lowest-bidder process).

OTHER FACTORS IN A COMPLIANCE AUDIT

Assessing Audit Risk

A compliance audit is subject to the same audit risk assessment that is made in a financial audit. Therefore, an auditor would rely on the audit risk formula established by *SAS No. 47, Audit Risk and Materiality in Conducting an Audit.* The audit risk formula used there is:

$$AR = IR \times CR \times DR \quad \text{where } AR = \text{Audit Risk}$$
$$IR = \text{Inherent Risk}$$
$$CR = \text{Control Risk}$$
$$DR = \text{Detection Risk}$$

In every case, the risk being assessed is the risk that a material misstatement may exist that would not be detected by the audit procedures.

Inherent risk is the "susceptibility of an assertion to a material misstatement, assuming that there are no related internal control structure policies or

---

[16]Ibid., sec. 4.43.

procedures."[17] Risk factors associated with program-related compliance requirements include such items as: (1) prior experience with the activity or program; (2) total receipts, revenues, or expenditures at risk; (3) subrecipient involvement in carrying out the program; (4) the extent of independent oversight or audit review in addition to the compliance audit; or (5) changes in economic or programmatic conditions.

The risk that a material misstatement that could occur in an assertion will not be prevented or detected on a timely basis under normal operating circumstances is the **control risk.** This risk is associated with and a function of the effectiveness of the internal control structure. As *SAS No. 47* makes clear, some control risk is always present simply because no internal control structure is foolproof. In a compliance audit this risk probably would be assessed at something more than minimum because the inherent risk of errors, irregularities, and illegal acts for compliance with laws and regulations normally would be high.

Detection risk relates to the auditor rather than to the entity being audited. It is a function of the effectiveness of an auditing procedure and the auditor's application of that procedure. Such risk will always exist because an auditor does not audit 100 percent of the transactions.

The combined **audit risk** assessment determines the nature, timing, and extent of audit procedures. For example, if the inherent risk and the control risk are both very high, the combined risk will be high. On the other hand, if both are low, the combined risk will be low. The difficulty, of course, is making the assessment when one is high and the other low, or when one is low and the other moderate. Limited authoritative guidance is available.

Two statements on auditing standards provide guidance, as does the GAO's publication on compliance auditing. *SAS No. 56* indicates that analytical procedures may be sufficient and appropriate evidential matter in areas of low risk. Under *SAS No. 55,* the auditor may consider performing minimal substantive tests (analytical procedures) when the control risk is assessed as low. It follows that for auditors to use only analytical procedures, the combined risk has to be low. As Exhibit 12-2 indicates, testing can be limited or moderate even when inherent risk is high.[18]

Questioned Costs

Under OMB Circular A-128, auditors are required to report all questioned costs. The nature of the questioned costs as well as the amounts involved determine whether the grantor agency will ultimately disallow them. In assessing questioned costs, auditors should consider the following criteria:

a. *Unallowable costs:* certain costs specifically unallowable under the general and special award conditions or agency instructions (including, but not limited to, pre-grant and post-grant costs and costs in excess of the approved grant budget either by category or in total)

---

[17]AICPA, *Codification,* sec. 312.20.

[18]General Accounting Office, *Assessing Compliance with Applicable Laws and Regulations* (Washington, D.C.: GAO, 1989), Table 3.1.

| Exhibit 12-2 |

Relationship Between Inherent Risk, Internal Controls, Vulnerability, and Testing Extent

Inherent Risk X	Internal Controls	Vulnerability/Testing Extent
High	Weak	High
	Adequate	Moderate to High
	Strong	Low to Moderate
Moderate	Weak	Moderate to High
	Adequate	Moderate
	Strong	Low
Low	Weak	Low to Moderate
	Adequate	Low
	Strong	Very Low

b. *Undocumented costs:* costs charged to the grant for which adequate detailed documentation does not exist (for example, documentation demonstrating their relationship to the grant or the amounts involved)

c. *Unapproved costs:* costs that are not provided for in the approved grant budget, or for which the grant or contract provisions or applicable costs principles require the awarding agency's approval, but for which the auditor finds no evidence of approval

d. *Unreasonable costs:* costs incurred that may not reflect the actions a prudent person would take in the circumstances, or costs resulting from assigning an unreasonably high valuation to in-kind contributions.[19]

Auditors do not have to include a projection of questioned costs to the universe in their report. Auditors also do not have to expand the scope of their audit to determine with greater precision the effect of questioned costs. Nonetheless, auditors or grantor agencies may use some specific questioned costs as a basis for determining that all costs charged to a federal program are questioned. For example, if eligibility criteria were not met by a recipient, the entire amount expended in connection with the affected programs may be questioned by the auditor and subsequently disallowed by the federal agency.

Subrecipient Considerations

As indicated in Chapter 11, many primary recipients of federal financial assistance make subawards and disburse their own funds to subrecipients. For example, a state's human resources division may receive a grant to enhance training opportunities for low-income individuals. It may disburse this money to the individual counties. If a primary recipient disburses more than $25,000, it has certain single audit responsibilities related to the subrecipient.

[19] AICPA, *SOP 92-7*, sec. 5.28.

Disbursements to subrecipients are usually based on properly completed and approved applications. The award to the subrecipient would include a provision that the awardee has to comply with federal conditions as well as any the primary recipient might attach to the award.

OMB Circular A-128 requires that any primary recipient disbursing more than $25,000 in federal financial assistance to subrecipients should:

a. determine that the subrecipients have adhered to the audit provisions of OMB Circular A-128
b. determine whether the subrecipients spent federal financial assistance funds provided in accordance with applicable laws and regulations
c. ensure that reported instances of noncompliance with federal laws and recommendations have been corrected
d. consider whether subrecipients' audits necessitate adjustment of the recipient's own records
e. require each subrecipient to permit independent auditors to have access to their records and financial statements as necessary to comply with the federal requirements[20]

These responsibilities are very broad and necessitate others. For example, to meet these responsibilities, a primary recipient must include in control policies and procedures attributes that allow it to determine a subrecipient's noncompliance with applicable federal laws and regulations. To make sure that corrective action has been taken by the subrecipient, a primary recipient has to review subrecipient audits and other reports. A primary recipient also will pursue the resolution of questioned costs to ensure prompt and appropriate corrective action is taken.

Auditors must consider subrecipients when planning and conducting a compliance audit of the primary recipient. Because part of a primary recipient's control structure pertains to subrecipient compliance, auditors should obtain an understanding of the design of control policies and procedures for monitoring subrecipients. Auditors should also make sure the control policies and procedures have been put into effect. The assessment of control risk involves evaluating the effectiveness of the primary recipient's monitoring system pertaining to the subrecipient. In addition, auditors have to assess the effects of reported noncompliance by the subrecipient on each of the recipient's major federal financial assistance programs.

REPORTING ON A COMPLIANCE AUDIT

One of the most confusing aspects of a single audit is the required reporting.

Explaining the federal compliance reports to a city council or members of the governing board of a local government . . . can be an extremely difficult job for the auditor. Generally, non-accountant readers of the federal compliance reports are usually completely mystified by the impressive (but to them almost

---

[20]Ibid., sec. 4.18.

incomprehensible) attempts by the auditors to communicate the results of their work on federal compliance.[21]

One reason for the confusion is the fact that auditors' reporting responsibilities are governed not only by generally accepted auditing standards but also by generally accepted governmental auditing standards and by the specific requirements of the Single Audit Act and OMB Circular A-128. These latter two include reports on compliance with general and specific requirements. They also require a report on the internal control structure. Depending on how the auditor combines these individual reports, the total number prepared may vary from one audit to the next. Exhibit 12-3 shows the levels of reporting and the different reports that are required for satisfying the provisions of the Single Audit Act and OMB Circular A-128. These same reporting requirements may be illustrated in a slightly different fashion, as in Exhibit 12-4.

As Exhibit 12-4 indicates, apart from the report on financial statements, seven individual reports may be required. In addition, a report on illegal acts may be required. Auditors sometimes combine the compliance reports, for example, they put the GAGAS report on compliance with the three compliance reports required under OMB Circular A-128. This combination would mean a total of four reports in addition to the one on financial statements. Although not done as commonly, an auditor could combine the report on the entity's internal control structure with the report on internal controls over

Exhibit 12-3

Single Audit Reporting Matrix*

| | | | Required by | |
| | | | Government Auditing | Single Audit Act/OMB |
Report	Type of Report	GAAS	Standards	Circular A-128
General-purpose financial statements	Opinion	X	X	X
Internal control structure based on GAAS procedures	SAS No. 60 type		X	X
Compliance based on GAAS procedures	Positive and negative		X	X
Federal financial assistance:				
Supplementary Schedule of Federal Financial Assistance	In relation to general-purpose financial statements			X
Compliance with general requirements	Positive and negative			X
Compliance with specific requirements:				
Major program	Opinion			X
Nonmajor (when selected)	Positive and negative			X
Internal control structure related to FFA	Results of procedures			X
Illegal acts (issued only when instances are detected)	See discussion in SAS No. 54		X	X

*This matrix summarizes the auditor's reports required by *Government Auditing Standards* and by the Single Audit Act and OMB Circular A-128. All reports should be tailored to individual circumstances (a report on illegal acts is required only when instances are detected).

Source: Adapted from Government Accounting and Auditing Committee, American Institute of Certified Public Accountants, *Statement of Position 92-7, Audits of State and Local Governmental Entities Receiving Federal Financial Assistance* (New York: AICPA, 1992), Chapter 5, Exhibit 5.1.

[21]R. P. Foltz and G.W. Crain, "A Proposed Change in Emphasis: Federal Compliance Reporting," *Line Items* (June/July 1993): 7.

Exhibit 12-4

Levels of Reporting in Governmental Single Audits

GAAS Audit vs. *Government Auditing Standards* Audit vs. Single Audit

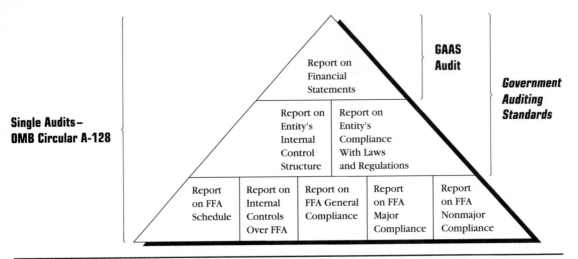

Source: Adapted from Government Accounting and Auditing Committee, American Institute of Certified Public Accountants, *Statement of Position 92-7, Audits of State and Local Governmental Entities Receiving Federal Financial Assistance* (New York: AICPA, 1992), Chapter 1, Exhibit 1.1.

federal financial assistance. This reporting structure reduces the total number of reports, including the one on financial statements, to four, or to five if a report on illegal acts is required.

▲   **OBSERVATION**

Most financial statement users are accustomed to a single opinion, and therefore need some assistance from the auditor in understanding the need for and precise nature of each of these reports. Further, the more that similar topics can be grouped in a single report, the easier the explanation. Nonetheless, because the level of assurance and nature of the reports varies, the extent to which they can be combined may be limited.

Report on General Purpose Financial Statements

As shown in Exhibit 12-5, the report on general purpose financial statements is similar to that found in the private sector and in a comprehensive annual report of a governmental entity that is not required to have a single audit. The Single Audit Act does not require financial statements prepared according to GAAP, but an auditor is required to report on whether the statements were prepared in accordance with the GAAP. An auditor may also indicate that the audit was conducted in accordance with generally accepted governmental auditing standards.

Exhibit 12-5

Unqualified Opinion on General-Purpose or
Component-Unit Financial Statements Only

Independent Auditor's Report

We have audited the accompanying general-purpose financial statements of City of Example, Any State, as of and for the year ended June 30, 19X1. These general-purpose financial statements are the responsibility of City of Example, Any State, management. Our responsibility is to express an opinion on these general-purpose financial statements based on our audit.

We conducted our audit in accordance with generally accepted auditing standards. Those standards require that we plan and perform the audit to obtain reasonable assurance about whether the general-purpose financial statements are free of material misstatement. An audit includes examining, on a test basis, evidence supporting the amounts and disclosures in the general-purpose financial statements. An audit also includes assessing the accounting principles used and significant estimates made by management, as well as evaluating the overall general-purpose financial statement presentation. We believe that our audit provides a reasonable basis for our opinion.

In our opinion, the general-purpose financial statements referred to above present fairly, in all material respects, the financial position of City of Example, Any State, as of June 30, 19X1, and the results of its operations and cash flows of its proprietary fund types and nonexpendable trust funds for the year then ended in conformity with generally accepted accounting principles.

[Signature]

[Date]

Source: Adapted from Government Accounting and Auditing Committee, American Institute of Certified Public Accountants, *Statement of Position 92-7, Audits of State and Local Governmental Entities Receiving Federal Financial Assistance* (New York: AICPA, 1992), Appendix D, Example 1.

Report on Compliance— Government Auditing Standards

Government auditing standards require a compliance report regardless of whether the auditor can determine the full effect of noncompliance. Auditors must express positive and negative assurance on compliance based on procedures conducted under generally accepted auditing standards. A report of this type is illustrated in Exhibit 12-6.

Any material violations or possible violations of laws or regulations should be considered for disclosure in the notes to the financial statements. If an auditor cannot determine whether the entity has complied with laws and regulations and whether any potential effect of noncompliance could be material, a scope limitation may exist. If so, the report on financial statements would be modified accordingly.

Internal Control Structure Report— Government Auditing Standards

No opinion is expressed in this report. An auditor describes the work performed as required by GAAS and identifies the significant internal control structure categories. "When federal financial assistance is material to the government's financial statements, the control categories identified include the controls over the general and specific compliance requirements."[22] A standard language report is displayed in Exhibit 12-7.

[22]Ibid., sec. 5.8.

Exhibit 12-6

Report on Compliance Based on an Audit of General-Purpose or Basic Financial Statements Performed in Accordance With *Government Auditing Standards*

We have audited the general-purpose financial statements of City of Example, Any State, as of and for the year ended June 30, 19X1, and have issued our report thereon dated August 15, 19X1.

We conducted our audit in accordance with generally accepted auditing standards and *Government Auditing Standards*, issued by the Comptroller General of the United States. Those standards require that we plan and perform the audit to obtain reasonable assurance about whether the financial statements are free of material misstatement.

Compliance with laws, regulations, contracts, and grants applicable to City of Example, Any State, is the responsibility of City of Example, Any State's management. As part of obtaining reasonable assurance about whether the financial statements are free of material misstatement, we performed tests of City of Example, Any State's compliance with certain provisions of laws, regulations, contracts, and grants. However, the objective of our audit of the general-purpose financial statements was not to provide an opinion on overall compliance with such provisions. Accordingly, we do not express such an opinion.

The results of our tests indicate that, with respect to the items tested, City of Example, Any State, complied, in all material respects, with the provisions referred to in the preceding paragraph. With respect to items not tested, nothing came to our attention that caused us to believe that City of Example, Any State, had not complied, in all material respects, with those provisions.

This report is intended for the information of the audit committee, management, and [*specify legislative or regulatory body*]. However, this report is a matter of public record and its distribution is not limited.

[*Signature*]

[*Date*]

Source: Adapted from Government Accounting and Auditing Committee, American Institute of Certified Public Accountants, *Statement of Position 92-7, Audits of State and Local Governmental Entities Receiving Federal Financial Assistance* (New York: AICPA, 1992), Appendix D, Example 17(A).

Exhibit 12-7

Single Audit Report on the Internal Control Structure Used in Administering Federal Financial Assistance Programs

---

We have audited the general-purpose financial statements of City of Example, Any State, as of and for the year ended June 30, 19X1, and have issued our report thereon dated September 8, 19X1. We have also audited the compliance of City of Example, Any State, with requirements applicable to major federal financial assistance programs and have issued our report thereon dated September 8, 19X1.

We conducted our audits in accordance with generally accepted auditing standards; *Government Auditing Standards*, issued by the Comptroller General of the United States; and Office of Management and Budget Circular A-128, *Audits of State and Local Governments*. Those standards and OMB Circular A-128 require that we plan and perform the audit to obtain reasonable assurance about whether the general-purpose financial statements are free of material misstatement and about whether City of Example, Any State, complied with laws and regulations, noncompliance with which would be material to a major federal financial assistance program.

In planning and performing our audits for the year ended June 30, 19X1, we considered the internal control structure of City of Example, Any State, in order to determine our auditing procedures for the purpose of expressing our opinions on the general-purpose financial statements of City of Example, Any State, and on the compliance of City of Example, Any State, with requirements applicable to major programs, and to report on the internal control structure in accordance with OMB Circular A-128. This report addresses our consideration of internal control structure policies and procedures relevant to compliance with requirements applicable to federal financial assistance programs. We have addressed internal control structure policies and procedures relevant to our audit of the general-purpose financial statements in a separate report dated September 8, 19X1.

(continued)

Exhibit 12-7　*(continued)*

The management of City of Example, Any State, is responsible for establishing and maintaining an internal control structure. In fulfilling this responsibility, estimates and judgments by management are required to assess the expected benefits and related costs of internal control structure policies and procedures. The objectives of an internal control structure are to provide management with reasonable, but not absolute, assurance that assets are safeguarded against loss from unauthorized use or disposition, that transactions are executed in accordance with management's authorization and recorded properly to permit the preparation of general-purpose financial statements in accordance with generally accepted accounting principles, and that federal financial assistance programs are managed in compliance with applicable laws and regulations. Because of inherent limitations in any internal control structure, errors, irregularities, or instances of noncompliance may nevertheless occur and not be detected. Also, projection of any evaluation of the structure to future periods is subject to the risk that procedures may become inadequate because of changes in conditions or that the effectiveness of the design and operation of policies and procedures may deteriorate.

For the purpose of this report, we have classified the significant internal control structure policies and procedures used in administering federal financial assistance programs in the following categories: [*identify internal control structure categories*].

For all of the internal control structure categories listed above, we obtained an understanding of the design of relevant policies and procedures and determined whether they have been placed in operation, and we assessed control risk.

During the year ended June 30, 19X1, City of Example, Any State, expended X percent of its total federal financial assistance under major federal financial assistance programs.

We performed tests of controls, as required by OMB Circular A-128, to evaluate the effectiveness of the design and operation of internal control structure policies and procedures that we considered relevant to preventing or detecting material noncompliance with specific requirements, general requirements, and requirements governing claims for advances and reimbursement and amounts claimed or used for matching that are applicable to each of City of Example, Any State's major federal financial assistance programs, which are identified in the accompanying Schedule of Federal Financial Assistance. Our procedures were less in scope than would be necessary to render an opinion on these internal control structure policies and procedures. Accordingly, we do not express such an opinion.

We noted certain matters involving the internal control structure and its operation that we consider to be reportable conditions under standards established by the American Institute of Certified Public Accountants. Reportable conditions involve matters coming to our attention relating to significant deficiencies in the design or operation of the internal control structure that, in our judgment, could adversely affect City of Example, Any State's ability to administer federal financial assistance programs in accordance with applicable laws and regulations. [*Include paragraphs to describe the reportable conditions noted.*]

A material weakness is a reportable condition in which the design or operation of one or more of the internal control structure elements does not reduce to a relatively low level the risk that noncompliance with laws and regulations that would be material to a federal financial assistance program may occur and not be detected within a timely period by employees in the normal course of performing their assigned functions.

Our consideration of the internal control structure policies and procedures used in administering federal financial assistance would not necessarily disclose all matters in the internal control structure that might be reportable conditions and, accordingly, would not necessarily disclose all reportable conditions that are also considered to be material weaknesses as defined above. However, we believe none of the reportable conditions described above is a material weakness.

We also noted other matters involving the internal control structure and its operation that we have reported to the management of City of Example, Any State, in a separate letter dated September 8, 19X1.

This report is intended for the information of the audit committee, management, and [*specify legislative or regulatory body*]. However, this report is a matter of public record and its distribution is not limited.

[*Signature*]

[*Date*]

Source: Adapted from Government Accounting and Auditing Committee, American Institute of Certified Public Accountants, *Statement of Position 92-7, Audits of State and Local Governmental Entities Receiving Federal Financial Assistance* (New York: AICPA, 1992), Appendix D, Example 26(A).

Report on Schedule of Federal Financial Assistance

This is an opinion-type report specifically required by the Single Audit Act. It references the related audit on the general purpose financial statements and, as Exhibit 12-8 indicates, it notes the purposes of the accompanying schedule of federal financial assistance. Most important, the report on the schedule of federal financial assistance relates the schedule to the fair presentation of the financial statements as a whole.

Report on Internal Control Structure for Federal Financial Assistance

More specialized than the general report on the internal control structure, the report on internal control for federal financial assistance assesses the internal control procedures as they affect the administration of federal financial assistance. The report should indicate that the audit was made in accordance with GAAS, GAGAS, and OMB Circular A-128.

As many as sixteen other elements must be contained in the report, as applicable. For example, the report should include a statement about management's responsibility for the internal control structure. It should also describe the entity's significant internal control structure policies and procedures, and the scope of the auditor's work conducted in gaining an understanding

---

Exhibit 12-8

Report on Supplementary Schedule of Federal Financial Assistance

Independent Auditor's Report

We have audited the general-purpose financial statements of City of Example, Any State, as of and for the year ended June 30, 19X1, and have issued our report thereon dated August 15, 19X1. These general-purpose financial statements are the responsibility of City of Example, Any State's management. Our responsibility is to express an opinion on these general-purpose financial statements based on our audit.

We conducted our audit in accordance with generally accepted auditing standards and *Government Auditing Standards* issued by the Comptroller General of the United States. Those standards require that we plan and perform the audit to obtain reasonable assurance about whether the general-purpose financial statements are free of material misstatement. An audit includes examining, on a test basis, evidence supporting the amounts and disclosures in the general-purpose financial statements. An audit also includes assessing the accounting principles used and significant estimates made by management, as well as evaluating the overall financial statement presentation. We believe that our audit provides a reasonable basis for our opinion.

Our audit was made for the purpose of forming an opinion on the general-purpose financial statements of City of Example, Any State, taken as a whole. The accompanying Schedule of Federal Financial Assistance is presented for purposes of additional analysis and is not a required part of the general-purpose financial statements. The information in that schedule has been subjected to the auditing procedures applied in the audit of the general-purpose financial statements and, in our opinion, is fairly presented in all material respects in relation to the general-purpose financial statements taken as a whole.

[*Signature*]

[*Date*]

Source: Adapted from Government Accounting and Auditing Committee, American Institute of Certified Public Accountants, *Statement of Position 92-7, Audits of State and Local Governmental Entities Receiving Federal Financial Assistance* (New York: AICPA, 1992), Appendix D, Example 16.

of the internal control structure. Exhibit 12-7 provides an example of a standard report that covers both the internal control structure discussed earlier as well as the compliance aspects. Other elements that could be covered are detailed in *SOP 92-7*.[23]

Reports on Compliance Applicable to Federal Financial Assistance

Three reporting requirements relate specifically to compliance applicable to federal financial assistance: (1) compliance with general requirements; (2) compliance with specific requirements; and (3) compliance with requirements applicable to nonmajor programs. The third report would not be required if no nonmajor program transactions were selected as part of the tests for the audit of financial statements or the review of the internal control structure. If a report is required, positive assurance is expressed for those items tested and negative assurance for the ones not tested, as indicated in Exhibit 12-9.

Exhibit 12-9

Single Audit Report on Compliance With Specific Requirements Applicable to Nonmajor Federal Financial Assistance Program Transactions

---

Independent Auditor's Report on City of Example, Any State's Compliance With Its Nonmajor Federal Financial Assistance Programs

---

We have audited the general-purpose financial statements of City of Example, Any State, as of and for the year ended June 30, 19X1, and have issued our report thereon dated August 15, 19X1.

In connection with our audit of the general-purpose financial statements of City of Example, Any State, and with our consideration of City of Example, Any State's control structure used to administer federal financial assistance programs, as required by Office of Management and Budget Circular A-128, *Audits of State and Local Governments*, we selected certain transactions applicable to certain nonmajor federal financial programs for the year ended June 30, 19X1. As required by OMB Circular A-128, we have performed auditing procedures to test compliance with the requirements governing [*list requirements tested*] that are applicable to those transactions. Our procedures were substantially less in scope than an audit, the objective of which is the expression of an opinion on City of Example, Any State's compliance with these requirements. Accordingly, we do not express such an opinon.

With respect to the items tested, the results of those procedures disclosed no material instances of noncompliance with the requirements listed in the preceding paragraph. With respect to items not tested, nothing came to our attention that caused us to believe that City of Example, Any State, had not complied, in all material respects, with those requirements. However, the results of our procedures disclosed immaterial instances of noncompliance with those requirements, which are described in the accompanying Schedule of Findings and Questioned Costs.

This report is intended for the information of the audit committee, management, and [*specify legislative or regulatory body*]. However, this report is a matter of public record and its distribution is not limited.

[*Signature*]

[*Date*]

Source: Adapted from Government Accounting and Auditing Committee, American Institute of Certified Public Accountants, *Statement of Position 92-7, Audits of State and Local Governmental Entities Receiving Federal Financial Assistance* (New York: AICPA, 1992), Appendix D, Example 24.

---

[23]Ibid., sec 5.11.

The report on compliance with general requirements expresses positive assurance on items tested and negative assurance on the ones not tested. This report must contain a summary of findings of noncompliance and an identification of any amounts questioned, by federal award, and regardless of materiality. As described earlier, findings refer to instances of noncompliance.

▲   **OBSERVATION**

The placement of findings is confusing. Circular A-128 indicates that a summary of all findings of noncompliance and total amounts questioned for each federal program should be in the auditor's report on compliance. The same document, as well as *SOP 92-7,* also indicates that these findings and amounts should be *reported in the appropriate auditor's report or identified in the schedule of findings and questioned costs.* Based on a review of a few actual reports, the author concludes that if the summary contained in the compliance report is detailed, no other reference is made in other reports. The other option is a summary in one place with the detail appearing in the report to which the instance of noncompliance pertains.

An illustration of this report when a material noncompliance exists is found in Exhibit 12-10.

Specific requirements tested should be identified in the report on compliance with specific requirements. The audit opinion addresses whether noncompliance, if any, has a material effect on any major programs. Immaterial instances of noncompliance that are included in the schedule of findings and

---

Exhibit 12-10

Single Audit Report on Compliance With the General Requirements Applicable to Federal Financial Assistance Program When Material Noncompliance Is Identified

---

**Independent Auditor's Report on Compliance
With General Requirements**

We have audited the general-purpose financial statements of [*name of entity*] as of and for the year ended June 30, 19X1, and have issued our report thereon dated September 8, 19X1.

We have applied procedures to test City of Example, Any State's compliance with the following requirements applicable to its federal financial assistance programs, which are identified in the Schedule of Federal Financial Assistance, for the year ended June 30, 19X1: [*List general requirements tested*].

Our procedures were limited to the applicable procedures described in the Office of Management and Budget's *Compliance Supplement for Single Audits of State and Local Governments* [*or describe alternative procedures performed*]. Our procedures were substantially less in scope than an audit, the objective of which is the expression of an opinion on City of Example, Any State's compliance with the requirements listed in the preceding paragraph. Accordingly, we do not express such an opinon.

Material instances of noncompliance consist of failures to follow the general requirements that caused us to conclude that the misstatements resulting from those failures are material [*indicate program(s) or financial statements*]. The results of our tests of compliance disclosed the following material instances of noncompliance that are described in the accompanying Schedule of Findings and Questioned Costs.

We considered these material instances of noncompliance in forming our opinon on whether City of Example, Any State's 19X1 general-purpose financial statements are presented fairly, in all material respects, in conformity with generally accepted accounting principles, and this report does not affect our report dated September 8, 19X1, on those financial statements.

(continued)

Exhibit 12-10 *(continued)*

Except as described above, the results of our procedures to determine compliance indicate that, with respect to the items tested, City of Example, Any State, complied, in all material respects, with the requirements listed in the second paragraph of this report. With respect to items not tested, nothing came to our attention that caused us to believe that City of Example, Any State, had not complied, in all material respects, with those requirements. However, the results of our procedures also disclosed immaterial instances of noncompliance with those requirements, which are described in the accompanying Schedule of Findings and Questioned Costs.

This report is intended for the information of the audit committee, management, and [*specify legislative or regulatory body*]. However, this report is a matter of public record and its distribution is not limited.

[*Signature*]

[*Date*]

Source: Adapted from Government Accounting and Auditing Committee, American Institute of Certified Public Accountants, *Statement of Position 92-7, Audits of State and Local Governmental Entities Receiving Federal Financial Assistance* (New York: AICPA, 1992), Appendix D, Example 23(B).

questioned costs also are referenced in the report. Exhibit 12-11 provides one example of this report.

The report on specific requirements may be difficult for readers to interpret. The auditor is giving an opinion on compliance related to each major program, yet these specific requirements are presented in a single report.

Exhibit 12-11

Single Audit Opinion on Compliance With Specific Requirements Applicable to Major Federal Financial Assistance Programs

We have audited the general-purpose financial statements of City of Example, Any State, as of and for the year ended June 30, 19X1, and have issued our report thereon dated August 15, 19X1.

We have also audited City of Example, Any State's compliance with the requirements governing [*list specific requirements tested*] that are applicable to each of its major federal financial assistance programs, which are identified in the accompanying schedule of federal financial assistance, for the year ended June 30, 19X1. The management of City of Example, Any State, is responsible for City of Example, Any State's compliance with those requirements. Our responsibility is to express an opinion on compliance with those requirements based on our audit.

We conducted our audit of compliance with those requirements in accordance with generally accepted auditing standards; *Government Auditing Standards,* issued by the Comptroller General of the United States; and OMB Circular A-128, *Audits of State and Local Governments.* Those standards and OMB Circular A-128 require that we plan and perform the audit to obtain reasonable assurance about whether material noncompliance with the requirements referred to above occurred. An audit includes examining, on a test basis, evidence about City of Example, Any State's compliance with those requirements. We believe that our audit provides a reasonable basis for our opinion.

The results of our audit procedures disclosed immaterial instances of noncompliance with the requirements referred to above, which are described in the accompanying Schedule of Findings and Questioned Costs. We considered these instances of noncompliance in forming our opinon on compliance, which is expressed in the following paragraph.

In our opinion, City of Example, Any State, complied, in all material respects, with the requirements governing [*list requirements tested*] that are applicable to each of its major federal financial assistance programs for the year ended June 30, 19X1.

This report is intended for the information of the audit committee, management, and [*specify legislative or regulatory body*]. However, this report is a matter of public record and its distribution is not limited.

[*Signature*]

[*Date*]

Source: Adapted from Government Accounting and Auditing Committee, American Institute of Certified Public Accountants, *Statement of Position 92-7, Audits of State and Local Governmental Entities Receiving Federal Financial Assistance* (New York: AICPA, 1992), Appendix D, Example 18(A).

If the entity has several major programs and each one has specific requirements, readers cannot tell which specific requirements relate to which major programs.

Other Reporting Factors

All reports are filed with the governmental entity's cognizant agency. The governmental entity also has to send copies of reports to each federal agency or department that provides financial assistance. If an entity receives $100,000 or more in funding, a copy of the reports must be sent to an audit clearinghouse.

Because the report on the supplementary schedule describes the relationship with the general purpose financial statements, both should carry the same date. Although not preferable, the other reports usually carry a later date; ordinarily, an auditor would conduct some of the work on the single audit after completing the work for the financial statement audit.

Auditors may prepare additional reports for the governmental entity. Nonreportable conditions may be reported to management, as would any incidents or indications of fraud, abuse, or illegal acts.

If the auditors discover instances or indications of illegal acts that could result in criminal prosecution, they are required to report them. Auditors generally do not know which ones may result in criminal prosecution, so they report all instances or indications. Reporting of illegal acts or indications of illegal acts may be covered in the other audit reports or in a separate one.

Government auditing standards indicate that auditors will have discharged this reporting responsibility by informing "the top official of the entity."[24] The entity being audited has a responsibility to report to the funding agencies if any illegal acts affect those programs. If the auditee does not report to the funding agencies within a reasonable length of time, the auditors should do so.

The schedule of findings and questioned costs referred to earlier is an important part of a single audit. It should be written clearly and concisely, and contain specific elements as described in the Yellow Book. Auditors should describe the condition relating to the questioned cost, what criteria were used in determining its classification as a questioned cost, the effect of the item, and the cause. The extent to which the auditor is able to develop each factor depends on the specific scope and how the questioned item arose in that context.

SOP 92-7 provides excellent guidance in preparing the schedule of findings and questioned costs. The auditors should consider the following guidelines:

a. The findings should be organized so that they can be readily related back to the Supplementary Schedule of Federal Financial Assistance.
b. Findings that produce questioned costs should be described completely and clearly.
c. Current-year findings should be distinguished from the discussion of the status of material prior-year findings.
d. The status of known but uncorrected material or significant prior-year findings should be discussed.

[24]Ibid., sec 6.15.

e. If...the auditor becomes aware of audits made by others, the schedule should refer to the reports of other auditors...that present material findings of other auditors that remain unresolved.[25]

FUTURE DIRECTIONS OF FEDERAL COMPLIANCE AUDITING

The Governmental Auditing Standards Board of the GAO is currently revising the Yellow Book, and an organization of Inspectors General from the various federal government agencies is recommending changes that would affect Circular A-128. These revisions and recommended changes appear designed to (1) make the reporting and auditing process clearer, and (2) ease the burden of the Single Audit Act.

One change would raise the threshold for a single audit from $25,000 to $100,000. Under the proposal, entities with federal financial assistance expenditures between $100,000 and $250,000 would be required to have an audit done in accordance with the terms of the grant agreement. Any entity with expenditures exceeding $250,000 would be required to have a single audit.

Other changes would simplify the reporting process. Auditors would be allowed to combine certain reports and to eliminate the positive/negative assurance wording when reporting on internal controls and compliance with laws and regulations. In some cases, auditors also would have the freedom to depart from "boilerplate" language in reporting on audited financial statements, allowing for a combined financial statement opinion, a compliance report, and an internal control report.

A number of the proposed revisions would require greater risk assessment. For example, auditors would be required to assess audit risk associated with assets vulnerable to loss or misappropriation. In addition, "the proposed changes would require auditors to assess whether the control environment contributes to or diminishes effectiveness of controls."[26]

SUMMARY

Conducting compliance auditing for governmental entities receiving federal financial aid is complex and specialized. Auditors have to conduct the audit in accordance not only with generally accepted auditing standards but also with government audit and single audit standards. In other words, two additional layers of auditing standards are superimposed on the basic audit considerations when a governmental entity expends over $25,000 in federal financial assistance.

Despite the complexity, the audit engagement involves the same basic aspects as any financial audit: planning the audit; conducting the audit; and

[25]Ibid., sec. 5.37.

[26]Loren W. Randall, "Forum Concentrates on Yellow Book Changes," *Line Items* (June/July, 1993): 18.

reporting on the audit findings. A compliance audit usually will be conducted along with an audit of the general purpose financial statements. Consequently, auditors do not start over when doing a single audit; rather, they build upon the work done in connection with the financial audit.

The "add-on" portions relate to compliance with federal laws and regulations, which in turn requires a review of the internal control structure from that vantage point. This also means examining the entity's compliance with respect to the general and specific requirements related to federal financial assistance. The general requirements pertain to broad social and political concerns; most general requirements affect all federal programs. The specific requirements, on the other hand, trace to a specific federal program. Typically, these latter requirements concern allowable services or expenditures, matching, level of effort, or special tests.

In addition to the report on general purpose financial statements, seven reports are required for a single audit: a report on the entity's internal control structure; a report on an entity's compliance with laws and regulations; a report on the federal financial assistance schedule; a report on internal controls over federal financial assistance; a report on general compliance; a report on major financial assistance compliance; and, if appropriate, a report on non-major compliance. A report on illegal acts may also be required.

A single audit also encompasses a schedule of findings and questioned costs. The auditor needs to describe the finding, how it was determined that the item is a finding, the cause of the finding, and possible corrective action. On a subsequent audit engagement, the auditor would examine the extent to which findings of a previous auditor had been corrected.

The complexity of a single audit, not to mention the number of different reports, leaves many oversight boards confused and frustrated. They are overwhelmed with the variety of opinions and technical language. The federal government, with input from the profession, is proposing changes that would make the auditor's reports more streamlined and, it is hoped, better understood.

QUESTIONS

12-1 Why is compliance auditing more important for governmental entities than for businesses?

12-2 Briefly describe each of the three elements of internal control.

12-3 What is the role (if any) of the cognizant agency in planning a single audit?

12-4 Explain why compliance with the general requirements cannot be tested by testing transactions. How is compliance verified?

12-5 How does compliance auditing under GAAS differ from compliance auditing under GAGAS? Under a single audit?

12-6 How much responsibility does an auditor have for the compliance of the governmental entity he or she is auditing?

12-7 Why do auditors have to be concerned with the compliance of a subrecipient?

12-8 How would an auditor determine the specific requirements for compliance with a major federal assistance program?

12-9 An audit performed in 19X1 resulted in some questioned costs. What should be the response of the entity under audit? The cognizant agency? The CPA who performs the audit in 19X2?

12-10 How are tests of controls for nonmajor programs different from those for major programs? Tests for compliance?

12-11 What are the three components of audit risk? How does each affect the audit?

12-12 A governmental entity has purchased a new mainframe computer with grant funds. Explain how a good internal control system would relate to the compliance audit of this transaction.

12-13 During a recent single audit, several material weaknesses in the internal control system of a governmental entity were uncovered. Which of the reports would reference these weaknesses?

12-14 What is the difference between the responsibility of the primary recipient for a subrecipient and the responsibility of the cognizant agency?

CASES

12-1 Your firm is about to conduct a single audit of the local county. You have been asked to explain to the less experienced associates why the usual planning activities will have to be somewhat different from those for a business audit. Following is a partial list of planning activities from the AICPA auditing standards that your firm usually uses as a basis for its planning:

1. Review last year's working papers, financial statements, and the related report.
2. Inquire about current business developments affecting the entity.
3. Read the current year's interim financial statements.
4. Discuss the type, scope, and timing of the audit with management of the entity, the board of directors, or its audit committee.
5. Consider the effects of applicable accounting and auditing pronouncements, particularly new ones.

REQUIRED

For each of the activities, explain what differences will exist between an audit of a business entity and a compliance audit of a governmental entity. Also explain why the differences occur.

12-2 The City of Noxin has a federal grant to provide low-income housing. The grant provides for abandoned buildings to be purchased, remodeled, and then rented to qualified families at rates based on their disposable income. The City of Noxin is required to match the grant with its own funds or with in-kind services. The following transactions were among those that occurred this year:

1. Gilbert O'Sullivan, a former mayor who is now disabled, has moved into the first completed low-income unit.
2. The city added 6 mills to its property tax levy in order to secure half the required matching funds; the other half is being supplied by work performed by the maintenance staff and a charge for the indirect costs of administration.
3. A local contractor was hired to do all the remodeling jobs.
4. The city does not maintain any special revenue funds; all transactions relating to the grant are being accounted for in the general fund.

REQUIRED

For each of the preceding transactions, determine what the auditor should consider in testing compliance. State how the auditor would determine if an instance of noncompliance had occurred.

12-3   Sam Johnson is conducting a single audit for Wave County. The county has a manual that outlines the procedures and policies designed to maintain good internal control. Specific safeguards are spelled out for all conceivable circumstances and all aspects of the county's operations. It is the most complete manual of its type that Sam has seen in his many years of auditing. He is so impressed that he has decided to assess control risk very low and conduct very few audit tests.

REQUIRED

1. Is Sam justified in deciding that Wave County's internal control can be relied on? Why or why not?
2. Without prejudice to your answer in Item 1, assume that control risk for this entity is very low. Does that justify a decision to limit audit tests? Why or why not?

12-4   A friend from college has called asking for your help. She is about to sign a major contract with the City of Remo. As is her usual practice with large contracts, she has asked for a set of financial statements to review. She was presented with a "book" that the city called its CAFR. She has waded through all the statements and thinks she has a handle on them, but she is still confused by all the audit reports. She has the following specific concerns:

1. At the beginning of the CAFR is a report on the financial statements. It is similar to the audit reports she is used to seeing. Why are so many other reports also included in the annual report?
2. Some of the reports do not seem to have an opinion. What is the use of an audit report without an opinion? How is she supposed to tell if any problems were uncovered during the audit?
3. Her major concern is that the contract be adhered to once the details are firm. Where can she look in the audit reports for some clue about whether the city can be counted on to do so?

4. She noted several reports on internal control. They state that no material weaknesses have been found. Is she safe in equating good internal control with a well-run city?

REQUIRED

Prepare an answer for each of your friend's questions.

EXERCISES

12-1 Select the best answer for each question.

1. The Yellow Book refers to:
   a. the AICPA's Audit Guide for state and local governments
   b. the codification of generally accepted governmental auditing standards
   c. the OMB's Circular A-128
   d. the codification of generally accepted auditing standards
2. Good internal control requires proper monitoring of any subrecipients. Which element of internal control is affected?
   a. the control environment
   b. the accounting system
   c. the control policies and procedures
   d. all of the above
3. General requirements include:
   a. budgetary and administrative constraints imposed by the oversight board
   b. broad goals as defined by the current political administration
   c. cost principles and administrative requirements
   d. all of the above
4. Compliance includes adherence to:
   a. budgetary and administrative constraints imposed by the oversight board
   b. broad limits on activities as defined by state or local laws and regulations
   c. specific programmatic parameters imposed by the agency granting federal financial assistance
   d. all of the above
5. Planning a single audit:
   a. requires a review of prior years' questioned costs
   b. should involve the cognizant agency and any affected subrecipients
   c. is conducted after the engagement letter has been signed by all parties
   d. all of the above
6. Under a single audit, testing of internal controls for a nonmajor program is:
   a. not required
   b. the same as testing of internal controls for a major program

  c. required, but not to the extent that it is required for a major program

  d. none of the above

7. The opinion on compliance:

  a. is only required for a single audit

  b. may carry a different date than the opinion on the general purpose financial statements

  c. is issued only if an entity has major federal assistance programs

  d. none of the above

8. Which of the components of audit risk relate more to the auditor than to the entity under audit?

  a. detection risk

  b. control risk

  c. inherent risk

  d. none of the above

9. Testing the internal control structure should:

  a. help the auditor determine the types of noncompliance that may be found during the compliance testing portion of the audit

  b. be done only if instances of noncompliance are found

  c. be done before the audit plan is finalized

  d. none of the above

10. An opinion on compliance must be issued:

  a. as a result of an audit conducted under GAAS

  b. only when material instances of noncompliance are noted

  c. only with respect to those items tested

  d. none of the above

12-2 Select the phrase that best answers the question.

1. If, as a result of the audit, an auditor notes evidence of illegal acts, he should:

  a. notify the highest level of management of the auditee

  b. notify the agency supplying the funding

  c. do nothing unless certain the acts could have a material effect on the financial statements

  d. none of the above

2. The opinion on internal control is issued in connection with:

  a. an audit conducted under GAAS

  b. an audit conducted under GAGAS

  c. a single audit

  d. none of the above

3. Compliance auditing has increased in importance in recent years as a result of:

  a. increasingly complicated and restrictive laws and regulations

  b. the need to assess performance of governmental units

  c. taxpayers' desires to limit the influence of government

  d. all of the above

4. For an audit conducted under GAAS:

   a. the auditor has no responsibility to test compliance

   b. the responsibility to test compliance is the same as that under an audit conducted under GAGAS

   c. the report on compliance offers only negative assurance

   d. none of the above

5. The auditor's responsibility in a compliance audit:

   a. has been increased by recent AICPA auditing standards

   b. will be decreased to some extent by the changes contemplated by the OMB

   c. can be quantitatively analyzed using the audit risk formula

   d. none of the above

6. In an audit of a governmental entity, materiality:

   a. is not an issue, because all uses of public funds are material

   b. is assessed in relation to the entity as a whole just as it is in business

   c. depends on the auditor's subjective assessment of detection risk

   d. none of the above

7. The extent of compliance testing that must be performed is higher in an audit in which:

   a. control risk and inherent risk are both low

   b. control risk is high and inherent risk is low

   c. control risk and inherent risk are both high

   d. none of the above — compliance testing must occur regardless of the level of risk

8. When an auditor determines that a particular cost should be questioned:

   a. the scope of the audit should be expanded to determine the extent of the noncompliance

   b. an estimate should be made of the total amount that was improperly spent

   c. it may be reported in a separate schedule attached to the audit report

   d. none of the above

9. Reports on single audits may be difficult for the lay reader to understand because:

   a. so many different sets of standards apply

   b. a single audit is more complex than most audits

   c. the language in the many reports may be quite technical

   d. all of the above

10. If a subrecipient receives over $100,000 in federal funds, the primary recipient must:

   a. determine that the subrecipient complies with federal audit provisions

   b. conduct a single audit of the subrecipient

   c. arrange a single audit for the subrecipient

   d. ensure the quality of the single audit of the subrecipient

CHAPTER 13

Governmental Accounting and Reporting: Issues and Problems

Governmental financial statements were, until recently, based on a nineteenth-century accounting model used in the United Kingdom. They were essentially on the cash basis with little recognition of accruals, and they recorded only current assets and liabilities. Beginning in the 1930s, the Municipal Finance Officers Association (MFOA) addressed the basic deficiencies of the cash-basis model. Although several improvements were made, most of them involved patchwork changes, such as accruing some receivables in certain circumstances, and keeping a separate record of long-lived assets. Progress was slow. It took over 30 years to move from the cash basis to the modified accrual basis.

Financial crises during the 1970s created the impetus to change financial accounting and reporting in the governmental sector. New York City, Chicago, Detroit, and several other large cities almost went bankrupt, but their financial statements did not reveal the true state of affairs. Indeed, most people could not understand the financial statements, much less assess the financial position or performance of the governmental entity.

The Governmental Accounting Standards Board (GASB) was created in 1984 in response to widespread dissatisfaction with financial accounting and reporting practices of state and municipal governments. More than 15 organizations representing key aspects of state and municipal governments—from the National Association of State Auditors, Comptrollers and Treasurers to the Municipal Finance Officers Association[1]—finally acquiesced to the formation of the GASB.

Since 1984 significant improvements have been made in governmental accounting and financial reporting. The GASB has eliminated one fund, reexamined the basis of accounting, and issued several pronouncements addressing specific accounting and reporting issues. The Board has undertaken major research into the informational needs of financial statement users, the basis for evaluating governmental units, and financial reporting.

This chapter provides historical perspective on the GASB's progress and examines the basic underlying issues in a number of current projects and future agenda items, including the financial reporting project, services efforts and accomplishments reporting, and pensions. Jurisdictional issues related to the FASB and the GASB also are discussed.

---

[1]Now called the Government Finance Officers Association.

STANDARD-SETTING IN THE GOVERNMENTAL SECTOR: A HISTORICAL PERSPECTIVE

The nineteenth-century governmental accounting model had three basic characteristics: (1) it focused on the measurement of current assets and current liabilities, basically excluding noncurrent assets and noncurrent liabilities; (2) it was essentially on a cash basis; and (3) the accounts for the entity were segregated into funds that were never aggregated to obtain a report for the entity as a whole. Little was done to change the measurement focus, the cash basis, or the fund structure used by governmental entities until 1930.

Beginning in the 1930s, the MFOA's National Council on Governmental Accounting (NCGA) addressed these characteristics, trying to modify each one enough to address current issues and financial developments. Because noncurrent assets and liabilities began to represent a material element of governments' financial picture, the NCGA (then called the National Committee on Municipal Accounting) added a long-term asset and a long-term debt account group. These two account groups were not integrated into the accounting model, however. Instead, they were single-entry accounts that were reported as "add-on" columns in the financial statements. Nonetheless, financial statement users could at least identify the costs of an entity's total assets.

The cash basis was modified to accrue those revenues "susceptible to accrual." Property tax revenues were about the only revenue items susceptible to accrual under the NCGA definition. In order to be recognized, the amount had to be received within 60 days after the end of the accounting period. Liabilities were likewise infrequently accrued. Accounts payable were recognized only if they were incurred to acquire current assets.

The basic fund structure remained intact, but certain changes were made by the NCGA. It required the use of enterprise funds to account for businesslike activities. Such funds used the full accrual basis of accounting. NCGA also changed the accounting for special assessments by requiring that (1) they be accounted for in a separate fund, and (2) the portion of the assessment receivable not currently due would be treated as a deferred revenue.

The Contributions of the GASB

In the brief period since 1984, the GASB has made significant changes in accounting and reporting principles for governmental entities. Although most of the changes were covered in the relevant chapters, a review of the major changes will give a better perspective of the magnitude of the task undertaken by the GASB.

Changes in Accounting Practices Under the GASB   GASB *Concepts Statement No. 1* on financial reporting objectives will have significant long-term effects on accounting practices. In that statement, the GASB deemphasizes compliance as a primary reporting objective; instead it focuses attention on the broader criterion of accountability as a basis of measuring performance.

The statement also is the first authoritative source to spell out the importance of maintaining interperiod equity, the concept that each generation should pay for the services it receives.

The most important of the practice statements issued to date is *Statement No. 11* on the measurement focus/basis of accounting. Moving from a modified accrual basis of accounting for governmental funds to an accrual basis is a gigantic leap. By prescribing accrual accounting, the GASB has stated boldly that overall performance is measured by the change in financial resources rather than by cash flows.

Another significant GASB statement is *No. 6* on special assessments. Previously, when projects were financed by special assessments, a separate fund accounted for the bond proceeds, the construction activities, and the debt service. Because any assessments not due were treated as deferred revenue (a liability) and because construction costs were shown as expenditures when incurred, large deficit balances occurred in the early years of a project. Many felt that an accounting methodology that resulted in these artificial deficits confused statement users. Therefore, the GASB eliminated the special assessment fund for financial reporting purposes. Under the GASB pronouncement, the construction phase of special assessment capital projects is treated like any other capital project: the expenditures and bond proceeds are reported in a capital projects fund, and the bonds payable are shown in the account group. If the governmental entity is not liable for the underlying long-term debt, the debt service activity is reported in an agency fund instead of in the debt service fund. In this case, the debt is not shown in the account group.

Statement No. 7 on defeased debt responds to a critical hot topic in the governmental area. Debt defeasance, or advance refunding, is the practice of retiring debt before its maturity, usually by issuing other long-term debt. Due to favorable bond market conditions, a large number of advance refundings occurred in the mid-1980s. These refundings were accounted for and reported in various ways. The GASB statement clarifies that the defeased issue must be reported in the notes until maturity. It also prescribes the conditions under which both the new debt and the defeased debt are reported in the general long-term debt account group. The GASB stopped short of making the refunding entity show the economic gain or loss in the financial statements.

Other statements address more narrowly focused issues. *Statement No. 12,* for example, sets the disclosure standards for postemployment benefits other than pensions. *Statement No. 9* requires a cash flow statement for proprietary funds; a statement of changes in financial position had been prepared previously. Accounting for risk financing and insurance-related activities in enterprise funds is spelled out in *Statement No. 10.* Recognizing and reporting compensated absences is addressed in *Statement No. 16.* Other statements address interim reporting standards for colleges and universities and proprietary funds.

These new accounting practices have three overriding consequences: (1) they move governmental accounting nearer to the business model of full accrual accounting; (2) they place less emphasis on the fund structure for reporting purposes and, as a result, simplify financial statement preparation;

and (3) they increase a government's responsibility for maintaining interperiod equity.

Impact of the GASB Pronouncements   Adoption of each new accounting pronouncement signals a marked change in the way practitioners must view governmental accounting and reporting practices. A fund has been eliminated, with the possibility of several more eliminations on the horizon. Long-term liabilities related to operations may eventually be reported on the balance sheet of the operating fund. Revenues will be accrued whenever practicable. Taken together, these changes represent a major upheaval for preparers, auditors, and users.

Because each one brings the governmental accounting model closer to the business model, the GASB pronouncements have been far more palatable to auditors than to preparers and those users who are not familiar with business accounting. Auditors deal with business entities daily and are generally comfortable with the notion that accrual-basis accounting results in financial statements that enable users to measure performance and financial position. In contrast, some users of governmental financial statements still believe that the traditional cash basis is preferable to any other model. To them, each change in the direction of accrual accounting has been a step backward rather than an advancement.

The pronouncements issued thus far have not been free from compromise. The GASB has recognized the difficult adjustments facing practitioners, not to mention the costly changes for governments. Like the experience in the private sector, a number of compromise positions have been adopted that do not appear to reflect the goals and objectives in the underlying concepts statement. Assuring governments that moving some long-term liabilities to the general fund would be done in such a way as to avoid a current fund balance deficit is one such compromise. This compromise may have material consequences and may have been politically motivated. Without such assurance, the accrual basis of accounting might not be accepted.

Understandably, the GASB's work is unfinished. Whenever a standards-setting board tries to develop fundamental accounting principles while simultaneously issuing pronouncements on hot accounting issues, some inconsistencies are bound to surface. Moving governmental accounting from the nineteenth to the twenty-first century meant overcoming much inertia. In the process of developing consensus in certain areas, the GASB has not moved as rapidly nor as far as it might have liked or as implied by basic tenets adopted in its early pronouncements.

ISSUES AND AGENDA ITEMS

Governmental accounting and reporting issues are diverse and numerous. They include, among others, the essence of financial reporting, pensions, evaluating governmental unit performance, and analyzing the implications of statements already issued. Capital asset (and the related debt) reporting and the more general project pertaining to financial reporting are probably the most important issues facing the GASB. Accordingly, they will receive the most attention here.

While trying to research and sort through these issues, the GASB has been forced to defend its jurisdiction and pacify its detractors. Although the Board has survived its first major review, an understanding of the review process and its outcomes adds an important dimension to the GASB's future work.

Capital Accounting and Reporting

When *Statment No. 11* becomes effective, the most significant distinction remaining between business and governmental accounting will be the treatment of general fixed assets and the related long-term debt. Governmental entities will use the flow of total financial resources/accrual accounting for governmental fund types, and fixed assets are not reported in these funds.

A related issue concerns depreciation. Unless one considers the principal portion of the debt service payments as a surrogate for depreciation, recognizing the cost of using these assets has not been fully resolved. Despite adoption of accrual recognition of most expenditures, GASB *Statement No. 11* on the measurement focus/basis of accounting (MFBA) project did not prescribe new standards for general capital debt service expenditure recognition. Presumably, this issue will be resolved as part of the capital reporting project.

Omitting the treatment of general capital assets from the MFBA statement gave the GASB additional time for research and deliberation. It also explains one reason why the effective date for *Statement No. 11* was deferred. Until the treatment of capital assets and related debt is resolved, the Board really has not completely defined the basis of accounting for governmental funds.

The *treatment of capital assets and related debt* encompasses four accounting issues:

- Recognizing the cost of the asset and recording debt service payments
- Determining where the assets should be reported, for example, in the general fixed asset account group, a capital fund, a capital account group, or a plant fund
- Deciding which assets will be reported; that is, should infrastructure assets be reported
- Determining whether to record depreciation of fixed assets

Recognizing the Cost of the Asset and Recording Debt Service Payments   The basic issue is whether the cost of the asset should be recognized when it is purchased or throughout its life. Under the flow of total financial resources model adopted by the GASB, the outflow of cash (or use of debt) to purchase a capital asset affects net financial resources. Therefore, an expenditure or other financing use will be debited when the asset is purchased. If debt (a financial liability) is issued, net financial resources decline by the net cash paid for the asset. To illustrate, assume capital assets of $14,000 were purchased. If the entire amount was paid in cash, net financial resources declined by $14,000, representing the amount of the expenditure:

| Capital Expenditure | 14,000 | |
| Cash | | 14,000 |

If $12,000 was paid in cash and bonds were issued for the remaining $2,000, the entries are:

Cash	2,000	
Other Financing Sources—Bond Proceeds		2,000
Expenditures	14,000	
Cash		14,000

Net financial resources decline by $12,000 ($14,000 − $2,000) rather than $14,000 because the debt issuance represents a source of financial resources. As long as the financial resources model is applied consistently, the cost of the asset will be recognized somewhere as an expenditure or other financing use when it is purchased. The issuance of capital debt will be a financial source. The only questions are where to report the expenditure and whether to keep a record of the asset and the debt. Under the current model, the assets and related debt are reported in account groups.

Debt service payments are uses of financial resources. The entire amount—principal and interest—represents an outflow of cash, which is a financial resource. Whether the entire amount is treated as an expenditure, however, depends on if the debt was reported and if the debt service payments take place in the same fund. To continue the previous example, assume that in the following year $1,000 principal and $1,100 interest was paid on the $2,000 debt incurred to buy the asset. The entire $2,100 is a use of financial resources under the current model:

| Expenditures | 2,100 | |
| Cash | | 2,100 |

Under the current model, an entry also is made reducing the principal amount of the debt in the account group. Because the account groups are single entry, the entry made is nothing more than gradually erasing the $2,000. It has no effect on operating results, which will show a decline in financial resources of $2,100.

Deciding Where to Report the Asset   As described earlier, capital assets and the related debt are reported in individual account groups. The results would change markedly if governments used one fund to reflect the asset, the liability, and the debt service payments. The fund could be called a capital fund.[2] Issuance of the debt would be recorded as:

[2]The March 1989 Discussion Memorandum on capital reporting shows several different fund/account group combinations that would produce the same results. The others, however, involve dual entries: one set of entries records the flow of financial resources and the other, the same single-entry system for two account groups as currently exists. The GASB refers to these other options as the dual focus of a fund or account group.

Cash	2,000	
Capital Debt		2,000

▲ **OBSERVATION**

An entity that involves double-entry rather than single-entry accounting is called a *fund.* Thus, creating an entity that includes both fixed assets and the related debt results in a title such as capital *fund,* rather than capital *account group.*

Assuming that the capital fund had a cash balance of $12,000, the entry made to record the asset purchase in the capital fund is:

Capital Asset	14,000	
Cash		14,000

The debt payment entry would be:

Expenditures	1,100	
Capital Debt	1,000	
Cash		2,100

Under this methodology, a $3,000 capital asset purchase made directly by the general fund would be recorded in the general fund as:

Expenditures	3,000	
Cash		3,000

The entry in the capital fund would be:

Capital Asset	3,000	
Transfers In		3,000

Given the preceding facts, the operating statement for the capital fund would look much like that in private industry:

Hypothetical Governmental Entity
Capital Fund
Statement of Revenues and Expenditures

Revenues and Other Financing Sources:		
Operating Revenues	$ -0-	
Transfers In	3,000	
Total Revenues and Other Financing Sources		$3,000
Expenditures:		
Operating	$ -0-	
Debt Service	1,100	
Total Expenditures		1,100
Revenues in Excess of Expenditures		$1,900

If this approach were used, the bottom line would differ significantly from what is shown on today's financial statements. Currently, the total debt service payment (interest and principal) and the total amount paid for capital assets are shown as expenditures, whereas only the interest portion would be shown as an expenditure when a combined fund is used. Also, under current GAAP, the amount generated from issuing debt would be shown as an "other financing source." Once the element of debt is introduced into the same fund in which debt service activities are reported, a liability would be reduced rather than showing an expenditure.

The only difference between this statement and one for a business is the transfer. Because businesses do not use funds, there are no transfers. However, taking the entity as a whole the bottom line will be the same as it is in business: the $3,000 expenditure in the general fund will be offset by the $3,000 transfer reflected in the capital fund for a net change of zero.

Deciding Which Assets Should Be Reported   General capital assets take several forms: machinery and equipment, buildings, and improvements other than buildings. The broad classification of "improvements other than buildings" includes a host of immovable assets, including curbs, gutters, roads, bridges, streets and sidewalks, drainage systems, lighting systems, and similar assets. These **infrastructure** assets involve large sums of money and pose accounting and reporting issues for governmental entities.

Standard-setting bodies have long maintained that the primary purpose of recording capital assets is to maintain stewardship. In other words, if there is a record of these assets, a governmental entity can maintain control over them. Responsibility can be assigned for periodic verification that the asset has not been stolen, destroyed, or misappropriated. As long as the focus is on stewardship, a convincing argument is hard to make supporting the importance of recording infrastructure assets. They are immovable and usually of value only to the government. A governmental entity does not have to check on them to make sure they still exist. Therefore, reporting them adds little to the informational content of a financial statement.

The GASB's concepts statement notes that financial reporting should provide:

> information about a governmental entity's physical resources having useful lives that extend beyond the current year, including information that can be used *to assess the service potential of those resources* [emphasis added].[3]

Infrastructure assets take on importance once attention shifts from stewardship to service potential. Unless governmental entities keep a record of all assets, their cost, and date of acquisition or construction, they are unable to assess service potential related to these assets.

Reporting capital assets has a number of benefits. The governmental entity can, among other things: (1) assess the adequacy of future capital plans;

[3] Governmental Accounting Standards Board, *Concepts Statement No. 1, Objectives of Financial Reporting* (Norwalk, Conn.: GASB, 1987), ¶79.

(2) determine total program or service costs; and (3) determine adequacy of insurance against potential losses.

Arguments against reporting infrastructure assets center around the cost of obtaining the information and the basic inconsistency with the flow of total financial resources model. The expenditure is reported when the asset is purchased; that is, the entire cost of that asset is charged against revenues of the current period. The expenditure of financial resources does not result in a reportable asset. To require governmental entities to report any capital assets, much less infrastructure assets, ignores the basic accounting model and the substantial costs involved, say the opponents. The problem with such arguments is that they ignore the benefits provided to future generations from capital assets.

Which approach the GASB will select is uncertain at this time. Clearly, it is mindful of the cost argument. Nonetheless, the GASB also seems to take a broad view of the objectives relating to accountability and the measurement of interperiod equity. If so, the GASB will be inclined to adopt a fund structure that reports the initial expenditure as an asset in a fund.

Depreciation of Fixed Assets   Governmental entities currently do not take depreciation on fixed assets. The practice is inconsistent with a flow of total financial resources model, under which the assets are shown as expenditures when acquired:

> The using up of capital assets, as measured by a periodic charge to operations such as depreciation, is not a use of financial resources, and therefore is not recognized in governmental funds.[4]

Although the GASB probably will not include depreciation as an operating expense in whatever capital model is adopted, governmental units will be allowed to show accumulated depreciation as a deduction from capital assets in the fund or account group in which the fixed assets are recorded. Even if depreciation is not formally recognized in the operating statement, it will be used to calculate program costs, particularly for cost-reimbursable federal grants.

Pension Accounting

When the GASB was formed, both the FASB and the NCGA were addressing pension issues. The FASB was considering changes to its previous pronouncements that would limit the number of actuarial costing methods, require financial statement disclosure of any unfunded pension liability, and force a closer tie between the employer's and the plan's financial status. The NCGA also was examining all aspects of pension accounting and reporting; it was both reexamining its *Statement No. 1* and determining whether it might use FASB *Statement No. 35* for pension plan accounting and reporting.

---

[4]Governmental Accounting Standards Board, *Discussion Memorandum, Accounting and Financial Reporting for Capital Assets of Governmental Entities* (Norwalk, Conn.: GASB, 1989), 13.

The NCGA concluded that the FASB *Statement No. 35* was not applicable to governmental entities. Instead, it issued its own *Statement No. 6,* which dealt with accounting and reporting issues for the employer entity and the plan. Because there were significant differences between the FASB and the NCGA statements, and the GASB was in the formative stage, both bodies agreed to defer application of their respective statements to governmental entities.

Subsequently, the FASB and the GASB determined that their views on pension accounting and disclosure differed. The FASB issued *Statement No. 87,* a comprehensive statement on accounting and financial disclosures related to employers. The GASB followed by stating that until it had fully addressed the issue, the FASB *Statement No. 87* would not apply to governmental units. The GASB chose to address disclosure requirements first, later issuing *Statement No. 5* on this subject. The project on employer accounting for pension costs and the related liabilities has not been finalized.

A preliminary views document issued in late 1988 revealed that the GASB had as much trouble as the FASB in resolving major pension accounting issues. A preliminary views document usually contains the Board's view of the accounting issue. The fact that the Board had not reached a consensus was obvious because a discussion of both majority and minority alternatives was presented.

OBSERVATION ▲

The basic disagreement of the Board over accrual-based accounting is reflected in the pension project. Those Board members supporting accrual-based accounting represent the majority view and those opposed represent the minority view.

The Preliminary Views Document Primary differences between the two views center on the extent to which governmental accounting will parallel the approach used in private industry. As Exhibit 13-1 illustrates, the majority view expressed in the preliminary views document would define a minimum periodic pension cost and minimum liability for governmental employers basically as in FASB *Statement No. 87.* The majority of the Board would permit governments to use any actuarial funding method to measure the periodic pension cost as long as the employer's required contribution equals or exceeds the amount prescribed under *Statement No. 87.*

Other minor differences exist between the GASB majority view and FASB *Statement No. 87.* The FASB requires employers to use a current discount rate in measuring their minimum pension liability and pension cost. If the majority view had prevailed, employers could use the FASB approach or use a market-related discount rate that reflects changes in the discount rate over five or fewer years.

Another difference concerns those plans that call for variable-rate or step-rate benefit formulas. Some plans vary the benefits to employees depending upon certain employment or market factors. *Statement No. 87* requires these benefits to be considered to accumulate in proportion to the ratio of the number of completed years of service to the number that will have been

---

Exhibit 13-1
_____

Major Provisions of GASB Proposals and FASB Statements

| ACCOUNTING ISSUE | FASB TREATMENT | GASB PROPOSALS | |
		Majority View	Minority View
Minimum Periodic Pension Cost	Increase in actuarial present value of pension obligation	Three options: (1) Apply FASB 87 with minor modification; (2) Option 1, but use market-related discount rate; (3) Select 1 or 2 as a minimum, but use another cost method	Use any systematic and rational basis, so any one of five popular funding methods could be used to determine the expense
Minimum Liability	Difference between accumulated benefit obligation and fair value of plan assets	Same as the FASB	None unless entity not making contribution by an acceptable method; then accrual for three prior years under an acceptable method
Intangible Asset	Upper limit is the unrecognized prior service cost	Same as the FASB	Not applicable
Bonds Payable Used to Fund Pension Liability	Not applicable	Fund liability with matching intangible asset	Same as majority view
Budgeting and Accounting Amounts for Pension Cost	Not applicable	Would differ if total cost was not funded	Amount budgeted equals pension cost

completed when the benefit is fully vested. The majority view adopts this approach in calculating the accumulated benefit obligation, but permits employers the option of using proration in calculating the minimum pension cost.

Under the minority view, proposed parameters are included to define _systematic and rational,_ as well as a methodology to be used for measuring the periodic cost when the plans are not being funded in a systematic and rational manner. Basically, the parameters would say that any one of five popular funding methods could be used for accounting and funding.

**Evaluation of the Majority View**   The majority view would have meant, with a few minor exceptions, that pension accounting for governmental units would be the same as for business. Knowledgeable people argue that "a pension is a pension"; that is, given similar plan provisions and funding formulas, the liability and periodic pension costs should not differ simply because one employer is in the government and another is in the private sector. The majority view is consistent with this reasoning.

Adoption of the majority view might have had a tremendous impact on a governmental entity's general fund. If all noncapital long-term liabilities were recorded in the general fund, general-fund liabilities would have increased markedly under the majority view. Some who oppose adoption of the majority view may be more concerned about this effect than with measuring "true" pension costs and related liabilities.

OBSERVATION ▲

It is difficult to evaluate the arguments of those opposing the notion that "a pension is a pension." Some of these arguments seem to be based on fundamental differences between government and business. Others sound more like general discontent with the GASB's movement away from a budgetary basis for governmental accounting practices.

Some disclosure requirements of the GASB's *Statement No. 5* would have changed if the majority view had been adopted. The major difference relates to the use of a specified discount rate in measuring the pension obligation. *Statement No. 5* continued the long-standing practice of using the expected return on plan assets for this purpose. Adoption of the majority view would replace this discount factor with a "risk-free" rate — that is, the rate available on long-term government obligations.

Response to the Preliminary Views and Subsequent Board Action An overwhelming number of those responding to the preliminary views document opposed the majority view. Of the 14 groups appearing at the Board's two public hearings, 13 were opposed to the majority view. The opponents represented such prestigious groups as the Government Finance Officers Association, the Association of Government Accountants, and the National Association of State Comptrollers. The written comments also supported the minority view by a wide margin.

The primary argument against the majority view revolves around the role of accounting in the budgetary process. Under the majority view, governmental units might budget an amount for funding purposes that is less than the periodic pension cost reported in the operating statement. At issue is whether public policy is better served by an accounting approach consistent with the budget or by one in which the actuarially determined contribution requirement is also the periodic pension expenditure/expense. The Board majority argued that, although accounting may influence funding issues, the transactions are recorded when they occur and not when cash is exchanged; the minority view argued that public policy is enhanced if the accounting and budgeting yield the same results.

The GASB has accepted the minority view. Based on the one-sided results of the hearings and comment letters, the GASB issued an exposure draft in 1990 that basically adopted the minority view. Although this decision satisfied many constituent groups, some were still unhappy about the document.

Various constituent groups identified several problems associated with the exposure draft. For example, it would significantly reduce the amortization periods for unfunded liabilities. Under the proposed standard, transition liabilities could be amortized over 40 years, but subsequent unfunded liabilities would be amortized over much shorter periods.

Two other major problems were noted. Many employers would be unwilling to recognize a pension asset or liability on their balance sheets because they used a methodology for financial statement purposes different from that allowed under state statutes. Another problem pertained to multiple-employer cost-sharing programs. Participants in such plans currently do not recognize any pension asset or liability as long as they are fully funding their required contributions as billed by the plan. A pension asset or liability might have been required under the exposure draft if the amount billed was more or less than the calculations required by the exposure draft. Also, the exposure draft left many unanswered questions about the reporting aspects of pension programs.

Three and one-half years later, after untold hours of research, debate, and discussion, the GASB has tentatively adopted the rudiments of a pension plan accounting and reporting framework. Because so many changes have been made since the original exposure draft was issued and because the Board has addressed reporting as well as accounting issues, a second exposure draft is necessary. On most of the accounting issues, the GASB has either adopted or moved toward industry practices. For example, the traditional accounting method for multiple-employer cost-sharing programs has been adopted.

In terms of the reporting aspects, the GASB has determined the basic statements that will be required as well as many display aspects of those statements. Defined benefit plans would present a balance sheet, a statement of changes in net assets available for benefits, and two supplementary schedules. One schedule would show the funding progress. The other schedule would display the employer's contribution rates as a percentage of payroll.

A number of display characteristics have been determined: (1) assets would be reported at market values, except for fixed assets used in plan operations, which would be at depreciated cost; (2) the schedule of funding progress would include any unfunded actuarial accrued liability; and (3) the schedule of funding progress would be prepared as of the actuarial valuation date, which need not coincide with the balance sheet date. The Board also has tentatively decided how the market values of investments (for balance sheet purposes) and the actuarial value of assets (for the schedule of funding progress) should be determined.

After other accounting and reporting issues have been resolved, the Board will issue the second exposure draft. Because many industry concerns have been addressed, observers do not expect major opposition to the proposed standard. A statement could be adopted as early as 1994 and implemented in 1995.

Financial Reporting Project

The GASB has had an item related to governmental financial reporting on its agenda almost from its inception. After issuing *Statement No. 11,* the Board also needed to decide, as explained in a previous section, on how to report capital assets—an issue known as the capital reporting project. Both the capital reporting project and a portion of the financial reporting project had to be completed prior to implementing the MFBA pronouncement. Further, capital reporting is one aspect of overall financial reporting. The two projects, therefore, are interrelated.

In 1991, the Board decided that the focus of the financial reporting project needed broadening from what had been described as "those aspects necessary for implementation of *Statement No. 11*," to include the long-range objectives of financial reporting. Including longer-range objectives meant examining such issues as the following:

- the relationship between the general purpose financial statements and the comprehensive annual financial report
- whether the financial statements, as currently defined, meet user needs and satisfy the objectives set forth in GASB's *Concepts Statement No. 1*
- the need for a conceptual framework that would include defining basic elements of the financial statements, such as fund balance

Later, after a reexamination of these issues, the Board decided to restructure the financial reporting project. The Board concluded that, in addition to a broad-scope project, a narrower scope project was also needed that would address *Statement No. 11* issues.

OBSERVATION ▲

This series of events makes the Board appear indecisive. Part of the problem traces to a change in the composition of the Board. The outgoing board did not have time to analyze responses and prepare an exposure draft on the financial reporting and capital reporting models. The new board is split regarding the whole issue of accrual accounting, so any topic that involves this issue even tangentially is difficult to resolve.

The primary issue needing attention before implementation of the new accrual-based accounting model was the appropriate balance sheet reporting of accrued liabilities (claims and judgments, compensated absences, and so on). The accrual-based model as defined by the Board made it clear that the debit should be an expenditure; however, *Statement No. 11* does not indicate how the credit is classified. In keeping with the accrual concept, the credit side ought to be a liability, but the Board also considered a direct credit to equity, like a prior-period adjustment. If the credit side is classified as a liability, financial statement preparers also need to know whether both the long- and short-term portions of those accruals should be in the governmental funds. *Statement No. 11* is silent on this subject too.

In terms of the implementation issues project, the Board issued a preliminary views document with both majority and minority views. The majority view wants the long-term operating liabilities on the balance sheet of the governmental funds. The minority, or alternate, view wants them in the general long-term debt account group. Mixed reaction to the preliminary views document, together with the Board's own failure to reach a consensus, led to the indefinite deferral of the effective date for *Statement No. 11*. Since then the Board has concentrated its efforts on the broader financial reporting project.

▲ **OBSERVATION**

The Board tentatively decided in the process of this discussion that long-term claims related to claims, judgments, compensated absences, and unfunded pension liabilities should continue to be reported in the general long-term debt account group. This clearly marks a major departure from the original concept of the measurement focus/basis of accounting model adopted by the Board and as explained in earlier chapters. Interestingly, the GASB decided, again tentatively, that the general long-term debt account group would be positioned closer to the governmental funds in the balance sheet. Together, these decisions suggest that the Board is saying, we are not going to record the liabilities, but we will put them in close proximity so users can at least see them!

The Board decided that, based on its earlier work, the broader financial reporting project should comprise six categories of basic financial data: (1) cash flows, (2) budgetary resources, (3) capital resources, (4) interperiod equity, (5) financial resources, and (6) financial condition. Both the staff and the Board have since been occupied in researching, debating, and developing tentative conclusions related to these six areas. Important observations or tentative conclusions include the following:

- A separate report may be necessary in order to assess an entity's financial condition because of the nature, complexity, and amount of data related to financial condition.
- Financial condition may be assessed at a highly aggregated level.
- Financial reporting should provide information on some areas not now included, such as the strength of the revenue base, revenue/expenditure trends, and the cost of infrastructure maintenance.
- Financial reporting objectives for capital assets should concentrate on how a governmental entity maintains and uses its capital assets.
- A primary reporting objective would be to provide information enabling users to determine whether an entity's financial position improved based on the current year's performance.
- Governmental entities should continue to report budget (both original and amended budgets) to actual comparisons, at least for the general fund.
- Financial statement users need both aggregated data and the more detailed information currently included in the CAFR financial section.
- How aggregations are achieved is significant and a model that will aggregate all governmental fund types into one set of data and all proprietary fund types into another has considerable appeal to the Board.

These conclusions are tentative, and the ultimate shape and configuration of the Board's financial reporting model is unknown. However, as long as the Board is split on basic recognition and display aspects of the accrual-based model, users can expect less rather than more change in the overall appearance of the comprehensive annual financial report. One aspect that does seem likely to change pertains to the inclusion of some nonfinancial performance measures in the comprehensive annual financial report. This inclusion is referred to as service efforts and accomplishments reporting.

SERVICE EFFORTS AND ACCOMPLISHMENTS (SEA) REPORTING

Shortly after its inception, the GASB passed a resolution encouraging governmental entities to experiment with various types of performance measures. Although some governments have long published certain indicators of their service efforts or accomplishments, the resolution had little effect on reporting. Even those governments that do publish performance measures in the statistical section of their CAFRs have few standards on which to base their work. Consequently, the Board decided to play a more active role in this area.

The GASB singled out 12 government functions to study for ways to inform citizens about performance:

- elementary and secondary education
- mass transit
- fire protection
- police protection
- public health
- water and wastewater treatment
- garbage collection and disposal
- public assistance
- colleges and universities
- road maintenance
- hospitals
- economic development

Most of these research reports are now completed and each provides a vast array of SEA indicators that can be used to evaluate performance.

The GASB has issued two other documents important to SEA reporting. One is an overview report that describes the purposes, problems, and approaches associated with SEA reporting. It summarizes the primary issues for a governmental entity and presents selected SEA indicators for all 12 functional areas. Both the overview report and the research reports on the individual functions are designed to facilitate experimentation. They even contain suggestions on **how** the service indicators might be reported.

SEA indicators are grouped into four broad classifications:

- Inputs: Measures of the resources used during the period, for example, costs of providing the services, hours needed to provide the services, capacity of the facilities.
- Outputs: Measures of what was accomplished during the period, for example, number of students graduated, miles of road maintained, number of residents served.
- Outcomes: Measures of the quality of services provided, for example, number of days pollution levels were higher than federal standards, performance on examinations, percentage of total population served on time or with uninterrupted service.
- Efficiency: Measures of the efficiency of the services provided, or indicators that relate service efforts to accomplishments (that is, inputs to outputs

or outcomes), for example, the cost per mile of laying underground pipe, improvement in exam scores as a result of additional staff.

The GASB also is working on a concepts document that would be part of the underlying conceptual framework for governmental accounting and financial reporting. The Board began with a preliminary views document in which it encouraged comments on whether (1) the Board was including the proper elements in SEA reporting considerations, (2) SEA reporting ought to be required, and (3) a distinction should be made between small and large governmental entities in terms of required reporting.

Even before the final draft of the preliminary views document was published, some segments of the GASB's constituency were opposing *any* required SEA reporting. Although most support the research effort undertaken by the GASB as well as its encouragement of SEA reporting in general, practitioners and preparers alike are opposed to mandatory reporting requirements. Excerpts from a *Government Finance Review* editorial illustrate the point:

> The GFOA is not persuaded . . . that it would be appropriate for the GASB to attempt to set standards for all types of SEA reporting . . . *nonfinancial* measures of the *quality* of service go beyond the purview of accounting and financial reporting, and thus beyong the competence and jurisdiction of the GASB. . . . The GASB's contribution to SEA should be directed toward those SEA measures that properly fall within the purview of accounting and financial reporting.[5]

Practitioners have cause for concern about SEA reporting. Financial statement preparers and governmental employees in general know that some will always abuse and misuse data, particularly if the performance measures depict deteriorating performance. Auditors have concerns as well. Depending on the specific placement of these data, attestation may be required. Auditors doubt that some of the databases can be adequately audited; they also are concerned about how lay readers will interpret an audit opinion on SEA indicators.

Preparer and auditor concerns aside, the GASB has made SEA reporting a priority. It also is a topic on which the Board seems to be able to develop a consensus. These factors, combined with general taxpayer unhappiness with the size and efficiency of government, suggest that SEA reporting, perhaps even mandatory reporting, will not disappear soon from the GASB's agenda.

THE STANDARD-SETTING PROCESS

The GASB's standard-setting power is another current issue. As explained in an earlier chapter, the GASB and the FASB jurisdictions overlap in the case of colleges and universities, hospitals, and utilities. Some are owned and operated by governmental entities; others are operated privately (some for profit and others on a nonprofit basis). Many argue that accounting and financial re-

[5]Jeffrey L. Esser, "Service Efforts and Accomplishments Reporting," *Government Finance Review* (October 1992): 3.

porting should be the same for all these entities, regardless of ownership. Each time the GASB issues a standard for governmental entities that differs from the prescribed treatment for nonprofit entities within the FASB purview, an uproar for changes in the standard-setting structure ensues.

A five-year review of the structure for governmental accounting standards was completed in 1989. In its report, the Structure Committee noted that

> the GASB has performed well in the public interest and should continue to function under the FAF. It is structurally sound, has produced effective standards, and has won an impressive measure of respect from its constituents.[6]

The Committee also reported that it had considered and rejected the idea of combining the FASB and the GASB into one standard-setting body. It also rejected the notion of having the GASB report to an independent foundation separate from the FAF. It did, nonetheless, make several recommendations with far-reaching consequences.

Some of the Committee's findings and recommendations concern day-to-day operations. It recommended that all Board members should be employed full-time with staggered terms. This meant that the Research Director held a separate position. Other operational recommendations involved:

- establishing a computerized system for handling technical inquiries
- having the FAF formally evaluate Board members before the end of their first term
- developing a conceptual framework
- improving communications with constituents on the procedures and goals of the GASB
- obtaining additional input from small governments and user groups[7]

Control over the standard setting of "special entities" (colleges and universities, hospitals, and utilities) also was addressed by the Structure Committee. As the report states, the Committee's primary task was to determine the jurisdictional arrangements between the GASB and the FASB that best satisfy the public interest with regard to the separately issued general purpose financial statements of special entities.[8] A number of options were possible: (1) give jurisdiction for all special entities to the FASB, regardless of ownership; (2) give jurisdiction for all special entities to the GASB; (3) continue the arrangement under which government ownership means GASB standards and private ownership means FASB rules apply; or (4) give certain powers to the GASB and others to the FASB regardless of ownership.

The Committee decided on the last option. The report states:

> We recommend that jurisdiction for the separately issued general purpose financial statements of special entities be determined by ownership except for

---

[6]Financial Accounting Foundation. *The Structure for Establishing Governmental Accounting Standards, Report of the Committee to Review Structure for Governmental Accounting Standards* (Norwalk, Conn.: FAF, 1989), 3.

[7]Ibid.

[8]Ibid., 22.

jurisdiction over the separately issued general purpose financial statements of hospitals; gas, water, and electric utilities; and colleges and universities (other than two-year colleges with the power to tax). The FASB should be the standard-setting body for the separately issued general purpose financial statements of these three groups of special entities, and the GASB should be the standard-setting body for additional data the GASB believes governmentally owned members of these three special entity groups should provide when separately issuing general purpose financial statements.[9]

In making its recommendation, the Structure Committee placed heavy emphasis on comparability and a broad definition of industry. It argued that financial statement users should have the ability to compare core financial statements of like entities, regardless of differences in ownership. **Like entities** are those in the same industry. As the Committee noted,

> the industry concept here . . . is rooted in accounting practices and the interests and practices of users of financial statements. For many years, hospitals; gas, water, and electric companies; and colleges and universities (other than two-year colleges with the power to tax) each have sought and applied common accounting standards and found it useful to do so.[10]

The Committee also recommended that a continuing process be established to deal with other jurisdictional problems as they arise. It recommended establishing a standing committee to determine proper jurisdiction when unclear from the original structural agreement. Although it believed that the number of additional jurisdictional issues would be few, those issues should be dealt with expeditiously and formally.

Following the report by the Structure Committee, the FAF established a special committee to deal with the recommendations concerning jurisdiction. The FAF accepted the recommendations of the special committee, which differ somewhat from those of the Structure Committee. The major differences follow.

- Separately issued financial statements of all colleges and universities would be placed under the FASB's purview, except that the *governing board of a governmental entity could make an irrevocable decision to select the GASB as its standard setter.*
- The special committee broadened the hospital industry to include *all health care* entities, but gave the governing board of governmental entities within the industry the option to select the GASB as the standard setter.
- Utilities under the FASB were confined to gas and electric entities, whereas the Structure Committee had included water utilities as well. The same option for choice of the appropriate standard-setting body was to be available to governmentally owned utilities as described above for health care entities and colleges and universities.
- The option to select the GASB as the standard setter was to be a permanent election to be made by the end of 1990.

[9]Ibid., 21.
[10]Ibid., 22.

Reactions to the FAF decision were mixed. Some affected entities were delighted that all like entities would have the same standards. Audit firms and other external bodies, such as bond rating agencies, also supported the decision.

The governmental bodies that had been the primary force behind establishing the GASB were furious. Ten of the original 14 supporting groups threatened to withdraw from the GASB and form their own standard-setting body. On November 17, 1989, *The Wall Street Journal* reported that, faced with this threat, the FAF conceded defeat and was willing to reconsider its decision. Later in 1989, the decision was formally reversed, giving the GASB jurisdiction over all governmental entities. With this reversal, the GASB had won its biggest battle since its inception, and the status quo was maintained.

IMPLICATIONS OF THE CURRENT ISSUES

Considering that the GASB has had such a brief history, these issues—particularly the jurisdictional questions—are to be expected. Even if all the research had been completed before the GASB was established, analyzing the conceptual issues and developing a broad understanding of governmental entities takes time. The Board members must have some experience in working together and in understanding one another's point of view before a consensus can be reached on an issue. To many observers, the GASB has been more successful at this point in its history than the FASB.

Some fundamental operational problems remain. Many issues being addressed by the GASB are interrelated, which causes inevitable delays. For example, the capital reporting project affects the measurement focus and basis of accounting decisions and vice versa. Either project is incomplete without final resolution of issues addressed in the other.

Continuity also is a problem. Addressing such a broad spectrum of issues at one time is an extraordinarily complicated task. For example, when the GASB began the measurement focus/basis of accounting project, it indicated that the resulting standards would apply to all governmental funds. As the Board conclusions evolved toward a total financial resources model and accrual accounting, the incongruity of applying such a model to some governmental funds became obvious. For example, how would preparers apply such a model to agency funds? Those funds have only financial resource flows. Further, trying to prepare an operating statement for agency funds seems nonsensical since they lack operating activities. This explains why the Board later decided to remove agency funds from the measurement focus/basis of accounting project.

Other difficulties surfaced as the Board continued its work on the project. Applying a total financial resources model to expendable trust funds may pose as many problems as it did with agency funds. Expendable trust funds may have fixed assets. Including these nonfinancial resources in a fund whose focus is supposed to be on financial resources is inconsistent. Because those assets are not "general governmental fixed assets," they cannot be placed in the general fixed asset account group. The GASB has indicated that it will address this problem, but in the meantime accounting and reporting may be inconsistent and therefore confusing to readers of financial statements. Such problems might be lessened if the Board could complete an underlying conceptual framework for governmental accounting before it determines all the related accounting principles.

Many proposals being considered by the GASB represent marked change for governmental entities. Because, for understandable reasons, practitioners tend to resist change, the GASB can anticipate resistance to proposed accounting principles. The GASB cannot afford to change the accounting and financial reporting so dramatically that it loses support from its constituency. Lack of support for several specific GASB accounting proposals may be interpreted as a lack of support for the GASB itself. Those who opposed GASB's formation might use any strife between the GASB and its constituency as a basis for getting all standard setting under a single board.

In summary, governmental accounting and reporting issues are complex. Many are interrelated and consistent application of any given solution may not always result in meaningful financial statements. Also, improvements in financial reporting usually mean change. The GASB not only has to overcome basic inertia but also political gainsayers for whom any disagreement between the GASB and its constituency can be used as an argument for its demise.

SUMMARY

Until the GASB was formed, governmental accounting and reporting practices were based largely on a model that focused on current assets/liabilities and cash flows. Founded on legal precedents instead of accounting logic, it also involved a complicated fund structure overlaying the basic chart of accounts. The resulting financial statements, although complex and overwhelming to some, allowed statement users to evaluate individual activities and to compare budgetary amounts with actual cash flows.

Although the nineteenth-century model served some purposes, it made an overall evaluation of the entity's performance and financial solvency almost impossible. Separating activities into numerous funds and placng noncurrent assets and liabilities in single-entry account groups rather than as part of the double-entry system created serious problems when trying to evaluate financial stability of the governmental unit. From about 1930 to 1984, practicing professionals within the governmental sector tinkered with the basic model to address some of these problems.

Since formation of the Governmental Accounting Standards Board in 1984, a concerted effort has been made to reevaluate the basic model. The GASB changed the focus to total financial resources and the basis to accrual accounting. It reduced the number of funds, with more eliminations possible. Governmental entities no longer use a special assessments fund for projects funded by a specific group of taxpayers. The GASB may eliminate some of the funds and/or account groups that currently account for the capital assets and their financing—that is, debt service, capital projects, general fixed asset account group, and general long-term debt account group.

Financial reporting has been both simplified and expanded under the GASB. Although governmental units can account for pension funds in a number of ways, consistent disclosures are required in the notes.

Despite its progress, the GASB's work is far from complete. There is no comprehensive conceptual framework. The single conceptual statement deals with the objectives of financial reporting. The second one will deal with the narrow, although very important, issue of service efforts and accomplishments reporting. Both will be very helpful in providing a basis for accounting promulgations. However, the GASB also needs some underlying foundation for measurement and recognition issues. Most of the major compromises made to date deal with measurement and recognition issues. Perhaps some will need to be reevaluated if the GASB issues other conceptual statements.

The project on capital assets is unfinished. The GASB needs to decide what capital assets should be recorded as well as how and where acquisition, disposal, and use of these assets will be reported. A number of options are available, some of which would further simplify governmental accounting and financial reporting.

Although much work remains, the GASB has accomplished a great deal. How much it is able to accomplish in the future depends as much upon its ability to develop an internal consensus and acceptance by its constituents as it does on solid research, clear exposition, and consistent application of an underlying conceptual framework.

QUESTIONS

13-1 Explain why the GASB has encouraged governmental units to experiment with SEA reporting.

13-2 Describe, in general, the ways in which the GASB has changed accounting and financial reporting for governmental entities.

13-3 Before the formation of the GASB, the National Council on Governmental Accounting (NCGA) developed accounting and reporting standards for governmental entities. Explain the developments that led to the formation of the GASB as the standard setter.

13-4 Why does the elimination of the special assessments fund have significance for governmental accounting and reporting?

13-5 Briefly contrast the several proposals for reporting capital assets.

13-6 Explain the rationale for including infrastructure assets in the financial statements. Also, explain the reasons for excluding infrastructure assets.

13-7 Some argue that depreciation is inconsistent with the financial resources model of accounting. Explain.

13-8 What were some of the major recommendations of the Structure Committee that examined the GASB at the end of its fifth year of operations?

13-9 Describe some of the major pronouncements issued by the GASB since its inception. What are some of the consequences of these pronouncements?

13-10 Briefly describe two major accounting and reporting issues remaining on the GASB's agenda.

13-11 If the GASB follows its current path, accounting for governmental pensions will differ from the accounting treatment used in business entities. Explain how this difference affects the jurisdictional dispute between the GASB and the FASB.

13-12 Why would governmental accountants be inclined to support the minority view expressed in the GASB preliminary views document on pensions?

13-13 What are the major differences between the recommendations of the Structure Committee and those of the Special Committee appointed to deal with the recommendations concerning jurisdiction?

CASES

13-1 Assume that the Financial Accounting Foundation has established an advisory council to examine the differences between the Structure Committee and the Special Committee regarding the jurisdiction of the Governmental Accounting Standards Board. At its first meeting the council had a heated discussion about the appropriate division of standard-setting authority between the FASB and the GASB. As a member of the council, you have been asked to summarize the major arguments for and against the GASB having jurisdiction over colleges and universities, selected public utilities, and healthcare organizations.

REQUIRED
Prepare a statement that could be circulated to council members summarizing the major arguments for and against GASB's jurisdiction over governmental colleges and universities, selected public utilities, and healthcare organizations.

13-2 School District 1 of the City of Portscar has agreed to be one of the test cases for the GASB in reporting SEA data pertaining to primary and secondary schools in its comprehensive annual financial report. Your CPA firm has agreed to assist the school district in this effort.

REQUIRED
1. Prepare a list of items that you think the firm should consider in preparing for the engagement and in assisting the school district.
2. Given your knowledge of primary and secondary education, provide a list of SEA indicators, grouped by the four classes explained in the text, that your firm could recommend to the school district.

13-3   A city council member comes to you for advice regarding the implications of the different proposals affecting the accounting for pensions.

REQUIRED
Answer the following questions raised by the city council member:
1. Under the majority view, where would the pension liability of a governmental entity have been shown?
2. Are there differences between the pension costing provisions contained in the FASB's *Statement No. 87* and the majority view as expressed in the preliminary views document? If so, explain the differences.

13-4   One recommendation made by the Structure Committee involved establishing a conceptual framework for governmental accounting. The GASB already has issued one conceptual framework document; it concerns the reporting objectives of governmental entities and was described in Chapter 2. Another concepts statement is planned for SEA reporting.

REQUIRED
Based on your understanding of the conceptual framework for financial accounting in the business sector and your knowledge of the GASB's first conceptual statement and the one being proposed, explain how the GASB should proceed to complete the conceptual framework for governmental accounting.

EXERCISES

13-1   Select the best answer for each question.

1. When first established, the GASB had jurisdiction over:
    a. all governmental entities
    b. all governmental entities, hospitals, and colleges and universities
    c. all governmental and nonprofit entities
    d. all nonprofit entities
2. SEA indicators describe:
    a. substitute evaluation attributes
    b. nonfinancial performance measures
    c. financial performance measures
    d. performance measures relating to services efforts and accomplishments
3. Under the majority view of the GASB's preliminary views document on pensions:

    a. governmental entities could use several methods to calculate pension costs

    b. pension costs of governmental entities would be calculated much the same as they are in private industry

    c. pension cost would be the difference between the actuarial present value of the obligation and the amount funded

    d. a current discount rate must be used in discounting the pension obligation

4. An important argument against maintaining records for infrastructure assets is:

    a. the resulting information would not be useful

    b. the amount of work necessary to record the assets would not be offset by the resulting benefits

    c. depreciation expense on these assets would be necessary if they were formally recorded in the accounting records

    d. federal granting agencies could not establish use rates if these assets were recorded

5. If the recommendations of the FAF Structure Review Committee had been adopted, the GASB would no longer be the standard setter for:

    a. general purpose financial statements of all hospitals, colleges and universities, and selected public utilities

    b. general purpose financial statements of governmental hospitals, colleges and universities, and selected public utilities

    c. all public financial information developed for governmental hospitals, colleges and universities, and selected public utilities

    d. none of the above

6. If the capital projects and debt service funds and the two account groups were combined under the flow of total financial resources model, the following entry or entries would be made when an asset was purchased by the fund:

a. expenditures		xxx	
cash			xxx
b. expenditures		xxx	
capital asset		xxx	
other financing sources			xxx
cash			xxx
c. capital assets		xxx	
cash			xxx
d. expenditures		xxx	
other financing sources			xxx

7. Under the same model and fund structure as described in Item 6, the operating statement would show:

    a. debt service expenditures for the total interest and principal payment

    b. debt service expenditures for the total principal payment

    c. debt service expenses for the total principal and interest payment

    d. debt service expenses for the amount of the interest payment

8. Which of the following is not a trend being set by the GASB?
    a. gradual movement toward accrual accounting
    b. establishing a model that incorporates the practice of taking depreciation
    c. the elimination of some funds
    d. the expansion of disclosure requirements for pensions
9. One of GASB's tentative conclusions regarding the financial reporting project is:
    a. budget and actual comparisons are not as meaningful as they once were and will be moved from the financial section to the statistical section of the CAFR
    b. aggregated data will be confined to the statistical section of the CAFR
    c. capital asset reporting should focus on how a governmental entity maintains and uses its assets
    d. a separate report definitely will not be needed to assess the financial condition of a governmental entity
10. The GASB's *Statement No. 5* establishes the:
    a. disclosure requirements for pensions
    b. accounting and reporting requirements for pensions
    c. accounting and reporting requirements for risk pools
    d. accounting requirements for pension trust funds

13-2 Here is a condensed version of Skyway County's general fund:

Skyway County
Condensed Balance Sheet
As of December 31, 19X1

Assets		
Cash	$ 5,000	
Receivables	101,000	
Short-Term Investments	85,000	
TOTAL ASSETS		$191,000
Liabilities and Fund Balance		
Accrued Payables	$ 17,200	
Compensated Absences, Current Portion	23,100	
Tax Anticipation Notes	89,000	
Total Liabilities		$129,300
Fund Balance		61,700
TOTAL LIABILITIES AND FUND BALANCE		$191,000

In reviewing other funds and account groups, you learn that Skyway has its own pension fund and the total long-term liability related to the pension is $240,000. Skyway also has long-term compensated absences of $160,000. Assume Skyway is planning to adopt the GASB's new measurement focus/ basis of accounting pronouncement as of December 31, 19X1.

REQUIRED

Discuss the effect of Skyway's decision to adopt the measurement focus/basis of accounting project.

13-3 Mandavia County has been considering the capital reporting and the financial reporting projects currently on the GASB's agenda. The county finance officer calls your firm indicating that she is confused about the relationship between the two projects and, in turn, the relationship between both of those projects and the measurement focus/basis of accounting pronouncement, application of which is being deferred indefinitely.

REQUIRED

1. Explain the relationship between the GASB's capital reporting and financial reporting projects. Be specific.
2. Is there any relationship between either or both of these projects and *Statement No. 11?* Explain.

13-4 Fenway County has been asked to test one of the GASB models for capital reporting. The proposed model combines the capital projects fund, the debt service fund, and the two account groups. It uses the accrual basis of accounting. The following activities occurred during 19X3:

1. Fenway issued $850,000 of long-term 9 percent bonds to finance an addition on the civic center. The bonds were issued on July 1, 19X3, and interest is payable July 1 and January 1. The budget for 19X3 includes the January 1, 19X4, interest payment.
2. Construction costs of $750,000 were incurred during Fiscal 19X3 to complete the project well under budget.
3. The general fund incurred capital expenditures for equipment of $5,000.
4. Interest costs were accrued on December 31, 19X3.
5. Because the project was completed under budget, the remaining debt funds were earmarked to apply to debt service payments.
6. Closing entries were made.

REQUIRED

Using a spread sheet, prepare the entries under current GAAP (modified accrual) and under the GASB proposed model. The spreadsheet should be formatted as follows:

Entry Description	Current GAAP										Proposed Model	
	GF		CPF		DSF		GFAAG		GLTDAG		Cap.	Fund
	Dr.	Cr.	Dr.	Cr.	Dr.	Cr.	Dr.	Cr.	Dr.	Cr.	Dr.	Cr.

13-5 Using the information provided in exercise 13-4, prepare a comparative operating statement for the appropriate funds under current GAAP and the proposed model.

PART II

Introduction to Nonprofit Section

Chapters 14, 15, and 16 describe the accounting practices of nonprofits: health care organizations, colleges and universities, voluntary health and welfare entities, and other nonprofit organizations. The Financial Accounting Standards Board (FASB) is responsible for setting financial accounting and reporting standards for all nonprofit organizations. While two of its concepts statements affect nonprofits, only recently has the FASB begun issuing specific standards pertaining to nonprofits. The areas selected by the FASB have been carefully chosen to enhance comparability among nonprofit financial statements. All of the standards also should make it easier to understand nonprofit financial statements, either because they simplify the statements or because they make the statements appear more like the ones prepared in the business sector.

To date, the FASB has issued three standards applicable to all nonprofits: *Statement No. 93* requiring depreciation of long-lived assets; *Statement No. 116* describing the appropriate accounting and reporting treatment of contributions; and *Statement No. 117* pertaining to the appropriate financial statements for nonprofits. The FASB has other projects on its agenda related to nonprofits, including investments (classification and valuation issues) and consolidations (what entities should be included in the primary unit's financial statements).

The standard dealing with financial statements and acceptable display practices has far-reaching implications for the accounting systems necessary to produce the required financial information. It also has implications for the fund structure currently being used by some nonprofits, most notably colleges and universities. Because the standard became effective after this textbook was published, specific applications were not always available in published financial reports. In those cases, the author reverted to illustrations based on the FASB statements.

Because some provisions have applicability across all three chapters, needless repetition has been avoided by explaining certain provisions in only those chapters describing the nonprofit most affected by the particular provisions. For example, handling endowment income is emphasized in the chapter on colleges and universities because they are most apt to have large endowments. Similarly, the required cash flow statement is illustrated only in

Chapters 14 and 16 because it would have similar application to all types of nonprofits.

Because the FASB has only recently become actively involved in setting standards for these organizations, accounting and financial reporting practices of nonprofits also derive from the audit guides issued by the American Institute of Certified Public Accountants and the professional organizations serving these nonprofits. The audit guides were issued at different times, and each professonal organization has different accounting and reporting goals. Thus, with the exception of the FASB standards, which are applicable to *all* nonprofits, each type of nonprofit has different accounting and reporting practices and is therefore described in a separate chapter.

Under these prior accounting standards, fund accounting was used to distinguish various types of activities, much as governmental entities do. Certain of the funds reported operating activities, for example, the activities that were associated with providing services and raising money to support those service offerings. Other funds were used to account for and report nonoperating activities, sometimes referred to as capital-related activities. Such activities included endowments, loans, and activities related to the acquisition and disposal of long-lived assets. Transfers between these two basic divisions were clearly illustrated in the financial statements. For example, the portion of endowment earnings used to fund current operations was separately identified in the operations section of the operating statement. As another example, any money transferred to endowments or put aside for capital acquisitions was clearly noted.

The FASB standards no longer allow fund accounting for external reporting purposes. The FASB's *Statement No. 117* requires reporting for the entity as a whole. It also requires that various types of equity will be displayed separately. More specifically, the FASB requires reporting by three classes of net assets (equity): unrestricted, temporarily restricted, and permanently restricted. The various funds used by nonprofits under an operating/nonoperating structure cannot be "rolled up" to equate to reporting by equity class. The standard neither requires nor prohibits fund accounting. Thus, nonprofits might choose to abandon fund accounting or to change it to coincide with the three equity classes. Only time and experience with the standard will make the choice evident.

These asset classes do not reflect an important historical accounting and reporting premise of nonprofits: distinguishing between operating and capital transactions. To mitigate complaints about the resulting lack of an "operating statement," the FASB included one paragraph in the standard allowing nonprofits to report an operating statement. The paragraph "neither encourages nor discourages" such a statement. If an operating statement is prepared, it

> shall be in a financial statement that, at a minimum reports the change in unrestricted net assets [that is, equity] for the period. If an organization's use of the term *operations* is not apparent from the details provided on the face of the statement, a note to the financial statements shall describe the nature of the reported measure of operations or the terms excluded from operations.[1]

[1] Financial Accounting Standards Board, *Statement No. 117, Financial Statements of Not-for-Profit Organizations* (Norwalk, Conn.: FASB, 1993), ¶23.

Although applauded by many in the nonprofit sector, this provision makes even more difficult the job of deciding the best way to respond to the new standards. The author believes that this permissive language will increase the likelihood that some nonprofits, again most notably colleges and universities, will retain their existing fund structure and simply maintain enough additional information to meet the FASB reporting standards, for example, the reporting by equity class. Readers should bear in mind these uncertainties related to financial reporting as they affect the information in the following chapters.

Even with some uncertainty about the specific response to these standards, the opportunity to become knowledgeable about nonprofit accounting standards in evolution is extraordinary. *Statement No. 117* does not simply change the accounting or reporting of a single asset, liability, or equity element (which is how one could characterize the standard setting in the business sector during the last 20 years). It changes the very essence of financial reporting in the nonprofit sector. It also will have a significant impact on audit procedures for nonprofits. This is indeed a period of rapid change for nonprofits. In addition to explaining nonprofit accounting and financial reporting, the next three chapters capture some of the excitement of this evolution.

CHAPTER 14

Accounting and Financial Reporting for Health Care Organizations

Health care organizations, such as hospitals, clinics, home health agencies and continuing care facilities for the elderly or the incapacitated, are operating in a rapidly changing environment. Ever larger investments in diagnostic and treatment facilities have greatly increased fixed costs. Some governing boards have created separate foundations to raise and hold funds for health care organizations. States have enacted laws creating financing authorities to obtain financing through tax-exempt bonds that use revenues and defined assets of health care providers as collateral for the debt. Many health care institutions use long-term debt to finance acquisition of the latest technology.

New entities are entering the health care field. Health maintenance organizations (HMOs) combine delivery and financing functions, while preferred provider organizations (PPOs) arrange health care packages for marketing to employers. Increased competition from these new health care providers places added financial strain on some hospitals and clinics, particularly in rural areas.

This chapter describes the impact of this changing environment on accounting and reporting for health care organizations. The evolution of accounting practices and standard setting for health care organizations, particularly hospitals, is also discussed. Generally accepted accounting principles are explained and applied to transactions of health care organizations. Accounting entries and financial statements are described and illustrated. Also, selected audit considerations are discussed.

As pointed out in the Introduction to the Nonprofit Section, some accounting and reporting standards affecting health care organizations change under FASB *Statement No. 116* and *Statement No. 117*. The standards in *Statement No. 116* pertain to recognition of contributions and pledges; accordingly on the effective date, health care entities simply apply the new standards. Those new standards are integrated into the appropriate sections of this chapter.

The transition will not be as easy under *Statement No. 117*. Because some of the provisions pertain **only** to external reporting, health care and other nonprofits may still prepare internal reports using some of the "old" standards. Therefore, both the reporting standards in effect before and after the effective date of *Statement No. 117* need to be explained.

THE CHANGING NATURE OF HEALTH CARE INSTITUTIONS

Technological changes and increased competition have forced hospitals to develop sophisticated operating systems. Capital needs must be projected several years into the future. Specialists necessary to operate the latest technology must be hired and their skills upgraded continuously. Facility use must be managed effectively and coordinating agreements established among health care organizations. These developments all tend to increase operating costs.

As the costs of facilities and specialists increase, so do prices charged to the public for health care services. Health care costs are beyond the financial abilities of many individuals so a large portion of the bills are paid by third parties, such as Medicare, Medicaid, Blue Cross, and private insurance carriers. Many third-party payers use cost-based formulas for reimbursement. The third-party payers either require substantiation of the costs necessary to provide particular health care services, or they base reimbursement on a system that resembles standard costing. Therefore, health care organizations must provide data on occupancy, patient type, nature of illnesses, and other information related to the costs of providing service to particular patient groups. Sophisticated internal accounting and reporting systems are necessary to document costs for third-party payments and for management control of organizations.

Changes in the source of investment and patient-care financing also focus considerable attention on health care accounting and external financial reporting. Investors and lenders usually require detailed cost analyses and audited financial statements before supplying long-term financing. Third-party payers not only require detailed cost accounting reports, but many also audit to determine which costs are allowable and require cost containment programs. Unless the health care providers can document their costs—or, if required, containment of costs—they may not be reimbursed for some costs. Health care organizations are therefore under great pressure to find ways to increase their efficiency.

The American Hospital Association (AHA) and the Healthcare Financial Management Association (HFMA) provide considerable assistance to health care financial managers. Charts of accounts, preferred accounting and reporting practices, and techniques for preparing detailed cost analyses enable health care managers to keep abreast of changing financial requirements.

Other assistance is available as well. In 1972, the AICPA issued an audit guide for hospitals that has been updated on a regular basis; the 1990 version refers to all health care organizations, not just hospitals, and provides comprehensive guidance for auditors of health care organizations. More recently, the FASB has issued three pronouncements affecting health care organizations. One statement has had little effect while the other two may significantly change the accounting and financial reporting of health care organizations.

Health care organizations have been depreciating fixed assets for many years. Therefore, FASB *Statement No. 93* requiring all nonprofit organizations to depreciate long-lived assets except works of art and historical treasures did not affect health care providers.

FASB *Statement No. 116* on recognizing contributions and pledge revenues will affect those health care organizations that have significant fund-raising activities. The statement requires nonprofits to record contributions and unconditional promises to pay (commonly called pledges) as revenue when received, regardless of when the organization receives the cash or other asset.[1]

Like the previous standard, whether the FASB standard on financial reporting, *Statement No. 117,* impacts health care organizations will depend on their operating characteristics. This standard requires nonprofits to prepare a statement of financial position, an activity statement (statement of revenues, expenses, and changes in net assets or equity), and a cash flow statement. Most health care organizations currently prepare these three statements but do not structure them around net asset class. Instead, most such displays show comingled assets and liabilities but fund balances are by major fund type. As noted in the Introduction to the Nonprofit Section, nonprofits will be unable to maintain their current fund structure for external financial reporting purposes. Health care organizations may retain fund accounting for internal reporting and decision making. Therefore, a conceptual understanding of both the recently adopted and the "old" standards is necessary. An understanding of the "old" also is important because only **selected** accounting and reporting practices change with the new FASB standards; this means that much of the "old" still represents GAAP.

Because fund accounting has been a major theme of the preceding thirteen chapters, long-standing accounting and financial reporting concepts, including fund accounting, will be presented first. A later section of this chapter will explain which of those accounting and reporting practices are changed by the FASB's *Statement No. 117.*

HEALTH CARE OPERATING AND ACCOUNTING CONCEPTS

The AICPA has published an audit guide for health care organizations, as it has for other types of nonprofit organizations.[2] Because the FASB has not taken a very active role in standard setting until recently, much of the accounting, as well as audit, guidance for health care entities has come from this audit guide.

The *Health Care Audit Guide* classifies health care organizations as voluntary, governmental, or investor owned.[3] Voluntary organizations include those affiliated with religious organizations or educational institutions, or operated independently on a nonprofit basis. If a health care unit is operated by

---

[1]As mentioned previously, many health care organizations, particularly hospitals, set up foundations for fund-raising purposes. For any health care organization using this approach, the statement will affect the foundation, which is also a nonprofit, and not the health care organization directly. Foundations are classed as "other" nonprofits and are discussed in Chapter 16.

[2]American Institute of Certified Public Accountants, *Audit and Accounting Guide, Audits if Providers of Health Care Services* (New York: AICPA, 1990). The guide is referred to in this chapter as the *Health Care Audit Guide.* It will, of course, be revised to reflect the requirements of *Statement No. 116* and *Statement No. 117* as discussed later in the chapter. The operative word is **revised** because much of the accounting and auditing guidance will not change; only practices related to recognizing income from contributions and external financial reporting will change.

[3]Ibid., 2.

the federal government or a state, a city, or a county, it is a governmental organization. Investor-owned organizations operate to earn a profit. At last count by the American Hospital Association, over 50 percent of the total number of hospitals were of the voluntary type. The next largest number are governmental hospitals. Investor-owned hospitals comprise the smallest portion.

The Financial Accounting Standards Board (FASB) sets accounting and reporting standards for general purpose financial statements prepared by all voluntary and investor-owned health care entities. The Governmental Accounting Standards Board (GASB) sets financial accounting and reporting standards for hospitals associated with governmental units.

Investor-owned and governmental health care units are not discussed further in this chapter. Their accounting and reporting are governed by standards applicable to other business enterprises or to governmental units and require no further explanation. Nonetheless, the revenue and expense classifications depicted later in this chapter for nonprofit health care providers can be applied to investor-owned and governmental facilities.

Accounting Directives from the Health Care Audit Guide

The primary purposes of an audit guide are to (1) explain the accounting practices used by particular organizations and (2) guide the audit of those practices. In the absence of an active standard-setting body, audit guides for nonprofits have tended to become de facto accounting standards. This has certainly been the case with the *Health Care Audit Guide*. While much of what is described in the following sections is detailed in the guide as standard practice, it also has set the practice of accounting in those areas.

Fund Accounting   The *Health Care Audit Guide* does not prescribe a particular fund structure for nonprofit health care providers. Rather, it identifies the general types of funds and the appropriate classification of resources obtained by health care entities.

OBSERVATION ▲

Interestingly, the 1988 and 1990 versions of the *Health Care Audit Guide* not only extend the purview from hospitals to all health care organizations, but also come much closer than any previous edition to requiring a specific fund structure. Undoubtedly, that will change in the next version.

As the *Health Care Audit Guide* points out, "fund accounting is an accounting technique used by some not-for-profit and governmental health care entities for purposes of internal recordkeeping and managerial control . . . Many individual funds may be established for that purpose."[4]

Implicit in the description of hospital accounting procedures is a fund structure that has two categories: unrestricted (general) funds and restricted

[4]Ibid., 17

funds. Restricted funds are used to account for financial resources (and re-lated liabilities) restricted *externally* for specified operating, capital outlay, or endowment purposes. Funds set aside for specific purposes by governing boards are classified as unrestricted and are designated in financial state-ments as "assets whose use is limited." They are not truly restricted because what the governing board can restrict today, it can "unrestrict" tomorrow.

Unrestricted resources can be spent at the governing board's discretion. The *Health Care Audit Guide* states that the amounts of restricted and unre-stricted funds should be disclosed separately to enable financial statement readers to understand which resources can be spent for general operating purposes and which must be spent for specified purposes.

The existence of a fund structure has the same accounting implications as it does for governmental units: each fund is a separate accounting entity with its own asset, liability, and equity accounts. Unlike governmental entities, however, many nonprofit health care entities have not used fund accounting for external reporting. Instead, all funds have been combined in a single statement, in which only the fund balances for individual funds are shown to allow readers to distinguish among the types of funds being used.

Those Health care units that use fund accounting typically open several types of unrestricted (general) funds and several types of restricted funds. All unrestricted transactions and the related assets and liabilities *pertaining to general operations* are classified as general funds. General funds include agency funds and property and equipment used for general operations.

Donor funds or other third-party restricted funds generally fall into five fund types: (1) specific purpose funds, (2) replacement and expansion funds, (3) endowment funds, (4) loan funds, and (5) annuity and life income funds. Health care units generally report one restricted fund for each type, but for management purposes a fund is operated for each specific restricted purpose.

A **specific purpose fund** resembles a governmental special revenue fund. Federal, state, or foundation grants, or contracts for research or educa-tion are accounted for in these restricted funds.

Funds restricted by donors for property, plant, and equipment additions or improvements are accounted for in the **plant replacement and expansion fund,** which resembles a governmental unit's capital projects fund.

When a donor specifies that gift principal cannot be spent, an **endow-ment fund** is opened. According to the *Health Care Audit Guide,* endowed resources include both term and permanent endowments. Under a term en-dowment, the principal can be spent after a specified period has elapsed or a condition has been met. Under a permanent endowment, the restriction on principal remains in perpetuity.

Loan and **annuity and life income funds** are used for the same pur-poses as in governmental entities. A third party provides money to a health care entity for purposes of loaning the principal or for eventually providing a corpus to add to an endowment or to earnings. Exhibit 14-1 summarizes the typical fund structure for health care organizations.

Reporting Focus and Basis of Accounting   Health care organizations, including those operated by governments, must report externally to third-

Exhibit 14-1

Fund Structure for Health Care Organizations

Fund Category	Fund Type	Purpose
Unrestricted Funds	General Funds	To account for the major operations of the entity, including general fixed assets
Restricted Funds	Specific Purpose	To account for resources whose purposes are specified by those external to the organization, for example, donors, federal or state government
	Endowment	To account for resources the principal of which cannot be spent in perpetuity or for a certain period (term endowment); it may be that the earnings cannot be spent for a certain length of time as well
	Plant Replacement and Expansion	To account for the resources restricted by donors for the acquisition or construction of fixed assets
	Loan and Annuity and Life Income	To account for resources restricted for making loans to identified parties or for eventually providing a residual interest to add to an endowment

[handwritten marginalia: S E P L; LALF; FOCUS - cap maint. - operating perf. accrual basis; revenue from contributions; PV of promise]

party payers and, in many cases, to investors and creditors. Accordingly, health care accounting and reporting systems focus on capital maintenance and operating performance. Revenues must be sufficient to cover all *expenses,* not just expenditures, if capital is to be maintained. Not surprisingly, then, health care units use the accrual basis of accounting.

Under health care units' generally accepted accounting principles, the accrual basis reflects some anamolies when used in conjunction with fund accounting. For example, although revenues and expenses are recognized according to the accrual basis, net income may be called the Excess of Revenues Over (Under) Expenses; the account balance is closed into Net Assets (Fund Balance) not retained earnings. These are differences in terminology only, not in the substance of the resulting financial statements.

Accounting Directives from FASB Statement No. 116

FASB *Statement No. 116* does not affect any of the *Health Care Audit Guide* provisions discussed above. Rather, the standard focuses on the timing and measurement of revenue from contributions, whether in the form of pledges, contributed services, or long-lived assets.

The standard indicates that these revenues should be recognized when the promise is received. Thus, when a health care organization gets an unconditional promise for a future sum, the revenue is recognized in the current period. The amount of revenue is determined by discounting the amount of the promise (or the stream of payments) to the present using current market rates.

The standard contains special provisions for donated services and contributed fixed assets. Donated services are recognized if the services received (1) create or enhance nonfinancial assets or (2) require specialized skills, are provided by individuals possessing those skills, and would typically need to be purchased if not provided by donation. Services requiring specialized skills include those provided by architects, carpenters or other craftspeople, nurses, accountants, and so forth.[5]

Statement No. 116 requires nonprofits to capitalize all gifts of long-lived assets except art objects and historical treasures; when the gift is received, the credit would be to revenues. Nonprofits are just "encouraged" to capitalize art objects and historical treasures. The standard reads "encourages" rather than "requires" for these types of long-lived assets because some nonprofits, particularly museums, objected strenuously to reporting revenue for works of art and historical treasures that would not be used for operating purposes but rather placed on permanent display. Gifts of long-lived assets to health care organizations are likely to be operating assets, not art objects. Such gifts will be recorded by a debit to an asset account and a credit to revenue in the unrestricted area.

APPLICATION OF ACCOUNTING PRINCIPLES

Several accounting conventions are unique to health care organizations; they are described in the following sections.

Operating and Other Revenues

Many health care providers, particularly hospitals, have three major activities: patient care, nonpatient services, and fund-raising. Consistent with major activities, health care providers distinguish between operating revenue, other revenue, and gains or losses. A major source of **operating revenue** is patient service revenue, which may be further classified as routine charges (for example, room, board, and general nursing) and professional service revenue (physician's care, pharmacy, and radiology).[6] Operating revenue for continuing care facilities is resident service revenue, which includes rental fees.

Other revenue is derived from sales and services to people other than patients. It includes revenues from educational programs, research grants, rentals, snack bars, gift shops, newsstands, and parking facilities. Donated medicines, linen, supplies, and other materials that would normally be purchased by health providers are included as other revenue (the debit is to inventory).

Gains and losses are unrelated to a unit's principal operations and include the results of fund-raising efforts: unrestricted gifts, investment in-

[5]Financial Accounting Standards Board, *Statement of Financial Accounting Standards No. 116, Accounting for Contributions Received and Contributions Made* (Norwalk, Conn.: FASB, 1993), ¶9.

[6]AICPA, *Health Care Audit Guide,* 110.

come (interest, dividends, gains, and losses), and unrestricted income from endowment funds. Any donated services recognized as support are classified as gains.

[handwritten: donated services = gains]

The *Health Care Audit Guide* indicates that if contributions, tax support, and other similar sources of support are ongoing or central sources, they are classified as other revenue, not gains. Consequently, both preparers and auditors must first examine the extent and importance of such activities to a health care provider's mission before classifying the amount generated as revenue or a gain.

OBSERVATION ▲

An obvious query is why donated materials are recognized as other revenues, and donated services as gains, particularly when in both cases the expense is recognized as an operating expense. This odd classification seems to result from historical happenstance, not a justifiable accounting convention.

Expenses Versus Revenue Deductions

The HFMA and the AICPA have long had a difference of opinion regarding the classification of two income statement items: uncollectibles (that is, bad debts) and uncompensated services. Uncompensated services include contractual adjustments from third-party payers, charity services, and discounts or free care given to employees and their families. Early editions of the *Hospital Audit Guide* described both uncollectibles and uncompensated services as *deductions from revenues.* The HFMA has argued repeatedly that they should be classified as *expenses.* In the *Health Care Audit Guide,* the AICPA makes a clear distinction between charity services and uncollectibles related to contract adjustments.

> Provisions recognizing *contractual adjustments* and other adjustments are recorded on an accrual basis and deducted from gross service revenue to determine net service revenue. For financial reporting purposes, gross revenue does not include charity care and service revenue is reported net of contractual and other adjustments in the statement of revenue and expenses.[7]

The *Health Care Audit Guide*'s sample hospital financial statements show *net patient service revenue* with a note detailing gross revenue and provisions for uncompensated services. The *Health Care Audit Guide* also depicts financial statements for a continuing care retirement community; the provision for its bad debts is included among the operating expenses. Therefore, a health care provider must carefully distinguish between charity services and bad debts.

[handwritten: Charity services deducted from revenues]

[handwritten: uncollectibles are an expense]

[handwritten: service rev. is net of contractual adjustments]

Cost Accounting

Due to pressures from third-party payers and rising health care costs, many providers have developed cost accounting systems.[8] In 1983, Medicare

[7]AICPA, *Health Care Audit Guide,* 13–14.

[8]For a more detailed discussion, see Robert Anthony and David Young, *Management Control in Nonprofit Organizations,* 5th ed. (New York: Richard D. Irwin, 1994), Chapter 4.

introduced a diagnosis-related group (DRG) reimbursement system. Under this system, diagnoses are classified into several hundred groups. Providers are reimbursed at a fixed amount per diagnosis group regardless of the costs incurred in treating an individual patient.

Resembling a job order cost system, DRG-based systems require a determination of the services provided for each diagnosis group; for example, a heart attack patient requires laboratory work, physician care, and room and board. Isolating individual services for each diagnosis group, in turn, requires elaborate cost accumulation and allocation procedures.

Costs are first collected in cost centers, such as radiology, cardiac care, and housekeeping. These cost centers are of two broad types: mission centers and service centers. **Mission centers** relate directly to the organization's primary purpose, while **service centers** are supportive in nature. In a hospital, intensive care and radiology are mission centers. Medical records and housekeeping are service centers.

The cost allocation process occurs at two levels after direct costs are collected in appropriate centers. Indirect costs are allocated to each center, and service center costs are allocated to mission centers. Exhibit 14-2 depicts the allocation process.

Costs accumulated in mission centers are then assigned to DRGs. Health care providers can use these cost accounting data to identify inefficiencies or to estimate unrecoverable costs under existing reimbursement formulas.

Formerly some states required third-party payers to reimburse health care providers on a per-diem basis. Closely paralleling a process cost approach, the entire entity is treated as a mission center. All costs are summed and divided by the number of patient days delivered for an average cost per day. Under this approach, all patients served are assumed to receive similar services.

Valuing Assets[9]

Most health care organization assets are valued the same as in businesses: property, plant, and equipment is recorded at cost unless received as a gift, when it is valued at fair market value. Depreciation is recorded in conformity with generally accepted accounting principles used in business.

Valuation of Securities and Selected Other Assets   Marketable equity securities are valued according to FASB *Statement No. 12,* at lower of cost or market. Debt securities are reported at amortized cost if the health care provider intends to hold them for the foreseeable future; if debt securities are held as short-term investments, they are reported at lower of cost or market. Receivables, including pledges, are shown at realizable values: gross amounts less provisions for uncollectibles. The *Health Care Audit Guide* in-

[9]The FASB has a topic on its agenda related to nonprofits' investments. Therefore, many of the practices described here may change.

Exhibit 14-2

Allocation of Costs to Mission and Service Centers

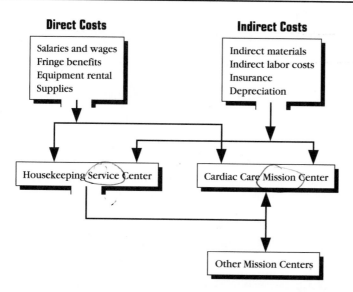

dicates that accounting for supplies is similar to methods used by other business organizations.[10]

Marketable Securities   Although valuation and reporting conventions for health care accounting are similar to those for business enterprises, there are unique applications, such as those for investments in marketable equity securities. The *Health Care Audit Guide* provides detailed guidance for nonprofit health care providers in applying FASB *Statement No. 12,* which covers the valuation of marketable equity securities.[11]

In applying the lower of cost or market valuation method to marketable equity securities, aggregate cost and market figures are used. Because nonprofit health care organizations may have investments in several different fund types, some interpretation of the word *aggregate* is needed. Does aggregate mean all investments? All investments in a single fund? All investments in a particular fund type? The *Health Care Audit Guide* indicates that all marketable equity securities of a particular fund type should be grouped together. For valuation purposes marketable equity securities of all special purpose funds would be grouped together but not combined with marketable equity securities of endowment funds.

For example, assume a hospital had investments in a general fund, in each of two specific purpose funds, and in each of two endowment funds. For purposes of comparing cost and market, the following aggregations would be made:

[10]AICPA, *Health Care Audit Guide,* 69.

[11]For a more detailed discussion, readers should refer to FASB *Statement No. 12,* ¶43.

```
┌─────────────────────────────┐  ┌──────────────────────────────────────────────────────────┐
│        General Fund         │  │   Specific Purpose          Specific Purpose               │
│  Cost      $22,000          │  │      Fund A                    Fund B                      │
│                             │  │  Cost     $15,000    +     Cost     $ 9,000 = $24,000       │
│  Market    $25,000          │  │                                                            │
│                             │  │  Market   $13,000    +     Market   $12,000 = $25,000       │
│  LCOM  =   $22,000          │  │                                                            │
│                             │  │            LCOM = $24,000                                   │
└─────────────────────────────┘  └──────────────────────────────────────────────────────────┘
```

```
        ┌──────────────────────────────────────────────────────────┐
        │      Endowment               Endowment                    │
        │       Fund A                  Fund B                       │
        │  Cost     $57,000    +     Cost   $101,000 = $158,000      │
        │                                                           │
        │  Market   $59,000    +     Market  $ 93,000 = $152,000     │
        │                                                           │
        │            LCOM = $152,000                                 │
        └──────────────────────────────────────────────────────────┘
```

If financial statements include more than one unit, such as a hospital and a nursing home, marketable equity securities in all funds of a particular type would be grouped together for purposes of measuring aggregate cost and market value.

When aggregate market value and cost are determined by fund type, recognized losses or recoveries must be allocated to individual funds. For general funds, recognized losses are shown as losses; recoveries are gains. For restricted funds, the loss or recovery is debited or credited to fund balance and shown as part of the Statement of Changes in Fund Balance. Realized gains or losses on securities are gains or losses for most health care units. However, when investment income is directly related to a unit's principal operations, as it is with health maintenance organizations, the income (loss) should be classified in the operating section. If several funds pool their securities for investment purposes, realized gains and losses must be allocated to the appropriate funds. The market value method is used to accomplish an equitable allocation among participating funds.[12]

Measuring Liabilities

The *Health Care Audit Guide* indicates that liabilities, such as accounts and notes payable, compensated absences, accruals, advance refunding of long-term debt, and pensions, are recorded and measured according to FASB standards. Occasionally, guidance is needed to apply those standards to the particular circumstances of health care providers. Uninsured and unasserted malpractice claims and prepaid health care services represent two important areas where additional guidance is necessary.

Malpractice Claims   The rising cost and declining availability of malpractice insurance have forced some health care providers to drop their coverage or increase their deductible limit. Others are purchasing policies that cover

---

[12] Each fund has a certain percentage of the total pool, which is expressed as the number of "units" held by each. When money is added to the pool, the participating fund receives additional units based on the market value at the time of the addition. The units are also used to determine appropriate allocations when equity is withdrawn from the pool and to calculate a fund's share of investment income.

only claims reported to the insurance carrier during the term of the policy. An important accounting issue is whether a health care provider should accrue the ultimate cost of uninsured malpractice claims when incidents occur. Other accounting issues include determining the amount to report as an accrued loss and classifying the losses in the financial statements.

Preferred accounting practices follow from the general guidance provided by the FASB's statements on accounting for contingencies and estimating losses.[13] The FASB has concluded that if it is *probable* that the liabilities have been incurred and if the losses can be *reasonably estimated*, the ultimate cost of malpractice claims should be accrued when the incidents giving rise to the claims occur.[14] Health care providers are required to disclose their program of medical malpractice insurance and the basis for determining any related loss accrual. In addition, a representation letter from the provider or its attorney should indicate the extent to which asserted or unasserted claims will likely be covered by insurance.

malprac. claim probable reas est then accrued malpractice claims.

Prepaid Health Care Services   With rapidly rising health care costs, many employers now offer employees a choice between ordinary medical coverage and prepaid health care plans. Diverse accounting practices have developed to account for health care costs by the providers of prepaid health care services. An important accounting issue is when to recognize the cost of prepaid health care services as expenses, either (1) as those services are rendered or (2) on the date of initial service.[15] Although the FASB has not addressed the issue, the Accounting Standards Division of the AICPA has ruled that health care costs should be accrued as the services are rendered, including estimates of the cost of services rendered but not yet reported.[16] Further, if the contract with the provider is terminated by the employer, costs that will be incurred after termination should be accrued upon notice of termination. Providers also must disclose the basis upon which the services were accrued.

accrued as services rendered.

RELATED ORGANIZATIONS

A health care organization may have a close relationship with other entities, such as foundations, guilds, or auxiliaries. The *Health Care Audit Guide* establishes certain conditions that define a **related unit;** if a unit is related but not consolidated the *Guide* requires certain disclosures.

[13] Financial Accounting Standards Board, *Accounting Standards Current Text as of June 1, 1993* (Homewood, Ill.: Irwin, 1993), sec. C59.

[14] American Institute of Certified Public Accountants, *Accounting for Unasserted Malpractice Claims of Health Care Providers and Related Issues, Statement of Position No. 87-1* (New York: AICPA, 1987). The coverage of these accounting practices is necessarily brief; the SOP provides considerably more detail on estimating the amount of the loss and the required disclosures.

[15] American Institute of Certified Pulic Accountants, *Financial Accounting and Reporting by Providers of Prepaid Health Care Services, Statement of Position No. 89-5* (New York: AICPA, 1989), 30.

[16] Ibid.

A separate organization is considered to be related...if...(a) the health care entity controls the separate organization...and (b) the entity is, for all practical purposes, the sole beneficiary of the organization.[17]

Control is defined in much the same way as for governmental entities: the entity has authority to direct the related organization's activities, determine organizational policies, and appoint managers. Determining whether the entity is the sole beneficiary requires satisfying one or more of the following conditions:

- The organization has solicited funds in the entity's name with the express or implied approval of the entity, and substantially all of the funds will be transferred to the entity.
- The entity has transferred some of its resources to the organization, and substantially all of the orgnization's resources are held for the entity's benefit.
- The entity has assigned certain of its functions to the organization, which is operated primarily for the entity's benefit.[18]

Required disclosures for related organizations include summarized information about the related unit's assets, liabilities, operations, and equity changes. The reporting entity must also explain the nature of the relationship and disclose material transactions between the two units. For example, the amount of contributions raised by the related organization as well as the amounts transferred to the reporting unit during the year should be disclosed.

ILLUSTRATED FINANCIAL TRANSACTIONS USING FUND ACCOUNTING

Financial transactions and the resulting financial statements illustrated here are not appropriate for **external financial reporting** after the effective date of FASB *Statement No. 117.* However, they would be appropriate, if desirable, for internal reporting and/or supplemental reporting.

Typical financial transactions are illustrated for each fund type. A hypothetical nonprofit hospital is used because hospitals usually have a broader range of transactions that reflect many accounting practices common to all health care organizations.

General Funds

During the year, revenue from patient services totaled $7,200,000. The hospital anticipated that 1 percent of the total billing would not be received because of unwillingness to pay; another $100,000 relates to charity services, and $220,000 to contract adjustments from third-party payers. The hospital distinguishes clearly between a refusal to pay and charity services.

[17]*Health Care Audit Guide,* 127.
[18]Adapted from the *Health Care Audit Guide,* 128.

The hospital also operated a cafeteria for patients and public use; revenues totaled $220,000.

1.	Cash	220,000	
	Accounts Receivable ($7,200,000 − $100,000)	7,100,000	
	Patient Service Revenue		7,100,000
	Other Operating Revenue—Cafeteria		220,000

2.	Provision for Bad Debts *(expenses)*	72,000 *(1% of total billing)*	
	Contractual Adjustments	220,000	
	Allowance for Uncollectible Receivables		72,000
	Allowance for Contract Adjustments		220,000

insurance company, care
negotiated that contractual revenue account 68

If some contractual adjustments had been recovered later, the hospital would have recorded the cash and reduced contractual adjustments.

The hospital collected $5,000,000 on account during the period and wrote off $50,000 in accounts receivable:

3.	Cash	5,000,000	
	Allowance for Uncollectible Receivables	50,000	
	Accounts Receivable		5,050,000

Several donations were received during the year; $10,000 was unrestricted and received directly from donors for general operations. It is assumed that fund-raising is central to the nonprofit hospital's mission. Another $87,000 was transferred from the hospital's specific purpose fund for educational programs. After receiving the transfer, the hospital incurred $87,000 of expenses related to the educational program.

charity
contributions
other Rev - if
ongoing or
central sources

4.	Cash	97,000	
	Transfers from Restricted Funds *(Other Revenue)*		87,000
	Other Revenue		10,000

The $87,000 transfer from the restricted fund would be classified as other revenue because it was derived from a specific purpose fund established for the hospital's educational program.

| 5. | Public Education Expense | 87,000 | |
| | Accounts Payable | | 87,000 |

Contributed services of $8,000 were recognized. A local company also contributed supplies and other materials totaling $1,500 for laboratory work.

6.	Laboratory Services *supplies inv*	1,500	
	Other Operating Expense—Cafeteria	8,000	
	Other Revenue		1,500
	Gain		8,000

During the year $316,000 of supplies were purchased for cash.

| 7. | Supplies Inventory | 316,000 | |
| | Cash | | 316,000 |

Other expenses incurred by major function included the following:

Nursing Administration	200,000
Nurses' Stations	1,200,000
Central Services	1,150,000
Laboratory Services	1,800,000
Radiology	116,000
Pharmacy	210,000
Social Services	82,000
Medical Records/Library	62,000
Dietary Services	187,000
Plant Operation and Maintenance	365,000
Housekeeping	210,000
General Administration	290,000
Cafeteria Expense	88,000

Ordinarily the listed expenses would be entered first by object code, such as salaries and wages and supplies, and then allocated to the functional classifications shown above. The allocation process is not unique to hospitals, so that step was omitted.

Inventories of supplies were used by major functions as follows:

Nurses' Stations	75,000
General Administration	7,000
Laboratory Services	33,000
Dietary Services	58,000

Other expenses that are typically not assigned to functional areas included:

Interest	12,000
Depreciation	29,000
Insurance	105,000
Employee Benefits	520,000
Taxes	63,000

Accounting for the functional expenses and others listed above is shown in entries 8 and 9.

8.	Nursing Administration	200,000	
	Nurses' Stations ($1,200,000 + $75,000)	1,275,000	
	Central Services	1,150,000	
	Lab Services ($1,800,000 + $33,000)	1,833,000	
	Radiology	116,000	
	Pharmacy	210,000	
	Social Services	82,000	
	Medical Records/Library	62,000	
	Dietary Services ($187,000 + $58,000)	245,000	
	Plant Operation and Maintenance	365,000	
	Housekeeping	210,000	
	General Admin. ($290,000 + $7,000)	297,000	
	Cafeteria	88,000	
	Accounts Payable		5,960,000
	Supplies Inventory		173,000

9.	Interest Expense	12,000	
	Depreciation Expense	29,000	
	Insurance Expense	105,000	
	Employee Benefits	520,000	
	Tax Expense	63,000	
	Accumulated Depreciation		29,000
	Accounts Payable		105,000
	Payable to State and Federal Governments		520,000
	Accrued Taxes Payable		63,000
	Interest Payable		12,000

Payments on accounts payable and other liabilities, including a mortgage payment of $72,000, are illustrated in entry 10.

10.	Interest Payable	12,000	
	Accounts Payable	3,900,000	
	Mortgage Payable	72,000	
	Payable to State and Federal Governments	390,000	
	Accrued Taxes Payable	55,000	
	Cash		4,429,000

Unrestricted earnings on endowment fund investments totaled $15,000; $10,000 was received in cash and an additional $5,000 will be transferred from the endowment fund. Investment earnings are assumed to be peripheral to this hospital's primary mission.

11.	Due from Endowment Fund	5,000	
	Cash	10,000	
	Gains from Investments		15,000

To record $180,000 of capital outlays made from the general funds, $30,000 of which was derived from funds restricted for capital outlays, the hospital made entries 12, 13, and 14.

12.	Land	60,000	
	Buildings	100,000	
	Equipment	20,000	
	Mortgage Payable		120,000
	Cash		60,000
13.	Due from Property Replacement and Expansion Fund	30,000	
	Contributed Capital—Transfers from the Property Replacement and Expansion Fund		30,000
14.	Cash	30,000	
	Due from Property Replacement and Expansion Fund		30,000

Capital assets costing $45,000 were sold for $10,000 during the year; accumulated depreciation totaled $32,000.

15.	Cash	10,000	
	Accumulated Depreciation—Equipment	32,000	
	Loss on the Disposal of Fixed Assets	3,000	
	Equipment		45,000

The governing board designated $25,000 toward an education project that would complement a similar program established by donors (see entry 4 for the transactions related to the restricted fund program). Because board designations are not classified as restricted funds, no entry is required. If the hospital wanted to show the results of the board action, the following entry could be made:

16.	Fund Balance	25,000	
	Fund Balance Designated for		
	Educational Purposes		25,000

Entries 17 and 18 show the year-end closing entries:

17.	Patient Service Revenue	7,100,000	
	Other Revenue ($11,500 + $220,000)	231,500	
	Gains ($15,000 + $8,000)	23,000	
	Transfers from Restricted Funds	87,000	
	Cafeteria Expense ($8,000 + $88,000)		96,000
	Public Education Expense		87,000
	Nursing Administration		200,000
	Nurses' Stations		1,275,000
	Central Services		1,150,000
	Laboratory Services ($1,833,000 + $1,500)		1,834,500
	Radiology		116,000
	Pharmacy		210,000
	Social Services		82,000
	Medical Records/Library		62,000
	Dietary Services		245,000
	Plant Operation and Maintenance		365,000
	Housekeeping		210,000
	General Administration		297,000
	Depreciation		29,000
	Insurance Expense		105,000
	Employee Benefits		520,000
	Tax Expense		63,000
	Interest Expense		12,000
	Provision for Bad Debts		72,000
	Contractual Adjustments		220,000
	Loss on Disposal of Fixed Assets		3,000
	Excess of Revenue Over Expenses		188,000
18.	Excess of Revenue Over Expenses	188,000	
	Fund Balance—Undesignated		188,000

To simplify the illustration, all patient service revenue was recorded in one account. Normally, patient service revenue would be broken down into functional categories. The income statement based on these transactions is shown as Exhibit 14-3. This exhibit is based on fund accounting concepts and is not acceptable for external financial reporting purposes after the effective date of FASB's *Statement No. 117*.

Specific Purpose Funds

The hospital has two specific purpose funds. One was established to account for an educational program. When $87,000 was transferred to the general fund (see entry 4), the following entry was made in the specific purpose fund:

Exhibit 14-3

Hypothetical Nonprofit Hospital
Statement of Revenues and Expenses
For the Period Ending June 30, 19X1

Patient Service Revenue		$7,100,000
Less: Contractual Adjustments		220,000
Net Patient Revenue		$6,880,000
Other Revenue		318,500
Total Operating Revenue		$7,198,500
Operating Expenses:		
Public Education Expense	$ 87,000	
Laboratory Services	1,834,500	
Cafeteria Expense	96,000	
Nursing Administration	200,000	
Nurses' Stations	1,275,000	
Central Services	1,150,000	
Radiology	116,000	
Pharmacy	210,000	
Social Services	82,000	
Medical Records/Library	62,000	
Dietary Services	245,000	
Plant Operation and Maintenance	365,000	
Housekeeping	210,000	
General Administration	297,000	
Interest Expense	12,000	
Depreciation	29,000	
Insurance	105,000	
Employee Benefits	520,000	
Taxes	63,000	
Bad Debt Expense	72,000	
Total Operating Expenses		7,030,500
Net Operating Income		$ 168,000
Gains (Losses):		
Loss on Disposal of Assets	$ (3,000)	
Gain on Sale of Investments	15,000	
Other Gains	8,000	
Gains (net)		20,000
EXCESS OF REVENUES OVER EXPENSES		$ 188,000

| 19. | Fund Balance | 87,000 | |
| | Cash | | 87,000 |

Another restricted fund was established to account for the restricted earnings from a permanent endowment; the endowment finances research on infectious diseases, and earnings on the endowed resources totaled $8,760 during the year:

| 20. | Due from Endowment | 8,760 | |
| | Fund Balance | | 8,760 |

If a hospital accounts for more than one specific purpose program in a single fund, the fund balance must be labeled to alert financial statement readers of the various special purpose activities. In entry 20, the credit would be Fund Balance — Infectious Diseases.

Investments in the educational program fund earned $51,000:

| 21. | Cash | 51,000 | |
| | Fund Balance | | 51,000 |

When a local government agency contributed $20,000 toward the hospital's educational program, the following entry was made in the specific purpose fund related to the educational program:

| 22. | Cash | 20,000 | |
| | Fund Balance | | 20,000 |

Because the hospital spent only $87,000 on the educational program, the investment earnings and additional contributions for this program were invested.

| 23. | Investments | 71,000 | |
| | Cash | | 71,000 |

As these entries illustrate, a specific purpose fund acts as a receiving, investing, and disbursing fund for the general funds. Operating performance is measured in the general fund, not in the restricted funds. Because the funds are restricted, not endowed, no distinction is made between principal and earnings.

Endowment Funds

The hospital has two endowment funds: in one, donors have specified that the income be used at the discretion of the governing board; in the other, the income must be directed toward research related to infectious diseases. The hospital has not begun the research program, so endowment earnings have not been transferred to the general fund.

Unrestricted income totaled $5,000 for the period (see entry 11 for the related entry in the general fund). These earnings had not been transferred by period end.

24.	Cash	5,000	
	Due to General Funds		5,000

A local fund drive yielded another $60,000 to be added to the endowment, the income from which is unrestricted. These amounts were invested.

25.	Cash	60,000	
	Fund Balance — Unrestricted Income		
	Endowment		60,000
26.	Investments	60,000	
	Cash		60,000

Because the permanent endowment sold investments costing $800,000 at par and purchased additional investments costing $915,000, entries 27 and 28 were made.

27.	Cash	816,000	
	Investments		816,000
28.	Investments	915,000	
	Cash		915,000

Earnings on permanently restricted funds totaled $8,760 for the period (see entry 20 for the related entry in the specific purpose fund).

29.	Accrued Interest Receivable	8,760	
	Due to Specific Purpose Fund		8,760

One fund balance designation was used for each separate endowment fund. Whenever a number of transactions occur in an endowment fund, the designations should be expanded to include the nature of the fund balance change: earnings, transfers, gifts, and so forth. Adding the descriptive information simplifies preparation of the cash flow statement.

Plant Replacement and Expansion Funds

Assets restricted specifically for the acquisition or construction of fixed assets are recorded in plant replacement and expansion funds. Entries 12 and 13 reflected the effect of purchasing assets on the hospital's general fund. Entry 30 was made in the plant replacement and expansion fund for the portion funded by restricted assets.

30.	Fund Balance—Purchase of Fixed Assets	30,000	
	Due to General Fund		30,000

If the $30,000 had been transferred before period end, the "due to" would be debited and cash credited in the plant replacement and expansion fund. At the same time, cash would be debited and the "due from" credited in the general fund.

During the year, a local philanthropist died leaving $1,000,000 for future capital outlays. The money was invested and the accrued interest of $20,000 shown in entry 33 was earned during the year.

31.	Cash	1,000,000	
	Fund Balance—Capital Program		1,000,000
32.	Investments	1,000,000	
	Cash		1,000,000
33.	Accrued Interest Receivable	20,000	
	Fund Balance—Capital Program		20,000

EFFECT OF FASB STATEMENT NO. 117 ON HEALTH CARE ACCOUNTING AND FINANCIAL REPORTING

Some health care accounting and reporting practices change under FASB *Statement No. 117*.[19] This section explains the specific features of the standard that affects health care entities and the next illustrates the financial statements resulting from those changes.

The effect of *Statement No. 117* on health care entities is easily stated: the required financial statements change and the external financial statements must be prepared for the entity as a whole, in other words, **not by fund.** Previously, health care entities prepared a balance sheet (statement of financial position), a statement of revenue and expenses of general funds, a statement of changes in fund balances, and a statement of cash flows of general funds. *Statement No. 117* requires an activity statement, a statement of financial position, and a cash flow statement.

In terms of type of statement, the differences between pre and post *Statement No. 117* is more form than substance. A balance sheet is required in both cases. An operating statement is required; before the new standard, it was called a statement of revenue and expenses and after the new standard it is referred to as an activity statement. A cash flow statement is required pre and post *Statement No. 117.*

In terms of content, the differences between pre and post *Statement No. 117* are striking indeed. Fund accounting will no longer be used for external financial reporting purposes. Instead, all nonprofits, including health care entities, will report by **net asset class.**

[19]*Statement No. 93* had no effect on health care entities because they already were depreciating fixed assets and the effects of *Statement No. 116* have been incorporated into the material in the previous sections.

The three asset classes were first identified in *Concepts Statement No. 6* and are based on the presence or absence of donor-imposed restrictions:

Permanently restricted net assets are those resulting from: (1) contributions and other inflows of assets whose use by the organization is limited by donor-imposed stipulations that neither expire by passage of time nor can be fulfilled or otherwise removed by actions of the organization; (2) other asset enhancements and diminishments subject to the same kinds of stipulations; and (3) reclassifications from (or to) other classes of net assets as a consequence of donor-imposed stipulations.

Temporarily restricted net assets result from: (1) contributions and other inflows of assets whose use by the organization is limited by donor-imposed stipulations that either expire by passage of time or can be fulfilled and removed by actions of the organization pursuant to those stipulations; (2) other asset enhancements and diminishments subject to the same kinds of stipulations; and (3) reclassifications to (or from) other classes of net assets as a consequence of donor-imposed stipulations, their expiration by passage of time, or their fulfillment and removal by actions of the organization pursuant to those stipulations.

Unrestricted net assets are those that are neither permanently restricted nor temporarily restricted by donor-imposed stipulations.[20]

With a few important exceptions, the term *unrestricted* is similar to what used to be called *operating,* the general fund activity. It includes the general revenues and expenses that an organization generates or expends for its daily activities. For health care providers, *unrestricted* would include patient revenues and related expenses, and the income from such peripheral activities as gift shops, parking facilities, or coffee shops.

Illustration of Selected Transactions under Statement No. 117

Instead of recording transactions in funds, nonprofits will make the entries in a single entity and identify the net asset class affected by the event. Futher *Statement No. 117* requires that while revenues are recorded by asset class, expenses are recorded only in the unrestricted asset class. A few transactions already illustrated using fund accounting are recorded using the *Statement No. 117* guidance to assist in making the transition.

Entry 1 illustrated the receipt of $7,200,000 in patient service revenue, $100,000 of which related to charity services. Another $220,000 in revenue was received from operating a cafeteria.

1(a).			
	Cash	220,000	
	Accounts Receivable	7,100,000	
	Patient Service Revenue—		
	Unrestricted		7,100,000
	Other Operating Revenue—		
	Unrestricted		220,000

[20] Adapted from the FASB's *Statement of Financial Accounting Standards No. 117, Financial Statements of Not-For-Profit Organizations* (Norwalk, Conn.: FASB, 1993), Appendix D.

Entry 7, recording the supplies inventory, does not affect any net asset class until the supplies are used. When the supplies are purchased, the supplies inventory is increased and cash is decreased.

7(a).	Supplies Inventory	316,000	
	Cash		316,000

"Due Tos" and "Due Froms" are common under fund accounting because each fund is a separate entity. Following the new FASB standard, only one entity exists, and none of these interfund relationships exist. Recognition of the unrestricted and restricted earnings on endowment assets (entries 11, 20, and 24) can all be recorded in one entry.

11(a).	Cash ($15,000 + $8,760)	23,760	
	Gains—Temporarily Restricted		
	Investment Income		8,760
	Gains—Unrestriced Investment Income		15,000

The implications for income recognition are evident from this entry. The entire $23,760 is recognized as income (gain) in the current period, regardless of how much is actually spent. In contrast, under fund accounting the restricted income is not recognized as a gain until the related expenditures are incurred. Similarly, earlier in entry 21, the investment earnings on the specific purpose fund assets were credited to fund balance until the related expenditures were incurred. *Statement No. 117* simplifies the process considerably.

21(a).	Cash	51,000	
	Gains—Temporarily Restricted		
	Investment Income		51,000

Income also is recognized when contributions are received for an endowment. Entry 25 reflected a gift of $60,000 to the endowment; the amount was recorded as an increase in cash and in the fund balance of the endowment fund. Under *Statement No. 117*, the gift is recognized as a premanently restricted gift.

25(a).	Cash	60,000	
	Gains—Permanently Restricted		60,000

The income is classified as a gain in accordance with the classification scheme used in the *Health Care Audit Guide*. *Statement No. 117* did nothing to change those classification schemes. However, a more descriptive classification scheme could be used. The income received and reflected by entries 11(a) and 21(a) could be designated simply as investment income, without the reference to gains. The income shown in 25(a) could be recorded as a contribution, which would be more descriptive of its nature.

The Activity Statement Under the FASB Standards

Statement No. 117 requires that the activity statement depict the three asset classes identified in *Concept Statement No. 6*—unrestricted, temporarily restriced, and permanently restricted—based on the existence or absence of donor-imposed restrictions.

> **OBSERVATION**
>
> As the standard's requirements are detailed, the reason for the title "activity statement" instead of some reference to "operations" becomes clear. Not only did the FASB need a title broad enough to cover the activities of a myriad of nonprofits, but it also had to reflect the fact that the term *operations* is no longer relevent.

Asset Reclassifications   The unrestricted class also includes any increases or decreases that result from expired restrictions. For example, if a health care organization received a contribution last year that could not be spent until this year, the unrestricted class would increase this year and the temporarily restricted class would decrease, hence the term *asset reclassification* in the definition. A reclassification is necessary because in the year in which the money was received, it was an increase in the temporarily restricted class (see entry 21(a) as an example). The term *reclassification* is used to avoid overstating "revenues," while still reflecting the movement from one asset class to another. Expenses always are shown as unrestricted because the Board concluded that "identifying or designating sources of donor-restricted revenues to be used to finance specific expenses does not make an expense donor restricted.[21]

Two reclassifications are particularly cumbersome and difficult to reconcile with the concept of "operations." The first relates to contributions restricted for fixed asset purchases. When received, the contribution increases temporarily restricted assets, for example, contribution revenue. In the year in which the contribution is spent for the intended purpose, namely the purchase of fixed assets, the temporarily restricted asset class would be reduced by a reclassification and the unrestricted class would be increased by the amount of the purchase. An alternative also is permitted. The asset remains in the temporarily restricted class, depreciation is recorded as an expense in the unrestricted class, and an amount equal to depreciation is reclassified as unrestricted support.

The accounting for fixed assets is even more complex if the donor restricts the purpose for which the asset must be used, for example, for some specific program such as cardiac care. In this case, the donation would be reported in the permanently restricted class, even after the asset is purchased. In following years, the asset would be depreciated as required by *Statement No. 93;* the depreciation expense would be recorded in the unrestricted section of the activity statement, with a corresponding decrease in the permanently restricted asset class and an increase in the unrestricted asset class. Both of the

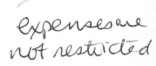

Expenses are not restricted

[21]Ibid., ¶135.

latter changes would be reflected in the reclassification section of the activity statement. The net result is that depreciation on gifted assets whose use is permanently restricted has no net effect on unrestricted net assets: depreciation decreases the net assets but the reclassification increases net assets by the same amount each year.

The second area difficult to visualize relates to endowments. Typically, endowments are contributions that cannot be spent but the income from which can be used either for specific purposes or general unrestricted use. The endowment will remain indefinitely in the permanently restricted asset class. All earnings, including gains and losses, on the endowment will be reported either in the unrestricted, temporarily restricted, or permanently restricted class depending on donor intent or, if the donor or gift document is silent, on industry practices.

Many nonprofit organizations use the spending-rate (total return) method of measuring annual earnings from endowments. Under this method, endowment earnings are measured at a specified percentage of the average market value of the endowment, rather than on the actual earnings for the period. The percentage is set below the actual earning rate so that the difference between actual earnings and the spending amount can be added to the endowment to preserve its purchasing power. If the spending-rate method is used and provided state law supports its use, the FASB standard requires total actual earnings for the period to be shown as unrestricted revenue.[22]

The extent to which this requirement affects the financial statements of health care organizations depends on the relative importance of the endowment to overall operations and whether the spending-rate method is used.

Reporting Expenses   The standard also requires expenses to be shown by functional class, for example, major classes of program services and supporting services, such as administration and fund-raising. This functional expense classification may be shown either on the face of the statement or in the notes to the financial statements. The standard encourages but does not require health care organizations also to depict the natural classification for expenses, for example, salaries, rent, insurance.

When discussing expense reporting, the FASB points out that nonprofits could enhance their financial reporting by showing the interrelationship between program expenses and program revenues. This sounds much like the idea of services efforts and accomplishments reporting being developed for governmental entities. In fact, the subtitle for the paragraph in which this notion is discussed includes the words *service efforts.*

Alternative Reporting Formats   The Board made a point of indicating that it is not requiring a specific format for a financial statement any more than it does for the private sector. Further, the Board recognizes difficulties posed by the fact that many nonprofits use fund accounting and try to distinguish between "operating" and "nonoperating" activities.

---

[22]Some of the nuances of this particular part of the standard are discussed further in Chapter 16.

Classifying revenues, expenses, gains, and losses within classes of net assets does not preclude incorporating additional classifications within a statement of activities. ... An organization may classify items as *operating* and nonoperating, expendable and nonexpendable, earned and unearned, recurring and nonrecurring, or in other ways. This Statement neither encourages nor discourages those further classifications.[23]

However, the standard does seem to preclude reporting by fund because it indicates that the statement should focus on the organization as a whole.

Exhibit 14-4 illustrates an approach to depicting the information for one type of health care organization, a nursing home, in an activity statement. As stated earlier, whether nonprofits will retain fund accounting for internal reporting and then prepare a reconciliation to obtain the information necessary for the financial statements or abandon fund accounting entirely is unclear.

Exhibit 14-4

Sample Care Nursing Home, Inc.
Statement of Activity
Year Ended December 31, 19X5
($000)

	Unrestricted	Temporarily Restricted	Permanently Restricted	Total
Revenues, Gains, and Other Support:				
Patient Service Revenue	$2,071			$2,071
Contributions	100	$ 60	$ 9	169
Investment Income	4		1	5
Unrealized Gains	66			66
Net Assets Released from Restrictions:				
Satisfaction of Program Restrictions	20	(20)		
Satisfaction of Equipment Restrictions	9	(9)		
Total Revenues, Gains, and Other Support	$2,270	$ 31	$10	$2,311
Expenses and Losses:				
Nursing Services	$1,370			$1,370
Dietary Services	220			220
General Services	260			260
Administrative Services	180			180
Fund-Raising	30			30
Fire Loss	20			20
Total Expenses and Losses	$2,080			$2,080
Change in Net Assets	$ 190	$ 31	$10	$ 231
Net Assets, January 1, 19X5	200	49	7	256
Net Assets, December 31, 19X5	$ 390	$ 80	$17	$ 487

[23]Ibid., ¶23.

The Statement of Financial Position

Statement No. 117 imposes few special restrictions on the display elements of the statement of financial position. The statement must show totals for each of the three net asset classes—permanently restricted, temporarily restricted, and unrestricted. Because the statement says "net asset classes," health care providers do not have to show separately permanently restricted assets and permanently restricted liabilities and then the net asset for that class. The other specific requirement is that the statement should focus on the entity as a whole; that is, it seems to preclude reporting by fund.

Other requirements pertaining to the statement of financial position reflect those applied in the private sector:

1. The statement should provide information about liquidity, financial flexibility, and the interrelationship of an organization's assets and liabilities.
2. Assets and liabilities should be grouped into homogeneous classes.
3. The statement should reflect liquidity by the display on the face of the statement or by appropriate notes. Most probably will put the information on the face of the statement by listing the most liquid assets first, for example, "sequencing" the assets; the same requirement applies to liabilities, except those that will be paid first are displayed first and so forth.
4. Understanding of financial flexibility is enhanced by appropriate notes and by explaining important restrictions imposed by donors on the use of contributed assets.

Exhibit 14-5 shows a statement of financial position for a health care provider. The information about the assets whose use is limited would not have to be depicted in the body of the statement. Such assets are common items on health care entity financial statements. They are assets set aside by the oversight board or other assets limited to use for identified purposes by an outside party other than a donor or a grantor. These assets could be described in the notes to the financial statements.

The Cash Flow Statement

Understanding the cash flow statement of health care entities is easy. The FASB simply amended *Statement No. 95* to extend its provisions to nonprofits. For example, the section of the statement referring to business enterprises has been amended to include nonprofits. One sentence is added to specifically address restricted contributions. The definition of cash flows from financing activities was changed to include:

> receipts from contributions and investment income that by donor stipulation are restricted for the purposes of acquiring, constructing, or improving property, plant, equipment, or other long-lived assets or establishing or increasing a permanent endowment or term endowment.[24]

---

[24]Ibid., ¶30.

Exhibit 14-5

Sample Care Nursing Home, Inc.
Balance Sheet
December 31, 19X5 and 19X4
($000)

	19X5	19X4
Assets		
Current Assets:		
Cash	$ 56	$ 57
Investments, at cost which approximates market	150	—
Assets whose use is limited and that are required for current liabilities	50	50
Patient Accounts Receivable less allowance for uncollectible accounts:		
19X5—$6.7; 19X4—$5.3	162	152
Estimated third-party payer settlements	71	62
Interest receivable	7	—
Supplies	59	57
Prepaid expenses	3	2
Total Current Assets	$ 558	$ 380
Property and Equipment:		
Land	$ 205	$ 205
Land improvements	37	32
Buildings	1,399	1,399
Major movable equipment	129	97
Furniture and fixtures	88	81
Automotive equipment	11	11
	$1,869	$1,825
Less Accumulated Depreciation	210	141
Total Plant Assets	$1,659	$1,684
Other Assets:		
Note receivable	$ 81	$ 72
Unamortized bond issuance cost	42	48
Other	19	—
Investments	181	157
Total Other Assets	$ 323	$ 277
TOTAL ASSETS	$2,540	$2,341
Liabilities and Net Assets		
Current Liabilities:		
Current maturities of long-term debt	$ 50	$ 50
Accounts payable	78	52
Accrued expenses	225	233
Total Current Liabilities	$ 353	$ 335
Long-Term Debt, Less Current Maturities	1,700	1,750
Total Liabilities	$2,053	$2,085
Net Assets:		
Unrestricted	$ 390	$ 200
Temporarily restricted	80	49
Permanently restricted	17	7
Total Net Assets	$ 487	$ 256
TOTAL LIABILITIES AND NET ASSETS	$2,540	$2,341

This provision makes it clear that temporarily or permanently restricted contributions for the purchase of fixed assets or additions to the endowment are financing activities. Otherwise, the required statement of cash flow does not have to be segregated by asset class. Exhibit 14-6 illustrates a cash flow statement for a nursing home that had only one contribution restricted for the purchase of long-lived assets.

Notes to the Financial Statements

Notes are always an important part of the financial statements. They will be particularly critical for nonprofits until users become accustomed to the requirements of *Statement No. 117.* One important aspect will be a clear exposition of the various asset classes. The policy notes should explain the treatment of restricted contributions and the reclassification of these amounts once the restriction has been satisfied. Identifying gifts reported as unre-

---

Exhibit 14-6

Sample Care Nursing Home, Inc.
Cash Flow Statement
Years Ended December 31, 19X5 and 19X4
($000)

	19X5	19X4
Cash Flows from Operating Activities:		
Changes in Net Assets	$ 231	$ 71
Add (Deduct) Items Not Affecting Cash:		
Depreciation	69	57
Amortization	—	6
Unrealized gains	(66)	
Loss from fire	20	11
Add (Deduct) Changes in:		
Patient accounts receivable	(10)	(17)
Estimated third-party payer settlements	(9)	2
Interest receivable	(7)	—
Supplies	(2)	(4)
Prepaid expenses	(1)	1
Accounts payable	26	12
Accrued expenses	(8)	10
Contributions restricted for fixed asset purchases	(9)	—
Interest restricted for fixed asset purchases	(1)	—
Net Cash Provided by Operating Activities	$ 233	$149
Cash Flows from Investing Activities:		
Purchase of investments	$(150)	$ —
Purchase of property and equipment	(44)	(77)
Proceeds from sale of property	—	2
Net Cash Used for Investing Activities	$(194)	$ (75)
Cash Flows from Financing Activities:		
Proceeds from contributions restricted for investment in plant	$ 10	$ —
Other Financing Activities:		
Repayment of long-term debt	(50)	(50)
Total Net Cash Used for Financing Activities	$ (40)	$ (50)
Net Change in Cash	$ (1)	$ 24
Beginning Cash Balance	57	33
Ending Cash Balance	$ 56	$ 57

See accompanying notes to financial statements.

stricted also will be important. One note should be devoted to detailing amounts received in the temporarily and permanently restricted classes; another should give the necessary detail for the reclassifications.

Investments also will require considerable detail in the notes to the financial statements, particularly if the entity uses the spending-rate or total return method of deciding how much of endowment earnings to spend. The amounts appropriated for the current period must be evident, as should the amounts returned to the endowment to maintain its purchasing power. Sample notes for a few of these areas are illustrated in Exhibit 14-7.

Exhibit 14-7

Sample Care Nursing Home, Inc.
Selected Notes to Financial Statements
December 31, 19X5 and 19X4

---

(1) Organization and Summary of Significant Accounting Policies

    (a) Organization

        Sample Care Nursing Home (Home) is a nonprofit corporation that operates a nursing home consisting of 50 skilled and 130 intermediate care beds.

    (b) General and Donor-Restricted Net Assets

        The Home reports gifts of cash and other assets as restricted support if they are received with donor stipulations that limit the use of the donated assets. When a donor restriction expires—that is, when a stipulated time restriction ends or a purpose restriction is accomplished—temporarily restricted net assets are reclassified to unrestricted net assets and reported in the statement of activities as net assets released from restrictions.

        The Home reports gifts of land, buildings, and equipment as unrestricted support unless explicit donor stipulations specify how the donated assets must be used. Gifts of long-lived assets with explicit restrictions that specify how the assets are to be used and gifts of cash or other assets that must be used to acquire long-lived assets are reported as restricted support. Absent explicit donor stipulations about how those long-lived assets must be maintained, the Home reports expirations of donor restrictions when donated or acquired long-lived assets are placed in service.

    (c) The Home uses fund accounting for internal reporting purposes; the accounting system also keeps track of transactions on the three asset classifications basis required by current accounting standards. The general purpose financial statements are prepared from this latter classification and are reconciled annually with the fund accounting records.

(2) Temporarily restricted net assets are available for the following purposes or periods:

Nursing Services	
Purchase of Equipment	$xx
Research	xx
Dietary Services	
Educational Seminars and Publications	$xx
Home Health Care	xx
Buildings and Equipment	xx
Annuity Trust Agreements	xx
For Periods After December 31, 19X5	xx

(3) Permanently restricted net assets are restricted to:

Investment in perpetuity, the income from which is expendable to support:

Nursing Services	$xx
Dietary Services	xx
Any Home Activities	xx

(4) Net assets were released from donor restrictions by incurring expenses satisfying the restricted purpose or by occurrence of other events specified by donors.

Purpose restrictions accomplished:
    (An explanation would be included here.)

Total restrictions released:
    (An explanation would be included here.)

Note: The FASB standards encourage other note disclosures for nonprofits, some of which can be better illustrated in connection with colleges and universities or other nonprofits. For example, most nonprofits would explain the investment valuation methods used as well as the interpretation of state law related to the total return or spending-rate methodology used by the reporting organization. These have more applicability to colleges and universities and will be illustrated in Chapter 15.

SELECTED AUDIT CONSIDERATIONS

Auditing a health care unit presents some particular challenges. Even though the audit standards are the same as those for other businesses, the auditor is typically asked to examine special-purpose reports necessary to obtain reimbursement from third-party payers. Usually special-purpose reports have prescribed forms, including the form of the auditor's report. Sometimes the special-purpose reports are prepared on a non-GAAP basis. The auditors must understand not only the basic accounting practices but also the complex rate-setting methods used by third-party payers. In some cases, auditing standards may require a special opinion paragraph if these other data are incorporated into the audit report.

prepaid plans

Auditors must pay particular attention to reporting risks associated with prepaid health care plans and uninsured malpractice losses and obligations. In the case of prepaid plans, health care costs may have been incurred but not yet reported to plan providers. Accordingly, a liability for these costs must be estimated, which requires a high degree of management judgment and skilled auditor review.[25]

malprac

Risks associated with uninsured malpractice losses and obligations require complex analyses before financial statements can be prepared. Sometimes, management and the legal staff may be unable to estimate the ultimate cost of resolving particular claims, in which case no provision can be made in the financial statements. Auditors must then provide a qualified opinion, usually a "subject to" qualification.

Audit objectives related to assets must be tailored to the three net asset classes. As illustrated earlier, the unit's net assets may be composed of unrestricted, temporarily restricted, and permanently restricted amounts. Auditors must verify that the restrictions have been maintained and that appropriate disclosures inform readers about the restrictions.

Donations

Donated services and materials, some restricted bequests, and receivables from third-party payers also present some audit review and disclosure requirements peculiar to health care organizations. A good understanding of accounting for health care providers, the *Health Care Audit Guide*, and general audit standards is necessary before the audit scope can be defined or the planning process begun.

SUMMARY

Hospitals and other health care organizations use many accounting practices common to other businesses. Nevertheless, application of generally accepted accounting principles depends on the ownership or affiliation of the organization. Investor-owned units use business GAAP. Nonprofits fall within the purview of the FASB but use different accounting practices. Health care providers affiliated with governmental entities look to the GASB for their ac-

---

[25]*Statement of Position No. 89-5* provides some guidance in this regard.

counting practices; normally, they would be operated as an enterprise fund of the governmental entity.

The FASB has issued three standards that specifically affect nonprofits under its purview: one requiring depreciation, another describing the accounting and reporting of contributions, and a third on financial statement display. The latter standard will not mesh with current accounting practices related to fund accounting. How health care entities will resolve the differences is unclear. Thus, current fund accounting practices and financial statements consistent with the financial display requirements were illustrated in the chapter.

Nonprofit health care entities have been using both restricted and general funds. Specific purpose, plant expansion and replacement, loan, annuity and life income, and endowment funds fall within the restricted category. For financial statement purposes, however, health care entities must report by net asset class after the effective date of *Statement No. 117.*

Particular account titles, recognition principles, and statement presentations differ from those used by businesses. Payments for services provided come largely from third-party payers and require detailed functional cost records. Revenues are recognized at billed rates and adjusted for contract changes. Such differences between accounting for health care organizations and for businesses are a matter of form, not substance.

Characteristics of health care providers that lead to specialized accounting practices also raise special audit considerations. With third-party payments, auditors must review special-purpose reports that require keen analytical skills. Auditing related claims is also a demanding job. Malpractice suits are commonplace; estimating these liabilities is a difficult and sometimes impossible task.

QUESTIONS

14-1 Identify some of the changes in the health care field; explain how they affect the accounting and reporting system.

14-2 Why has the AICPA had considerable influence over the accounting practices of health care organizations?

14-3 Describe three types of health care organizations and briefly explain how their accounting and reporting practices are determined.

14-4 The Healthcare Financial Management Association argues that all health care providers should have the same accounting and reporting standards. Explain why this is important.

14-5 Drawing on the material in earlier chapters, what fund would be used to account for a governmentally owned hospital? Explain.

14-6 In analyzing the performance of a hospital, what are the advantages of showing the gross "anticipated" revenues and the deductions from those revenues, rather than the net amount billed?

14-7 Contrast the accounting for donated services and donated materials.

14-8 Why is cost accounting important for health care organizations?

14-9 Explain the valuation procedures used by health care organizations for valuing investments.

14-10 Describe the fund structure currently used by health care organizations.

14-11 How are health care pooled investments accounted for and valued?

14-12 Define and give examples of operating revenues, other revenues, and gains or losses.

14-13 In what major area will the new standard on contributions affect the health care industry?

14-14 In determining whether two health care units are "related," what does it mean if one unit is described as a sole beneficiary of the other?

14-15 Is special accounting and reporting guidance required for malpractice claims? Why or why not?

14-16 Describe the recognition principles for temporarily restricted donations of health care organizations under *Statement No. 117.*

14-17 What disclosures are required for "related" health care organizations?

14-18 What are asset reclassifications? Where are they shown?

CASES

14-1 The president of Good Service Hospital presented highlights from the hospital's operating results to members of the press and local chamber of commerce executives. She explained that operating revenues totaled $17,000,000 for the past year; deductions from revenues were approximately $1,300,000, and total operating expenses were $15,400,000. The net excess of revenues over expenses was $480,000.

A local reporter asked the president to explain the deductions from revenues. He also wondered why the president distinguished between deductions from revenues and operating expenses. Finally, he wondered what the president left out in her explanation; according to his calculations, the excess of revenues over expenses should have been $300,000, not $480,000.

REQUIRED

1. Discuss the reason for distinguishing between deductions from revenues and operating expenses. Under what circumstances could the president classify some of the deductions as operating expenses and still prepare financial statements according to GAAP?

2. What explanation would you give for the difference between the $480,000 and the $300,000?

3. Draft a statement that the president could have used to avoid the confusion she created in addressing the press.

14-2 Charlestown's largest clinic is worried about its operating performance. The following condensed statement indicates that although gross revenues exceed operating expenses, deductions from revenues are averaging about 16 percent of gross revenues, almost twice the national average.

Charlestown EverReady Clinic
Condensed Operating Statement
For Year Ending June 30, 19X8

Operating Revenues	$11,700,000
Less: Deductions from Revenues	1,860,000
Net Revenues from Patient Services	$ 9,840,000
Other Revenues	150,000
Total Operating Revenues	$ 9,990,000
Total Operating Expenses	10,100,000
Excess of Operating Expenses Over Revenues	$ (110,000)
Total Gains	280,000
Net Excess of Revenues	$ 170,000

REQUIRED

1. Assuming the national average cited for deductions from revenue is correct, should the clinic be concerned about its performance? Why or why not? Are there areas of potential concern besides the high percentage for deductions from revenue? Explain.
2. Presuming the clinic has reason to be concerned about its performance, explain what analysis you would make to determine the cause(s) for that concern.
3. Does the amount shown for gains have any bearing on your analysis? Explain.

14-3   The following statement appeared in the audited financial statements of a small nursing home:

Various legal proceedings and claims are outstanding against the home that have arisen from patient use of facilities and alleged malpractice suits by residents or their families. Based on information available to management and counsel at this time, the ultimate disposition of these legal proceedings should not have material adverse effects on the financial statements of the nursing home. Management is unable to estimate the ultimate cost, if any, of the resolution of such potential claims and, accordingly, no accrual has been made for them.

The nursing home received an unqualified opinion.

REQUIRED

1. Is the preceding note disclosure adequate? If so, explain why. If not, indicate what else should have been included in the note.
2. Presuming these claims were the only issue facing the auditors, do you agree with the decision to issue an unqualified opinion? Explain your answer.

14-4   The Rogers Medical Institute is a nonprofit health care provider established in 19X1 to finance research for diabetes. Until this year when it purchased land and buildings suitable for its purposes, it leased facilities.

To make sure that the maximum amount of research money is available, the Institute intends to operate the plant property as a self-supporting entity.

The Institute uses fund accounting for internal reporting purposes and wants to establish a separate fund to account for this entity, as well as establish a rate structure that will fund all operating costs. The Institute's general operating fund will reimburse the separate fund at the preestablished rates.

REQUIRED

1. Given the Institute's goal, what kind of fund should be established for operating the property? What accounting basis will the fund use? Is the fund restricted or unrestricted?
2. If the property has the following components, how would you establish a rate structure to cover the costs? (Hint: There will be other operating costs, such as heat, lights, insurance, and maintenance.)

Land	$ 186,000
Building	3,760,000
Furniture	53,000
Equipment	1,600,000

3. Assuming the Institute issued bonds to cover the cost of acquiring the facility, make the entries to establish the fund.

14-5   An analysis of the Jasper voluntary hospital's patient accounts reveals that under the current billing system, accounts are held for three days after discharge so that late charges and credits may be posted. The analysis also indicates that the unbilled accounts are broken down in the following manner:

	NUMBER OF ACCOUNTS UNBILLED			
Principal Payer	**Awaiting Diagnosis**	**Benefits Missing**	**Ready to Bill**	**Other**
Medicare	40	83	285	24
Blue Cross	52	76	141	27
Welfare	36	82	115	68
Commercial Insurance	38	26	197	22
Self-Pay	—	—	53	27
	166	267	791	168

REQUIRED

1. Prepare a brief description of the situation for the hospital's administration.
2. Outline the corrective actions to be taken giving particular attention to (a) the number of accounts ready to bill and (b) the normal billing activities.
3. Explain the steps necessary to prevent a recurrence of this situation.

(Adapted from a Fellowship Examination of the Hospital Financial Management Association, now Healthcare Financial Management Association)

EXERCISES

14-1 Select the best answer for each question.

Questions 1–3 are based on the following information pertaining to Abbey Hospital.

Under Abbey Hospital's established rate structure, the hospital would have earned patient revenue of $6,000,000 for the year ended December 31, 19X3. However, Abbey did not expect to collect this amount because of charity allowances of $1,000,000 and discounts and contract adjustments of $500,000. In May 19X3, Abbey purchased bandages from Lee Supply Co. at a cost of $1,000. However, Lee notified Abbey that the invoice was being canceled and that the bandages were being donated to Abbey. At December 31, 19X3, Abbey had board-designated assets consisting of cash of $40,000 and investments of $700,000.

1. For the year ended December 31, 19X3, how much should Abbey report as gross patient service revenue?
   a. $6,000,000
   b. $5,500,000
   c. $5,000,000
   d. $4,500,000

2. For the year ended December 31, 19X3, Abbey should record the donation of bandages as:
   a. a $1,000 reduction in operating expenses
   b. a gain of $1,000
   c. other revenue of $1,000
   d. a memorandum entry only

3. How much of Abbey's board-designated assets should be included in the unrestricted net asset grouping?
   a. $0
   b. $40,000
   c. $700,000
   d. $740,000
   (Adapted from the May 1984 CPA Exam, Practice II, #41–43)

4. Which of the following would be included in the unrestricted class of a health care provider?
   a. permanent endowments
   b. term endowments
   c. board-designated resources originating from previously accumulated income
   d. donations for fixed asset purchases
   (Adapted from the May 1984 CPA Exam, Theory #59)

5. Which of the following normally would be included in Other Revenues of a volunteer clinic?

	Revenue from Educational Programs	Unrestricted Gifts
a.	yes	no
b.	yes	yes

c.	no	yes
d.	no	no

(Adapted from the May 1987 CPA Exam, Theory #59)

6. Which of the following health care providers would receive accounting and reporting guidance from the GASB?
   a. a clinic associated with a private university
   b. a county medical center
   c. a hospital owned by local community investors
   d. none of the above

7. Under *Statement No. 117* pledges restricted for a specific use should be recognized:
   a. as deferred revenue
   b. as income when the pledge is made
   c. in the period in which the related expenditure is made
   d. none of the above

8. The distinction between unrestricted, temporarily restricted, and permanently restricted net asset class must be shown on:
   a. the income statement
   b. the statement of cash flows
   c. the balance sheet
   d. both a and c

9. Long-term investments in debt securities by health care providers would be valued at:
   a. amortized cost
   b. cost
   c. lower of cost or market
   d. market value

10. Reporting of uninsured malpractice claims of health care providers requires:
    a. a reservation of net assets
    b. determining and reporting the average loss for the past 10 years
    c. detailed disclosures regarding anticipated impact on the financial statements
    d. none of the above

14-2 Esperanza, a nonprofit hospital, wants to use fund accounting practices for internal reporting purposes. Effective January 1, 19X7, Esperanza's board of trustees voted to adjust the December 31, 19X6, general ledger balances, and to establish separate funds for the general (unrestricted) funds, the endowment fund, and the plant replacement and expansion fund. The hospital's unadjusted post-closing trial balance at December 31, 19X6, appears below:

Esperanza Hospital
Unadjusted Post-Closing Trial Balance
As of December 31, 19X6

Cash	$ 60,000
Investment in U. S. Treasury Bills	400,000

(continued)

Investment in Corporate Bonds	500,000	
Interest Receivable	10,000	
Accounts Receivable	50,000	
Inventory	30,000	
Land	100,000	
Building	800,000	
Equipment	170,000	
Allowance for Depreciation		$ 410,000
Accounts Payable		20,000
Notes Payable		70,000
Endowment Fund Balance		520,000
Other Fund Balances		1,100,000
	$2,120,000	$2,120,000

ADDITIONAL INFORMATION

1. Investment in corporate bonds pertains to the amount required to be accumulated to invest cash equal to accumulated depreciation until the funds are needed for asset replacement. The $500,000 balance at December 31, 19X6, is less than the full amount required because of errors in computation of building depreciation in past years. Included in the allowance for depreciation is a correctly computed amount of $90,000 applicable to equipment. The assets were originally gifted to Esperanza Hospital.

2. Endowment fund balance has been credited with the following:

Donor's Gift of Cash	$300,000
Gains on Sales of Securities	100,000
Interest and Dividends Earned in 19X4, 19X5, and 19X6	120,000
Total	$520,000

The terms of the gift specify that the principal plus all gains on sales of investments are to remain fully invested in U.S. government or corporate securities. At December 31, 19X6, $400,000 was invested in U.S. Treasury bills. The gift document further specifies that interest and dividends on investments are to be used for payment of current operating expenses.

3. Land comprises the following:

Donation of land in 19X0, at appraised value	$ 40,000
Appreciation in fair value of land as determined by independent appraiser in 19X5	60,000
Total	$100,000

4. Building comprises the following:

Hospital building completed 40 years ago, when operations were started (estimated useful life of 50 years), at cost	$720,000
Installation of elevator 20 years ago (estimated useful life of 20 years), at cost	80,000
Total	$800,000

REQUIRED

Prepare a worksheet with the following headings and enter the adjustments necessary to restate the general ledger account balances properly. Distribute the adjusted balances to establish separate fund accounts, and complete the worksheet. Formal journal entries are not required, but supporting computations should be referenced to the worksheet adjustments.

Trial Balance	Adjustments	General Funds	Endowment Fund	Plant Replacement and Expansion Fund

(Adapted from the May 1987 CPA Exam, Practice II)

14-3 The Lincoln Nursing Home had the following transactions during 19X8:

1. Gross revenues from nursing home services and nearby parking facilities owned by the nursing home were:

Room and Board	$860,000
Nursing	280,000
Other Professional Services	135,000
Parking Facility	90,000

(All but the parking facility revenues were on account; the parking facility represented cash collections from the meters.)

2. The clinic was able to distinguish between charity services and unwillingness to pay, and the amounts for those items and contract adjustments were:

Provision for Uncollectibles (estimated)	$37,000
Charity Services (actual for room and board)	18,000
Contract Adjustments (estimated)	9,000

3. Vouchers totaling $980,000 were issued for the following expenses:

Administrative Services	$ 87,000
Fiscal Services	47,000
Nursing Services	611,000
Other Professional Services	140,000
Rehabilitation Services	8,000
Medical Record and Library Services	5,000
Other Operating Expenses	34,000
Supplies Inventory	48,000

4. Collections on accounts receivable totaled $850,000, and cash payments on vouchers payable during the year were $680,000.
5. Accounts written off as uncollectible totaled $15,000.
6. The Lincoln Nursing Home received $65,000 in unrestricted gifts during the year; it also received $15,000 in investment earnings from the endowment fund. The use of these endowment earnings was unrestricted.
7. The endowment fund whose earnings were unrestricted received $80,000 as an addition to its principal from a local philanthropist.

8. The nursing home still owes $160,000 on the mortgage covering its operating facilities; it paid $10,000 in principal and $15,200 in interest during the year.

9. At the beginning of the year, a donor provided corporate securities valued at $5,000 to the Lincoln Nursing Home. The donor specified that the donation was to be used for acquisition of fixed assets. That donation earned $400 during the year.

10. Supplies of $30,000 were issued to nursing services during the year.

11. The nursing home purchased $1,000 of equipment during the year; the purchase was made from money restricted for that purpose. It also sold equipment, which had a cost of $3,000 and had accumulated depreciation of $1,800, for $500. Depreciation on unsold equipment was $6,000 for 19X8. You may assume that the entire amount is reclassified in the year of purchase.

REQUIRED

1. Make the necessary journal entries for 19X8 under *Statement No. 117.* Each entry should be keyed to the transaction.

2. Prepare a statement of activity for the year ending December 31, 19X8, using the net asset classification required by the FASB.

14-4 The Keystone Retirement Community, which provides housing, health care, and related services to residents, has 320 apartments and a 60-bed continuous health care facility.

Residents pay an advance fee upon entering into the contract for continuing care. The fees vary, depending on the type of apartment and services rendered once the individual is moved to the continuous-care facility. Any fees paid, less the amount refundable to the resident, are recorded as deferred revenue and are amortized on a straight-line basis over the estimated remaining life expectancy of the resident.

Family members may visit and stay in the apartments for a nightly charge, which varies depending on the length of stay. No pets of any kind are allowed, and residents are expected to observe common courtesies related to extracurricular activities. Residents may assume responsibility for the flower bed in front of their apartments, and recreational facilities are provided at no charge.

Property and equipment are stated at cost, and depreciation is computed using the straight-line method and the following estimated useful lives:

Land Improvements	20 years
Buildings	40 years
Equipment	5–10 years

Keystone is exempt from federal income tax pursuant to Section 501(a) of the Internal Revenue Code, and it maintains its accounting records according to GAAP.

Because of its successful operations, Keystone has over $1,000,000 in government and corporate securities. Of this amount, $800,000 was donated by a wealthy benefactor with the stipulation that it be used to provide services to needy people who could not otherwise afford the care. The principal of the gift may not be spent, but any earnings are available for the stated purpose.

Total gifts received by Keystone this period were $340,000. Of this amount, $125,000 was unrestricted and the rest was the result of a campaign to secure funds for new diagnostic equipment.

Annually, Keystone calculates the present value of estimated future services to current residents and compares that amount to the balance of deferred revenues from advance fees. If the present value of the costs exceeds the deferred revenue amount, a liability is recorded.

Keystone has $6,500,000 in long-term debt. Of that total, $5,800,000 is a 9½ percent mortgage payable. The remainder is an unsecured note payable at the local bank.

REQUIRED

1. Given the preceding information and based on information in this chapter, particularly the exhibit showing notes, draft the required disclosures for financial statement purposes. For some notes, insufficient information may have been provided to complete the note, in which case you should indicate what other information pertinent to that item should be disclosed. Assume that Keystone operates under *Statement No. 117.*

2. Considering the type of organization Keystone is, what significant items would require disclosure that were not mentioned in the information provided above?

14-5 Select the phrase that best answers the question.

1. Under *Statement No. 116* an unrestricted pledge from an annual contributor to a nonprofit health care provider made in December 19X1 and paid in cash in March 19X2 would generally be credited to:

   a. a gain in 19X1
   b. nonoperating revenue in 19X2
   c. operating revenue in 19X1
   d. operating revenue in 19X2

   (Adapted from the November 1982 CPA Exam, Theory, #60)

2. When can the provision for uncollectible accounts be included as an operating expense of a health care organization?

   a. when the account cannot be paid
   b. when the governing board authorizes the action
   c. when it is possible to accurately estimate the amount that will be uncollectible
   d. when the organization can distinguish between unwillingness and inability to pay

3. In applying lower of cost or market to security valuation of a health care provider, the term *aggregate* is applied to

   a. all investments of a given fund
   b. all investments of a given fund type
   c. all investments of the entity
   d. all investments of the entity and its related organizations

4. Prepaid health care fees should be

   a. allocated in a rational way to resident's expected life
   b. recognized as revenue when received

   c. recognized on a straight-line basis over a period not to exceed
     five years

   d. recognized as a prior-period adjustment when the resident dies

5. On May 1, 19X4, Lila Lee established a $50,000 endowment fund; the income is to be paid to Waller Clinic for general operating purposes. Waller is to invest the fund's principal in perpetuity. If Waller Clinic uses fund accounting for internal purposes, what journal entry is required on Waller's books?

	Debit	Credit
a. a memo entry only	—	—
b. Nonexpendable Endowment Fund	50,000	
Endowment Fund Balance		50,000
c. Cash	50,000	
Endowment Fund Balance		50,000
d. Cash	50,000	
Unrestricted Fund Balance		50,000

   (Adapted from the May 1984 CPA Exam, Practice II, #56)

6. Revenue from an educational program of a health maintenance organization (HMO) would be included in
   a. gains
   b. other revenue
   c. patient service revenue
   d. professional services revenue
   (Adapted from the May 1985 Exam, Theory, #60)

7. On July 2, 19X1, Lilydale Hospital's Board of Trustees designated $200,000 for expansion of outpatient facilities. The $200,000 is expected to be expended in the fiscal year ending June 30, 19X4. In Lilydale's balance sheet at June 30, 19X2, the equity related to the Casa would be classified as:
   a. permanently restricted net assets
   b. unrestricted net assets
   c. temporarily restricted net assets
   d. unrestricted or temporarily restricted net assets
   (Adapted from the May 1982 CPA Exam, Practice II, #40)

[handwritten margin note: internal restriction only]

8. When operating equipment is purchased with cash held in the plant replacement and expansion fund, the entry in the plant fund is
   a. debit equipment, credit cash
   b. debit transfers to unrestricted fund, credit cash
   c. debit fund balance, credit cash
   d. none of the above

9. Under *Statement No. 117* an asset may be reclassified from temporarily restricted to unrestricted when
   a. the conditions of the restriction are met
   b. the governing board decides it would be more appropriate
   c. the general fund borrows money from a restricted fund
   d. none of the above

10. An asset purchased with temporarily restricted funds
    a. is shown on the balance sheet as an asset whose use is limited
    b. is considered an increase in temporarily restricted net assets
    (c.) would normally cause a reclassification of the temporarily restricted amounts to the unrestricted net asset class
    d. none of the above

14-6   The Roily Community Hospital has just begun operations. It is interested in knowing what minimum average billed charges per day must be experienced in order to recover the total cost of care for 19X8. The following information was taken from the pro forma documents prepared by the hospital.

Operating Expenses:	
Payroll	$1,320,000
Supplies	880,000
Depreciation	110,000
Total	$2,310,000
Number of Charges (in days), by type:	
Charity Cases	660
Contractual Cases	1,320
Uncollectible Accounts	220
Full-Pay Patients	8,800
Total Patient Care Days	11,000
Projected Daily Collections, by type:	
Charity Cases	none
Contractual Cases	$264
Uncollectible Accounts	none
Full-Pay Patients	as billed

REQUIRED

1. Compute the minimum average billed charges per day to recover total costs of care for 19X8 (show your computations in schedule form).
2. Summarize the data from Item 1 and present them in the following form:

> Patient Service Revenue
> Deductions from Revenue
> Net Patient Service Revenue
> Less: Operating Expenses
> Excess of Revenues Over Expenses

(Adapted from the FHFMA Exam)

14-7

Hinsdale Nursing Home
Comparative Balance Sheets
As of December 31, 19X6 and 19X7

	19X6	19X7
Assets		
Cash	$ 195,000	$ 510,000
Receivables (net)	1,600,000	1,430,000
Pledges Receivable—Restricted	20,000	350,000
Inventories	175,000	180,000
Prepaid Expenses	60,000	70,000
Investments	7,300,000	6,360,000
		(continued)

(continued)	19X6	19X7
Property, Plant, and Equipment (net)	7,000,000	7,500,000
Other	1,300,000	1,600,000
TOTAL ASSETS	$17,650,000	$18,000,000

Liabilities and Net Assets

	19X6	19X7
Liabilities		
Accounts Payable	$ 540,000	$ 550,000
Accrued Expenses	150,000	145,000
Notes Payable	100,000	300,000
Advances from Third-Party Payers	390,000	430,000
Deferred Revenue	210,000	100,000
Long-Term Debt	1,700,000	1,800,000
Total Liabilities	$ 3,090,000	$ 3,325,000
Net Assets		
Unrestricted	7,178,000	7,485,000
Permanently Restricted	7,382,000	7,190,000
TOTAL LIABILITIES AND NET ASSETS	$17,650,000	$18,000,000

Hinsdale Nursing Home
Condensed Statement of Activity
For the Year Ending December 31, 19X7

Patient Service Revenue		$8,500,000
Less: Deductions		1,800,000
Operating Revenue		$6,700,000
Other Revenue		200,000
Gains		797,000
Total Revenue		$7,697,000
Operating Expenses:		
Provision for Depreciation	$ 300,000	
Other Patient Service Expenses	6,810,000	
Other Expenses	472,000	7,582,000
Total Change in Net Assets		$ 115,000

ADDITIONAL INFORMATION

1. Other assets include nondepreciable long-term assets whose use is limited by the governing board.
2. When the restricted investments were sold, the portion representing the gain was classified as unrestricted.
3. Restricted pledges outstanding at the first of the year were all collected. New pledges were made, but no cash has been collected. Fundraising is not considered central to this entity's operations.
4. The third-party payers include Medicare, Medicaid, and Blue Cross.
5. Hinsdale has no temporarily restricted net assets.

REQUIRED

Prepare a statement of cash flow for the Hinsdale Nursing Home. The statement should distinguish among operating, financing, and investing activities as required by *Statement No. 117.*

14-8 During 19X9, the following events and transactions were recorded by Dexter Hospital:

1. Gross charges for hospital services, charged to accounts and notes receivable, were:

Revenue from Nursing Services	$780,000
Revenue from Other Professional Services	351,000

2. Actual deductions from revenues were:

Discounts for Medical Staff	$30,000
Charity Services	15,000

3. The general funds paid $18,000 to retire mortgage bonds payable; the bonds had an equivalent face value.
4. Provision for bad debts was estimated at $30,000.
5. During the year, the general fund received unrestricted cash contributions of $50,000 and restricted income from endowment fund investments of $6,500.
6. New equipment costing $26,000 was acquired with donor-restricted cash. An x-ray machine with an original cost of $24,000 and an undepreciated cost of $2,400 was sold for $500 cash.
7. Vouchers totaling $1,191,000 were issued for the following items:

Fiscal and Administrative Services Expenses	$215,000
General Services Expenses	225,000
Nursing Services Expenses	520,000
Other Professional Services Expenses	165,000
Inventory	60,000
Expenses Accrued at December 31, 19X8	6,000

8. Collections of accounts receivable totaled $985,000. Accounts written off as uncollectible amounted to $11,000.
9. Cash payments on vouchers payable during the year were $825,000.
10. On December 31, 19X9, accrued interest income on plant replacement and expansion fund investments was $800.
11. Supplies of $37,000 were issued to nursing services.
12. Depreciation on buildings was $73,000 and on equipment, $44,000.
13. On December 31, 19X9, an accrual of $6,100 was made for interest on mortgage bonds payable.

REQUIRED

Prepare journal entries to reflect the transactions for Dexter Hospital for the year ending December 31, 19X9, assuming the use of fund accounting. Number your entries to correspond with the transaction number and indicate in which fund each transaction takes place.

(Adapted from the AICPA Exam)

14-9 The Happy Home Maintenance Organization was incorporated in 19X5 as a nonprofit corporation to provide comprehensive health care services on a prepaid basis and to establish and operate organized health care maintenance and health care delivery systems. The post-closing trial balance as of June 30, 19X8, appears below:

Happy Home Maintenance Organization
Post-Closing Trial Balance
June 30, 19X8

Cash	$	2,000
Temporary Cash Investments		2,900,000

(continued)

Premiums Receivable	360,000	
Other Receivables	265,000	
Inventories of Supplies	190,000	
Prepaid Expenses	195,000	
Property, Plant, and Equipment	7,600,000	
State Guaranty Fund Deposit	150,000	
Unamortized Debt Issuance Costs	18,000	
Accumulated Depreciation		$ 1,800,000
Unsecured 12% Note Payable		44,000
Current Installment of Long-Term Debt		110,000
Accounts Payable—Medical Services		2,250,000
Other Accounts Payable and Accrued Expenses		829,000
Unearned Premium Revenue		140,000
Long-Term Debt (excludes short-term portion)		4,300,000
Net Unrestricted Assets		2,207,000
	$11,680,000	$11,680,000

The following transactions or events occurred in 19X9:

1. Premiums received, including the receivable on June 30, 19X8, totaled $28,400,000. Another $250,000 of unearned premium income was received on June 30, 19X9.
2. Other earned revenues included reinsurance recoveries of $600,000 and coinsurance proceeds of $690,000. One-half of these amounts was received in cash. Interest income on temporary investments totaled $230,000, all of which was received during the year.
3. Interest income of $40,000 was accrued at year end.
4. The following expenses were paid:

Wages and Salaries	$14,000,000
Supplies	1,800,000
Contracted Services	5,400,000
Interest	530,000
Insurance	1,000,000
Equipment Rental	300,000
Laboratory Services	3,100,000

These expenses are allocated to functional areas as follows: 32 percent to health centers—medical services; 32 percent to hospitalization; 8 percent to other outside services; 8 percent to health centers—administration; 15 percent to administration; and 5 percent to membership services.

Accounts payable of $2,250,000 and other payables of $829,000 were paid during the year.

5. Depreciation totaled $370,000.
6. The current installment of long-term debt was paid, and an equal amount reclassified from long-term to short-term liabilities.
7. At year end 19X9, other accounts payable were $500,000 and accrued expenses totaled $160,000; of that amount $530,000 pertained to contracted services, $60,000 to supplies, and $70,000 to interest on short-term debt. These items all related to health centers—medical.
8. Supplies inventory at year end was $185,000; supplies consumed pertained to health centers—medical.
9. Malpractice claims have been asserted against Happy Home by various claimants. The claims are in various stages of processing, and some may be brought to trial. In the opinion of legal counsel, the

outcome of these actions will not have a significant effect on the financial position or the results of operation of Happy Home. Other claims may be asserted, but management believes that these claims, if asserted, would be settled within the limits of insurance coverage.

10. Prepaid expenses totaled $100,000 at year end. The decline pertained to the unassigned portion of insurance costs.
11. Unamortized debt issuance costs of $1,000 were amortized to administration.

REQUIRED

Prepare a worksheet, beginning with the 19X8 post-closing trial balance, and record the transactions, including any adjustments, for the year. Then complete the worksheet presentation for an income statement and a balance sheet. Happy Home has no temporarily or permanently restricted assets.

Formal journal entries are not necessary, but your working papers should provide detailed documentation for all calculations.

14-10 The Rocky Point Hospital pooled its investments to obtain the best possible return. Money from two of Rocky's endowment funds was deposited on July 1, 19X7, in the following amounts:

Educational Endowment	$1,100,000
Operating Expense Endowment	500,000

Transactions occurring during the 19X7–19X8 fiscal year included the following:

1. On September 30, 19X7, investment earnings of $36,000 were distributed to the two funds.
2. On October 1, 19X7, the plant replacement and expansion fund added $800,000 not needed for current construction to the pooled investment account. On that date and before the addition, the market value of the fund was $1,620,000.
3. Investment earnings of $71,000 were distributed to the funds on December 31, 19X7.
4. On March 30, 19X8, the plant replacement and expansion fund withdrew $600,000 from the fund; this transaction occurred after interest earnings of $71,000 had been distributed to the three funds. The market value at the date of withdrawal was $2,400,000.
5. On June 30, 19X8, investment earnings of $50,000 were distributed to the three funds.

REQUIRED

1. Prepare journal entries to record the above transactions in the endowment and plant replacement and expansion funds (round pool shares to the nearest whole percent).
2. Prepare a schedule showing the lower-of-cost-or-market valuation for the three funds on June 30, 19X8. The market value of the pooled investments on that date was $1,810,000.

CHAPTER 15

Colleges and Universities: Their Accounting and Reporting Practices

In the broad sense, "higher education" refers to all educational organizations beyond high school. There are approximately 4,000 such organizations. They can be divided into two main categories—proprietary and nonprofit. Proprietary schools include trade schools, secretarial schools, and the like. They are for-profit organizations, and their accounting is the same as that for business. Nonprofit schools include independent schools and colleges and universities. Independent schools do not grant degrees; they are often called preparatory schools.

The second category of nonprofit institutions—colleges and universities—provide most of the postsecondary education for the U.S. population and for numerous people from other countries. The nation's colleges and universities also conduct a large portion of the research funded by the federal government. The scope of some colleges and universities is confined to liberal arts. Others offer programs in professional endeavors such as medicine, law, and business in addition to the liberal arts.

Colleges and universities grant degrees, ranging from the two-year Associate of Arts degree to the PhD and various professional degrees. Some are public; that is, they are owned by states or municipalities. Others are independently owned, and managed by independent boards of trustees.

Standards for public institutions are set by the Governmental Accounting Standards Board (GASB). The GASB has issued very few standards for colleges and universities, and even then it allows, as an option, the accounting treatment contained in the AICPA *Audit Guide*. The Financial Accounting Standards Board (FASB) establishes standards for private nonprofit colleges and universities. As pointed out in the Introduction to Nonprofit Section, only three standards have direct applicability to colleges and universities: the statements on depreciation, contributions, and financial statements. Consequently, these institutions also rely heavily on the AICPA's audit guide for colleges and universities.

Annually, the United States spends over $100 billion on higher education. A large portion of that is spent by the nation's colleges and universities. Revenue sources include student fees and tuition, state, local, and federal funding, and philanthropic contributions. Since the early 1900s an organization now called the National Association of College and University Business Officers (NACUBO) has been assisting college and university administrators in accounting and reporting for educational activities. Through its paid staff and volunteers from colleges and universities, NACUBO has published and updated accounting and reporting manuals that have greatly influenced college and university accounting and reporting practices, including the guidance contained in the *Audit Guide.*

This chapter identifies the different types of colleges and universities and describes the nature of their operations, performance criteria, and acceptable accounting and reporting practices. Selected financial transactions and the resulting statements are illustrated.

NATURE AND OPERATIONS OF COLLEGES AND UNIVERSITIES

Colleges and universities are classified according to funding sources. **Proprietary** institutions are like any other business. Stockholders invest in the endeavor in order to earn a return. Students pay tuition and fees that cover the cost of providing the education and also provide a return on investment to the stockholders. These institutions, such as business colleges, architectural design centers, and computer technology training centers, provide specialized training needs.

Private independent nonprofit institutions historically were funded by religious orders or by philanthropic benefactors. They vary in size from small liberal arts colleges with a few hundred students to universities with thousands.

Public colleges and universities comprise the bulk of the institutions, accounting for about 75 percent of total postsecondary enrollment. Within the ranks of public institutions are state colleges and universities. Other than tuition and fees, resources for state institutions come in large part from state legislatures, while community colleges are funded by both state and local tax dollars. Tribal colleges are funded by the federal government and by the Native American tribe establishing the college.

Organizational Structure and Oversight Responsibility

Most colleges and universities have an organizational structure patterned after private business. The chief executive officer is referred to as the *president* or *provost.* A number of vice presidents report to the president. Usually, there is a chief academic officer and a chief financial officer. Other vice presidential positions include student services, public relations, and planning. The size and complexity of the institution usually determine how many positions are included in the organizational structure. Below the vice presidential positions are deans and directors who are responsible for particular functions or groupings of academic programs. These would be equivalent to division heads in business. The next level, similar to plant managers, are the department chairs who are responsible for individual academic programs.

In a private institution, the president reports to a Board of Trustees. Public institution presidents typically report to a Board of Regents or a coordinating commission. Regardless of the exact title, the functions of the oversight board are the same as those in industry: to establish overall policy, to select key administrators, and to exercise oversight. Public education has become so complex in recent years that most boards or coordinating commissions have paid staff, some of which are very large and resemble a governmental department. The staff spend considerable time measuring institutional performance and persuading legislatures to increase or maintain funding for their schools.

Sources and Uses of Funds

Public institutions obtain resources from four major areas: state legislatures; tuition and fees; federal, state, and local contracts or grants; and private donations. With the exception of legislative appropriations, the same funding sources are used by private institutions. For most public institutions, the largest single source of funds is the legislative appropriation.

Colleges and universities classify resource outflows according to **function.** The major function is, of course, education. The educational and general function includes the subcategories of instruction, research, and public service, and various activities necessary to support these functions (see Exhibit 15-1). Support activities range from student services to plant operation and maintenance. Other major functions include auxiliary services—the largely self-supporting activities, such as dormitories, food service, health service, and other student activities—hospitals, and independent operations.

Classifying outflows by function is useful for comparative purposes, but this classification system is too broad for managerial uses. An administrator wants to know how much the botany, business, or biology program costs rather than the total instruction costs for all programs. Much of the internal management data are reported by program, which may cut across functional lines. Within the program areas, expenditures are classified by **natural class:** salaries and wages, supplies, rent, insurance, and so on, regardless of function.

Sometimes colleges and universities classify resource outflows by **organizational unit.** With this classification scheme, academic and support programs are grouped under the responsible administrator. For example, the accounting, finance, marketing, economics, and management programs could be grouped within an organizational unit referred to as the school of business administration. Similarly, a number of programs providing a liberal arts focus may be located within a college of arts and sciences.

Measuring Performance

Public colleges and universities lack a profit motive. Their purpose is to provide the best possible education with the available resources. Educators and the public have been trying to define and measure "the best possible education" for centuries. Almost everyone has a general sense of what it means to be educated—literate, knowledgeable about human relations and the universe, able to perform duties requiring application of general knowledge. However, opinions about education do not help much in evaluating the comparative or absolute performance of a college or university program.

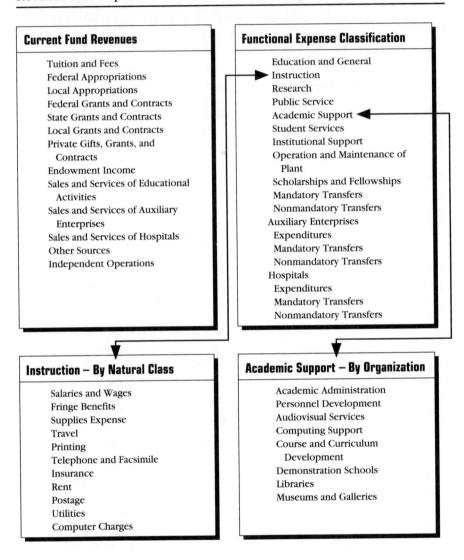

Exhibit 15-1

Revenue and Expense Classifications for Colleges and Universities

Unable to define and measure specific attributes of "being educated," educators settle for certain output indicators, such as employment opportunities or pay scales available to graduates. In some fields, national exams reveal the relative positions of college or university graduates. Some institutions even follow up on their graduates to determine how many achieve prominent positions, such as corporate presidencies or high-ranking political or civil jobs. In other words, postgraduate achievements are used as indicators of the quality of the education.

Research capabilities and accreditation standings also add to an institution's credibility. Research provides practical experiences for students and, therefore, adds to the students' marketability and to institutions' ability to attract additional resources. Achieving full accreditation means an institution has met certain minimal educational standards.

As the public outlays for higher education increase, in some cases at alarming rates, taxpayers are becoming increasingly preoccupied with evaluating the quality of higher education. Associations responsible for accrediting public and private institutions are trying to develop assessment methodologies and outcomes measures. Although aimed at a specific type of nonprofit, these efforts to measure quality are similar to the services efforts and accomplishments reporting project of the GASB.

Funding Issues In the eyes of many legislators and contributors, educational institutions never seem to have sufficient funding. Part of the reason educators always seem to be asking for additional resources traces to the difficulty of establishing funding priorities. Educators have a general belief that quality education involves both depth and breadth of academic programs. Students need a strong liberal arts background to function as literate adults. They also need in-depth training in a specific discipline that will facilitate their employment. Educators cannot determine which programs contribute most to the bottom line and put emphasis in those areas. Even if demand is strong for engineers, as an example, a good engineer needs a broad liberal arts background. An educator would, therefore, argue for both programs, not one or the other. Legislators and other resource providers, most of whom come from a business environment, are understandably frustrated by this seeming unwillingness to establish clear funding priorities.

The same struggle occurs within an institution. Deans and department chairs constantly argue that quality education in their discipline costs more than administrators are willing or able to allocate. In comprehensive institutions the arguments often become the most heated between professional programs (law, medicine, business, pharmacy, and so on) and the more traditional liberal arts programs. Because measures of quality are inadequate, the arguments become largely rhetorical.

Determining Funding Levels With only a general notion of what it means to be educated, legislators and contributors have difficulty assessing how much funding is needed to achieve or maintain certain standards of excellence. Legislatures try to finance some *acceptable* norm within funding constraints. Acceptable norms are sometimes determined by analyzing comparable institutions. Statistical analyses are made of institutions grouped by size, geographic location, and scope of program. A particular grouping of these institutions will be analyzed to see what it costs, on a per-student or per-credit-hour basis, to educate students. The average is used as a norm and then adjusted to fit the specific character of an institution. If an institution has a medical program, for example, either the grouping will be expanded to include medical schools or the statistics adjusted to reflect the high cost of medical education.

Tradition and physical characteristics also affect an institution's nature and its average costs. For example, a campus located on 200 acres will not cost the same to maintain as one located on three square city blocks. An emphasis on intercollegiate athletics serves as an example of tradition. The budget for intercollegiate athletics is much larger at a Big Ten than at a Pacific Conference school.

Implications for Accounting and Reporting   Unable to measure performance according to generally accepted criteria, educators and resource providers spend a lot of time measuring details. To compare the cost of an academic program in two similar institutions requires detailed cost records and general agreement on what costs should be accounted for in which programs. For example, comparing the business programs in two different institutions requires an understanding of which academic programs are encompassed in the term *business*. It also requires knowledge of whether certain costs, such as plant maintenance or academic support, are allocated to academic programs. Because graduate education is more costly than undergraduate, the reviewer also needs to know if the institutions being compared have both graduate and undergraduate programs.

To facilitate these comparisons, published reports must reflect the administrative and academic peculiarities of the institution. For example, detailed reporting of revenues is necessary to enable users to analyze the funding status of an institution. Only by knowing the proportion of total revenue derived from tuition and fees can comparisons of tuition levels be analyzed. A legislative user needs to know how much of the total research budget is funded by outside agencies and how much by general appropriations. Similarly, the proportion of total expenditures supported by unrestricted gifts and grants tells contributors how their institution fares compared to others in the state, region, or nation.

Uniform accounting is critical for valid comparative analyses. States can pass legislation mandating comparability of financial reports among all institutions in the state. However, comparisons are frequently made among institutions in several states. Therefore, educators have had to agree on certain accounting and reporting practices that enhance comparability. Uniformity has been achieved largely by agreements among fiscal administrators through the National Association of College and University Business Officers.

STANDARD-SETTING PROCESS

Ever since NACUBO published its first manual on preferred accounting practices, this organization has had a significant influence on college and university accounting and reporting practices. Through volunteers and an effective committee structure, NACUBO has continued to update and revise manuals that explain and depict accounting practices appropriate for colleges and universities. The manuals have influenced both practice and teaching related to college and university accounting.

The 1982 revision of *College and University Business Administration*[1] (CUBA), kept current by a loose-leaf service, carries the endorsement of the AICPA. *Audits of Colleges and Universities*[2] recognized CUBA as an authoritative source of generally accepted accounting principles in 1975.

The American Council on Education (ACE) has also influenced the direction of college and university accounting. ACE not only supported NACUBO's work on several occasions, but also published a series of studies and helpful interpretations concerning preferred accounting practices.

FASB Influence

A 1978 pronouncement stated that the FASB was assuming responsibility for standard setting for nonprofits, including nonprofit colleges and universities. The FASB did little immediately to address the major accounting issues of colleges and universities. Its *Statement No. 32*, effective in 1979, established that the *Audit Guide* reflected preferable accounting principles for purposes of justifying a change in acounting practice. None of the three statements issued since then officially retract *Statement No. 32* guidance. However, anything in the *Audit Guide* that conflicts with standards contained in the three FASB pronouncements will not constitute GAAP. The AICPA is working on a new audit guide for all nonprofits; no doubt it will reflect the new FASB standards for nonprofit colleges and universities. Because of the broad latitude permitted in *Statement No. 117*, an institution could ignore reporting practices described in the new guide and still receive an unqualified opinion.

GASB Jurisdiction

Colleges and universities are among those nonprofits affected by the jurisdictional squabble between the Financial Accounting Standards Board and the Governmental Accounting Standards Board. Governmentally operated colleges and universities fall within the GASB's purview. The accounting practices for private and all other colleges and universities are determined by the FASB. If the two organizations issue different accounting guidelines, users will not be able to compare financial statements among types of colleges and universities.

The issue of depreciation illustrates the problem. The FASB issued *Statement No. 93* requiring depreciation of almost all fixed assets; the GASB followed with a statement that governmentally operated colleges and universities should not change their accounting practices, which did not include depreciation. After 1990, financial statements for private and nonprofit colleges and universities were no longer comparable to those of public colleges and universities.

[1]Lanora F. Weizenbach, ed. *College and University Business Administration*, 4th ed. (Washington: NACUBO, 1982), 390, referred to in this chapter as the *NACUBO Manual.*

[2]Committee on College and University Accounting and Auditing, *Audits of Colleges and Universities* (New York: AICPA, 1975), 7, referred to in this chapter as the *Audit Guide.*

With the exception of depreciation, the GASB has avoided most significant comparability issues by indicating that colleges and universities may use the "AICPA model." GASB *Statement No. 15* allows public institutions of higher education to use one of two different reporting models: the one used by general-purpose local governments (and discussed in Chapters 1 through 13) or the one implicit in the AICPA's 1975 edition of the college and university audit guide. When the GASB issues a standard for local governments that does not appear to fit colleges and universities, it includes as part of the standard permission for governmentally owned colleges and universities to use the *Audit Guide* model instead of adopting the new standard.

What worked in the past to avoid conflicting standards for the same class of nonprofits will apparently not work in the future. Presumably the FASB standards will be used as a basis for the new nonprofit audit guide, effectively changing the very essence of the "AICPA model" option. The GASB will have to decide whether it will adopt FASB standards for governmentally owned colleges or universities or issue its own standards for these entities.

▲   **OBSERVATION**

The GASB would always have the option of saying that the "AICPA model" was no longer acceptable accounting practice and all standards pertaining to general-purpose governmental entities were applicable to colleges and universities. Most governmentally owned colleges and universities would be as unhappy with that pronouncement as they are with the FASB standards. The GASB also could ask the AICPA to include governmental colleges and universities within the scope of the proposed audit guide. Although the outcome is uncertain, the GASB actions to date suggest that it is wedded to the notion of fund accounting. A third option would be to allow colleges and universities to be treated like an enterprise fund and indicate which FASB standards would be applicable to enterprise fund accounting.

GENERAL ACCOUNTING PRACTICES

Two operating characteristics govern most accounting practices of colleges and universities. Providing a service rather than earning a profit is one important operating characteristic. Assessing whether the resources were used effectively in providing the service is a major concern to colleges and universities. The National Association of College and University Business Officers and the American Institute of CPAs agree that effectiveness is best measured by using the accrual basis of accounting. Nonetheless, colleges and universities apply some unique accounting practices that fit their particular accounting and reporting needs.

The other operating characteristic that has greatly affected college and university accounting is the diversity of operating funds. To properly account for many different sources of funds, the principles and practices of fund accounting are generally used for internal accounting and for external reporting purposes. Thus, a major issue since the issuance of the FASB standard on reporting, at least for nongovernmentally owned colleges and universities, is whether to abandon fund accounting or to continue it for internal accounting purposes and prepare some type of reconciliation statement to achieve the reporting requirement related to net asset class. Deciding which avenue to pursue is necessary because, just as was the case for health care entities, the funds used by colleges and universities cannot be conveniently "rolled up" to equate to the three types of net assets. Both because the FASB's standards apply only to the nongovernmental institutions of higher education and because the GASB has not shown any inclination toward adopting the FASB standards for governmentally owned colleges and universities, this author sees no clear pattern emerging. Fund accounting probably will continue to be an integral part of governmentally owned college and university accounting practices. On the other hand, large nonprofit institutions may well abandon fund accounting and try to accommodate the FASB standards within a general context of a separation between operational activities and endowment activities. Accordingly, this chapter discusses both fund accounting and possible display options for reporting by the three net asset classes. A discussion of both is necessary not only because of the uncertainty of future developments, but also because it is difficult to understand the dilemmas posed by the FASB standards without first seeing how colleges and universities have been reporting.

OBSERVATION ▲

An understanding of accounting by fund and net asset class is further necessitated by the fact that the GASB thinks it will be some time—maybe not until the year 2000—before it fully addresses college and university accounting and reporting practices. In the meantime, public institutions may be using the 1975 version of the *Audit Guide* for guidance.

Fund Accounting

As is true for governments, colleges and universities have **fund groupings.** College or university fund groups are of two broad types: current funds and noncurrent funds. **Current funds,** the operating funds, are in turn broken down into restricted and unrestricted funds. The **noncurrent fund** grouping includes loan funds, endowment and similar funds, annuity and life income funds, plant funds, and agency funds. Exhibit 15-2 summarizes the fund groups.

Current Funds Current funds can be either unrestricted or restricted. The unrestricted fund is used to account for general resources of the institution. Any resource that is not restricted for some specific purpose—general legislative appropriations, unrestricted gifts and bequests, and fees and tuition—is accounted for in the current unrestricted fund. Funds designated by an oversight board for specific purposes are reported in an unrestricted fund. Funds designated by the board one day may be undesignated the next; therefore, by definition they are unrestricted. All expenses related to general operations of the institution would be recorded in the current unrestricted fund.

Exhibit 15-2

Summary of Fund Groups
Colleges and Universities

Current Funds

[handwritten: × quasi endowments]

Current Unrestricted Fund: all funds available for any lawful operating purpose.

Current Restricted Fund: funds available for specific operating purposes. Purpose is defined by external donor or grantor.

Noncurrent Funds

Endowment and Similar Funds: funds whose principal remains inviolate are available for producing income that is to be spent for unrestricted or restricted purposes. Term endowments represent alternatives to the regular endowment. Quasi-endowments, those established by the oversight board or management, are classified in the current unrestricted area.

Annuity and Life Income Funds: annuity funds are used to pay stipulated amounts periodically in exchange for assets. Life income funds account for remainder trusts; after income from assets is paid to the beneficiary for life, the institution receives the remaining assets.

Agency Funds: funds held in custody on behalf of groups related to the institution, such as student organizations.

[handwritten: 5]

Plant Funds:
1. *Unexpended Plant Funds* account for resources used to finance the acquisition or construction of long-lived plant assets and associated liabilities.
2. *Renewal and Replacement Funds* account for resources used to finance renewals and replacements rather than additions and improvements of long-lived assets and associated liabilities. Usually renewals and replacements are not capitalized.
3. *Retirement of Indebtedness Funds* are used to accumulate resources for interest and principal payments related to plant fund indebtedness.
4. *Net Investment in Plant Funds* contain all long-lived assets used by the institution and the associated liabilities. Construction in progress may be carried here or in the unexpended plant fund.

Loan Funds: money provided by donors to be held for the purpose of making loans to students, faculty, or staff.

Current restricted funds are established for those resources that can be spent on general operations but which are restricted for specific purposes, such as research and public service activities, by *external* providers. For example, the legislature may appropriate a specific amount for scholarships, library books, or a particular public service project. Also, federal or state agency contracts or grants to conduct research activities are accounted for in restricted funds, as are restricted gifts from donors.

Sometimes laws or trustee policies require public colleges and universities to maintain separate accounting for auxiliary enterprises. Auxiliary enterprises include all those activities, such as residence halls, food services, and health services, whose physical facilities typically are financed by bonds and whose debt servicing is paid by student fees rather than by state appropriations or general operating funds. In order to satisfy bond indenture requirements and trustee policy or state law, such facilities and the related services must be accounted for separately and revenues must equal or exceed expenditures (including reserves to maintain the facilities). Such activities, therefore, are *self-supporting*. This becomes a difficult management as well as accounting issue. For example, if an activity funded by general appropriations occupies auxiliary space, the activity must be charged rent. The reverse is also true. Sometimes managers have split responsibilities: some cover auxil-

[handwritten margin notes: Auxiliary enterprises / Self-supporting from student fees]

iary activities and some cover state-appropriated activities. The associated salaries and wages would have to be allocated to the respective activities.

Noncurrent Funds The noncurrent fund group encompasses all fund types the resources of which cannot be used for day-to-day operations.

Loan Funds. These funds are established to account for resources available for student, faculty, and staff loans. Some grantors may establish permanent loan funds that are operated on a revolving basis, in which case the interest earned on the loan is added to the corpus (principal amount) or used to pay administrative expenses. In other cases, the loan may be established temporarily; the principal and interest (usually after administrative expenses) are returned to the grantor after a specified period of time.

Endowment Funds. Like similar funds for other nonprofits, endowments may be permanent or term. Donors or other external parties stipulate the purpose and term of the endowment. Endowments typically are established to fund scholarships, loans, or specific academic programs. Under a **permanent endowment,** the principal remains inviolate forever. The income received from the endowed assets may be restricted or unrestricted and is accounted for accordingly.

If a donor establishes a **term endowment,** the principal must be maintained during the term of the endowment. After the term expires, the principal may be spent. Income received from assets held under a term endowment may be restricted or unrestricted, as in the case of a permanent endowment.

Quasi-endowment funds are established by oversight boards for the same purposes as other endowments. The only difference is the money has been set aside by the board, so the principal may be used at any time for other purposes. Such endowments therefore should be reported in the current unrestricted area.

Annuity and Life Income Funds. Occasionally, donors who want to provide money to colleges and universities after some other purpose has been served use annuity or life income contracts. Under an **annuity** contract, an institution is obligated to pay stipulated amounts periodically to the donor's beneficiary. When the agreement terminates, any remaining funds become the property of the institution.

A **life income fund** is established when a college or university is the trustee and remainderman for a charitable remainder trust. The trust document specifies that the income, less expenses, is paid to the beneficiary for life. The principal becomes the property of the institution when the beneficiary dies. If neither annuity nor life income funds are material, they typically are combined for reporting purposes.

Plant Funds. Unlike most other nonprofits, colleges and universities have four separate plant funds. They account for money being held for acquisition separately from the completed fixed assets. Two funds are used to account for the construction, acquisition, or remodeling of capital facilities. A third fund is used to retire the related debt, and a fourth for accounting for the net investment in plant and the related debt.

Colleges and universities' use of several plant funds traces to the need to segregate financing sources. For example, construction could be financed by external agencies, student assessments, transfers from unrestricted funds, earnings from endowments, or loans. Putting the various construction proceeds in the same fund with completed assets might confuse readers. Thus, construction activity is segregated into a fund resembling the capital projects fund in a governmental entity. Also, readers of financial statements find it useful to see how much money is being set aside for new construction or purchases as distinguished from money allocated for major repairs. Therefore, replacements and renovations are accounted for in a separate fund.

The **unexpended plant fund** is used to account for resources held to finance the acquisition or construction of long-lived assets. It is called "unexpended" because once the resources have been spent or the facility constructed, the asset is accounted for in another fund. This fund also accounts for any related liabilities during the construction or acquisition period. For example, if the legislature provided $1,000,000 to complete a wing on a building, the money would be placed in the unexpended plant fund. The construction activity also could be accounted for in this fund.

Money set aside for asset replacement or refurbishing is placed in the **fund for renewals and replacements.** Ordinarily, only those replacements or repairs that are not capitalized would be accounted for in this fund. However, the distinction between renewals and replacements and improvements (accounted for in the unexpended plant fund) is not always clear. Sometimes renewals and replacements may be capitalized.

The **investment in plant fund** is used to account for completed capital construction or acquired assets. Unlike the treatment in governmental entities, the related liabilities are accounted for in the same fund. For example, if a building is purchased for $800,000 with a mortgage of $300,000 and the remainder in cash, the $300,000 mortgage and the $800,000 asset would both be reported in the investment in plant fund. If construction activity is not reported in the unexpended plant fund, it would be accounted for in the net investment in plant fund.

Similar to the debt service fund in governmental units, the **fund for the retirement of indebtedness** includes the accumulated resources for interest and principal payments and other debt service charges relating to plant indebtedness. Typically, money for principal and interest payments is transferred from the current unrestricted fund group to the fund for the retirement of indebtedness. However, direct charges to students for debt repayment may be deposited directly into this fund.

Agency Funds. Colleges and universities may hold assets as a fiscal agent or as a custodian. Such funds are reported in agency funds unless they are immaterial, in which case they are reported as part of the current unrestricted fund group. Student and faculty organizations frequently have the institution maintain their accounting records, hold deposits, and make disbursements on their behalf. Just as in governmental entities, agency funds do not have a fund balance.

Accrual Accounting

Colleges and universities use the accrual basis of accounting. Revenues are recognized when earned and expenditures when the materials or services are used. This means that unearned revenues are deferred, and all expenses incurred at the balance sheet date are accrued. It also means that tuition revenues are reported in total; tuition fee waivers or scholarships and bad debts are expenditures. Only refunds of tuition or other fees are debited to the revenue account.

OBSERVATION ▲

Colleges and universities do not use accrual accounting terminology consistently. Outflows are described as expenditures, not expenses. However, prepaids are reported as "prepaid expenses." No explanation is provided in either the *Audit Guide* or the *NACUBO Manual*.

Some colleges and universities also use encumbrance accounting. However, any outstanding encumbrances for materials or services not received as of the reporting date should not be reported as expenditures or included in liabilities on the balance sheet. If the encumbrances are material, a reservation of fund balance is required.

Special Accounting Conventions

Like most other nonprofit organizations using accrual accounting, colleges and universities use certain accounting practices that cannot be described strictly as accrual accounting. For example, some colleges and universities enter the budgetary accounts into the general ledger; some also report comparisons between budget and actual in their financial statements. Other important college and university accounting conventions are described in the following sections.

Revenue and Expenditure Recognition   Revenues and expenditures are recognized only in the current funds. Any earnings or expenditures from an endowment, loan, or other noncurrent fund are credited or debited directly to fund balance. As in governmental entities, capital expenditures made from the current fund group are reported as such. An entry is made simultaneously in the investment in plant fund to capitalize the asset.

Valuing and Recording Fixed Assets   Fixed assets are reported at cost unless received as a gift, in which case they are reported at the fair market value on the date of the gift. If the asset is constructed, a construction in progress account is debited for all expenditures until the asset is completed, at which time it is capitalized in the net investment in plant fund. Any related debt is transferred to the net investment in plant account at the same time. For example, if construction expenditures totaled $1,000,000 and were financed by issuing bonds in the same amount, the unexpended plant fund would record the receipt of the bond proceeds and the construction:

Cash	1,000,000	
Bonds Payable		1,000,000
Construction in Progress	1,000,000	
Cash		1,000,000

When the asset is transferred to the net investment in plant fund, the following entries would be made in the unexpended plant fund and the net investment in plant fund:

Unexpended Plant Fund:

Bonds Payable	1,000,000	
Construction in Progress		1,000,000

Net Investment in Plant Fund:

Building	1,000,000	
Bonds Payable		1,000,000

The fund balance would be debited or credited for any difference between the amount of debt and the cost of the project.

When fixed assets are sold, the carrying value (cost less accumulated depreciation if accumulated depreciation is recorded) is removed from the accounts, and the net investment in plant reduced accordingly. For example, if an asset costing $200,000 with accumulated depreciation of $160,000 were sold, the entry in the net investment in plant fund would be:

Net Investment in Plant	40,000	
Accumulated Depreciation	160,000	
Fixed Asset		200,000

[handwritten annotation: No gain or loss reported on sale of asset.]

The proceeds from the sale typically are used to reduce any debt associated with the asset or added to the unexpended fund balance. Thus, no gain or loss is reported on the sale of the asset.

Depreciation of Fixed Assets   Colleges and universities under the FASB's jurisdiction are required to depreciate all fixed assets, even though these organizations have long opposed this convention. Neither the 1975 *Audit Guide* nor the 1988 update of the *NACUBO Manual* required colleges and universities to report depreciation expense in their operating statements. Considerable justification is provided for this departure from accrual basis accounting practices. For example, earlier additions of the *NACUBO Manual* noted:

> Unlike businesses, colleges and universities are not faced with the same requirements of profit and loss determination. . . . They do not pay taxes based on income; their fixed assets are not directly related to their general credit and debt-incurring capacity. . . . Any recording of depreciation on capital assets in the current operating accounts would not only fail to serve any essential informational purpose in the financial statements and reports, but could actually be misleading to users of such statements and reports.[3]

The GASB allows colleges and universities to follow the 1975 edition of the *Audit Guide;* therefore, depreciation is not required for governmentally owned colleges and universities. This represents the first significant diver-

[3] Weizenbach, *NACUBO Manual,* 391.

gence in accounting standards between the two types of colleges and universities. It also means that when the new audit guide is issued reflecting current FASB standards, the GASB will have to issue some kind of statement. The statement will indicate whether it is still acceptable for governmentally owned colleges and universities to use the "AICPA model" of accounting and financial reporting, or whether they should continue to use the guidance in the "old" audit guide, a more likely possibility.

OBSERVATION ▲

With such strong admonitions concerning depreciation, colleges and universities were naturally disturbed when the FASB issued its pronouncement requiring depreciation on all fixed assets. Some colleges and universities opted to receive a qualified audit opinion rather than conform to FASB *Statement No. 93*.

Although not reported in the financial statements for governmentally owned institutions, depreciation may be calculated and used for managerial purposes. Sometimes academic and service departments are charged for centralized services, such as computer processing. Full costing, including depreciation, may provide an appropriate transfer price basis. Also, auxiliary enterprises may include depreciation expense as a basis for determining unit costs. Just as for governmental entities, these colleges and universities are not precluded from showing accumulated depreciation in the plant funds.

Fixed assets held by endowment funds are depreciated. Depreciation is one of the expenses deducted from revenues in determining the net income to be allocated to the uses specified by the donor.

Gains and Losses on Endowed Assets   Historically, colleges and universities treated gains and losses on endowment funds as adjustments to the principal. This view was based on the legal precedent that colleges and universities are not the absolute owners, merely the managers, of the gifts and bequests placed in the endowment. Beginning about 1969, considerable support has been generated for a sharply contrasting view of endowments. Those embracing the new philosophy argue that colleges and universities are the absolute owners of the endowed assets and, therefore, the allocation of investment gains and losses to principal or income is an administrative decision. This view is based on a corporate law rather than a trust law concept.

Following the corporate law concept, many colleges and universities have adopted some version of the **total return concept.** Under this approach, total investment return, including traditional yield plus or minus gains and losses, is emphasized. The basic rationale for using a total return approach is that interest is a good measure of the return on debt securities, but dividends are not a good measure of the return on equity securities. Investment managers invest in equities primarily to get appreciation in market value. Thus, the total return on equities also includes the change in market value.

Several variations of the total return concept are used. A common one is to allocate enough of the gains or losses to the principal to maintain the purchasing power of the endowment. The remainder is allocated to income. If the total endowment was $100,000, the inflation rate was 5 percent, and the total return (appreciation plus dividends and interest) $12,500, $5,000 would be added to the principal. The remaining $7,500 would be classified as income and transferred to a restricted or unrestricted fund to be spent.

Another common approach is to estimate the average yield expected on the portfolio. The average yield is allocated to income and any remaining net gains or losses are allocated to the principal. Using the same endowment of $100,000, if the governing board thought the assets would consistently yield $11,000, this amount would be transferred from the endowment to the current restricted or unrestricted fund to be spent as income. Any remaining earnings—in this case $1,500—would be added to the principal.

Neither the *Audit Guide* nor the *NACUBO Manual* prescribe specific treatment of endowment yields. The *Audit Guide* mentions, however, that the method used should be objectively determined and consistently applied. The *NACUBO Manual* notes that until a general practice has evolved, any appreciation used as income should be reported separately from the traditional income of endowments. Thus, a careful review of an institution's policies is in order before accountants can assess whether the accounting entries have been made correctly.

A specific accounting treatment pertaining to investment gains and losses is implicit in FASB's *Statement No. 117* on financial statements. The sample financial statements show *all* gains and losses as unrestricted income unless specifically restricted by the donor or state law. Thus, the portion of the total return added to the endowment in order to maintain its purchasing power would be shown as income in the unrestricted net asset class, and reclassified to the permanently restricted class.

OBSERVATION

The FASB standard on financial statements was not meant to be a recognition and measurement document. However, because one of the statements shows "operating results," implicit in the display guidelines are recognition and measurement directives related to the operating elements.

Revenue Recognition in Restricted Funds   Under accrual accounting, revenues are recognized when earned. In accounting for restricted funds, when is the earnings process complete? As with some other nonprofits, colleges and universities have determined that restricted fund revenues are earned when the related expenditures are made.

Under acceptable accounting practices for governmentally owned colleges and universities, and consistent with the total return concept explained in the preceding section, any capital gains or losses used for operating purposes (whether restricted or unrestricted) would be reported as transfers rather than as revenues. In other words, any revenues reported in restricted funds from an endowment would include only dividends and interest. For example, if $1,500 representing portfolio gains in the endowment were being spent currently in a restricted fund, the entries would be:

Endowment:

Fund Balance	1,500	
Cash		1,500

Restricted Fund:

Cash	1,500	
Transfer from Endowment		1,500

(gain)

Calling it a transfer instead of revenue enables the accountant to segregate dividends and interest from capital gains and losses.

Under the FASB standard, colleges and universities could use the same accounting as described above for internal reporting purposes. However, for external reporting, the revenue would be reported as an increase to the unrestricted net asset class unless temporarily or permanently restricted by the donor. The expenditure also would be reported as unrestricted because the standard says that all expenditures will be shown in the unrestricted class on the activity statement.

No 117?
all expend
all unrestricted

Transfers Among Funds   Colleges and universities classify transfers among funds as either mandatory or nonmandatory. Whenever a college or university has no choice about whether the transfer is made, it is called a **mandatory transfer.** Discretionary transfers are called **nonmandatory transfers.**

Mandatory transfers include provisions for debt service and transfers to match loan money gifted by donors. When principal and interest payments on debt are transferred, the mandatory transfers account is debited in the transferring fund. The same account is debited when the current unrestricted fund is required to match loan funds received from donors.

Nonmandatory transfers are "allocations of unrestricted resources between fund groups which are not required either by the terms of the loan or by other agreements with outside persons or agencies."[4] If a college or university decides to increase the amount available in the renewal or replacement, or unexpended plant funds from current resources, the transfer would be nonmandatory. Additions to quasi-endowment funds or voluntary payments of debt principal also would qualify as nonmandatory transfers.

The FASB *Statement No. 117* eliminates the notion of transfers because fund accounting is not necessary. Further, the changes from one asset class to another are *reclassifications,* not transfers.

FASB
nonmandatory
transfers

Indirect Cost Reimbursement on Federal Contracts   A college or university applying for federal funds submits a budget for the proposed research or public service project. The budget will show the estimated direct costs by natural classification, for example, salaries and wages, fringe benefits, supplies, travel, or rent. In order to obtain reimbursement for indirect costs, such as wear and tear on assets, electricity, and computer services, the institution must have an approved **indirect cost rate.**

The indirect cost rate shows the relationship between the institution's indirect costs and its total costs. Formulas are applied to detailed asset and cost

[4]*Audit Guide,* 30.

records to determine the appropriate rate. (Actually there is one rate for applied research and another for public service projects; there may be others as well but for the purposes of this discussion, one rate is sufficient to demonstrate the point.) The institution and the federal government finally negotiate a rate acceptable to both parties. It is applied to all federal contracts during the succeeding fiscal period(s). The approved indirect cost rate is multiplied by the total direct costs in the budget and added for a total project cost.

The indirect cost reimbursements received by an institution are typically recorded as revenues and spent in the current unrestricted fund. When the reimbursement is received by the restricted fund, the entry made is:

Cash	xxx
Fund Balance	xxx

This entry is reversed when the transfer is made to the current unrestricted fund. The current unrestricted fund makes the following entry:

Cash	xxx
Revenues—Indirect Cost Reimbursements	xxx

ILLUSTRATED TRANSACTIONS

Selected transactions are illustrated for funds frequently used by colleges and universities. Transactions requiring an entry in more than one fund are so noted. The illustrated transactions, along with others not shown, form the basis of the financial statements depicted in a later section. Current fund transactions are shown first, followed by entries for plant, endowment, and loan funds. Because their accounting is similar to other college and university or governmental unit funds, annuity and life income, and agency funds are not illustrated.

Current Funds

The illustrated transactions pertain to a state university that receives a legislative appropriation. Funding also is derived from tuition and fees, state and federal contracts and grants, and contributions. No separate fund has been established for auxiliary enterprises, but revenues and expenditures for these activities have been identified in the appropriate entries.

Current Unrestricted Fund   The following revenues were received during the year:

Legislative appropriation	$20,100,000
Tuition and fees	9,900,000
Auxiliary sales and services	3,200,000
Unrestricted gifts	360,000
Total	$33,560,000

Revenues from the legislature, auxiliary charges, and gifts were received in cash. Of the $9,900,000 representing tuition and fees charged to students, $7,300,000 was received in cash.

1.	Cash	30,960,000	
	Accounts Receivable	2,600,000	
	Legislative Appropriation		20,100,000
	Auxiliary Sales and Services		3,200,000
	Tuition and Fees		9,900,000
	Unrestricted Gifts		360,000

The college estimated that $38,000 of the receivables would not be collected, and the institution granted $226,000 in tuition scholarships and fee waivers.

2.	Bad Debt Expense	38,000	
	Tuition Fee Waivers and Scholarships *exp.*	226,000	
	Accounts Receivable		226,000
	Allowance for Uncollectible Accounts		38,000

As noted earlier, tuition and fee revenue is reported gross. Bad debt expense and tuition offsets represent expenditures, just as bad debts would be reflected in a business operation.

Pursuant to the bond indenture, a transfer was made to the Fund for the Retirement of Indebtedness for principal and interest payments totaling $206,000 (see also entry 1 in the Retirement of Indebtedness Fund).

3.	Mandatory Transfers *out*	206,000	
	Cash		206,000

In addition to supply purchases of $3,100,000 of which $338,000 was for Auxiliaries, the following expenditures were incurred:

	Education & General	Auxiliaries
Salaries and Wages, Including Fringe Benefits	$23,856,500	$2,551,500
Insurance	1,069,000	131,000
Interest	80,000	10,000
Rent	76,500	9,500
Other Operating Expenses	1,915,500	234,500
Total	$26,997,500	$2,936,500

Ordinarily, subsidiary ledgers would be used for natural classification, and the general ledger would show either expenditures by major function (education and general, and auxiliaries) or by subfunction (instruction, public service, student services, research, operation and maintenance of plant, and so on). For convenience, only the natural classification is used here. Also, numerous additional natural classifications would be used; many of those are combined in the "other operating expense" classification to conserve space and simplify the presentation.

Entry 4 shows the amounts for general and educational expenditures, while entry 5 shows the auxiliary expenditures (the designation E&G is used to distinguish educational and general expenditures from auxiliary expendiures [Aux]).

4.	Inventory of Supplies	2,762,000	
	Salaries and Wages—E&G	23,856,500	
	Insurance—E&G	1,069,000	
	Interest—E&G	80,000	
	Rent—E&G	76,500	
	Other Operating Expenditures—E&G	1,915,500	
	Accounts Payable		29,759,500
5.	Salaries and Wages—Aux	2,551,500	
	Inventory of Supplies	338,000	
	Insurance—Aux	131,000	
	Interest—Aux	10,000	
	Rent—Aux	9,500	
	Other Operating Expenditures—Aux	234,500	
	Accounts Payable		3,274,500

No distinction is made between balance sheet accounts for auxiliaries and education and general because all current unrestricted funds are normally combined for balance sheet presentations. However, separate operating statements are usually prepared.

The administration allocated $200,000 of its current-year budget for financing renewals and replacements, and $300,000 for plant additions (see also entry 2 in the renewal and replacement fund and entry 6 in the unexpended plant fund).

6.	Nonmandatory Transfers	500,000	
	Cash		500,000

Unrestricted current funds of $80,000 were spent for equipment (see also entry 5 in the net investment in plant fund).

7.	Expenditures—Equipment—E&G	80,000	
	Cash		80,000

An alternative treatment may be used for entry 7, particularly if the expenditure is large. The $80,000 would be transferred to the unexpended plant fund, as illustrated for the renewal and replacements in entry 6. The cash outlay would be made from the unexpended plant fund and a transfer would be reflected in the current unrestricted fund. Under either circumstance, the entry in the net investment in plant fund would be the same.

Tuition revenues totaling $625,000 for the summer session were received in cash. The majority of the summer program falls in the next fiscal period; therefore, all of the revenue will be recognized at that time.

| 8. | Cash | 625,000 | |
| | Deferred Revenue—Tuition & Fees | | 625,000 |

Of the supply inventory purchased (see entry 4), $2,100,000 was spent in the educational area and $236,000 in auxiliaries.

9.	Supplies Expense—E&G	2,100,000	
	Supplies Expense—Aux	236,000	
	Inventory of Supplies		2,336,000

Accounts payable totaling $26,000,000 were paid and excess cash of $1,000,000 was invested in short-term securities.

10.	Investments	1,000,000	
	Accounts Payable	26,000,000	
	Cash		27,000,000

In the previous period, $300,000 was borrowed from the restricted funds for current operating purposes. This type of borrowing is expressly permitted by state law. The interest incurred was $18,000 (see also entry 3 in the restricted funds).

11.	Due to Restricted Funds (Payable)	300,000	
	Interest Expense—E&G	18,000	
	Cash		318,000

Had the borrowing been done from an external source, the debit would have been to notes payable.

Unrestricted earnings on endowed assets totaled $56,000 (see also entry 3 in the endowment fund). The entire amount was allocated for research projects to be undertaken next year. None of the earnings pertained to auxiliaries.

| 12. | Cash | 56,000 | |
| | Endowment Income—E&G | | 56,000 |

| 13. | Fund Balance—Unallocated | 56,000 | |
| | Fund Balance—Allocated | | 56,000 |

The funds are not transferred to the restricted fund group because the restriction has been placed internally rather than externally. The reservation of the fund balance makes the oversight board's intent clear. The nominal accounts are closed in entries 14 and 15.

14.	Revenues—E&G	30,416,000	
	Supplies Expense—E&G		2,100,000
	Tuition Fee Waivers—E&G		226,000
	Bad Debt Expense—E&G		38,000
	Expenditures—Equipment—E&G		80,000
	Nonmandatory Transfers		500,000
			(continued)

Mandatory Transfers		206,000
Salaries and Wages—E&G		23,856,500
Insurance—E&G		1,069,000
Interest—E&G (80,000 + 18,000)		98,000
Rent—E&G		76,500
Other Operating Expenditures—E&G		1,915,500
Excess of Revenues Over Expenditures		250,500

15.	Revenues—Aux	3,200,000	
	Supplies Expense—Aux		236,000
	Salaries and Wages—Aux		2,551,500
	Insurance—Aux		131,000
	Interest—Aux		10,000
	Rent—Aux		9,500
	Other Operating Expenditures—Aux		234,500
	Excess of Revenues Over Expenditures		27,500

Current Restricted Fund   Restricted revenues are derived, in large part, from state and federal contracts and grants and from endowed assets. Because the sphere of activity is small, general ledger accounts are used to illustrate the accounting convention of maintaining a separate fund balance for each identifiable activity. Ordinarily the distinction would be made by maintaining subsidiary ledgers for each activity.

Restricted endowment earnings were received for the following activities:

Student Scholarships/Aid	$ 6,000
Academic Department Travel Subsidies	13,000
Library Outreach Program	4,500

1.	Cash	23,500	
	Fund Balance—Student Scholarships		6,000
	Fund Balance—Departmental Travel		13,000
	Fund Balance—Library Outreach		4,500

Other cash payments received during the year are reflected in entry 2:

2.	Cash	41,000	
	Fund Balance—State Research Contracts		8,800
	Fund Balance—Federal Research Grants		23,700
	Fund Balance—Handicap Accessibility		8,500

Payment was received from the current unrestricted fund for the amount borrowed in an earlier year; the funds were borrowed from the departmental travel subsidy fund.

3.	Cash	318,000	
	Due from Unrestricted Fund		300,000
	Fund Balance—Departmental Travel		18,000

One of the institution's endowments provides matching support, up to $10,000 annually, for the handicap accessibility project. The funds earned in this period were not received (see also entry 3 in the endowment funds).

4. Due from Endowment Funds	3,200	
Fund Balance—Handicap Accessibility		3,200

Expenditures incurred for all restricted programs totaled $48,500, of which $40,000 was paid in cash. A breakdown follows and entries 5 and 6 reflect the transactions in the current restricted funds.

Program	Amount
Scholarship Aid	$ 4,000
Departmental Travel	10,000
Library Outreach	4,500
Contracts—State Research	8,800
Grants—Federal Research	18,000
Gifts—Handicap Accessibility	3,200
Total	$48,500

5. Expenditures—E&G	48,500	
Cash		40,000
Accounts Payable		8,500
6. Fund Balance—Student Scholarships	4,000	
Fund Balance—Departmental Travel	10,000	
Fund Balance—Library Outreach	4,500	
Fund Balance—State Research Contracts	8,800	
Fund Balance—Federal Research Grants	18,000	
Fund Balance—Handicap Accessibility	3,200	
Revenues—E&G		48,500

For simplicity, all expenditures were classified as educational and general. In some circumstances, expenditures would have been incurred for auxiliary enterprises and other related activities, such as a university hospital. Note also that revenues are recognized only to the extent of expenditures incurred during the period. This means that the fund balance reflects the amount of cash received or receivables accrued in excess of expenditures. Further, the closing entry shown below reflects revenues equal to expenditures:

7. Revenues—E&G	48,500	
Expenditures—E&G		48,500

Idle cash of $340,000 was invested.

8. Investments	340,000	
Cash		340,000

Plant Funds

This state university uses all four plant funds. Where appropriate, entries in these funds are cross-referenced to entries discussed earlier.

Unexpended Plant Fund   During the year, obsolete computer equipment costing $1,000,000 and having accumulated depreciation of $640,000 was sold for $300,000. The proceeds were deposited in the unexpended plant fund and earmarked for a significant computer installation project scheduled for the following year (see also entry 1 in the investment in plant fund).

1.	Cash	300,000	
	Fund Balance—Restricted		300,000

To expand campus parking, the university purchased three homes on the perimeter of the campus. The purchases cost $380,000; the institution paid $100,000 cash and issued a mortgage for the balance. The buildings were immediately torn down, and bonds in the amount of $200,000 were issued to complete the parking lots.

2.	Construction in Progress	380,000	
	Cash		100,000
	Mortgage Payable		280,000
3.	Cash	200,000	
	Bonds Payable		200,000

Because the purchase represents part of the total cost of the parking facilities, the cost is shown as construction in progress; when completed, the entire facility will be capitalized in the net investment in plant fund. Had the buildings been purchased for office use, as an example, no entry would have been made in this fund. The entire cost would have been entered directly in the net investment in plant fund.
Construction on the parking facility was completed and the asset capitalized (see also entry 2 in the net investment in plant fund).

4.	Construction in Progress	200,000	
	Cash		200,000
5.	Mortgage Payable	280,000	
	Bonds Payable	200,000	
	Fund Balance—Unrestricted	100,000	
	Construction in Progress		580,000

The cash was received from the current unrestricted fund (see also entry 6 in the current unrestricted fund).

6.	Cash	300,000	
	Fund Balance—Unrestricted		300,000

Renewal and Replacement Fund   The institution received a donation to replace the directories and signs in several buildings.

1.	Cash		28,000	
		Fund Balance—Restricted		28,000

The cash was received from the current unrestricted fund (see also entry 6 in the current unrestricted fund).

2.	Cash		200,000	
		Fund Balance—Unrestricted		200,000

The institution undertook a series of renewal projects, none of which was large enough to warrant capitalizing the expenditures. Of the total $115,000 spent on these projects, $12,000 met the requirements of the donor's gift reflected in entry 1.

3.	Fund Balance—Restricted	12,000	
	Fund Balance—Unrestricted	103,000	
	Cash		115,000

The primary difference between the renewal and replacement and the unexpended plant fund is that expenditures in the latter are capitalized. Renewal and replacement items do not extend the life of the asset or increase its value; consequently, they should not be capitalized. Nonetheless, some state laws establish expenditure limits above which an asset should be capitalized regardless of whether it meets the test of increasing the asset's life or value. If this institution had been operating under a state law that required capitalization of any amounts in excess, say, of $50,000, an entry would have been made in the net investment in plant fund.

Fund for the Retirement of Indebtedness   The required payment from the current unrestricted fund was received. Of the total $206,000 paid on an outstanding bond, $12,000 represented interest and $194,000 represented principal (see also entry 3 in the current unrestricted fund and entry 3 in the net investment in plant fund).

1.	Cash		206,000	
		Fund Balance—Restricted		206,000
2.	Fund Balance—Restricted		206,000	
		Cash		206,000

One installment of the mortgage incurred in buying the buildings for the parking facilities became due and payable. The institution was successful in obtaining donations sufficient to meet the $21,000 payment (see also entry 4 in the net investment in plant fund).

3.	Cash		21,000	
		Fund Balance—Restricted		21,000

4.	Fund Balance—Restricted	21,000	
	Cash		21,000

Most conceivable transactions for this fund would involve the same types of entries. Sometimes the fund may receive the cash payment or donation in advance of the due date, thus affording the opportunity to invest the money on a short-term basis. Any interest earned on such deposits would be added to the fund balance of the retirement of indebtedness fund.

Net Investment in Plant Fund   As is true for governmental entities, almost all entries made in this fund are triggered by entries in other funds. The sale of the computer equipment described in entry 1 of the unexpended plant fund was entered.

1.	Net Investment in Plant	360,000	
	Accumulated Depreciation	640,000	
	Equipment		1,000,000

The parking facility construction was recorded (see also entry 4 in the unexpended plant fund).

2.	Land Improvements	580,000	
	Mortgage Payable		280,000
	Bonds Payable		200,000
	Net Investment in Plant		100,000

The payment of bond principal of $194,000 and the interest of $12,000 was made (see also entry 2 in the retirement of indebtedness fund). Interest payments do not affect the total liabilities shown in this fund.

3.	Bonds Payable	194,000	
	Net Investment in Plant		194,000

The mortgage payment of $21,000 was made (see also entry 4 in the retirement of indebtedness fund). Of the total amount, $16,800 was for interest and $4,200 was for principal.

4.	Mortgage Payable	4,200	
	Net Investment in Plant		4,200

The direct expenditure by the current unrestricted funds (see also entry 7 in the current unrestricted fund) increases the net investment in plant.

5.	Equipment	80,000	
	Net Investment in Plant		80,000

Because depreciation is used for determining the indirect cost rate and for internal management purposes, the institution reflects the accumulated depreciation in the net investment in plant fund. Before the transactions of the current period, the institution showed the following balances in the asset and accumulated depreciation accounts:

	Assets	Accumulated Depreciation
Land	$ 5,470,000	
Land Improvements	810,000	
Buildings	86,000,000	$29,000,000
Equipment	24,300,000	8,900,000
Structures Other Than Buildings	1,500,000	860,000
Library Books	855,000	
Total	$118,935,000	$38,760,000

Just as in business, land and land improvements are not depreciated. In addition, because library books have an indefinite life, they sometimes are not depreciated. Depreciation for the year, including half-year depreciation of new assets, was:

(handwritten margin note: not depreciated — land, land improv, books)

Buildings	$2,150,000
Equipment	1,620,000
Structures Other Than Buildings	100,000

5.	Net Investment in Plant	3,870,000	
	Accumulated Depreciation		3,870,000

The entries related to depreciation shown above are for governmentally owned colleges and universities. Other nonprofit colleges and universities that use fund accounting would actually show depreciation expense as a change in fund balance in the plant funds. Thus, the internal statement of changes in fund balance would show a reduction to the net investment in plant as one of the decreases in that account during the year. For these institutions, the external financial statements would show depreciation as an expense in the unrestricted net asset class.

Endowment Funds

The institution has two primary endowments: one is an unrestricted endowment, which means the earnings can be used for any lawful operating purpose, and the other is a restricted endowment, which provides matching support for the handicap accessibility project.

At the beginning of the year, the endowment providing unrestricted resources had a balance of $700,000. The restricted endowment had a balance of $127,000. Earnings on the endowments were $57,000 and $10,160, respectively.

1.	Cash	67,160	
	Fund Balance—General Support		57,000
	Fund Balance—Handicap Accessibility		10,160

Premiums pertaining to the general support endowment were amortized.

2.	Fund Balance—General Support	1,000	
	Unamortized Premiums		1,000

The money was disbursed to the current unrestricted fund and shown as owing but not transferred to the current restricted funds (see also entry 12 in the current unrestricted fund and entry 4 in the current restricted fund).

3.	Fund Balance—General Support	56,000	
	Fund Balance—Handicap Accessibility	3,200	
	Cash		56,000
	Due to Restricted Fund		3,200

As illustrated in entry 2, amortization is charged to the income of the fund; therefore, only $56,000 of the $57,000 remained to be distributed to the current unrestricted fund. No amortization was applicable to the investments held for the handicap accessibility project, so the entire amount spent by the restricted fund or $3,200 is shown as due to the restricted fund (see entry 6 in the current restricted fund).

If the institution had several large endowments, the approach taken here would be altered. For one thing, the investments probably would be pooled, and the income reported first in an "income from pooled investments account," from which the net amount would be distributed to the other funds. Any amount not distributed, such as the $6,960 ($10,160 − 3,200) for the handicap accessibility project, would be closed to the fund balance of the appropriate endowment. The effect is the same, but using an income account for distribution makes it easier to keep track of the increases and decreases.

If the investments are pooled, the same accounting procedures used for governmental entities (see Chapter 9) apply. Distributions are made on the basis of each fund's share of the fund reflected at market value. Market values are used for pooled investment distributions even though colleges and universities may use either cost or market value for financial statement purposes.

Investments pertaining to the general support endowment with a cost of $29,000 were sold for $37,000, and the proceeds were reinvested.

4.	Cash	37,000	
	Investments		29,000
	Fund Balance—General Support		8,000
5.	Investments	37,000	
	Cash		37,000

At year end, a contributor provided an additional $5,000 for the handicap accessibility endowment.

6.	Cash	5,000	
	Fund Balance—Handicap Accessibility		5,000

Loan Fund

Prior to the current period, the loan fund had a fund balance of $35,000, a combination of contributions and earnings on loans. About one-half of the prior-period balance is invested in loans and one-half in short-term securities. A contributor provided an additional $15,000 for the fund. The funds were invested temporarily.

1.	Cash	15,000	
	Fund Balance—Restricted		15,000

2.	Investments	15,000	
	Cash		15,000

Earnings on investments totaled $1,260.

3.	Cash	1,260	
	Fund Balance—Restricted		1,260

Student loan payments totaling $5,800 were received, along with interest payments of $850. Of the $850 total interest, $300 had been accrued at the end of last period.

4.	Cash	6,650	
	Loans Receivable		5,800
	Accrued Interest Receivable		300
	Fund Balance—Restricted		550

After several unsuccessful attempts to collect a $1,000 loan from a student, the university decided to write off the bad debt. The college uses an allowance for doubtful loans.

5.	Allowance for Uncollectible Loans	1,000	
	Loans Receivable		1,000

New loans totaling $7,000 were made; the appropriate allowance is calculated at 1 percent of total loans.

6.	Loans Receivable	7,000	
	Fund Balance—Restricted	70	
	Allowance for Uncollectible Loans		70
	Cash		7,000

COLLEGE AND UNIVERSITY FINANCIAL STATEMENTS

Financial Statement Requirements

The financial statements required depend on the type of college or university. After December 15, 1994, nonprofit colleges and universities required to adopt FASB *Statement No. 117* will prepare a balance sheet, an activity statement, and a cash flow statement. Because the GASB has not said whether the FASB standard will be allowed for governmentally owned institutions, their requirements after 1994 are uncertain. Currently, those institutions that follow the *Audit Guide* prepare a balance sheet, a statement of changes in fund balance, and a statement of current funds revenues, expenditures, and other changes. As current accounting conventions dictate, only the *current funds* have an operating statement. Revenues or expenditures are not reported in the endowment, plant, and other noncurrent funds; therefore, no operating statement is prepared. The statement of changes in fund balance takes the place of both an operating statement and a cash flow statement for these types of institutions.

None of the standards prescribe the precise format of the statements. The FASB makes it clear in its standard that it will not provide any more specificity in that regard than it does for for-profit entities. The same is true of the current *Audit Guide*. However, *Statement No. 117* does requires that the display attributes achieve certain reporting objectives:

1. To provide the reader with adequate information concerning the details of the sources and uses of current funds
2. To enable the institution to report the total of unrestricted and restricted current funds expended for each of the functional categories so that the total level of financial activity for each function is disclosed
3. To facilitate the presentation of a comparison with prior years[5]

The second reporting objective refers to the disclosure of each function. This means the educational and general function, auxiliaries, hospitals, and any independent operations need to be separated in the financial statements. It also means showing the subfunctions of the educational and general area: instruction, research, public service, academic support, student services, institutional support, and plant operation and maintenance. Scholarships and fellowships as well as mandatory and nonmandatory transfers are detailed whenever the amounts are material.

Frequently, colleges and universities provide several supporting schedules in their annual reports. Included among them might be a schedule of long-term debt, schedules of auxiliary enterprise operations, summary of investments, and summary of gifts received by source and purpose. These schedules should follow the financial statements and the related notes.

Illustrated Financial Statements

Numerous uncertainties surround the financial reporting of nonprofit and governmentally owned colleges and universities. One unknown is whether nonprofit colleges and universities will abandon or change their fund accounting practices to ease the transition to the new standard on financial statements. Another is what the GASB will do in response to the FASB standard. Will it permit governmentally owned colleges and universities to use the FASB standard? Will it require all colleges and universities to adopt the "governmental" model (as described in the earlier chapters of this text)? Or, will it permit the 1975 *Audit Guide* as GAAP until it establishes a financial reporting structure specifically for colleges and universities? These uncertainties make illustration of college and university financial statements difficult at best. The author has chosen to (1) illustrate the financial statements common to all colleges and universities prior to the effective date of the FASB

---

[5]*Audit Guide*, 56.

standard, and (2) depict how two of the statements for nonprofit colleges and universities might appear under the FASB standard.

Statements Prior to the FASB Standard Exhibit 15-3 shows the typical format for a current funds statement of revenues, expenditures, and other

---

Exhibit 15-3

Hypothetical University
Statement of Current Fund Revenues,
Expenditures, and Other Changes
For the Period Ending June 30, 19XX

	UNRESTRICTED		RESTRICTED	TOTAL Current Year	TOTAL Prior Year
	Operating	Auxiliary			
REVENUES:					
Tuition and Fees	$ 9,900,000			$ 9,900,000	$ 9,600,000
State Appropriation	20,100,000			20,100,000	20,800,000
State and Local Contracts and Grants			$ 8,800	8,800	9,700
Private Gifts, Grants, and Contracts	360,000		3,200	363,200	298,000
Federal Contracts and Grants			18,000	18,000	60,000
Land Grant Income					160,000
Investment Income					16,000
Sales and Service		$3,200,000		3,200,000	3,060,000
Endowment Income	56,000		18,500	74,500	80,000
Total Revenues	$30,416,000	$3,200,000	$48,500	$33,664,500	$34,083,700
EXPENDITURES AND MANDATORY TRANSFERS					
Educational and General:					
Instruction	$15,616,500			$15,616,500	$14,175,000
Research	1,473,000		$26,800	1,499,800	1,480,700
Public Service	294,500			294,500	305,000
Student Services	2,356,900		3,200	2,360,100	2,387,600
Academic Support	2,946,000		14,500	2,960,500	3,750,000
Institutional Support	2,651,500			2,651,500	2,860,000
Operation and Maintenance of Plant	3,830,000			3,830,000	3,800,000
Scholarships and Fellowships	295,100		4,000	299,100	560,000
Total Educational and General	$29,463,500		$48,500	$29,512,000	$29,318,300
Mandatory Transfers for Plant Funds					500,000
Principal and Interest	206,000			206,000	
Total Educational and General	$29,669,500		$48,500	$29,718,000	$29,818,300
Auxiliary Enterprises:					
Expenditures		$3,172,500		$ 3,172,500	$ 2,980,000
Mandatory Transfers for Retirement of Indebtedness					1,000,000
Total Auxiliary Enterprises		$3,172,500		$ 3,172,500	$ 3,980,000
Total Expenditures and Mandatory Transfers	$29,669,500	$3,172,500	$48,500	$32,890,500	$33,798,300
Other Transfers and Additions (Deductions):					
Excess of Restricted Receipts over Transfers to Revenues			$37,200	$ 37,200	$
Nonmandatory Transfers to Plant Funds	$ (500,000)			(500,000)	(600,000)
Total Transfers and Additions	$ (500,000)		$37,200	$ (462,800)	$ (600,000)
Net Increase (Decrease) to Fund Balance	$ 246,500	$ 27,500	$37,200	$ 311,200	$ (314,600)

changes. The auxiliary enterprises have been shown separately, although not all colleges and universities retain the distinction by type of current unrestricted funds when preparing this statement. Rather than applying the object code classification used for the illustrated transactions, the expenditures have been reported by function. However, the total for educational and general expenditures is the same as the total for all object codes given earlier in the illustrated transactions.

The comparative column for the prior year is typical of the display used by many colleges and universities. Most find that any attempt to provide comparisons by fund type is confusing to readers.

The statement of changes in fund balance, Exhibit 15-4, is prepared for all funds. Even though transactions for an agency fund and annuity and life income funds were not illustrated, column headings are depicted on this statement. Although most entries for the noncurrent funds involved a debit or credit to the fund balance, the detail provided in Exhibit 15-4 is far greater than the illustrated transactions would suggest. Subsidiary ledgers are often used to facilitate preparation of this statement.

The current fund shows a deficit. Depending on state law and the funding cycle, a deficit may not be allowed. If, on the other hand, this hypothetical institution was funded on a biennial basis, it could have a surplus in the first year and a deficit in the second, as long as the deficit did not exceed the previous surplus.

Exhibit 15-5 is a balance sheet based, in part, on the illustrated transactions for the hypothetical university. To give the full depth of the statement, some prior period amounts were assumed.

Possible Statements After FASB Standard   Exhibit 15-6 illustrates one possible format of a statement of activity for a nonprofit college or university, using the FASB standard as a guide and the same data depicted earlier. Numerous assumptions and explanations are necessary to translate one statement to another.

- Eliminating the requirement to report by fund eliminates the section of Exhibit 15-4 that pertains to the plant funds. The only exception is the $180,000 that was presumed to be spent from resources restricted for the purpose of plant acquisitions. When expended for the intended purpose, the temporarily restricted amounts are reclassified as increases to the unrestricted net assets. Said differently, the $180,000 was a gift in a prior year; it is recognized as a reclassification when the asset is placed in service.
- Loan funds were considered permanently restricted, as were the additional gifts to the loan and endowment fund.
- Of the $97,660 total investment income related to endowments ($61,000 + $26,700 + $1,960 + $8,000), $1,960 was required by donors to be added to the endowment, and $26,700 was temporarily restricted for a specific purpose. The remainder of the realized gains and endowment income ($61,000 + $8,000) is shown as unrestricted revenue as required by the standard.

Exhibit 15-4

Hypothetical University
Statement of Changes in Fund Balance
For the Year Ended June 30, 19XX

ITEM	CURRENT FUNDS		Loan	Endowment	Agency Fund	Annuity and Life Income	PLANT FUNDS			
	Unrestricted	Restricted					Unexpended	Renewal and Replacement	Retirement of Indebtedness	Investment in Plant
Revenues and Other Additions:										
Unrestricted Current Fund Revenues	$13,100,000									
Private Gifts, Grants, and Contracts	360,000	$ 8,500	$15,000	$ 5,000				$ 28,000	$ 21,000	
Federal and State Contracts/Grants		32,500								
State Appropriations	20,100,000									
Endowment Income	56,000	26,700								
Realized Gains on Investments				6,960						
Expended for Plant Facilities										$ 180,000
Retirement of Indebtedness				8,000						198,200
Interest on Loans Renewable		18,000	550							
Proceeds from Disposal of Plant Assets							$300,000			
Investment Income			1,260							
	$33,616,000	$ 85,700	$16,810	$ 19,960			$300,000	$ 28,000	$ 21,000	$ 378,200
Expenditures and Other Deductions:										
Expenditures	$32,636,000	$ 48,500								
Provision for Uncollectible Loans			70							
Expended for Plant Facilities							$100,000	$115,000		
Retirement of Indebtedness									$198,200	
Interest on Indebtedness									28,800	
Disposal of Plant Facilities										$ 360,000
Provision for Depreciation										3,870,000
Premium Amortization										
	$32,636,000	$ 48,500	$ 70	$			$100,000	$115,000	$227,000	$ 4,230,000
Transfers Among Funds—Additions/(Deductions):										
Mandatory:										
Principal and Interest	$ (206,000)								$206,000	
Nonmandatory:										
Additions to Plant	(500,000)						$300,000	$200,000		
	$ (706,000)						$300,000	$200,000	$206,000	
Net Increase (Decrease) for Year	$ 274,000	$ 37,200	$16,740	$ 19,960			$500,000	$113,000	$ -0-	$ (3,851,800)
Fund Balance at Beginning of Year	(300,000)	300,000	35,000	700,000			100,000	60,000	16,000	29,320,000
Fund Balance at End of Year	$ (26,000)	$337,200	$51,740	$719,960			$600,000	$173,000	$ 16,000	$25,468,200

Exhibit 15-5

Hypothetical University
Balance Sheet
As of June 30, 19XX

ITEM	CURRENT FUNDS Unrestricted	CURRENT FUNDS Restricted	Loan	Endowment	Agency Fund	Annuity and Life Income	PLANT FUNDS Unexpended	PLANT FUNDS Renewal and Replacement	PLANT FUNDS Retirement of Indebtedness	PLANT FUNDS Investment in Plant
Assets										
Cash	$3,537,000	$ 2,500	$ 1,010	$116,160			$500,000	$113,000	$ 16,000	
Investments	1,000,000	340,000	28,800	598,000			100,000	60,000		
Unamortized Premium				9,000						
Accounts Receivable	2,374,000									
Less: Allowance for Uncollectible Accounts	(38,000)									
Inventory of Supplies	764,000									
Prepaid Expenses										
Loans Receivable			22,200							
Less: Allowance for Uncollectible Accounts			(270)							
Due from Other Funds		3,200								
Land and Improvements										$ 6,860,000
Buildings and Other Structures										87,500,000
Equipment										23,380,000
Library Books										855,000
Less: Accumulated Depreciation										(41,990,000)
TOTAL ASSETS	$7,637,000	$345,700	$51,740	$723,160			$600,000	$173,000	$ 16,000	$ 76,605,000
Liabilities and Fund Balances										
Accounts Payable	$7,034,000	$ 8,500					$300,000	$ 76,000		
Due to Other Funds				$ 3,200						
Deferred Revenue	625,000									
Long-Term Notes Payable							300,000			
Bonds Payable										$ 50,861,000
Mortgage Payable										275,800
Fund Balances										
Allocated	56,000									
Unallocated	(78,000)									
Restricted		337,200	51,740	719,960				97,000	16,000	
Unrestricted										
Net Investment in Plant										25,468,200
TOTAL LIABILITIES AND FUND BALANCES	$7,637,000	$345,700	$51,740	$723,160			$600,000	$173,000	$ 16,000	$ 76,605,000

Exhibit 15-6

Hypothetical University
Statement of Activities
(Under *Statement No. 117*)
For the Period Ending June 30, 19XX

	Unrestricted	Temporarily Restricted	Permanently Restricted	Total
REVENUE, GAINS, AND OTHER SUPPORT:				
Current Fund Revenues	$13,100,000			$13,100,000
Private Gifts, Grants, and Contracts	360,000	$ 49,000	$ 20,000	429,000
Federal and State Grants		32,500		32,500
State Appropriations	20,100,000			20,100,000
Endowment Income	61,000	26,700	1,960	89,660
Realized Gains on Investments	8,000			8,000
Interest on Loan Renewals		18,000	550	18,550
Investment Income			1,260	1,260
Net Assets Released from Restrictions:				
Satisfaction of program restrictions	32,000	(32,000)		
Satisfaction of equipment acquisition restrictions	180,000	(180,000)		
Expiration of time restriction	16,500	(16,500)		
Total Revenues, Gains, and Other Support	$33,857,500	$(102,300)	$ 23,770	$33,778,970
EXPENSES AND LOSSES:				
Instruction	$15,616,570			15,616,570
Auxiliaries	3,172,500			3,172,500
Research	1,505,000			1,505,000
Public Service	311,000			311,000
Student Services	2,356,900			2,356,900
Academic Support	2,946,000			2,946,000
Institutional Support	2,651,500			2,651,500
Operation and Maintenance of Plant	3,830,000			3,830,000
Scholarships and Fellowships	295,100			295,100
Loss on Asset Disposal	60,000			60,000
Total Expenses and Losses	$32,744,570	$	$	$32,744,570
Changes in Net Assets	1,112,930	(102,300)	23,770	1,034,400
Net Assets at Beginning of Year	25,114,700	460,000	735,000	26,309,700
Net Assets, June 30, 19XX	$26,227,630	$ 357,700	$758,770	$27,344,100

- All restricted current funds were presumed to meet the definition of temporarily restricted assets; thus, the $48,500 shown in Exhibit 15-4 as expenditures represents a reclassification of temporarily restricted assets ($32,000 from satisfaction of program restrictions and $16,500 from expiration of time restrictions).
- Expenditures made from these reclassifications were assumed to represent research activities ($32,000) and public service ($16,500). The $70 provision for bad debts in the loan fund was added to the instruction function.
- If fund accounting is not maintained, there can be no mandatory or nonmandatory transfers among funds. Interest expense would be shown in the unrestricted fund.

- The illustration ignores depreciation expense, which would be shown in the unrestricted column. If the asset was premanently restricted, depreciation expense in the unrestricted column would be matched by an asset reclassification from the permanently restricted class to the unrestricted class of the same amount.[6] This translates to recognition of the original contribution as an increase in unrestricted net assets as the fixed asset is used up. Under this option, the effect on net unrestricted assets is zero in any one year: depreciation decreases net assets but the reclassification increases net assets.
- The loss on the asset (calculations are based on entry 1 in the unexpended plant fund) is shown in the unrestricted asset class.

Exhibit 15-7 is a balance sheet for the same university. The FASB standard does not require a separate asset and liability section for each asset class. Only net assets must be separated into the three classes.

Exhibit 15-7

Hypothetical University
Balance Sheet
(Under *Statement No. 117*)
As of June 30, 19XX

Assets

Cash	$ 4,285,670
Investments	2,126,800
Unamortized Premium	9,000
Accounts Receivable, net	2,336,000
Inventory of Supplies	764,000
Prepaid Expenses	10,000
Loans Receivable, net	11,930
Land and Improvements, net	6,860,000
Buildings and Other Structures, net	59,500,000
Equipment, net	9,480,000
Library Books	765,000
Total Assets	$86,148,400

Liabilities and Net Assets

Accounts Payable	$ 7,042,500
Deferred Revenue	625,000
Long-Term Notes Payable	
Bonds Payable	50,861,000
Mortgage Payable	275,800
Total Liabilities	$58,804,300
Unrestricted Net Assets	$26,227,630
Temporarily Restricted Net Assets	357,700
Permanently Restricted Net Assets	758,770
Total Net Assets	$27,344,100
Total Liabilities and Net Assets	$86,148,400

---

[6]The other option under the standard, the one used for the $180,000 spent in the current year, is to show the entire amount of the asset as a reclassification in the year in which the asset is placed in service. The asset would be depreciated over its useful life and the depreciation expense would be shown each year in the unrestricted net asset class.

As before, some assumptions were made in translating the information in Exhibit 15-5 and Exhibit 15-7. The loan and endowment funds were assumed to be permanently restricted. The $100,000 beginning balance in the unexpended plant fund and the $60,000 beginning balance in the renewal and replacement fund were assumed to be temporarily restricted—that is, money given by a donor that must be spent for fixed assets or to replace fixed assets. The beginning fund balance in the restricted fund also was classified as temporarily restricted. Again, the elimination of fund accounting means that the interfund receivables and payables are eliminated. Existing fixed assets were assumed to be purchased with unrestricted funds and therefore classified as unrestricted.

A cash flow statement is not illustrated. It would look much like the cash flow for a business, except that the financing section would have two parts. The proceeds from restricted contributions for the endowment, plant assets, and other funds, such as loan funds, would comprise one section. The other part of the financing section would contain the items traditionally classified as financing and interest and dividends restricted for reinvestment.

COMPARISON OF THE FINANCIAL STATEMENTS

Shifting to the FASB standard on financial statements represents a marked change for nonprofit colleges and universities. The statement of revenues, expenditures, and changes in fund balance and the statement of activities have few visual or substantive similarities. The former best illustrates what happened to numerous activities during the year, while the latter focuses on the overall change in net assets. Also noteworthy are the differences in the amounts that financial statement users will see. The change in unrestricted net assets is $1,172,930 whereas the change in the unrestricted fund is $274,000 ($246,500 + $27,500). Although the difference in magnitude will vary, the results under the new standard usually will tend to be larger, both because of the treatment of endowment earnings and because asset reclassifications are included in the change in net assets. Also, the larger the mandatory transfers, the greater the difference between the two numbers. Financial statement readers will no doubt need detailed notes to understand the character of the asset reclassifications.

Great care must be taken in interpreting the results under the new standards. Financial statement users must understand that the term *unrestricted* is not the same as under previous standards, and that temporarily restricted net assets are similar to the restricted fund assets under some but not all circumstances. Generally, permanently restricted assets will include what was in the endowment and loan funds before. It will also include any money for fixed assets or permanently restricted fixed assets; these items would come from amounts previously shown in the plant funds.

The balance sheet also looks very different under the new standard. It contains much less detail. Most noticeably, unless additional disclosures are made in the notes to the financial statements, readers will not be able to identify specific assets with specific activities. For example, which investments are associated with the endowed assets will not be observable. To what extent money is available for fixed asset acquisition or improvement also will be unavailable without additional disclosures. Nonetheless, as illustrated by comparing Exhibits 15-5 and 15-7, the total of all fund balances does equal the total for the three net asset classes.

One question facing financial statement preparers will be how to help readers make the transition from the old to the new standard. Preparers may have a natural tendency to put statements under the "old" standard in the annual report as supplementary information. This approach may not help users make the transition but rather continue to rely on a presentation that may not be provided indefinitely. Users may benefit more from supplementary information that explains the new statements in terms of the old, much the same way as those unaccustomed to the metric system first learned metric units in terms of equivalencies.

SUMMARY

Some colleges and universities are operated for profit. Others are nonprofit colleges and universities, which are either private or governmental. Most colleges and universities are organized after the business model, with a chief executive officer, various vice presidents, and the equivalent of division heads.

A critical problem facing universities is performance measurement. The goal is to provide quality education within resource limitations. Few agree on what constitutes a quality education, at least in terms specific enough to enable an institution to measure its own performance. The difficulty in evaluating performance leads to a constant search for better measurement criteria and a periodic struggle for adequate funding.

Colleges and universities are also entering a period of rapid change in terms of their accounting and financial reporting. Until recently, all have used accrual accounting conventions blended with the anomalies of fund accounting. Now, the private nonprofits are required to prepare three financial reports—a balance sheet, a statement of activity, and a cash flow statement—all by net asset class. These net asset classes are unrestricted, temporarily restricted, and permanently restricted. They do not mesh with the current fund structure. Therefore, fund accounting may be on its way out as an accounting convention for these institutions. Governmental colleges and universities are uncertain about what their requirements may be, although most speculate that the GASB will continue to require fund accounting at least for the foreseeable future.

Under fund accounting, governmental colleges and universities use six primary fund groups. They are current funds, loan funds, agency funds, endowment funds, annuity and life income funds, and plant funds. The current group is composed of the restricted and unrestricted funds. The unrestricted funds are used for general operating purposes while the restricted funds are used for federal and state contracts or grants, and restricted gifts.

The publicly owned colleges and universities prepare a balance sheet (all funds), a statement of revenues, expenditures, and other changes (current funds), and a statement of changes in fund balance (all funds). Alternative formats are possible for most statements, but the distinction between restricted and unrestricted must be preserved. Also, the statements must provide enough detail to be helpful to statement users.

The diverging accounting and reporting practices will make comparability among institutions more difficult. But, as some college and university representatives are beginning to observe, maybe this sector of the economy has over-emphasized the importance of comparability.

QUESTIONS

15-1 Explain why you think depreciation should or should not be taken on all fixed assets of colleges and universities.

15-2 Describe the various types of colleges and universities and indicate to what organization each looks for standard-setting guidance.

15-3 How are endowment gains and losses shown for nonprofit colleges and universities when restricted by the donor?

15-4 Describe the several expenditure classification schemes used by colleges and universities.

15-5 If an institution decides to spend indirect cost reimbursements on items generating the reimbursement, to what functional areas would the reimbursements likely be allocated?

15-6 Explain the difficulties in measuring the performance of governmental colleges and universities. What causes these performance measurement difficulties?

15-7 A legislator wants to pass a resolution requiring all state institutions to be compared to "similar" institutions in the region. She feels that she will then have some basis for evaluating funding requests. What characteristics should be examined to determine "similar" institutions? Explain.

15-8 Describe the four plant funds. What distinguishes the unexpended plant fund from the renewal and replacement fund?

15-9 Describe in general terms the accounting basis for colleges and universities.

15-10 What is the primary difference between a term endowment and a quasi-endowment?

15-11 Describe the typical organizational structure of a college or university. Is the organizational structure reflected in the expenditure classification scheme?

15-12 Under what circumstances would a donor be likely to establish a life income fund?

15-13 Distinguish between a mandatory and a nonmandatory transfer. List some typical transactions that would be denoted as nonmandatory transfers.

15-14 A comprehensive university is preparing its financial report and asks for guidance in determining what schedules to include. List several schedules and describe the circumstances under which each would be included.

15-15 With the adoption of the FASB statements on contributions, depreciation, and financial statements, what will be the key differences in the accounting and financial reporting between nonprofit and governmental colleges and universities?

15-16 A statement of cash flows is required under FASB *Statement No. 117.* Why do you suppose this statement was not required previously?

15-17 A college president observes that auxiliary enterprises belong in the current unrestricted fund area. This being the case, she wants to know why a separate column has been used for these activities in the financial statements. Explain.

15-18 Describe the financial statements required for each type of college and university.

15-19 Why are college and university revenues reported gross before bad debt expense or tuition and fee waivers and scholarships?

CASES

15-1 Legislatures in two states decided to complete a comparative analysis of the colleges and universities in both states. The object of the comparative analysis was to see which state funded higher education better and to establish norms for future appropriations. Some of the comparative statistics follow:

	State 1	State 2
Educational and General Costs:		
Instruction	$ 76,500,000	$33,000,000
Research	22,500,000	1,200,000
Public Service	3,000,000	300,000
Academic Support	15,000,000	6,000,000
Student Services	8,500,000	6,600,000
Institutional Support	11,000,000	5,400,000
Plant Operation and Maintenance	19,500,000	7,000,000
Scholarships and Fellowships	1,000,000	500,000
Total	$157,000,000	$60,000,000

The total number of students served in all institutions in state 1 was 29,500, and in state 2, 9,600. In state 1, total cost per student credit hour ranged from a low of $147 to a high of $153. In state 2, the range was from $144 to $196.

Climates are similar in the two states. State 1 is dominated by large metropolitan campuses, whereas most institutions in state 2 are located in rural areas. State 1 has three campuses and state 2 has only two.

The student-to-faculty ratio in state 1 is 19:1 and the ratio in state 2 is 16:1.

REQUIRED

Prepare a report describing which state has provided the best funding for higher education. Some specific questions you will need to address are: Which state is providing the greatest amount of funding? How have the institutions chosen to allocate the funding among the major functions of education? What could account for the differences in allocating money to the various functions? As part of the report, explain why it is difficult to make judgments about "best funding" or "best education" from these data.

15-2 George Paely, a new member of a state university's board of regents, is confused by the financial statements prepared for his review. He indicates that he has been a county commissioner before and that part of the statements seem familiar. George notes, however, that in some respects college and university accounting appears very different from that used by governmental units.

REQUIRED

Explain the important similarities and differences between the accounting used by public colleges and universities and that used by governmental units.

15-3 As a newly formed institution, Torrence College will provide college-level training in selected fields for students interested in a two-year, associate degree program. Located in a metropolitan area, it will rent acceptable facilities for the foreseeable future. Students will commute rather than live on campus.

Financial support will be provided by a local mill levy, a state appropriation, and contributions from benefactors. Certain members of the faculty already hired have broad expertise in scientific research.

Because it is only a two-year program, no intercollegiate athletics will be offered. Instead, Torrence will offer an intramural sports program for all students. Student government will collect fees and help manage the sports program. Torrence intends to use fund accounting for internal purposes.

REQUIRED

Indicate which funds, if any, Torrence's fiscal administrators should establish. If a fund is needed, explain why. Also explain why certain funds may not be needed.

15-4 Jeffries State University has launched a major building expansion program. New to the job, the controller has placed all activities in a single fund. The various projects are described below:

1. Land and buildings on the perimeter of the campus were purchased for $260,000. The buildings are being torn down to make room for a parking structure, estimated to cost $510,000. Bonds were issued for the total project cost, but construction has not yet begun.

2. An alumnus provided investments with a total market value of $1,400,000 to be earmarked for partial construction costs related to an intramural sports center. The campus already owns the land upon

which the facility is being built; its original cost was $80,000. By year end, construction was half-completed and $700,000 was borrowed from another fund to avoid selling the investments durng a market slump. The investments yielded $87,000 during the year and interest on the loan amounted to $70,000 (it was not paid).

3. Contributions totaling $37,000 for replacing windows and doors in a classroom buildng were received. Because construction was not contemplated soon, the money was invested.

4. The student union building operated by auxiliaries was renovated at a cost of $600,000. Revenue bonds were sold to finance the project. The bond payments will be made by revenue generated from the facility and from a student-union use fee paid by students at registration. Fees collected totaled $11,600 during the year; no revenue was generated from the facility because the renovation was completed just before year end. The first interest and principal payment is not due until next year.

5. At the beginning of the year, Jeffries State had the following plant assets:

Land and Improvements	$ 235,000
Buildings	15,426,000
Other Structures	118,000
Equipment	1,200,000
Library Books	916,000

REQUIRED

Prepare a year-end balance sheet for each plant fund needed by Jeffries State University. (Hint: Prepare T-accounts for the year's transactions before completing the assignment.)

15-5 As a member of a student organization designed to promote the university, Debra Meekin has encountered a particularly recalcitrant legislator. The legislator cannot understand why the university needs so much funding. To him the question is simply a matter of priorities: determine the programs in highest demand, fund those adequately, and close down the remainder of the programs. He notes that this is how it works in business; either there is a demand for your product or you go out of business.

REQUIRED

Provide Ms. Meekin with arguments to present to the legislator. What would happen if your institution followed his suggestions? Why do universities maintain programs and activities for which there is limited demand? Do you think universities can achieve economies of scale in certain programs? Explain.

15-6 Presume that you were recently appointed to a GASB task force that will advise the Board on future accounting practices for colleges and universities. As the Board has explained, with the FASB's adoption of the standard on financial reporting and contributions and with the pending revision of the *Audit Guide,* the GASB needs to issue some interim guidance, at the very least, for governmental colleges and universities.

REQUIRED

Prepare a report advising the GASB of your opinions and substantiating arguments. The following questions may help you frame your report. Should governmental colleges and universities adopt the same model as the nonprofits? Should fund accounting be preserved? What will be the impact on governmental institutions if they continue to follow the guidance in the "old" audit guide? Should the GASB issue comprehensive standards pertaining to the public institutions?

EXERCISES

15-1 Select the best answer for each question.

1. The plant fund group of a governmental university includes which of the following subgroups?

	Investment in Plant Funds	Unexpended Plant Funds
a.	no	yes
b.	no	no
c.	yes	no
d.	yes	yes

(Adapted from the November 1986 CPA Exam, Theory #59)

2. For the spring semester, Lane University assessed its students $3,400,000 (net of refunds), covering tuition and fees for educational and general purposes. Only $3,000,000 was expected to be realized because scholarships totaling $300,000 were granted to students, and tuition and fee waivers of $100,000 were allowed to faculty members' children attending Lane. How much should Lane include in educational and general current fund revenues from student tuition and fees?
   a. $3,400,000
   b. $3,300,000
   c. $3,100,000
   d. $3,000,000
   (Adapted from the May 1984 CPA Exam, Practice #51)

3. Which of the following accounting conventions would be used by an endowment fund of a public college or university? *GASB*
   a. the operating statement shows revenues and expenses
   b. fixed assets would be reported at the lower of cost or market
   c. depreciation would be reflected by a decrease in fund balance
   d. none of the above

   endowment fixed assets are depreciated

4. Under *Statement No. 93*, nonprofit private colleges and universities are required to take depreciation on:
   a. only fixed assets held by endowments
   b. artifacts and museum pieces of historical significance

     c. fixed assets, except artifacts and museum pieces of historical significance

     d. assets used only in auxiliary enterprises

5. If a public institution allocated gains and losses from the endowment fund to a restricted purpose, the amount would be shown in the restricted fund as a:

     a. transfer from endowment

     b. revenue from endowments

     c. gain or loss on the sale of endowed assets

     d. none of the above

6. During the years ended June 30, 1990 and 1991, Sonata State University conducted a cancer research project financed by a $2,000,000 gift from an alumna. This entire amount was pledged by the donor on July 10, 1989, although she paid only $500,000 on that date. The gift was restricted to the financing of this particular research project. During the two-year research period, Sonata's related gift receipts and research expenditures were as follows:

| | YEAR ENDED JUNE 30 | |
	1990	1991
Gift Receipts	$1,200,000	$ 800,000
Cancer Research Expenditures	900,000	1,100,000

     How much gift revenue should Sonata report in the restricted column of its statement of current funds revenues, expenditures, and other changes for the year ended June 30, 1991?

     a. $0

     b. $800,000

     c. $1,100,000

     d. $2,000,000

     (Adapted from the May 1982 CPA Exam, Practice #24)

7. Delhi State University had current unrestricted fund revenues of $28,000,000 and expenditures of $27,850,000, mandatory transfers of $1,200,000, and nonmandatory transfers of $210,000. Its increase (or decrease) in the fund balance of the current unrestricted fund was:

     a. $150,000

     b. ($1,050,000)

     c. ($1,260,000)

     d. none of the above

8. On January 2, 19X1, Mary Todd established a $500,000 life income fund for Murray State University. Her beneficiary is expected to live 1 year and will receive the income for that period. If the expected earnings are 8 percent per year and the inflation rate is 5 percent, what amount will Murray State receive at the end of the 1 year?

a. $515,000
b. $500,000
c. $475,000
d. $0

9. The following funds were among those on Kery State University's books at April 30, 19X8:

Funds to be used for acquiring additional properties	$3,000,000
Funds set aside for debt service charges	$5,000,000

How much of these funds should be included in plant funds?
a. $0
b. $3,000,000
c. $5,000,000
d. $8,000,000
(Adapted from the May 1984 CPA Exam, Practice #55)

10. Current unrestricted fund revenues would not include which of the following?
a. tuition and fees
b. grant or contract revenue
c. state appropriation
d. none of the above

11. The current funds group of a governmental university includes which of the following:

	Annuity Funds	Loan Funds
a.	yes	yes
b.	yes	no
c.	no	no
d.	no	yes

(Adapted from the May 1986 CPA Exam, Theory #59)

12. Souny University, a nonprofit institution, has elected to use the total return concept for its endowed assets. On December 31, 19X1, the market value of the endowment was $1,000,000 and $70,000 was earned during the year. Souny projects that over the long run the portfolio will yield 9 percent, and it plans to add 4 percent on average to the endowment to maintain its purchasing power. If the state law under which Souny operates allows the total return concept, how much will be shown as income in the unrestricted fund?
a. $70,000
b. $90,000
c. $40,000
d. $50,000

13. John Jones pledged $60,000 to a nonprofit college during 19X1; he says that he will make the payment in early 19X2 and that the college can spend $20,000 in 19X1, 19X2, and 19X3. How much revenue will

the college show in its unrestricted and temporarily restricted net asset classes in 19X ℓ?

	Unrestricted	**Temporarily Restricted**
a.	$60,000	$ 0
b.	$20,000	$40,000
c.	$40,000	$20,000
d.	$ 0	$60,000

14. After the effective date of FASB's *Statement No. 117,* what statements are required for nonprofit colleges and universities?
    a. balance sheet, statement of revenues, expenditures, and changes in net assets, and a cash flow statement
    b. a cash flow statement, an activity statement, and a statement of changes in net assets
    c. an activity statement, a statement of financial position, and a cash flow statement
    d. the answer varies depending on the purpose of the audited financial statements

15-2 Select the best answer for each question.

1. Money set aside by the Board of Trustees for scholarships should be recorded in:
    a. restricted fund
    b. endowment fund
    c. current unrestricted fund
    d. none of the above
2. A donor gave $100,000 to Bliss State University for support of academic programs. The principal remained inviolate and the earnings could be used for supporting travel and research within academic departments. What funds would be affected?
    a. restricted and endowment funds
    b. restricted and unrestricted funds
    c. restricted, unrestricted, and endowment funds
    d. endowment funds
3. A restricted fund incurred expenditures of $250,000 on a grant supporting state tourism research. The entry (entries) required is (are):

a. Expenditures	250,000	
Cash		250,000
b. Fund Balance	250,000	
Cash		250,000
c. Expenditures	250,000	
Cash		250,000
Due from Endowments	250,000	
Fund Balance		250,000

d. Expenditures	250,000	
Cash		250,000
Fund Balance	250,000	
Revenues		250,000

4. Use of a functional expense classification would involve use of which of the following account titles?
   a. research, public service, maintenance of plant
   b. salaries, wages, supplies, rent, utilities
   c. business administration, law, anthropology
   d. public affairs, finance, academic programs, athletics

5. One operating characteristic affecting college and university accounting practices is:
   a. the combination of academic and nonacademic departments
   b. providing a service rather than earning a profit
   c. the variety of funding sources, from appropriations to gifts
   d. both b and c

6. Which of the following would best describe the fund groupings used by public colleges and universities?   (GASB)
   a. maintain a distinction between operating and nonoperating resources
   b. establish funds by revenue source
   c. maintain distinctions between operating and nonoperating, and between restricted and unrestricted resources
   d. establish funds for each major operating function

7. Which of the following should be included in the current fund revenues of a public college or university?   GASB

	Tuition Waivers	**Unrestricted Bequests**
a.	yes	no
b.	yes	yes
c.	no	yes
d.	no	no

(Adapted from the May 1985 CPA Exam, Theory #59)

8. Current funds are of which two types?
   a. endowment and restricted
   b. restricted and unrestricted
   c. operating and nonoperating
   d. unrestricted and operating

9. Which of the following is *not* a characteristic consistent with the total return concept?
   a. the actual return is used as a basis for income distribution
   b. all gains and losses in the amount necessary to retain the purchasing power are added to the principal amount
   c. colleges and universities are the absolute owners of the assets
   d. gains and losses are recognized as transfers when spent by the restricted or unrestricted funds

10. Required matching funds for a loan fund established by a donor would be reported in the current unrestricted funds as:
    a. expenditures
    b. mandatory transfers
    c. nonmandatory transfers
    d. liquidation of a liability

11. After the effective date of FASB *Statement No. 117,* nonprofit colleges and universities will:
    a. prepare external financial statements that reflect fund accounting but use net asset classes for internal reporting
    b. recognize pledges when the cash is received
    c. "roll up" fund balances to equate to net asset classes
    d. none of the above

12. Depreciation of fixed assets is required for:
    a. all college and university long-lived assets
    b. all college and university long-lived assets that do not have historical significance and are maintained for educational or research purposes
    c. all public college and university long-lived assets
    d. all nonprofit college and university long-lived assets that do not have historical significance and are maintained for educational or research purposes

13. If a nonprofit college received a gift restricted for the acquisition of fixed assets, what accounting is appropriate when the money is expended for the acquisition of fixed assets?
    a. the asset would be debited and cash credited
    b. the amount of the gift would be reclassified from temporarily restricted to the unrestricted class
    c. depreciation would be reported in the activity statement of the unrestricted asset class from the acquisition date to the end of the year
    d. all of the above

15-3   A partial balance sheet of Ratan State University as of the end of its fiscal year follows:

Ratan State University
Current Funds Balance Sheet
July 31, 19X9

ASSETS		LIABILITIES AND FUND BALANCES	
Unrestricted		**Unrestricted**	
Cash	$200,000	Accounts Payable	$100,000
Accounts Receivable (tuition and fees less allowance for uncollectible accounts of $15,000)	360,000	Due to Other Funds	40,000
		Deferred Revenue—Tuition and Fees	25,000
Prepaid Expenses	40,000	Fund Balance	435,000
Total	$600,000		$600,000

(continued)

(continued)

ASSETS		LIABILITIES AND FUND BALANCES	
Restricted		**Restricted**	
Cash	$ 10,000	Accounts Payable	$ 5,000
Investments	210,000	Fund Balance	215,000
Total Current Funds	$820,000	Total Current Funds	$820,000

The following information pertains to the succeeding year, the one ended July 31, 19Y0:

1. Cash collected from students' tuition totaled $3,000,000. Of this amount, $362,000 represented accounts receivable outstanding at July 31, 19X9; $2,500,000 was for the current year's tuition; and $138,000 was for tuition applicable to the quarter beginning in August 19Y0.
2. Deferred revenue at July 31, 19X9, was earned during the year ended July 31, 19Y0.
3. Accounts receivable at July 31, 19X9, that were not collected during the year ended July 31, 19Y0, were determined to be uncollectible and were written off against the allowance account. At July 31, 19Y0, the allowance account was estimated at $10,000.
4. An unrestricted appropriation of $460,000 was made by the state. This state appropriation was to be paid to Ratan sometime in August 19Y0.
5. Unrestricted cash gifts of $80,000 were received from alumni. Ratan's board of trustees allocated $30,000 of these gifts to the student loan fund.
6. Investments costing $25,000 were sold for $31,000. Restricted fund investments were purchased at a cost of $40,000. Investment income of $18,000 was earned and collected.
7. Unrestricted general expenses of $2,500,000 were recorded in the voucher system. At July 31, 19Y0, the unrestricted accounts payable balance was $75,000.
8. The restricted accounts payable balance at July 31, 19X9, was paid.
9. The $40,000 due to other funds at July 31, 19X9, was paid to the plant fund.
10. One quarter of the prepaid expenses at July 31, 19X9, expired during the current year and pertained to general education expense. No additions to prepaid expenses were made during the year.

REQUIRED

Prepare journal entries to record the foregoing transactions for the year ended July 31, 19Y0. Number each entry to correspond with the number indicated in the description of its respective transaction and identify the fund in which the entry is made. (19Y0 designates the year following 19X9.) (Adapted from the November 1983 CPA Exam, Practice)

15-4 On January 1, 19X9, a wealthy donor gave Delany College $500,000 to establish a variety of programs. Make the journal entries in the appropriate funds, and identify the fund in which each entry is made, assuming fund accounting is used by Delany.

1. The donor required that one-half of the donation be maintained in perpetuity, the income from which was to be used for the following:
   a. 20 percent to research on biochemistry (if no viable project was approved, the income would be added to the principal)
   b. 50 percent to scholarships and fellowships for students in scientific programs
   c. 30 percent to be spent as the institution saw fit
2. The remaining one-half was to be used for an addition on the microbiology laboratory; any earnings generated on this portion before the building was constructed would be used for repairing an existing biochemistry structure.
3. All gift money was invested immediately.
4. Earnings for the first six months totaled $10,000. No construction or research was undertaken during the first six months, but the cash for the research project was held, pending submission of grant proposals from faculty.
5. Investments made in connection with the microbiology gift of $100,000 were sold for $110,000; the proceeds were reinvested. Delany College does not use the total return concept in determining earnings versus principal additions.
6. Earnings for the second six months totaled $11,200, of which 10 percent was accrued and the remainder received in cash.
7. A proposal for biochemistry research totaling $2,000 was approved; the money was spent. No other viable projects were presented during the entire calendar year ending December 31, 19X9.
8. The windows on the west wing of the biochemistry building were replaced at a cost of $8,000.

15-5   Palace Verde University pools its investments. It also uses the total return concept in which it allocates an amount necessary to maintain the purchasing power of each endowment portfolio to principal and the remainder to income. The pooled investments are broken down as follows:

	Market Value 7/1/X8
Endowment A	$ 88,000
Endowment B	116,000
Endowment C	59,000
Total	$263,000

The total realized return for the fiscal period ending 6/30/X9 was $31,560 ($21,040 represented dividends and interest and $10,520 was realized gains and losses). The principal amounts pooled did not change during the period, and the total market value (before any additions due to the application of the total return concept) at year end 6/30/X9 was $265,000. The inflation rate was 3 percent.

REQUIRED

1. Calculate the amount that can be spent by Palace Verde and the amount that must be added to the corpus for the year.
2. Assuming the income is spent, what is the total investment value for each fund involved in the pool by year end?

15-6 The transactions for Frailing State University for the period ending June 30, 19X9, are described in the materials that follow. Prepare a six-column worksheet for each fund, keying each entry to the number of the transaction. The first two columns of each worksheet should contain the post-closing trial balance information summarized below. The next two columns should contain the transactions for the period ending June 30, 19X9, and the final two the pre-closing trial balance at year end.

Frailing State University
Post-Closing Trial Balance
June 30, 19X8

	CURRENT FUNDS				PLANT FUNDS			
	Unrestricted	Restricted	Agency Fund	Endowment Funds	Unexpended	Renewal and Replacement	Retirement of Indebtedness	Investment in Plant
Assets								
Cash	$2,500,000	$ 300,000	$145,000	$ 15,000	$ 60,000	$ 76,000	$ 180,000	
Investments		600,000	500,000	1,100,000	430,000	578,000	5,404,500	
Accounts Receivable	650,000	370,000	150,000					
Less Allowance for Uncollectible Accounts			(4,100)					
Inventories	2,300,000							
Prepaid Expenses	95,000		1,200					
Due from Other Funds		31,000		1,100,000				
Land and Land Improvements								$ 4,100,000
Buildings								61,160,000
Equipment								17,500,000
Library Books								14,600,000
Construction in Progress					9,800,000			
Accumulated Depreciation								(38,500,000)
Total Assets	$5,545,000	$1,301,000	$792,100	$2,215,000	$10,290,000	$654,000	$5,584,500	$ 58,860,000
Liabilities and Fund Balances								
Accounts Payable	$3,600,000	$ 540,000	$325,000		$ 2,118,000	$ 17,200		
Accrued Liabilities	210,000	39,000	9,000					
Students' Deposits	129,000							
Due to Other Funds	1,000,000		131,000					
Deposits Held in Custody for Others			327,100					
Current Bonds/Notes Payable					5,000,000			$ 202,000
Long-Term Notes Payable								272,000
Long-Term Leases								45,000
Long-Term Bonds								5,300,000
Fund Balances:								
Unallocated	606,000							
Restricted		722,000		$2,215,000	3,100,000		$5,584,500	
Unrestricted					72,000	636,800		
Net Investment in Plant								53,041,000
Total Liabilities and Fund Balances	$5,545,000	$1,301,000	$792,100	$2,215,000	$10,290,000	$654,000	$5,584,500	$ 58,860,000

1. Current fund revenues were as follows:

	Unrestricted	Restricted
Tuition and Fees	$ 9,000,000	
State Appropriation	27,500,000	
Federal Grants and Contracts		$6,200,000
State and Local Grants and Contracts		1,345,000
Private Gifts, Grants, and Contracts	52,000	
Land Grant Income	235,000	
Investment Income	168,000	153,000
Endowment Income	55,000	45,000
Other Sources	580,000	
Total	$37,590,000	$7,743,000

Tuition and fees of $350,000 were not paid by year end; all other revenues had been received in cash by then. An allowance for doubtful accounts was established for $22,000, the first time the institution established such an account for tuition and fee revenue.

2. Unrestricted education and general expenses, including those for auxiliary enterprises, totaled $35,595,600. Mandatory transfers from auxiliary enterprises for the retirement of indebtedness totaled $1,400,000. The amount of $37,500,000 was paid on accounts payable.

3. The accounts receivable outstanding at year end 19X8 were collected for the current funds. Of the receivables for the agency funds, $85,000 was collected, and one account totaling $1,500 was written off for the agency funds.

4. Inventories of $250,000 were expensed, and one-fifth of the prepaid expenses were used.

5. The current unrestricted fund repaid one-fourth of its loan to the endowment fund (with interest of $79,400), and all its accrued liabilities by year end.

6. The restricted fund paid $300,000 on its accounts payable and all its accrued liabilities. The entire amount of $131,000 due to other funds (in the agency fund) remained outstanding on June 30, 19X9, and interest of $10,400 was accrued at year end. Of that amount, $2,460 was due to the restricted fund. (All interfund loans were assessed the same rate of interest.)

7. The agency fund liquidated $200,000 of investments, at par, to garner enough cash to pay off the accounts payable, which was done. The accrued liabilities also were paid. The prepaid expenses were used up during the year.

8. The endowment fund was established in 19X8 by a $2,200,000 gift from one donor and a $15,000 gift from another. In addition to the interest on loans, the endowment earned $100,000 on its investments during 19X9. The investment earnings were distributed to the current unrestricted and restricted fund but the loan interest was added to the principal per the donor's intent.

9. Construction on a major fine arts facility was completed, adding another $300,000 to the construction in progress (on account). Additional long-term debt in the amount of $2,000,000 was issued. The $430,000 investments were sold for $437,000 and, together with the cash on hand and the bond proceeds, were used to pay off the accounts payable. The asset was capitalized. All debt in the unexpended plant fund pertained to the fine arts facility. In addition to this major capital item, the current unrestricted fund spent $50,000 on equipment.

10. Renewal and replacement projects of $82,000 were undertaken; none were capitalized. The accounts payable, including the $82,000, were paid. Investment earnings totaled $46,240. All cash balances were invested.

11. The following amounts were paid on outstanding debts:

	Principal	Interest
Current Portion of Bonds	$ 202,000	$ 12,000
Long-Term Notes	42,000	2,500
Long-Term Leases	5,000	4,000
Long-Term Bonds	2,500,000	318,000
Total	$2,749,000	$336,500

As a matter of policy, the retirement of indebtedness fund invests any excess cash above $50,000.

12. Earnings of $486,000 were received by the fund for the retirement of indebtedness and investments of $1,200,000 were sold for $1,350,000.

13. Buildings are depreciated on a straight-line basis over 40 years; the half-year convention is used. The equipment has a 15-year life.

14. The excess of restricted receipts over restricted expenditures was $19,200, which applied totally to federal contracts and grants.

15-7 Using the information provided in exercise 15-6, prepare a balance sheet for the current funds. Also, prepare a current funds statement of revenues, expenditures, and other changes.

15-8 Following is the current funds balance sheet of Burnsville State University as of the end of its fiscal year.

Burnsville State University
Balance Sheet
June 30, 19X1

Assets		*Liabilities and Fund Balances*	
Current Funds:		Current Funds:	
Unrestricted:		Unrestricted:	
Cash	$210,000	Accounts Payable	$ 45,000
Accounts Receivable		Deferred Revenues	66,000
(student tuition and		Fund Balances	515,000
fees, less allowance			
for doubtful accounts			
of $9,000)	341,000		*(continued)*

(continued)

Assets		Liabilities and Fund Balances	
State Appropriation			
Receivable	75,000		
	$626,000		$626,000
Restricted:		Restricted:	
Cash	$ 7,000	Fund Balances	$ 67,000
Investments	60,000		
	$ 67,000		$ 67,000
Total Current Funds	$693,000		$693,000

The following transactions occurred during the fiscal year ended June 30, 19X2:

1. On July 7, 19X1, a gift of $100,000 was received from an alumnus. The alumnus requested that one-half of the gift be used for the purchase of books for the university library and the remainder be used to endow a scholarship fund. The alumnus further requested that the income generated by the scholarship fund be used annually to award a scholarship to a qualified disadvantaged student. On July 20, 19X1, the board of trustees resolved that the money of the newly established scholarship fund would be invested in certificates of deposit. On July 21, 19X1, the certificates were purchased.

2. Revenues from student tuition and fees applicable to the year ended June 30, 19X2, amounted to $1,900,000. Of this amount, $66,000 was collected in the prior year, and $1,686,000 was collected during the year ended June 30, 19X2. In addition, at June 30, 19X2, the university received cash of $158,000 representing fees for the session beginning July 1, 19X2.

3. During the year ended June 30, 19X2, the university had collected $349,000 of the outstanding accounts receivable at the beginning of the year. The balance was determined to be uncollectible and was written off against the allowance account. At June 30, 19X2, the allowance account was increased by $3,000.

4. During the year, interest charges of $6,000 were earned and collected on late student fee payments.

5. During the year, the state appropriation was received. An additional unrestricted appropriation of $50,000 was made by the state but had not been paid to the university as of June 30, 19X2.

6. An unrestricted gift of $25,000 cash was received from alumni of the university.

7. During the year, unrestricted operating expenses of $1,777,000 were recorded. At June 30, 19X2, $59,000 of these expenses remained unpaid.

8. Restricted investments costing $21,000 were sold for $26,000. Interest earnings of $1,900 on restricted investments were received.

9. Restricted current funds of $13,000 were spent for authorized purposes during the year.

10. The accounts payable at June 30, 19X1, were paid during the year.

11. During the year, $7,000 in interest was earned and received on the certificates of deposit purchased in accordance with the board of trustees resolution (see item 1).

REQUIRED

1. Prepare journal entries to record in summary the preceding transactions for the year ended June 30, 19X2. Each journal entry should be numbered to correspond with the transaction described. The answers should be displayed as follows:

	CURRENT FUNDS				Endowment Fund	
	Unrestricted		Restricted			
Accounts	**Dr.**	**Cr.**	**Dr.**	**Cr.**	**Dr.**	**Cr.**

2. Prepare a statement of changes in fund balance for Burnsville for the period ending June 30, 19X2.

(Adapted from the May 1978 CPA Exam, Practice)

15-9 Your firm has been engaged to review the financial statements for a small two-year nonprofit junior college, Bainsville Junior College. The fiscal vice president indicates that the institution needs financial statements prepared in "good form" in order to apply for a particular federal grant. She is concerned that not all of their accounting practices are in accord with college and university accounting standards, and has asked you to make a preliminary review of the records before undertaking the engagement.

The balance sheet and operating statement prepared for your review follow:

Bainsville Junior College
Balance Sheet
As of December 31, 19X1

Assets	
Cash	$ 50,000
Tuition and Fees Receivable	229,900
Supplies Inventory	118,000
Endowment Fund Investments:	
Rental Property	180,000
Less Accumulated Depreciation	(9,000)
Stocks	15,000
Bonds	300,000
Land and Improvements	1,800,000
Buildings	3,600,000
Equipment	580,000
TOTAL ASSETS	$6,863,900

Liabilities and Equity	
Bank Loans	$ 150,000
Accounts Payable	90,000
Bonds Payable	445,000
Equity, Including Income Over Expenses for Current Year	6,178,900
TOTAL LIABILITIES AND EQUITY	$6,863,900

Statement of Revenues and Expenses
For the Year Ended December 31, 19X1

Revenues:			
Tuition		$690,000	
Contracts and Grants		12,000	
Endowment Income:			
Rentals	$19,400		
Stocks	1,600		
Bonds	14,300	35,300	
Net from Auxiliaries		(5,000)	
Unrestricted Donations		18,000	
Other Sources		3,000	
			$753,300
Expenses:			
Educational and General		$556,000	
Contracts and Grants		10,000	
Rental Property Depreciation		9,000	
Premium Amortization		300	
Other Expenses of Endowment Stock and Bond Investments		1,500	
Bond Interest		26,700	
			603,500
Excess of Revenues Over Expenses			$149,800

The vice president's staff also provided the following information:

1. This was the first year that the college had received any federal contract and grant support for research. Revenues reflect the amounts received on the grant.
2. Unamortized premium on endowment bonds has a balance of $1,200 on December 31, 19X1, which is not reflected on the financial statements.
3. Auxiliary enterprise expenses totaled $96,000 for the year.
4. Completed 15 years ago, the campus buildings were originally constructed from gifts totaling $1,000,000 and a $2,000,000, 6 percent bond issue. A $600,000 student union was built 5 years ago and was financed entirely by unrestricted gifts. The land upon which the campus is built was given by the state and had a market value of $1,800,000 on the date of the gift. Through gifts and annual payments, the total debt has been reduced to $445,000 on December 31, 19X1.
5. Net endowment income related to the rental property is restricted to building improvements and additions; other endowment income is unrestricted. Revenues are paid promptly on the due date, and there were no accruals related to the endowments at year end.
6. Bainsville calculates depreciation only on endowed assets. The buildings are expected to last 40 years. The equipment purchased 10 years ago is expected to have a life of 15 years.
7. Other than the items noted above, Bainsville appears to follow generally accepted accounting principles for nonprofit colleges and universities.
8. All endowments are restricted in perpetuity.

REQUIRED
Prepare an activity statement and balance sheet for Bainsville. Identify any additional information necessary to properly complete the statements, and any assumptions made in the preparation of these statements.

CHAPTER 16

Accounting for All Other
Nonprofit Organizations

Chapter 14 was devoted to nonprofit health care organizations and Chapter 15 to nonprofit colleges and universities. All remaining nonprofits are discussed in this chapter. These nonprofits are of two types: voluntary health and welfare organizations (VHWOs) and all other nonprofit organizations (ONPOs).

Voluntary health and welfare organizations are defined as "organizations that derive their revenue primarily from voluntary contributions from the general public to be used for general or specific purposes connected with health, welfare, or community services."[1] They include such organizations as the United Way, the American Heart Association, various mental or physical health organizations, child care facilities, counseling centers, halfway houses, drug and alcohol abuse centers, and facilities for the underprivileged or handicapped.

Distinguishing between voluntary health and welfare organizations and health care providers is not always easy. Voluntary health and welfare organizations provide funding and organizational assistance to match a health or welfare need with a particular service. They also provide health support services, whereas the health care providers discussed in an earlier chapter actually deliver health care services. Although the distinction between the two types of organizations is not clear, they currently have different accounting conventions and are covered in different AICPA audit guides.

The AICPA audit guide pertaining to "all other" nonprofits lists about 20 specific entity types that fit into the "all other" category. They include private schools, museums, foundations, trade associations, religious organizations, political parties, and labor unions. Some, such as professional and trade associations, confine their services largely to members, whereas others, such as museums and libraries, offer service to the public at large.

This chapter begins with a discussion of the purpose and structure of other nonprofits followed by an explanation of their unique accounting and reporting practices. The chapter highlights the differences between the two types of organizations and depicts selected financial transactions and statements.

---

[1] Committee on Voluntary Health and Welfare Organizations, American Institute of Certified Public Accountants, *Audits of Voluntary Health and Welfare Organizations* (New York: AICPA, 1988), v.

PURPOSE AND STRUCTURE OF NONPROFITS

Societal issue

Nonprofit voluntary health and welfare organizations and other nonprofits are organized around a common bond or concern for a societal issue: a forgotten group, a health concern, a research aim, common beliefs, community problems, or public needs unfulfilled by private or governmental organizations. Many continue indefinitely because the bond or cause remains; religious organizations, trade associations, and political parties fall into this category. Others go out of existence as government or private organizations begin to address the problem. In recent years, for example, governments have taken over many libraries, museums, mental health groups, and cultural institutions.

Organizational Structure

Different purposes and affiliations tend to overshadow the strong organizational similarities among other nonprofit organizations. Although the purpose of an organization that campaigns for improved mental health service is quite different from that of a political party, the organizational structures are quite similar. Nevertheless, the similarities in organizational structure and operations are far more important than the diversity of purpose in determining appropriate management and accounting practices.

Governing Boards   A good way to involve a broad segment of the community in a nonprofit's activities is to appoint representatives from diverse constituencies to the governing board. Some possess the skills necessary to manage and secure financing for the nonprofit. Others, however, may know little about the organization's central purpose or how to manage such an organization. These honorary appointments are designed to demonstrate the organization's importance.

Although the appointments help to achieve visibility, they sometime hinder the development of a strong management organization. Honorary appointees may lend their names only, leaving traditional board functions of developing policies and financial controls to the staff.

Staff and Volunteers   Frequently, staff members are chosen for either their fund-raising skills or their training in the particular service provided by the entity. Both aspects are necessary for the organization to remain viable and provide credible service. However, good fund-raisers and service experts are not necessarily good managers. Their primary interest is to obtain resources for providing services. Good management is viewed by many of them as nothing more than unnecessary "red tape."

Although critically important to VHWOs and ONPOs, part-time volunteer help does not strengthen a nonprofit's organizational structure. Volunteers usually focus on specific duties for short periods of time. They teach Sunday School one day a week or help raise money during a telethon, for example. Their primary interests lie elsewhere. They have little opportunity to provide management direction and may be unwilling to accept direction from the staff.

Limited Financial Resources   Many nonprofits have severely limited resources. Even if resources are plentiful, the basic priority will be the societal concern that brought the group together. Personnel or systems that would strengthen the organizational structure or the overall management are of much less concern.

As long as nonprofits operate in a community or neighborhood environment and remain small, personal dedication usually compensates for organizational weaknesses. The trend, however, is toward growth of large, broad-based organizations that conduct regional or national fund-raising campaigns. The larger the organization and the broader its scope, the greater the need for organizational talents. As titular boards, fund-raising executives, and volunteer help expand in scope and number, accounting and auditing concerns become more important.

NONPROFIT ACCOUNTING AND REPORTING ISSUES

Increased sophistication of contributors and the general public has heightened interest in the financial operations of VHWOs and ONPOs. Twenty years ago, a donor's request for audited financial statements would have been most unusual. Now it is common. Abuses of public contributions have also spawned greater government control and more reporting requirements. For example, in many jurisdictions, nonprofits that solicit money from the public must provide audited financial statements to a regulatory agency. Some VHWOs and ONPOs encounter difficulties in meeting these growing demands for financial information. The organizational structure and operating characteristics discussed earlier lead to problems with internal control, budgeting, and investments. Unless these problems can be addressed effectively, little is gained by an understanding of the accounting and reporting procedures.

Internal Control

Limited staff support and a mixture of volunteers and employees participating in the operations pose difficult internal control problems. There may be too few staff members to ensure a separation of duties, particularly in receiving, depositing, and disbursing funds. Rather than define daily tasks according to some pattern and with internal control issues in mind, nonprofits tend to assign those responsibilities to whoever is available. If it is time to open the mail, the staff member or volunteer present gets the job without much consideration for what other tasks the person will be doing. As a consequence, receiving, depositing, and disbursing funds may all be done by the same person. This is contrary to the principle that no one person should be responsible for all aspects of a transaction.

The accounting system must be carefully designed to compensate for the problems of limited staff and expertise. The staff must be trained to follow certain procedures that assign functional duties to specific persons rather than to those available at the time. Just because a certain staff member is present when the mail is delivered, for example, does not mean that he or she should open it. Internal control is also strengthened by using prenumbered multicopy forms for both receiving and disbursing funds, asking managers to assist in verifying and observing certain activities, and developing work schedules with some overlap for dual verification.

Budgeting

Nonprofit employees and volunteers tend to be very optimistic about the fund-raising potential of their organization. Sometimes they lack understanding about the costs of doing business. As a result, governing boards and supporters are often disappointed by the small net amount that can be spent directly on the organization's primary mission.

Budgeting is crucial for the board and management. It forces them to develop realistic goals and to evaluate performance. A budget also helps all concerned focus on the proportion of total funds spent on the mission versus funds spent on administration, an important issue with most contributors.

A budget may be prepared either on a functional or an object basis. If expenses and revenues are classified on a functional basis, each significant program and support service is presented separately. Program expenses are those relating to the central mission (education, research, community development, for example); support services are those necessary to fulfill the central mission (fund-raising, membership development, administration, and so forth).

A budget based on expenditure object is easier to develop than is a function-based budget. Such a budget shows a listing of salaries and wages, fringe benefits, other personnel costs, supplies, rent, insurance, depreciation, and other operating expenses. Although easier to prepare, it may not be as meaningful to governing boards. Governing boards realize that the success of nonprofits depends on whether the bulk of their resources are spent on the primary mission. Budgeting only by object code does not disclose information about the proportion of the total being budgeted for program services.

The distinction between restricted and unrestricted resources must be maintained in the budgeting process. Because restricted contributions cannot be spent for general operations, the distinction between support and program funds is very important, even when an object code classification is used.

The budget should be formally approved by the governing board. Without formal board commitment, employees and volunteers alike will have a tendency to ignore the budget. A formally adopted budget not only helps guide the staff's daily activities, but it also can be used effectively as a fund-raising device, by showing prospective donors the plan for the year.

Investments

VHWOs and ONPOs with large endowments typically invest the principal portion of the gift. Some spend only the income from these investments, while others use the total return concept. Some try to manage their own investment portfolios, while others hire outside advisers to select and manage the investments. In either case, the governing board has a fiduciary responsibility to invest wisely. Building an endowment is of little consequence unless it is invested prudently with specific investment goals in mind.

Determining investment goals often tests a governing board's ability to work together. Some board members believe firmly that the primary goal ought to be safety and long-run maintenance of capital while others believe that more risks should be accepted in order to obtain higher yields. Statutes and court precedents have not helped much in clarifying trustees' responsibilities; most simply reiterate the "prudent-man rule": if the decision would have been made by a "rational and prudent investor," it cannot be judged later as malfeasant.

Whether investment decisions are made by a counselor, the governing board, or the professional staff, certain operating procedures are critical:

- The governing board should develop a written statement of investment goals. The goals should include general ranges for fixed-income versus growth-oriented securities, the approximate overall return expected, and the grade of securities acceptable to the board.
- If an external adviser is selected, the selection procedure should be well defined before solicitations begin. Selected parts of the investment objectives should be included in the solicitation. A critical aspect of the solicitation ought to be the basis upon which the adviser will be evaluated: return on investment; appreciation in the principal; ability to respond appropriately to requests for information, withdrawals, and deposits; and so on.
- If investment decisions are made internally, procedures for monitoring and evaluating the investment function must be clearly defined. Evaluation criteria are as important for an internally managed fund as they are for one managed by an investment counselor.
- If the invested funds are only quasi-endowments (the governing board has set aside the funds), the board should determine what portion of the income and principal will be spent each year. Without such a policy, a tendency may develop to value investments for investment sake rather than as a vehicle to accomplish the nonprofit's mission.
- The governing board must decide whether it will use trust principles or the total return convention to determine the amount of endowed income to spend annually.

Investment earnings may constitute the lifeblood of a mature VHWO or ONPO. Unless carefully monitored, the investments may represent the organization's greatest risk.

ACCOUNTING AND REPORTING STANDARDS FOR NONPROFITS

Limited official guidance has been provided to VHWOs and ONPOs. Before 1979 most of the available guidance came from professional associations. As

Exhibit 16-1 illustrates, the body of knowledge for other nonprofits is much smaller than that for business organizations and relatively little of it is derived from either the AICPA or the FASB.

In 1979, when the FASB assumed responsibility for standard setting in the nonbusiness sector, it announced that the audit guides and other specific publications listed in *Statement No. 32* were *preferable* for purposes of justifying a change in accounting principle.[2] This advisory gave the nonprofits some accounting and reporting guidance while the FASB was studying their operations to develop appropriate standards.

Between 1979 and 1993, the FASB published a conceptual framework for nonprofit accounting and reporting and has issued standards on selected topics, including depreciation, pledges, and financial statements. *Concepts Statement No. 4* on the objectives of financial reporting by nonbusiness organizations was published in 1980. *Concepts Statement No. 3* on the elements of financial statements for business enterprises was replaced in 1985 by *Concepts Statement No. 6,* which deals with both business and nonprofit organizations.[3]

Reporting Objectives

In *Concepts Statement No. 4,* the FASB makes it clear that, with few exceptions, the financial reporting objectives of businesses and nonprofits ought to be similar. Differences relate to resource providers and their expectations.

Exhibit 16-1

Source and Distribution of Accounting and Reporting Standards

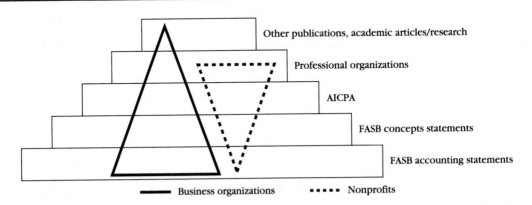

Other publications, academic articles/research

Professional organizations

AICPA

FASB concepts statements

FASB accounting statements

—— Business organizations   ▪▪▪▪ Nonprofits

---

[2]Financial Accounting Standards Board, *Statement on Financial Accounting Standards No. 32, Specialized Accounting and Reporting Principles and Practices* (Stamford, Conn.: FASB, September 1979), ¶11.

[3]Financial Accounting Standards Board, *Statement of Financial Accounting Concepts No. 4, Objectives of Financial Reporting by Nonbusiness Organizations* and *Statement of Financial Accounting Concepts No. 6, Elements of Financial Statements* (Stamford Conn.: FASB, December 1980 and December 1985).

Investors and creditors are the primary resource providers for businesses; they expect an economic return on the resources they provide and eventual repayment. Resource providers for nonprofits either expect no return or a return that is less than the resources provided.

Because nonprofits rely on contributions to sustain their operations, they have a more direct relationship with their resource providers than do businesses. Businesses provide an annual report, invite shareholders to an annual meeting, and most pay dividends. Not much additional contact with shareholders is expected. Maintaining a donor's interest usually requires frequent financial updates, progress reports pertaining to the donor's interests, and appropriate recognition of major donors.

The financial accomplishments of a business are reported on the bottom line of its income statement. As a rule, the higher the profit, the greater the accomplishment. Because by definition nonprofits do not have a profit objective, and because their accomplishments cannot be measured entirely in financial terms, the bottom line of their operating statement does not measure accomplishment. It does measure the extent to which the organization has maintained its financial capital—that is, lived within its means. With this exception, the financial reporting objectives for nonprofits and businesses differ only in terminology and emphasis.

[handwritten margin note: NP — Bottom line doesn't measure accomplishment — capital maintenance]

OBSERVATION ▲

The FASB's *Concepts Statement No. 4* went largely unheralded when published. It contained nothing to really alarm nonprofits and so attracted little attention. Now that the FASB has issued specific standards based on those concepts, nonprofits are spending more time debating the basic precepts of *Concepts Statement No. 4.*

Concepts Statement No. 3, which describes the elements—assets, liabilities, and equity—of financial statements, was revised specifically to encompass nonprofits and was renamed *Concepts Statement No. 6.* For the most part, the new statement only adds the words *not-for-profit organizations* to much of the earlier language. The FASB included a section on the net assets (assets minus liabilities) of nonprofits and applied the concept of "capital maintenance" to these organizations.

[handwritten margin note: Concepts St. No. 6 → elements of financial statements]

Net Assets

The FASB points out that nonprofits have no ownership interests corresponding to *owners' equity* in a business. The difference between assets and liabilities is referred to as *net assets* or simply *equity.* Net assets increase in two ways: (1) by receipts from providers who do not expect to receive either repayment or economic benefits in proportion to their contributions; and (2) by revenues from the sale of goods and services. The FASB states that there are three classes of net assets: (1) permanently restricted; (2) temporarily restricted; and (3) unrestricted. Although the first and second classes of assets do restrain the organization's uses of those resources, the FASB makes it clear that restrictions do not create liabilities.

[handwritten margin note: ↑ Net Assets (1) receipts (2) revenues]

▲   **OBSERVATION**
_____

If the FASB had decided that donor restrictions create liabilities, it would have revolutionized nonprofit accounting and reporting. Imagine the implications of debiting cash and crediting a liability each time someone donated restricted resources to a nonprofit! Under such circumstances, a nonprofit's equity would increase only with an excess of revenues over expenses.

No 6

Donations restrictions affect aggregate net assets

Concepts Statement No. 6 also makes it clear that donor's restrictions affect aggregate, not particular, net assets. For example, a donation of $100,000 in government securities restricted to capital improvements loses its identity upon receipt; the nonprofit only keeps track of the amount of the restricted gift ($100,000 in this case) and its intended purpose (capital additions), not the form of the donation (government securities). Without this flexibility, nonprofit accounting would be terribly complex and nonprofits would be unable to manage assets prudently.

Capital Maintenance

Capital maintenance in each asset class

One other significant accounting concept is applied to nonprofits in *Concepts Statement No. 6:* even though they have no ownership interests, nonprofits have a responsibility to maintain their capital (net assets). Because donor restrictions affect the types and levels of services that nonprofits can provide, "whether an organization has maintained certain classes of net assets may be more significant than whether it has maintained net assets in the aggregate."[4] For example, knowing that a nonprofit's net assets include $100,000 related to an endowment and $50,000 related to unrestricted net assets may be more important than knowing that net assets of $150,000 have been maintained between this period and last. This conceptual statement assures an accrual-based accounting system.

STANDARDS FOR VOLUNTARY HEALTH AND WELFARE ORGANIZATIONS

Development of formal accounting and reporting standards for voluntary health and welfare organizations began in 1964 when the National Health Council and the National Social Welfare Assembly published an accounting and reporting guide. It was followed by the AICPA's publication of an audit guide in 1966.[5] The guide was revised in 1974 and again in 1988 by the Institute's Committee on Voluntary Health and Welfare Organizations.

Uniformity of VHWOs' accounting and reporting practices has increased markedly since 1980. The FASB has endorsed the *Audit Guide* as represent-

---

[4]FASB, *Concepts Statement No. 6*, 37.

[5]Committee on Voluntary Health and Welfare Organizations, American Institute of Certified Public Accountants, *Audits of Voluntary Health and Welfare Organizations* (New York: AICPA, 1988).

ing "preferred accounting practices," and the *Guide* makes reference to generally accepted accounting principles as defined by authoritative publications. If some particular accounting application is not discussed in the *Guide,* VHWOs should apply GAAP of businesses unless "they are inapplicable." As a further push toward uniformity, the National Health Council and the National Social Welfare Assembly revised their instructions to complement the *Guide.* The material presented in this chapter is based on the *Audit Guide* and the FASB concept statements and standards.

STANDARDS FOR ALL OTHER NONPROFITS

Accounting and reporting standards for other nonprofits were slow to develop. Until 1981, when the AICPA published the *Audit Guide* for "certain" nonprofits, each type of organization took its accounting and reporting cues from affiliated professional associations or business organizations. A foundation manager, for example, looked to its national association for guidance; churches looked to denominational sources or the National Assembly of Churches, and so on. Pre-1981 audit judgments were based, in large part, on industry standards and on the basis of whether the financial statements made sense to contributors and financiers.

The *Audit Guide* for other nonprofits is limited to nonprofits not covered by other audit guides (health care organizations, colleges and universities, VHWOs, and governmental units). It also excludes those that operate essentially as businesses, such as pension plans and mutual insurance companies.[6] *Statement of Position No. 78-10 (SOP 78-10)* provides additional detail on the accounting principles and reporting practices of the nonprofits covered by the *Audit Guide.*[7] Both the *Audit Guide* and the statement of position as well as applicable FASB pronouncements are used as a basis for the principles and illustrations for ONPOs presented in this chapter.

SOP 78-10

THE IMPACT OF THE LATEST FASB STANDARDS

As was the case for health care organizations and colleges and universities, volunteer health and welfare organizations and other nonprofits will be greatly affected by the FASB standards on accounting for contributions and on financial statements. Their accounting practices were similar and these two statements will have the effect of making them converge even further. Also, neither volunteer health and welfare organizations nor other nonprofits were required to use fund accounting and consequently some did not. Therefore,

[6]Subcommittee on Nonprofit Organizations, American Institute of Certified Public Accountants, *Audit Guide for Certain Nonprofit Organizations* (New York: AICPA, 1981), 1.

[7]Accounting Standards Division, American Institute of Certified Public Accountants, *Statement of Position 78-10, Accounting Principles and Reporting Practices for Certain Nonprofit Organizations* (New York: AICPA, 1978).

fund accounting might disappear almost entirely from their accounting practices. Any separate identification of assets, liabilities, or net assets will reflect the temporarily restricted, the unrestricted, and the permanently restricted net asset classes required by the FASB statement on financial reporting.

ACCOUNTING AND REPORTING PRACTICES OF VHWOs AND ONPOs

Most differences in the accounting and reporting practices of VHWOs and ONPOs are minor. For example, some fund types used by nonprofits that use fund accounting have names different from those used by some voluntary health and welfare organizations. Valuation of investments also differs depending on whether the organization is a VHWO or an ONPO. These differences can be easily identified, and consequently VHWOs and ONPOs are discussed together in the remaining sections.

▲ **OBSERVATION**

Treating VHWOs and ONPOs together not only makes sense conceptually, but also better reflects the approach being taken by the FASB in setting accounting and reporting standards. No distinction was made among nonprofits by the FASB in discussing reporting objectives or in the three subsequent pronouncements.

Basis of Accounting

Both VHWOs and ONPOs use accrual accounting. Although many small nonprofits may operate on a cash basis throughout the year, the records are adjusted to the accrual basis for financial statement purposes. The accrual basis is required only for financial statement presentation and not necessarily for daily record keeping.[8] If the encumbrance system is used for outstanding purchase orders and other commitments, the encumbrances do not represent expenses or liabilities in the financial statements. *SOP 78-10* does, however, require that all material commitments be disclosed in the financial statement notes.[9]

Revenue Recognition

VHWOs and ONPOs characterize resource inflows as public support or revenues. **Public support** includes current contributions to fund drives, bequests, and so forth. Public support resources from specific events are shown gross and the related costs as expenses. VHWOs' and ONPOs' **revenues** have the same meaning as in business: increases in assets or decreases in liabilities (or both) from providing goods or services. Dues, ticket sales, fees, interest, rent, and so forth, are classified as revenues.

[8]AICPA, *Statement of Position No. 78-10*, 10.
[9]Ibid.

Revenues and public support are recognized as they are in business — when earned. Because resources classified as public support often carry donor restrictions, determining when they are earned poses some problems. Determining when it is appropriate to recognize contributed services and in what amount also creates some accounting problems.

Revenues when earned

Contributions and Pledges   Under *Statement No. 116,* all nonprofits recognize contributions, including unconditional promises to give (pledges), as revenue when received. Conditional promises to give are not recognized until they become unconditional. Contributions are recognized at their fair value at the date of the gift. Unconditional promises to give are valued at the present value of the future cash flows.[10] The FASB requires using a discount rate that is commensurate with the risk involved. Subsequent interest amounts, based on the effective interest method, are recognized as support in the same net asset class in which the pledge was recorded.

Contributions - FMV
Uncond. pledges - PV of amount

Ordinarily, contributed tangible assets are capitalized and recognized as revenue at their fair value at the date of the gift. However, the statement allows the recipient organization to neither capitalize nor recognize the revenue associated with such items if they are added to collections, such as those held by a museum, and if the collections meet the following conditions:

Tangible assets
↓
capitalized at FMV except museum collections

1. they are held for public exhibition, education, or research in furtherance of public service rather than financial gain
2. they are protected, kept encumbered, cared for, and preserved
3. they are subject to an organization policy that requires the proceeds from the sales of collection items to be used to acquire other items for the collections[11]

The preceding provision primarily affects museums although foundations and churches may have substantial "collections" as well. If the provision applies, subsequent sale of a collection item would be recorded as a debit to an asset account and a credit to the appropriate net asset class. Purchase of another collection item to replace the one sold would result in a debit to the appropriate net asset class.

OBSERVATION   ▲

Museums, colleges and universities, churches, and other nonprofits that receive material amounts of art, artifacts, and other collection items fought hard for this provision. Otherwise, they would have had to credit revenue each time they received such a gift. These organizations felt that it would give financial statement users an inflated view of the revenues because most of those assets would be maintained indefinitely.

---

[10] If the unconditional promises are expected to be collected or paid within a year or less, they may be valued at net realizable value (the amount that will be received).

[11] Financial Accounting Standards Board, *Statement of Financial Accounting Standards No. 116, Accounting for Contributions Received and Contributions Made* (Norwalk, Conn.: FASB, 1993), ¶5.

must depreciate!

Operating Assets, Collection Assets, and Depreciation   As mentioned in earlier chapters, nonprofits must capitalize and depreciate their operating assets, including buildings, equipment, and improvements other than buildings. In addition, they must disclose (1) depreciation expense for the period, (2) book value balances by major classes of depreciable assets, (3) accumulated depreciation by major asset class, and (4) a general description of the depreciation method(s) used for major asset classes.[12]

The FASB exposure draft on depreciation for nonprofits created considerable controversy. It required nonprofits to systematically catalog and depreciate operating assets, works of art, statues, artifacts, historical monuments, and so forth. The FASB's final pronouncement responded in a limited way to concerns about the additional record keeping that would be imposed on some nonprofits: if verifiable evidence exists, works of art or historical treasures with *extraordinarily long lives* need not be depreciated.[13] These same assets are accorded similar treatment in the pronouncement on contributions.

Under *Statement No. 116,* nonprofits are encouraged to capitalize their collection items retroactively or, if that is not practical, prospectively. If nonprofits decide not to capitalize such assets, they must report the following information on the face of their statements of activities:

1. costs of collection items purchased as a decrease in the appropriate class of net assets
2. proceeds from sale of collection items as an increase in the appropriate class of net assets
3. proceeds from insurance recoveries of lost or destroyed collection items as an increase in the appropriate class of net assets[14]

Fund Accts not required

must segregate restricted assets on fin. St.

Fund Accounting

Fund accounting is not required for either VHWOs or ONPOs. Both the *Audit Guide* for VHWOs and *SOP 78-10* describe fund accounting as a method of observing limitations on a nonprofit's resources, particularly in segregating unrestricted from restricted resources. Whether fund accounting is used or not, these pronouncements require nonprofits to clearly identify all restricted resources in the financial statements.

The FASB standard on financial statements requires reporting for the entity as a whole in the financial statements, although it does not preclude more detailed reporting if desired by the organization. Given the fact that fund accounting was not previously required, most VHWOs and ONPOs are likely to abandon traditional fund accounting. If any funds are established, they likely will represent the three net asset classes.

Because some VHWOs and ONPOs may continue using fund accounting initially, a description of the appropriate funds follows. However, the transac-

---

[12] Financial Accounting Standards Board, *Statement of Financial Accounting Standards No. 93, Recognition of Depreciation by Not-For-Profit Organizations* (Stamford, Conn.: FASB, 1987), ¶5.

[13] Ibid., ¶6.

[14] FASB, *Statement No. 116,* ¶26.

tions illustrated later in the chapter are not categorized by fund. If fund accounting is being used for internal management purposes by an organization, the accounting system must be designed to also keep track of transactions by the three net asset classes.

The *Audit Guide* for VHWOs describes several fund types commonly used by these nonprofit organizations:[15]

- **Current unrestricted funds** are used to account for resources that can be used in the general operation of the organization. Any board-designated funds are shown as unrestricted funds.
- Resources that are expendable only for operating purposes specified by the donor or grantor are accounted for in **current restricted funds.**
- A **land, building and equipment** (or plant) **fund** is used to accumulate the net investment in fixed assets and to account for contributed resources not yet expended for capital assets. Any related liabilities are included in the fund. Depreciation also is recorded in this fund.
- **Endowment funds** are used to segregate the principal amount of gifts and bequests restricted in perpetuity or for specific periods of time.
- Assets held for others or disbursed only on external instructions are accounted for in **custodian funds,** which are similar to the agency funds of governments.
- Assets restricted for loans or resulting from annuity arrangements should be held in **loan and annuity funds.**

OBSERVATION ▲

The strong similarity between these fund types and those of colleges and universities probably traces to the historically close affiliation between the two types of organizations. Despite this similarity, VHWOs (and ONPOs) record revenues and expenses in all funds. Colleges and universities record them only in the current funds.

ONPOs also may use fund accounting to segregate assets whose purpose or use is restricted. The *Audit Guide* recognizes that although some ONPOs may use fund accounting, specific funds are not required. Funds commonly used by ONPOs include restricted and unrestricted operating funds, endowment funds, plant funds, and annuity, life income, and loan funds.

OBSERVATION ▲

Both VHWOs and ONPOs will be incorporated into the new AICPA audit guide. The AICPA will most likely eliminate any reference to fund accounting because it no longer has any real relevance for financial reporting. To what extent the AICPA will discuss segregation of transactions by the net asset classes is uncertain. Future audit guides are only **guides;** an organization does not have to adhere to them.

---

[15]Adapted from the AICPA's *Audits of Voluntary Health and Welfare Organizations* (New York: AICPA, 1988), 2–3.

Restricted Support   Restricted gifts, bequests, or grants are common for many ONPOs and VHWOs. *Statement No. 116* specifically addresses the revenue recognition issues related to restricted support. When received, contributions with donor-imposed restrictions are shown as revenue in either the temporarily or permanently restricted asset class. Then, when the restrictions are satisfied, the unrestricted asset class is increased and the restricted class is decreased by a reclassification. A restriction is satisfied when the time stipulated by the donor has elapsed or when the intended use of the contribution has been satisfied. In the case of grants, for example, the reclassification to the unrestricted net asset class would take place when expenses satisfying the grant requirements are made.

Contributions restricted for the acquisition of long-lived assets are more complicated. The FASB permits either of two alternatives. Ordinarily, a donor stipulation that the contributions be spent for long-lived assets would be satisfied when the long-lived assets are placed in service.

▲ | **OBSERVATION**

This recognition rule results in an unusual accounting convention. When the contribution is received, it will be recorded as revenue in the temporarily restricted asset class in the statement of activity. When an asset is placed in service, the asset account is debited and cash credited. The statement of activity for this period shows a reduction in the temporarily restricted asset class and an increase in the unrestricted asset class. Thus, the asset class is increased **by the entire amount of the gift** when the asset is placed in service, even though the asset may be depreciated over many years.

However, if the organization has a policy that restrictions related to such contributions are satisfied as the asset is used, only an amount equal to the annual depreciation expense would be reclassified. Thus, depreciation expense for the period decreases the unrestricted asset class while the reclassification increases this asset class by the same amount; thus, there is no change in net assets.

How a gift of a long-lived asset is treated depends on the organization's policy for cash contributions restricted for the acquisition of long-lived assets.

Gifts of long-lived assets received without stipulations about how long the donated asset must be used shall be reported as restricted support if it is an organization's policy to imply a time restriction that expires over the useful life of the donated assets. Organizations that adopt a policy of implying time restrictions also shall imply a time restriction on long-lived assets acquired with gifts of cash or other assets restricted for those acquisitions.[16]

In other words, an organization has to be consistent. Either the reclassification from restricted to unrestricted occurs over the life of the asset as it is depreciated or the entire reclassification occurs when the asset is placed in service, regardless of whether the original contribution is the cash to purchase the long-lived asset or the asset itself.

[16]FASB, *Statement No. 116*, ¶16.

OBSERVATION ▲

This policy issue is important to nonprofits. If they have a policy of implying that the time restriction occurs over the useful life of the asset, the annual change in the unrestricted asset class is zero. If they do not have such a policy, the unrestricted net asset class increases markedly in the first year and declines every year thereafter until the asset is fully depreciated. Financial statement users might make significantly different assessments about a single nonprofit depending on which treatment is used.

Donated Materials and Services   VHWOs and ONPOs use similar criteria to determine when and in what amount to recognize donated materials and services in their activity statement. The VHWO *Audit Guide* and *SOP 78-10* (ONPOs) use slightly different language to describe recognizing donated *materials,* but in substance the following conditions govern the recognition:

1. the amount is significant
2. an objective, clearly measurable basis exists to determine the value of the donation

Donated *services* are difficult to value. The FASB pronouncement on contributions indicates that material amounts of contributed services are recognized as revenue and as an expense or asset if the services received: "(a) create or enhance nonfinancial assets or (b) require specialized skills, are provided by individuals possessing those skills, and would typically need to be purchased if not provided by donation."[17] Services provided by doctors, lawyers, accountants, electricians, architects, and other professionals are among those requiring specialized skills.

The Board believes that recognizing only those services meeting the conditions described above will "provide information that is clearly relevant, clearly measurable, and obtainable at a cost that does not exceed the benefits of the information provided."[18] This guidance reflected a significant change from the exposure draft. The exposure draft would have required nonprofits to recognize almost all services as long as they met the materiality criterion. Whatever else it does or does not accomplish, the statement certainly eliminates the inconsistencies among nonprofits.

[handwritten margin note: Only significant amounts recognized.]

OBSERVATION ▲

Many nonprofits are pleased with the narrowing of the definition of what services will be recognized. On the other hand, the pronouncement does seem a bit snobbish, leaving out the most frequent in-kind contributions, such as clerical duties and telethon assistance. In small nonprofits where everyone knows everyone else, some will find it difficult to understand why their contributed services are not recognized while those of other in-kind contributors are recognized.

---

[17]Ibid., ¶9.
[18]Ibid., ¶121.

Endowment Income   The accounting treatment for endowment income depends on the document establishing the endowment and on state law. If the donor stipulates that the income from the endowment is restricted for a specific use or time period, the income would be reported as income in the temporarily restricted asset class. If the donor makes it clear that the income may be used in any period for any purpose, the income would be shown as an increase in unrestricted net assets. Finally, if the donor indicates that the income must be added to the endowment until the endowment reaches a certain level, the entire income would be classified as permanently restricted until that level is reached.

State law helps define what is meant by income. At least 29 states have adopted some form of the Uniform Management of Institutional Funds Act, which allows institutions to use the total return concept. As described earlier, the total return concept permits only a specified fraction of the total return to be classified as income.[19] Without the sanction of this act, nonprofits may feel obliged to follow trust law, which requires adding the realized and unrealized gains and losses to the principal, and recognizing all other income as unrestricted revenue.

The FASB guidance takes both donor intent and state law into consideration in its financial statement document. If the donor is silent and state law allows the total return concept, the total return on endowed assets would be reported as revenue in the unrestricted asset class. If the donor is silent and there is no enabling law, both VHWOs and ONPOs probably would report the realized and unrealized gains and losses in the permanently restricted asset class and the remaining income as unrestricted. As the Board states, "because donor stipulations and laws vary, not-for-profit organizations must assess the relevant facts and circumstances for their endowment gifts and their relevant laws to determine if net appreciation on endowments is available for spending or is permanently restricted."[20]

Expense Recognition and Classification

Expenses when incurred.

Expenses are recognized in the unrestricted asset class when incurred. Many nonprofit expenses are the same as those incurred by business organizations, among them salaries and wages, rent, repairs, cost of goods sold, and insurance.

Most financial statement users, including contributors, are interested in how much the nonprofit organization is spending on **program services** (the social service activities) as opposed to **support services.** Governing boards and contributors alike want to ensure that the organization is operating efficiently—that a large portion of every dollar received is spent on the organization's primary mission. With so much emphasis placed on the dis-

---

[19] For a more exhaustive discussion, see Robert N. Anthony and David W. Young, *Management Control in Nonprofit Organizations,* 5th ed. (Homewood, Ill.: Irwin, 1994), 100. The pioneer work on the total return concept was done by Richard M. Ennis and J. Peter Williamson, *Spending Policy for Educational Endowments* (New York: The Common Fund, 1976).

[20] FASB, *Statement No. 116,* ¶125.

tinction between program and support services, the proper classification is a primary accounting problem associated with expenses.

Functional Expense Classifications The FASB standard on financial statements requires that functional expenses be shown in the activity statement. The pronouncement also requires VHWOs to report this information as well as the natural expense classifications, such as rent, salaries, and repairs, *in a matrix format in a separate financial statement.* ONPOs are encouraged but not required to provide this information about natural expense classifications.

OBSERVATION

The FASB does not explain why it imposed special requirements on VHWOs, but presumably the decision related to past practices. Prior to *Statement No. 117,* VHWOs had to prepare a statement of functional expenses, and a number of respondents felt that "a separate statement" is necessary for these organizations.

How detailed functional expenses are shown depends on the services rendered by an ONPO or a VHWO. At a minimum, the classification scheme should distinguish among program services, management and general activities, and fund-raising efforts. If a nonprofit has several different programs, each program's revenues and expenses should be reported separately. For example, a trade association (ONPO) might have member services, technical services, continuing education programs, fund-raising, and administration. Revenue from each source and expenses associated with each program should be depicted in the activity statement.

Presenting natural classifications may be helpful for complex nonprofits. Continuing the example of the trade association, the activity statement would show continuing education expenses, for example, broken down by salaries and wages, equipment rentals, speaker fees, travel, and so on.

The growing complexity of fund-raising activities and the greater sophistication of contributors sometimes suggests a further breakdown of expenses. Showing support from and expenses associated with each *type* of fund-raising event is a common practice for large organizations.

Allocating Expenses to Functions Reporting direct costs by functional classification is easy; allocating indirect costs to each functional classification is not. The task of allocating personnel and other costs to the fund-raising function is particularly difficult. Fund-raising programs should be assigned a portion of personnel, supplies, occupancy, printing, mailing, and other solicitation costs. Because fund-raising is so intertwined with daily activities, managers have a difficult time determining what portion of numerous costs to allot to the fund-raising function: How much of the director's luncheon with a local business group was to provide technical assistance versus solicitation? How much of an organization's brochure costs should be assigned to fund-raising versus membership development?

Limited guidance is available for developing cost allocation procedures. The VHWO and ONPO audit guides refer to "reasonable bases" of allocation, "allocating all applicable" costs, and "according to procedures that...determine the portion of the costs related to each function." They provide few examples of acceptable bases. In *SOP 78-10* (ONPOs), the AICPA acknowledges the difficulty of the task and mentions that it is not the division's intent to force ONPOs into "overly meticulous allocation."

The *Audit Guide for Volunteer Health and Welfare Organizations* illustrates costs that would and would not be allocated to particular programs. In the AICPA illustration, a public education program would include such expenses as direct costs of educational symposia; salaries and wages of employees working on the symposia or other public lectures; costs of pamphlets, letters, posters, and films; and costs of educational materials distributed to select groups. The illustration also indicates that certain partially related costs should not be allocated to the public education function, including postage for mass mailings, public meetings to kick off fund-raising solicitations, or informational materials containing general information regarding health or welfare problems.[21]

Allocating Joint Material Costs   The AICPA also provides guidance for allocating joint costs of informational materials and activities that include a fund-raising appeal. The statement of position (SOP) issued by the AICPA on this subject in 1987 was difficult to apply because it did not give specific guidance on the types of costs to be considered and because no allocation formulas were provided. A revised SOP is being considered. Joint costs are clearly defined in the proposed SOP to include costs of conducting, producing, and distributing materials and activities that include both a fund-raising appeal and program or administrative costs. According to the proposed statement, all joint costs will be reported as fund-raising costs unless the organization can demonstrate that a bona fide program or management and general function also has been conducted.

A bona fide program or management and general function is conducted if:

1. the joint purpose can be established, for example, the program or management and general function will still be conducted without a fund-raising activity, or compensation to professional fund-raisers in connection with the activities is not based solely on amounts raised
2. the audience is broad enough to benefit from or act on the other (management or general) function, for example, audience members are not selected primarily for their ability to contribute
3. the costs support bona fide program or management and general functions, for example, the materials must contain messages that relate to broad organizational goals, such as "stop smoking," or "say no to drugs."

If the so-called purpose criterion (Item 1) is not met, the activity may still qualify as a joint activity if other tangible evidence supporting the true joint

---

[21]AICPA, *Audits of Voluntary Health and Welfare Organizations* (1988), 25–26.

nature of the activity can be obtained, for example, board minutes that clearly indicate the joint nature of the project.

The proposed SOP requires that the joint costs be systematically and rationally allocated. It provides three alternative methodologies, all of which involve determining the *proportion* of the total cost allocable to each function. For example, the physical units method involves allocating joint costs in proportion to the number of units of output. Examples of output are lines on a paper and square inches. Another methodology, the stand-alone-joint-cost method, allocates the costs based on the ratio of the stand-alone costs for each function to total stand-alone costs times the total cost of the activity. As an example, if the mailing costs of a joint-message are $100,000 and it contains both a fund-raising appeal (stand-alone cost of $40,000) and a program message (stand-alone cost of $80,000), the allocation of joint costs is:

Fund-raising	$40,000/$120,000 × $100,000 = $33,333
Program	$80,000/$120,000 × $100,000 = $66,667

The third method allocates the joint costs based on their respective direct costs.

OBSERVATION ▲

The allocation of joint costs is a significant issue for all nonprofits. Donors want to give to organizations that are able to spend a large portion of every dollar on their program functions, rather than on fund-raising and administration. Reported fund-raising costs can be reduced, in part, by allocating a portion of the cost to program efforts.

Investments

VHWOs or ONPOs may receive stocks, bonds, or other investments as contributions. They also acquire investments by investing idle cash that will be used for operating or restricted purposes. Initial valuations are the same as for business and governmental units. Purchased investments are recorded at cost, and donated securities are recorded at fair market value on the date of the acquisition. From acquisition date forward, optional valuation procedures are available to VHWOs and ONPOs.

Valuation Subsequent to Acquisition   VHWOs and ONPOs may value investments at either cost or market; in some cases, the lower of cost or market may be used as well. To further confuse matters, VHWOs and ONPOs do not always have the same options. *SOP 78-10* prescribes the following valuation basis for ONPOs' investments.

- Marketable debt securities that likely will be held until maturity should be reported at amortized cost, market value, or the lower of amortized cost or market value.
- Marketable equity securities and other marketable debt securities should be reported at market value or the lower of cost or market.

• All other investments should be reported at either fair market value or the lower of cost or market.[22]

Whatever valuation basis is selected for each group should apply to all investments in that group. ONPOs using the lower-of-cost-or-market basis report declines below market on noncurrent investments as a direct addition to or deduction from net equity. Recoveries are reported only to the extent of raising the investment value to cost. Declines below market on current investments are reported in the statement of activity, as are recoveries.

Volunteer health and welfare organizations have fewer valuation options: most use cost, but lower-of-cost-or-market is also an acceptable valuation basis. The *Audit Guide* points out that when the market value falls below cost — for investments carried at the lower of cost or market — the loss should be recognized. Any recoveries, up to original cost, should be recognized as income in the periods realized. VHWOs must use the same valuation basis for all funds, which means for all investments. The basis must be clearly disclosed in the financial statements.

With this confusing array of rules for nonprofit investments, it is not surprising that the FASB is now considering a project on investments. Although a final pronouncement is several years away, all nonprofits probably will account for investments in the same manner when the FASB completes its work in this area. *Statement No. 117* implies that investments be reported at market value: unrealized gains and losses are recognized, so the effect would seem to be reporting the asset at market.

Investment Pools   VHWOs and ONPOs often pool investments from various sources. They use the **unit value method** to allocate net investment earnings (dividends, interest, and realized and unrealized gains and losses) equitably. Under the unit value method, "each fund is assigned a number of units based on the relationship of the market value of all investments at the time they are pooled."[23] To illustrate, if funds A and B initiated a pooled account by contributing $100,000 and $50,000 respectively, and $1,000 was the initially assigned value per unit, fund A would have 100 units or 67 percent of the total units, and fund B would have 50 units or 33 percent of the total. When the pool is revalued — usually when a fund enters or withdraws from the pool — new unit values are assigned.

To continue the example, if one year later the pooled investments had a total market value of $200,000, the new unit value would be $1,333 ($200,000/150). Fund A's investments are worth $133,333 and fund B's are worth $66,667.

Transfers Among Funds

Interfund transfers are used only if a nonprofit uses fund accounting. They represent asset and fund balance shifts from one fund to another or capital-

---

[22] Adapted from AICPA, *Statement of Position No. 78-10,* 27.

[23] AICPA, *Statement of Position No. 78-10,* ¶116 and ¶117; and *Audits of Voluntary Health and Welfare Organizations* (1988), 8.

izations of fixed assets in the plant funds that were purchased from current unrestricted funds. Both VHWOs and ONPOs draw a distinction between interfund transfers and revenues and expenses. VHWOs report interfund transfers under "other changes in fund balances," while ONPOs show them after the beginning fund balance in the activity statement.

ILLUSTRATED FINANCIAL TRANSACTIONS

Selected financial transactions are presented for Carlton Community Research Foundation, a private nonprofit foundation (ONPO). The foundation does not use fund accounting. Selected transactions for 19X8 are illustrated, some of which depict operating activities; others show entries pertaining to the organization's endowment and plant. Descriptors are used to facilitate an understanding of the various net asset classes, for example, Revenues—Temporarily Restricted, but no doubt a nonprofit would use subsidiary accounts for this purpose. The entries that do not have any descriptors relate to unrestricted net assets.

Operating Activities   *19 X8*

The Carlton Foundation received $87,000 in unrestricted pledges from its annual fund drive. In a typical year, about 4 percent of the pledges will not be received. Also, contributions of $18,000 received in 19X7 but designated for 19X8 were reclassified to unrestricted net assets at year end. If separate cash accounts are maintained for each asset class, the entry would be a debit to Cash—unrestricted and a credit to Cash—temporarily restricted.

1.	Pledges Receivable	87,000	
	Support—Contributions		83,520
	Allowance for Uncollectible Pledges		3,480

no bad debt expense as dr.

In 19X8, pledges of $80,000 were received in cash; in addition, one person made a $6,000 contribution designated for 19X9. A $1,000 19X8 pledge was considered uncollectible.

2.	Cash	86,000	
	Allowance for Uncollectible Pledges	1,000	
	Pledges Receivable		81,000
	Support—Temporarily Restricted		6,000

A donor contributed equipment to the foundation. The donor indicated that the foundation was free to use the equipment or to sell it and use the proceeds to benefit the organization's goals. The donor's basis in the property was $100,000 and the fair market value was $150,000. The foundation decided to sell the property; it was sold at fair market value and the proceeds were earmarked by the governing board for research on native habitat.

FMV

| 3. | Equipment Held for Resale | 150,000 | |
| | Support—Contributions | | 150,000 |

| 4. | Cash | 150,000 | |
| | Equipment Held for Resale | | 150,000 |

The foundation solicited grant requests for conducting research on native habitat; in the meantime, it invested the proceeds in short-term securities.

| 5. | Short-Term Investments | 150,000 | |
| | Cash | | 150,000 |

(internal)

A research grant for $65,000 was approved by the foundation's board, but disbursement was not made during 19X8.

| 6. | Awards and Grants Expense—Research | 65,000 | |
| | Awards and Grants Payable | | 65,000 |

Either Board designation does not affect restricted net assets but at year end unrestricted net assets would show an $85,000 ($150,000 − $65,000) designation for habitat research.

In-kind contributions for the year totaled $11,800: legal services on one of the foundation's research projects ($4,000); a consultant's time on reorganizing the foundation's committee system ($6,000); and supplies worth $1,800 that were used in a fund-raising drive.

7.	Supplies Inventory	1,800	
	Expenses—Research	4,000	
	Expenses—Administration	6,000	
	Support—Donated Materials		1,800
	Support—Donated Services		10,000

Other operating expenses for the year totaled $55,000:

Salaries and Wages	$20,000
Payroll Taxes and Employee Benefits	4,000
Supplies	1,500
Facilities Rental	9,000
Conferences	8,000
Printing and Publication	5,700
Utilities and Telephone	2,700
Postage	1,900
Equipment Rental	800
Miscellaneous Expenses	1,400

Of the total costs 60 percent was spent for research, 20 percent for fund-raising, and 20 percent for administration. All except $10,500 of the expenses, excluding inventory, were paid by year end. The entries recording the expenses will be illustrated for a program classification, but not by object code:

8.	Expenses—Research	33,000	
	Expenses—Fund-Raising	11,000	
	Expenses—Administration	11,000	
	Cash		43,000
	Accrued Expenses Payable		10,500
	Supplies Inventory		1,500

In addition to the pledges and contributions shown earlier, the following unrestricted amounts were received in cash:

9.	Cash	66,000	
	Revenue—Investment Income		8,200
	Support—Legacies		21,000
	Support—United Giving		33,800
	Revenue—Public Sales		3,000

The foundation sponsored a local marathon event, the net proceeds to be used for its general research efforts. The fees generated by participants totaled $8,000, and the expenses for prizes and organizing the marathon were $5,100.

10.	Cash	8,000	
	Support—Special Events		8,000
11.	Expenses—Fund Raising	5,100	
	Cash		5,100

For many years, ONPOs and VHWOs debited such expenses directly to the revenue account and therefore showed only the net support provided by special events. Guidance provided by *Statement No. 117* changes this practice. Now, nonprofits must report the gross revenue and the related expenses, unless the activity is peripheral to the organization.

An endowment instrument allowed the foundation to utilize realized endowment gains as unrestricted resources. Realized gains totaled $3,200 in 19X8.

| 12. | Cash | 3,200 | |
| | Revenue—Investment Income | | 3,200 |

The foundation's board decided to utilize $15,000 of unrestricted resources to purchase equipment needed for the research program.

| 13. | Equipment | 15,000 | |
| | Cash | | 15,000 |

Carlton Foundation's operating activities also involve education on the importance of broad-based nonpartisan community research and research on community problems. The education program is supported, in large part, from an endowment established for that purpose by a local philanthropist (see the later section on Other Activities). Specific research projects are funded almost entirely from local contributions and governmental grants.

Support received during the year included pledges of $71,000, all of which was earmarked by the donors for research. The foundation estimates that all but $1,800 will be collected. Investment income totaled $33,000; $13,000 was earned on investments held for the education program and the remainder was earned on investments restricted for research.

14.	Cash	33,000	
	Pledges Receivable	71,000	
	Allowance for Uncollectible Pledges		1,800
	Contributions—Temporarily Restricted		69,200
	Investment Income—Temporarily Restricted		33,000

As the expenses are incurred related to the research and education programs, the foundation would reclassify assets from the temporarily restricted to the unrestricted net asset class. The foundation probably would segregate the cash to assure availability when the expenses are incurred.

By year end, the foundation collected $65,000 of the pledges.

15.	Cash	65,000	
	Pledges Receivable		65,000

The endowment fund restricted for education earned $8,000 during the year. Since the donor has restricted the earnings, they would be recorded as revenue in the temporarily restricted net asset class until actually spent for the intended purpose. Had the donor not specified the use of the income, it would be reported as revenue in the unrestricted net asset class regardless of whether it was spent during the year.

revenue in temp restr NAC until related expense made Then reclassified to unrestr NAC

16.	Cash	8,000	
	Investment Income—Temporarily Restricted		8,000

Research and education program expenses for the year totaled $79,200 and $21,000 respectively. The foundation also purchased $10,000 of equipment for the research program from temporarily restricted resources. To simplify the transaction, all expenses are assumed to be paid in cash.

17.	Expenses—Research	79,200	
	Expenses—Education	21,000	
	Equipment	10,000	
	Cash		110,200

These expenses would be reported in the unrestricted net asset class; the equipment would be reported there as well. Depreciation expense on the asset would be included in the unrestricted expenses. A reclassification from the temporarily restricted to the unrestricted class of $110,200 would be reported in the activity statement for the year.

On December 31, 19X8, the Carlton Foundation was notified of a $30,000 governmental grant award to research the effect of the proposed highway by-pass on the city of Carlton and surrounding communities. The research is scheduled for 19X9.

(external))

18.	Grants Receivable	30,000	
	Revenue—Temporarily Restricted		30,000

Because the earlier temporarily restricted expenses/capital purchases equaled total temporarily restricted revenues, the grant and related net equity (asset) are the only amounts in the temporarily restricted net asset class at year end.

Other Activities

The Carlton Foundation also has an endowment that was established by a local donor. One-half the earnings from the $200,000 endowment are restricted to education about the importance of community research; the related operating activities were described earlier. The remaining one-half of investment earnings must be added to the endowment base. The endowment was invested immediately.

19.	Cash	200,000	
	Contributions—Permanently Restricted		200,000
20.	Investments	200,000	
	Cash		200,000

Another donor contributed $5,000 to the endowment (the gift was made with the same stipulations as those of the first donor); this donation also was invested.

21.	Cash	5,000	
	Contributions—Permanently Restricted		5,000
22.	Investments	5,000	
	Cash		5,000

Investments with a book value of $15,000 were sold for $15,900; the proceeds were reinvested. Because the donor explicitly stated that one-half of all earnings should be added to the endowment, the sale affects both permanently restricted and temporarily restricted assets.

23.	Cash	15,900	
	Investments		15,000
	Gain on Sale—Permanently Restricted		450
	Gain on Sale—Temporarily Restricted		450
24.	Investments	15,900	
	Cash		15,900

Investment income of $16,000 was earned during the year. One-half or $8,000 already was reflected as temporarily restricted income in the operating section (see entry 16). Pursuant to the donors' instructions, the remaining $8,000 represents a permanent increase in the endowment or permanently restricted assets:

25.	Cash	8,000	
	Investment Income—Permanently Restricted		8,000

One wing of a research facility was constructed at a total cost of $420,000. Carlton has been accumulating funds for this purpose during the past ten years. Accumulated funds totaled $300,000, and the balance was financed by a 20-year mortgage.

26.	Building	420,000	
	Cash		300,000
	Mortgage Payable		120,000

As Carlton accumulated the funds for this research facility, the contributions were recorded as revenue in the temporarily restricted fund. As explained earlier, depreciation on the facility would affect unrestricted net assets. Carlton has no policy of recognizing gifts on long-lived assets as they are used; thus, a reclassification from the temporarily restricted to the unrestricted net asset class equal to the total cost of the asset is made at the time it is placed in service. Although the depreciation entry is not illustrated, depreciation would be taken annually and shown in the unrestricted net asset class. Because this purchase represents a substantial sum, the foundation probably would have designated a portion of the temporarily restricted net assets in prior years to alert readers to the building plans. If so, the designation would be removed:

27.	Temporarily Restricted Net Assets		
	Designated for Capital Additions	300,000	
	Temporarily Restricted Net Assets		300,000

Other activities related to the permanently restricted assets might include recording the unrealized gains and losses on investments, recording amortization of premium or discounts associated with the investments, and making payments related to the mortgage. No doubt Carlton would try to obtain contributions to make the annual mortgage payment or to pay it off entirely. None of these activities poses accounting problems not already discussed. The only one that reflects differences between an ONPO and a VHWO is the recording of unrealized gains and losses. Providing the entities do not use the total return convention, ONPOs and VHWOs would use different valuation bases for some investments. Thus, the amount of unrealized gains or losses recognized by each type of entity likely could vary in any given period.

Depreciation and other expenses that can be reasonably allocated should be recorded on a functional basis. Depreciation on facilities or equipment used by Carlton's research program should be recorded as Depreciation Expense—Research, for example. Interest expense ordinarily is not allocated, or the entire amount is allocated to the general and administrative area. For Carlton, however, debt can be associated with a particular program and therefore so can the related interest.

ILLUSTRATED FINANCIAL STATEMENTS

With the issuance of *Statement No. 117,* financial statements used by VHWOs and ONPOs are almost identical. Both prepare a balance sheet, a statement of activity, and a cash flow statement. The activity statement must provide information about expenses reported by their functional classification, such as education, research, general and administrative, and fund-raising. In addition, VHWOs must report information about their expenses by natural classification (rent, supplies, salaries and wages), and by functional classification "in a matrix format in a separate statement."[24] The FASB encourages other nonprofits to report the information about the natural classification of expenses.

OBSERVATION ▲

As discussed previously, VHWOs were required by the earlier audit guide to show expenses by both functional and natural class. Although the FASB does not explain fully the reason for the additional requirement for VHWOs in *Statement No. 117,* it does indicate that specialized reporting practices are not inconsistent with the requirements of this standard. Thus, the special requirement for VHWOs remains in effect.

The audit guides and the FASB pronouncement allow organizations flexibility in formatting their statements. Therefore, the statements depicted here should be viewed only as one possible version. To the extent possible and to illustrate the flexibility allowed, the statements shown in this chapter were purposely designed differently than those in earlier chapters. These illustrated statements reflect the transactions described in the chapter. However, to illustrate the full breadth of these statements, other transactions are assumed to have occurred as well. All three required statements are presented. Exhibit 16-2 depicts a statement of activity. A balance sheet is presented in Exhibit 16-3, and a cash flow statement in Exhibit 16-4. The additional matrix statement required of VHWOs is presented in Exhibit 16-5.

The statement of activity displayed in Exhibit 16-2 shows the changes in the net asset classifications in a "stacked" rather than a columnar approach. It tends to emphasize the increase in net assets, the $307,280, rather than the various component parts of that change.

Assets reclassified require explanation. As would be explained in the notes to the financial statements, assets released from restrictions and shown

---

[24] FASB, *Statement No. 117,* ¶26.

Exhibit 16-2

Carlton Foundation
Statement of Activity
For the Year Ended June 30, 19X1

Changes in Unrestricted Net Assets:

Support, Revenues, and Gains:	
Support—Contributions	$ 233,520
Support—Other	74,600
Investment Income	11,400
Net Unrealized and Realized Gains[a]	10,000
Other	3,000
Total Unrestricted Revenues and Gains	$ 332,520
Net Assets Released from Restrictions:	
Satisfaction of Program Restrictions	$ 100,200
Satisfaction of Equipment Restrictions	430,000
Expiration of Time Restrictions[a]	21,000
Total Net Assets Released from Restrictions	$ 551,200
Total Unrestricted Revenues, Gains, and Other Support	$ 883,720
Expenses and Losses:	
Education[a]	$ 190,000
Research[a]	125,200
Fund-raising	16,100
Administrative and General[a]	54,040
Total Expenses and Losses	$ 385,340
Increase in Unrestricted Net Assets	$ 498,380

Changes in Temporarily Restricted Assets:

Contributions	$ 75,200
Income on Investments	41,000
Revenues	30,000
Net Realized and Unrealized Gains	450
Net Assets Released from Restrictions[a]	(420,000)
Increase in Temporarily Restricted Assets	$ (273,350)

Changes in Permanently Restricted Net Assets:

Contributions	$ 205,000
Income on Investments	8,000
Net Realized and Unrealized Gains	450
Net Assets Released from Restrictions[a]	(131,200)
Decrease in Permanently Restricted Net Assets	$ 82,250
Increase in Net Assets	$ 307,280
Net Assets, Beginning of the Year	697,520
Net Assets, End of the Year	$1,004,800

[a]Other transactions were assumed in the derivation of this number.

as a decrease in the temporarily restricted and permanently restricted assets equal the amount reclassified and added to unrestricted net assets. The entire amount of equipment reclassifications was shown in this year because the

Exhibit 16-3

Carlton Foundation
Statements of Financial Position
June 30, 19X1 and 19X0

	19X1	19X0
Assets		
Cash and Cash Equivalents[a]	$ 28,900	$200,000
Accounts and Interest Receivable[a]	8,000	7,000
Prepaid Expenses[a]	2,100	—
Inventory of Supplies	300	—
Contributions Receivable, net[a]	73,720	66,000
Grants Receivable	30,000	—
Short-Term Investments[a]	112,200	30,500
Land, Buildings, and Equipment, net[a]	545,000	116,000
Long-Term Investments[a]	415,630	323,920
Total Net Assets	$1,215,850	$743,420
Liabilities and Net Assets		
Accounts Payable[a]	$ 12,850	$ 18,500
Accrued Expenses Payable[a]	10,500	18,000
Refundable Advance[a]	—	1,600
Grants Payable	65,000	—
Notes Payable[a]	—	5,000
Annuity Obligations[a]	2,700	2,800
Mortgages Payable	120,000	—
Total Liabilities	$ 211,050	$ 45,900
Net Assets		
Unrestricted	$ 714,640	$216,260
Temporarily Restricted	84,350	68,900
Permanently Restricted	205,810	412,360
Total Net Assets	$1,004,800	$697,520
Total Liabilities and Net Assets	$1,215,850	$743,420

[a]The 19X1 figures cannot be calculated with only the 19X0 balances and the transactions shown in the chapter.

Exhibit 16-4

Carlton Foundation
Statement of Cash Flow
For the Year Ending June 30, 19X1

Cash Flows from Operating Activities:	
Change in Net Assets	$ 307,280
Adjustments to Reconcile Change in Net Assets to	
Net Cash Provided by Operating Activities:	
Depreciation	16,000
Gain on Sale of Investments	(900)
Increase in Receivables	(1,000)
Increase in Inventory	(300)
Increase in Prepaid Expenses	(2,100)
Increase in Grants Receivable	(30,000)
Increase in Contributions Receivable	(7,720)

(continued)

Exhibit 16-4   *(continued)*

Decrease in Refundable Advance	(1,600)
Decrease in Payables	(13,150)
Increase in Grants Payable	65,000
Decrease in Annuity Obligations	(100)
Contributions Restricted for Long-Term Investments	(205,000)
Interest and Dividends Restricted for Reinvestment	(8,000)
Net Cash Provided by Operating Activities	$ 118,410
Cash Flows from Investing Activities:	
Purchase of Land, Buildings, and Equipment	$(445,000)
Proceeds from Sale of Investments	15,900
Purchase of Investments	(188,410)
Net Cash Used by Investing Activities	$(617,510)
Cash Flows from Financing Activities:	
Proceeds from Contributions Restricted for:	
Investment in Endowment	$ 205,000
Investment in Plant	—
Investment Subject to Annuity Agreements	—
Other Financing Activities:	
Interest and Dividends Restricted for Reinvestment	8,000
Payment on Notes Payable	(5,000)
Proceeds from Mortgage	120,000
Net Cash Used by Financing Activities	$ 328,000
Net Decrease in Cash and Cash Equivalents	$(171,100)
Cash and Cash Equivalents at Beginning of the Year	200,000
Cash and Cash Equivalents at the End of the Year	$ 28,900

Exhibit 16-5

Hypothetical Volunteer Health and Welfare Organization
Statement of Functional Expenses
For the Period Ending December 31, 19X8

	PROGRAM SERVICES			SUPPORT SERVICES		
	Research	Educa-tion	Total	Manage-ment	Fund-Raising	Total
Salaries and Wages	$ 22,000	$185,000	$207,000	$421,000	$134,000	$555,000
Employee Benefits	2,000	7,000	9,000	11,000	7,500	18,500
Payroll Taxes	4,000	37,000	41,000	84,200	26,800	111,000
Total Salaries and Related Expenses	$ 28,000	$229,000	$257,000	$516,200	$168,300	$684,500
Contracted Services	500	5,000	5,500	13,000	4,000	17,000
Supplies	1,000	6,500	7,500	9,000	8,500	17,500
Utilities	500	2,000	2,500	1,500	500	2,000
Communication Expenses	1,000	5,500	6,500	7,500	11,500	19,000
Occupancy	2,500	13,500	16,000	15,000	14,500	29,500
Conferences and Meetings	4,000	9,500	13,500	19,300	6,500	25,800
Printing and Publications	2,000	32,100	34,100	7,000	32,000	39,000
Awards and Grants	332,000	7,000	339,000	—	—	—
Miscellaneous	4,100	2,000	6,100	5,300	2,700	8,000
Total Expenses Before Depreciation	$375,600	$312,100	$687,700	$593,800	$248,500	$842,300
Depreciation of Buildings and Equipment	1,000	2,500	3,500	3,500	2,000	5,500
Total Expenses	$376,600	$314,600	$691,200	$597,300	$250,500	$847,800

foundation does not have a policy of recognizing permanently restricted capital gifts as the assets are used. Therefore, the entire cost of the asset is recognized as a reclassification when the asset is placed in service. If the foundation had such a policy, only an amount equal to the depreciation would be reclassified annually. Some argue that this requirement tends to distort the statement of activity. Certainly the net increase in assets would be substantially different in the latter case.

SUMMARY

Other nonprofit organizations include voluntary health and welfare organizations and a myriad of other organizations ranging from churches to labor unions. Despite the broad spectra of services provided by nonprofits, their organizational structures, operating characteristics, and accounting and reporting practices are remarkably similar. Characterized by lay boards and volunteer help, other nonprofits must respond not only to those needing their services but also to an increasingly sophisticated philanthropic community. The accounting system must provide both managerial and financial data; accounting reports must be understandable and concise.

The FASB is responsible for establishing accounting and reporting standards for other nonprofits. Nonprofits are covered in *Concepts Statement Nos. 4 and 6.* Implicit in the conceptual framework is a focus on capital maintenance and an ability to identify restricted assets. Nonprofits use accrual accounting and many of their entries and financial statements mirror those of business organizations. To assure that restricted resources are used for their intended purposes and to help clarify accounting reports, some nonprofits blend industrial and fund accounting practices.

With the issuance of FASB's *Statement No. 116* and *Statement No. 117,* the accounting for volunteer health and welfare organizations and other nonprofits has converged considerably. Now major revenue sources — contributions and pledges — are recognized identically by both types of organizations. Recognition occurs when the contribution is received or the pledge is made. Also, both types of organizations now prepare the same basic financial statements: a balance sheet, a statement of activity, and a cash flow statement. In addition, VHWOs must prepare a matrix showing expenses by both natural and functional classifications. All required statements are prepared for the entity as a whole; however, VHWOs and ONPOs are not precluded from using fund accounting for internal accounting purposes or supplementary reporting purposes.

Other than the fact that VHWOs prepare one additional statement, the primary difference between VHWO and ONPO accounting is in the area of valuing investments, a topic the FASB has on its agenda for nonprofits. Also, VHWOs may have had a greater reliance on fund accounting and therefore may find the transition to the requirements of FASB *Statement No. 116* more difficult than will ONPOs. The accounting for VHWOs and ONPOs will become even more similar, perhaps even identical, when the FASB completes other projects on its nonprofit agenda and when the AICPA completes the audit guide for nonprofits.

QUESTIONS

16-1   Characterize the organizational structure and governance of other nonprofit organizations.

16-2   What organization is responsible for establishing the accounting and reporting standards for other nonprofit organizations?

16-3   Under FASB *Statement No. 117*, what is the role of fund accounting in accounting and financial reporting for VHWOs and ONPOs?

16-4   Is budgeting important for other nonprofits? Explain why or why not.

16-5   How have accounting and reporting standards for voluntary health and welfare organizations been established? Contrast this development with that for businesses.

16-6   Identify and briefly describe the other nonprofit accounting and reporting standards issued by the FASB since 1979.

16-7   What are "net assets" of a nonprofit? Why is the concept of net assets important for nonprofit organizations?

16-8   Explain how donor restrictions are reflected in the accounting for nonprofit organizations.

16-9   Describe the nature of financial statements required for VHWOs and ONPOs.

16-10   What basis of accounting is used by other nonprofit entities for financial statement purposes? Do nonprofits use the same basis for managerial purposes?

16-11   Explain the accounting for pledges by VHWOs and ONPOs.

16-12   What is the "unit value" method used to allocate investment earnings to participating funds in an investment pool?

16-13   Contrast the investment valuation practices for VHWOs and ONPOs.

16-14   The board of directors of a local athletic support group decides to set aside some money for athletic scholarships. If the organization uses fund accounting, how is this money classified? Why is the classification necessary?

16-15   Describe the circumstances under which an ONPO can record donated materials as public support.

16-16   What fund types are commonly used by VHWOs and ONPOs? Are there significant differences between the fund structures for the two types of organizations?

16-17   Explain how the total return concept is applied to the endowments of other nonprofits.

16-18   A local foundation values all investments at cost. Would an auditor accept this practice? Explain.

16-19   Describe the statement of cash flows for VHWOs and ONPOs, and contrast its contents and format with those of a business cash flow statement.

16-20 Explain how an accountant would determine whether joint costs existed under the exposure draft statement of position on allocating joint material costs in nonprofits.

16-21 Bella Donny donated $1,000,000 to the Oldtown Foundation. Of this amount, $100,000 may be used at management's discretion, $200,000 is restricted for mounting an educational program, $200,000 goes to the building fund for a future new wing, and the remaining $500,000 is for the Bella Donny endowment. How should these amounts be accounted for under *Statement No. 116?*

16-22 The Bella Donny endowment (see question 16-21) has the following conditions: two-thirds of the income may be used for any current activity; the other third must be added to the endowment. How is the investment income recorded?

CASES

16-1 A group representing the Zook County Preservation Club, an unincorporated entity, has requested accounting advice. The club's membership has been growing steadily for the past several years, drawing together individuals from several states to work for the preservation of bighorn sheep. Currently, the club has about 5,000 members located in five states. It has been loosely organized. The elected president deposits checks in a local bank account and pays the bills, most of which are for ads and for travel to meetings on behalf of the Preservation Club. All mail is sent to the president's home, and he uses part of his house for club office space. The group indicates that it has approximately $10,000 in the local account. To build a stronger identity, local representatives have decided to rent facilities and separate completely the club's operations from those of elected officials. They also explain that if they can prepare financial statements according to generally accepted accounting principles, the club would be eligible for state grants supporting its efforts.

REQUIRED

1. In broad and understandable terms, explain the accounting and reporting practices required to prepare GAAP financial statements.
2. Outline each step the club must take to get from its current position of a loosely organized, unincorporated entity to an incorporated, functioning nonprofit organization. If the services of other professionals are required, please identify those for the club representatives.
3. Identify key management issues that the club must address, and explain how these issues should be addressed.

16-2 The United Nondenominational Church has not been formally reporting many of its fixed assets in its financial statements. The church recently received notification from its national affiliate that depreciation is required on all fixed assets. Church staff members search their records for invoices to document previously unreported assets; the following information is available:

Church structure (the church operates out of a historic mission established in the early 1800s and no cost records are available)	?
Repaired stained-glass windows, 1955	$ 6,900
Resurfaced cobblestone walkways, 1937	4,200
New roofing, 1929	8,100
New roofing, 1977	18,600
Redid ceilings and nave, 1980	11,000
Removed hand-carved church pews and replaced with wrought-iron/wood pews that were manufactured locally, 1987	23,200
Statues (two religious figures mark the church entrance; they were donated in the early 1900s by local sculptors)	?
Recasted and surfaced one statue, 1950	16,000
Recasted and surfaced second statue, 1983	26,200

REQUIRED

1. What advice would you give the United Nondenominational Church regarding the capitalization and depreciaiton of the assets listed above?
2. Without prejudicing your answer to part 1, presume that the church decided to ignore the accounting mandate related to depreciation and that an independent CPA gave a qualified opinion on the audited statements. Is the CPA correct? Explain why or why not.

16-3   The KayMay Community Center is a voluntary health and welfare organization. Recently, it issued financial statements and provided copies to its board of directors. One board member requires help in interpreting certain items on the statements and asks you to explain further the following items:

1. The statement of activity includes $7,200 entitled "support from special activities." The board member wants to know how to determine how much support was generated compared to the costs to produce that support.
2. The balance sheet shows an allowance for uncollectible pledges. She does not understand why it is in the balance sheet and what it means.
3. The notes explain that KayMay uses the total return concept for recognizing endowment earnings. The board member knows that $5,000 was received on the investments in the endowment fund, and that the earnings are unrestricted. She wants to know where the $5,000 is shown and what it means to use the total return concept.
4. The board member worked on a brochure used in KayMay's fund-raising drives during the year. She remembers that the brochure cost $3,110 but she cannot find that expense anywhere in the operating statement. Brochure costs shown under the fund-raising function total $1,800, not $3,110. Where, she asks, is the rest of the expenses?

REQUIRED

Prepare a written statement that KayMay's executive director can use to respond to the board member's concerns. Answer each specific question raised by the board member.

16-4   The Fernville Health Assistance (FHA) organization has not used fund accounting in the past. FHA gets federal and state grants to support its services to incapacitated elderly people. Some money also comes from the local city and county governments. Still other revenues are derived from investments donated by a local donor and from fees charged at local fund-raising events, including bingo parties. The person who donated the investment stipulated that the income be used for medical aid to the elderly.

FHA rents its office space and a local restaurant prepares the meals delivered to the elderly. Volunteers make the deliveries in vans provided by FHA.

For the last two years, contributions and other support has exceeded current operating costs. The board has designated that the accumulated excess be used to provide temporary housing (usually in an older hotel) for any elderly homeless people.

REQUIRED

1. Should the Fernville Health Assistance organization use fund accounting for internal purposes? Explain.
2. If FHA decides to implement fund accounting, which funds should it establish? Justify the recommendation.

16-5 The accounting and reporting practices of voluntary health and welfare organizations differ in certain respects from those of state or local governmental units.

REQUIRED

1. Describe the major differences and similarities between the use of fund accounting by VHWOs and governmental units.
2. Describe the major differences in financial statements between VHWOs and governmental entities.
3. Describe significant differences in revenue recognition between VHWOs and governmental entities.

16-6 Alfred May responded to the public library's 19X1 appeal for funds to create a video department. He contributed $2,000 in 19X1 but told the library to use it in 19X2.

REQUIRED

1. How should Mr. May's contribution be treated on the activity statement?
2. Would the answer be different if he told the library to spend it only on a specific type of video equipment? Explain.

EXERCISES

16-1 Select the best answer for each question.

1. A voluntary health and welfare organization received a cash donation in 19X3 from a donor specifying that the amount donated is to be used in 19X5. The cash donation should be accounted for as:
   a. unrestricted support in 19X3
   b. temporarily restricted support in 19X3, 19X4, and 19X5, and as a deferred credit in the balance sheet at the end of 19X3 and 19X4

c. support in 19X5, and no deferred credit in the balance sheet at the end of 19X3 and 19X4

d. temporarily restricted support in 19X3, and a reclassification in 19X5

2. Cura Foundation, a voluntary health and welfare organization supported by contributions from the general public, included the following costs in its statement of functional expenses for the year ended December 31, 19X8:

Fund-Raising	$500,000
Administrative (including data processing)	300,000
Research	100,000

Cura's functional expenses for 19X8 program services totaled:

a. $900,000

b. $500,000

c. $300,000

d. $100,000

(Adapted from the May 1984 CPA Exam, Practice #46)

3. Securities donated to an other nonprofit organization should be recorded at the:

a. fair market value at the date of the gift, or the donor's cost, whichever is less

b. donor's cost

c. fair market value at the date of the gift

d. fair market value at the date of the gift, or the donor's cost, whichever is higher

Items 4 and 5 are based on the following: Community Service Center is a voluntary welfare organization funded by contributions from the general public. During 19X1, unrestricted pledges of $900,000 were received, half of which were payable in 19X1, with the other half payable in 19X2 for use in 19X2. Ten percent of the pledges are estimated as uncollectible. In addition, Zelma Zorn, a registered social worker on Community's permanent staff earning $20,000 annually for a normal workload of 2,000 hours, contributed an additional 800 hours of her time to Community, at no charge.

4. How much should Community report as net unrestricted contribution revenue for 19X1 with respect to pledges?

a. $0

b. $405,000

c. $810,000

d. $900,000

5. How much should Community record in 19X1 for contributed service expense?

a. $8,000

b. $4,000

c. $800

d. $0

(Adapted from the May 1984 CPA Exam, Practice #44 and #45)

6. An other nonprofit's priorities probably would not include:
   a. fund-raising events
   b. providing program service
   c. separation of duties in cash receiving and disbursement
   d. appointment of a prestigious person as chairman of the board
7. Court precedents guiding the investment decisions of nonprofit organizations typically are based on:
   a. the "balanced portfolio" concept
   b. the concept of overall return on investment
   c. the prudent-man rule
   d. both b and c
8. The net assets of nonprofits are defined as:
   a. permanently restricted assets
   b. temporarily restricted assets
   c. assets that are not pledged for program services
   d. the difference between total assets and total liabilities
9. If a nonprofit organization issued a brochure that described the general program services as well as a fund-raising appeal, the costs to develop and publish the brochure would be:
   a. allocated to both fund-raising and program services
   b. charged solely to fund-raising functions
   c. charged solely to the program services
   d. either a or b depending on the circumstances
10. Accounting and reporting guidance for VHWOs has come largely from:
    a. the GASB and the FASB
    b. National Health Council and the AICPA
    c. the GASB
    d. the Committee on Accounting Practice

16-2 Select the best answer for each question.

1. Which basis of accounting should an other nonprofit organization use?
   a. cash basis
   b. modified accrual basis
   c. accrual basis
   d. none of the above
   (Adapted from the May 1984 CPA Exam, Theory, #60)
2. The following expenditures were among those incurred by a non-profit botanical society during 19X9:

Printing of Annual Report	$10,000
Merchandise Sent to Encourage Contributions	20,000

What amount should be classified as fund-raising costs in the society's activity statement?
   a. $0
   b. $10,000
   c. $20,000
   d. $30,000
   (Adapted from the May 1988 CPA Exam, Practice #56)

3. In an activity statement of a voluntary health and welfare organization, depreciation expense should:
   a. not be included
   b. be included as an element of support
   c. be included as an element of other changes in fund balance
   d. be included as an element of expense

4. Under *Statement No. 117*, VHWOs and ONPOs must use the fund accounting for:
   a. audited financial statements
   b. internal management statements
   c. published financial statements
   d. none of the above

5. Which of the following is not a common fund for a VHWO using fund accounting?
   a. special purpose fund
   b. endowment fund
   c. loan fund
   d. current restricted fund

6. Recognition of restricted pledges as support for VHWOs and ONPOs occurs:

	VHWOs	ONPOs
a. when received	yes	yes
b. when cash is received	no	yes
c. when an appropriate expense is incurred	yes	no
d. when the liability is incurred	no	yes

7. Two common expense classification schemes for VHWOs are:
   a. natural and functional
   b. program and departmental
   c. functional and accrual
   d. object and departmental

8. Which entry would a foundation make for recognizing investment gains on endowment assets?
   a. debit cash, credit fund balance
   b. debit recognized gain, credit endowment earnings
   c. debit investments, credit endowment earnings
   d. none of the above

9. Nonprofit organizations establish investment pools to:
   a. simplify the accounting requirements
   b. satisfy audit objectives
   c. enhance earnings
   d. develop better accountability for assets

10. The operating statement is entitled:

	VHWO	ONPO
a. functional expense statement	yes	no
b. statement of activity	yes	yes
c. income statement	yes	no
d. statement of revenues and expenditures	no	yes

16-3 The Art Appreciation Society operates a museum for the benefit and enjoyment of the community. During hours when the museum is open to the public, two clerks positioned at the entrance collect a $5 admission fee from each nonmember patron. Members of the Art Appreciation Society are permitted to enter free of charge upon presentation of their membership cards.

At the end of the day, one clerk delivers the proceeds to the treasurer. The treasurer counts the cash in the presence of the clerk and places it in a safe. Each Friday afternoon, the treasurer and one of the clerks deliver all cash held in the safe to the bank, and receive an authenticated deposit slip, which provides the basis for the weekly entry in the cash receipts journal.

The board of directors of the Art Appreciation Society has identified a need to improve their system of internal control over cash admission fees. The board has determined that the cost of installing turnstiles, sales booths, or otherwise altering the physical layout of the museum will greatly exceed any benefits that may be derived. However, the board has agreed that the sale of admission tickets must be an integral part of its improvement efforts.

Smith has been asked by the board to review the internal control over cash admission fees and provide suggestions for improvement.

REQUIRED
Indicate weaknesses in the existing system of internal control over cash admission fees that Smith should identify, and recommend one improvement for each of the weaknesses identified.
(Adapted from AICPA exam)

16-4 A local pastor seeks your advice. He must report to his board soon on the status of the church's finances. His treasurer quit two months ago and, as near as he can tell, the following represents the activities since the last financial statements were prepared.

Contributions from parishioners, of which $300 represented collections of earlier pledges	$1,100
Interest on investments, source of the investments is unknown	500
Collections from parishioners on behalf of a summer Bible camp that is offered by a community group	900
Supplies for Sunday School	50
Office salaries	100
Other expenses	800
Gift for a row of new pews in the church; the pews will be purchased next year	5,000
Balance in the checking account at the time financial statements were last prepared	650

REQUIRED
1. Compute the amount of *revenue and support* received in the last two months.
2. Assuming that all cash received was deposited and all expenses were paid by check, how much cash is available to be spent for operating activities of the church?
3. Describe what additional information is necessary before Items 1 and 2 can be answered definitively.

16-5 Following are the adjusted trial balances for the unrestricted and temporarily restricted assets of the Community Association for Handicapped Children, a voluntary health and welfare organization, at June 30, 19X9:

	UNRESTRICTED		TEMPORARILY RESTRICTED	
	Dr.	Cr.	Dr.	Cr.
Cash	$ 40,000		$ 9,000	
Bequest Receivable			5,000	
Pledges Receivable	12,000			
Accrued Interest Receivable	1,000			
Investments (at cost, which approximates market)	100,000			
Accounts Payable and Accrued Expenses		$ 52,000		$ 1,000
Allowance for Uncollectible Pledges		3,000		
Net Assets, July 1, 19X8:		38,000		3,000
Contributions		300,000		15,000
Membership Dues		45,000		
Program Service Fees		30,000		
Investment Income		10,000		
Deaf Children's Program	120,000			
Blind Children's Program	150,000			
Management and General Services	45,000		4,000	
Fund-Raising Costs	8,000		1,000	
Provision for Uncollectible Pledges	2,000			
	$478,000	$478,000	$19,000	$19,000

REQUIRED

1. Preapre an activity statement for the year ended June 30, 19X9.
2. Prepare a balance sheet as of June 30, 19X9.

16-6 For the past three years, TaxPac, a political organization operating in a three-state area, has amassed a large endowment. The endowment earnings are all restricted by the donors to support research and political stands on proposed state and national tax legislation. Brochures describing TaxPac's work suggest that investment earnings have averaged approximately 8 percent on the $1,200,000 portfolio. TaxPac officials see no reason why that average is not achievable during the next five years as well. For the past several years, 90 percent of the earnings have been used to support the research effort, and 10 percent to support specific legislation. Actual revenues and expenses for the past three years are summarized below:

	19X6	19X7	19X8
Investment Earnings	$84,300	$92,800	$111,000
TaxPac Legislative Program Costs	51,000	77,000	90,000
Realized Gains (Losses)	4,000	2,000	(500)
TaxPac Research Program Costs	22,000	6,000	7,000
General and Administrative Costs	7,500	7,900	8,700

REQUIRED

1. Under trust principles, what are the total revenues and expenses for the unrestricted and temporarily restricted net asset classes for each of the three years?

2. If TaxPac adopted a total return concept, what would total revenues and expenses be for the temporarily restricted and unrestricted net asset classes for each of the three years (asume that state law permits the total return approach but requires a 3 percent annual addition to the endowment for maintaining its purchasing power)? For purposes of calculations, assume the portfolio value is constant at $1,200,000 for the three-year peiod.

3. What are the advantages and disadvantages of adopting the total return concept to an organization such as TaxPac?

16-7 Prepare journal entries to record the following transactions for the A-Z Community Service Group, a voluntary health and welfare organization. The A-Z Community Service Group diagnoses various health and welfare needs of individuals, provides referral services, and allocates a portion of its total budget to direct aid. Denote the appropriate net asset class for each entry. This is A-Z's first year of operations.

1. The following gifts and pledges were received (an estimated 12 percent of all pledges will be uncollectible):

Cash for:	
General Operations	$380,000
Diagnostic Equipment	310,000
Aid to the Disadvantaged	50,000
Fixed Assets	35,000
Pledges for:	
General Operations	$ 35,000
Diagnostic Program	31,000
Aid to the Disadvantaged	5,000
Donated Services and Materials:	
Diagnostic Services	$ 3,000
X-rays for Diagnosis	1,100
Vitamins for Disadvantaged	800

(handwritten annotations: 775,000 ; .88 X ; 71,000)

In addition, a local donor established an $800,000 endowment, the income of which was to be used for medical aid and dietary supplements for the disadvantaged. The sum of $500,000 was paid in cash, and the balance will be paid ratably over the next three years.

2. The following expenses were incurred and paid:

Fund-Raising	$177,000
General Administrative	165,000
Diagnostic Treatment	62,000
Aid to the Disadvantaged	98,000

3. A $50,000 restricted matching grant was approved by the federal government. As the dollar-for-dollar matching funds are raised, A-Z can spend the federal portion and request reimbursement. During the year,

$10,000 was raised to match the grant, and the total available amount was used to purchase sophisticated diagnostic equipment. The reimbursement was received before the payment on the equipment was due. The equipment had a useful life of ten years; the half-year convention was used with the straight-line method of depreciation.

4. Unrestricted earnings from temporary investments during the year totaled $11,000. At year end, excess cash in each net asset class was invested in a money market account. Any amount above $40,000 is categorized as excess.

5. A local dental group that moved to new quarters gave their old facilities to A-Z; the fair market value of the property was $1,000,000, and it had a $600,000 mortgage note payable that was assumed by A-Z. The gift was to be used entirely by the diagnostic services program. The expected useful life of the building is 25 years, and the equipment 7 years. The half-year convention and the straight-line method were used for depreciating buildings and equipment. The appraiser estimated the following allocations:

Land	$100,000
Building	830,000
Equipment	70,000

6. The local hospital gave diagnostic equipment to A-Z on the condition that it would be sold and the proceeds would be split evenly between the two programs. The estimated fair market value of the equipment was $78,000.

7. The equipment was sold for $78,000. A-Z has a policy that recognizes reclassification as the asset is used.

16-8 The A-Z Community Service Group (see exercise 16-7) uses fund accounting for internal management purposes. It uses both current funds (current operating and current restricted) and, unless otherwise noted, the diagnostic program and the direct aid programs are operated out of the current restricted fund. A-Z also uses a land, buildings, and equipment fund and an endowment fund. Using fund accounting, prepare the journal entries for the transactions indicated in exercise 16-7, denoting the appropriate fund for each entry. For Item 4, assume any amount of cash above $10,000 is excess.

16-9 Senora Valley Developmental Center is a nonprofit voluntary health and welfare association organized to provide food and shelter for individuals on a prerelease program from state institutions. Local donations are sought for basic program needs; state and federal grants provide another source of revenue. Also, each prerelease person pays a membership fee that is computed as a percentage of the person's ability to pay: those employed, for example, pay a certain proportion of their monthly salary for room and board; those receiving veteran's aid would contribute a part of the VA payment; and so forth.

At the end of Fiscal 19X1, the trial balance for the three funds used internally by Senora Valley Developmental Center were as shown:

Senora Valley Developmental Center
Trial Balances
June 30, 19X1

	UNRESTRICTED		RESTRICTED		ENDOWMENT	
	Dr.	Cr.	Dr.	Cr.	Dr.	Cr.
Cash	$ 40,000		$ 9,000		$ 1,000	
Pledges Receivable	100,000		5,000		2,000	
Allowance for Uncollectible Pledges		$ 5,000		$ 250		$ 200
Advance to Restricted Fund	20,000					
Investments	55,000				110,000	
Interest Receivable	2,200				2,000	
Land	45,000					
Buildings	218,000				108,000	
Accumulated Depreciation		54,500				16,200
Equipment	25,000		62,000			
Accumulated Depreciation		10,710		17,720		
Accounts Payable		45,000		6,500		
Accrued Expenses		5,000				
Advance from Unrestricted Fund				20,000		
Deferred Revenue				5,000		
Mortgage Payable						65,000
Fund Balance		384,990		26,530		141,600
	$505,200	$505,200	$76,000	$76,000	$223,000	$223,000

During Fiscal 19X2, the following transactions took place in the unrestricted fund:

1. Unrestricted pledges received during the year totaled $210,000, of which 7 percent was not expected to be collected. Total cash received from Fiscal 19X1 and Fiscal 19X2 unrestricted pledges was $280,000; unrestricted pledges totaling $6,000 were written off.

2. Membership dues from prerelease people totaled $65,000, all of which was received in cash.

3. Dividend and interest payments received were $4,400, and $1,100 was accrued at Fiscal 19X2 year end. Investments are carried at cost, which approximates market value.

4. Expenses incurred during the year were:

Payroll Expenses	$108,000
Food and Shelter Supplies	49,000
Office Supplies	4,000
Transportation	2,700
Utilities	16,000
Brochures, Hosted Socials, and Other Fund-Raising Expenses	27,000
Other Operating Expenses	5,200

5. Senora estimates that its buildings have a 20-year life, while equipment is depreciated over 7 years.

6. Accrued salaries at year end totaled $4,100; other accrued expenses amounted to $1,100.

7. Accounts payable was reduced to $21,000 during the year, and the accrued expenses balance from Fiscal 19X1 was paid entirely.
8. The advance to the restricted fund was repaid.

Transactions occuring in the restricted fund for Fiscal 19X2 are as follows:

1. A local individual contributed $13,200 to the restricted fund for training and education of prerelease individuals.
2. The net pledges expected to be received were collected, and the portion set aside in the allowance was written off.
3. A state grant of $45,000 was approved; $32,000 was received during the current year, and the balance will be received and spent in 19X3.
4. The deferred revenue balance at year-end 19X1 was earned.
5. Training contracts for prerelease individuals totaled $28,500; one-half of the required training was paid by year end.
6. Other expenses related to training included part-time salaries of $12,000, supplies of $1,200 (one-half of which remained at year end), and the depreciation on the equipment, which has the same useful life as other center equipment.
7. Accounts payable were reduced to $10,000, and the advance was repaid to the unrestricted fund.
8. A transfer of earnings was made from the endowment to the restricted fund (see Item 6 in the endowment transactions).

The following transactions occurred during Fiscal 19X2 in the endowment fund:

1. Pledges of $8,000 were made, but no cash was received before year end; 19X1 pledges of $1,800 were received in cash; the remainder was written off. Fifteen percent of the pledges were expected to be uncollectible.
2. Dividends and interest payments received during the year totaled $8,900. No amounts were accrued at Fiscal 19X2 year end.
3. Rents received on the building held in the endowment totaled $10,000; the building is leased on a net-net basis so no expenses other than depreciation were incurred to operate the rental property. The building has a 20-year life, and straight-line depreciation is used.
4. Investments costing $20,000 were sold for $15,000. The sum of $5,000 was reinvested. The accrued interest was received.
5. A mortgage payment of $15,200 was made; of that amount, $5,200 was interest.
6. One-half of the net excess of income over expenses from the endowment is added to the principal each year; the remainder is transferred to the restricted fund for educational purposes.
7. Any additions to the endowment corpus were invested.

REQUIRED

Prepare a worksheet for each fund, showing the beginning trial balance, the transactions for the year, and a trial balance; extend the appropriate amounts from the trial balance to the operating statement and the balance sheet.

16-10 In 19X8 a group of civic-minded merchants in Albcary City organized the "Committee of 100" for the purpose of establishing the Community Sports Club, a nonprofit sports organization for all youth. Each member contributed $1,000 toward the club's capital, and in turn received a participation certificate. In addition, each participant agreed to pay dues of $200 a year for the club's operations. All dues have been collected in full by the end of each fiscal year, ending March 31. Members who have discontinued their participation have been replaced by an equal number of new members through transfer of the participation certificates from the former members to the new ones. Following is the club's trial balance at April 1, 19X8:

	Debit	Credit
Cash	$ 9,000	
Investments (at market which is equal to cost)	58,000	
Inventories	5,000	
Land	10,000	
Building	164,000	
Accumulated Depreciation—Building		$130,000
Equipment	54,000	
Accumulated Depreciation—Equipment		46,000
Accounts Payable		12,000
Participation Certificates (100 × $1,000)		100,000
Cumulative Excess of Revenue Over Expenses		12,000
	$300,000	$300,000

Transactions for the year ended March 31, 19X9, were as follows:

1. Collections from Participants for Dues — $20,000
2. Snack Bar and Soda Fountain Sales — 28,000
3. Interest and Dividends Received — 6,000
4. Additions to Voucher Register:
   House Expenses — 17,000
   Snack Bar and Soda Fountain — 26,000
   General and Administrative — 11,000
5. Vouchers Paid — 55,000
6. Assessments for Capital Improvements Not Incurred (assessed on March 20, 19X8; none collected by March 31, 19X9; deemed 100% collectible during year ending March 31, 19X0) — 10,000
7. Unrestricted Bequest Received — 5,000

Adjustment data:

8. Investments are valued at market, which amounted to $65,000 on March 31, 19X9.
9. Depreciation for the Year:
   Building — 4,000
   Equipment — 8,000
10. Allocation of Depreciation:
    House Expenses — 9,000
    Snack Bar and Soda Fountain — 2,000
    General and Administrative — 1,000
11. Actual physical inventory on March 31, 19X9, was $1,000, and it pertains to the snack bar and soda fountain.

REQUIRED

1. Prepare an activity statement for the year ended March 31, 19X9.
2. Analyze the statement you prepared in Item 1, and comment on the financial condition of the Committee of 100's Sports Club

16-11 Salias County citizens have organized a voluntary health and welfare organization to aid trauma victims. The board of directors understands that accrual accounting is required for the organization; it also understands which financial statements must be prepared. However, the board does not have all the special revenue and expense recognition and valuation procedures clearly in mind. Described below are several transactions or circumstances occurring during the first year of operations. The board wants advice on the proper reflection of these events in the accounts or financial statements.

1. A local physician called the Trauma Center's director informing her he had provided an in-kind contribution by treating (free of charge) a county resident who had experienced trauma. He estimated that his contribution was worth $295.
2. Investments valued at $100,000 and costing the donor $85,000 were gifted to the center. Earnings from the investment were restricted to treating child abuse cases. At the end of the year, the investments were worth $110,000.
3. A local hospital donated sheets and blankets to the center for use when the center's personnel provided temporary sleeping quarters for flood victims. The estimated value of these supplies was $800.
4. The Trauma Center helped finance a brochure on the health and welfare services available in the community. The brochure described the services of various organizations. The last part of the brochure was a contribution form that could be used for any organization described in the brochure. The Trauma Center's share of the costs totaled $5,000.
5. Earnings on permanently restricted investments totaled $10,000 during the year.
6. Pledges of $100,000 were made.
7. The facilities used by the Trauma Center cost the county $180,000; they have a 20-year remaining useful life (based on a 30-year total life). They are used rent-free by the Trauma Center. Before occupied by the Trauma Center, the facilities were rented to another organization for $6,000 per year.
8. The federal Health and Human Services Department made a grant of $55,000 to the center to be used specifically for care and counseling for family members of AIDS patients. A total of $25,000 was spent for this purpose during the current year; the total grant had been received by the Trauma Center before year end.

REQUIRED

Prepare a report for the Trauma Center director outlining the generally accepted accounting principles for each item. Indicate the appropriate fund, if applicable, as well as the year in which the event should be recognized or reported.

APPENDIX

Excerpts from the City of Raleigh,
North Carolina, Comprehensive
Annual Financial Report
for the Year Ended June 30, 1992[1]

---

[1]With the exception of the various auditor opinions and reports, all of the appendix is exactly as it appeared in the comprehensive annual financial report. The auditor would not permit the author to print the opinions/reports; any similarities between those issued by the auditors and the ones appearing in this appendix are purely coincidental and result from the fact that such a large part of most opinions is simply boilerplate language.

City of Raleigh Organizational Chart

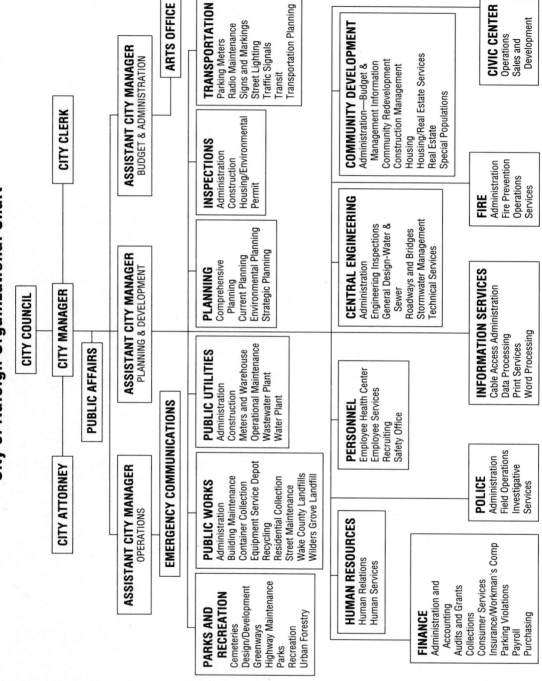

CITY COUNCIL

CITY ATTORNEY

CITY CLERK

CITY MANAGER

PUBLIC AFFAIRS

EMERGENCY COMMUNICATIONS

ASSISTANT CITY MANAGER
OPERATIONS

ASSISTANT CITY MANAGER
PLANNING & DEVELOPMENT

ASSISTANT CITY MANAGER
BUDGET & ADMINISTRATION

ARTS OFFICE

TRANSPORTATION
Parking Meters
Radio Maintenance
Signs and Markings
Street Lighting
Traffic Signals
Transit
Transportation Planning

INSPECTIONS
Administration
Construction
Housing/Environmental
Permit

PLANNING
Comprehensive Planning
Current Planning
Environmental Planning
Strategic Planning

PUBLIC UTILITIES
Administration
Construction
Meters and Warehouse
Operational Maintenance
Wastewater Plant
Water Plant

PUBLIC WORKS
Administration
Building Maintenance
Container Collection
Equipment Service Depot
Recycling
Residential Collection
Street Maintenance
Wake County Landfills
Wilders Grove Landfill

PARKS AND RECREATION
Cemeteries
Design/Development
Greenways
Highway Maintenance
Parks
Recreation
Urban Forestry

HUMAN RESOURCES
Human Relations
Human Services

PERSONNEL
Employee Health Center
Employee Services
Recruiting
Safety Office

FINANCE
Administration and Accounting
Audits and Grants
Collections
Consumer Services
Insurance/Workman's Comp
Parking Violations
Payroll
Purchasing

POLICE
Administration
Field Operations
Investigative Services

INFORMATION SERVICES
Cable Access Administration
Data Processing
Print Services
Word Processing

CENTRAL ENGINEERING
Administration
Engineering Inspections
General Design–Water & Sewer
Roadways and Bridges
Stormwater Management
Technical Services

FIRE
Administration
Fire Prevention
Operations
Services

COMMUNITY DEVELOPMENT
Administration—Budget & Management Information
Community Redevelopment
Construction Management
Housing
Housing/Real Estate Services
Real Estate
Special Populations

CIVIC CENTER
Operations
Sales and Development

City Of Raleigh
North Carolina

October 31, 1992

The Honorable Mayor and Members of the City Council
City of Raleigh, North Carolina

The Comprehensive Annual Financial Report of the City of Raleigh, for the fiscal
year ended June 30, 1992, is herewith submitted. This report was prepared by the
City Finance Department. Responsibility for both the accuracy of the presented
data and the completeness and fairness of the presentation, including all
disclosures, rests with the City. We believe the data, as presented, is accurate
in all material aspects; that it is presented in a manner designed to fairly set
forth the financial position and results of operations of the City as measured
by the financial activity of its various funds; and that all disclosures
necessary to enable the reader to gain the maximum understanding of the City's
financial affairs have been included.

The Comprehensive Annual Financial Report is presented in four principal
sections; Introductory, Financial, Statistical and Single Audit.   The
Introductory Section provides a brief overview of the objectives of the report,
the operations and organization of the City and a copy of the Certificate of
Achievement for Excellence in Financial Reporting.   The Financial Section
includes the Independent Auditors' Report, combined statements, notes to the
financial statements and more detailed combining and individual fund statements
and schedules. The Statistical Section includes selected financial and general
information, much of which is presented on a multi-year comparative basis. The
Single Audit Section includes the Independent Auditors' Reports on internal
control and compliance with laws and regulations as well as all schedules and
exhibits necessary to satisfy the requirements of the single audit grant
regulations.

Reporting Entity and Services

This report includes all the funds and account groups of the City and includes
all activities and entities which are controlled by or dependent upon the City
executive or legislative branches. Financial control by or dependence on the
City was determined on the basis of budget adoption, taxing power, outstanding
debt secured by revenues or general obligations of the City, obligation of the
City to finance any deficits that may occur, or receipt of significant subsidies
from the City. Based on these criteria, the Walnut Creek Amphitheatre Financing
Assistance Corporation, a non-profit corporation established   to issue
certificates of participation for an amphitheatre, is included in the reporting

entity as a blended component unit. The Raleigh Convention and Visitors Bureau
is also treated as a blended component unit through December 31, 1991, at which
time it became a City-County joint venture under the name The Greater Raleigh
Convention and Visitors Bureau. Other entities, including a for-profit
corporation established to issue certificates of participation for the
construction of a parking deck, the Raleigh Housing Authority and the Raleigh
Durham Airport Authority have not met the established criteria for inclusion in
the reporting entity and accordingly, are excluded from this report. Each
organization's relationship to the City and the specific criteria used in
evaluating their potential for inclusion in the City's entity is described in the
Notes to the Financial Statements.

The City

The City of Raleigh is a thriving metropolitan city located in central North
Carolina, 150 miles from the sandy Atlantic beaches and 190 miles from the Great
Smoky Mountains. It is 370 miles north of Atlanta and 250 miles south of
Washington, D. C.

The central North Carolina climate is relatively mild with moderate winters and
warm summers. The annual mean temperature of the City of Raleigh is 60.2 degrees
Fahrenheit. January, with a mean temperature of 43.4 degrees Fahrenheit is the
coolest month and July, with a mean temperature of 80.6 degrees Fahrenheit is the
warmest month. The average annual precipitation is 38.71 inches including
average yearly snowfall of 8.01 inches. On the average, the last spring frost
occurs April 6th and the first frost of fall November 4th.

The City prides itself in the quality of life of its citizens, in its attention
to natural beauty, in its efforts at downtown and urban renewal and in its role
as the government center of the entire state. In all that it has to offer, the
City warmly welcomes its visitors and its new residents alike.

The North Carolina General Assembly purchased land for the original site of the
City for the specific purpose of being the Capital of North Carolina. The City
was incorporated in 1792 by an act of the General Assembly and now operates under
a Council-Manager form of government. The City Council is comprised of the Mayor
and seven Councilors who are responsible for the legislative affairs of the City.
It also makes appointments to various statutory and advisory boards and appoints
the City Manager, City Attorney, and the City Clerk. As chief administrative
officer, the City Manager is responsible for enforcement of laws and ordinances
and delivery of all City services.

The City provides the full range of governmental services including police and
fire protection, street, solid waste disposal, water, sanitary sewer, parks,
recreation and cultural services. The City is constantly aware of the
infrastructure needs of providing such services and accordingly, has installed
and maintained such in the highest manner. Presently the infrastructure of the
City is in excellent condition.

The estimated 1992 population for the City was 222,403 compared to the official 1990 census of 211,008. The population growth from the census count is expected to be consistent with historical trends. The City presently encompasses an area of 93.94 square miles and uses the services of 2,401 permanent employees. We anticipate that FY 1992-93 and subsequent years will result in the continuing growth of the City.

Economic Condition and Outlook

The economy of the City is stabilized by the presence of state and local government employment markets, the college and university employment markets, and the Research Triangle Park research facilities, all of which offer substantial employment opportunities to the City's population. No major specialized industry dominates the economy of the City; and, as a result, the June 1992 unemployment rate was 4.6 percent as compared to 6.6 percent statewide and 7.8 percent nationwide (according to the N. C. Employment Security Commission). The unemployment rate continues to reflect stability in the local economy while also reflecting the effects of the national recession. Economic recovery is anticipated in the Raleigh area consistent with expectations statewide and nationally. Such recovery will result in a return to unemployment rates below 3 percent, we believe.

The most recent statistical analysis by the North Carolina Office of State Budget and Management shows that the Raleigh metropolitan area leads the entire state in per capita income and substantially exceeds that of the nation as well. This position in per capita income also positively affects the strength of the private and government sections of the local economy.

With the attractiveness of the Research Triangle Park and its proximity to three major research universities, it is no accident that medical and electronic industries flourish in the region. Glaxo, Burroughs Wellcome and Ajinomoto lead the medical research and production industry with IBM, Northern Telecom, the Microelectronics Center of North Carolina and Memorex-Telex leading the electronics research and production industry, giving both industries major presence in the region. It is expected that these major corporations and centers will continue to thrive, and offer employment opportunities to the City's citizens.

The City's taxable property base and its economic base are felt to be strong due in part to the quality of life which has attracted industry and citizens to Raleigh and the region. The level of fees associated with new construction and the use of City services are expected to continue to increase. We are continuing to strive for a balanced tax base with adequate commercial and industrial base complementing residential base. Again, the recession continues to slow the construction industry and consequently affects the rate of growth of tax base.

There is every reason to anticipate a continuation of financing resources including intergovernmental revenues except for possible additional losses of federal funding. On the other hand, the City has encountered and managed the negative effects of the national recession, including the reduction in growth of tax base as mentioned above. Over the last several years, various revenue sources have been impacted such as retail sales taxes, building permits, inspection fees, impoundment of state-shared revenues, etc. Due to these circumstances, required cost containment controls were imposed in fiscal years 1991 and 1992 to allow the City to end the 1991-92 fiscal year in a strong financial position.

Additionally, in the adopted budget the City has focused on adequately increasing existing revenues, creating new revenue sources and implementing additional cost containment measures to insure the maintenance of the City's traditionally strong financial position while continuing to deliver quality basic services. There is every reason to believe the direction of the City and its fiscal capacity will continue to be quite positive.

Major Initiatives

For the Year

The 1991-92 Operating Budget reflected operating growth of just 2.9 percent and a minimal increase in the property tax rate of one cent. This small increase in the total operating budget and the limited number of expanded programs reflected a continuing response to general economic conditions as well as reductions in certain economic-sensitive revenues, as indicated above. All basic service programs provided the residents of the City were continued. The most significant adjustments to the City's operating programs for 1991-92 included the following:

(1)   Expansion of the curbside recycling program from one-half of the City to a City-wide program.

(2)   Expansion of the drop-off recycling program.

(3)   Two new pilot recycling programs.

(4)   Expansion of transit services.

(5)   Continued priority funding of housing for low and moderate income residents and the operations of a homeless shelter.

The Capital Budget for 1991-92 included a number of major facility improvements consistent with the City's ten-year Capital Improvements Program. Included were major street improvements, water and sewer annexation and replacement projects, and completion of a new Aquatics Center and Softball Complex. Revenue sources for such capital improvements included general obligation bonds, intergovernmental revenues, sales tax funds, and other designated sources.

For the Future

The budget for fiscal year 1992-93 was adopted, again with a "hold the line" approach, characterized by continuing efforts to reduce costs through improved efficiency, the evaluation of general staffing levels throughout the City, and the use of employee generated projects to contain costs. All traditional City services were continued at their present level.

In 1992-93, a number of enhancements and service expansions are being implemented, including the following:

(1)   Public safety programs are being given increased focus in order to give additional attention to "at risk" neighborhoods.

(2)   The Fire Prevention Inspections program is being expanded.

(3)   The Aquatics Center and Softball Complex are becoming operational.

(4)   A new Yard Waste Center is opening in compliance with state legislation mandating that no yard wastes go into the landfills after January 1, 1993.

(5)   Other solid waste management programs are being implemented and refined to meet state requirements for reduced landfill volumes and to plan for federal mandates on landfill closures.

(6)   Housing initiatives under the $20 million Housing Bond Program are underway to improve housing for low and moderate income residents of the City. These initiatives complement the Community Development Block Grant federal funding.

In keeping with the EPA mandate to reduce or eliminate phosphorus from the waste water stream, the City has undertaken improvements to its sanitary waste water treatment plant. The improvements will increase capacity to treat waste water to 60 million gallons per day and to also remove phosphorus from the effluent which in turn enhances the quality of the natural waterways into which the effluent is released. This improvement is consistent with state interests to combat the algae bloom found in coastal waterways.

Capital improvements for the future will focus on a wide range of very key projects. These include major street improvements, various utility extensions and annexation projects, park improvements and acquisitions, a new communications tower, and continued development of the geographical information system.

The downtown area also remains a key focal area for improvement and expansion. The City is participating in the private development of a 576 space public parking deck near the Two Hannover Square building and the construction of a 725 space public parking deck near the First Union Capital Center is scheduled for completion in late 1992. Streetscape beautification is continuing throughout the downtown area. The plans of the City for public projects are complemented by a major capital improvements program by the State of North Carolina. These improvements include phase I and II parking facilities with 2,386 spaces, a new museum of history, and a new revenue building. A new museum of natural sciences building has been authorized for statewide bond referendum and a new visitor center is being pursued by the state with legislative authority yet to be provided.

FINANCIAL INFORMATION

Accounting System and Budget Control

The diverse nature of governmental operations and the necessity of assuring legal compliance preclude recording and summarizing all governmental financial transactions and balances in a single accounting entity. Therefore, from an accounting and financial management viewpoint, a governmental unit is a combination of several distinctly different fiscal and accounting entities, each having a separate set of accounts and functioning independently of each other.

Each accounting entity is accounted for in a separate "fund." A fund is defined as a fiscal accounting entity with a self-balancing set of accounts recording cash and other financial resources together with all related liabilities and residual equities or balances, and changes therein, which are segregated for the purpose of carrying on special activities or attaining certain objectives in accordance with special regulations, restrictions, or limitations.

The various funds and account groups of the City have been classified into fund categories and types as follows:

Category	Type
Governmental	General
	Special Revenue
	General Capital Projects
Proprietary	Enterprise
	Internal Service
Fiduciary	Trust and Agency
Account Groups	General Fixed Assets
	General Long-Term Obligations

A brief description of each fund type is found in Note 1 to the Financial Statements.

The City's accounting records for general governmental operations are reported on the modified accrual basis whereby revenues are recognized when measurable and available, and expenditures are recognized when goods and services are received. Accounting records for the City's proprietary and pension trust operations are reported on the full accrual basis.

In developing and evaluating the City's accounting system, consideration is given to the adequacy of internal accounting controls. Internal accounting controls are designed to provide reasonable, but not absolute, assurance regarding: (1) the safeguarding of assets against loss from unauthorized use or disposition; and (2) the reliability of accounting records for preparing financial statements and maintaining accountability for assets. The concept of reasonable assurance recognizes that: (1) the cost of a control should not exceed the benefits likely to be derived; and (2) the evaluation of costs and benefits requires estimates and judgment by management.

All internal control evaluations occur within the above framework. We believe that the City's internal accounting controls adequately safeguard assets and provide reasonable assurance of proper recording of financial transactions.

North Carolina General Statute 159-8 requires the adoption of an annual balanced budget. It is the intent of that article that all money received and expended be included in the budget ordinance. Any unanticipated resources or expenditures may be added to the original budget ordinance by official legal amendment as provided in G. S. 159-15, Amendments to the Budget Ordinance. The City operates in accordance with both of these statutes. Budgetary control is maintained at the line-item object level by the encumbrance of estimated purchase amounts prior to the release of purchase orders to vendors. Purchase orders which would over-obligate account balances are not released until additional appropriations are made available by Council. Open encumbrances at June 30, 1992 are reported either as accounts payable or are rebudgeted and reported as appropriated fund balance.

1991–92 Annual Budget

Total: $205,589,826

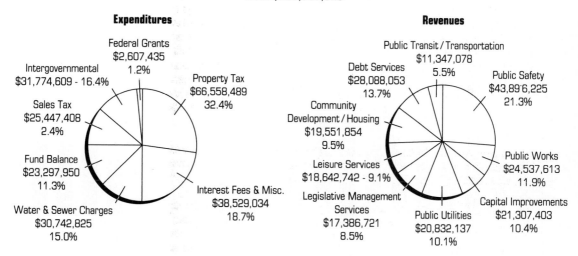

Expenditures

Federal Grants
$2,607,435
1.2%

Intergovernmental
$31,774,609 - 16.4%

Property Tax
$66,558,489
32.4%

Sales Tax
$25,447,408
2.4%

Fund Balance
$23,297,950
11.3%

Water & Sewer Charges
$30,742,825
15.0%

Interest Fees & Misc.
$38,529,034
18.7%

Revenues

Public Transit / Transportation
$11,347,078
5.5%

Debt Services
$28,088,053
13.7%

Public Safety
$43,896,225
21.3%

Community
Development / Housing
$19,551,854
9.5%

Leisure Services
$18,642,742 - 9.1%

Public Works
$24,537,613
11.9%

Legislative Management
Services
$17,386,721
8.5%

Public Utilities
$20,832,137
10.1%

Capital Improvements
$21,307,403
10.4%

General Governmental Functions

Revenues for general governmental functions (General, Special Revenue, and General Capital Projects Funds) amounted to $146,287,621 for the fiscal year ended June 30, 1992.

Revenues from various sources and the changes from last year are shown in the following tabulation (stated in thousands):

Revenue Sources	1992 Amount	Percent of Total	Increase (Decrease) Over 1991
Ad Valorem Taxes	$ 68,750	47.0%	$ 3,382
Intergovernmental	24,959	17.1	(536)
Sales Taxes	21,218	14.5	(577)
Licenses, Fees & Permits	17,906	12.2	1,617
Interest on Investments	5,803	4.0	(1,253)
Other	7,652	5.2	(2,444)
Total	$146,288	100.0%	$ 189

City property tax bills are mailed by Wake County in July and August each year and become due and payable on September 1st. These billings become delinquent after the following January 5th if not paid. Gross tax collections are up 5.9 percent over last year again reflecting rigorous efforts at collecting and also reflecting the desire of Council to provide a sufficient levy to raise resources for necessary governmental services, to provide debt service capacity for authorized bonds and to provide substantial pay-as-you-go capital financing. The tax collection rates over the past five years have averaged in excess of 98 percent of levy.

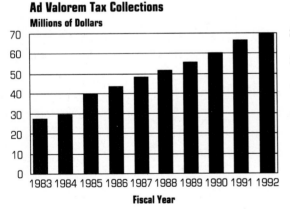

Ad Valorem Tax Collections
Millions of Dollars

Fiscal Year

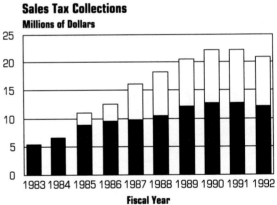

Sales Tax Collections
Millions of Dollars

Fiscal Year

☐ Half-Cent Increments
■ 1-Cent Local Option

Assessed valuation of all taxable property (100 percent assessment ratio) of approximately $8.9 billion represents an increase of 4.5 percent compared to the preceding year. The North Carolina General Assembly exempted all manufacturers, wholesalers and retailers inventory values from taxation in its 1988 session.

The City has found it necessary to require periodic small increases in its tax rate in order to meet the growing demands for expanded governmental services brought on by continuing community growth and the need to keep pace with capital requirements in maintaining modern efficient infrastructure. A recapitulation of such rates is found in the statistical section of this report.

Intergovernmental revenues continue to represent a significant portion of total general governmental revenues at 17.1 percent compared to 17.5 percent for the preceding year. This important class of revenue has remained steady in the last several years; however, further cuts in federal and possibly state assistance are anticipated.

Local sales taxes are collected and redistributed by the State of North Carolina. The current year collection was 2.6 percent less than the preceding year. Sales tax levels indicate a leveling out of retail activity in the region.

Resources for general capital projects consist of residual balances remaining from the issuance of general obligation bonds, proceeds from new general obligation bonds, allocations from the property tax, proceeds from the state gasoline tax and the investment return associated with each, as applicable. These resources are accounted for in the General Capital Projects Funds exclusive of all enterprise capital resources. These resources are for streets, sidewalks, parks, downtown mall, civic center and other miscellaneous capital projects.

Expenditures for general governmental purposes total $160,088,845, an increase of 2.5 percent over the preceding year. Changes in levels of expenditure for major functions of the City over the preceding year are shown in the following table (stated in thousands):

Functions of Expenditure	1992 Amount	Percent of Total	Increase (Decrease) Over 1991
General Government	$ 21,489	13.4%	$1,135
Public Safety	34,876	21.8	776
Public Works	19,140	12.0	502
Leisure Services	14,567	9.1	693
Capital Outlay	32,228	20.1	(873)
Debt Service	11,327	7.1	2,707
Other	26,462	16.5	(976)
Total	$160,089	100.0%	$3,964

Fund equities in the general governmental funds have remained steady and continue to complement financial position, credit worthiness and capacity against substantial unforeseen emergencies. The General Fund Equity totals $54,539,875 of which $15,370,846 is undesignated, the Special Revenue Fund Equity totals $15,202,013 of which $2,439,870 is undesignated, and the General Capital Projects Fund Equity totals $39,248,617 all of which is designated or appropriated.

General Fund Balance

The City has established a goal for General Fund unobligated fund balance of 10 percent of the succeeding year expenditure budgets. At that level an expenditure equivalent to 26 working days is established. Such fund balance is needed to insure exemplary credit ratings, to insure against unexpected emergencies and to provide cash position to allow foregoing short-term borrowings. The unobligated fund balance for FY 1991-92 was 10.4 percent of succeeding year budgeted expenditures.

Proprietary Activities

There are three separate proprietary activities accounted for in enterprise funds: Water and Sewer Utilities, Transit and Parking. The Water and Sewer Fund had fund equity of $236,157,425 as of June 30, 1992 compared to $220,768,724 the preceding year. Of that total $116,721,925 represented contributed capital primarily from the federal and state governments. Operating income after depreciation totaled $6,802,821 for the year ended June 30, 1992. The Water and Sewer Fund is self-supporting and provides resources to general government operations only sufficient to fund its associated costs.

The steady growth of the City and its metropolitan area has required expansion of the water and sewer systems. Water consumption is now placed at an annual average daily amount of 38 million gallons for 75,975 users. The water system capacity is 62.5 million gallons per day which provides for anticipated growth. Sewage treatment is at an average daily volume of 28 million gallons for 71,337 customers. Expansion plans now underway will increase sewage treatment capacity to 60 million gallons per day. These plans will provide capacity for the City's anticipated growth.

The Mass Transit Fund had fund equity of $9,724,978 as of June 30, 1992 compared to $10,558,102 the preceding year. Of that total $9,603,191 or 99 percent represented contributed capital primarily from the Federal Transit Administration (formerly UMTA). Operating subsidies from FTA were $901,816 and $1,010,581 for FY 1991-92 and FY 1990-91 respectively, with the decrease representing a smaller percentage of operating deficit currently funded by FTA.

The Parking Facilities Fund had fund equity at June 30, 1992 of $14,804,142. The City has three decks in operation and is planning and/or constructing others. All of these facilities are located downtown.

During 1992, the City established an internal service fund to account for the activities of its Print Shop and Office Supply Room. Internal service funds are reported within the proprietary fund-type since the full costs of the operations are recouped through user charges to City Departments. At June 30, 1992, the Print and Supply Shop Fund had fund equity of $188,426, including $185,421 of contributed capital from the General Fund.

Fiduciary Funds

The City's Fiduciary Funds account for resources received and held by the City as trustee or for which the City acts as agent for individuals. At June 30, 1992, the following amounts were reported under programs in which the City provided custodial responsibilities.

Supplemental Money Purchase Pension Plan	$ 1,657,932
Law Enforcement Officers' Special Separation Allowance	2,576,675
Employee Health Insurance	600,559
Deferred Compensation	5,402,567
Supplemental Retirement Savings Plan	3,000,113
Occupancy Tax	4,576
	$13,242,422

Pension Trust Fund Operations

The operations of the Law Enforcement Officers' Special Separation Allowance Plan for the year resulted in the accumulated funding for obligations in excess of current year needs to the extent that $2,576,675 remains available for future periods. It is the intent of the City to continue to fund this program such that future unfunded liabilities will be funded at the time such obligations are required to be liquidated. The annual actuarial valuation reflects funding requirements which the City fully expects to fund on an ongoing basis.

The Supplemental Money Purchase Pension Plan for all other employees has accumulated employer share contributions of $1,657,932. It is expected that this plan will continue to accumulate values over time consistent with employer levels of participation.

Debt Administration

The City has found it necessary to use tax-exempt bond financing for a number of its capital programs. Use of bonded debt capital has allowed the City to modernize its sewer system to efficiency standards established by the U. S. Environmental Protection Agency, to expand its treated water capacity, to develop major parks facilities, to provide needed street improvements and construction, to provide off-street parking facilities and to construct the downtown Civic Center Complex. These programs have been accomplished while imposing reasonable debt burdens within the capacity of taxpayers. As well, the City has issued taxable certificates of participation to finance an amphitheatre. Principal and interest requirements on the certificates will be provided by appropriation in the year in which they become due.

Outstanding general obligation bonds at June 30, 1992 totaled $154,545,000 of which $70,765,000 were issued for enterprise facilities and structures. The remaining $83,780,000 represents obligations related to general governmental operations.

The General Statutes of North Carolina provide that net debt may not exceed eight percent of the present market value of taxable property as certified by the county tax assessor. Such a provision, when compared to the net debt of the City, provides a legal debt margin for the City at June 30, 1992 of $533,473,121.

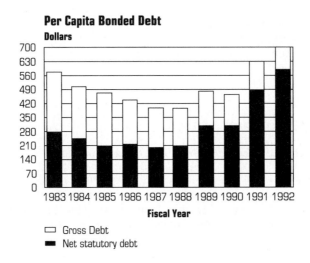

Per Capita Bonded Debt

Gross Debt
Net statutory debt

The debt service requirements to retire the indicated debt are adequately funded and anticipated increases in such requirements have been identified with incremental additional funding already programmed into future annual budgets.

Even though the outstanding bonded debt of the City has increased substantially over the past few years, proper management of the debt program along with the provision for necessary financial position has allowed continuation of the Aaa credit rating by Standard and Poor's and the AAA credit rating by Moody's Investors Services.

Cash Management

Effective forecasting of cash requirements and cash management have allowed utilization of available cash resources to the extent that investments for FY 1991-92 have resulted in investment earnings of $8,700,058, excluding Fiduciary Funds' earnings. This utilization of resources has resulted in reduced current property tax requirements, supplemented capital project resources, and has aided in reduced debt levels, minimizing short-term and long-term borrowing costs.

The investment policy of the City is guided in large part by State Statute whereby, investments in certificates of deposit, repurchase agreements, secured time deposits, banker's acceptances, commercial paper, United States government and agency securities and the North Carolina Cash Management Trust are made.

The City's policy stipulates that investments be fully secured by pledged collateral, delivered securities or United States government guarantee with all securities, including repurchase agreements and pledged collateral being delivered to a third party safekeeping account in the name of the City.

General Fixed Assets

The general fixed assets of the City are those fixed assets used in the performance of general governmental functions and exclude the fixed assets of Enterprise Funds. As of June 30, 1992 the general fixed assets of the City amounted to $408,742,532. This amount represents the historical cost of the assets and is considered to be less than their present value. Depreciation of general fixed assets is not required in the City's accounting system.

Risk Management

The City provides a comprehensive and varied plan of risk management. It has undertaken a special renewed effort in loss control through safety and has a broad plan for insuring against risk exposure. Workers' compensation is self insured up to $250,000 per accident and public officials liability is fully self insured. Other major lines of insurance are provided through participation in the Interlocal Risk Financing Fund of North Carolina, offered as a pooled insurance program through the North Carolina League of Municipalities on a statewide basis. The League pool is six years old, and has made significant progress and presently has strong financial position with the ability to offer reduced premiums in the future to its participants unless extraordinary losses occur. Employee health and medical coverage is provided by a medical insurance trust that was established by the City as a self-insurance fund to pay the claims of City employees and their covered dependents.

OTHER INFORMATION

Independent Audit

This report includes financial statements and supplemental schedules which have been audited by Deloitte & Touche, a firm of independent Certified Public Accountants, as required by North Carolina General Statute 159-34. The auditors' report of Deloitte & Touche specifies the scope of their audit, the use of generally accepted auditing standards and the use of generally accepted accounting principles and concludes that these financial statements present fairly the financial position of the City.

In addition, Deloitte & Touche has provided auditors' reports related specifically to the Single Audit in compliance with the federal Single Audit Act of 1984 and related OMB Circular A-128 and the State Single Audit Implementation Act. Those reports are found in the Single Audit Section.

Reporting Standards

The accounting policies of the City conform to generally accepted accounting principles as applicable to governments and as set forth by the Governmental Accounting Standards Board (GASB), the accepted standard-setting body for establishing governmental accounting and financial reporting principles.

The City has participated in the Government Finance Officers Association of the United States and Canada (GFOA) Certificate of Achievement for Excellence in Financial Reporting Program since 1980. GFOA recognizes governmental units that issue their comprehensive annual financial reports substantially in conformity with the standards developed by GASB. The City has received favorable recognition for its comprehensive annual financial reports for 1980 and each consecutive year thereafter, including the 1991 report.

To be awarded a Certificate, a governmental unit must publish an easily readable and effectively organized comprehensive annual financial report, whose contents conform to program standards. Such reports must satisfy both generally accepted accounting principles and applicable legal requirements.

A Certificate of Achievement for Excellence in Financial Reporting is valid for one year only. It is felt that the current report continues to conform to Certificate requirements, and it is being submitted to GFOA to determine its eligibility for another award.

Acknowledgements

The preparation of this report on a timely basis has been accomplished by the efficient and dedicated services of the staff of the Finance Department who have been assisted by the independent auditors, Deloitte & Touche. The contribution of all are invaluable and sincerely appreciated and clearly reflect the high standards we have set for ourselves.

It is also appropriate to thank the Mayor and members of the City Council for making possible the excellent financial position of the City through their interest and support in planning and conducting the financial affairs of the City.

Respectfully submitted,

Dempsey E. Benton, Jr.
City Manager

Z. B. Hill
Finance Director

Certificate of Achievement for Excellence in Financial Reporting

Presented to

City of Raleigh, North Carolina

For its Comprehensive Annual
Financial Report
for the Fiscal Year Ended
June 30, 1991

A Certificate of Achievement for Excellence in Financial
Reporting is presented by the Government Finance Officers
Association of the United States and Canada to
government units and public employee retirement
systems whose comprehensive annual financial
reports (CAFRs) achieve the highest
standards in government accounting
and financial reporting.

President

Executive Director

GENERAL PURPOSE FINANCIAL STATEMENTS

(COMBINED STATEMENTS—OVERVIEW)

THE COOPERATIVE CPA FIRM

Fancy Suite 101
Any Street
Anywhere, USA 00000-0000

Independent Auditors' Report

To the Honorable Mayor and Members
    of the City Council
City of Raleigh, North Carolina

We have audited the accompanying general purpose financial statements of City of Raleigh, North Carolina, as of June 30, 1992, and for the year then ended, as identified in the table of contents. These general purpose financial statements are the responsibility of the management of the City of Raleigh, North Carolina. Our responsibility is to express an opinion on these general purpose financial statements based on the audit.

We conducted our audit in accordance with generally accepted auditing standards. Those standards require that we plan and perform the audit to obtain reasonable assurance about whether the general purpose financial statements are free of material misstatement. An audit includes examining, on a test basis, evidence supporting the amounts and disclosures in the general purpose financial statements. An audit also includes assessing the accounting principles used and significant estimates made by management, as well as evaluating the overall general purpose financial statement presentation. We believe that our audit provides a reasonable basis for our opinion.

In our opinion, the general purpose financial statements present fairly, in all material respects, the financial position of the City of Raleigh, North Carolina, as of June 30, 1992, and the results of its operations and cash flows of its proprietary fund types for the year then ended in conformity with generally accepted accounting principles.

Our audit was made for the purpose of forming an opinion on the general purpose financial statements taken as a whole. The combining and individual fund and account group financial statements and schedules, which are also the responsibility of the management of the City of Raleigh, are presented for purposes of additional explanation, and are not a required part of the general purpose financial statements. Such information has been subjected to the auditing procedures applied in the audit of the general purpose financial statements and, in our opinion, is fairly presented in all material respects in relation to the general purpose financial statements taken as a whole.

City of Raleigh

COMBINED BALANCE SHEET
ALL FUND TYPES AND ACCOUNT GROUPS
June 30, 1992

	Governmental Fund Types			Proprietary
	General	Special Revenue	General Capital Projects	Enterprise
ASSETS				
Cash and Cash Equivalents/Investments	$ 48,899,793	$ 13,156,111	$ 42,486,478	$ 52,729,187
Taxes Receivable, Net of Allowance for Uncollectibles of $3,677,638 in 1992 and $3,325,612 in 1991	846,186	-	-	-
Assessments Receivable, Net of Allowance for Uncollectibles of $205,471 in 1992 and $131,882 in 1991	239,112	-	836,804	2,828,042
Customer Receivables, Net of Allowance for Uncollectibles of $1,210,622 in 1992 and $1,112,339 in 1991	-	-	-	2,761,935
Due from Other Governmental Agencies	607,629	347,077	505,640	21,859
Accrued Interest Receivable	630,013	173,448	275,702	870,486
Other Receivables and Assets	1,977,880	96,023	380,140	476,214
Sales Tax Receivable	4,186,650	2,221,116	-	-
Due from Other Funds	592,329	64,397	-	7,734
Inventories	1,269,868	-	-	3,026,568
Resources to be Provided in Future Years for Retirement of General Long-Term Obligations	-	-	-	-
Deferred Charges	-	-	-	74,782
Loans Receivable	242,901	10,940,057	-	-
Cash and Cash Equivalents - Restricted Deposits	-	-	-	7,248,365
	59,492,361	26,998,229	44,484,764	70,045,172
Fixed Assets:				
Land	-	-	-	9,010,996
Water and Sewer Systems	-	-	-	206,700,604
Buildings and Machinery	-	-	-	63,428,154
Streets and Sidewalks	-	-	-	-
Buses	-	-	-	9,089,251
Equipment	-	-	-	9,157,205
Furniture and Fixtures	-	-	-	164,319
Improvements	-	-	-	460,833
Construction in Progress	-	-	-	42,610,603
	-	-	-	340,621,965
Less: Accumulated Depreciation	-	-	-	63,941,494
Fixed Assets, Net	-	-	-	276,680,471
Total Assets	$ 59,492,361	$ 26,998,229	$ 44,484,764	$ 346,725,643

The accompanying notes are an integral part of the financial statements.

Fund Types Internal Service	Fiduciary Fund Type Trust and Agency	Account Groups General Fixed Assets	General Long-Term Obligations	Total (Memorandum Only) June 30, 1992	June 30, 1991
$ 46,039	$ 13,214,304	$ -	$ -	$ 170,531,912	$ 158,820,936
-	-	-	-	846,186	716,040
-	-	-	-	3,903,958	2,505,762
-	-	-	-	2,761,935	2,872,899
-	-	-	-	1,482,205	3,988,652
-	28,118	-	-	1,977,767	1,662,114
254	-	-	-	2,930,511	3,698,633
-	-	-	-	6,407,766	6,353,061
-	-	-	-	664,460	518,379
31,025	-	-	-	4,327,461	3,756,351
				-	
-	-	-	107,989,866	107,989,866	94,397,144
-	-	-	-	74,782	83,091
-	-	-	-	11,182,958	7,769,265
-	-	-	-	7,248,365	6,723,204
77,318	13,242,422	-	107,989,866	322,330,132	293,865,531
-	-	53,547,938	-	62,558,934	57,538,929
-	-	-	-	206,700,604	196,285,511
-	-	70,910,306	-	134,338,460	101,374,433
-	-	157,692,809	-	157,692,809	151,370,631
-	-	-	-	9,089,251	9,972,889
150,245	-	39,979,373	-	49,286,823	45,187,436
6,832	-	3,306,027	-	3,477,178	3,381,761
-	-	34,693,734	-	35,154,567	31,612,878
-	-	48,612,345	-	91,222,948	92,094,757
157,077	-	408,742,532	-	749,521,574	688,819,225
26,827	-	-	-	63,968,321	58,212,904
130,250	-	408,742,532	-	685,553,253	630,606,321
$ 207,568	$ 13,242,422	$ 408,742,532	$ 107,989,866	$ 1,007,883,385	$ 924,471,852

City of Raleigh

COMBINED BALANCE SHEET
ALL FUND TYPES AND ACCOUNT GROUPS
June 30, 1992

	Governmental Fund Types			Proprietary
	General	Special Revenue	General Capital Projects	Enterprise
LIABILITIES, EQUITY AND OTHER CREDITS				
Liabilities:				
Accounts Payable	$ 1,261,984	$ 339,877	$ 3,011,429	$ 3,318,076
Arbitrage Rebate Payable	-	-	507,988	68,699
Accrued Salaries and Employer Payroll Taxes	1,119,965	-	-	58,811
Accrued Liabilities	-	-	879,926	58,024
Due to Other Governmental Agencies	-	-	-	80
Accrued Interest Payable	-	9,527	-	1,535,508
Rehabilitation Loans Escrow	-	252,929	-	-
Due to Other Funds	7,734	219,837	-	436,889
Unearned Grant Proceeds	-	-	-	-
Other Liabilities	976,920	97	-	-
Deferred Revenue for Taxes, Assessments and Other Receivables	1,585,883	10,973,949	836,804	-
Deferred Contributions from Other Funds for Capital Projects	-	-	-	81,922
Deferred Benefits Payable	-	-	-	-
Customer Deposits Payable from Restricted Assets	-	-	-	7,248,365
Current Portion of Long-Term Obligations:				
Bonds Payable	-	-	-	6,360,000
Contracts Payable	-	-	-	1,020,178
General Long-Term Obligations:				
Bonds Payable	-	-	-	64,405,000
Contracts and Other Notes Payable	-	-	-	1,066,009
Earned Vacation Pay	-	-	-	381,537
Certificates of Participation Payable	-	-		-
Total Liabilities	4,952,486	11,796,216	5,236,147	86,039,098
Equity and Other Credits:				
Contributed Capital	-	-	-	137,322,559
Retained Earnings	-	-	-	123,363,986
Investment in General Fixed Assets	-	-	-	-
Fund Balances:				
Reserved for Inventories	1,269,868	-	-	-
Reserved by State Statute	7,559,111	82,023	-	-
Reserved for Encumbrances	1,636,075	-	-	-
Unreserved:				
Designated for Subsequent Year's Appropriation	12,704,197	12,680,120	35,879,009	-
Designated for Specific Purposes	15,999,778	-	3,369,608	-
Undesignated	15,370,846	2,439,870	-	-
Total Equity and Other Credits	54,539,875	15,202,013	39,248,617	260,686,545
Total Liabilities, Equity and Other Credits	$ 59,492,361	$ 26,998,229	$ 44,484,764	$ 346,725,643

The accompanying notes are an integral part of the financial statements.

Fund Types	Fiduciary Fund Type	Account Groups		Total (Memorandum Only)	
Internal Service	Trust and Agency	General Fixed Assets	General Long-Term Obligations	June 30, 1992	June 30, 1991
$ 13,332	$ -	$ -	$ -	$ 7,944,698	$ 10,211,976
-			-	576,687	529,685
-	-	-	-	1,178,776	2,423,887
870	-	-	-	938,820	205,809
-	4,576	-	-	4,656	-
-	-	-	-	1,545,035	1,472,985
-	-	-	-	252,929	235,875
-	-	-	-	664,460	518,379
-	-	-	-	-	11,692
-	-	-	-	977,017	2,388,805
-	-	-	-	13,396,636	9,643,251
-	-	-	-	81,922	34,929
-	9,003,239	-	-	9,003,239	7,349,679
-	-	-	-	7,248,365	6,723,204
-	-	-	-	6,360,000	5,590,000
-	-	-	-	1,020,178	1,071,760
-	-	-	83,780,000	148,185,000	124,525,000
-	-	-	7,693,128	8,759,137	10,383,875
4,940	-	-	5,016,738	5,403,215	5,268,571
-	-	-	11,500,000	11,500,000	11,500,000
19,142	9,007,815	-	107,989,866	225,040,770	200,089,362
185,421	-	-	-	137,507,980	132,922,071
3,005	-	-	-	123,366,991	112,531,818
-	-	408,742,532	-	408,742,532	371,277,902
-	-	-	-	1,269,868	1,126,769
-	-	-	-	7,641,134	7,529,072
-	-	-	-	1,636,075	1,575,910
-	-	-	-	61,263,326	57,636,053
-	4,234,607	-	-	23,603,993	25,346,729
-	-	-	-	17,810,716	14,436,166
188,426	4,234,607	408,742,532	-	782,842,615	724,382,490
$ 207,568	$ 13,242,422	$ 408,742,532	$ 107,989,866	$ 1,007,883,385	$ 924,471,852

City of Raleigh

COMBINED STATEMENT OF REVENUES, EXPENDITURES
AND CHANGES IN FUND BALANCES
ALL GOVERNMENTAL FUND TYPES
For the Fiscal Year Ended June 30, 1992

	Governmental Fund Types			Total (Memorandum Only)	
	General	Special Revenue	Capital Projects	June 30, 1992	June 30, 1991
Revenues:					
Ad Valorem Taxes	$ 68,749,965	$ -	$ -	$ 68,749,965	$ 65,367,860
Intergovernmental	17,986,422	6,841,409	130,914	24,958,745	25,495,000
Assessments	96,747	-	544,277	641,024	454,470
Local Sales Tax	12,921,883	8,296,138	-	21,218,021	21,795,353
Transient Occupancy Tax	1,948,715	-	-	1,948,715	1,760,435
Licenses	5,325,109	-	-	5,325,109	4,202,908
Interest on Investments	3,087,331	778,647	1,937,190	5,803,168	7,056,390
Inspection Fees	1,643,800	-	-	1,643,800	1,386,408
Highway Maintenance Refunds	507,960	-	-	507,960	657,752
Miscellaneous Fees and Charges	9,551,034	-	-	9,551,034	8,690,481
Facility Fees	-	-	1,386,567	1,386,567	2,030,370
Tenant's Capital Investment	-	-	-	-	3,500,000
Miscellaneous Other	1,453,785	2,479,483	620,245	4,553,513	3,701,344
Total Revenues	123,272,751	18,395,677	4,619,193	146,287,621	146,098,771
Other Financing Sources:					
Operating Transfers In	4,910,300	2,087,225	8,498,838	15,496,363	16,174,270
In-kind Contribution from City	-	36,238	-	36,238	36,228
Proceeds of General Obligation Bonds, Bond Anticipation Notes and Premium	-	8,300,030	10,700,000	19,000,030	20,959,469
Proceeds of Capital Lease and Other Installment Obligations	1,487,050	-	-	1,487,050	4,340,206
Proceeds of Certificates of Participation	-	-	-	-	11,500,000
Total Other Financing Sources	6,397,350	10,423,493	19,198,838	36,019,681	53,010,173
Total Revenues and Other Financing Sources	129,670,101	28,819,170	23,818,031	182,307,302	199,108,944
Expenditures:					
Current:					
General Government	21,135,196	353,849	-	21,489,045	20,354,110
Personnel	1,017,604	-	-	1,017,604	984,397
Finance	3,040,169	-	-	3,040,169	2,897,518
Information Services	2,061,058	-	-	2,061,058	2,297,646
Community Development Services	13,395,789	-	-	13,395,789	13,101,300
Public Safety	34,876,166	-	-	34,876,166	34,099,923
Public Works	19,139,800	-	-	19,139,800	18,637,374
Leisure Services	14,566,801	-	-	14,566,801	13,874,336
Public Service and Economic Development Programs	-	3,114,588	-	3,114,588	4,381,599
Planning, Management, Relocation and Services	-	1,687,418	-	1,687,418	1,455,825
Other	18,296	2,126,699	-	2,144,995	2,319,481
Capital Outlay	-	3,234,616	28,993,321	32,227,937	33,100,550
Debt Service:					
Principal Retirement	3,980,000	130,000	874,526	4,984,526	3,979,133
Interest and Fiscal Charges	4,446,575	12,600	244,464	4,703,639	3,364,073
Capital Leases, Including Interest	1,439,075	-	-	1,439,075	1,105,865
Other	200,235	-	-	200,235	171,324
Total Expenditures	119,316,764	10,659,770	30,112,311	160,088,845	156,124,454

City of Raleigh

COMBINED STATEMENT OF REVENUES, EXPENDITURES
AND CHANGES IN FUND BALANCES
ALL GOVERNMENTAL FUND TYPES
For the Fiscal Year Ended June 30, 1992

	Governmental Fund Types			Total (Memorandum Only)	
	General	Special Revenue	Capital Projects	June 30, 1992	June 30, 1991
(Continued):					
Less: Administrative Costs Charged to Water and Sewer Fund	$ 3,930,060	$ -	$ -	$ 3,930,060	$ 3,258,838
	115,386,704	10,659,770	30,112,311	156,158,785	152,865,616
Other Financing Uses:					
Operating Transfers Out	10,064,102	8,301,262	231,456	18,596,820	17,994,559
Transfer to New Joint Venture	-	55,115	-	55,115	-
Total Other Financing Uses	10,064,102	8,356,377	231,456	18,651,935	17,994,559
Total Expenditures and Other Financing Uses	125,450,806	19,016,147	30,343,767	174,810,720	170,860,175
Excess (Deficiency) of Revenues and Other Financing Sources Over Expenditures and Other Financing Uses	4,219,295	9,803,023	(6,525,736)	7,496,582	28,248,769
Fund Balances - Beginning of Year	50,348,924	8,046,448	45,774,353	104,169,725	81,731,248
Residual Transfer of Equity	(28,344)	(2,647,458)	-	(2,675,802)	(5,810,292)
Fund Balances - End of Year	$ 54,539,875	$ 15,202,013	$ 39,248,617	$ 108,990,505	$ 104,169,725

The accompanying notes are an integral part of the financial statements.

City of Raleigh

COMBINED STATEMENT OF REVENUES, EXPENDITURES AND
CHANGES IN FUND BALANCES - ANNUAL BUDGET AND ACTUAL -
GENERAL AND SPECIAL REVENUE FUND TYPES
For the Fiscal Year Ended June 30, 1992

	Actual
Revenues:	
Ad Valorem Taxes	$ 68,749,965
Intergovernmental	17,986,422
Assessments	96,747
Local Sales Tax	12,921,883
Transient Occupancy Tax	1,948,715
Licenses	5,325,109
Interest on Investments	3,087,331
Inspection Fees	1,643,800
Highway Maintenance Refunds	507,960
Miscellaneous Fees and Charges	9,551,034
Miscellaneous Other	1,453,785
Total Revenues	123,272,751
Other Financing Sources:	
Operating Transfers In	4,910,300
Proceeds of Capital Lease and Other Installment Obligations	1,487,050
Total Other Financing Sources	6,397,350
Total Revenues and Other Financing Sources	129,670,101
Fund Balance Appropriated	-
	129,670,101
Expenditures:	
Current:	
General Government	21,135,196
Personnel	1,017,604
Finance	3,040,169
Information Services	2,061,058
Community Development Services	13,395,789
Public Safety	34,876,166
Public Works	19,139,800
Leisure Services	14,566,801
Other Expenditures	18,296
Capital Outlay	-
Debt Service:	
Reserve for Future Debt	-
Principal Retirement	3,980,000
Interest and Fiscal Charges	4,446,575
Capital Leases	1,439,075
Other Expenditures	200,235
Total Expenditures	119,316,764
Less: Administrative Costs Charged to Water and Sewer Fund	3,930,060
	115,386,704
Other Financing Uses:	
Operating Transfers Out	10,064,102
Transfer to New Joint Venture	-
Total Other Financing Uses	10,064,102
Total Expenditures and Other Financing Uses	125,450,806

The accompanying notes are an integral part of the financial statements.

	General		Special Revenue		
	Budget	Over (Under) Budget	Actual	Budget	Over (Under) Budget
$	66,558,489	$ 2,191,476	$ -	$ -	$ -
	14,467,685	3,518,737	5,077,379	5,267,000	(189,621)
	40,000	56,747	-	-	-
	16,906,408	(3,984,525)	-	-	-
	1,652,300	296,415	-	-	-
	4,973,174	351,935	-	-	-
	3,406,000	(318,669)	249,587	90,000	159,587
	1,395,000	248,800	-	-	-
	472,000	35,960	-	-	-
	9,692,209	(141,175)	-	-	-
	1,139,499	314,286	-	-	-
	120,702,764	2,569,987	5,326,966	5,357,000	(30,034)
	5,410,300	(500,000)	556,526	556,526	-
	1,595,980	(108,930)	-	-	-
	7,006,280	(608,930)	556,526	556,526	-
	127,709,044	1,961,057	5,883,492	5,913,526	(30,034)
	16,086,355	(16,086,355)	-	-	-
	143,795,399	(14,125,298)	5,883,492	5,913,526	(30,034)
	24,021,227	(2,886,031)	-	-	-
	1,170,346	(152,742)	-	-	-
	3,370,293	(330,124)	-	-	-
	2,541,466	(480,408)	-	-	-
	14,563,742	(1,167,953)	-	-	-
	37,634,794	(2,758,628)	-	-	-
	21,700,150	(2,560,350)	-	-	-
	17,536,810	(2,970,009)	-	-	-
	-	18,296	502,773	546,586	(43,813)
	-	-	108,380	125,700	(17,320)
	2,538,217	(2,538,217)	-	-	-
	3,980,000	-	-	-	-
	5,539,057	(1,092,482)	-	-	-
	1,725,978	(286,903)	-	-	-
	236,651	(36,416)	-	-	-
	136,558,731	(17,241,967)	611,153	672,286	(61,133)
	3,878,923	51,137	-	-	-
	132,679,808	(17,293,104)	611,153	672,286	(61,133)
	11,115,591	(1,051,489)	5,232,300	5,232,300	-
	-	-	55,115	8,940	46,175
	11,115,591	(1,051,489)	5,287,415	5,241,240	46,175
	143,795,399	(18,344,593)	5,898,568	5,913,526	(14,958)

City of Raleigh

COMBINED STATEMENT OF REVENUES, EXPENDITURES AND
CHANGES IN FUND BALANCES - ANNUAL BUDGET AND ACTUAL -
GENERAL AND SPECIAL REVENUE FUND TYPES
For the Fiscal Year Ended June 30, 1992

	Actual
(Continued):	
Excess (Deficiency) of Revenues and Other Financing Sources Over Expenditures and Other Financing Uses	$ 4,219,295
Fund Balances - Beginning of Year	50,348,924
Residual Equity Transfer	(28,344)
Budgeted on a Project Ordinance Basis	-
Fund Balances - End of Year	$ 54,539,875

The accompanying notes are an integral part of the financial statements.

General			Special Revenue		
Budget		Over (Under) Budget	Actual	Budget	Over (Under) Budget
$ -		$ 4,219,295	$ (15,076)	$ -	$ (15,076)
34,262,569		16,086,355	720,689	720,689	-
-		(28,344)	-	-	-
-		-	14,496,400	14,496,400	-
$ 34,262,569		$ 20,277,306	$ 15,202,013	$ 15,217,089	$ (15,076)

City of Raleigh

COMBINED STATEMENT OF REVENUES, EXPENSES
AND CHANGES IN RETAINED EARNINGS/FUND BALANCE
ALL PROPRIETARY FUND TYPES AND PENSION TRUST FUNDS
For the Fiscal Year Ended June 30, 1992

	Proprietary Fund Types		Fiduciary Fund Type	Total (Memorandum Only)	
	Enterprise	Internal Service	Pension Trust	June 30, 1992	June 30, 1991
Operating Revenues:					
User Charges	$ 34,441,301	$ 537,996	$ -	$ 34,979,297	$ 33,158,742
Employer Contributions	-	-	842,570	842,570	1,359,008
Interest	-	-	243,595	243,595	181,078
Other	750,957	52,732	-	803,689	1,366,227
Total Operating Revenues	35,192,258	590,728	1,086,165	36,869,151	36,065,055
Operating Expenses:					
Administration	1,432,678	-	-	1,432,678	1,360,816
Water Supply and Treatment	6,111,561	-	-	6,111,561	6,623,154
Sewer System and Treatment	5,522,730	-	-	5,522,730	5,236,521
Warehousing and Maintenance	1,706,250	-	-	1,706,250	1,975,715
Other Administrative Services	3,149,878	-	-	3,149,878	3,058,013
Non-Departmental Charges	2,909,152	-	-	2,909,152	2,402,558
Management Contract Charges	5,133,622	-	-	5,133,622	4,856,127
Depreciation	6,820,651	26,827	-	6,847,478	6,333,382
Other	13,427	598,396	332,532	944,355	265,505
Total Operating Expenses	32,799,949	625,223	332,532	33,757,704	32,111,791
Operating Income (Loss)	2,392,309	(34,495)	753,633	3,111,447	3,953,264
Nonoperating Revenues:					
Interest on Investments	2,896,890	-	-	2,896,890	3,784,167
Subsidy Income - Federal and State	901,816	-	-	901,816	1,010,581
Other	149,664	-	-	149,664	50,268
Total Nonoperating Revenues	3,948,370	-	-	3,948,370	4,845,016
Nonoperating Expenses:					
Interest Expense on Long-Term Obligations	2,110,471	-	-	2,110,471	3,212,563
Other	76,324	-	-	76,324	102,828
Total Nonoperating Expenses	2,186,795	-	-	2,186,795	3,315,391
Income (Loss) Before Operating Transfers	4,153,884	(34,495)	753,633	4,873,022	5,482,889
Operating Transfers In	3,847,282	37,500	-	3,884,782	3,572,703
Operating Transfers Out	(784,325)	-	-	(784,325)	(1,752,414)
Net Income	7,216,841	3,005	753,633	7,973,479	7,303,178
Add: Amortization of Contributed Capital	3,615,327	-	-	3,615,327	3,165,108
Retained Earnings/Fund Balance - Beginning of Year	112,531,818	-	3,480,974	116,012,792	105,544,506
Retained Earnings/Fund Balance - End of Year	$ 123,363,986	$ 3,005	$ 4,234,607	$ 127,601,598	$ 116,012,792

The accompanying notes are an integral part of the financial statements.

City of Raleigh

COMBINED STATEMENT OF CASH FLOWS
ALL PROPRIETARY FUND TYPES
For the Fiscal Year Ended June 30, 1992

	Proprietary Fund Types		(Memorandum Only)	
Reconciliation of Operating Income to Net Cash Provided by (Used in) Operating Activities	Enterprise	Internal Service	June 30, 1992	June 30, 1991
Operating Income (Loss)	$ 2,392,309	$ (34,495)	$ 2,357,814	$ 2,678,683
Adjustments to Reconcile Operating Income (Loss) to Net Cash Provided by Operating Activities:				
Depreciation and Amortization	6,820,651	26,827	6,847,478	6,333,382
Bad Debt Expense	99,524	-	99,524	147,116
Loss on Sale of Fixed Assets	13,427	-	13,427	14,776
Cash Receipts from Other Nonrevenue Sources	525,161	-	525,161	305,678
Capitalized City Forces	(477,572)	-	(477,572)	(620,975)
Other Adjustments	593	-	593	(70,867)
Changes in Assets and Liabilities:				
Operating Receivables	21,091	(254)	20,837	(846,194)
Inventories	(396,986)	(2,681)	(399,667)	(104,732)
Accounts Payable - Operating Accounts	(447,908)	13,332	(434,576)	170,447
Salaries Payable	(84,042)	-	(84,042)	4,891
Accrued Liabilities - Operating Accounts	(4,962)	870	(4,092)	29,355
Earned Vacation Pay	18,287	4,940	23,227	23,781
Net Cash Provided by Operating Activities	8,479,573	8,539	8,488,112	8,065,341
Cash Flows from Noncapital Financing Activities:				
Operating Grants Received	978,506	-	978,506	1,018,065
Operating Transfers In	3,347,470	37,500	3,384,970	3,213,081
Operating Transfers Out	(784,325)	-	(784,325)	(2,323,970)
Other	229,984	-	229,984	(26,805)
Net Cash Provided by Noncapital Financing Activities	3,771,635	37,500	3,809,135	1,880,371
Cash Flows from Capital and Related Financing Activities:				
Proceeds from Sale of Bonds and Other	15,333,950	-	15,333,950	20,797,553
Acquisition and Construction of Capital Assets	(20,245,904)	-	(20,245,904)	(32,483,433)
Principal Paid on General Obligation Bonds and Lease Contracts	(6,061,545)	-	(6,061,545)	(5,933,738)
Interest Paid on General Obligations Bonds, Lease Contracts and Other Obligations	(3,577,838)	-	(3,577,838)	(2,885,975)
Capital Debt Service Provided by General Fund Transfer In	505,270	-	505,270	600,299
Contributed Capital Provided by Governmental Funds	2,947,795	-	2,947,795	5,548,669
Other Contributed Capital	4,121,570	-	4,121,570	1,798,588
Proceeds from Sale of Equipment	52,528	-	52,528	9,441
Net Cash Used in Capital and Related Financing Activities	(6,924,174)	-	(6,924,174)	(12,548,596)
Cash Flows from Investing Activities:				
Interest on Investments	2,789,647	-	2,789,647	4,055,689
Net Cash Provided by Investing Activities	2,789,647	-	2,789,647	4,055,689

The accompanying notes are an integral part of the financial statements.

City of Raleigh

COMBINED STATEMENT OF CASH FLOWS
ALL PROPRIETARY FUND TYPES
For the Fiscal Year Ended June 30, 1992

	Proprietary Fund Types		(Memorandum Only)	
	Enterprise	Internal Service	June 30, 1992	June 30, 1991
(Continued):				
Net Increase in Cash and Cash Equivalents	$ 8,116,681	$ 46,039	$ 8,162,720	$ 1,452,805
Cash and Cash Equivalents, Beginning of Year	51,860,871	-	51,860,871	50,408,066
Cash and Cash Equivalents, End of Year	$ 59,977,552	$ 46,039	$ 60,023,591	$ 51,860,871

Noncash Capital and Related Financing Activities:

During the fiscal year ended June 30, 1992, the City received donated water and sewer assets of $2,662,823, entered into a note agreement for the purchase of land for water and sewer operations for $200,000 and entered into a capital lease agreement for water and sewer equipment for $133,950.

Also, during the fiscal year ended June 30, 1992, the Internal Service Fund received inventories and fixed assets in the amount of $185,421 as contributed capital from the General Fund.

The accompanying notes are an integral part of the financial statements.

CITY OF RALEIGH

NOTES TO THE GENERAL PURPOSE FINANCIAL STATEMENTS

FOR THE FISCAL YEAR ENDED

JUNE 30, 1992

Note 1. Summary of Significant Accounting Policies

The City of Raleigh was incorporated in 1792 by an Act of the North Carolina General Assembly. The City operates under a Council-Manager form of government and provides the following general services: public safety, highways and streets, sanitation, culture-recreation, public improvements, transportation, water and sewer service, human resource programs, community development, planning and zoning, and general administrative services.

The accounting policies of the City of Raleigh conform to generally accepted accounting principles (GAAP) as applicable to governments. The Governmental Accounting Standards Board (GASB) is the accepted standard-setting body for establishing governmental accounting and financial reporting principles. The following is a summary of the more significant policies:

A. Reporting Entity

The financial statements of the City of Raleigh include all funds and account groups of the City (the primary government) and its component units. One blended component unit is included in the City's reporting entity because of the significance of its operational or financial relationship with the City. The criteria used in this evaluation focuses on the financial accountability of potential component units (i.e. ability of the City to impose its will on an organization, appointment of the organization's governing board, and financial benefits or burdens on the City) as well as other unique relationships between the City and an organization.

Blended component unit included with the reporting entity:

Walnut Creek Amphitheatre Financing Assistance Corporation (WCAFAC). The WCAFAC is governed by a five-member board appointed by the City Council. Although it is legally separate from the City, the WCAFAC is reported as if it were part of the primary government because its main purpose is to finance an amphitheatre for the City. Financial transactions of the WCAFAC are audited and reported through the City's annual audit. No separate financial statements are prepared.

Other potential component units excluded from the reporting entity:

Related Organizations:

The Raleigh Housing Authority. The Raleigh Housing Authority (Authority) assists in providing housing for low income, elderly and disabled residents of the City. The City Council appoints all members of the Authority's governing body, but the

Authority is not otherwise financially accountable to the City. The City has no responsibility in selecting the management of the Authority. The primary revenue sources for the Authority are federal grants and program revenues. Financial transactions between the City and the Authority reflect contractual agreements between the parties for the provision of specific services by the Authority for the City. The City is not responsible for financing any deficits of the Authority nor is it entitled to any surpluses. In addition, the City does not guarantee any debt of the Authority and such debt is not included in the City's statutory debt limits.

Raleigh-Durham Airport Authority. The Raleigh-Durham Airport Authority is the board appointed to plan and conduct operations of the Raleigh-Durham International Airport. This eight-member governing body is jointly appointed by the City of Durham, City of Raleigh, County of Durham and County of Wake, with each member government appointing two members. The Authority Board selects the management and determines the budget and financing requirements of the Authority. Each member government contributes $12,500 annually for administration of the Authority. Neither the City nor the other appointing jurisdictions exercise management control or are responsible for budget and financing requirements for the Authority. A Special Airport Tax District of Durham and Wake Counties was created to aid in the financing of major airport facilities and is governed by two members each from the respective County Boards of Commissioners. Because of its limited role in the Raleigh-Durham Airport Authority and the related Special Tax District, the City does not consider its participation to be a joint venture and accordingly, further disclosure of the Airport entity is not included.

Raleigh Parking Deck Associates, Inc. A for-profit corporation established to finance and construct a parking deck does not technically meet the criteria of a component unit, but is reflected in substance through a capital lease with the City. Full inclusion of the Corporation would not have any further material effect on the City's financial statements.

Joint Venture:

The Greater Raleigh Convention and Visitors Bureau. The Greater Raleigh Convention and Visitors Bureau (Bureau) is a continuation of the Raleigh Convention and Visitors Bureau which was previously a component unit of the City of Raleigh. The Bureau, whose objective is to promote and solicit business, conventions, meetings and tourism in Wake County, receives it primary revenue from a county-wide 6 percent occupancy tax. Beginning on January 1, 1992, the Bureau is a joint venture of the City of Raleigh and Wake County. The governing body of the Bureau is a Board of Directors appointed by the Raleigh City Council and the Wake County Board of Commissioners. The County is required to distribute monthly a percentage of the tax collected with a minimum aggregate annual distribution of $1,000,000. If tax revenues are not sufficient to fully fund the Bureau's minimum annual distributions, the City and County must fund the deficiency equally to ensure that the Bureau receives its minimum distribution of $1,000,000 in any fiscal year. All unexpended funds of the Bureau revert to the County and City at the end of each fiscal year. Except for an investment in fixed assets previously recorded by the City, the only equity in the fund at year-end is for encumbrances which will be expensed in the subsequent year. Based on this, no additional equity interest in the Bureau is recorded at June 30, 1992.

B. Fund Accounting

The City's accounting system is operated on a fund basis. A fund is an independent accounting entity with a self-balancing set of accounts for recording its assets, liabilities, revenues, expenditures and fund balance. The various funds are maintained for the purpose of carrying on specific activities or to obtain certain objectives. The various funds are grouped by type in the financial statements. An account group is a financial reporting device designed to provide accountability for certain assets and liabilities that are not recorded in the funds because they do not directly affect net expendable available financial resources. The following fund types and account groups are used by the City:

GOVERNMENTAL FUNDS

The General Fund - to account for all unrestricted resources except those required to be accounted for in other funds.

Special Revenue Funds - to account for the proceeds of specific revenue sources that are restricted by law or to account for administrative action to expend funds for specified purposes.

General Capital Projects Funds - to account for financial resources segregated for the acquisition of major capital facilities (other than those financed by enterprise funds).

PROPRIETARY FUNDS

Enterprise Funds - to account for operations that are financed and operated in a manner similar to private business enterprises where the determination of net income is necessary or useful to sound financial administration and where the costs of providing such services are typically recovered to varying extents through user charges. The City of Raleigh has three enterprise funds: the Mass Transit Fund, the Water and Sewer Fund, and the Parking Facilities Fund.

Internal Service Fund - to account for the centralized services of the City's Print Shop and Office Supply Room which are provided City departments on a cost-reimbursement basis.

FIDUCIARY FUNDS

The fiduciary funds are used to account for resources received and held by the City as trustee or for which the City acts as agent for individuals. These funds are expended or invested in accordance with agreements or applicable prescribed procedures. The fiduciary funds are comprised of two pension trust funds (the Supplemental Money Purchase Plan Fund and the Law Enforcement Officers' Special Separation Allowance Fund) and four agency funds (the Employee Health Insurance Fund, the Deferred Compensation Fund, the Supplemental Retirement Savings Plan Fund and the Occupancy Tax Fund).

ACCOUNT GROUPS

General Fixed Assets Account Group - This group of accounts is established to account for all fixed assets of the City, other than those accounted for in the proprietary fund type.

General Long-Term Obligations Account Group - This group of accounts is established to account for all long-term obligations of the City other than those accounted for in the proprietary fund type.

C. Basis of Accounting

The accounting and financial reporting treatment applied to a fund is determined by its measurement focus. All governmental funds are accounted for using a current financial resources measurement focus. With this measurement focus, only current assets and current liabilities generally are included on the balance sheet. Operating statements of these funds present increases (i.e., revenues and other financing sources) and decreases (i.e., expenditures and other financing uses) in net current assets.

All proprietary funds and pension trust funds are accounted for on a flow of economic resources measurement focus. With this measurement focus, all assets and all liabilities associated with the operation of these funds are included on the balance sheet. Fund equity (i.e., net total assets) is segregated into contributed capital and retained earnings components. Proprietary fund type operating statements present increases (e.g., revenues) and decreases (e.g., expenses) in net total assets.

The modified accrual basis of accounting is used by all governmental fund types and agency funds. Under the modified accrual basis of accounting, revenues are recognized when susceptible to accrual (i.e., when they become both measurable and available). "Measurable" means the amount of the transaction can be determined and "available" means collectible within the current period or soon enough thereafter to be used to pay liabilities of the current period. The City considers revenues as available if they are collected within 60 days after year-end. Expenditures are recorded when the related fund liability is incurred. Principal and interest on general long-term debt are recorded when due. Encumbrances are recognized during the year but outstanding encumbrances at the end of the year which do not represent incurred expenditures are either charged to an appropriation in the following year or are cancelled.

Those revenues susceptible to accrual are sales tax collected and held by the state at year-end on behalf of the City, investment earnings, landfill tipping fees, cable franchise fees, Civic Center charges to customers, property taxes collected and held by the county at year-end on behalf of the City, and earned grant proceeds. Assessments, property taxes (other than amounts on hand at the county), hotel occupancy tax and certain other intergovernmental revenues are not susceptible to accrual because generally they are either not available or not measurable until received in cash.

The accrual basis of accounting is utilized by proprietary fund types and pension trust funds. Under this method, revenues are recorded when earned and expenses are recorded at the time liabilities are incurred.

The City reports deferred revenue on its combined balance sheet. Deferred revenues arise when a potential revenue does not meet both the "measurable" and "available" criteria for recognition in the current period. Deferred revenues also arise when resources are received by the City before it has legal claim to them, as when grant monies are received prior to the incurrence of qualifying expenditures. In subsequent periods, when both revenue recognition criteria are met, or when the City has a legal claim to the resources, the liability for deferred revenue is removed from the combined balance sheet and revenue is recognized.

D. Budgets

Budgetary control is exercised in all funds except the trust and agency funds. The budget shown in the financial statements is the budget ordinance as amended at the close of the day of June 30, 1992. The City is required by the General Statutes of the State of North Carolina to adopt an annual balanced budget by July 1 of each year. The General Statutes also provide for balanced project ordinances for the life of projects, including both capital and grant activities, which are expected to extend beyond the end of the fiscal year. The City Council officially adopts the annual budget ordinance and all project ordinances and has the authority to amend such ordinances as necessary to recognize new resources or reallocations of budget. At June 30, 1992, the effect of such amendments, less eliminating transfers, was as follows:

	Original Budget	Total Amendments	Budget June 30, 1992
General Fund	$142,228,123	$ 1,567,276	$143,795,399
Special Revenue Funds	39,898,750	11,726,520	51,625,270
General Capital Projects Funds	128,167,011	3,490,342	131,657,353
Proprietary Funds	150,665,314	2,475,975	153,141,289
Internal Service Fund	762,300	25,678	787,978

All budgets are prepared on the modified accrual basis of accounting as is required by North Carolina law. Appropriations for funds that adopt annual budgets lapse at the end of the budget year. Project budgeted appropriations do not lapse until the completion of the project.

Budget control on expenditures is limited to departmental totals and project totals as specified in the budget ordinances. Administrative control is maintained through the establishment of more detailed line-item budgets, which correspond to the specific object of the expenditure. All budget transfers, both at the ordinance and the line-item levels, are approved by the City Council. The City Manager is authorized to transfer line-item budgeted amounts up to $1,000 within a fund prior to their formal approval by the City Council.

Encumbrances represent commitments related to unperformed contracts for goods or services. Encumbrance accounting--under which purchase orders, contracts, and other commitments for the expenditure of resources are recorded to reserve that portion of the applicable appropriation--is utilized in all funds. Outstanding encumbrances at year-end for which goods or services are received are reclassified to expenditures and accounts payable. All other encumbrances in the annual budgeted funds are reversed at year-end and are either cancelled or are included as reappropriations of fund balance for the subsequent year. Encumbrances at year-end in funds which are budgeted on a project basis automatically carry forward along with their related appropriations and are not subject to an annual cancellation and reappropriation.

The Combined Statement of Revenues, Expenditures and Changes in Fund Balances - Annual Budget and Actual - General and Special Revenue Fund Types includes all governmental fund types for which annual budgets have been legally adopted. This presentation, accordingly, does not include any of the general capital projects funds and certain of the special revenue funds that have budgets which are adopted on a project basis, spanning more than one year. The Raleigh Convention and Visitors Bureau Fund and the Powell Bill Fund are the only special revenue funds which had annual budgets and are, therefore, the only special revenue funds presented on the above referenced financial statement.

E. Investments

State Statutes authorize the City to invest in securities of the U. S. Government, U. S. Government Agencies, high quality commercial paper, banker's acceptances, repurchase agreements, obligations of the State of North Carolina and the North Carolina Cash Management Trust.

Investments are stated at cost or amortized cost, except for investments in the deferred compensation agency fund which are reported at market value.

F. Ad Valorem Taxes Receivable

City ad valorem taxes are billed for the City by the Wake County Revenue Collector after July 1 of each fiscal year based upon the assessed value listed as of the prior January 1 lien date. The City Council is required to approve the tax levy no later than August 1, although this traditionally is in the month of June. Taxes are due on September 1 but do not begin to accrue penalties for nonpayment until the following January 5. Collections of City taxes are made by the County and are remitted to the City as collected.

Ad valorem taxes receivable at year-end are not considered to be available as a resource that can be used to finance the current year operations of the City, and therefore, are not susceptible to recognition as earned revenue. The amount of the recorded receivable for ad valorem taxes has been reduced by an allowance for uncollectible accounts and the net receivable is offset by deferred revenue in an equal amount.

G. Other Receivables

Other accounts receivable reported in governmental funds which represent amounts considered measurable and available are recorded as revenue but, based on state law restrictions, are restricted in fund balance at year-end.

Any other accounts receivable which represent amounts not subject to accrual as earned revenue are recorded as assets and are offset by deferred revenue in an equal amount. Assessment receivables have been reduced by an amount deemed to be uncollectible.

The amounts due from other governmental agencies are grants and participation agreements which are reserved for specific programs and capital projects. Program grants, primarily accounted for in the special revenue funds, are recognized as receivables and revenue in the period benefitted, i.e., at the time reimbursable program costs are incurred.

Capital project grants are recorded as receivables and revenues at the time reimbursable project costs are incurred.

H. Inventories

Inventories in the governmental, enterprise and internal service funds consist primarily of expendable supplies held for consumption. Inventories are recorded as an expenditure at the time an item is used and are available at cost, using the first-in, first-out (FIFO) method.

I. Fixed Assets

Enterprise and Internal Service funds fixed assets are accounted for within the respective funds and are recorded as expenditures at the time of purchase to satisfy statutory budgetary requirements. At year-end these assets are capitalized at historical cost for financial statement presentation. Such cost includes capitalized interest on long-term obligations during the construction period of fixed assets, when material. Depreciation on these assets is calculated under the straight-line method and is charged to operations. The estimated useful lives of the assets for determining depreciation charges are as follows: Water and Sewer Systems and Improvements - 50 years, Buildings and Machinery - 45 years, Buses - 15 years, Equipment, Furniture and Fixtures - 3 to 10 years.

The values of fixed asset additions contributed to the Water and Sewer, Mass Transit and Parking Facilities Funds are recorded in the enterprise funds as contributed capital at their estimated fair value at time of acquisition.

All other fixed assets of the City are recorded as expenditures at the time of purchase and capitalized at year-end at historical cost in the General Fixed Assets Account Group. These assets are not depreciated. They are funded primarily by local ad valorem taxes, state shared revenues, bonded debt proceeds, local sales taxes and state or federal funding. Others are acquired through donations and gifts and are assigned a value equal to the fair market value at the date of receipt. Public domain ("infrastructure") general fixed assets consisting of such improvements as roads, bridges, sidewalks and curbs and gutters are capitalized along with other general fixed assets.

(Portions of report not shown here)

	Balance June 30, 1991	Additions	Payments and Retirements	Balance June 30, 1992
For Retirement of Other Installment and Contractual Obligations	$ 8,432	$ 1,570	$2,308	$ 7,694
For Retirement of Earned Vacation Pay	4,905	111	-	5,016
	$93,597	$20,681	$6,288	$107,990
General Long-Term Obligations Payable: Serial Bonds	$68,760	$19,000	$3,980	$ 83,780
Other Long-Term Obligations	24,837	1,681	2,308	24,210
	$93,597	$20,681	$6,288	$107,990

Note 5. Employee Retirement Plans

North Carolina Local Government Employees' Retirement System

All permanent full-time City employees participate in the statewide North Carolina Local Government Employees' Retirement System (System), a multiple-employer, cost-sharing, defined benefit pension plan. The City's payroll for employees covered by the System for the fiscal year ended June 30, 1992 was $72,290,325; the City's total payroll was $76,124,343.

The System provides retirement and disability benefits. After five years of creditable service, employees qualify for a vested deferred benefit. Employees not engaged in law enforcement may retire with unreduced retirement benefits under the following conditions:

1) complete 30 years of creditable service, or
2) reach age 65 with 5 years creditable service, or
3) reach age 60 and complete 25 years of creditable service.

Law enforcement officers may retire with unreduced retirement benefits after completing 30 years of creditable service or after reaching age 55 and completing 5 years of creditable service. Employees retiring under any of these conditions are entitled to annual retirement benefits equal to 1.64 percent of their average final compensation times their years of creditable service. Average final compensation is the average of an employee's salary during the employee's four highest paid years in a row.

Employees may retire with reduced retirement benefits under the following conditions:

1) employees not engaged in law enforcement who reach age 50 and complete 20 years of creditable service or reach age 60 and complete 5 years of creditable service, or

2) law enforcement officers who reach age 50 and complete 15 years of creditable service, or

3) firemen who reach age 55 and complete 5 years of creditable service.

Covered employees are required by State Statute to contribute 6 percent of their salary to the System. The City is required by the same statute to contribute the remaining amounts necessary to pay benefits when due. The actuarially determined contribution requirement for the fiscal year ended June 30, 1992 was $7,717,678, which consisted of $3,380,239 from the City and $4,337,439 from employees. The City's required contributions for employees not engaged in law enforcement and for law enforcement officers represented 4.80 percent and 4.24 percent of covered payroll, respectively.

The "pension benefit obligation" is a standardized disclosure measure of the present value of pension benefits, adjusted for the effects of projected salary increases and step-rate benefits, estimated to be payable in the future as a result of employee service to date. The measure, which is the actuarial present value of credited projected benefits, is intended to help users assess the System's funding status on a going-concern basis, assess progress made in accumulating sufficient assets to pay benefits when due, and make comparisons among public employee retirement systems and employers. The System does not make separate measurements of assets and pension benefit obligations for individual employers. The pension benefit obligation for the System as a whole at December 31, 1991, the date of the latest available actuarial valuation was $3,326,299,000. The System's net assets available for benefits on that date (at cost) were $3,576,973,000, leaving net assets in excess of the pension benefit obligation of $250,674,000. The City's 1992 contribution represented 3.0 percent of total contributions required of all participating employers.

Ten year historical trend information showing the System's revenues by source and expenses by type will be presented in the State of North Carolina's June 30, 1992 Comprehensive Annual Financial Report (CAFR). The State's CAFR will also present prospective trend information showing the System's progress in accumulating sufficient assets to pay benefits when due.

Law Enforcement Supplemental Plans

401-K Retirement Plan

All law enforcement officers employed by the City participate in the Supplemental Retirement Income Plan, a defined contribution pension plan. Participation begins at the date of employment. In a defined contribution plan, benefits depend solely on amounts contributed to the plan plus investment earnings. State

Statute requires that the City contribute each month an amount equal to five percent of each officer's salary, and all amounts contributed are vested immediately. Also, the law enforcement officers may make voluntary contributions to the plan.

The City's contributions were calculated using a covered payroll amount of $15,958,480. Total contributions for the fiscal year ended June 30, 1992 were $923,163 which consisted of $797,924 from the City and $125,239 from the law enforcement officers. The City's required contributions and the officers' voluntary contributions represented 5.0 percent and 0.8 percent of the covered payroll amount, respectively.

Law Enforcement Officers' Special Separation Allowance

A. Description

The City of Raleigh is the administrator of a single-employer, defined benefit, public employee retirement system (System), established by the City to provide special separation benefits to its law enforcement officers. The City's annual compensation for full-time employees covered by the System for the fiscal year ended June 30, 1992 was $15,473,511; the City's total payroll was $76,124,343.

All full-time City law enforcement officers are covered by the System. At December 31, 1991, the date of the latest available actuarial valuation, the System's membership consisted of:

Retirees currently receiving benefits	31
Current employees:	
Vested	0
Nonvested	433
Total	464

The System provides separation benefits to all full-time City law enforcement officers who meet the following:

1) have (1) completed 30 or more years of creditable service, or (2) have attained 55 years of age and completed 5 or more years of creditable service, and
2) have not attained 62 years of age, and
3) have completed at least 5 years of continuous service as a law enforcement officer immediately preceding a service retirement.

The qualified law enforcement officers are entitled to an annual retirement benefit of .85 percent of the annual equivalent of the base rate of compensation most recently applicable to the covered employee for each year of creditable service. The retirement benefits are paid monthly in equal installments. Payments to retired officers cease at their death or on the last day of the month in which the officer attains 62 years of age or upon the first day of re-employment by any state department, agency or institution.

(Portions of report not shown here)

A summary of interfund operating transfers by fund type for the fiscal year ended June 30, 1992, is as follows:

Fund Type	Amount
Transfers from Other Funds	
General Fund	$ 4,910,300
Special Revenue Funds	2,087,225
General Capital Projects Funds	8,498,838
Enterprise Funds	3,847,282
Internal Service Fund	37,500
	$19,381,145
Transfers to Other Funds	
General Fund	$10,064,102
Special Revenue Funds	8,301,262
General Capital Projects Funds	231,456
Enterprise Funds	784,325
	$19,381,145

The following residual equity transfers were made for the fiscal year ended June 30, 1992:

From	To	Amount
General Fund	Internal Service Fund	$ 28,344
Special Revenue Funds:	Proprietary Funds:	
Sales Tax Fund	Sewer Bond Fund	2,358,000
	Water Bond Fund	284,000
Housing Development Fund	Parking Facilities Fund	5,458
Proprietary Funds:		
Parking Facilities Fund	Mass Transit Fund	53,654
		$2,729,456

Note 7. Contributed Capital

Grant proceeds and other contributions received for the purchase or construction of fixed assets and the fair market value of property donated or annexed by the City are accounted for as contributed capital within the applicable proprietary fund type. Contributed capital from grants, entitlements and shared revenues which are externally restricted for capital acquisitions or construction is amortized over the useful life of the related asset and transferred to retained earnings. The changes in contributed capital during the fiscal year 1991-92 are as follows:

Enterprise Funds:

Mass Transit Fund	Amount
Balance, Beginning of Year	$10,436,315
Additions	52,634
Amortization	(885,758)
Balance, End of Year	$ 9,603,191

Water and Sewer Fund	
Balance, Beginning of Year	$111,440,117
Additions	8,011,377
Amortization	(2,729,569)
Balance, End of Year	$116,721,925

Parking Facilities Fund	
Balance, Beginning of Year	$ 11,045,639
Additions	-
Other	(48,196)
Balance, End of Year	$ 10,997,443

Internal Service Fund:

Print and Supply Shops Fund	
Balance, Beginning of Year	$ -
Additions	185,421
Balance, End of Year	$ 185,421

Note 8. Segment Information - Enterprise Funds

The City maintains three enterprise funds which provide transit, water and sewer, and parking services. Segment information for the fiscal year ended June 30, 1992, is as follows (stated in thousands):

	Mass Transit Fund	Water and Sewer Fund	Parking Facilities Fund	Total Enterprise Funds
Operating Revenues	$ 1,524	$ 32,689	$ 979	$ 35,192
Depreciation Expense	865	5,649	307	6,821
Operating Income (Loss)	(4,911)	6,802	501	2,392
Operating Grants and Shared Revenues	902	-	-	902
Operating Transfers In (Out)	3,124	(553)	491	3,062
Net Income (Loss)	(886)	7,377	725	7,216
Contributed Capital: Contributions	53	8,011	-	8,064
Fixed Assets: Additions	53	19,795	4,391	24,239
Deletions	906	251	-	1,157
Total Assets	10,281	311,467	24,978	346,726
Bonds and Other Long-Term Obligations: Payable from Operating Revenues	-	64,599	8,634	73,233
Total Equity	9,725	236,157	14,804	260,686

Note 9. Mass Transit Fund

The City established the Mass Transit Fund to account for the operations and capital acquisitions of the City-wide transit system which is operated and managed by ATC Management Corporation under an agreement with the City. In 1991-92, the City paid ATC Management Corporation a fee of $134,950 and reimbursed all losses incurred.

All operating losses subsidized by the City were shared by the U. S. Urban Mass Transportation Administration (UMTA) to the extent of 20.8 percent of the losses, contingent on the City's share being at least equal to the average of the City's contributions in the prior two fiscal years.

Note 10. Commitments and Contingencies

Claims and Legal Actions

The City generally follows the practice of recording liabilities resulting from claims and legal actions only when they become fixed or determined in amount. At June 30, 1992, the City was a party to the usual number of such claims and legal actions; however, no provision has been made in these financial statements for the contingent liabilities incident thereto. In the opinion of the City's legal counsel and management, the outcome of legal matters referred to above will not significantly impact the overall financial position of the City of Raleigh.

GENERAL FUND

City of Raleigh

BALANCE SHEET
GENERAL FUND
June 30, 1992

ASSETS	Total June 30, 1992	June 30, 1991
Cash and Cash Equivalents	$ 48,899,793	$ 46,393,255
Taxes Receivable, Net of Allowance for Uncollectibles of $3,677,638 in 1992 and $3,325,612 in 1991	846,186	716,040
Assessments Receivable, Net of Allowance for Uncollectibles of $12,585 in 1992 and $9,023 in 1991	239,112	171,442
Due from Other Governmental Agencies	607,629	-
Accrued Interest Receivable	630,013	507,763
Other Receivables	1,900,531	2,368,656
Sales Tax Receivable	4,186,650	4,200,482
Due from Other Funds	592,329	454,962
Inventories	1,269,868	1,126,769
Other Assets	77,349	65,838
Loans Receivable	242,901	243,310
Total Assets	$ 59,492,361	$ 56,248,517

LIABILITIES AND FUND EQUITY		
Liabilities:		
Accounts Payable	$ 1,261,984	$ 1,297,557
Accrued Salaries and Employer Payroll Taxes	1,119,965	2,423,887
Due to Other Funds	7,734	-
Other Liabilities	976,920	978,551
Deferred Revenues for Taxes, Assessments and Other Receivables	1,585,883	1,199,598
Total Liabilities	4,952,486	5,899,593
Fund Equity:		
Fund Balance:		
Reserved for Inventories	1,269,868	1,126,769
Reserved by State Statute	7,559,111	7,463,057
Reserved for Encumbrances	1,636,075	1,575,910
Unreserved:		
Designated for Subsequent Year's Appropriation	12,704,197	13,386,386
Designated for Specific Purposes	15,999,778	14,383,383
Undesignated	15,370,846	12,413,419
Total Fund Equity	54,539,875	50,348,924
Total Liabilities and Fund Equity	$ 59,492,361	$ 56,248,517

City of Raleigh

STATEMENT OF REVENUES, EXPENDITURES
AND CHANGES IN FUND BALANCE
GENERAL FUND
For the Fiscal Year Ended June 30, 1992

	Total	
	June 30, 1992	June 30, 1991
Revenues:		
Ad Valorem Taxes	$ 68,749,965	$ 65,367,860
Intergovernmental	17,986,422	17,519,980
Assessments	96,747	71,041
Local Sales Tax	12,921,883	13,613,425
Transient Occupancy Tax	1,948,715	1,760,435
Licenses	5,325,109	4,202,908
Interest on Investments	3,087,331	3,735,538
Inspection Fees	1,643,800	1,386,408
Highway Maintenance Refunds	507,960	657,752
Miscellaneous Fees and Charges	9,551,034	8,690,481
Miscellaneous Other	1,453,785	1,473,967
Total Revenues	123,272,751	118,479,795
Other Financing Sources:		
Operating Transfers In	4,910,300	3,879,778
Proceeds of Capital Lease and Other Installment Obligations	1,487,050	1,820,996
Total Other Financing Sources	6,397,350	5,700,774
Total Revenues and Other Financing Sources	129,670,101	124,180,569
Expenditures:		
General Government	21,135,196	20,058,953
Personnel	1,017,604	984,397
Finance	3,040,169	2,897,518
Information Services	2,061,058	2,297,646
Community Development Services	13,395,789	13,101,300
Public Safety	34,876,166	34,099,923
Public Works	19,139,800	18,637,374
Leisure Services	14,566,801	13,874,336
Debt Service	10,065,885	7,836,442
Other	18,296	48,539
Total Expenditures	119,316,764	113,836,428
Less: Administrative Costs Charged to Water and Sewer Fund	3,930,060	3,258,838
	115,386,704	110,577,590
Other Financing Uses:		
Operating Transfers Out	10,064,102	11,199,407
Total Expenditures and Other Financing Uses	125,450,806	121,776,997
Excess of Revenues and Other Financing Sources Over Expenditures and Other Financing Uses	4,219,295	2,403,572
Fund Balance - Beginning of Year	50,348,924	48,011,511
Residual Transfer of Equity	(28,344)	(66,159)
Fund Balance - End of Year	$ 54,539,875	$ 50,348,924

SPECIAL REVENUE FUNDS

SPECIAL REVENUE FUNDS

Raleigh Convention and Visitors Bureau Fund - The Raleigh Convention and Visitors Bureau Fund accounts for the operations of the Raleigh Convention and Visitors Bureau which was considered part of the City of Raleigh entity through December 31, 1991. At that time it became the Greater Raleigh Convention and Visitors Bureau (GRCVB) funded by a county-wide six percent room occupancy tax. The GRCVB is accounted for as a joint venture of the City of Raleigh and Wake County.

Grants Fund - The Grants Fund accounts for activities to which federal, state, and other aid is contributed, with the exception of capital projects, Federal Community Development, and transportation assistance. This fund centralizes all funding sources for these activities and provides for full budgetary accountability.

Sales Tax Fund - The Sales Tax Fund accounts for revenue from the two one-half cents local option sales tax proceeds. Forty percent of the total one cent, which is in addition to the regular one cent sales tax levied by counties in North Carolina, must be used for water and sewer purposes.

Housing Development Fund - The Housing Development Fund accounts for City housing development programs, which are funded from City tax revenues.

Housing Bond Fund - The Housing Bond Fund accounts for City housing development programs which are financed by a $20 million bond issue.

Community Development Fund - The Community Development Fund accounts for United States Department of Housing and Urban Development (HUD) block grant proceeds allocated to the City for community development programs.

Powell Bill Fund - The Powell Bill Fund accounts for the receipts of the one cent sales tax on motor fuel, which is distributed to municipalities for local street improvement and maintenance. Allocation of this state tax is on the basis of local street mileage and population data.

City of Raleigh

COMBINING BALANCE SHEET
ALL SPECIAL REVENUE FUNDS
June 30, 1992

ASSETS	Grants Fund	Sales Tax Fund	Housing Development Fund
Cash and Cash Equivalents	$ -	$ 3,045,176	$ 2,179,215
Due from Other Governmental Agencies - Grant Agreements	196,137	-	3,930
Accrued Interest Receivable	-	77,348	14,077
Other Receivables and Assets	-	-	-
Sales Tax Receivable	-	2,220,436	680
Due from Other Funds	-	1,550	62,847
Loans Receivable	-	3,550,387	2,863,449
Total Assets	$ 196,137	$8,894,897	$ 5,124,198

LIABILITIES AND FUND EQUITY

	Grants Fund	Sales Tax Fund	Housing Development Fund
Liabilities:			
Accounts Payable	$ 26,863	$ 116,284	$ 134,086
Accrued Interest Payable	-	-	-
Rehabilitation Loans Escrow	-	-	67,743
Due to Other Funds	156,990	-	-
Unearned Grant Proceeds	-	-	-
Deferred Revenue - Grants	-	-	-
Deferred Revenue - Loans	-	3,550,387	2,863,449
Other Liabilities	-	-	-
Total Liabilities	183,853	3,666,671	3,065,278
Fund Equity:			
Fund Balances:			
Reserved by State Statute	-	-	-
Unreserved:			
Designated for Subsequent Year's Appropriation	-	3,531,497	1,972,964
Undesignated	12,284	1,696,729	85,956
Total Fund Equity	12,284	5,228,226	2,058,920
Total Liabilities and Fund Equity	$ 196,137	$ 8,894,897	$ 5,124,198

	Housing Bond Fund	Community Development Fund	Powell Bill Fund	Total June 30, 1992	June 30, 1991
	$ 7,175,659	$ 101,633	$ 654,428	$ 13,156,111	$ 6,230,119
	-	147,010	-	347,077	409,795
	21,311	-	60,712	173,448	126,779
	-	96,023	-	96,023	154,480
	-	-	-	2,221,116	2,152,579
	-	-	-	64,397	50,606
	-	4,526,221	-	10,940,057	7,525,95
	$ 7,196,970	$ 4,870,887	$ 715,140	$ 26,998,229	$ 16,650,3

					88
	$ -	$ 62,644	$ -	$ 339,877	$ 506
	-	-	9,527	9,527	,875
	-	185,186	-	252,929	,814
	-	62,847	-	219,837	,692
	-	-	-	-	36,903
	-	33,892	-	33,892	25,955
	-	4,526,221	-	10,940,057	232
	-	97	-	97	,603,865
	-	4,870,887	9,527	11,796,216	

					66,01
	21,311	-	60,712	82,023	5,957,6
	7,175,659	-	-	12,680,120	2,022
	-	-	644,901	2,439,870	8,04
	7,196,970	-	705,613	15,202,013	
					$ 16,6 3
	$ 7,196,970	$ 4,870,887	$ 715,140	$ 26,998,22	

City of Raleigh

COMBINING STATEMENT OF REVENUES, EXPENDITURES
AND CHANGES IN FUND BALANCES
ALL SPECIAL REVENUE FUNDS
For the Fiscal Year Ended June 30, 1992

	Raleigh Convention and Visitors Bureau Fund (Six Months)	Grants Fund	Sales Tax Fund	Housing Development Fund
Revenues:				
Intergovernmental	$ -	$ 725,400	$ -	$ 3,930
Local Sales Tax	-	-	8,296,138	-
Interest on Investments	1,775	-	354,507	79,245
Miscellaneous Other	-	5,112	47,165	1,228,437
Total Revenues	1,775	730,512	8,697,810	1,311,612
Other Financing Sources:				
Operating Transfers In	556,526	407,171	262,278	1,318,417
In-Kind Contribution from City	-	36,238	-	-
Proceeds of General Obligation				
Bonds and Premium	-	-	-	-
Proceeds of Capital Lease	-	-	-	-
Proceeds of Other Installment				
Obligations	-	-	-	-
Total Other Financing Sources	556,526	443,409	262,278	1,318,417
Revenues and Other Financing Sources	558,301	1,173,921	8,960,088	2,630,029
Expenditures:				
General Government	-	-	-	-
Service and Economic Development Programs	-	-	962,736	953,484
Management and Conservation Services	-	-	-	513,374
Outlay	413	42,617	2,299,862	-
Debt Expenditures	502,773	1,131,689	69,668	422,569
Principal	-	-	-	130,000
Interest	-	-	-	12,600
Total Expenditures	503,186	1,174,306	3,332,266	2,032,027
Other Financing Operating Uses:				
Transfer to Out	-	-	3,559,829	44,481
Total Other Venture	55,115	-	-	-
Expenditures Uses	55,115	-	3,559,829	44,481
Expenditures and Other Financing	558,301	1,174,306	6,892,095	2,076,508
(Deficiency) of Revenues and Other Financing over Expenditures and Other Financing Uses	-	(385)	2,067,993	553,521
Balances - Beginning of Year	-	12,669	5,802,233	1,510,857
Transfer of Equity	-	-	(2,642,000)	(5,458)
Balances - End of Year	$ -	$ 12,284	$ 5,228,226	$ 2,058,920

	Housing Bond Fund	Community Development Fund	Powell Bill Fund	Combining Eliminations	Total June 30, 1992	June 30, 1991
	$ -	$ 1,034,700	$ 5,077,379	$ -	$ 6,841,409	$ 7,319,798
		-	-	-	8,296,138	8,181,928
	95,308	-	247,812	-	778,647	870,371
	-	1,198,769	-	-	2,479,483	1,604,559
	95,308	2,233,469	5,325,191	-	18,395,677	17,976,656
	-	78,181	-	(535,348)	2,087,225	3,154,053
	-	-	-	-	36,238	36,228
	8,300,030	-	-	-	8,300,030	-
	-	-	-	-	-	355,050
	-	-	-	-	-	75,000
	8,300,030	78,181	-	(535,348)	10,423,493	3,620,331
	8,395,338	2,311,650	5,325,191	(535,348)	28,819,170	21,596,987
	-	353,849	-	-	353,849	295,157
	1,198,368	-	-	-	3,114,588	4,381,599
	-	1,174,044	-	-	1,687,418	1,455,825
	-	783,757	107,967	-	3,234,616	2,270,942
	-	-	-	-	2,126,699	1,718,600
	-	-	-	-	130,000	210,000
	-	-	-	-	12,600	15,339
	1,198,368	2,311,650	107,967	-	10,659,770	10,347,462
	-	-	5,232,300	(535,348)	8,301,262	6,688,874
	-	-	-	-	55,115	-
	-	-	5,232,300	(535,348)	8,356,377	6,688,874
	1,198,368	2,311,650	5,340,267	(535,348)	19,016,147	17,036,336
	7,196,970	-	(15,076)	-	9,803,023	4,560,651
	-	-	720,689	-	8,046,448	7,996,704
	-	-	-	-	(2,647,458)	(4,510,907)
	$ 7,196,970	$ -	$ 705,613	$ -	$ 15,202,013	$ 8,046,448

City of Raleigh

SCHEDULE OF REVENUES AND EXPENDITURES
COMPARED WITH BUDGET
HOUSING DEVELOPMENT FUND
For the Fiscal Year Ended June 30, 1992

	Actual				Over
	Prior Years	Current Year	Total	Budget	(Under) Budget
Revenues:					
Intergovernmental	$ -	$ 3,930	$ 3,930	$ 101,500	$ (97,570)
Interest on Investments	-	79,245	79,245	-	79,245
Miscellaneous Other	906,494	1,228,437	2,134,931	1,970,783	164,148
Total Revenues	906,494	1,311,612	2,218,106	2,072,283	145,823
Other Financing Sources:					
Operating Transfers In:					
Downtown Parking Deck Fund	-	932	932	932	-
General Fund	-	803,000	803,000	803,000	-
Sales Tax Fund	-	490,867	490,867	490,867	-
Park Improvement Fund	-	23,618	23,618	23,618	-
Total Other Financing Sources	-	1,318,417	1,318,417	1,318,417	-
Total Revenues and Other Financing Sources	$ 906,494	$2,630,029	$3,536,523	3,390,700	$ 145,823
Fund Balance Appropriated				3,927,649	
				$7,318,349	
Expenditures:					
Program Administration	$ 11,431	$ 388,302	$ 399,733	$ 365,004	$ 34,729
Rental Incentive Program	277,806	458,357	736,163	818,278	(82,115)
Second Mortgage Loans	46,228	167,021	213,249	369,364	(156,115)
Home Ownership Assistance	790,325	375,165	1,165,490	1,368,682	(203,192)
Emergency Rehabilitation	102,687	16,459	119,146	138,270	(19,124)
Housing Initiatives	-	-	-	211,828	(211,828)
Low Income Rental Assistance	897,963	-	897,963	974,065	(76,102)
Public Owned Housing	727,261	7,476	734,737	745,000	(10,263)
Triangle Investment Housing Program	2,352	20,000	22,352	22,500	(148)
Transitional Housing Program	170,241	38,558	208,799	681,556	(472,757)
Downtown East Development	359,961	379,892	739,853	1,072,973	(333,120)
King Subdivision Project	-	3,930	3,930	101,500	(97,570)
State Housing Grant Study	110	-	110	4,000	(3,890)
Debt Service:					
Principal	-	130,000	130,000	130,000	-
Interest	-	12,600	12,600	12,600	-
Other	58,236	34,267	92,503	182,626	(90,123)
Total Expenditures	3,444,601	2,032,027	5,476,628	7,198,246	(1,721,618)
Other Financing Uses:					
Operating Transfers to Community Development Fund	11,913	44,481	56,394	114,645	(58,251)
Residual Equity Transfer to Wilmington Street Parking Fund	-	5,458	5,458	5,458	-
Total Expenditures, Other Financing Uses and Residual Equity Transfer	$3,456,514	$2,081,966	$5,538,480	$7,318,349	$(1,779,869)

GENERAL CAPITAL PROJECTS FUNDS

Street Improvement Fund - The Street Improvement Fund accounts for all street improvement programs to be financed from applicable street assessment proceeds and other non-bond street improvement resources.

Street Bond Fund - The Street Bond Fund accounts for all bond proceeds and capital project costs for the installation of bond-funded street improvements within the City.

Sidewalk Fund - The Sidewalk Fund accounts for all bond proceeds and capital project costs for the installation of sidewalks within the City.

Park Improvement Fund - The Park Improvement Fund accounts for transfers from the General Fund and other revenues and allocations, and all project costs in the construction of park improvements or park land acquisition.

Walnut Creek Amphitheatre Fund - The Walnut Creek Amphitheatre Fund accounts for all certificate of participation proceeds, tenant's capital investment and other resources, and all project costs in the construction and financing of the Walnut Creek Amphitheatre.

Facility Fees Fund - The Facility Fees Fund accounts for facility fees collected from developers to be expended for street and park capital purposes within designated zones in the City.

Park Bond Fund - The Park Bond Fund accounts for all bond proceeds and capital project costs related to the construction of park improvements or park land acquisition.

Miscellaneous Capital Improvements Fund - The Miscellaneous Capital Improvements Fund accounts for all capital improvement costs not applicable to other capital improvement programs. These improvements are financed from non-bond resources.

Civic Center Fund - The Civic Center Fund accounts for all capital project costs related to the Raleigh Civic and Convention Center complex.

City of Raleigh

COMBINING BALANCE SHEET
ALL GENERAL CAPITAL PROJECTS FUNDS
June 30, 1992

	Street Improvement Fund	Street Bond Fund	Sidewalk Fund	Park Improvement Fund
ASSETS				
Cash and Cash Equivalents	$ 6,669,056	$ 25,320,125	$ 365,601	$ 2,305,820
Assessments Receivable, Net of Allowance for Uncollectibles of $44,042 in 1992 and $46,358 in 1991	836,804	-	-	-
Due from Other Governmental Agencies	243,000	262,640	-	-
Accrued Interest Receivable	63,459	145,629	3,788	32,041
Other Receivables and Assets	231,315	31,735	2,034	15,825
Total Assets	$ 8,043,634	$ 25,760,129	$ 371,423	$ 2,353,686
LIABILITIES AND FUND EQUITY				
Liabilities:				
Accounts Payable	$ 282,424	$ 1,212,049	$ 1,896	$ 88,438
Arbitrage Rebate Payable	-	368,131	-	-
Other Liabilities	89,636	-	-	-
Deferred Revenue for Assessments Receivable	836,804	-	-	-
Total Liabilities	1,208,864	1,580,180	1,896	88,438
Fund Equity:				
Fund Balance:				
Unreserved:				
Designated for Subsequent Year's Appropriation	5,914,625	23,526,897	345,973	2,161,927
Designated for Specific Purposes	920,145	653,052	23,554	103,321
Total Fund Equity	6,834,770	24,179,949	369,527	2,265,248
Total Liabilities and Fund Equity	$ 8,043,634	$ 25,760,129	$ 371,423	$ 2,353,686

	Walnut Creek Amphitheatre Fund	Facility Fees Fund	Park Bond Fund	Miscellaneous Capital Improvements Fund	Civic Center Fund	Total June 30, 1992	Total June 30, 1991
	$ 1,585,828	$ 2,538,664	$ 2,469,829	$ 693,324	$ 538,231	$ 42,486,478	$ 50,229,242
	-	-	-	-	-	836,804	880,795
	-	-	-	-	-	505,640	736,826
	-	19,413	3,688	7,010	674	275,702	270,808
	33,812	-	64,604	815	-	380,140	371,655
	$ 1,619,640	$ 2,558,077	$ 2,538,121	$ 701,149	$ 538,905	$ 44,484,764	$ 52,489,326
	$ -	$ -	$ 1,426,622	$ -	$ -	$ 3,011,429	$ 3,956,692
	-	-	95,657	-	44,200	507,988	467,464
	-	790,290	-	-	-	879,926	1,410,022
	-	-	-	-	-	836,804	880,795
	-	790,290	1,522,279	-	44,200	5,236,147	6,714,973
	1,619,640	732,456	816,250	685,594	75,647	35,879,009	38,291,981
	-	1,035,331	199,592	15,555	419,058	3,369,608	7,482,372
	1,619,640	1,767,787	1,015,842	701,149	494,705	39,248,617	45,774,353
	$ 1,619,640	$ 2,558,077	$ 2,538,121	$ 701,149	$ 538,905	$ 44,484,764	$ 52,489,326

City of Raleigh

COMBINING STATEMENT OF REVENUES, EXPENDITURES
AND CHANGES IN FUND BALANCES
ALL GENERAL CAPITAL PROJECTS FUNDS
For the Fiscal Year Ended June 30, 1992

	Street Improvement Fund	Street Bond Fund	Sidewalk Fund	Park Improvement Fund	Walnut Creek Amphitheatre Fund
Revenues:					
Intergovernmental					
State of North Carolina	$ 39,654	$ 71,640	$ -	$ 8,100	$ -
Wake County	-	-	-	11,520	-
Assessments	544,277	-	-	-	-
Interest on Investments	312,232	995,539	19,414	178,363	186,418
Facility Fees	-	-	-	-	-
Tenant's Capital Investments	-	-	-	-	-
Miscellaneous Other	168,142	237,473	56,291	28,992	33,812
Total Revenues	1,064,305	1,304,652	75,705	226,975	220,230
Other Financing Sources:					
Operating Transfers In	3,309,683	3,571,765	85,000	1,150,140	534,448
Proceeds of General Obligation Bonds, Bond Anticipation Notes and Premium	-	10,700,000	-	-	-
Proceeds of Capital Lease and Other Installment Obligations	-	-	-	-	-
Proceeds of Certificates of Participation	-	-	-	-	-
Total Other Financing Sources	3,309,683	14,271,765	85,000	1,150,140	534,448
Total Revenues and Other Financing Sources	4,373,988	15,576,417	160,705	1,377,115	754,678
Expenditures:					
Public Improvements:					
Street Paving/Sidewalk Projects	2,997,943	12,203,618	121,166	-	-
Parks and Recreation Projects	-	-	-	1,572,930	-
Memorial Auditorium	-	-	-	-	-
City Market Projects	-	-	-	-	-
Public Safety Projects	-	-	-	-	-
Walnut Creek Amphitheatre	-	-	-	-	5,349,510
Other	-	-	-	-	-
Debt Service:					
Principal	-	-	-	-	-
Interest	-	-	-	-	-
Total Expenditures	2,997,943	12,203,618	121,166	1,572,930	5,349,510
Other Financing Uses:					
Operating Transfers Out	-	50,185	10,171	854,028	-
Total Expenditures and Other Financing Uses	2,997,943	12,253,803	131,337	2,426,958	5,349,510
Excess (Deficiency) of Revenues and Other Financing Sources Over Expenditures and Other Financing Uses	1,376,045	3,322,614	29,368	(1,049,843)	(4,594,832)
Fund Balances - Beginning of Year	5,458,725	20,857,335	340,159	3,315,091	6,214,472
Residual Transfer of Equity	-	-	-	-	-
Fund Balances - End of Year	$ 6,834,770	$ 24,179,949	$ 369,527	$ 2,265,248	$ 1,619,640

	Facility Fees Fund	Park Bond Fund	Miscellaneous Capital Improvements Fund	Civic Center Fund	Combining Eliminations	Total June 30, 1992	Total June 30, 1991
	$ -	$ -	$ -	$ -	$ -	$ 119,394	$ 484,227
	-	-	-	-	-	11,520	170,995
	-	-	-	-	-	544,277	383,429
	109,232	94,991	40,608	393	-	1,937,190	2,450,481
	1,386,567	-	-	-	-	1,386,567	2,030,370
	-	-	-	-	-	-	3,500,000
	-	77,485	18,050	-	-	620,245	622,818
	1,495,799	172,476	58,658	393	-	4,619,193	9,642,320
	662,000	853,249	229,200	-	(1,896,647)	8,498,838	9,140,439
	-	-	-	-	-	10,700,000	20,959,469
	-	-	-	-	-	-	2,089,160
	-	-	-	-	-	-	11,500,000
	662,000	853,249	229,200	-	(1,896,647)	19,198,838	43,689,068
	2,157,799	1,025,725	287,858	393	(1,896,647)	23,818,031	53,331,388
	221,580	-	-	-	-	15,544,307	14,752,481
	40,578	6,145,226	-	-	-	7,758,734	5,602,401
	-	-	-	15,404	-	15,404	273,881
	-	-	-	-	-	-	7,435
	-	-	115,774	-	-	115,774	81,409
	-	-	-	-	-	5,349,510	10,192,793
	-	-	205,793	3,799	-	209,592	471,550
	874,526	-	-	-	-	874,526	434,133
	244,464	-	-	-	-	244,464	124,481
	1,381,148	6,145,226	321,567	19,203	-	30,112,311	31,940,564
	954,773	8,680	250,266	-	(1,896,647)	231,456	106,278
	2,335,921	6,153,906	571,833	19,203	(1,896,647)	30,343,767	32,046,842
	(178,122)	(5,128,181)	(283,975)	(18,810)	-	(6,525,736)	21,284,546
	1,945,909	6,144,023	985,124	513,515	-	45,774,353	25,723,033
	-	-	-	-	-	-	(1,233,226)
	$ 1,767,787	$ 1,015,842	$ 701,149	$ 494,705	$ -	$ 39,248,617	$ 45,774,353

City of Raleigh

SCHEDULE OF REVENUES AND EXPENDITURES
COMPARED WITH BUDGET
PARK BOND FUND
For the Fiscal Year Ended June 30, 1992

| | Actual | | | | Over |
	Prior Years	Current Year	Total	Budget	(Under) Budget
Revenues:					
Interest on Investments	$ -	$ 94,991	$ 94,991	$ 108,680	$ (13,689)
Miscellaneous Other	-	77,485	77,485	12,681	64,804
Total Revenues	-	172,476	172,476	121,361	51,115
Other Financing Sources:					
Operating Transfers In:					
General Fund	-	22,839	22,839	22,839	-
Park Improvement Fund	-	830,410	830,410	830,410	-
Total Operating Transfers In	-	853,249	853,249	853,249	-
Proceeds of General Obligation Bonds	-	-	-	3,800,000	(3,800,000)
Total Other Financing Sources	-	853,249	853,249	4,653,249	(3,800,000)
Total Revenues and Other Financing Sources	-	$1,025,725	$1,025,725	4,774,610	$ (3,748,885)
Fund Balance Appropriated				7,980,313	
				$12,754,923	
Expenditures:					
Fund Reserve	$ -	$ -	$ -	$ 250	$ (250)
East West Park Drive	3,836	631	4,467	5,000	(533)
Roberts Park	528,051	92,545	620,596	621,439	(843)
Apollo Heights Center	20,899	6,690	27,589	30,089	(2,500)
Glen Eden Park	5,780	109,513	115,293	123,675	(8,382)
Southgate Park	18,951	-	18,951	45,788	(26,837)
Raleigh Little Theatre	51,471	321	51,792	51,800	(8)
Tarboro Road Daycare	-	2,413	2,413	2,700	(287)
Nash Square	6,586	33,700	40,286	75,000	(34,714)
Mordecai Park	77,057	54,571	131,628	131,934	(306)
Eastgate Park	47,715	(3,127)	44,588	175,000	(130,412)
Chavis Park	21,318	-	21,318	50,000	(28,682)
Campbell Center	-	8,013	8,013	25,000	(16,987)
Method Center	129	79,129	79,258	316,397	(237,139)
Aquatics Facility	293,836	3,641,705	3,935,541	5,604,720	(1,669,179)
Softball Complex	341,143	1,638,230	1,979,373	2,070,720	(91,347)
Spring Forest Park	5,400	18,872	24,272	1,000,000	(975,728)
Laurel Hills	764,304	277,366	1,041,670	1,086,585	(44,915)
Lake Lynn Park	21,583	29,804	51,387	1,000,000	(948,613)
Carolina Pines	-	-	-	150,000	(150,000)
Cedar Hills Park	15,296	154,850	170,146	170,146	-
Other	1,415	-	1,415	10,000	(8,585)
Total Expenditures	2,224,770	6,145,226	8,369,996	12,746,243	(4,376,247)
Other Financing Uses:					
Operating Transfer to General Fund	-	8,680	8,680	8,680	-
Total Expenditures and Other Financing Uses	$2,224,770	$6,153,906	$8,378,676	$12,754,923	$ (4,376,247)

ENTERPRISE FUNDS

Mass Transit Fund - The Mass Transit Fund accounts for the user charges, fees, federal contributions and all operating costs associated with the operation of the transit system of the City. This fund also accounts for all capital projects financed by transit grant proceeds.

Water and Sewer Fund - This fund combines the operating, debt service and capital projects fund as follows:

Water and Sewer Operating Fund - The Water and Sewer Operating Fund accounts for the user charges, fees, other resources and all operating costs associated with the operation of the water and sewer systems of the City.

Water Bond Fund - The Water Bond Fund accounts for all water bond proceeds and capital project costs in the construction of water capital improvement projects.

Sewer Bond Fund - The Sewer Bond Fund accounts for all sewer bond proceeds and capital project costs in the construction of sewer capital improvement projects.

Parking Facilities Fund - The Parking Facilities Fund accounts for the parking fee charges and all operating costs associated with the operation of all parking decks and lots owned by the City. This fund combines two operating and capital projects funds as follows:

Downtown Parking Deck Fund - The Downtown Parking Deck Fund accounts for the operations, debt service and capital costs of three downtown parking decks.

Wilmington Street Parking Fund - The Wilmington Street Parking Fund accounts for the capital costs of parking facilities on Wilmington Street and nearby lots.

City of Raleigh

COMBINING BALANCE SHEET
ALL ENTERPRISE FUNDS
June 30, 1992

	Mass Transit Fund	Water and Sewer Fund	Parking Facilities Fund	Total June 30, 1992	June 30, 1991
ASSETS					
Cash and Cash Equivalents	$ 536,762	$ 46,473,390	$ 5,719,035	$ 52,729,187	$ 45,137,667
Assessments Receivable, Net of Allowance for Uncollectibles of $148,844 in 1992 and $76,501 in 1991	-	2,828,042	-	2,828,042	1,453,525
Customer Receivables, Net of Allowance for Uncollectibles of $1,210,622 in 1992 and $1,112,339 in 1991	-	2,761,935	-	2,761,935	2,872,899
Due from Other Governmental Agencies	18,205	3,654	-	21,859	2,842,031
Accrued Interest Receivable	-	855,804	14,682	870,486	756,764
Other Receivables and Assets	122,427	213,727	140,060	476,214	738,004
Due from Other Funds	-	7,734	-	7,734	12,811
Inventories	-	3,026,568	-	3,026,568	2,629,582
Deferred Charges	-	74,782	-	74,782	83,091
Cash and Cash Equivalents - Restricted Deposits	-	7,248,365	-	7,248,365	6,723,204
	677,394	63,494,001	5,873,777	70,045,172	63,249,578
Fixed Assets:					
Land	988,989	5,314,608	2,707,399	9,010,996	6,086,036
Water and Sewer Systems	-	206,700,604	-	206,700,604	196,285,511
Buildings and Machinery	3,948,845	47,551,124	11,928,185	63,428,154	47,565,096
Buses	9,089,251	-	-	9,089,251	9,972,889
Equipment	484,731	8,548,645	123,829	9,157,205	8,874,149
Furniture and Fixtures	50,546	113,570	203	164,319	154,852
Improvements	178,139	52,340	230,354	460,833	194,118
Construction in Progress	-	36,555,772	6,054,831	42,610,603	48,408,672
	14,740,501	304,836,663	21,044,801	340,621,965	317,541,323
Less: Accumulated Depreciation	5,137,310	56,863,781	1,940,403	63,941,494	58,212,904
Fixed Assets, Net	9,603,191	247,972,882	19,104,398	276,680,471	259,328,419
Total Assets	$ 10,280,585	$ 311,466,883	$ 24,978,175	$ 346,725,643	$ 322,577,997

	Mass Transit Fund	Water and Sewer Fund	Parking Facilities Fund	Total June 30, 1992	Total June 30, 1991
LIABILITIES AND FUND EQUITY					
Accounts Payable	$ 36,716	$ 2,000,953	$ 1,280,407	$ 3,318,076	$ 4,433,939
Arbitrage Rebate Payable	-	68,699	-	68,699	62,221
Accrued Liabilities	-	-	58,024	58,024	52,038
Accrued Salaries and Payroll Taxes	-	58,811	-	58,811	153,771
Due to Other Governmental Agencies	80	-	-	80	-
Accrued Interest Payable	-	1,333,806	201,702	1,535,508	1,463,379
Due to Other Funds	436,889	-	-	436,889	258,565
Deferred Contributions from Other Funds for Capital Projects	81,922	-	-	81,922	34,929
Customer Deposits Payable from Restricted Assets	-	7,248,365	-	7,248,365	6,723,204
Current Portion of Long-Term Obligations:					
Bonds Payable	-	5,985,000	375,000	6,360,000	5,590,000
Contracts Payable	-	1,006,015	14,163	1,020,178	1,071,760
Long-Term Obligations:					
Bonds Payable	-	56,600,000	7,805,000	64,405,000	55,765,000
Contracts and Other Notes Payable	-	626,272	439,737	1,066,009	1,152,052
Earned Vacation Pay	-	381,537	-	381,537	363,250
Total Liabilities	555,607	75,309,458	10,174,033	86,039,098	77,124,108
Fund Equity:					
Contributed Capital	9,603,191	116,721,925	10,997,443	137,322,559	132,922,071
Retained Earnings	121,787	119,435,500	3,806,699	123,363,986	112,531,818
Total Fund Equity	9,724,978	236,157,425	14,804,142	260,686,545	245,453,889
Total Liabilities and Fund Equity	$ 10,280,585	$ 311,466,883	$ 24,978,175	$ 346,725,643	$ 322,577,997

City of Raleigh

COMBINING STATEMENT OF REVENUES, EXPENSES
AND CHANGES IN RETAINED EARNINGS
ALL ENTERPRISE FUNDS
For the Fiscal Year Ended June 30, 1992

	Mass Transit Fund	Water and Sewer Fund	Parking Facilities Fund	Total June 30, 1992	June 30, 1991
Operating Revenues:					
User Charges	$ 1,437,015	$ 32,024,883	$ 979,403	$ 34,441,301	$ 33,158,742
Other	86,652	664,305	-	750,957	1,366,227
Total Operating Revenues	1,523,667	32,689,188	979,403	35,192,258	34,524,969
Operating Expenses:					
Administration	254,911	1,005,768	171,999	1,432,678	1,360,816
Water Supply and Treatment	-	6,111,561	-	6,111,561	6,623,154
Sewer System and Treatment	-	5,522,730	-	5,522,730	5,236,521
Warehousing and Maintenance	-	1,706,250	-	1,706,250	1,975,715
Other Administrative Services	168,459	2,981,419	-	3,149,878	3,058,013
Non-Departmental Charges	-	2,909,152	-	2,909,152	2,402,558
Management Contract Charges	5,133,622	-	-	5,133,622	4,856,127
Depreciation	864,594	5,649,487	306,570	6,820,651	6,333,382
Loss on Disposal of Fixed Assets	13,427	-	-	13,427	-
Total Operating Expenses	6,435,013	25,886,367	478,569	32,799,949	31,846,286
Operating Income (Loss)	(4,911,346)	6,802,821	500,834	2,392,309	2,678,683
Nonoperating Revenues:					
Interest on Investments	-	2,746,790	150,100	2,896,890	3,784,167
Subsidy Income - Federal and State	901,816	-	-	901,816	1,010,581
Other	-	112,565	37,099	149,664	50,268
Total Nonoperating Revenues	901,816	2,859,355	187,199	3,948,370	4,845,016
Nonoperating Expenses:					
Interest Expense on Long-Term Obligations	-	1,678,540	431,931	2,110,471	3,212,563
Other	-	53,617	22,707	76,324	102,828
Total Nonoperating Expenses	-	1,732,157	454,638	2,186,795	3,315,391
Income (Loss) Before Operating Transfers	(4,009,530)	7,930,019	233,395	4,153,884	4,208,308
Operating Transfers In	3,123,772	223,698	499,812	3,847,282	3,572,703
Operating Transfers Out	-	(776,393)	(7,932)	(784,325)	(1,752,414)
Net Income (Loss)	(885,758)	7,377,324	725,275	7,216,841	6,028,597
Add: Amortization of Contributed Capital	885,758	2,729,569	-	3,615,327	3,165,108
Retained Earnings - Beginning of Year	121,787	109,328,607	3,081,424	112,531,818	103,338,113
Retained Earnings - End of Year	$ 121,787	$ 119,435,500	$ 3,806,699	$ 123,363,986	$ 112,531,818

INTERNAL SERVICE FUND

Print and Supply Shops - The Print and Supply Shops Fund accounts for the operations of the City's Print Shop and the Office Supply Room.

City of Raleigh

BALANCE SHEET
INTERNAL SERVICE FUND - PRINT AND SUPPLY SHOPS
June 30, 1992

	June 30, 1992
ASSETS	
Cash and Cash Equivalents	$ 46,039
Customer Receivables	254
Inventories	31,025
	77,318
Fixed Assets:	
Equipment	150,245
Furniture and Fixtures	6,832
	157,077
Less: Accumulated Depreciation	26,827
Fixed Assets - Net	130,250
Total Assets	$ 207,568
LIABILITIES AND FUND EQUITY	
Liabilities:	
Accounts Payable	$ 13,332
Accrued Liabilities	870
Earned Vacation Pay	4,940
Total Liabilities	19,142
Fund Equity:	
Contributed Capital	185,421
Retained Earnings	3,005
Total Fund Equity	188,426
Total Liabilities and Fund Equity	$ 207,568

City of Raleigh

STATEMENT OF REVENUES, EXPENSES AND CHANGES IN RETAINED EARNINGS
For the Fiscal Year Ended June 30, 1992

	June 30, 1992
Operating Revenues:	
User Charges	$ 537,996
Other	52,732
Total Operating Revenues	590,728
Operating Expenses:	
Operations and Administrative - Printing and Photocopy	500,164
Office Supply Purchases - Supply Room	98,232
Depreciation	26,827
Total Operating Expenses	625,223
Operating Loss	(34,495)
Operating Transfer In	37,500
Net Income	3,005
Retained Earnings - Beginning of Year	-
Retained Earnings - End of Year	$ 3,005

ACCOUNT GROUPS

General Fixed Assets Account Group - The General Fixed Assets Account Group accounts for all fixed assets of the City other than those accounted for in the Proprietary Funds.

General Long-Term Obligations Account Group - The General Long-Term Obligations Account Group accounts for all long-term obligations of the City other than those accounted for in the Proprietary Funds.

City of Raleigh

SCHEDULE OF CHANGES IN GENERAL FIXED ASSETS
For the Fiscal Year Ended June 30, 1992

	Balance June 30, 1991	Additions	Transfers	Deletions	Balance June 30, 1992
Land	$ 51,452,893	$ 1,911,934	$ 983,111	$ 800,000	$ 53,547,938
Buildings and Machinery	53,809,337	5,417,184	11,684,657	872	70,910,306
Streets and Sidewalks	151,370,631	3,567,086	2,755,092	-	157,692,809
Improvements - General and Parks	31,418,760	1,478,046	1,835,167	38,239	34,693,734
Equipment	36,313,287	5,125,127	14,488	1,473,529	39,979,373
Furniture and Fixtures	3,226,909	107,045	-	27,927	3,306,027
Construction in Progress	43,686,085	22,198,775	(17,272,515)	-	48,612,345
Total Fixed Assets	$ 371,277,902	$ 39,805,197	$ -	$ 2,340,567	$ 408,742,532

City of Raleigh

SCHEDULE OF GENERAL FIXED ASSETS BY FUNCTION AND ACTIVITY
June 30, 1992

	Land	Buildings	Streets and Sidewalks
General Government:			
City Council	$ -	$ -	$ -
City Clerk & Treasurer	-	-	-
City Attorney	-	-	-
City Manager	-	-	-
Planning and Budget	-	-	-
Arts Commission/Grants	372,178	-	-
Public Affairs	-	-	-
Personnel	-	-	-
Finance:			
Administration/Accounting	-	-	-
Collections	-	-	-
Consumer Services	-	-	-
Purchasing	-	-	-
Parking Violations	-	-	-
Internal Audits	-	-	-
Payroll	-	-	-
Information Services:			
Information Services Administration	-	-	-
Data Processing	-	-	-
Word Processing	-	-	-
Cable Office	-	-	-
Public Access Studio	-	-	-
Print Shop	-	-	-
Community Development Services:			
Real Estate	-	-	-
Central Engineering	-	-	-
Construction Management	-	-	-
Planning	-	-	-
Transportation	9,547,302	954,450	157,301,292
Inspections	-	-	-
Human Services	5,521,636	872	-
Public Safety:			
Emergency Communications Center	-	11,770	-
Police Administration	-	-	-
Special Services	-	930,767	-
Field Operations	-	-	-
Investigations	-	-	-
Fire Administration	3,001	1,883,768	-
Fire Prevention	-	-	-
Fire Fighting	156,781	2,080,936	-
Public Works:			
Administration	-	-	2,250
Street Maintenance	-	371,018	-

Improvements	Equipment	Furniture and Fixtures	Construction in Progress	Total
$ -	$ 10,212	$ 44,640	$ -	$ 54,852
-	14,551	8,386	-	22,937
-	12,288	13,562	-	25,850
-	80,941	35,438	-	116,379
-	20,226	8,654	-	28,880
800	83,512	33,677	-	490,167
-	31,330	17,459	-	48,789
-	49,195	25,927	-	75,122
-	48,446	40,546	-	88,992
-	240,100	14,133	-	254,233
-	193,932	23,048	-	216,980
-	39,316	7,561	-	46,877
-	8,546	5,578	-	14,124
-	6,863	1,535	-	8,398
-	1,441	4,364	-	5,805
-	27,967	4,044	-	32,011
15,850	119,238	24,696	-	159,784
-	8,737	15,422	-	24,159
-	68,187	9,441	-	77,628
-	137,282	9,963	-	147,245
-	95,208	6,513	-	101,721
-	6,894	9,250	-	16,144
-	709,631	55,201	-	764,832
-	12,680	4,127	-	16,807
-	104,940	79,670	-	184,610
902,896	2,094,581	34,830	36,191,090	207,026,441
-	809,398	132,919	-	942,317
2,515,402	47,717	15,775	636,178	8,737,580
-	451,663	10,159	666,512	1,140,104
-	31,326	13,570	-	44,896
10,942	6,258,499	91,335	-	7,291,543
1,950	148,839	43,539	-	194,328
-	181,974	58,717	-	240,691
127,290	393,901	2,291	-	2,410,251
-	19,236	6,823	-	26,059
40,975	4,827,822	150,503	53,198	7,310,215
-	118,364	5,702	-	126,316
-	3,395,382	10,520	-	3,776,920

City of Raleigh

SCHEDULE OF GENERAL FIXED ASSETS BY FUNCTION AND ACTIVITY
June 30, 1992

	Land	Buildings	Streets and Sidewalks
Public Works (Continued):			
Sanitation	$ 30,680	$ 588,000	$ -
Buildings - Municipal	6,670,808	17,313,028	28,834
Landfill	1,086,297	-	-
Equipment Service Depot	-	88,939	-
Leisure Services:			
Civic Center	9,100,881	19,710,757	-
Parks and Recreation Administration	-	580	-
Recreation	3,406,307	8,251,588	267
Parks	17,507,817	18,717,688	360,166
Highway Park Maintenance	-	-	-
Cemeteries	-	6,145	-
Greenway	144,250	-	-
Urban Trees	-	-	-
Design/Development	-	-	-
Total General Fixed Assets	$53,547,938	$70,910,306	$157,692,809

Improvements	Equipment	Furniture and Fixtures	Construction in Progress	Total
$ -	$ 6,929,314	$ 14,843	$ -	$ 7,562,837
5,775,723	219,992	17,285	-	30,025,670
4,147	5,233,008	193,770	-	6,517,222
-	593,915	12,511	-	695,365
8,721,273	1,114,799	1,631,541	209,347	40,488,598
1,404	142,591	38,484	-	183,059
7,341,085	1,931,550	282,011	-	21,212,808
9,089,777	2,084,257	34,042	10,856,020	58,649,767
-	345,232	-	-	345,232
3,219	43,050	62	-	52,476
141,001	339,206	-	-	624,457
-	75,811	-	-	75,811
-	16,283	1,960	-	18,243
$34,693,734	$39,979,373	$3,306,027	$48,612,345	$408,742,532

City of Raleigh

SCHEDULE OF GENERAL FIXED ASSETS BY SOURCES
June 30, 1992

General Fixed Assets:	
Land	$ 53,547,938
Buildings	70,910,306
Streets and Sidewalks	157,692,809
Improvements - General and Parks	34,693,734
Equipment	39,979,373
Furniture and Fixtures	3,306,027
Construction in Progress	48,612,345
Total	$408,742,532

Investment in General Fixed Assets From:	
General Revenue	$ 31,718,915
State Revenue	5,776,543
Federal Grants	6,311,257
General Obligation Bonds	145,827,372
Donations	1,503,552
Contributed Property	34,334,802
Amount Prior to 1987 for Which Source is Unknown	183,270,091
Total	$408,742,532

City of Raleigh

SCHEDULE OF CHANGES IN GENERAL
LONG-TERM OBLIGATIONS
For the Fiscal Year Ended June 30, 1992

	Balance June 30, 1991	General Long-Term Obligations Incurred	General Long-Term Obligations Retired	Balance June 30, 1992
Resources to be Provided in Future Years for Retirement of General Obligation Bonded Debt	$68,760,000	$19,000,000	$3,980,000	$ 83,780,000
Resources to be Provided in Future Years for Retirement of Certificates of Participation	11,500,000	-	-	11,500,000
Resources to be Provided in Future Years for Retirement of Other Installment and Contractual Obligations	8,431,823 (1)	1,569,784	2,308,479	7,693,128
Resources to be Provided in Future Years for Retirement of Earned Vacation Pay	4,905,321	111,417	-	5,016,738
Total Available and to Be Provided	$93,597,144	$20,681,201	$6,288,479	$107,989,866
General Long-Term Obligations Payable:				
Serial Bonds	$68,760,000	$19,000,000	$3,980,000	$ 83,780,000
Other Long-Term Obligations	24,837,144	1,681,201	2,308,479	24,209,866
Total General Long-Term Obligations Payable	$93,597,144	$20,681,201	$6,288,479	$107,989,866

Note:

(1) During 1991-92, one installment obligation was reclassified from General Long-Term Obligations to Enterprise Long-Term Obligations.

City of Raleigh

SCHEDULE OF GENERAL GOVERNMENTAL LONG-TERM OBLIGATIONS
For the Fiscal Year Ended June 30, 1992

Description	Interest Rate	Date of Issue	Maturities Amount	Date Due	Amount Outstanding 6/30/91
GENERAL OBLIGATION					
BONDS PAYABLE					
Recreation - Series A	4.60%	3/1/73	$ 90,000	3/1/92-93	$ 180,000
Recreation - Series A	4.50	3/1/73	95,000	3/1/94	95,000
Recreation - Series A	4.50	3/1/73	100,000	3/1/95	100,000
Recreation - Series A	4.50	3/1/73	75,000	3/1/96	75,000
Redevelopment - Series A	4.60	3/1/73	50,000	3/1/92-93	100,000
Redevelopment - Series A	4.50	3/1/73	50,000	3/1/94-98	250,000
Redevelopment - Series A	4.50	3/1/73	25,000	3/1/99	25,000
Grade Crossing - A	4.60	3/1/73	10,000	3/1/92-93	20,000
Grade Crossing - A	4.50	3/1/73	5,000	3/1/94	5,000
Recreation - Series B	5.00	4/1/74	75,000	4/1/92-94	225,000
Recreation - Series B	4.00	4/1/74	75,000	4/1/95-96	150,000
Civic Center - Series A	5.00	4/1/74	175,000	4/1/92-94	525,000
Civic Center - Series A	4.00	4/1/74	175,000	4/1/95-96	350,000
Civic Center - Series A	4.00	4/1/74	100,000	4/1/97	100,000
Civic Center - Series B	5.70	3/1/75	275,000	3/1/92-93	550,000
Civic Center - Series B	4.00	3/1/75	150,000	3/1/94	150,000
Public Improvement	5.70	3/1/75	300,000	3/1/92	300,000
Public Improvement	5.70	3/1/75	250,000	3/1/93	250,000
Civic Center - Series C	6.00	12/1/75	400,000	6/1/92	400,000
Civic Center - Series C	6.10	12/1/75	450,000	6/1/93	450,000
Civic Center - Series C	6.25	12/1/75	700,000	6/1/94	700,000
Civic Center - Series C	6.25	12/1/75	850,000	6/1/95	850,000
Civic Center - Series C	5.00	12/1/75	875,000	6/1/96	875,000
Civic Center - Series C	5.00	12/1/75	725,000	6/1/97	725,000
Street Improvement - 77	4.75	3/1/77	100,000	3/1/92-93	200,000
Street Improvement - 77	4.75	3/1/77	225,000	3/1/94-95	450,000
Street Improvement - 77	4.00	3/1/77	225,000	3/1/96	225,000
Street Improvement - 77	4.00	3/1/77	375,000	3/1/97	375,000
Civic Center - Series D	4.75	3/1/77	100,000	3/1/92-95	400,000
Civic Center - Series D	4.00	3/1/77	100,000	3/1/96-97	200,000
Recreation Refunding	6.25	5/1/86	605,000	7/1/91	605,000
Recreation Refunding	6.25	5/1/86	600,000	7/1/92	600,000
Recreation Refunding	6.25	5/1/86	565,000	7/1/93	565,000
Recreation Refunding	6.25	5/1/86	560,000	7/1/94	560,000
Recreation Refunding	6.30	5/1/86	550,000	7/1/95	550,000
Recreation Refunding	6.30	5/1/86	540,000	7/1/96	540,000
Recreation Refunding	6.30	5/1/86	530,000	7/1/97	530,000
Recreation Refunding	6.30	5/1/86	500,000	7/1/98	500,000

Issued During Year	Payments During Year		Amount Outstanding 6/30/92	Due Fiscal 1992-93	
	Principal	Interest		Principal	Interest
$ -	$ 90,000	$ 8,280	$ 90,000	$ 90,000	$ 4,140
-	-	4,275	95,000	-	4,275
-	-	4,500	100,000	-	4,500
-	-	3,375	75,000	-	3,375
-	50,000	4,600	50,000	50,000	2,300
-	-	11,250	250,000	-	11,250
-	-	1,125	25,000	-	1,125
-	10,000	920	10,000	10,000	460
-	-	225	5,000	-	225
-	75,000	11,250	150,000	75,000	7,500
-	-	6,000	150,000	-	6,000
-	175,000	26,250	350,000	175,000	17,500
-	-	14,000	350,000	-	14,000
-	-	4,000	100,000	-	4,000
-	275,000	31,350	275,000	275,000	15,675
-	-	6,000	150,000	-	6,000
-	300,000	17,100	-	-	-
-	-	14,250	250,000	250,000	14,250
-	400,000	24,000	-	-	-
-	-	27,450	450,000	450,000	27,450
-	-	43,750	700,000	-	43,750
-	-	53,125	850,000	-	53,125
-	-	43,750	875,000	-	43,750
-	-	36,250	725,000	-	36,250
-	100,000	9,500	100,000	100,000	4,750
-	-	21,375	450,000	-	21,375
-	-	9,000	225,000	-	9,000
-	-	15,000	375,000	-	15,000
-	100,000	19,000	300,000	100,000	14,250
-	-	8,000	200,000	-	8,000
-	605,000	18,906	-	-	-
-	-	37,500	600,000	600,000	18,750
-	-	35,312	565,000	-	35,313
-	-	35,000	560,000	-	35,000
-	-	34,650	550,000	-	34,650
-	-	34,020	540,000	-	34,020
-	-	33,390	530,000	-	33,390
-	-	31,500	500,000	-	31,500

City of Raleigh

SCHEDULE OF GENERAL GOVERNMENTAL LONG-TERM OBLIGATIONS
For the Fiscal Year Ended June 30, 1992

Description	Interest Rate	Date of Issue	Maturities Amount	Maturities Date Due	Amount Outstanding 6/30/91
GENERAL OBLIGATION					
BONDS PAYABLE					
Street/Sidewalk Refunding	6.25%	5/1/86	$ 450,000	7/1/91	$ 450,000
Street/Sidewalk Refunding	6.25	5/1/86	445,000	7/1/92-93	890,000
Street/Sidewalk Refunding	6.25	5/1/86	440,000	7/1/94	440,000
Street/Sidewalk Refunding	6.30	5/1/86	435,000	7/1/95	435,000
Street/Sidewalk Refunding	6.30	5/1/86	430,000	7/1/96	430,000
Street/Sidewalk Refunding	6.30	5/1/86	630,000	7/1/97	630,000
Street/Sidewalk Refunding	6.30	5/1/86	620,000	7/1/98	620,000
Street/Sidewalk Refunding	6.30	5/1/86	610,000	7/1/99-2000	1,220,000
Street/Sidewalk Refunding	6.30	5/1/86	590,000	7/1/2001	590,000
Street/Sidewalk Refunding	6.30	5/1/86	650,000	7/1/2002	650,000
Public Improvement Series 1989	6.70	2/1/89	750,000	2/1/92-93	1,500,000
Public Improvement Series 1989	6.80	2/1/89	750,000	2/1/94-96	2,250,000
Public Improvement Series 1989	6.80	2/1/89	1,000,000	2/1/97	1,000,000
Public Improvement Series 1989	6.80	2/1/89	1,500,000	2/1/98	1,500,000
Public Improvement Series 1989	6.80	2/1/89	2,000,000	2/1/99-2008	20,000,000
Public Improvement Series 1989	6.90	2/1/89	1,550,000	2/1/2009	1,550,000
Public Improvement Series 1991	6.30	3/1/91	600,000	3/1/92-97	3,600,000
Public Improvement Series 1991	6.30	3/1/91	1,200,000	3/1/98-99	2,400,000
Public Improvement Series 1991	6.30	3/1/91	1,350,000	3/1/2000	1,350,000
Public Improvement Series 1991	6.40	3/1/91	1,350,000	3/1/2001	1,350,000
Public Improvement Series 1991	6.40	3/1/91	1,675,000	3/1/2002	1,675,000
Public Improvement Series 1991	6.40	3/1/91	1,750,000	3/1/2003	1,750,000
Public Improvement Series 1991	6.40	3/1/91	1,925,000	3/1/2004-07	7,700,000
Public Improvement Series 1991	6.50	3/1/91	1,030,000	3/1/2008	1,030,000
Housing - Series 1991	6.00	12/1/91	150,000	6/1/93-2003	-
Housing - Series 1991	6.10	12/1/91	150,000	6/1/2004	-
Housing - Series 1991	6.20	12/1/91	150,000	6/1/2005	-
Housing - Series 1991	6.30	12/1/91	150,000	6/1/2006	-
Housing - Series 1991	6.40	12/1/91	150,000	6/1/2007	-
Housing - Series 1991	6.50	12/1/91	600,000	6/1/2008	-
Housing - Series 1991	6.50	12/1/91	150,000	6/1/2009	-
Street/Sidewalk - Series 1992	6.00	4/1/92	550,000	4/1/93-99	-
Street/Sidewalk - Series 1992	6.10	4/1/92	550,000	4/1/2000-11	-
Street/Sidewalk - Series 1992	6.10	4/1/92	250,000	4/1/2012	-
Housing - Series 1992A	6.00	4/1/92	150,000	4/1/93-99	-
Housing - Series 1992A	6.10	4/1/92	150,000	4/1/2000-11	-
Housing - Series 1992A	6.10	4/1/92	200,000	4/1/2012	-
Housing - Series 1992B Taxable	7.90	4/1/92	100,000	4/1/93	-
Housing - Series 1992B Taxable	8.10	4/1/92	100,000	4/1/94-96	-
Housing - Series 1992B Taxable	8.20	4/1/92	100,000	4/1/97-2011	-
Housing - Series 1992B Taxable	8.25	4/1/92	350,000	4/1/2012	-
Total General Obligation Bonded Debt					68,760,000

Issued During Year	Payments During Year		Amount Outstanding 6/30/92	Due Fiscal 1992-93	
	Principal	Interest		Principal	Interest
$ -	$ 450,000	$ 14,062	$ -	$ -	$ -
-	-	55,625	890,000	445,000	41,719
-	-	27,500	440,000	-	27,500
-	-	27,405	435,000	-	27,405
-	-	27,090	430,000	-	27,090
-	-	39,690	630,000	-	39,690
-	-	39,060	620,000	-	39,060
-	-	76,860	1,220,000	-	76,860
-	-	37,170	590,000	-	37,170
-	-	40,950	650,000	-	40,950
-	750,000	100,500	750,000	750,000	50,250
-	-	153,000	2,250,000	-	153,000
-	-	68,000	1,000,000	-	68,000
-	-	102,000	1,500,000	-	102,000
-	-	1,360,000	20,000,000	-	1,360,000
-	-	106,950	1,550,000	-	106,950
-	600,000	226,800	3,000,000	600,000	189,000
-	-	151,200	2,400,000	-	151,200
-	-	85,050	1,350,000	-	85,050
-	-	86,400	1,350,000	-	86,400
-	-	107,200	1,675,000	-	107,200
-	-	112,000	1,750,000	-	112,000
-	-	492,800	7,700,000	-	492,800
-	-	66,950	1,030,000	-	66,950
1,650,000	-	49,500	1,650,000	150,000	99,000
150,000	-	4,575	150,000	-	9,150
150,000	-	4,650	150,000	-	9,300
150,000	-	4,725	150,000	-	9,450
150,000	-	4,800	150,000	-	9,600
600,000	-	19,500	600,000	-	39,000
150,000	-	4,875	150,000	-	9,750
3,850,000	-	-	3,850,000	550,000	231,000
6,600,000	-	-	6,600,000	-	402,600
250,000	-	-	250,000	-	15,250
1,050,000	-	-	1,050,000	150,000	63,000
1,800,000	-	-	1,800,000	-	109,800
200,000	-	-	200,000	-	12,200
100,000	-	-	100,000	100,000	7,900
300,000	-	-	300,000	-	24,300
1,500,000	-	-	1,500,000	-	123,000
350,000	-	-	350,000	-	28,875
19,000,000	3,980,000	4,436,115	83,780,000	4,920,000	5,307,317

City of Raleigh

SCHEDULE OF GENERAL GOVERNMENTAL LONG-TERM OBLIGATIONS
For the Fiscal Year Ended June 30, 1992

Description	Interest Rate	Date of Issue	Maturities Amount	Date Due	Amount Outstanding 6/30/91
OTHER GENERAL GOVERNMENTAL LONG-TERM OBLIGATIONS					
Certificates of Participation					$ 11,500,000
Other Installment Obligations					7,951,525 (2)
Reimbursement Contracts - Streets					480,298
Earned Vacation Pay					4,905,321
Total Other General Governmental Long-Term Obligations					24,837,144
Total General Governmental Long-Term Obligations					$ 93,597,144

Notes:

(1) The amount of vacation pay to be paid in any fiscal year cannot be determined. The total amount of accrued vacation pay outstanding at any point in time is not expected to materially increase or decrease from the amount shown.

(2) During 1991-1992, one installment obligation was reclassified from General Long-Term Obligations to Enterprise Long-Term Obligations.

Issued During Year	Payments During Year		Amount Outstanding 6/30/92	Due Fiscal 1992-93	
	Principal	Interest		Principal	Interest
$ -	$ -	$ 565,168	$ 11,500,000	$ -	$ 1,695,503
1,487,050	2,221,820	511,344	7,216,755	2,229,983	447,656
82,734	86,659	21,386	476,373	77,839	19,055
111,417	- (1)	-	5,016,738	- (1)	-
1,681,201	2,308,479	1,097,898	24,209,866	2,307,822	2,162,214
$ 20,681,201	$ 6,288,479	$ 5,534,013	$107,989,866	$ 7,227,822	$ 7,469,531

City of Raleigh

GENERAL GOVERNMENTAL EXPENDITURES BY FUNCTION
LAST TEN FISCAL YEARS

Fiscal Year Ended June 30	General Government	Public Safety	Public Works	Leisure Services	Debt Service
1983	$ 10,277,003	$ 16,748,966	$ 8,552,177	$ 6,639,146	$ 3,335,969
1984	10,862,572	18,221,492	7,753,108	7,480,519	4,112,617
1985	11,956,937	18,787,866	9,175,809	8,155,363	3,529,091
1986	16,616,470	20,388,164	10,444,556	9,514,263	3,766,570
1987	18,668,882	24,463,428	11,696,850	10,276,028	3,179,783
1988	19,375,690	25,885,967	12,989,793	10,898,805	4,764,389
1989	22,619,380	28,530,054	13,495,171	12,006,703	5,009,621
1990	15,340,096	32,375,713	15,728,241	12,874,478	7,704,024
1991	17,095,272	34,099,923	18,637,374	13,874,336	8,061,781
1992	17,558,985	34,876,166	19,139,800	14,566,801	10,208,485

Notes:

(1) Includes General and Special Revenue Funds. Administrative costs charged to Water and Sewer Fund are netted to General Government.

(2) Community Development category reflects reclassifications of certain activities in 1991 and 1992 previously reported as General Governmental Expenditures.

Highways and Streets	Community Development Services	Capital Outlay	Manpower Services	Other	Total
$ 2,905,684	$ 1,109,238	$ 5,036,877	$ 746,567	$ 1,180,259	$ 56,531,886
2,929,582	1,213,882	6,880,651	386,493	2,467,115	62,308,031
3,465,869	943,810	2,273,681	-	2,881,524	61,169,950
3,916,057	1,039,874	5,220,741	-	3,280,338	74,187,033
3,897,981	1,264,464	3,827,025	-	4,556,047	81,830,488
3,938,733	1,092,516	2,627,293	-	6,998,200	88,571,386
4,139,876	1,702,827	1,936,442	-	6,671,926	96,112,000
4,246,942	12,615,733	3,318,220	-	7,575,515	111,778,962
4,475,475	14,613,588	1,718,600	-	8,348,703	120,925,052
4,764,881	13,432,914	3,234,616	-	8,263,826	126,046,474

City of Raleigh

GENERAL GOVERNMENTAL REVENUES BY SOURCE
LAST TEN FISCAL YEARS

Fiscal Year Ended June 30	Ad Valorem Taxes	Inter-governmental	Local Sales Tax	Transient Occupancy Tax
1983	$ 27,902,297	$ 15,497,947	$ 5,966,975	$ -
1984	29,637,325	16,549,722	7,177,024	-
1985	39,499,391	16,251,837	11,098,800	-
1986	43,662,052	17,541,709	12,744,676	-
1987	48,006,795	18,191,595	15,441,036	1,207,488
1988	51,180,194	19,008,552	17,978,680	1,656,355
1989	55,102,853	23,118,591	20,540,537	1,609,401
1990	58,218,190	27,244,670	21,893,144	1,638,982
1991	65,367,860	24,839,778	21,795,353	1,760,435
1992	68,749,965	24,827,831	21,218,021	1,948,715

Notes:

Includes General and Special Revenue Funds.

Licenses and Fees	Interest on Investments	Fines, Forfeits, and Penalties	Other	Total
$ 2,309,487	$ 3,230,272	$ 409,462	$ 4,231,794	$ 59,548,234
3,329,605	3,031,603	447,139	3,925,543	64,097,961
3,983,959	3,449,960	500,997	4,940,780	79,725,724
4,446,360	3,608,981	476,212	5,801,692	88,281,682
4,111,196	3,110,395	608,016	5,153,609	95,830,130
4,228,464	3,403,324	657,642	6,591,781	104,704,992
4,191,714	4,779,941	661,081	6,873,761	116,877,879
5,368,042	4,644,565	704,334	7,500,152	127,212,079
5,589,316	4,605,909	702,474	11,795,326	136,456,451
6,968,909	3,865,978	762,866	13,326,143	141,668,428

City of Raleigh

PROPERTY TAX LEVIES AND COLLECTIONS
LAST TEN FISCAL YEARS

Fiscal Year Ended June 30	Year of Levy	Gross Levy	Gross Collected Current	Percent Collected Current	Collected Prior Levies	Total Collected	Percent Total Collected to Levy
1983	1982	$29,828,655	$29,209,621	97.9%	$405,240	$29,614,861	99.3%
1984	1983	32,400,121	31,374,170	96.8	419,876	31,794,046	98.1
1985	1984	39,335,023	38,728,229	98.4	962,956	39,691,185	100.9
1986	1985	43,916,816	43,256,839	98.5	490,632	43,747,471	99.6
1987	1986	48,641,329	47,789,356	98.2	369,805	48,159,161	99.0
1988	1987	51,701,112	50,838,443	98.3	596,456	51,434,899	99.5
1989	1988	55,589,702	54,693,751	98.4	686,690	55,380,441	99.6
1990	1989	58,852,248	57,804,391	98.2	652,785	58,457,176	99.3
1991	1990	66,068,070	64,853,739	98.2	923,978	65,777,717	99.6
1992	1991	70,174,457	68,730,530	97.9	961,755	69,692,285	99.3

City of Raleigh

ASSESSED VALUE OF ALL TAXABLE PROPERTY
LAST TEN FISCAL YEARS

Fiscal Year Ended June 30	Real Property	Personal Property	Corporate Excess	Total
1983	$ 1,960,412,130	$ 965,442,116	$200,026,880	$ 3,125,881,126
1984	2,108,328,235	1,194,548,401	163,243,854	3,466,120,490
1985	4,327,763,484	1,484,351,032	213,343,764	6,025,458,280
1986	4,743,881,294	1,729,856,611	245,616,674	6,719,354,579
1987	5,159,543,470	1,879,239,303	297,117,923	7,335,900,696
1988	5,672,369,022	1,847,609,870	281,566,066	7,801,544,958
1989	5,943,043,148	1,427,718,095*	328,025,022	7,698,786,265
1990	6,229,525,113	1,526,282,748	282,693,391	8,038,501,252
1991	6,473,218,892	1,728,801,643	306,679,030	8,508,699,565
1992	6,671,172,417	1,903,355,991	314,713,468	8,889,241,876

Notes:

(1) This schedule does not include valuations on property owned by the State of North Carolina, United States Government, eleemosynary institutions, etc., not subject to taxation.

(2) Assessed valuations are established at 100% of estimated market value for real property and 100% of actual value for personal property.

*Decrease due to legislative elimination of manufacturers and wholesale/retail inventories from personal property base.

City of Raleigh

ANALYSIS OF CURRENT TAX LEVY
For the Fiscal Year Ended June 30, 1992

Property Valuation:

Real Property	$ 6,671,172,417
Personal Property	1,903,355,991
Corporate Excess	314,713,468
Total Subject to Tax	$ 8,889,241,876

Tax Rate per $100 of Value	$ .785

Gross Levy (1)	$ 70,174,457
Add: Interest	138,251
Less: Rebates	1,100,701
Net Levy	69,212,007

Uncollected, Current Tax Levy, at June 30, 1992	1,443,927

Net Current Year Taxes Collected on Net Levy	$ 67,768,080

Percent of Current Taxes Collected to Net Levy	97.9%

Note:

(1) Gross Levy includes taxes levied on discovered properties of prior periods at tax rates applicable to those periods.

City of Raleigh

SCHEDULE OF DIRECT AND OVERLAPPING DEBT
June 30, 1992

	Bonded Debt	Percentage Applicable to City	City's Share of Debt
Direct Debt - City of Raleigh (a)	$ 91,960,000	100.00%	$ 91,960,000
Overlapping Debt: (b)			
Wake County General Improvement Bonds (c)	190,275,000	44.25 (d)	84,196,688
Total Direct and Overlapping Debt	$282,235,000		$176,156,688

Notes:

(a) This total does not include $62,585,000 of water and sewer bonds.

(b) Overlapping debt does not include the debt of the Special Airport Tax District of Durham and Wake Counties as these bonds are payable by the Airport Authority out of airport revenues.

(c) This total includes $163,772,700 of Wake County School Bonds; but does not include Hospital bonds, as these bonds are payable solely from hospital revenues.

(d) Percentage of Direct and Overlapping Debt is based on June 30, 1992, Assessed Valuation of Wake County ($ 20,088,603,859) as compared to the June 30, 1992, Assessed Valuation of the City of Raleigh ($8,889,241,876).

City of Raleigh

STATEMENT OF LEGAL DEBT MARGIN
June 30, 1992

Appraised Valuation - June 30, 1992		$ 8,889,241,876
Debt Limit - Eight (8%) Percent of Appraised Valuation	$711,139,350	

Gross Debt

Outstanding General Obligation
  Bonded Debt:

General Governmental Bonds	$ 83,780,000	
Water Bonds	22,437,000	
Sewer Bonds	40,148,000	
Parking Deck Bonds	8,180,000	
	154,545,000	

General Obligation Bonds
  Authorized not Issued:

Sewer	4,100,000	
General Governmental	23,345,000	
	27,445,000	

Other

Certificates of Participation	11,500,000	
Lease Purchase Obligations	8,820,133	
Installment Notes - Parking Deck	453,900	
Reimbursement Contracts - Streets	476,373	
Reimbursement Contracts - Water and Sewer	28,908	
	21,279,314	
Gross Debt	203,269,314	

Statutory Deductions

Bonded debt included in gross debt incurred or authorized for water	22,437,000	

Uncollected special assessments levied
  for local improvements for which gross
  debt was incurred to the extent to be
  applied to the payment of such gross
  debt
	3,166,085	

	25,603,085	

Net Debt		177,666,229
Legal Debt Margin		$ 533,473,121

(Portions of report not shown here)

THE COOPERATIVE CPA FIRM

Fancy Suite 101
Any Street
Anywhere, USA 00000-0000

Independent Auditors' Report on the Internal Control Structure Based on the Audit of General Purpose Financial Statements Conducted in Accordance with Government Auditing Standards

To the Honorable Mayor and Members
        of the City Council
City of Raleigh, North Carolina

We have audited the general purpose financial statements of the City of Raleigh, North Carolina, as of and for the year ended June 30, 1992, and issued our report dated Sometime, 1992.

We conducted our audit in accordance with generally accepted auditing standards and *Government Audit Standards*, issued by the Comptroller General of the United States. Those standards require that we plan and perform the audit to obtain reasonable assurance about whether the general purpose financial statements are free of material misstatement.

In planning and performing our audit of the general purpose financial statements of the City of Raleigh, North Carolina, for the year ended June 30, 1992, we considered its internal control structure in developing our audit procedures for the purpose of expressing our opinion on the general purpose financial statements and not to provide assurance on the internal control structure.

The management of the City of Raleigh, North Carolina, is responsible for establishing and maintaining an internal control structure. In satisfying this responsibility, estimates and judgments by management are required to assess the expected benefits and related costs of internal control structure policies and procedures. The purpose of an internal control structure is to provide management with reasonable, but not absolute, assurance that assets are safeguarded against loss from unauthorized use or disposition and that transactions are executed in accordance with management's authorization and recorded properly for the preparation of general purpose financial statements in accordance with generally accepted accounting principles. Because of the inherent limitations in any internal control structure, errors or irregularities may nevertheless occur and not be detected. Also, projection of any evaluation of the structure to future periods is subject to the risk that procedures may become inadequate because of changes in conditions or that the effectiveness of the design and operation of policies and procedures may change.

To the Honorable Mayor and Members
of the City Council
City of Raleigh, North Carolina

For the purpose of this report, we have classified the significant internal control structure policies and procedures in the following categories:

Revenues/Receipts
Purchases/Disbursements

(Many other categories would be listed, including the general requirements under the Single Audit Act)

For the internal control structure categories listed above, we obtained an understanding of the design of relevant policies and procedures and determined whether they have been placed in operation, and we assessed the control risk.

Our consideration of the internal control structure would not necessarily disclose all matters in the internal control structure that might be material weaknesses under standards established by the American Institute of Certified Public Accountants. A material weakness is a condition in which the design or operation of one or more of the internal control structure elements does not reduce to a relatively low level of risk that errors or irregularities in amounts that would be material in relation to the general purpose financial statements being audited may occur and not be detected within a timely period by employees in the normal course of performing their assigned functions. We noted no matters involving the internal control structure and its operation that we consider to be material weaknesses as defined above.

However, we noted certain matters involving internal control structure and its operation that we have reported to the management of the City of Raleigh, North Carolina, in a separate letter dated Sometime, 1992.

This report is intended for the information of the Mayor and members of the City Council, the cognizant agency, and other federal and State agencies. This restriction is not intended to limit the distribution of this report, which is a matter of public record.

Sometime, 1992

THE COOPERATIVE CPA FIRM

Fancy Suite 101
Any Street
Anywhere, USA 00000-0000

Independent Auditors' Report on the Compliance Based on the Audit of General Purpose Financial Statements Performed in Accordance with Government Auditing Standards

To the Honorable Mayor and Members
    of the City Council
City of Raleigh, North Carolina

We have audited the general purpose financial statements of the City of Raleigh, North Carolina, as of and for the year ended June 30, 1992, and have issued our report dated Sometime, 1992.

We conducted our audit in accordance with generally accepted auditing standards and *Government Audit Standards*, issued by the Comptroller General of the United States. Those standards require that we plan and perform the audit to obtain reasonable assurance about whether the general purpose financial statements are free of material misstatement.

Compliance with laws, regulations, contracts, and grants applicable to the City of Raleigh, North Carolina, is the responsibility of the management of the City of Raleigh, North Carolina. As part of obtaining reasonable assurance about whether the general purpose financial statements are free of material misstatement, we performed tests of the City's compliance with certain provisions of laws, regulations, contracts, and grants. However, the objective of our audit of the financial statements was not to provide an opinion on overall compliance with such provisions. Accordingly, we do not express such an opinion.

The results of our tests indicate that, with respect to the items tested, the City of Raleigh, North Carolina, complied, in all material respects, with the above-mentioned provisions. With respect to items not tested, nothing came to our attention that caused us to believe that the City had not complied, in all material respects, with those provisions.

This report is intended for the information of the Mayor and members of the City Council, the cognizant agency, and other federal and State agencies. This restriction is not intended to limit the distribution of this report, which is a matter of public record.

Sometime, 1992